Plant Behaviour and Intelligence

Plant Behaviour and Intelligence

Anthony Trewavas FRS FRSE

University of Edinburgh

To Val my light and life, to whom I owe so much and to three dearly loved children, Seren, Eira and Joseph, all of whom have made life worth living.

OXFORD
UNIVERSITY PRESS

Plant Behaviour and Intelligence. First Edition. Anthony Trewavas.
© Anthony Trewavas 2014. Published 2014 by Oxford University Press.

OXFORD
UNIVERSITY PRESS

Great Clarendon Street, Oxford, OX2 6DP,
United Kingdom

Oxford University Press is a department of the University of Oxford.
It furthers the University's objective of excellence in research, scholarship,
and education by publishing worldwide. Oxford is a registered trade mark of
Oxford University Press in the UK and in certain other countries

First published 2014
First published in paperback 2015

Impression: 1

Published in the United States of America by Oxford University Press
198 Madison Avenue, New York, NY 10016, United States of America

British Library Cataloguing in Publication Data
Data available

Library of Congress Cataloging in Publication Data
Data available

ISBN 978–0–19–953954–3 (Hbk.)
ISBN 978–0–19–875368–1 (Pbk.)

Printed and bound in Great Britain by
Clays Ltd, St Ives plc

Preface

This book takes as its theme the statement by the Nobel prize winning botanist Barbara McClintock in 1984; 'a goal for the future would be to determine the extent of knowledge the cell has of itself and how it uses that knowledge in a thoughtful manner when challenged'. The response to 'challenge' is behaviour and 'thoughtful' responses are intelligent behaviour. Thus, the title of this book is *Plant Behaviour and Intelligence*. The knowledge cells have of themselves derives from the complex self-organizing system that constructs the cell from its constituent molecules and directly implies self-recognition. There is a further issue less well recognized—intelligent behaviour is inextricably linked to fitness. This issue is largely overlooked by all who either discuss intelligence or behaviour.

This book in 26 chapters fleshes out McClintock's superb insight in the cells and organisms to which she was referring, plant cells and plant organisms. It describes the elements and processes that bring cells to life, their origin four billion years back, and why they became multicellular to form recognizable higher plants. Behaviour some of it surprising is shown to require integration through the cambium. A further chapter highlights how leaves control their internal temperature homeostat. The analogous organizational and behavioural properties between social insect colonies (swarm intelligence) and large plants are described. Furthermore, how plant roots adjust their sensing systems to deal with different predominant signals, and are able to self-recognize forms three critical chapters. Games that plants play are critically assessed. The phenomenon of intelligence is illustrated with a detailed discussion and reference to the numerous descriptions from those informed scientists that have spent time examining the question. Brains are not needed for intelligent behaviour and reflex behaviour is rejected. Intelligent genomes and intelligent foraging are outlined. Finally, in the context of McClintock's 'thoughtful', the vexed question of consciousness is discussed and in that context J. C. Bose's 'plant nervous system' receives its rightful recognition. Throughout the important issue of fitness is raised.

This book represents a suitable introduction for those who have an interest in the rapid developing areas of plant behaviour. Although some of the material is technical and molecular this has been kept to a minimum in favour of whole plant behaviour. Some overlap in idea and content between chapters is inevitable, but I have tried always to ensure that chapters can be read independently of others and that necessitates small amounts of occasional repetition for those that read right through. Much of the described material is fully referenced for those that seek to investigate further. For a more general readership, many of these chapters should be comprehensible and convey to them the excitement that encompasses our increasing understanding of McClintock's imaginative insight.

Foreword

The force that through the green fuse drives the flower.   **(Dylan Thomas, 1952)**

An author's justification for the organism

This book is concerned with behaviour and intelligence, but in plants, not animals and that makes it unusual. In this day and age, scientists are constantly required to justify what they research and, in this foreword, I have put some of the reasons that justify research on this group of organisms, rather than give personal reasons for the book, which come later in Chapter 1. It is my hope that, on reading this foreword, it will encourage the reader to delve further into other parts of the book.

Earth is a planet dominated by plants, a self-evident statement on any trip into the countryside. It is also the case that the words that describe some of our major ecosystems such as tundra, rainforest, prairie, etc., refer to the dominant plant life that characterizes such regions. Photosynthesis is responsible for the current composition and substantive presence of oxygen, a highly reactive gas, make this dominance very clear. It is one of those niceties of life that we require the oxygen that plants produce and they in turn require the carbon dioxide that we exhale.

One of the reasons that a Martian, if there were such, might conclude the possibility of life on earth is the potential greening of parts of the planet with the change in the seasons. He/she might also observe that with such a reactive gas, as oxygen, in the atmosphere that there must be an abundance of life on earth to produce it. By the same token, Professor James Lovelock FRS concluded that there was no life on Mars because its atmosphere was at chemical equilibrium. However, there are other more common reasons that account for the popularity of plant life with the public.

Plants are some of the most beautiful objects

'From fairest creatures we desire increase, that thereby beauty's rose might never die'. Many green plants and flowers have particular effects on our emotions as William Shakespeare (sonnet 1), the author of this quotation, was well aware. If it is beauty in biology we are looking for, then flowers must rank as some of the most beautiful objects on this planet. Burns compared his love 'to a red, red rose that's newly sprung in June'. The similar thrill generated by a perfect flower is surely familiar to many. Perhaps it is no accident that Van Gogh's 'Sunflowers' is currently one of the world's most highly priced paintings. Members of the orchid family come, in my mind, closest to perfection in beauty. Many orchids excite collectors and public alike, and rare orchids rank as some of the most expensive and sought after plants in the world by collectors. Expect to pay up to £100,000 for a particularly rare specimen. Surely orchids can equal some of the most beautiful pictures that artists have painted. I have been fortunate enough to attend two exhibitions of flowering orchids, one in Germany (Minau) and the other in Scotland. The enormous variety of shapes and colours is almost overpowering.

However, others will have different reasons; 'Beauty is bought by judgement of the eye'. Shakespeare again, as accurate as ever in *Loves Labours Lost*. Beautiful objects do have an extraordinary calming effect and with flowers being natural objects, the pleasure is greatly increased. Surely, this is the reason that we inundate those in hospital with flowers or decorate those that have died.

Biophilia is another reason

Many find enormous satisfaction to be gained from digging the soil—to nurturing plants from seed to flower, all the way to designing a garden. Certainly in the UK, this has become a tremendous industry and its popularity speaks of something quite basic in the human condition. Biophilia is a term coined by E. O. Wilson (1984) to describe the bond, the obvious kinship, between ourselves and other organisms. Orians (1980) has gone further and suggested that, in gardens and outdoor properties of all kinds, mankind attempts to construct a psychologically-satisfying environment that mimics the savannah with its open grassland, clumps of trees, and small areas of water. The evidence that early hominids evolved in such environments is quite strong and the implication is that this environment over millions of years became hard-wired into the brain. Carl Gustav Jung would have referred to this phenomenon as an aspect of the collective unconscious.

The evidence for this satisfying effect of plants has strong psychological support. Across different cultures there is a strong preference for natural over urban environments (Parsons 1991). Patients exposed to natural surroundings exhibit a much more rapid recovery with reduced dependence on drugs and better clinical assessment, than those who are not so exposed (Ulrich 1984, 1999; Franklin, 2012). The known effects of gardens on health, and direct measurements of brain alpha waves and EEGs indicate strong reductions of stress when looking at plants compared to other situations (Ulrich 2002).

The history of gardens seems lost in the mists of time. When did present mankind actually start to till the soil for purely decorative purposes, rather than food? The Hanging Gardens of Babylon and those in ancient Egypt, which can be seen carved on the walls of various temples and structures, speaks of a long history of biophilia.

Agriculture is the means whereby the hunter-gatherer changed his nomadic way of life to pastoral food collection, to living in villages and cities. Plants predominate in present-day agriculture, cereals and vegetables being the basis of most human diets. From slow beginnings, arable farming presently uses more than one billion hectares world-wide; about one-tenth of the earth's land surface. Crop production itself probably occupies at least half of mankind in one way or another. Could an early affinity with growing useful and highly decorative plants have been the first steps in crop domestication? The supposition has always been that food was the prime reason for domestication, but perhaps it was the other way round. We now know that early mankind decorated him/herself with simple ornaments and necklaces. Could flowers, although ephemeral, also have been used?

Trees excite a different kind of appreciation and are beautiful in an alternate way. Although many are enormous, compared with ourselves, they are completely benign. Again, trees are intimately involved in mankind's early history, providing wood as fuel, construction, and useful chemicals. The mature, deciduous trees of temperate climates or some of the splendid cedars, easily excite widespread admiration. My first visit to the Giant Redwoods and Sequoiadendrons of California induced in me an extraordinary feeling of rapture and awe similar to that of Darwin on his notable world-encompassing voyage when he first encountered the tropical forest; 'wonder, astonishment, and sublime devotion fill and elevate the mind'. Because of the high canopy, giant redwood forests are extraordinarily still and peaceful. Sound travels a considerable distance in these forests, no doubt reflected from the high canopy. These forests are one of the seven natural wonders of the world that everyone should visit. The sheer size of these trees dwarfs the observer; what is man, indeed, compared with trees and mountains?

Greater still is what goes on underground and unseen. The massive root system that anchors such enormous leviathans. The frenetic activity that drives water and minerals to the highest shoots a hundred metres up. 'The force that through the green fuse drives the flower . . . drives my red blood', Dylan Thomas (1952) echoing a common poetic sentiment of the oneness of nature, but with insight seeing a common thread to animals and plants. Although not seen, the growing root system is in a remarkably dynamic state. Sensing mechanisms operate that enable accurate navigation of the soil mosaic. Soil organisms, pockets of water and minerals, soil characteristics and crumb structure, pockets of gases, soil chemicals, and stones are all recognized, and action taken to exploit or avoid.

In temperate climates, plants accurately mark the seasons. 'A thousand branches flowering in due rotation, each has his season coming early or late but to all alike the fertile soil is kind; the red flowers hang like a heavy mist, the white flowers gleam like a fall of snow' Pang chu-I (819, translation published 1961).

Even sleep movements are recorded 'Now sleeps the crimson petal, now the white . . . Now folds the lily all her sweetness up' (Tennyson 1949). *Flora Poetica* contains many examples.

Many plant biologists find fascination in uncovering the hidden beauty that underpins plant life. It is obvious reading Keller's book on Barbara McClintock, who gained the Nobel Prize for plant transposons that she shared many of these sentiments—a love of life and an embrace of the natural world, but more on her views later. Plants in general enable that easy embrace where, in many respects, many animals do not. Elephants, tarantulas, and lions excite our attention but usually only at a distance, or on film, or behind bars.

Practical reasons for investigating plant life

There are, of course, practical reasons for science to investigate the plant world that are equally crucial. Could we have evolved without the services that plants provide? The green forests and the great expanse of oceanic plankton of the world act as its lungs. The origin of the use of wood in all sorts of human activities (houses, furniture, etc.), again, is lost in the mists of time, but the use in house construction is still a dominant feature. Plants supply a multiplicity of basic foods and nutritional/medicinal chemicals and fibres for paper and clothes. Plants are the basis of all food chains. The *Dictionary of Useful Plants* (Coon, 1974) lists 20,000 species out of about 300,000. Plants are inextricably linked with our survival.

So the justification for a book on plant behaviour finds its basis in an effective love of the organism. Plant behaviour is an enormous topic. Laboratory behaviour or physiology has, in the past, required 20 volumes to cover knowledge. Thus, this book contains merely subjects that interest me and I hope the reader, too. There are 26 chapters in this book, all of them relatively short and it is a book for dipping into, rather than reading through. The chapters describe the things that interest me—some are technical and may require some background knowledge, but the general reader will find plenty to get into. If nothing else it should increase respect for the organisms that are so much the unrecognized staff of life.

References

Coon, N. (1974). *The dictionary of useful plants: an organic farming and gardening book.* Rodale Press, New York.

Franklin, D. (2012). How hospital gardens help patients heal. *Scientific American*, **306**, 24–25.

Orians, G.H. (1980). Habitat selection: general theory and applications to human behaviour. In Lockard, J.S., ed., *The evolution of human social behavior*, pp. 86–94. Elsevier, New York.

Pang chu-I (819). *Chinese poems*, transl. Waley, A. (1961). Unwin Books, London.

Parsons, R. (1991). The potential influences of environmental perception on human health. *Journal of Environmental Psychology*, **11**, 1–23.

Tennyson, A.L. (1949). *Poems of Alfred Lord Tennyson.* Oxford University Press, London.

Thomas, D. (1952). *Collected poems.* J. M. Dent and Sons Ltd, London.

Ulrich, R.S. (1984). View through a window may influence recovery from surgery. *Science*, **224**, 420–421.

Ulrich, R.S. (1999). *Effects of gardens on health outcomes.* Available at: www.majorfoundation.org/pdfs/Effects%20of%20Gardens%20on%20Health%20Outcomes.pdf.

Ulrich, R.S. (2002). *Health benefits of gardens in hospitals.* Available at: http://www.greenplantsforgreenbuildings.org/news/health-benefits-of-gardens-in-hospitals/

Wilson, E.O. (1984). *Biophilia.* Harvard University Press, Cambridge, MA.

Contents

CHAPTER 1

A feeling for the organism

A goal for the future would be to determine the extent of knowledge the cell has of itself and how it uses that knowledge in a thoughtful manner when challenged.

(McClintock 1984)

⮑ Summary

This chapter starts with a brief introduction to Barbara McClintock's insights into cell behaviour, including her famous statement about cellular knowledge given above, which forms part of the basis for this book. It considers some of her insights into plant behaviour and describes my own reasons for writing this book. The basic problem with plant behaviour is its difficulty in general detection. The description of what is meant by the term 'plant', frequently used in this book, is described and justification given for using a dicot as an exemplar. The variety of types of plant in the plant kingdom are included, particularly those without roots, without a vegetative stem or leaves. The major tissues are indicated to provide a necessary background for the general reader. Finally, the problems of using domesticated plants for experimental purposes are raised since domestication usually involves elimination of numerous behaviours.

Introduction

This book is about plant behaviour and intelligence, terms rarely put together in a knowledgeable way. Behaviour is best described as what plants do and intelligence as a capacity for problem solving. I will justify those definitions of behaviour and intelligence in greater detail later, but accept them for the moment. To many, the notion that plants do anything at all is faintly ludicrous—are they not prime examples of still life or sculpture? However, the fact is that plants do many things and, for those plants in natural circumstances, there are plenty of problems to solve. To the extent that we come to understand the behaviour of all plants better, we will place a greater value on them and, in turn, on ourselves. A better and healthier perspective is gained of our position here on this earth and a more realistic assessment of our position in this extraordinary universe. 'Respect yourself first and then all that surrounds you' is a Navaho precept that I believe in and underpins this text. We live on a planet dominated by plants and, hopefully, this book will indicate why respect should be shown to many members of the plant kingdom, but remembering all the time, 'respect yourself first'. I have to state that at the beginning, because some may misinterpret notions of plant intelligence to try and justify placing plants as necessitating a legal protection accorded to higher mammals.

My own commitment to plant biology

Occasionally, someone raises the question as to where you were when some dramatic or apocalyptic event happened. I can certainly recall where

I was when I heard of President Kennedy's assassination, or when Armstrong put his foot on the moon. However, with less certainty of the precise date, I can identify what made me a plant biologist. My own entry into the plant world was determined by a superlative botanical teacher at school. Common enough reason, I can hear the reader say. Teachers often do not know the long-term effects of their teaching and in my case this teacher left as I was finishing my A levels. When young you are often too gauche to express your thanks and provide the appropriate plaudits that teachers need.

However it came about, my eyes were opened to the fascinating, but often still mysterious subjects of plant morphology, ecology, physiology, biochemistry, and everything plant-like. I can still recall the feeling of intense excitement in 1955 when joining the upper school that I was finally allowed to open the locked cupboard and to examine some of the books kept for advanced classes. They were full of mysterious terms and chapter headings and some remain as exciting mysteries. I acquired my own copies of some of these books in later years, but once bitten I never looked back. It has dominated my life as it has many others.

What had always interested me was the whole organism. However, when I finally entered postdoctoral research and later on as a lecturer at the University of Edinburgh, whole plant studies were no longer research priorities, so I spent a long research sojourn on things more molecular, but always to do with the signals (that is meaningful information) that plants sense and act upon. Plants continually react to the environment in which they live. My later investigations on how these signals do what they do in the responding plant, brought me back to my first compelling fascination—the behaviour of the whole plant itself.

The road to systems and plant intelligence

In 1972, I purchased a small book by Bertalanffy published in 1971 and entitled *General Systems Theory*. Although the material in the book was quite limited in amount, the way of thinking about cells, organism, and biology, and indeed economics and politics was quite radical. Biology, it indicated, was constructed from networks or systems. Understanding required identifying the connections between the network constituents, since it was the connections that generated the novel properties of biological organisms and populations. I, like many of my time had been typically reductionist, probing the bits and pieces of the network. To make a living as a scientist required, and still requires, that mode of investigation. However, that small book changed my way of thinking. Systems thinking taught one to think sideways, as it were, to see the connections and, thus, the surrounding context into which any network constituent is embedded. The connections could be straightforward or more complicated with negative feedback or feedforward devices.

There were precedents to Bertalanffy and I read as much as I could find at that time. Jan Smuts, for example, who first used the word holism; the developmental biologist Paul Weiss, '*The science of life*' (1973); Bernard Patten (1971), an ecologist who edited four volumes on systems thinking; Jay Forrester (1961), on economics systems theory; Stafford Beer (1972), management systems theory; Gregory Bateson (1972), systems approaches to mind. All of these were already on the shelves in 1972–73. In the University of Edinburgh, which I joined in 1970, Henrik Kacser and Jim Burns published the highly significant 'The control of flux' in 1973 and Conrad Waddington, *Tools for Thought* in 1977. I list these people in particular because, like many others at the time, they effectively educated me in systems approaches and understanding, and as others have said before, I stand on the shoulders of these superb intellects.

However, acquisition of the systems approach led me into serious controversy over plant growth regulation by hormones. I had written a long invited article (Trewavas 1981) emphasizing the context within which molecules worked as being crucial and no less important than the molecule itself. It countered the common research view of the time. I received over 600 reprint requests in 3 weeks (no websites at that time), so there was certainly interest, but there were subsequent meetings where what I had written was either damned or lauded as the new approach; my promotion was also temporarily blocked.

What directed me into the area of intelligence was not only a lifetime experience with plant behaviour (for so it turned out to be), but also McClintock's very challenging statement, published in 1984, which begins this chapter. What exactly did she mean by it? The words 'thoughtful' and 'knowledge' indicated someone with a profound understanding of plants and they resonated with conclusions that had slowly emerged from my own reading. Most of this book really is an exploration of McClintock's assessment of plant life. 'Thoughtful' directly implies intelligence and 'challenge' requires behaviour. As indicated in the preface to this book, its title, *Plant Behaviour and Intelligence* becomes an inevitable consequence of McClintock's insight. All self-organizing cells and organisms are very complex systems and the particular system structure at the time represents 'the knowledge it has of itself'. Chapter 3 amplifies the meaning of systems structure.

However, one consequence of controversy on plant hormones is that it led to numerous invitations to write articles for other scientific journals. In one of these subsequent invited articles, I illustrated a particular complex amino acid biosynthetic pathway in plants as a simple neural network (Trewavas 1986). It seemed to me that it was one way to use 'thoughtful' and 'knowledge' from McClintock's article. In turn, thinking about that led me to the realization that the complicated network inside every cell must have similar analogous organization and, thus, behaviour to the potentially more complicated ones found in brains. In fact, any self-organizing network of sufficient complexity, and capable of maintenance in the face of environmental perturbation and the active pursuit of food of any kind must be intelligent. Plants were certainly in that category. However, at the time, plants were the last organisms normally associated with intelligent behaviour. When I mentioned this possibility to some colleagues, the response was often ferociously negative. Thinking that way was obviously dangerous. The jottings on the issue went into the desk drawer and did not surface again until I was more confident, and could argue the case.

With time and data amassed in 1999 and 2002, I used the opportunities again of invited articles to float the idea of plant intelligence gradually (Trewavas 1999, 2002) and then in 2003 published another long invited article entitled 'Aspects of plant intelligence' (Trewavas 2003). Inevitably, controversy surfaced again and, immediately, some of those who agreed with me 20 years earlier now seemed opposed, but with a new band of supporters, some of whom had already started down this road. This book 8 years in occasional writing is a consequence of thinking around that theme and, of course, new information has now emerged from elsewhere, which is to be found in its pages.

Just as outstanding scientists provided me in the past with systems education, two others are Barbara McClintock, already mentioned, and Charles Darwin who will surface now and again. Darwin wrote the first book on plant behaviour. A third much less well known, but of remarkable stature is J. C. Bose whose contributions will find reasonable reference later on in Chapters 2 and 25.

In some sense, the more I look into plant biology, the more I see and the more I appreciate how little is actually understood. In that sense, exploration has magnified my ignorance, the expansion of knowledge is now much greater than when I graduated; thus, my knowledge in relative terms has diminished. Like so many scientists, I need two or more lifetimes to explore further, but nature in its wisdom does not permit us that luxury. Perhaps that is the most fortunate aspect of our biology; there are too many who have lived too long already.

'A feeling for the organism'

In 1984, Barbara McClintock, a plant biologist, received the Nobel Prize, the highest honour and accolade any scientist can receive from other scientists. For many years, her pioneering research, decades ahead of others, contradicted one of the then-current dogmas that assumed that the genome, the sequence of nucleotides in DNA was stable throughout the lifetime of the individual. When scientific dogma takes hold, life becomes difficult for any scientist whose research does not fit; for Barbara the penalty was to be ignored and her observations, clear though they were, misunderstood or even trivialized (Keller 1983).

It did not help that she worked with a plant, *Zea mays* or corn, a crop that produces the familiar yellow sweetcorn. Although plants can be popular with the public, they are not a particularly popular organism for biological study or grant money, although that may be changing. The fact is plants do not seem to do anything, and if they do not seem to do anything, what is there for any young scientist to be challenged to investigate? An abundance of food in western countries has not helped either; plant research in terms of food provision and security no longer seems publicly so important.

However, recent surges in the price of food have reawakened us to the fact that we have a problem. The population of the world, currently now over seven billion and predicted to rise to nine billion by 2050 needs more and plentiful food. There is no more land available unless we cut down rainforest, so two ears of wheat must be provided where one was grown before. We need more knowledge about plants and their behaviour.

Evelyn Keller has written a biography of Barbara McClintock, a readable and enjoyable text that gives substantial insight into McClintock's thinking and attitudes. Keller talked with McClintock at length, so that we often have direct quotes from her and I have used several below.

'But just because they sit there, anybody walking down the road considers just as if they're not really alive' (Keller 1983, p. 200). One reason for writing this book is to modify that undoubtedly common perspective of the ordinary public 'walking down the road'.

What exactly is meant when I refer to a plant?

This question will be examined again and again in this text, because it is seminal to any study of plants. The real question is 'what is the essence of being a plant', because through that question the phenomenon of behaviour is more obviously displayed. I will use the word 'plant' frequently, as a shorthand for plants we are familiar with. While it is generally true that plants are photosynthetic, not all organisms that photosynthesize are plants.

The living kingdom used to be divided into animals and plants. So far as I can ascertain, the division was based on the simple idea that all the interesting things moved and all the uninteresting ones did not. So, originally, both bacteria and fungi were classed as plants, together with the more obvious, algae, mosses, liverworts, ferns, gymnosperms, and finally, angiosperms. Once it was realized that bacteria caused disease and plants did not, attitudes changed. Microscopical studies established that bacteria lacked a nuclear membrane and thus a proper nucleus. Furthermore, obvious chromosomes during mitosis were absent and it is now known that, instead, bacteria possess a single circular chromosome containing their DNA. Bacteria are described as prokaryotes and placed in a kingdom all of their own. In contrast, virtually all other organisms, animals, the non-photosynthetic fungi, and plants are described as eukaryotes, meaning they have a true nucleus and obvious chromosomes.

More recent studies using genome and protein sequencing indicate that fungi left the main evolutionary tree at a different time to plants, so they, too, are now regarded as a kingdom of their own. If their present lifestyle of living off the decaying materials of other organisms was the same when the fungal branch occurred, then self-evidently they could only do so when there was sufficiently large number of dead organisms to provide the necessary substrate material. Yeast, truffles, and mushrooms are the public's main experience of fungi.

The reader should regard the word 'plant' in this book as synonymous with a higher plant, an angiosperm

In evolutionary terms, the first true plants are often regarded as members of the algae. The algae are eukaryotes, but these eukaryotes were preceded, probably by a billion years at least in photosynthetic terms, by photosynthetic bacteria and blue-green algae, both of which are part of the prokaryotic kingdom. Many algae live in marine conditions or in freshwater, and again, in evolutionary terms, are assumed to have preceded the mosses and liverworts; these, in turn, are assumed to have preceded the ferns. Tree ferns and horsetails, some 300 million years ago, formed the basis of the material that eventually became coal measures. The ancestors of gymnosperms appeared about the same time and present day representatives are mainly large trees. Finally, about 150–200 million years ago, the angiosperms, probably the most familiar of plants to the reader, were first detected in the fossil record.

When I use the word 'plant' throughout this book, it is simply a shorthand for an angiosperm, a higher (i.e. more recently evolved) plant. In contrast to algae, mosses, and ferns, which use a motile, fast-moving, male sperm for fertilization, which swims to the ovule or egg cell, gymnosperms and angiosperms use pollen containing the male cell for fertilization. The reproductive cells in angiosperms are found in flowers and about 70% of species are hermaphrodites; the same flower contains both male and female cells, although both types may mature at different times. Others contain male and female cells either on other individuals or on other flowers.

A variety of ways are used to transfer pollen to the female stigma, but once arrived, pollen tubes germinate and form a tube that grows with astonishing accuracy and speed (e.g. 5 cm/day by effectively a single cell) through the female tissues. The male cells move inside the pollen tube and eventual targeting of the female cell by the pollen tube permits fertilization to occur initiating a process of embryogenetic development that eventually culminates in seed formation. Because the pollen tube grows internally in the female tissues, the film of water required for motile sperm movement is no longer needed. It is assumed that pollen evolved (so-called siphonogamy) as a response to the requirement for fertilization of plants in a drier climate. Alternatively, the evolutionary progenitors of both gymnosperms and angiosperms attempted to expand their habitat into the drier regions of the land surface in response to increased competition for light or root resources.

The commonest version of survival in dry conditions is perhaps exemplified by members of the grass family. Stigmas of most angiosperms contain a sticky fluid to which the transferred pollen grain adheres and these moist conditions enable pollen germination to start. The grasses, which survive in drier conditions quite happily, have a dry stigma. Germination of the pollen on dry stigmas can take place through a drop of liquid provided by the pollen cell itself, once it senses contact with the stigma. The mechanism is extraordinary. The response to sensing may give rise to lipids synthesized by either stigma or pollen, and a number have been identified. Apply these chemicals to leaves and pollen tubes will penetrate and grow through the leaf, something it cannot ordinarily do (Wolters-Arts et al. 1998).

Gymnosperms (about a thousand species altogether) are largely distinguished from angiosperms by using cones instead of flowers as the reproductive organ. They, too, are wind pollinated. Photosynthesis takes place in needles instead of true leaves, although the Ginkgoales (e.g. *Gingko biloba*) have leaf-like structures, but are still recognizably gymnosperm. Reasonable numbers of the gymnosperms are important crop plants—larches, pines, and spruces, which are quick growing trees and efficient converters (relatively speaking) of light energy into wood. Among the gymnosperms are the Giant Redwoods and Sequoiadendrons found native in California. These gymnosperms contain individuals that are both the largest living things on earth (General Sherman, the largest Sequoiadendron weighing an estimated 6000–7000 tons) and the tallest still in existence is a coast redwood (*Sequoia giganteum*) at 362 feet.

The giant redwood forests are one of the greatest, jaw-dropping, and extraordinary wonders on planet Earth that all should make an effort to see. One's first view of any of these, simply instils wonder at what the natural world can produce. These giant trees are now protected, but a number were cut down in a typically unthinking act, perhaps similar in character to the virtual elimination of the bison in North America.

The bristlecone pines contain the longest living individual trees with estimated lives at 4500–5000 years. Sometimes these records of longevity are instead claimed for Pando, known as 'The Trembling Giant', that is actually a clonal colony of Aspen (*Populus tremuloides*). In total, Pando is estimated at over 6000 tons and believed germinated over 80,000 years ago. However, a clonal colony arises by vegetative suckers and the individual trees that arise could easily be isolated and live independently. As the older ones died new suckers took over. Thus, Pando consists of a set of joined individuals, but there is no evidence yet, that these individuals are in any way dependent on each other.

Some fern communities have a similar clonal relationship and grow outwards in a circle with the original individuals dying off in the middle; rather like a large fairy ring. Some of these have been estimated at 40,000 years old. These abilities reflect a major difference with most animals; many plants can reproduce vegetatively, as well as sexually. For some higher plants like the small members of the Lemnaceae (duckweeds) that cover the surface of ponds, flowering is uncommon and most growth is by replication of individuals that separate from each other. In good conditions doubling in numbers of some duckweeds takes less than a day. Other members of the Lemnaceae, the Wolffiellas, are the smallest flowering plants known. The vegetative body of Wolffiella is about 1–2 mm across and the flower can only be seen with magnification.

The overall evolutionary trend in plants seems to be directed towards survival in drier climates. The algae largely live in water; mosses and liverworts also prefer moist habitats. Reproduction in ferns usually requires moist conditions with a film of water on the surface of a haploid organ, the prothallus, in which motile sperm swims towards the egg cell. Evolutionary convergence is described in Chapter 6.

Survival in a very dry climate is surely best exemplified by lichens, a symbiotic relationship between algal and fungal partners. These can survive in exceptional dry and harsh climates, but they pay for this capability by a low rate of growth.

The term 'plant' will also be generally used for a young dicotyledonous species

The angiosperms themselves contain about 240–270,000 species and originated 150 million to possibly 200 million years ago (Cornet 2007). The real surprise has been the rapidity of speciation, thought to be the result of direct interactions with insect pollinators and insect herbivores that were themselves undergoing rapid evolutionary change (Cornet 2007). It looks as though speciation in both organism groups was synergized by this interaction.

Very early on, an evolutionary split gave rise to progenitors that have produced, over time, two main classes. First, there are the monocotyledonous angiosperms (monocots for short) and, secondly, the dicotyledonous angiosperms (dicots). The cotyledon refers to an embryonic leaf in the seed and whether there is one or two, but there are other differences. Many monocots use bulbs or corms for vegetative propagation, and these act as a food store for the plant to grow in springtime. In some bulbs the decision to form a flower is taken either one or more years ahead of time. Many bulbs/corms produce contractile roots that are used to pull the bulb down in the soil to a pre-determined level of safety. Monocot leaves are usually parallel-veined, in contrast to dicot leaves that use a network of veins.

Veins are composed of two tissues—xylem and phloem. These are the primary cell constituents of all vascular tissue in all angiosperms. As in animals, it is the function of vascular tissues to transport necessary materials around the plant. Leaves synthesize sugars (mainly sucrose), which is needed by non-photosynthetic tissues, while roots provide water and minerals from the soil. However, many other important chemicals are transported by the vascular tissues that act as carriers of information and initiate changes in behaviour. The critical concept of information is discussed later.

There is no need these days to provide simple diagrams of plants to illustrate the main parts, the web provides all. For those who do need a reminder, simply typing 'diagrammatic pictures of plants' into Google will summon up a large number; usually these are young dicot seedlings. Dicots contain about 170,000 species of which an estimated 100,000 are trees. The dicotyledonous tree life cycle is different in behaviour to annuals; many trees have juvenile periods that can range from 2 to 30 years before flowers are produced. Cycles of flowering can often appear, sometimes occurring every other year or even longer. As I write this section, all the local mature ash trees are covered in flowers; next year there will be hardly any.

Dicot trees contain a root and a shoot, and growth takes place at the tips of both in areas called meristems, which are basically undifferentiated embryonic areas, capable of generating new cell types by differentiation after division. Shoot and root meristems are the subjects of intense investigation at the present time. Branching occurs from buds (basically a dormant meristem) in the stem, located at what are called nodes. One common method of dicot propagation requires only the grafting of a single bud onto a recipient plant, usually of the same species, but a different variety. This grafting method, for example, is used by gardeners for propagating virtually all roses. Below ground, branch roots originate from a main root and are formed *de novo* from an internal cellular tissue in the main root called the pericycle.

Increases in stem and root girth result from the activities of the cambium, another embryonic meristematic tissue that in form is like an internal skin under the stem bark or under the outer epidermis of mature roots and surrounding other internal tissues. The cambium produces new cells both to the inside and outside of itself by mitosis, that then differentiate further. The inner cells form the xylem, a word derived from the Greek for wood. Xylem cells eventually become lignified then die, providing essential support tissues as the plant increases in height. The tubular structure of xylem acts as a conduit for active water and mineral translocation up the stem and branches to the leaves and other growth points. The differentiation process and, thus, the life cycle of xylem cells is an excellent example of programmed cell death, a process called apoptosis.

The second important tissue produced on the outer ring from cambial differentiation is the phloem (from the Greek for bark), the tissue that is involved in the transport of sugars and other chemicals. The main phloem cells are anucleate.

The mitotic activity of the cambium in trees is based on an annual cycle and it is the xylem cells that differ in characteristics of size through the season that give rise to the characteristic rings seen in transverse sections of the cut trunk of dicot trees. Since the activity of the cambium is a sensitive indicator of the growth conditions each year, the thickness of individual tree rings acts as a potential proxy of the experienced climate for that year. Since cambial activities are part of the process of development, everything that modifies development, including mineral access, rainfall, general weather, light conditions, predation, and disease affect the size of the ring, as well as temperature. Temperature might be only a weak contributor as described in Chapter 12.

The science of tree rings is called dendrochronology and can be used not only to check carbon dating methods to at least 10,000 years past. It has, of course, been used to measure the length of life of old trees. By this means, we know that giant redwoods and Sequoidendrons in California are several thousand years old.

The oldest trees in Europe are generally considered to be slow growing yews (*Taxus* species) and some have been identified as at least 3000 years old. The Fortingall yew in Scotland was measured by Linnaeus as having a girth of 16 m, but is now sadly decayed and partly vandalized. There is a drawing of the signing of the Magna Carta in 1215 at Runnymede under a yew tree. Recent photographs indicate the tree is still there and looks very similar to its drawing eight centuries ago.

As needed, other anatomical and tissue characteristics will be introduced in the text. It is dicot species that I will generally refer to in discussing behaviour and intelligence.

The monocots have only some 60,000 species, monocot tree species are rare, the most well-known being the palms, although large bamboos, at about 20 m high, could be regarded as trees. However, many monocots grow initially from the base of the shoot, either they grow from a bulb or, like grasses, grow from a basal meristem. Vascular elements are distributed through the stem, whereas in dicots they form a ring. Shoot branches are often called tillers and the root characteristics are fibrous, with many numerous branch roots that stabilize surface soil. In other long-lived monocots, like bamboos, growth takes places at the nodes in a less distinct fashion than dicots. Monocots lack cambium, and it is expansion and growth of cells throughout the trunk that enables lateral expansion to occur. The grass family (Gramineae) are the most well-known group of monocots because members of them (e.g. wheat, maize, rice, oats, etc.) act as staple foodstuffs.

Is a dicot really representative of the plant kingdom?

Having chosen a dicot as representative of a plant, it is now necessary to provide adequate justification. Most readers, when asked to name a specific representative animal, will probably say a dog or a cat, perhaps even a horse. There are only a few thousand species of mammals that, incidentally, did evolve at about the same time as angiosperms, but one of the least likely to be chosen will be an insect. By both species and numbers, insects are far and away the commonest animals (Hull 1988). There are probably at least 10 million insect species, of which only about a million have been classified. As for numbers, a single large locust swarm can contain nearly 10 billion individuals, more than the present human population—and locusts are large insects. How many aphids, small flies, or mosquitoes? Hull (1988) directs attention to the problems that arise from such biases in attempting to describe general biological attributes using only single organism examples.

In part, our choice of specimens of animal life is anthropic, biased by our own common-sense familiarity, rather than really trying to choose something meaningfully representative. It is difficult to emote with an insect, particularly those like mosquitoes that create annoyance or disease—we are indifferent to the fate of a fly in a web in a way that we would not be with a mammal in a gin trap. Quite simply insects (like plants) are not warm and cuddly; they do not respond to us as do our domesticated pets. However, that common sense approach is fraught with problems because it can mean ascribing properties and behaviour to our representative organism that, in reality, is not shared by any specific type.

If I use the term organism, in how many cases do prokaryotes, such as bacteria spring to mind? However, in numbers of individuals, species, and environments currently inhabited, bacteria undoubtedly reign supreme. They are found everywhere on the planet, in soils, in the air, in the oceans, on the surfaces on our own skin, and in all kinds of extreme environments, even in deep rock (Zhang et al. 2005; Rothschild and Mancinelli 2001). Probably, in terms of numbers that have ever existed, blue-green alga almost certainly can claim that title (Hull 1988). Yet it is doubtful if 99% of biologists could name one blue-green alga or even know its significance to their own existence, but those common (mis)conceptions bias the way we think about biology.

However, we are on somewhat surer ground in using an angiosperm plant as representative.

Compared with the 270,000 angiosperm species, ferns, liverworts and mosses, and algae, respectively, have only 12,000, 15,000, and 40,000 extant species in total. Most algal species are aquatic. Brown kelp (Macrocystis), a good example, can be extremely large, 50–60 m long has been recorded, with growth rates of 30 cm/day, although bamboo at 100 cm/day easily outperforms this speedy plant. Unicellular plants, some of which are motile, are only found in the algae. However, algal unicell activity cannot be ignored. The earth's annual primary photosynthetic productivity, i.e. the carbon dioxide fixed in excess to plant respiration is about 100 billion tons. Of this enormous amount, about half results from photosynthetic behaviour of single-celled, phytoplankton in the oceans. Very little is really known of these organisms, and any study of their natural behaviour is, to all intents and purposes, absent.

However, if we accept that the behaviour of a more interesting kind is to be found in multicellular plants, then choosing an angiosperm as representative is at least reasonable from the species numbers. However, the variety of structural morphological variation makes any complete summary of an angiosperm difficult. There are angiosperm plants, for example, that have no roots (Tillandsia, Wolffiella). There are others that have no vegetative stem (e.g. Streptocarpus) and quite a large number that have no leaves (numerous cacti); there are others that do not photosynthesize (parasitical plants, e.g. dodder) and some that hardly ever flower (Lemnaceae, duckweeds).

Dicots have the largest numbers of species, although it is likely that many more monocot individuals exist given the widespread occurrence of prairies and pampas dominated by various grasses. Arable farming covers about the 10% of the earth's land surface and another 20% is used for rough grazing and much of these are, again, covered by the grass family members. Be that as it may, most research is performed on dicot plants and their behaviour is more distinctive.

Because many dicots are temperate trees, they are more familiar to the reader as well, but in using dicots as the basic 'plant' designation, it must be admitted that bias of some kind can come into the discussion of behaviour—while some properties will be shared by monocots, others will not. The monocot lifestyle presumably arose through occupation of climatic areas in which either grazing was common or hurricanes a fact of life. Monocots lack secondary wood that limits the potential for generating trees. That says something about environmental conditions when the first monocot evolved.

Domestication can also mislead about plant behaviour

Another problem that emerges is that our plant may be a domesticated species. This is a complication often not recognized. Domestication involves selection of individual wild plants for breeding out of potential millions of wild progenitors, all of which are/were individual in genotype and behaviour, and distinguishable from each other. Inevitably, such domesticated plants exhibit a much lower degree of variation than the wild population. The selection of particular individuals was made because they had particular desirable characteristics that met human requirements either for crop yield, disease resistance, or decoration. Domestication has also involved elimination of some undesirable behaviours, such as photoperiodism (control of development through day length recognition) or vernalization (cold treatment required for induction of flowering).

Although the phenotype of a domesticated species may look superficially similar to its wild relatives, the phenotype is much more robust to change than genotypic variation might suggest. Domestication therefore involves a narrowing of perspective and without constant reiteration may mislead if too much conceptual dependence is placed on the behaviour of domesticated lines. As far as possible, the subject of this book deals with the more variable behaviour of non-domesticated 'wild' populations. Consequently, much of the literature in this text will refer to articles in ecological journals because ecologists are much more focused on the importance of natural selection and evolution of which behaviour is a crucial part.

References

Bateson, G. (1972). *Steps to an ecology of mind*. Chandler Publishing Company, New York.

Beer, S. (1972). *Brain of the firm*. Allen Lane the Penguin Press, London.

Bertalanffy, L., von (1971). *General system theory*. Allen Lane, London.

Cornet, B. (2007). When did angiosperms first evolve? Available at: www.sunstar-solutions.com/sunstar/Why02/why2.htm.

Forrester, J. (1961). *Industrial dynamics*. MIT Press, Cambridge.

Hull, D.L. (1988). Interactors versus vehicles. In Plotkin, H.C., ed. *The role of behaviour in evolution*, pp. 18–50. MIT Press, Cambridge, MA.

Kacser, H. and Burns, J.A. (1973). The control of flux. *Symposium of the Society of Experimental Biology and Medicine*, **27**, 65–104.

Keller, E.F. (1983). *A feeling for the organism*. The life and work of Barbara McClintock. W.H. Freeman and Company, New York.

McClintock, B. (1984). The significance of responses of the genome to challenge. *Science*, **226**, 792–801.

Patten, B.C. (1971) *Systems analysis and simulation in ecology*. Academic Press, New York.

Rothschild, L.J., and Mancinelli, R.L. (2001). Life in extreme environments. *Nature*, **409**, 1092–1101.

Trewavas, A. (1981). How do plant growth substances work. *Plant Cell and Environment*, **4**, 203–228.

Trewavas, A.J. (1986). Understanding the control of development and the role of growth substances. *Australian Journal of Plant Physiology*, **13**, 447–457.

Trewavas, A.J. (1999). Le calcium c'est la vie; calcium makes waves. *Plant Physiology*, **120**, 1–6.

Trewavas, A. (2002). Mindless mastery. *Nature*, **415**, 841.

Trewavas, A.J. (2003). Aspects of plant intelligence. *Annals of Botany*, **92**, 1–20.

Waddington, C.H. (1977). *Tools for thought*. Paladin, St Albans.

Weiss, P.A. (1973). *The Science of Life*. Futura Publishing Company, New York.

Wolters-Arts, M., Lush, W.M., and Mariani, C. (1988). Lipids are required for directional pollen-tube growth. *Nature*, **392**, 818–821.

Zhang, G., Dong, H., Xu, Z., Zhao, D., and Zhang, C. (2005). Microbial diversity in ultra-high-pressure rocks and fluids from the Chinese continental scientific drilling project in China. *Applied and Environmental Microbiology*, **71**, 3213–3227.

CHAPTER 2

Plant behaviour foundations

Intelligence is based on how efficient a species becomes at doing the things they need to survive.

(Darwin 1871)

⊃ Summary

This chapter provides for a very brief introduction to some aspects of plant behaviour, but more particularly the reasons for its common neglect and general failure to recognize it. Plant behaviour is very different to animal behaviour, but is easy to recognize as indicated by McClintock. The substantial early roles of Darwin and Pfeffer in recognizing and reporting plant behaviour are highlighted. In particular, Pfeffer correctly identified the obvious lack of movement now revealed to be present by time-lapse photography. Sachs described plant behaviour as purposeful. Darwin's role in demonstrating the transmission of information and, thus, coordinating responses is described, including the first demonstration of the involvement of memory in plant behaviour. The problems in recognizing plant behaviour result from using subjective human criteria for behaviour, rather than recognizing that plants behave, but in ways that are unfamiliar, because of slowness and also because, below ground, it cannot easily be seen. Plants have the same biological criteria for survival as animals—the need to obtain food, to see off competitors, deal with pests and disease, and access mates. The earliest description of plant intelligence recognized its inextricable link to fitness. Behaviour is essential to fitness. The contribution of Bose to understanding rapid plant movements is indicated and some brief outline of the mechanisms involved described.

Plant behaviour is unlike animal behaviour

Simple observation indicates the difference in animal and plant behaviour. Plant do not appear to do anything, or at least nothing obvious, and that in itself creates its own difficulties for defining what it is. An old expression *'saxa crescunt, plantae crescunt et vivunt; animalia crescunt, vivunt et sentient'* perhaps indicates the general attitude. Roughly, 'Rocks grow; plants grow and are alive; while animals grow, live and feel or think'.

To many biologists and many members of the public, the notion that plants actually have behaviour is entirely foreign. The term 'vegetable', commonly used to describe brain-dead human beings, perhaps exemplifies the public attitude. Vegetables lack any semblance of behaviour or intelligence. The words 'a carrot' was a comment thrown at me by one animal scientist when I was talking at one meeting about potential intelligent behaviour in plants. The implication again was that a vegetable organ, the root, domesticated in this case for human consumption, does not appear to do anything except be boiled and end up on a plate. One can question whether a domesticated, edible vegetable root is really representative of plant behaviour, just as one can question whether fat or muscle cells are representative of the behaviour of the domesticated cow. Carrots and cows are also kept in relatively controlled conditions that, again, remove the need for much behaviour that characterizes the wild equivalent. We control them to provide food for us, but they do not have to fight for the food that we give them.

Barbara McClintock's take on the difference between animal and plant behaviour is striking. 'Animals can walk around but plants have to stay still to do the same things with ingenious mechanisms—plants are extraordinary'. 'These organisms are beyond our wildest expectations'. 'There is no question that plants have all kinds of sensitivities-they do a lot of responding to their environment' (Keller, 1983, p. 199-200 quoting McClintock).

Most people's experience of corn plants, McClintock's favourite plant, is either passing fields of serried ranks of rather daunting 2-m high plants, or as the rather delightful and tasty yellow seeds on their dinner plate or as 'corn-on-the-cob'. Unfortunately, perhaps, corn doesn't run around, purr, bark, have a nice furry coat, or any of the other characteristics of animals that attract most students and most biologists to animal areas of study. Nor does corn double its number every 20 min, like *Escherichia coli*, a bacterium that lives normally in the human gut. Under the microscope *E. coli* can be observed to swim in a meaningful way towards food and away from danger. It is the speed of movement that impresses; something is happening, at least from a human perspective, and that means a problem for scientists to examine and uncover. Behaviour of that kind attracts many others into microbial research.

Charles Darwin wrote the first book on plant behaviour

Charles Darwin published some 25 books altogether. His most well-known text—*The Origin of Species by means of Natural Selection*—has been read, reread, and republished many times since its first issue in 1859. It is, of course, a direct antidote to the anthropomorphic view espoused in the biblical Genesis of mankind having dominion over every living thing, including 'every herb bearing seed . . . and every tree', and being some special sort of creation by a rather obviously anthropomorphized and often punitive God. A good first edition copy of Darwin's *Origin* can make the owner richer by £100,000 when sold, but if we discard the 10 books Darwin published on his long voyage to South America, the majority of his remaining books are on plants, not animals. While many biologists will have read the *Origin of Species*, how many will have read Darwin's botanical texts?

Darwin moved comfortably between animals and plants. Perhaps the paucity of knowledge at the time enabled polymaths to be reasonably common, but the present day sees enormous specialism, and one of those divisions is between those who work on higher animals and those who work on higher plants. There is little contact, unfortunately, between the two, although I find plant scientists are sometimes more aware of animal research than the other way round.

Many of Darwin's plant books were collections of his own experimental observations. Others were enormous collations of important information gained from a variety of sometimes obscure sources. *The Variation of Animals and Plants under Domestication* in two volumes published in 1875 is one such. Its immense value is that it refers to information on plants much of which is probably no longer available. Darwin's concern in these two volumes was to establish that domesticated species could exhibit much greater variation than those in the wild because of a lack of natural selection and competition. Of course, there was also artificial breeding of characteristics, which would never survive in wild circumstances. To this can be added the fact that domesticated species live in environments in which there is effectively no predation and disease is controlled. Using domesticated plants and controlled experimental circumstances is very likely to mislead over the potential for plant behavioural responses.

Darwin was also a patient, perceptive observer. He was well aware of the fact that plants moved and his *The Power of Movements of Plants*, published in 1880 and assisted by his son Francis, in 570 pages details numerous examples of stem movement in many plant species, and how these are modified by environmental challenges or signals. Darwin also demonstrated that shoot movements were often the result of transmission of a stimulus from sensory to motor tissues. He further made remarkably accurate observations on root movements in response to soil signals.

In the nineteenth and early twentieth centuries, plant biologists were inevitably much closer to the natural world. Controlled growth facilities were rare, and Darwin was very keen to try and establish general principles by using a huge variety of plants. Again, this would be frowned on now, with the current molecular genetic emphasis on the single *Arabidopsis* species.

The benefit of using *Arabidopsis* is the extremely rapid life cycle. The developmental programme that takes a seed through to its offspring seeds can be accomplished within 6–7 weeks. There are a few *Brassica* species that are even quicker. *Arabidopsis* is normally regarded as a weed, but in ecological terms, it is a pioneer. The plant is geared to occupy newly exposed bare soil, such as occurs in a forest when a mature tree falls. The life cycle is thus constructed to ensure maximum seed production before other taller annuals and biennials overgrow it. While recognizing the value of getting large numbers of plant scientists to concentrate on a single plant species, it has narrowed perception of the potential range of different plant behaviours.

Plant behaviour is purposeful

Purposeful behaviour is best seen when it is goal directed. Purposeful plant behaviour was recognized by another giant of Plant Physiology, Julius von Sachs. I quote:

I have had repeatedly had cause to refer to certain resemblances between the phenomena of irritability (i.e. response to external signals) in the vegetable kingdom and those of the animal body.

If then irritability is the reaction of the organs to the outside world, it follows thence that the phenomena of irritability both in the vegetable and animal world must be full of purpose. All those adaptations in the organism are purposeful which contribute to its maintenance and insure its existence. (Sachs 1887, p. 600).

Purposeful behaviour as goal-directed behaviour is discussed in Trewavas (2009) and many examples are described in this book.

Pfeffer identified the problem that obscures recognition of plant behaviour

The real problem of recognizing plant behaviour has been known for more than a century. Professor Wilhelm Pfeffer of Leipzig was one of the 'giants' of plant biology in the nineteenth century. He shared that standing with Charles Darwin and Julius von Sachs. In the late nineteenth and early twentieth century, German plant physiology was highly creative and progressive. Goebel, Haberlandt, Warburg (the Warburg manometer), and Meyerhof (the Embden–Meyerhof glycolytic pathway) were all plant scientists of enormous stature, who contributed hugely to knowledge. Books written by some of them were overflowing with information gained solely from their own investigations.

Pfeffer's contribution was a three-volume series on Plant Physiology, only translated into English in 1906. Volume 3 is nearly all about plant movements. Again, much of this section of his third volume summarized a wealth of information on many kinds of plants that I have not seen elsewhere. Wilhelm Pfeffer, like Charles Darwin, also investigated numerous different species of plants.

I quote from volume 3, p. 2 of Pfeffer.

The fact that in large plants the power of growth and movement are not strikingly evident has caused plants to be popularly regarded as 'still life'. Hence the rapid movements of *Mimosa pudica* were regarded as extraordinary for a plant.

Among plants it is only in small organisms that active locomotion is possible. A freely motile plant may travel towards a source of illumination, whereas a rooted plant responds in a less degree by growing and curving toward the illuminated side. In spite of the difference, the actual perception and stimulation may be identical in the two cases.

It was known at the time that some single-celled plants like *Euglena* and *Chlamydomonas* were capable of rapid movement; thus, the reference in the quote to 'motile plants' and to the necessity for magnification.

While Pfeffer was at Leipzig, he authored an article that suggested taking photographs at defined time intervals and then running them together as film. The quotation from Pfeffer (1906, p. 2) continues, 'If mankind from youth upwards were accustomed to view nature under a magnification of 100–1000 times or to perceive the activities of weeks and months performed in a minute, as is possible by the aid of a cinematograph, this erroneous idea would be entirely dispelled.' Such procedures were exceedingly difficult at the time and they were never carried out to the best of my knowledge. However, clearly, Pfeffer was presaging the 'recent' time-lapse photography that could be used to counter the 'still life' perception of plants by many of the public.

Time-lapse photography has opened a new world for plant behaviour studies

Time-lapse photography has enabled the speeding up of plant movements, bringing them into a time frame familiar to us. There are several that are easily available to the reader. There are some very interesting time-lapse observations to be found in part 1 of David Attenborough's, (1995) *Private Life of Plants* dvd series. The more recent series entitled 'Life', again from the BBC, devoted section 9 to plants (Attenborough 2009). The Internet, of course, has also helped, and the web site constructed by Roger Hangartner (2000) contains many interesting examples, unfortunately all of laboratory grown plants, but these films do reveal some quite extraordinary behaviour in certain instances.

The first identification of transmission of information in plants by Darwin

Darwin's experiments were conducted mainly in his front room at Down House, Kent, UK; less variable than the environment experienced outside by wild plants, but still not, in any way, meaningfully controlled. Much of Darwin's *The Power of Movement of Plants* is concerned with describing circumnutation in the shoots of numerous species. He was also interested in why young seedling shoots bend towards the light (phototropism) and why young seedling roots bent towards a gravity stimulus (gravitropism). His most interesting experiments used canary grass seedlings and a tissue that became extremely popular in the 1930s to 1960s—the coleoptile. There are many thousands of papers on this one tissue.

The coleoptile is a hollow, living sheath of cells that covers and protects the first pair of leaves in grass seedlings. It is part of a programme of development that occurs in darkness when some monocot seeds, particularly grasses, are buried in the soil and, thereafter, commence germination. The coleoptile, a product of this etiolation schedule, is serviced by only two vascular bundles. The coleoptile also exhibits the basic tropic responses to gravity (if placed on its side) by regaining the vertical orientation. Unilateral light from one side causes phototropic bending. The coleoptile has a limited life span. In natural conditions and once well above the soil, the coleoptile senses the light condition and simply ceases growth, allowing the first primary leaves to break through, expand, and commence photosynthesis.

Darwin's most memorable experiments concerned phototropism. Where, Darwin asked himself, were the cells located that sensed this unequal light distribution? Simple marking methods with Indian ink indicated that bending occurred in regions below the tip, was it these cells here that sensed phototropically active light? To answer this question, Darwin constructed very tiny caps from very thin sheet metal and placed these on the coleoptile tip. The sensitivity to a unilateral light source all but disappeared. Thus, was born the idea that the tip produced a substance that, when transported downwards, perhaps unequally, caused the coleoptile to bend.

Darwin performed many similar kinds of experiments on roots; removal of the tip prevented the familiar response to gravity. Although he was not the first to demonstrate that removal of the tip prevented the response to gravity, his extensive experiments led him to write a whole chapter, chapter 11, in his *The Power of Movements of Plants* that highlighted the transmission of stimuli in plants.

The transport of information identified by Darwin was really the first demonstration of a hormone in any organism

Phytohormones, written by Went and Thimann (1937), is a plant physiology classic. The observations initiated by Darwin had eventually given rise to the identification of the plant hormone, auxin, in the early 1930s. Within 6–7 years, virtually all the major physiology of auxin effects had been investigated and this book describes them, but more notable is the title of the book as 'Phytohormones' following what was, by then, the well-established field of animal hormones. The first identification of hormones as chemical messengers, having an effect remote from the site of synthesis, is generally attributed to Starling and Bayliss in 1905, but it was really Darwin, 25 years earlier, who established the potential of chemical communication and, thus, the hormone concept; but he did so in plants. This is not the first time that discoveries in plants remain unknown and uncredited!

Of the discoveries about auxin in the 1930s the most crucial was the demonstration that much auxin movement in plants is polar. This process takes place in cells outside the vascular tissue. Conjugates of auxin can be found in the vascular system as well. In a growing plant, biosynthesis of auxin is thought to be mainly located in young shoots and leaves, particularly in the developing vascular tissue, and is preferentially transported downwards. Much early investigation used the coleoptile to investigate the phenomenon and identified polar movement as being active secretion from the basal regions of cells, rather than passive movement. In developmental terms, plants are characteristically polar, stems are often vertically growing tubes, leaves are flat-bladed structures, for example. The polar movement of auxin is inextricably linked with this pronounced morphological polarity and can be expected to contribute to it.

Darwin's indication of memory in plant responses

Darwin also reported a clear instance of plant memory to a unidirectional light source. 'We found that if seedlings kept in a dark place were laterally illuminated by a small wax taper for only two or three minutes at intervals at about three quarters of an hour, they all become bowed to the point where the taper had been'. He concluded that 'In several of the above respects light seems to act on the tissues of plants in the same manner as it does on the nervous system of animals' (Darwin 1880, p. 566).

In stark contrast to the assumption that plant behaviour is akin to an unmoving 'vegetable' attitude, Darwin also continued 'the habit of moving at certain periods is inherited by both plants and animals; But the most striking resemblance is the localization of sensitiveness and the transmission of an influence from the excited part to another which consequently moves' (Darwin 1880, p. 572).

Tropic responses investigated by Darwin are described as intelligent behaviour

'In tropistic movements, plants appear to exhibit a sort of intelligence; their movement is of subsequent advantage to them' (Went and Thimann 1937, p. 151). This statement indicates the first recognition that fitness in plants is inextricably linked with intelligence and will recur later in this book.

Anthropomorphic thinking prevents recognition of plant behaviour

The problem with recognizing plant behaviour, as Pfeffer clearly indicated above, is one that will be met again when considering intelligence; it is anthropic or anthropomorphic suppositions. It is a common error to impose human expectations and restrictions on the behaviour of other organisms. As human beings, we identify visible movement with behaviour because that is how we recognize human behaviour. If it does not appear to move, then it is not behaving. The problem of anthropomorphic attitudes was supposed to have been eliminated centuries ago from science, but it is very difficult to disentangle in this area of work. Many scientists, through lack of knowledge commonly adopt public (i.e. unqualified) attitudes to behaviour and intelligence, and to these capabilities in plants.

When asked what biological behaviour actually is, the common answer will surely be made from our own perspective—'well it's . . . running, jumping, eating, throwing and so on'. The basic element is surely meaningful movement that we can see and understand the reason for. When animals are observed to move with meaningful intent, a lion racing after a zebra for example, that's behaviour, too. 'Meaningful intent' may be difficult to establish in wild organisms other than ourselves, but if any movement is genuinely pointless, then hard-won food, converted to energy, is wasted and the probable consequence will be a loss of fitness.

Fitness is crucial to an appreciation of plant behaviour

Even activity that initially seems pointless can usually be identified as part of a relentless search for food and in competitive circumstances, an abundance may be absent by definition. The ability to acquire substantial food is central to that biological goal. The problem is lack of recognition of the extent to which fitness governs all forms of behaviour, in particular, our own lack of fitness requirements in present day behaviour. For human beings, a weekly visit to a supermarket is all that is needed to get food. Fitness in large numbers of human beings, if it exists at all, no longer shares the behavioural drivers that move most other organisms on the planet; that is why we should not judge animal behaviour by our own standards. Since intelligence is an aspect of behaviour, the same argument holds.

However, plants are not immune to the requirement to gain food in competitive circumstances either and the same stipulations on fitness hold as above. What is needed is skill in acquiring more than the plant beside you and solving the problems that inevitably derive from that situation; that skill is, of course, intelligent behaviour. By the same token, it is unlikely that plant behaviour is pointless given the waste of resources that would result, even though it may not be obvious to us why plants are doing what they are doing.

The selective constraints of striving for ultimate fitness are just as real and just as important

The only situations in which the criterion, requiring 'meaningful intent', no longer applies are those in which food is abundantly provided. This situation is not uncommon for domesticated organisms and animals maintained in zoos or plants in greenhouses, laboratories, or gardens. This is one of the reasons that this book concentrates on the behaviour of wild plants and regards laboratory-gained observations with a grain of scepticism.

Subjective judgements about behaviour are always difficult to untangle

If movement is the criterion we like to employ to characterize behaviour then there is, of course, another subjective judgement to be avoided. We are limited by our own senses and many movements take place outside our simple ability to see them. We cannot see a bullet move with the naked eye—it is 'far too fast'—or the stars or planets move in the sky—'too slow'. Even the movement of the moon is difficult, but these latter events are actually 'running' at very substantial speeds. The moon moves around the earth at 2000 miles/hr, for example, about twice the speed of a bullet. A film runs at 50 frames/sec, but looks continuous; the individual frames are certainly not usually visible. The retinal image lasts about a tenth of a second and numerous vibratory movements are used to prevent retinal adaptation within this time frame. In addition, the brain compares a previous image with the present and predicts a future one, as well in assessing movement, thus providing continuity in vision. If, however, the movement within a second is very small relative to surrounding still objects, let us say 0.05 mm, our eyes will simply not be able to see it either. We then need a method of marking the position at time intervals to identify movement, even though, in several hours, this movement will have carried the object 18 cm (nearly 8 inches). In other words a judgement on behaviour, based on what we can see moving, is entirely suspect and needs to be discarded. Great oaks from little acorns grow—it may be difficult to see the changes day by day, but the final result is surely impressive.

Various plant organs, tendrils, stems, and roots certainly move position, often using forms and varieties of what is called circumnutation. Darwin (1880) in his book on plant movements recorded large numbers of these movements in shoots by the simple expedient of patiently marking the position on a glass plate held flat above the plant, at relatively frequent intervals. Many of these nutatory movements, Darwin observed, could move at a relatively fast 10–20 cm/hr. Again, this is just too slow for us to see with the naked eye.

The fastest growing plant, a bamboo, is often quoted as extending its height at a m/day, about

0.01 mm/sec on average. However, extension growth is usually confined to only a few hours a day and is controlled by circadian rhythms. During the actual period of growth, it might be 10 times faster. Impressive though this rate of growth actually is and probably only achievable in a steamy hot tropical jungle, it is still too slow for cursory observation. The simple fact is that fast movements relative to our timescale are not requirements of a successful plant lifestyle, but plants do move!

Because we are animals, too, it is easy to judge and observe animal behaviour

Because most animals move commensurate with our rate of movement, their behaviour in the wild is relatively easy to observe, although perhaps sometimes difficult to interpret. However, the behaviour can be recorded with little more than a pencil and paper or camera. It is easy to see a zebra running away from a lion and to make deductions about the behaviour, the sensing of threat, the need to assuage hunger by the predator and the desire not to be Sunday lunch by the prey. We can build in ideas about the evolution of such behaviours, about natural selection, the behaviourally weakest going to the wall and being weeded out. We can also make potential deductions about the ease with which such animals might be domesticated.

The speed of much animal behaviour results, in part, from the speed of action potentials through the nervous system. The speed is about 100 m/sec for large axons. Thus, most animals that use nervous systems for communication will operate their movement on a timescale familiar to ourselves because we also use a nervous system and equivalent action potentials to coordinate body activities and brain function.

Plants have no defined nervous system. The previously mentioned few plants that exhibit visible movement, such as *Mimosa pudica* or the Venus flytrap (*Dionea*), do actually use 'action potentials', sudden drops on membrane potential, and similar to action potentials in nerves. In plants, the action potential is used to provide for information flow from a point of stimulation to a point of response. However, the conducting tissue is thought to be part of the vascular system (the phloem) and the speed of 'action potential' movement may be much slower than the typical nerve axon.

Most plants do not show obvious movement and its slowness from our perspective has serious consequences for its assessment. Most plant behaviour cannot usually be seen without some special investigation and, therefore, much plant behaviour in the wild will have passed unnoticed and unrecorded. Add to that the difficulty that half of plant behaviour is in the root system underground, and thus, also unseen, and the reader might start to appreciate why plants are often regarded as not behaving at all. There is certainly room for the critically perceptive amateur to make a contribution here by observing what does happen over longer timescales to wild plants if they are frequent visitors to the countryside.

The world of biology is not constructed to enable any biologist to make rash judgements and simplification of behaviour based solely on a poverty of knowledge about all its splendid variety. Unfortunately many do.

Plants that exhibit fast movements: the contribution of J. C. Bose

Some insectivorous plants exhibit movements

Obvious, visible movement on our timescale does occur with some plants. There is the popular Venus fly trap (*Dionea*) that catches flies or other small insects. There are two hairs inside the fly trap leaf; provided these are both touched within a short 10–20-sec period, the trap then rapidly closes. The stimulus results in the movement of an action potential to motor cells that initiate trap closure through extremely rapid changes in turgor pressure. *Dionea* lives naturally in peat bogs, which are horrendously infertile, with little or no free nitrate. The captured insects die, or are anaesthetized and slowly digested. The juice is then absorbed to provide much sought-after nitrogen, enabling the plant to synthesize its own proteins. It is this rather gruesome aspect of the fly trap that appeals to so many. It is perhaps rather like some spiders. Tarantulas (I kept one for 6 years) kill their prey and then cover it with digestive juices. After several hours they simply suck up the juice and discard what is left. *Dionea* fortunately does not have the sudden movements and eight hairy legs of the Arachnid kingdom. Charles Darwin's 1875 book on *Insectivorous Plants* sold faster and better than his *Origin of Species by means of Natural Selection* (1859). The fascination with the macabre crosses generations.

There are other well-known insectivorous plants, such as the sundew and pitcher plants, the latter having an elaborate structure that causes the unwary insect to slip into the pitcher's fluid where, again, death is slow and so is digestion. The slipperiness of the surface on the top inclination of the pitcher varies in intensity and sometimes in circadian fashion. This is accomplished by the production of nectar that attracts water onto the slope's waxy surface and causes the doomed insect or even small amphibian to skid into the pitcher solution by repelling oily claws or feet. It has provided the inspiration for the development of an unusual liquid repellent surface (Wong et al. 2011).

Another popular 'moving' plant is the touch-sensitive *Mimosa pudica*. The leaves are compound, containing many leaflets. When a suitable touch stimulus is administered, the leaflets close on each other and usually do so in sequence from the point of stimulation. The sequential transmission of information, the result of movement of an action potential, leads to an obvious collapse that follows very shortly after the perceived signal. Action potentials transmit information along the long dendrites of nerve cells and the mechanism in *Mimosa* is similar, but not identical to these. If the stimulus is more vigorous, then the whole leaf droops substantially and takes some 30–45 min to recover if no further stimulus is received. The reasons for this kind of behaviour are not clear, but are surely to do with fitness.

It was Sir J. Chunder Bose (1858–1937), a remarkable Indian physicist and biologist, who first investigated in detail the electrical properties that underpin signalling in *Mimosa*. His contributions are little known, but Bose was one of those early, superb scientists that with almost no facilities to hand, constructed equipment that produced a wealth of scientific information far ahead of his times. Bose was Cambridge educated and, as a physicist, patented the first solid-state semiconductor diode. He constructed elegant equipment for generating

microwaves and developed the first use of a semi-conducting crystal to detect radio waves, thus anticipating the existence of p- and n-type semi-conductors, the basis of the transistor. All of these discoveries impressed the leading physicists of the time and they were all published in the *Proceedings of the Royal Society*. He was eventually elected to the Royal Society as a mark of recognition. Shepherd (2005) provides a good summary of Bose's contribution.

On his return to India, using the skill he had demonstrated in assembling physical apparatus, he constructed some superlative equipment for the measurement not only of electrical potential variation and action potentials, but of growth or leaf position changes within time periods of 0.005 sec. He constructed micro-electrode probes that could be inserted into plant tissues in 0.1-mm increments. His plant of choice was mainly *Mimosa pudica* that grew wild outside his laboratory, but he transferred the knowledge gained on this plant to many others. His results were summarized in a series of detailed books and in a later chapter, I will introduce more of his observations. Meanwhile, it is better to let Bose speak for himself. Some of his very early research was also performed in the Royal Institution, London and published in 1902. He returns in chapter 25.

My discovery of an excitatory polar action of an electrical current and its transmission to a distance proved that the conduction of excitation is fundamentally the same as that in the nerve of the animal.

Experiments are described showing that the response of isolated plant nerves is indistinguishable from that of the animal nerve throughout a long series of parallel variations of condition. (He identified correctly that the phloem acted as the tissue transmitting action potentials).

In *Mimosa* the velocity of nervous impulses in thin petioles is as high as 400 mm per second. (All taken from Bose 1926.)

It has been shown finally that there is no physiological response given by the most highly organised animal tissue that is not also to be met within the plant. This was proved in detail in the case of the identical polar effects induced in both by electrical currents; in the possibility of detecting the excitatory wave to a distance; in the possibility of detecting the excitatory wave in transit and measuring its rate; and in the appropriate modification of its velocity by different agencies even in the case of ordinary plants; in the passing of multiple into autonomous response in vegetable tissues; in the light thrown by this phenomenon on the causes of rhythmicity in animal tissues; in the similar effects of drugs on animal and plant tissues and in the modification introduced into these effects by the factor of individual 'constitution'. (Bose 1906, Preface)

It can only be by virtue of a system of nerves that the plant constitutes a single organised whole, each of whose parts is affected by every influence that falls on any other. (Bose 1926, p. 121)

Bose considered that plants had a nervous system, but no nerves or neurones, and he demonstrated both learning and memory in this system and regarded plants as intelligent organisms. Finally, Bose did not believe in commercialization, ownership, or patenting of scientific ideas, something I am in very broad agreement with.

Despite his extensive studies, Bose received little or no mention in western texts; the time was not right, so far as I can deduce, for what Bose had to offer. Plants, it was assumed, really did not do anything and *Mimosa* was an oddity that few scientists ever came across. However, the consequence is that present-day plant biologists are remarkably ignorant of his enormous investigations. A further difficulty was that Bose worked in effective isolation from the mainstream of scientists and at a time when transmission of information was still extremely slow.

Development of hormonal concepts side-lined Bose's contribution

In the early 1930s, the discovery of auxin changed the direction of botanical and agricultural research. It is much easier to experimentally manipulate plants by adding chemicals than by manipulating them electrically. There was also great agricultural interest and money to be gained in isolating chemicals that could be used by farmers to manipulate and increase crop growth and yield.

The isolation of auxin quickly gave rise to the development of the first useful herbicides. Even so, a quote from Went and Thimann perhaps indicates that they had read Bose too. They certainly reference one of his books, but that is almost the only reference I can find. 'However in tropistic movements, plants appear to exhibit a sort of intelligence; their movement is of subsequent advantage to them' (Went and Thimann 1937, p. 151). That rather important statement has been missed by so many, which is why I repeat it. For the first time, perhaps, plant behaviour was placed in the context of fitness and natural selection, as with all organisms. Major plant research directions continued with the concept of plant hormones and control of behaviour until the present; Bose and action potentials received only occasional interest. It is, however, an area that now needs investigation with modern approaches and with more advanced understanding that is different to when Bose contributed. Fortunately, that is now beginning to change with evidence that relates herbivore defence being initiated by electrical signalling, something that will be described later in this book.

Modern interpretation suggests that action potentials cause changes in cytoplasmic calcium. Thus, many of the phenomena that Bose described are now known to be mediated by changes in cytoplasmic calcium.

Many plants use tissue movements

Leaf and petal movements of many plants are not uncommon on the approach of dusk. About half the plants in my garden produce flowers that certainly close their petals around the central part of the flower at night. Clover, again common in my lawn, closes its leaflets either with bright light or at night. This is quite definitely a phenomenon related to light exposure and day/night variation in sunlight. These kinds of common movements gained a very early description as sleep movements of plants, but they must represent an aspect of fitness too.

These movements are controlled by a discrete set of motor cells. These cells have the capability to change turgor pressure very rapidly. Turgor pressure in plant cells is maintained by the presence of potassium chloride at a concentration of about 0.3 M. The simple analogy is a balloon whose expanded shape is determined by the differential air pressure inside and outside the balloon skin. Similarly, the plant cell maintains its shape within the constraints of the wall, by the differential osmotic pressure inside the cell as against that outside. To lose turgor rapidly, requires an enormous rate of flow of potassium and chloride ions out from the cell into the wall compartment and it can be initiated by action potentials and other means of changing the cell membrane potential. The motor cells contain proteins in their outer plasma membrane (potassium and chloride channels) that act as conduits for these ions. To re-establish turgor pressure, requires the active pumping using cellular energy of these ions back into the cell.

The ecological reason for such sleep movements being widespread may be to reduce frost damage—the delicate surface is no longer exposed to low temperatures. However, a more likely reason for petal closure around the central part of the flower at night is to reduce the loss of pollen that could be washed away by night rain, when there is no insect pollinator around to use what is available. The poppies, I grow every year, turn the flower downwards when the first few drops of rain land on them and return to the upright, open position only when the rain stops. This, again, reduces pollen loss. This response is clearly the result of a touch stimulus, although little recognized.

References

Attenborough, D. (1995). *The private life of plants* (dvd 1–5). BBC Natural History Unit. A BBC TV Production in association with Turner Broadcasting Systems, Inc.

Attenborough, D. (2009). *Life* (dvd). BBC Worldwide Limited, London.

Bose, J.C. (1906). *Plant response as a means of physiological investigation.* Longmans Green and Co Ltd, London.

Bose, J.C. (1926). *The nervous mechanism in plants.* Longmans, Green and Co. Ltd, London.

Darwin, C. (1859). *The origin of species by means of natural selection.* John Murray, London.

Darwin, C. (1868). *The Variation of Animals and Plants under Domestication.* Vols 1 and 2. John Murray, London.

Darwin, C. (1871). *The descent of man.* John Murray, London.

Darwin, C, (1875). *Insectivorous plants.* John Murray, London.

Darwin, C. (1880). *The power of movement in plants.* John Murray, London.

Hangartner, R (2000). Plants in Motion. Available at: http://plantsinmotion.bio.indiana.edu/plantmotion/start here.html

Keller, E.F. (1983). *A feeling for the organism the life and work of Barbara McClintock.* Freeman & Co., New York.

Pfeffer, W. (1906). *The physiology of plants,* Vols 1–3, transl. A.J. Ewart. Clarendon Press, Oxford.

Sachs, J., von (1887). *Lectures on the physiology of plants.* Clarendon Press, Oxford.

Shepherd, V.A. (2005). From semi-conductors to the rhythms of sensitive plants: the research of J.C. Bose. *Cellular and Molecular Biology,* **51**, 607–619.

Trewavas, A.J. (2009). What is Plant Behaviour. *Plant Cell and Environment,* 32, 606–616.

Went F., and Thimann, K.V. (1937). *Phytohormones.* Macmillan, New York.

Wong, T-S., Kang, S.H., Tang, S.K.Y., Smythe, E.J., Hatton, B.D., Grinthal, A., and 1 other (2011). Bioinspired self-repairing slippery surfaces with pressure stable omniphobicity. *Nature,* **477**, 443–447.

CHAPTER 3

The origins of photosynthesis: what are the salient characteristics of living systems?

Hierarchical organisation in biological systems is characterised by an array of delicately and intricately interlocked order, steadily increasing in level and complexity and thereby giving rise to neogenetically emergent properties.

(Grobstein 1973)

⊃ **Summary**

Organisms that developed independent existence had to rely on external sources of energy and, in plants, photosynthesis was probably the end of an evolutionary process that saw cells free living in sunlight. How did this process evolve? The earliest organisms thought to be bacteria are potentially detectable 3.5 billion years ago. Photosynthesis commenced about 3 billion years ago or so with oxygen-producing organisms in abundance 2.7 billion years ago. Fossil stromatolites, 2.2 billion years old, and containing blue-green algae and bacteria are well established, and, astonishingly, are very similar to present-day stromatolites. What provided the impetus for early molecular primordia to eventually generate a living cell? A robust energy supply is undoubtedly essential. Early chemical reactions would have to be coupled directly or indirectly to it. Providing the energy supply is sustained, Prigogine's dissipative mechanism, seeing order derive increasingly from continued energy flow, is the crucial underpin. The early molecular components would have to be connected to form an integrated, holistic system of low entropy and information flow between them. With increasing experimentation, a stabilizing hierarchical structure would come to dominate, initially, between molecules, then groups of molecules as modules. This early system had to become teleonomic; that is being purposive in maintenance and replication. Negative feedback would have helped stabilize the early structure by keeping the internal environment constant, but may have evolved to counteract destabilizing noise. Each of these criteria is discussed in this chapter to try and provide understanding of this vital event.

Introduction

In this chapter and the next one, I want to outline two subjects that continue to fascinate; how did life evolve and how did photosynthesis evolve. Photosynthesis, the process of capturing light energy and converting it into chemical energy, is the most obvious characteristic of all plants. Light energy from the sun was freely available on the early earth and basically still is. Whereas animals of most kinds had, by necessity, to move to acquire food, the ubiquitous presence of light provided no such strong evolutionary imperative for plant movement.

Plant Behaviour and Intelligence. First Edition. Anthony Trewavas.
© Anthony Trewavas 2014. Published 2014 by Oxford University Press.

Movement in most animals is a necessary accompaniment to their lifestyle, but like all things in biology there are exceptions. Corals, sponges, and some protozoans live in waters where currents waft large amounts of food past them, which they then capture. These organisms then exhibit no requirement of movement to find food, although they can sometimes exhibit rapid contractions. There is a further similarity to plants in that some sessile coelenterates, *Obelia* for example, exhibit tip growth accompanied by branching similar to that of higher plants. The goal is to occupy local space as it is in higher plants, enabling the capture of resources (food) and, by controlling the space, deny it to competitors.

Motile plant cells are largely but not completely found only in unicellular organisms. The behavioural problems associated with the fundamental biological necessities—acquiring resources (energy, minerals, and water), avoiding predators, and picking reproductive partners—have thus been solved in ways that do not require direct movement. When plant growth and development is recorded by time lapse, the behaviour can mimic movement.

Early animals depended heavily on plants for food. Predation, then, is a fact of life for plants, but predation threatens the biological imperative of survival, so a fairly continuous war has been waged between plants and their predators. For angiosperms this behavioural battle has lasted for some 200 million years and, fortunately, neither side has yet won. In biology, there are always costs and benefits to any evolutionary change. So all solutions to any biological problem have their limitations and these can then be exploited subsequently by the opponent. The term 'natural selection' or survival of the fittest can imply that one organism becomes superlatively good and eliminates all other competitors. I think a better description is 'it's a better living for now' might more accurately describe natural selection and at least does indicate why life is so diverse.

This chapter and the next tell a story, an intriguing one, but a story nevertheless, because like all history it is largely about unrepeatable events. However, my story no doubt is in conflict with many others and represents my own assessment of this question above all questions; from whence did life (and photosynthesis) come? Once that choice was made, the forms of behaviour found in plants follow naturally.

The time scale of events for the origin of life and photosynthesis

The age of the earth is generally agreed to be about 4.5 billion years old; not new in a universe believed to be just over 13 billion years old. The earth was formed from an accretion of dust, the residue from a previous supernova, which was captured by our present sun. Some theories suggest the sun might have been part of a binary system and it is the residue of the other partner that forms part of the planetary material as well. Current geological views stress that the early earth was extremely hot, the climate hostile and was bombarded frequently by asteroids (Nisbet and Sleep 2001). About 4 billion years ago bombardment markedly declined and the oceans condensed, although still remaining hot. The earliest atmosphere may have contained some methane and ammonia, but under intense UV light these will have quickly been degraded. The predominant atmospheric gases when life emerged are thought to be carbon dioxide, nitrogen, and water vapour.

It is believed that living organisms (bacteria) might have emerged before 3.8 billion years ago (Mojzsis et al. 1996). There are substantive microscopic data, suggesting that bacterial fossils are present in rocks at least 3.4 billion years old (Westall et al. 2001). However, these early bacteria surely had to be photosynthetic. Many elements have isotopic, but non-radioactive forms. Carbon, for example, has three forms, the abundant C^{12}, the less abundant but stable C^{13}, and a radioactive isotope, C^{14} (half-life about 5000 years), the number referring to its elemental weight. All exist naturally in our atmosphere and in carbon compounds in living systems. However, carbon compounds containing the heavier isotopes are metabolized more slowly by living organisms than the lighter isotope. Evidence of living activity can then be gained by measuring the natural abundance of C^{12} to C^{13} and comparing that with the ratio in material, which it is suspected may be remnants of living organisms. Certain rock strata identified as 3.4 billion years old, which it is thought contain potential bacterial fossils and an altered C^{12}/C^{13} ratio, also support this age for the existence of recognizable living organisms. However, there is disagreement about the actual identification of these as supposedly of bacteria (Brasier et al. 2002).

Clearer evidence identifies the origin of photosynthesis as earlier than 2.7–2.9 billion years ago and possible up to 3.4–3.5 billion years (Schopf 2000; Noffke et al. 2003, 2008; Schopf et al. 2007). Stromatolites are large, dome-like structures that consist of layers of photosynthetic prokaryotic blue-green algae and bacteria. In blue-green algae, the photosynthetic apparatus is located on sheets of membrane and not in a membrane-bound organelle, the chloroplast, as found in higher plants. Blue-green algae are so-called because of the presence of a photosynthetic blue-green accessory pigment (phycocyanin) used instead of chlorophyll b, as in present day higher plants. Blue-green algae oxidize water to oxygen during photosynthesis.

Present-day stromatolites can be found off the coast of Australia and microscopic sections through these reveal an internal structure effectively identical to fossil stromatolites over two billion years ago [pictures of stromatolites, both modern and ancient, and sections through the latter can be found in Barghoorn (1992)]. Stromatolites are formed from mats of mucilage-secreting bacteria and blue-green algae living in supersaturated silicates. Metabolic activity and excretion of H^+, changes the local pH and converts the mineral super-silicates to silica, forming an embedding matrix for the colonies and a structure resistant to decay, and thus easily forming fossils. New colonies are only added on the top of the growing stromatolite and the structure continues to grow, often to very large size—sometimes metres across. The earliest stromatolite fossils are dated at 2.7–2.9 billion years up to 3.5 billion years ago (Noffke et al. 2003, 2008; Nisbet et al. 2007; Schopf et al. 2007).

Other fossilized material has characteristics similar to present-day free-living blue-green algae. Use of Raman spectroscopy and three-dimensional reconstruction, as well as isotopic analysis does support a biogenic origin for these blue-green algal fossils (Schopf et al. 2007). This very early appearance of blue-green algae at this time, emitting oxygen is in agreement with a dated change in banded iron deposits, which show a definite shift from the reduced ferrous (Fe^{2+}) to the oxidized ferric (Fe^{3+}) during the period 2–3 billion years ago and reflecting the change in the atmosphere from an anaerobic composition to its present atmosphere containing 20% oxygen (Trouwborst et al. 2007; Konhauser et al. 2011).

While blue-green algae and bacteria are prokaryotes, the origin of eukaryotic cells is indicated to have occurred at about the same time (Brocks et al. 1999; Javaux et al. 2001) based on chemical analysis of molecules known to be unique to eukaryotes.

How did life originate?

The actual mechanisms that generated the first living things will probably always remain a mystery, because being an historical process, the intermediary events that underpinned it have long disappeared. Scientists and readers of this text, as I myself, will therefore have to be content with plausible possibilities. However, the problem continues to intrigue many scientists and there is no shortage of challenging suggestions to explain the origin of life. The views given below are not intended in any way to cover all suggestions, that would require a book to itself, but this is my version and is no more than a plausible possibility like any other, but does have differences!

Can we define what life actually is?

If we are to try and understand the origin of photosynthesis and, indeed, life itself with which it is intimately related, then the first point to establish is what exactly we are looking for; what exactly is meant by the word 'alive'. It is often easy to identify things that we think are alive, but far less easy to characterize precisely what it is that make us think so. If we can define one or two essential life characteristics then that simplifies the problem of trying to guess how it might have happened. However, even that is not as easy as it sounds.

Little agreement exists, as perhaps might be expected. Is it the presence of a cell membrane? Is it reproduction or movement, or the utilization of energy, i.e. some kind of respiration? Alternatively, is it the presence of some kind of irritability, a response to environmental challenges or is it a necessary internal stability—a kind of homeostasis involving negative feedback protecting early cellular chemistry against pH, salt, or temperature insults? Perhaps, it is all of them?

Freeman Dyson (1985) considers life was always complex, in contrast to numerous others who regard the origin as an orderly sequence of acquisitions. It is common to view replication as the essential criterion, but Dyson regards homeostasis as a critical step. Without this prior homeostatic capability, other processes could not evolve. It is generally agreed that the earliest cells were some kind of bacterium. However, complex does not mean a fully formed bacterial cell; only that some of the above life characteristics evolved together, rather than sequentially.

Davies (1989), an insightful physicist, has listed a more novel set of criteria of living than those above. His list comprises complexity, uniqueness, holism, emergence, interconnectedness, unpredictability, openness, organization, disequilibrium, evolution, and finally teleology (or as Pittendrigh coined it, teleonomy). Teleonomy causes problems for some biologists, if they even know of the term. I will add hierarchy, information, and self-organization to this list, then indicate what is meant by some of these properties. I have not placed these in the order in which they probably occurred; that is left to the end.

Fundamental to all, however, was the initial event, a source of energy preferably constant in supply and sufficiently long-lived to stabilize the evolution of our primitive molecular structures on their progress to independent life. That is considered in the next chapter.

Everything that biology studies is a system of systems. Our earliest life form must be a system

A system is a network of mutually dependent and, thus, interconnected components comprising a unified whole (Trewavas 2006). It is the connections and characteristics of these connections or interactions that determine the ultimate property of any system. Many natural systems and, indeed, some man-made ones are extremely complex (Strogatz 2001). Because the behaviour of individual constituents is altered by being connected, systems possess

what are called emergent properties; that is, properties that, to all intents and purposes, are not shared by the individual constituents, but only by the system as a whole. Simple interactions between parts of the system are usually synergistic when they interact and synergism is another emergent property.

Emergent properties result from the connections themselves. A very simple and familiar example of an emergent property is a clock; only the whole, constructed together of the individual parts, provides a measurement of time; none of the parts—the cogs, wheels, or springs—can accomplish this. In biological systems there are many other examples. Some proteins require an adjunct for activity. The property of the active protein is not shared by either the adjunct (usually a small molecule) or the inactive protein, but only by both together. Again, it is an excellent example of synergy between the two.

Larger numbers of proteins can interact with each other to form more complex organization and to express different discrete functions. These groups of proteins are called modules. Modules obviously express emergent properties. Sometimes modules are transiently formed as during signalling or during specific stages of development. Modules themselves combine together by interconnections to produce additional new and other emergent properties.

An important recognition is that modules are often arranged hierarchically (Grobstein 1973; Hartwell et al. 1999; Ravasz et al. 2002). When connected together in the hierarchy, larger modules appear. Some of the modules involved in gene regulatory networks have been detailed. These modules are sometimes constructed from common sub-modular circuits in different combinations and, thus, contain additional features that make their contribution to the whole system unique (Davidson 2010). Some of the simpler systems or modules are often enclosed by larger ones; the simple analogy is rather like the familiar Russian dolls, one inside the other.

All cells are extremely complex systems. Through the connections, everything is effectively connected to everything else, enabling the cell to act as a whole entity. The working elements of any cell are its proteins, and interactions between numerous proteins determine signalling and replicative modules, as well as those of metabolism. There are two other connection structures:

1. The strength of connection between any two proteins that normally interact with each other can be changed by other interacting molecules and proteins. The strength of connections between the constituents can then alter, constructing a different kind of network. However, changing the strength of connection will alter the rate at which information can flow through the network.
2. Proteins differ in the number of other proteins and molecules that they interact with. This has led to a description of cellular networks as 'small world' or 'scale free'. The terms differ little from each other, but the terminology is designed to recognize that proteins can be roughly divided into hubs with large numbers of linkages and connectors (edges) with only a few. This arrangement seems to provide relative stability and robustness to any network that forms, including ecological networks.

During development the constituent proteins change, too, thus breaking old connections as proteins disappear and forming new connections within the network as new ones are synthesized. More complex situations can arise and can be envisaged. The whole network can be envisaged as analogous to a complex surface in which folds and the surface structure are in constant dynamic change.

Most cells are subject to variable environmental influences. These influences impact initially on only part of the cellular network usually, and through proteins designed to detect and interpret the signal. However, in turn, the surrounding cellular context will influence that response because every molecule is ultimately connected to every other molecule. Thus, the same signal can be interpreted differently if the cellular context itself has changed previously.

The network of interactions is described as an interactome, and impressive pictures of these networks involving either sub-cellular (modular) groups of proteins or those of the whole cell can be found in the literature (Pennisi 2003; Li et al. 2004; Tarrasov et al. 2008; Yu et al. 2008; Costanzo et al. 2010). These maps are simplifications because cells contain numerous kinds of protein-modifying enzymes (e.g. phosphorylation) that enormously increase the numbers of actual protein species involved in cellular activity. Protein-modifying

enzymes can either change the strength of connection between proteins or provide for an all-or-nothing change in connection. These maps fail to provide for indications of the strengths of connections that are important for interpretation.

Finally, cells operate regulatory controls on connections via thousands of negative feedback and positive feedforward processes that enable cellular smooth running and initiate change. Negative feedback is very familiar, since it is also used in many devices around the house, controlling oven or room temperature, for example. Such systems are controlled through the transfer of information from the end process, through a control element that senses the output of the process and can modulate it usually at the beginning (Trewavas 2006). The aim of negative feedback is to control flux rates and, thus, the concentrations of small and large molecules and modular activity. The common example of negative feedback is to be found in organism homeostasis, first described in detail in by Cannon (1932). He also included the less obvious hunger and thirst in his discussion of homeostasis, processes that operate over much longer time scales than the well-known homeostatic temperature control in mammals and birds.

Feedforward processes are commonly used to amplify signals that arrive at very low intensity. The amplification through successive steps can be extremely large, thus enabling substantive change. Phosphorylation can provide for enormous amplification. Feedforward is also used to amplify weak outside signals, as well those inside. With a variety of such sensing mechanisms, cells can, in theory, construct a potential image, a three-dimensional picture of their local environment.

The value of being hierarchical

Hierarchical systems are far more stable than non-hierarchical systems, because of the constraint exerted by the various upper levels of the hierarchy on the levels below. Thus, we should expect living cells to be hierarchical. A non-hierarchical system rapidly disaggregates to its basic constituents (Simon 1969; Oyama 2000).

To explain how constraint operates, a very simple hierarchical system that is familiar to the reader can be used as an analogy. The notion can then be transferred to cells themselves. The base of this simple hierarchical system is all the letters of the alphabet. The next level on top of this base is words. Any word is constructed from a discrete selection of letters that are effectively joined together in a specific order. Compared with the potential number of possible combination of letters, meaningful words form a discrete and very small subset. Theoretically, with an alphabet of 26 letters the number of possible six-letter words is 26^6, somewhere in the order of 320 million possibilities. However, the maximum number of words in the major dictionaries is only half a million. The word thus constrains what letters can be used to spell it.

The final upper level in this simple system is the sentence. Meaningful sentences are constructed of a very limited number of words that are effectively joined together and usually in a particular order. The number of potential combinations of words in any order, but put together, is truly enormous; there are at least 500,000 words in the OUP dictionary. Meaningful sentences are, again, a very small subset of the possibilities. A sentence constrains what words can be used to convey its specific meaning. The meaning of a sentence is its emergent property, just as the particular order and choice of letters is the emergent property for any word. Emergent properties appear at every level as a result of the connections between the constituents, either letters or words in this case. A non-hierarchical system

here would simply be a random collection of spaces and letters. Kline (1995) provides a number of other hierarchical structures including those in biology.

The cellular hierarchy can be envisaged in ascending order as atoms, molecules, macromolecular complexes, modules, very large molecular conglomerates, organelles, cell.

Figure 3.1 arranges these in the shape of a pyramid to indicate the increasing constraint that higher levels have on those lower. This figure also includes time-dependent changes in development and morphogenesis arranged in similar fashion. In this hierarchical situation, constraint on the behaviour at every level is exerted by the next level above and finally by the unified cellular whole. The hierarchy can be continued through tissues, whole organisms, and ecosystems. At each level, the number of potential combinations is constrained by the level above. Each level imposes constraint on that lower.

Note, in our analogy, that there is slight room for variation in the order of the words in any sentence that still conveys the same meaning, 'The cat sat on the mat' is no different in meaning to 'on the mat the cat sat' or 'the cat was sitting on the mat'. There is some variation in the spelling of words, at least if we go back to early English and Chaucer. Thus, on this analogy there will be some flexibility in the behaviour and composition of the constituents in any cell too within certain tolerances. The consequence will be that what appear to be identical cells performing a similar function, will be able to do so

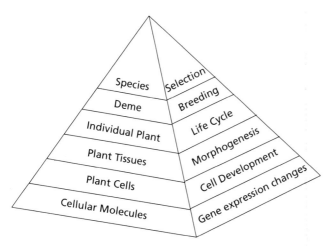

Figure 3.1 Biological systems arranged in a hierarchy of increasing organizational complexity. Each lower level through complex interactions of its constituents creates the level above as an emergent property. On the left is a static compositional hierarchy and on the right a dynamic developmental and evolutionary hierarchy incorporating time dependence of change.

with a degree of molecular variation between them. This is certainly commonly observed. The process is called noise and finds further discussion later.

Information and hierarchical constraint

Information is related to constraint—the higher the constraint on any system, the higher its intrinsic information content (Trewavas 2012)—but what exactly is information? All of us acquire information in the form of signals from our environment; we process these and act if necessary upon them. The present-day theory of information started with investigations of information transfer down phone lines and its potential destruction by noise (Shannon and Weaver 1949). Information is seen as messages and the more complex the message, the greater the information content. Information can be measured in bits and a bit is a yes/no situation, an either/or situation, and one commonly present in the simplest of transistors. However, two interacting cellular molecules also transfer information between them.

Information varies in complexity and, again, a simple analogous example makes the point. 'The cat sat on the mat' provides information, but of a fairly low order, it could apply to millions of cats. If instead the sentence goes 'After eating a bird, the black and white cat named Tommy sat on the mat and then went to sleep' the information conveyed is much larger and is much more constrained because it refers to only a very small subset of world cats. Information is, therefore, reciprocally related to the numbers of alternatives. Alternatively, the probability of occurrence of this particular combination of words can be assessed and will be extremely low compared with all other sentences that can be constructed and have relevant meaning. In the same way, meaningful information provides a constraint on what combination of letters actually can make a word and what words can make a sentence as previously indicated.

It was Shannon who drew attention to the possible relation of information to entropy (Vedral 2010). Highly ordered systems are improbable and have low entropy; disordered ones have high entropy. A meaningful sentence is of low probability because it consists of a rare selection out of all the potential words possible and meaningful sentences, of course, have high information content. Organization, complex systems, thus become a crucial property of living systems as they do of our language.

However, a crucial element in information transmission is the presence of a receiver able to interpret the information. Without a receiver, there can be no effective information present at all, and a particular combination of words and letters has no more information than a completely random jumble of letters and words. It is not enough to be improbable to provide information. A specific string of random numbers can represent a highly improbable event.

In fact, improbable events happen all the time. If I could measure to the exact angstrom, the precise place on the key pad that I had just typed the letter 'r' and then calculated the probability of hitting the key in precisely the same position, I would conclude that the probability was so low I could never have done it! A jumbled-up version of the words and letters in the sentences above is no less probable than the sentence itself, but a jumbled up version has no information to an intelligent receiver (the reader) able to interpret. Information is not simply related to the probability with which it might occur. The crucial issue lies in the ability to interpret.

Information is, therefore, a holistic phenomenon. The receiver of this sentence is the reader, the sentence is what is transmitted, but information only appears when the sentence is read. Sentence and reader together are what makes information, but, to the reader, the information must make sense, i.e. it must be meaningful and whole. In biological terms, we can regard the sentence as an environmental or internal signal, and the information it conveys must be meaningful to the cell itself. Signals in biological terms are, therefore, meaningful information, recognized and acted upon sensibly. It is evolution that has constructed organisms to recognize all the sources of information they need to perceive as meaningful and to construct appropriate responses. Again, information will be subject to greater discussion when we come to intelligence and the processing of meaningful information by different organisms.

Although the total information content of the environment has remained in one sense unchanging, the information gained by organisms about their environment has become much larger over evolutionary time. The facets of the environment are distinguished in much greater detail and with greater accuracy. There has been, during evolutionary time, an elaboration of both receptors and sensory tissues ensuring that the information content received can be acted upon with greater sensitivity and discrimination. Organisms are enabled to improve their survival rates and to increase the sum total of diversity of life itself. One consequence has been the inevitable evolutionary generation of multicellularity, thus enabling specific sets of cells to be demarcated to perform specific sensory functions or to contain specific receptors.

Thus, for our primordial origin of a cell, a hierarchical system should have developed early on along with homeostasis and with some capability of interpreting the information available from the environment.

Molecular noise is inevitable and living systems have to have the means to counteract it

Information theory commenced with Shannon and Weaver's (1949) attempts to estimate the accuracy of transmission of messages down phone lines. The degradation of information transmission is called noise and it is a disordering process that still threatens all living processes.

Noise is inevitable in all living processes and ways in the first living cells must have been present to provide for the overall supremacy of organization against its destruction by noise (Trewavas 2012). Present-day living cells use many thousands of reactions that are probabilistic in character requiring different molecules to come together. Present life survives because the tendency of randomizing processes is counterbalanced by correcting statistical forces. The connections within a system tend to counteract stochastic variation, but this will depend on the degree of complexity of the system itself and the controlling elements involved in its stability. Thus, a large number of molecules working together countermand the less frequent stochastic event that threatens to disrupt.

Many control circuits have been constructed in cells to offset or reduce noise, and the primary one here is the previously mentioned negative feedback.

Information is provided to an earlier part of the circuit to try and modulate or stabilize throughput. This control circuitry does provide for a kind of homeostasis and as indicated earlier must have been present in very early cells. However, one hazard of negative feedback is that a delay in the feedback conveyance of information can increase noise compared with others in which the feedback is fast.

The evidence for noise in present-day cellular systems is extensive (Trewavas 2012) and indicates the problems that must have faced early cells. Thus, in gene expression circuitry, DNA during transcription can change its structure; proteins necessary for transcription can drop off or change conformation, or become non-functional for periods of time. Signalling complexes have to be formed from large numbers of soluble proteins and a crowded cytoplasm can hinder movement, ion channels are inevitably noisy. All these difficulties speak of early complexity as being essential.

What is teleonomy?

Teleonomy is the apparent purposefulness and the obvious goal-directed nature of living organisms that derives from both adaptation and evolution. To see why teleonomy is important, try to imagine life without it. In any competitive scenario, only teleonomic organisms would survive.

Teleonomy was originally called teleology, but that was changed to teleonomy because of the mysticism associated with teleology when it was first introduced by Aristotle. Jacques Monod (1972, p. 20), Nobel Prize winner, comments:

One of the fundamental characteristics common to all living beings without exception, is that of being objects endowed with a purpose which they show in their structure and execute through their performances. Rather than reject this idea (as certain biologists try to do), it must be regarded as essential to the very definition of all living being. We shall maintain the latter are distinct from all other structures or systems present in the universe by this characteristic property which we shall call teleonomy.

Teleonomy, I regard, as the obvious drive to survive and reproduce.

Rosenbleuth et al. (1943) in a very early, but enlightening discussion of purpose, behaviour, and teleology identified negative feedback processes as obviously purposeful and what they viewed as the correct meaning to teleology, *viz.* teleonomy. Norbert Weiner, one of the authors in Rosenbleuth et al. (1943), was the originator of cybernetics and benefited from a shared student who worked for Cannon on homeostasis. With organisms that obviously move quickly, in response to critical environmental signals to acquire food before others or to avoid predators, the involvement of negative feedback is obvious. In due course it will be indicated that feedback is equally applicable to green plants.

Coupled with teleonomy is the word intention, raised in an animal context by Scott Turner (2007), Hull (1988) and by myself (Trewavas 2009). Hull states implicitly that animals do strive, they intend, to avoid predators and to find mates, a statement that observation makes obvious. Do plants strive to avoid predation or disease, or to spread their pollen and thus find mates? They certainly act as if they do and if they do not, they lose out to others that do! Often the simplest way to get a recalcitrant tree or shrub to flower and reproduce is to starve it of mineral resources. The intention in this case is a last ditch effort to spread its genes. As we will find with intelligence, refined nervous systems are not essential to enable these particular behaviours.

The openness of organisms and the generation of order

The cellular system is maintained far from chemical equilibrium and homeostatically controlled by an open flow of energy through the system gained from food. The acquisition of food (energy) by the whole organism and the drive for reproduction provides for purposive teleonomic behaviour. Our primordial cell will need access to a source of sustainable energy.

Two scientists raised particular awareness of this fundamental requirement of life. Bertalanffy (1971) in his proposal for a General Systems Theory called attention to organisms as open systems, and how a flux of energy enabled cellular growth as a consequence. Coincidentally, Schrodinger (1944), in his classic text, *What is Life*, argued that living systems survived only by consuming 'negative entropy'; implicitly the same concept as Bertalanffy and indicating that living organisms avoided the disorganizing principle issuing from the second law of thermodynamics of entropy increase by using energy.

Processes that are far from chemical equilibrium are known to generate order out of a chaotic situation; matter simply self-organizes when driven by a flux of energy. This can lead, in turn, to a progressive unfolding of organized complexity. The Nobel Prize winner Ilya Prigogine established this phenomenon clearly (Prigogine and Stengers, 1984). A good example is that of a simple negative feedback process constructed in bacteria that enables rings of density to develop in culture (Liu et al. 2011). As the population increases in size, it produces a ring-stripe pattern. The well-known Belousov–Zabotinski reaction involving simple chemicals mimics this process with clear organization into rings and waves, and pictures can be viewed of this reaction in the book by Winfree (1987).

Prigogine (1996) showed that, as the flux of energy increases and takes a reacting system further from chemical equilibrium, a bifurcation point is reached in which the system suddenly becomes unstable and at least two alternative pathways of change are opened up. No prediction can be made about which pathway will be taken, but whereas one pathway can lead to chaos, the other is a state of increased order or organization. Successive bifurcation points are reached as energy input continues to climb and one possible outcome is increasing order and thus the evolution of organization. Prigogine (1996) refers to these systems as dissipative to emphasize the contrast between the production of order, and the dissipation of both energy and entropy. Because order is created out of chaos, Prigogine describes dissipative systems as composed of 'active' matter (1996, p. 286) that seemingly has 'a will of its own'. The jumps to new forms of organization are the result of fluctuations amplified by positive feedback loops. There is no doubt that Prigogine's (1996) input has engendered a radical shift in the emphasis that classical science placed on the supposed pre-eminence of the second law of thermodynamics and the dominance of entropy increase.

The flux of continued energy through a primitive cell must have been essential, since the flux itself tends to drive organization and help to counteract the destruction wreaked by noise. I do see that process as essential in early life and something that must be present at the beginning.

What is needed for our primordial cell?

This brief discussion has indicated the necessity for a source of energy to drive chemical reactions that are coupled through the whole combination of molecules, to maintain a far-from-equilibrium state and, thus, high complexity, low entropy, and organization. These early systems required meaningful connections between the constituent molecules. That is, specific information transfer between them so that the system could act as an integrated whole. The early systems may originally have been simple, but an arrangement into meaningful groups or modules that are arranged hierarchically, stabilizes the system. Selection among the enormous number of primordial products that emerged would have been inevitable. Successful early organisms or molecular primordia would have been teleonomic, a systems property that seeks to maintain itself, replicate, and thus survive selection. Mechanisms that deal with noise and counteract it would have arisen early. Possibly statistical forces, i.e. reasonable numbers of molecules doing the same thing, may initially have been the mechanism, but other events, such as negative feedback, might have then originated to help reduce noise reduction. Once started, negative feedback would have been useful in stabilizing the internal environment. Finally, Prigogine's mechanism of dissipative structures provides for the basis for the enormous amount of experimentation that would have underpinned the evolution of a hierarchical, complex system capable of both survival and reproduction. It is difficult to see how one requirement of life would have survived without the others, but then the surrounding context, such as stability in energy supply and chemical milieu may have helped providing the necessary environment over a long enough period for Prigogine's mechanism to operate successfully.

References

Barghoorn, E.S. (1992). The antiquity of life. In Margulis, L. and Olendzenski, L., eds, *Environmental evolution. Effects of the origin and evolution of life on planet Earth*, pp. 71–87. MIT Press, Cambridge, MA.

Bertalanffy, L., von (1971). *General system theory*. Allen Lane, London.

Brasier, M., Green, D.R., Jephcoat, A.P., Kleppe, A.K., Krakendonk, M.J., van, Lindsay, J.F., and 2 others (2002). Questioning the evidence for Earth's oldest fossils. *Nature*, **416**, 76–81.

Brocks, J.J., Logan, G.A., Buick, R., and Summons, R.E. (1999). Archaen molecular fossils and the early rise of eukaryotes. *Science*, **285**, 1033–1036.

Cannon, W.B. (1932). *The wisdom of the body*. Norton, New York.

Costanzo, M., Baryshnivoka, A., Bellay, J., Kim, Y., Spear, E.D., Sevier, C.S., and 47 others (2010). The genetic landscape of a cell. *Science*, **327**, 425–432.

Davidson, E.H. (2010). Emerging properties of animal gene regulatory networks. *Nature*, **468**, 911–920.

Davies, P. (1989). *Cosmic blueprint*. Unwin-Hyman Ltd, London.

Dyson, F. (1985). *Origins of life*. Cambridge University Press, Cambridge.

Grobstein, C. (1973). Hierarchical order and neogenesis. In Pattee, H., ed. *Hierarchy Theory*, pp.29–48 Braziller, New York.

Hartwell, L.H., Hopfield, J.J., Liebler, S., and Murray, A.W. (1999). From molecular to modular cell biology. *Nature*, **402**, Suppl. C47–C52.

Hull, D.L. (1988). Interactors versus vehicles. In Plotkin, H.C., ed. *The role of behaviour in evolution*, pp.19–51. MIT Press, Cambridge, MA.

Javaux, E.J., Knoll, A.H., and Walter, M.R. (2001). Morphological and ecological complexity in early eukaryotic ecosystems. *Nature*, **412**, 66–69.

Kline, S.J. (1995). *Conceptual foundations for multidisciplinary thinking*. Stanford University Press, Redwood City, CA.

Konhauser, K.O., LaLonde, S.V., Planavsky, N.J., Pecoits, E., Lyons, T.W., Mojsis, S.J., and 6 others (2011). Aerobic bacterial pyrite oxidation and acid rock drain age during the great oxidation event. *Nature*, **478**, 369–372.

Li, S., Armstrong, C.M., Bertin, N.G.E., Ge, H., Milstein, S., Boxem, M., and 42 others (2004). A map of the interactome network of the metazoan, *C. elegans*. *Science*, **303**, 540–543.

Liu, C., Fu, X., Liu, L., Ren, X., Chau, C.K.L., Li, S., and 9 others (2011). Sequential establishment of stripe patterns in an expanding cell population. *Science*, **334**, 238–242.

Mojsis, S.J., Arrhenius, G., McKeegan, K.D., Harrison, T.M., Nutman, A.P., and Friend, C.E.L. (1996). Evidence for life on earth before 3,800 million years ago. *Nature*, **384**, 55–59.

Monod, J. (1972). *Chance and necessity*. Collins, London.

Nisbet, N.G., Grassinaeu N.V., Howe, C.J., Abell, P.I., Regelous, M., and Nisbet, R.E.R. (2007). The age of Rubisco: the evolution of oxygenic photosynthesis. *Geobiology*, **5**, 311–335.

Nisbet, E.G., and Sleep, N.H. (2001). The habitat and nature of early life. *Nature*, **409**, 1083–1091.

Noffke, N., Beukes, N., Bower, D., Hazen, R.M., and Swift, D.J.P. (2008). An actualistic perspective into Archaean worlds-(cyano)bacterially induced sedimentary structures in the siliciclastic Nhlazatse Section 2.9 Ga Pongola Supergroup, South Africa. *Geobiology*, **6**, 5–20.

Noffke, N., Hazen, R., and Nhelko, N. (2003). Earth's earliest microbial mats in a siliciclastic marine environment (2.9 Ga Mozaan Group, South Africa). *Geology*, **31**, 673–676.

Oyama, S. (2000). *The ontogeny of information*, 2nd edn. Duke University Press, Durham, NC.

Pennisi, E. (2003). Tracing life's circuitry. *Science*, **302**, 1646–1649.

Prigogine, I. (1996). *The end of certainty*. Free Press, New York.

Prigogine, I., and Stengers, I. (1984). *Order out of chaos; Man's new dialogue with nature*. Bantam Books, New York.

Ravasz, E., Somera, A.L., Mongru, D.A., Oltvai, Z.N., and Barabasi, A-L. (2002). Hierarchical organisation of modularity in metabolic networks. *Science*, **297**, 1551–1555.

Rosenbleuth, A., Wiener, N., and Bigelow, J. (1943). Behaviour purpose and teleology. *Philosophy of Science*, **10**, 18–24.

Schopf, J.W. (2000) Solution to Darwins dilemma: discovery of the missing Precambrian record of life. *Proceedings of the National Academy of Sciences USA*, **97**, 6947–6953.

Schopf, J.W., Kudryavtsev, A.B., Czaja, A.D., and Tripathi, A.B. (2007). Evidence of Archaean life: stromatolites and microfossils. *Precambrian Research*, **158**, 141–155.

Schrodinger, E. (1944). *What is life?* Cambridge University Press, Cambridge.

Scott Turner, J. (2007). *The Tinkerers accomplice: How design emerges from life itself*. Harvard University Press, Cambridge, MA.

Shannon, C.E., and Weaver, W. (1949). *The mathematical theory of communication*. University of Illinois Press, Urbana, IL.

Simon, H.A. (1996). *The sciences of the artificial*. MIT Press, Cambridge, MA.

Strogatz, S.H. (2001). Exploring complex networks. *Nature*, **410**, 268–276.

Tarrasov, K., Messier, V., Landry, C.R. Radinovic, S., Serna Molina M.M., Shames I., and 5 others (2008). An *in vivo* map of the yeast protein interactome. *Science*, **320**, 1465–1470.

Trewavas, A.J. (2006). A brief history of systems biology. *Plant Cell*, **18**, 2420–2430.

Trewavas, A.J. (2009). What is plant behaviour. *Plant Cell and Environment*, **32**, 606–616.

Trewavas, A.J. (2012). Information, noise and communication: Thresholds as controlling elements. In Witzany, G., and Baluska, F., eds, *Biocommunication of plants*, pp. 11–37. Springer-Verlag, Berlin.

Trouwborst, R.E., Johnston, A., Koch, G., Luther, G.W., and Pierson, B.K. (2007). Biogeochemistry of Fe (II) oxidation in a microbial mat: Implications for Precambrian Fe (II) oxidation. *Geochimica et Cosmochimica Acta*, **71**, 4629–4643.

Vedral, V. (2010). *Decoding reality the universe as quantum information*. Oxford University Press, Oxford.

Westall., F., Wit, de, M.J. Dann, J., Gaast, S., van der, Ronde, C.E.J., de, and Gerneke, D. (2001). Early fossil Archaen bacteria and biofilms from the Barberton greenstone belt, South Africa. *Precambrian Research*, **106**, 93–116.

Winfree, A.T. (1987). *Timing of biological clocks*. Scientific American Library, Portland, OR.

Yu, H., Braun, P., Yildirim, M.A., Lemmens I, Venkatesan K, Sahalie J., and 28 others (2008). High quality binary protein interaction map of the yeast interactome network. *Science*, **322**, 104–110.

CHAPTER 4

The origins of photosynthesis: the evolution of life and photosynthesis

From so simple a beginning, endless forms most beautiful and most wonderful have been and are being evolved.

(Darwin 1859)

⊃ **Summary**

This chapter deals with the continuation of life's origin leading eventually to photosynthesis. Two novel elements emerge here. Evolution in the deep oceans used pressure at depths as a novel additional energy source, and the Margulis mechanism for organelle evolution by cell fusion actually occurred much earlier, right at the beginning, enabling the rapid acquisition of complex systems. A potential origin of life at hydrothermal vents is envisaged using both temperature and high pressure as energy sources. The route is traced through peptide formation, rather than an RNA world, which is the alternative. Some early reactions formed peptides that aggregated to generate primordial membranes and, thus, formed a primitive vesicle enclosing some simple reactions. Vesicle fusion then becomes the main engine for increasing complexity. The fusion product has greater fitness and is thus selected on for further fusion. The first cells form with a transition to a simple system structure. Eventually, this primitive system or even cell generates its own energy source using sulphur-containing polypeptides or proteins, and becomes partly independent. Cell fusion, however, still remains the main engine driving complexity upwards. The earliest photosynthetic process may have evolved from light emitted by hydrothermal vents. Selection remains the main driver. Teleonomy was generated by selection only of those cells that contained the necessary processes to ensure continued independent survival.

Introduction

The process of the origin of life is often posed as a sequence of particular steps of increasing complexity. I doubt that this was ever the case. I would see the process more likely as parallel paths on which natural selection operated at every turn. Since selection is dependent on the precise environmental circumstances and we do not know what these were, we can never reconstruct what actually happened, only provide a plausible speculation—but one which continues to intrigue. One very important principle will be the fusion of discrete structures—primordial vesicles and, later, cells to increase and advance complexity. Fusion requires parts of the final cellular structure to evolve at different places and perhaps even different times; thus, life evolution occurred in a kind of parallel.

Plant Behaviour and Intelligence. First Edition. Anthony Trewavas.
© Anthony Trewavas 2014. Published 2014 by Oxford University Press.

What sources of energy were available on the early Earth; the geographical location of life's origin

The brief discussion in Chapter 3 has provided some suggested characteristics of life, but it was concluded that, for the origin of life, a sustainable source of energy was surely primary. Sources of energy were not only needed to generate organization, but also to catalyse the formation of the necessary molecules from which life was formed. The powerful sources of energy that might have been available are numerous, but which is crucial depends on where, if it can be ascertained, life originated.

The common assessment favours the earth's surface. Numerous sources of energy were apparently available here, UV light from the sun, lightning (world-wide there are still 30 lightning flashes every second), radioactivity, and possible higher temperatures than ambient, near volcanic activity. The early oceans were expected to be hot and the presence of carbon dioxide in the early atmosphere would have kept them warm through the greenhouse effect.

Using one or other of these sources of energy, laboratory experiments have examined whether life's constituent molecules could have been easily formed. The general conclusion is that formation of most of the known constituent amino acids, lipids, sugars, and nucleic acid bases are potentially possible if not relatively straightforward (Fitz et al. 2007). The classical Miller (1953) experiment used electrical discharge to mimic lightning flashes through a supposed primitive atmosphere of methane, ammonia, and water vapour, and demonstrated the formation of a few amino and organic acids. This experiment also reported on the formation of ammonium cyanide prior to the formation of amino acids. Later examination of the sludge produced by simply refluxing ammonium cyanide indicated the presence of polypeptides. It is thought that hydrolyses of these polypeptides might have accounted for Miller's amino acids (Matthews et al. 1984). Further examination indicated formation of the 5 nucleic acid bases (Kobayashi et al. 1986).

However, there are difficulties with a surface origin. Material formed in the atmosphere would presumably be washed into the oceans, but these might not have condensed from steam until 4 billion years ago. Furthermore, although the earliest atmosphere may have contained some ammonia and methane (as used by Miller 1953), these are likely to have disappeared by reactions catalysed by the intense UV light unencumbered by a protective ozone layer at that time. The remaining atmosphere would then probably have been carbon dioxide, water vapour, and nitrogen.

The major difficulty, however, is the dilution of material washed into the ocean. Hydrophobic material could concentrate on the ocean's surface, but the surface is very large and other soluble material would simply be too weak in concentration to have played any part. Others have suggested that material might have been concentrated in small ponds, as did Darwin, but evolution of life would have required a continuous supply of amino acids, polypeptides, or lipids if it was to survive at all. Furthermore, the weather conditions are variable enough in the present climate. In earlier times, they would probably have been much more variable and any surface reactions in a pond would still face the damaging effects of the sun. Surely stability of environmental conditions was essential as some form of living system was being constructed.

The deep ocean is a more likely place for life to get going

The obvious solution to the surface difficulties is the early deep ocean. Hydrothermal vents form, when cracks in the ocean floor allow seawater to penetrate directly onto hot magma below. The immensely hot seawater rises back through these vents carrying numerous chemicals. Among these chemicals are hydrogen sulphide, ammonia, hydrogen, methane, iron, copper, manganese, phosphates, and calcium in very substantial amounts (Butterfield et al. 1997). Limited vent size can give rise to roughly tubular, highly porous chimneys and, if black in colour, this results from a precipitation of iron sulphide.

The primary source of energy at these vents is obviously high temperature, but what is frequently omitted is the very high pressure on the ocean bed, not easy to replicate under laboratory conditions, but also an additional energy source (Gold 1999; Hazen et al. 2002). Under intense pressure at ocean depths, water remains liquid at several hundred degrees past its normal atmospheric boiling point. At these intense pressures, supercritical water can form an apolar environment that would concentrate other apolar molecules, such as methane, hydrogen, ammonia, nitrogen, carbon dioxide, and hydrogen sulphide, and trigger prebiotic chemistry (Bassez 2003). High pressure can stabilize many molecules once they are formed and, thus, a greater variety would be available (Daniel et al. 2006). Vent activity can last millions of years and conditions deep in the oceans are constant compared with the surface, with its daily temperature and seasonal fluctuations. Chimneys may be more ephemeral. The deep ocean is also protected from the disruptive effect of UV light from the sun.

Furthermore, the rocks on the ocean floor are porous and synthesized chemicals could easily accumulate, relatively undisturbed in warm, even hot, niches a slight distance from the very high temperatures of the vent itself. Gold (1999) on p. 171 calculates that the amounts of synthesized chemicals trapped in porous rocks could be of the order of 10^{44} molecules equating to 5.1×10^{16} tons in early conditions and possibly similar to what is present now.

If free amino acids were formed under these circumstances (although ammonium cyanide is surely inevitable), there is an additional problem not often faced. Present-day proteins are specifically composed of L-amino acids; the other enantiomers, D-amino acids, are only rarely used and not for proteins. However, the simplest method for forming simple polypeptides from all amino acids currently tested is the salt-induced peptide reaction (Fitz et al. 2007). The reaction forms polypeptides in a few days at moderate temperatures with small amounts of copper that were probably available at the time; certainly there was an abundance of salt (sodium and potassium chlorides) in seawater. The salt-induced reaction preferentially catalyses the formation of peptides in which the amino acids are all of the same enantiomeric form. Reactions using L-amino acids are favoured over their D counterparts! With even a slight bias towards L-amino acids, competition between the two forms would quickly edge out the D-forms.

Additional evidence for a deep ocean origin comes from two further observations. From DNA sequence analysis there was an early evolutionary split from the last universal common ancestor to form the archaebacteria and the eubacteria. Furthermore, sequence analysis suggests that the archaebacteria were on the direct evolutionary line that gave rise to the eukaryotes; the eubacterial line gave rise to most of the modern, familiar, largely mesophilic bacteria in soil and elsewhere. Hyperthermophilic, archaebacteria can live and replicate at $110°C$ and are found in the ocean deeps, usually near volcanic chimneys. Such bacteria can also survive at very high pressures (barophiles).

More recent information has emerged from modelling the proteins from these ancestral archaebacteria and they are heat stable in contrast to the mesophilic bacteria, which are unfolded by temperatures much over $25–40°C$ (Gouy and Chaussidon 2008). Further evidence that all life evolved from one common ancestor has been supported by using model selection theory (Theobald 2010).

Did life start with protein or nucleic acids: replication of peptides and criticality

There are many supporters of an early RNA world (e.g. Maynard-Smith and Szathmary 1999). Some RNA species have catalytic (enzymatic-like) activity and some oligonucleotides may self-replicate. However, RNA would not be stable in the early Earth's environment (Fitz et al. 2007). Alternative current evidence favours peptides and, eventually, proteins as the initial directions in life's origin.

It has been demonstrated frequently in the past that certain peptides have catalytic activity. More crucially, peptides with autocatalytic activity with respectable rates of reaction have been demonstrated (Lee et al. 1996). These peptides thus carry out the essential act of replication of themselves; surely, a process completely fundamental to life. A more recent advance is the observations that certain other peptides can catalyse the formation of others and ligate other peptides together (Yao et al. 1998; Isaac and Chmielewski 2002). A more familiar self-replicating protein is the prion, but what is replicated is a three-dimensional structure, rather than *de novo* synthesis. Intriguingly, the varieties of three-dimensional folding of proteins are much more limited than the amino acid sequence (Dok-holyan et al. 2002).

Given the availability of precursor peptides, a replicating system could rapidly increase their numbers. Even if a single polypeptide molecule only replicated itself once a day, within 21 days the numbers of such polypeptides could be 2^{20}, nearly a millimole. How much peptide would form would depend on the availability of precursors and its stability in these early conditions. However, since specific peptide precursors may not be present in large amounts, what will be required will be a peptide template that can replicate peptide precursors from free amino acids. Such capabilities have survived into present-day organisms (Kuraishi 1974). The biosynthesis of glutathione (a tripeptide) and numerous other peptide antibiotics are synthesized by what is described as a protein template mechanism; not through transcription/translation. Present-day organisms activate their amino acids for this protein template mechanism through attachment to pantotheine. In the early Earth, this may not have been necessary, particularly if the salt-induced peptide-synthetic mechanism previously described, operates (Fitz et al. 2007). An alternative using carbon monoxide and iron sulphide is described below.

More importantly, any particular strain of bacteria can produce various analogues of these small peptides in which some constituent amino acids are replaced by structurally related ones (Kuraishi 1974). Fidelity of replication through a protein template is weaker than the eventual method cells evolved, using nucleic acids. As indicated below, a trade-off between variation in synthesis as result of poor fidelity, and eventual accuracy and stability would mark a turning point in life's evolution.

Enclosure of this early set of peptide reactions would, at some stage, become essential, but the 'membranes' around the reactive mixtures could simply have been made of proteins or peptides initially. There is now evidence that particular peptides can undergo self-assembly to form micelles (vesicles). Such peptides would have hydrophobic amino acids concentrated at one side of the micelle and the charged amino acids at the other. The micelles (vesicles) that form have the hydrophobic ends projecting into the medium and hydrophilic amino acids internal (Vauthey et al. 2002). This hydrophobic

surface could attract lipid-like material to itself, thus helping construct an early membrane. The value of a predominantly peptide or protein membrane is that its leakiness would still permit entry of externally formed amino acids and other molecules. Present-day membranes have large amounts of proteins anywhere from 20% to 80%. Vesicles are also formed by treating pyruvic acid at high pressure and temperature (Hazen et al. 2002) mimicking conditions near hydrothermal vents.

An early idea attributed to Oparin was that life originated in a coacervate, a colloidal droplet, which could concentrate other organic molecules. However, coacervates are usually formed using gum Arabic as one of the constituents and it is not obvious that this specific material has any value to the origin of life, although the behaviour of coacervates can be extraordinarily life-like.

A self-organizing, critical system evolves

The onset of cross-replication and ligation of peptides together would have been important in beginning to construct a peptide network. The network would clearly be a self-organizing structure and each peptide network will have been tested many times until suitable network structures emerged, but could enough different peptides emerge within one primordial cell? Surely not.

The symbiotic theory of evolution has emphasized how increased complexity emerged through fusion of original symbiotic partners (Margulis 1970). Transferring this process to an earlier time, it can be envisaged that fusion of different vesicular structures containing different peptides and, thus, different reactions would have greatly accelerated the complexity of the primordial cell. No doubt, many combinations occurred, but of these, very few could have been successful. Only with many trials did more stable systems emerge with greater potential, reproduction, and organization, control, and system structure. Natural selection intervenes early.

Kaufmann (1995) provided a very simple scenario to cover this delicate region of the origin. Scatter thousands of buttons on a floor and start to stitch them together in pairs. Eventually, the pairs will be joined together and, in turn, as this process continues all the buttons will be eventually be connected together in one large web. Kaufmann sees the buttons as analogous to chemical reactions among the constituent molecules. Once the full network forms he regards the system as undergoing the quantum leap of emergence—it becomes both autocatalytic, and self-sustaining and alive. It becomes a complex system! Life becomes inevitable. Equate the buttons to vesicles and the analogy becomes complete.

However, the evolution of control and design structures will have accelerated the process of forming a system, too. Peptide–peptide interactions are obvious linkages; negative feedback might have started as product inhibition, but simple feedback loops in which one peptide controls the pH and/or ionic strength controlling its own replication would also help improve homeostasis. It is interlinked, fast and slow positive feedback loops that apparently drive reliable decisions in present-day cells, and we can expect such design features to make an early appearance (Brandman et al. 2005).

A critical situation develops

Continued generation of new auto- and cross-replicating peptides will, at some stage, reach a critical situation. Scale-free networks, constructed from hubs and connectors, should be well on the way. When a critical number of interactions is reached, a transition to a new ordered state becomes probable through what is termed a phase transition (Nykter et al. 2008, and references therein to biological examples). The phase transition might mark a change from a disorganized to an organized state, but a shift in the balance between stability and continued adaptability is equally possible. This situation is clearly similar to the bifurcation points illustrated by Prigogine (1996) in which the fate at a bifurcation point is either disorganization, or increased structure and order. What will generate this phase shift or does the critical state follow from the problems of accuracy in replication? At least two stages call for a jump in organization.

The first may simply have marked a change from a disorganized mixture of different peptides to a recognizably, interactive system. Secondly,

use of protein or peptide templates for replication will inevitably generate a variety of mutant peptides, with a probable variety of both function and replication. While this is advantageous to our primordial cell at the beginning, there is probably a trade-off between variation and eventual stability. If, for example, a spectrum of peptides or proteins appears with very desirable functions, then weak accuracy of replication becomes a disadvantage and vice versa. At this stage, a process of replication with much greater fidelity will be beneficial and it is here that nucleic acids perhaps enter the story in a phase shift. It can be envisaged that a short sequence of DNA might be synthesized by a protein template, which then, in turn, acts as a nucleic acid template for much greater accuracy of replication of this peptide. The replication rate by this means may have been slow at the beginning, but the much greater accuracy will be preferential, particularly if it is a peptide responsible for synthesizing a number of others.

Only later will RNA emerge as useable, and only when conditions are sufficiently stable for it to be used. In present-day organisms, interactions of particular proteins with specific short sequences of DNA are well-characterized, and this ability may well reflect the ancestral capability. Other organizing phase shifts can be envisaged as resulting in better homeostasis, and in generating systems that are more robust and resilient, enabling primordial cells to occupy different environmental features of the deep ocean.

The evolution of the eventual cell can be seen to have been beset by a series of crises, and the attempts were no doubt made millions of times before one successfully gained the right combination to be self-sustaining.

The earliest metabolic cycles

A metabolism became necessary once early primordial cells started to move away from the hydrothermal vent, and as temperatures diminished or as volcanic activity itself diminished. At this stage, some primordial cells might even have found their way to the surface with replicative, homeostatic properties, and a potential variety of metabolic reactions.

An old (and less likely) idea suggested that heterotrophic metabolism was the earliest form. All sorts of organic molecules were formed, it was assumed, in the primordial soup and as these were used up, early cells had to develop enzymes to synthesize and replace them.

A much more likely scenario was autotrophic metabolism as indicated by Wachtershauser (1990). The earliest forms of metabolism were probably of two kinds:

1. Some process that converted carbon dioxide into organic molecules as independent synthesis of carbon-containing compounds became essential.

2. Simple redox reactions so that chemical energy could replace temperature or heat energy that so far had provided the necessary energy input. Redox processes would also be essential for manipulating the pH and ionic strength of the primordial cell internal milieu, providing some form of homeostatic control.

The chemical energy available at the earliest stages for both carbon fixation and redox reactions is most likely to have been a combination of hydrogen sulphide and ferrous sulphide, in which the latter would have been oxidized to pyrites (Wachtershauser 1990). Ferrous sulphide and hydrogen sulphide would have been abundant at hydrothermal vents. As mentioned earlier, hydrothermal chimneys are often black because they contain abundant iron sulphide and the chimney surface now provides possible catalytic surfaces (Huber and Wachtershauser 1997, 1998; Wachtershauser 2000).

Using simple constituents and an iron sulphide surface as catalyst, the synthesis of activated acetic acid (analogous to acetyl CoA) and the formation of peptides have been demonstrated, the latter case using carbon monoxide as a condensation agent. Further studies (Cody et al. 2000) using an iron sulphide surface have detected the synthesis of organometallic compounds and the formation of pyruvic acid. These authors noted that some of the iron sulphide is solubilized during the reaction. Hazen et al. (2002) reported that pyruvic acid, under conditions of high temperature and pressure, condenses into compounds that display surface activity and form vesicles when placed in normal buffer solution, an alternative membrane-like material.

The first metabolic pathway

The earliest metabolic pathway suggested is the reductive tricarboxylic acid cycle, effectively the reverse of the normal tricarboxylic acid (TCA) cycle that underpins energy generation in present-day aerobic organisms. The reductive TCA cycle fixes carbon dioxide and synthesizes some carboxylic acids, which can be used as precursors for amino acids. Only with the onset of aerobic metabolism would the TCA cycle assume its normal decarboxylating and energy-generating direction. Aside from Wachtershauser's early analysis and support of the reductive TCA, other evidence that strongly supports his assessment and emphasis on iron sulphide catalysis is the ubiquitous presence of iron sulphide proteins that are found in all life forms containing clusters of varying proportions (modules) of iron and sulphur (Beinert et al. 1997). These proteins catalyse redox reactions and now act as sensors of iron, oxygen, superoxide, and nitric oxide.

Morowitz et al. (2000) used some very simple selection methods applied to some 3.5 million known chemicals. The aim was to find molecules using only C, H, and O that starts with CO_2 and uses reductants from iron sulphide and redox couples as an energy source, i.e. potential early metabolism. They found only 153 such molecules and among these were all 11 members of the reductive citric acid cycle, suggesting again the reductive TCA cycle as a potential first metabolic cycle. A small number of selection rules generate a very constrained subset of molecules, suggesting that this is the type of reaction model that will prove useful in the study of biogenesis. The model indicates that the metabolism shown in the universal chart of pathways may be central to the origin of life, is emergent from organic chemistry, and may be unique.

In protobacteria found near hydrothermal vents (and other more extreme environments that use the reductive carboxylic acid cycle), the critical carboxylation steps use a group of iron sulphur proteins (ferridoxins) as the source of reductant (Hugler et al. 2005). Ferridoxins also act as redox sources in the fixation of nitrogen to ammonia, a process that is strictly anaerobic and was probably required as sources of ammonia may have declined as organisms started to disperse.

The first photosynthetic process

An earlier intriguing suggestion is found in the report by Borowska and Mauzerall (1988) of the photoreduction of carbon dioxide catalysed by ferrous ions. Intriguingly, geothermal light is emitted by hydrothermal vents, although there may not be enough light in the ultraviolet (UV) wavelength for this reaction to proceed efficiently. However, there could be enough light to permit a potential photosynthetic reaction to occur, and supplement other chemical redox reactions or perhaps to develop chlorophylls that acted as sensors of nearness to the vent (Nisbet et al. 1995; White et al. 2000). Light is emitted from hydrothermal vents, both in the visible and infra-red ranges. An obligately photosynthetic bacterial anaerobe has been isolated from a deep-sea hydrothermal vent that uses light from the vent to supplement other chemical reactions, to provide energy to survive and reproduce (Beatty et al. 2005).

Movement to the surface: the start of surface photosynthesis

With the upwelling of hot water from deep ocean hydrothermal vents, early organisms will have been brought to the cooler regions on the ocean's surface. Two problems accompanied such movement. With lower temperatures, the incorporation of chemical energy of some kind would become crucial and only primordial organisms that had already developed such abilities would survive. Present-day chemoautotrophs can survive using ammonia, hydrogen sulphide, and hydrogen as redox sources, but fix carbon dioxide (via the iron sulphide-containing proteins, ferredoxin) and use sulphate as a final electron acceptor. On the surface, numerous volcanic areas would continue to provide some of these chemical materials for cellular energy, as they do today.

However, the second was much more crucial to the evolution of life—exposure to strong UV light from sunlight. In an anaerobic world, the density of UV light would have been damagingly high at the surface. Porphyrins are molecules composed of four pyrrole units, linked together in a ring, and which chelate single atoms of metal at their centre. If the metal is magnesium, the porphyrin represents the basic structure of chlorophyll, if iron, cytochromes, and if cobalt, vitamin B12. Although these molecules are crucial to present-day plants, animals, and bacteria, porphyrins were probably synthesized to act as sunshades to protect early cells against UV light. In this function, large numbers would be synthesized and, by attaching a phytol tail, could be lined up along membranes.

Present-day photosynthesis uses groups of about 700 chlorophylls aggregated together on a membrane to act as antennae for light absorption. Light quanta are absorbed by electrons in these antennae to reach a much higher energy level and thus generate strong reducing potential. These excited electrons can move between the different chlorophylls of the antenna in a process called exciton migration. The consequence is the separation of a strong reductant, energetic electron, from the hole left behind as the electrons move, which becomes a strong oxidant.

The electrons are finally deposited at a reaction centre or trap—holes end up at another trap. An alternative mechanism to actual electron movement is quantum coherence that might see immediate transfer of an energetic state to the trap without the need for electrons to physically move. However, at the reaction centre, these energetic electrons are transferred through several electron transfer and reducing compounds that are used to reduce CO_2. Finally, metabolic cycles can convert these first enzymatic products to carbohydrates or other useful metabolic intermediates, such as amino acid precursors.

The earliest extant photosynthetic organism may be *Chlorobium tepidum* an anaerobic, thermophile found near hot springs emitting hydrogen sulphide and a member of the green sulphur bacteria (Elsen et al. 2002). In this organism and because it is anaerobic, the strong oxidant converts hydrogen sulphide to sulphur. Significantly, and unlike other photosynthetic organisms that use an enzyme called Rubisco for CO_2 fixation, *C. tepidum* uses the more primitive reductive TCA cycle to reduce carbon dioxide.

If other completely different forms of photosynthesis evolved they have not survived, with one exception. *Halobacterium halobium*, a member of the archaebacteria, lives in extreme saline conditions (4M sodium chloride) and uses a rhodopsin-like pigment (bacteriorhodopsin), similar to the visual pigment in mammals to pump chloride out of the cell, a reaction from which it can gain cellular energy.

The cell fusion/symbiosis theory of cell complexity and the construction of a two-stage photosynthesis

Reference has already been made to the effects of fusion of vesicles containing simple reactions in the development of the primordial cell. The resulting conglomerate no doubt gained substantially in enhanced organization with continued energy flux and the Prigogine (1996) effect at bifurcation points and criticality. What started as accidental events would no doubt have continued with the simplest of cells so that vesicle fusion was now overtaken by cell fusion. While these processes on a per-cell basis may have been infrequent, with enough cells around, such crucial events leading to new critical states and the construction of new organization would have been sufficiently common for real experimentation to happen.

Cell fusion is similar to the symbiotic theory of evolution vigorously propagated by Margulis (1970). The only difference here is to see the process as continuous from the beginning—organization as a result of stochastic meanderings and fusion. That the symbiotic theory is correct for the origin of both eukaryotic mitochondria and angiosperm chloroplasts is established beyond reasonable doubt. Both chloroplasts and mitochondria contain their own DNA, which is used to act as templates for some of the organelle proteins. DNA sequencing clearly establishes the evolutionary origin of the chloroplast as from a blue-green alga and mitochondrion as from a bacterium.

The report by Bernhard et al. (2000) indicates that microbial mats in the Santa Barbara basin contain large numbers of protozoa and metazoa, which harbour prokaryotic symbionts. Ryan (2002), in his first chapter, describes observations of such eventual symbiont acquisition made by Kwang Jeon (Jeon and Jeon 1976; Jeon 1987). The original event

was an infection of amoeba by a bacterium, from which only a few individuals survived. With time and cultivation these pathogens changed into potential symbionts, then into required cell components. These interactions may not have occurred with great probability, but given the large number of single-celled organisms likely to be around, the 'symbiotic' event, occurred with sufficient frequency to ensure evolutionary development.

However, both mitochondria, as well as chloroplasts, are resident in eukaryotic cells. The origin of this cell organelle, the mitochondrion, seems likely from DNA sequence information to have actually resulted from a cell fusion between an archaebacterium and a proteobacterium. The unusual event here was a fusion of genomes with elimination of many unnecessary or even destabilizing genes (Simonson et al. 2005). Horizontal gene transfer is extremely common in present-day bacteria and the process has made decoding the actual event more difficult than anticipated.

Photosynthetic bacteria were almost certainly the earliest forms of photosynthetic organisms, but these organisms require a fairly strong reductant-like hydrogen sulphide or hydrogen to provide reducing potential. An extra fillip of 'reducing' light energy from a single set of chlorophyll antennae and, thus effectively, a single quantum of light is added in. However, the oxidant produced is relatively weak and sufficient only to convert hydrogen sulphide to sulphur or hydrogen to water.

In blue-green algae, and thus in the chloroplast of higher plants, two sets of chlorophyll antennae are joined together by a few electron-transferring compounds. The consequence is now that two quanta of light, instead of one, are injected into the system that produces both reductant and oxidant. The oxidant produced is now very much stronger and sufficient to ensure that water is directly oxidized to oxygen. Again, the most likely preceding event for the evolution of the blue-green algae was fusion of two photosynthetic bacteria. Together with consequent organizational changes, these two sets of chlorophylls were placed in sequence joined by several redox proteins and now producing an oxidant strong enough to oxidize water to oxygen.

The strong reductant was again used to provide reductive energy for metabolism. In particular a new enzyme, Rubisco (ribulose 1,5 bisphosphate carboxylase) evolved to fix CO_2 by combination with ribulose bisphosphate and forming phosphoglycerate. A novel cycle evolved that enabled regeneration of ribulose bisphosphate for CO_2 fixation. Coupled with a few additional enzymes this became the respiratory pentose phosphate pathway (Nisbet et al. 2007)

Metabolic methods also had to evolve for defusing the damaging effects of oxygen free radicals, formed inevitably as oxygen is being synthesized. These metabolic reactions may also have evolved from those that mitigated the damaging effects of UV light.

The consequences and the dating of the appearance of oxygen-releasing photosynthesis

The evolution of blue-green algae that synthesize oxygen during photosynthesis literally changed the face of the earth. The onset of oxygen production from blue-green algal photosynthesis is feasibly dated by examination of the age of the banded iron deposits that changed from the reduced ferrous form of iron to the oxidized ferric. This estimate of change is in reasonable agreement with the recognition of stromatolites that contain blue-green algal fossils as starting somewhere between 2.5 and 3 billion years ago (Nisbet et al. 2007; Trouwborst et al. 2007). The appearance of oxygen would have progressively eliminated most (95%) of anaerobic organisms at the time except those that had found how to manage local anaerobic environments, where they are now largely located.

It may have taken as long time for a eukaryotic cell to evolve, as it did for life itself, because of the very complex changes that were necessary—the packaging of DNA into chromatin, a nuclear envelope, the appearance of a cytoskeleton, and internal endoplasmic reticulum—but fossil evidence for the presence of such cells, 1.5 billion years ago, seems well established (Javaux et al. 2001; Poole and Penny 2001).

There is good fossil evidence for the existence of a red alga 1.2 billion years ago with clear sexual reproductive capabilities. This identification indicates the earliest date for this complex sexual process with the requirement for meiosis (reduction division) to evolve (Butterfield 2000).

Whatever the earliest eukaryotic cell was like, it contained many proteins and signal processes that are still held in common between plants and animals. However, the processes of generating individuality had to wait until multicellularity appeared extensively, only in the last billion years, and these are described in the next chapter.

The further evolution of plants is well known and much of it has been to generate plants that can deal with the transition from marine to land, and then to progress to inhabit the much drier areas of the land surface. During this process, new problems emerged that have resulted in the formation of a recognized behaviour. We start to look at these in details later, but the critical event, that of autotrophy through using visible light, was the first critical step.

References

Bassez, M.P. (2003). Is high pressure water the cradle of life? *Journal of Physics: Condensed Matter*, **15**, L353–L361.

Beatty, J.T., Ovemann, J., Lince, M.T., Manske, A.K., Lang, A.S., Blankenship, R.E., and 3 others (2005). An obligately photosynthetic bacterial anaerobe from a deep-sea hydrothermal vent. *Proceedings of the National Academy of Sciences USA*, **102**, 9306–9310.

Beinert, H., Holm, R.E., and Munck, E. (1997). Iron-sulfur clusters: natures modular multipurpose structure. *Science*, **277**, 653–659.

Bernhard, J.M., Buck, K.R., Farmer, M.A., and Bowser, S.S. (2000). The Santa Barbara basin is a symbiosis oasis. *Nature*, **403**, 77–80.

Borowska, Z., and Mauzerall, D. (1988). Photoreduction of carbon dioxide by aqueous ferrous ion. *Proceedings of the National Academy of Science USA*, **85**, 6577–6580.

Brandman, O., Ferrell, J.E., Li, R., and Meyer, T. (2005). Interlinked fast and slow positive feedback loops drive reliable cell decisions. *Science*, **310**, 496–498.

Butterfield, N.J. (2000). *Bangiomorpha pubescens* sp.: implications for the evolution of sex, multicellularity and the Mesoproterozoic/Neoproterozoic radiation of eukaryotes. *Paleobiology*, **26**, 386–404.

Butterfield, D.A., Jonasson, I.R., Massoth, G.J., Feely, R.A., Roe, K.K., Embley, R.E., and 5 others (1997). Seafloor eruptions and evolution of hydrothermal fluid chemistry. *Philosophical Transactions of the Royal Society. A. Mathematical, Physical and Engineering Sciences*, **355**, 369–386.

Cody, G.D., Boctor, N.Z, Filley, T.R., Hazen, R.M., Scott, J.H., Sharma, A., and 1 other (2000). Primordial carbonylated iron sulfur compounds and the synthesis of pyruvate. *Science*, **289**, 1337–1340.

Daniel, I., Oger, P., and Winter R. (2006). Origins of life and biochemistry under high pressure conditions. *Chemical Society Reviews*, **35**, 858–875.

Darwin, C. (1859). *The origin of species by means of natural selection*. John Murray, London.

Dokholyan, N.V., Shakhnovich, B., and Shakhanovich, E.I. (2002). Expanding protein universe and its origin from the big bang. *Proceedings of the National Academy of Sciences USA*, **99**, 14132–14136.

Elsen, J.A., Nelson, K.E., Paulsen, I.T. Heidelberg, J. F., Wu, M., Dodson, R. J., and 30 others (2002). The complete genome sequence of *Chlorobium tepidum* TLS a photosynthetic anaerobic green-sulfur bacterium. *Proceedings of the National Academy of Sciences USA*, **99**, 9909–9914.

Fitz, D., Reiner, H., and Rode, B.M. (2007). Chemical evolution towards the origin of life. *Pure and Applied Chemistry*, **79**, 2101–2117.

Gold T. (1999). *The deep hot biosphere*. Springer-Verlag, New York.

Gouy, M., and Chaussidon, M. (2008). Ancient bacteria liked it hot. *Nature*, **451**, 635–636.

Hazen, R.M., Boctor, N., Brandes, J.A., Cody, G.D., Hemley, R.J., Sharma, A., and 1 other. (2002). High pressure and the origin of life. *Journal of Physics-Condensed Matter*, **14**, 11489–11494.

Huber, C., and Wachtershauser, G. (1997). Activated acetic acid by carbon fixation on (Fe,Ni) S under primordial conditions. *Science*, **276**, 245–247.

Huber, C., and Wachtershauser, G. (1998). Peptides by activation of amino acids with CO on (Ni,Fe)S surfaces; implications for the origin of life. *Science*, **281**, 670–672.

Hugler M., Wirsen, C.O., Fuchs, G., Taylor, C.D., and Sievert, S.M. (2005). Evidence for autotrophic CO_2 fixation via the reductive tricarboxylic acid cycle by members of the ε subdivision of proteobacteria. *Journal of Bacteriology*, **187**, 3020–3027.

Isaac, R., and Chmielewski, J. (2002). Approaching exponential growth with a self replicating peptide. *Journal of the American Chemical Society*, **124**, 6808–6809.

Javaux, E.J., Knoll, A.H., and Walter, M.R. (2001). Morphological and ecological complexity in early eukaryotic ecosystems. *Nature*, **412**, 66–69.

Jeon, K.W. (1987). Change of cellular pathogen into required cell components. *Annals of the New York Academy of Sciences*, **503**, 359–371.

Jeon, K.W., and Jeon, M.S. (1976). Endosymbiosis in amoebae: recently established endosymbionts have become required cytoplasmic components. *Journal of Cell Physiology*, **89**, 337–344.

Kaufmann, S.A. (1995). *At home in the universe: the search for the laws of self organisation and complexity*. Oxford University Press, New York.

Kobayashi, K.L.H., Hare, P.E., Hobish, M.K., and Ponnamperuma, C. (1986). Abiotic synthesis of nucleosides by electric discharge in simulated Earth atmosphere. *Origins of Life*, **16**, 277–278.

Kuraishi, K. (1974). Biosynthesis of small peptides. *Annual Review of Biochemistry*, **43**, 445–459.

Lee, D.H., Granja, J.R., Martinez, J.A., Severin, K., and Ghadiri, M.R. (1996). A self-replicating peptide. *Nature*, **382**, 525–528.

Margulis, L. (1970). *Origin of the eukaryotic cell*. Yale University Press, New Haven, CT.

Matthews, C.N., Ludicky, R., Schaefer, J., Stesjskal, E.O., and McKay, R.A. (1984). Heteropolypeptides from hydrogen cyanide and water? Solid state N^{15} investigations. *Origin of Life*, **14**, 243–250.

Maynard-Smith, J., and Szathmary, E. (1999). *The origins of life*. Oxford University Press, Oxford.

Miller, S.L. (1953) A production of amino acids under possible primitive earth conditions. *Science*, **117**, 528–529.

Morowitz, H.J, Kostelnik, J.D., Yang, J., and Cody, G.D. (2000). The origin of intermediary metabolism. *Proceedings of the National Academy of Sciences USA*, **97**, 7704–7708.

Nisbet, E.G., Cann, J.R., and Dover, C.L., van (1995). Origins of photosynthesis. *Nature*, **373**, 479–480.

Nisbet, E.G., Grassinaeu, N.V., Howe, C.J., Abell, P.I., Regelous, M., and Nisbet, R.E.R. (2007). The age of Rubisco: the evolution of oxygenic photosynthesis. *Geobiology*, **5**, 311–335.

Nykter, M., Price, N.D., Aldana, M., Ramsey, S.A., Kauffman, S.A., Hood, L., and 2 others (2008). Gene expression dynamics in the macrophage exhibit criticality. *Proceedings of the National Academy of Science USA*, **105**, 1897–1900.

Poole, A., and Penny, D. (2001). Does endosymbiosis explain the origin of the nucleus? *Nature Cell Biology*, **3**, E173–174.

Prigogine, I. (1996). *The end of certainty*. Free Press, New York.

Ryan, F. (2002). *Darwin's blind spot*. Houghton Mifflin, New York.

Simonson, A.B., Servin, J.A., Skophammer, R.G., Herbold, C.W., Rivera, M.C., and Lake, J.A. (2005). Decoding the genomic tree of life. *Proceedings of the National Academy of Science. USA*, **102**, 6608–6613.

Theobald. D.L. (2010). A formal test of the theory of universal common ancestry. *Nature*, **465**, 219–222.

Trouwborst, R.E., Johnston, A., Koch, G., Luter, G.W., and Pierson, B.K. (2007). Biogeochemistry of Fe (II) oxidation in a photosynthetic microbial mat: implications for

Precambrian Fe (II) oxidation. *Geochimica et Geochimica Acta*, **71**, 4629–4643.

Vauthey, S., Santoso, S., Gong, H., Watson, N., and Zhang, S. (2002). Molecular self assembly of surfactant-like peptides to form nanotubes and nanovesicles. *Proceedings of the National Academy of Sciences USA*, **99**, 5355–5360.

Wachtershauser, G. (1990). Evolution of the first metabolic cycles. *Proceedings of the National Academy of Sciences USA*, **87**, 200–204.

Wachtershauser, G. (2000). Life as we don't know it. *Science*, **289**, 1307–1308.

White, S.N., Chave, A.D., Reynolds, G.T., Gaidos, E.J., Tyson, J.A., and Dover, C.L., van (2000). Variations in light emission from black smokers and flange pools on the Juan de Fuca ridge. *Geophysical Research Letters*, **27**, 1151–1154.

Yao, S., Ghosh, I., Zutshi, R., and Chmielewski, J. (1998). Selective amplification by auto- and cross-catalysis in a replicating peptide system. *Nature*, **396**, 447–480.

CHAPTER 5

Why did plants become multicellular?

When cells in a cluster cooperate, make sacrifices for the common good and adapt to change, that's an evolutionary transition to multicellularity.

(Ratcliff et al. 2012)

⊃ Summary

Most familiar plants are multicellular eukaryotes and the question arises as to how such a morphology and lifestyle evolved. The question is substantial because unicellular bacteria and unicellular eukaryotes are very successful in terms of numbers and habitats occupied. The original eukaryote combination is thought to have resulted from a fusion between two bacteria. It survived because it must have benefited from synergistic interactions between the fusion partners. Synergism implies communication and holistic behaviour. This first eukaryote cell must have acted as an individual to enable survival and replication. Various synergistic, and thus symbiotic, combinations are now known; some are highly unusual. The self-organized criticality hypothesis of Bak (1996) is described. Radical changes can take place with increased size and intensity of communication. Sexual reproduction in *Volvox*, cell clusters in yeast, and quorum sensing in bacteria, as well as day neutral plants are good examples. Communication between initial partners in multi-cells is essential to create an individual in which all partners are suborned to the benefit of the whole. Definite experimental evidence for communication between a three-celled plant stage is described. Modularity enables organisms to easily increase in size during evolution and it has occurred in plants which are intensely modular. Finally, one distinct fitness benefit that would accrue even to organisms that are combinations of two or more cells arises from the convoy principle. It is more difficult for predators to find a group of cells than to find the equivalent numbers of single cells uniformly distributed.

Introduction

In the two previous chapters, a sketch was provided of a plausible origin of life, and the appearance of single cells and photosynthesis. Whatever other description is used to characterize plants, photosynthesis is generally accepted as the salient feature. There are, of course, some exceptions to this rule. Biology cannot be defined in the same way as physical principles—generalized descriptions are the best that one can use. Parasitic plants, like mistletoe or dodder, for example, although sharing other characteristics that we recognize as plant-like, have usually disposed of photosynthesis either transiently or permanently. There are some 4000 species of parasitic plants altogether, found in 19 different angiosperm families—a kind of convergent evolution.

However, the previous chapter left life largely at the single-cell stage. Although single-celled marine plankton account for at least half of the photosynthetic fixation of carbon dioxide on Earth, few of these cell types, remarkably structured that they are, will

Plant Behaviour and Intelligence. First Edition. Anthony Trewavas.
© Anthony Trewavas 2014. Published 2014 by Oxford University Press.

be familiar to the reader. It is the multicellular plants that are most familiar, and it is those that present obvious behaviour and, as we shall see, intelligence. How or why plants became multicellular is what is considered in this chapter. There is no intention here of trying to detail the palaeontology of plants and the supposed evolution of individual forms.

Eukaryotic plants are most conveniently grouped into algae, bryophytes (mosses, liverworts), pteridophytes (ferns), gymnosperms, and angiosperms. Although it is thought that algal mats might have first appeared on land 1200 million years ago, the first proper multicellular land plants, the Lycopods (club mosses) and the Equisitales (horse tails) appear in the fossil record in the Silurian about 400 million years ago. Members of the lycopods and horsetails are still extant today, but are small compared with the tree-like lycopods and horsetails (and tree ferns) that were dominant and formed the basis of the coal measures in the Carboniferous period. The behaviour of these early plants, so far as can be deduced, was much more constrained in behaviour than present-day angiosperms. Early gymnosperm fossils are also reported as present in the carboniferous era.

Why become multicellular and eukaryotic? The role of synergism and fusion

As a group, bacteria are remarkably successful organisms

What might be considered the simplest of organisms, the bacteria, are remarkably successful and that creates a major difficulty. Why did anything more complex than bacteria evolve? The distribution and capabilities of bacteria highlight the problem. Microbes have found life situations virtually everywhere on earth. They can easily exchange genes with each other (a kind of sexual reproduction); they have elaborate signalling systems for dealing with environmental change with up to 50 different signals known to be sensed, although not all in the same species. Some members differentiate into different cell types. *Bacillus subtilis* can produce a highly resistant spore stage and *Caulobacter* can undergo an asymmetric division that into a stalk

cell and a highly motile swarmer. Many bacteria can live in colonies as biofilms and change gene expression according to colony size (quorum sensing). Others can form large highly structured morphologies when placed in unpalatable conditions improving survival. 50% of all bacteria are motile using flagellae to swim.

Bacteria survive on the outside and inside of virtually all plants and animals. In the termite gut they break down the resistant cellulose, and lignin to sugars and methane. Bacteria are found in all soils performing a multiplicity of essential reactions. Others can dispose of explosive or oil. Yet others contain minute bar magnets used for orientating their swimming. Some can grow at 110°C, or in extreme acidic or alkaline conditions, in solutions containing 4M salt or on the surface of glaciers, or under intense pressure at the bottom of the ocean (Rothschild and Mancinelli 2001). Some survive without oxygen, others can rot concrete or damage minerals. Furthermore, recent discoveries have shown them to survive several thousand metres or more, down in deep rocks (e.g. Zhang et al. 2005). They can even act as luminous beacons living in the pouches of fish that live in the darkest depths.

The free-living bacterial form of life has survived to this day and it may be possible to consider the bacterial lifestyle as the most successful of all life on this planet. Why then did organisms of greater complexity ever evolve? The problem is really compounded when we consider how successful eukaryotic, unicellular organisms actually are as well. Single-celled diatoms cover extensive areas of the surfaces of oceans. Diatoms are also able to produce really elaborate and complex cell wall structures made out of silica.

Why become eukaryotic? Synergistic interactions resulting from fusion would be crucial

The precise elements of fitness that accrued to the earliest eukaryote ancestor will probably never be known. Cell fusion between two different bacterial species is thought to have generated the eukaryote ancestor, based on examination of DNA sequences (Simonson et al. 2005). There is some controversy as to whether fusion is sufficient to account for eukaryotic features like the nucleus and the nuclear membrane (Poole and Penny 2001), but descent with modification was Darwin's view, and many additional and unusual modifications may have appeared millions of years after the original eukaryote fusion.

However, one important characteristic can be identified. The original cell fusion to construct a eukaryote must have led to new behaviour resulting from a synergistic cooperation between the two partners. Fitness would not have increased, but for synergism and the fusion organism would not have survived (Corning 2003). What cannot be known is the environmental conditions under which this synergistic fusion occurred and what other competitive organisms were present. Again, the critical point, it is the interaction between the organism and the environment in its totality that determines fitness. Organism and environment make for a holistic combination and fitness is a property of both elements interacting together.

Corning (2003) indicates that the strength of synergistic interactions and its positive effect on fitness probably underpins the evolution of many organisms. Synergism is basic to many aspects of improved fitness in evolutionary timescales. Just as behaviour is a holistic combination between environment and organism, so is fitness. In early vesicle fusion, for example (Chapter 4), the successful fusions would have to represent a synergistic fusion in order to more successfully compete. Synergistic selection or as Corning describes it, holistic Darwinism, represents a better understanding of evolutionary processes. Synergism, by its nature, also implies connection and thus an inter-connected system—two organism donors and the environment make for a three-way partnership in evolutionary endeavour.

Synergistic cell and organism interactions and fusions continue to this day

Synergism as a biological process continues to the present day, mainly between organisms and often as some kind of symbiotic state. However, once constructed such combinations enable the potential for unique accidents that could give rise to novel forms of life, such as required for further eukaryote evolution. Some examples illustrate the point.

Various nitrogen-fixing bacteria live in different degrees of symbiosis with plants. Methane oxidation in marine environments is performed by a consortium of different microbial species that cooperate to construct enormous chimneys from carbonate as a by-product (Hoffmeister and Martin 2003). Fusion of some of these, in due course, or gene exchange seems likely in time. Some oligochaete worms use endo-symbiont bacteria in their epidermis to metabolize a full set of nutrients and replace the digestive system that has now been lost. That pest of gardeners and farmers, the aphid, relies on bacterial symbionts for the synthesis of some essential amino acid acids. Mealy bugs contain endo-symbionts that are bacteria within another larger bacterium. There are sea slugs that acquire whole chloroplasts from marine eukaryotic algae by ingestion and incorporate them into their cells and use them to photosynthesize. It looks as though glyoxylate cycle enzymes in higher plants and found in a limited number of species were acquired from bacteria sometime in the past, implying a close interaction. Perhaps it was the other way round, plants providing bacteria with the necessary DNA sequences? Many other examples of bacteria living within animal cells are known. All of these situations provide the potential for transferring bacterial genes if not the whole micro-organism into host cells. How long before the sea slug finds the mechanism for replicating the chloroplasts it has incorporated and becoming permanently photosynthetic? Is there potential there for future human beings to reduce energy requirements by becoming literally green and sunbathing used to reduce energy requirements?

The issue that arises is that increased complexity can develop from such fusions. What needs further exploration is whether fusion could have contributed to the evolution of higher plants, a question that currently remains unanswered.

The costs and benefits of becoming eukaryotic

The subsequent benefits as eukaryotes evolved are thought to have come from a larger genome, greater internal differentiation and demarcation of cellular functions. However, these advantages could only appear once the initial cell fusion occurred; they could not have been predicted beforehand. Once gained, greater complexity in signalling, environmental sensing, and the occupation of new ecological niches could all evolve. The earliest synergistic interaction that enabled selection may have been no more than the ability to perform some new kind of metabolic reaction, such as the pentose phosphate pathway.

Could self-organized criticality explain the origin of multicellularity?

One possibility to explain the origin of multicellularity is to see it as an inevitable set of events in evolution, rather as Prigogine (1996) saw organization as resulting from a continued input of energy. There is discrete evidence for periods of apparent stability or even stasis followed by times of often intense change in evolution. Bursts of speciation and evolutionary change accompany critical points that develop naturally in ecosystems resulting from the continued flow of energy giving rise to greater organization or chaos (Prigogine 1996).

Apart from the evidence provided by Gould (2002, and references therein) of 'punctuated equilibria', there are the well-defined, very rapid, periods of speciation in eukaryotes in the Proterozoic and early Cambrian, animals in the Cambrian, insects in the carboniferous and flowering plants in the tertiary, the latter only about 120–140 million years ago. In the same way, multicellularity may have taken place in a burst of evolutionary change with many multicellular organisms developing at the same time. A model used to examine how such changes occur is the self-organized criticality model of Bak (1996) and Sneppen et al. (1995). Although this hypothesis was initially used as an analogy for evolutionary bursts, I think it has enormous relevance to understanding how and why multi-cells appear. Higher plants as will be indicated in a later chapter are self-organizing systems.

Bak (1996) studied very simple systems to help explain these apparent sudden changes. The most well-known is the growing sand pile. It is a common observation that by continually adding grains of sand to a pile for a time nothing seems to happen, except of course the pile gets bigger and the overall shape, a kind of pyramid, remains the same. Suddenly beyond a critical point, an avalanche happens and the shape is irreversibly changed.

Like cells and organisms, the sand pile system is analogously open with a flow of energy because sand grains are continually poured on top. The pile is initially stable because of the connections between the grains. Only when those connections exceed a critical number, do avalanches emerge. The pile just before an avalanche, just before the next sand grain is added, is clearly in a critical state: one extra grain is sufficient to precipitate obvious change. Bak performed large numbers of experiments on this very simple system to try and understand the system better, and so to understand avalanche-like changes in biology. Avalanches were of variable size and largely unpredictable as to when they would occur within a range of pyramid sizes, but the size of the avalanches obeyed a simple power relation—small avalanches were more frequent than large ones.

Bak's conclusion was that cells and organisms may operate on the edge between order and chaos. Thus, in evolving a multicellular organism, simply increasing the numbers of cells in a colony may, on its own, precipitate the change to interdependent interaction, pushing the colony in the direction of the individual. Furthermore, by analogy, it is the connections and probably the intensity of connection between the members of the colony that becomes the major issue generating the individual. The intensity of signalling can precipitate new emergent properties.

Transitions that occur with size

If we take Bak's (1996) idea as more than just an odd model, what it implies is that size can generate, very suddenly, radical change. Is there biological evidence for that point of view?

Size dependence of reproduction in Volvox

The Volvocales are fresh-water colonial algae consisting of groups of single photosynthetic cells held together in a matrix. Each vegetative cell possesses a flagellum, enabling the colony to be mobile. Each colony is derived from a single cell and, thus, the cells in the colony share kinship, but the numbers of individual cells that form a colony in each *Volvox* species vary from 32 up to several thousand. Only the species with the largest colonies reproduce sexually with the transition between 200 and 400 cells. Potential sexual cells lose their flagellae and differentiate. When this transition is exceeded, the *Volvox* clearly behaves as an individual with demarcation of functions between the daughter cells. At this stage certainly the *Volvox* behaves as an individual, instead of a conglomerate. Based on Bak's model this transition must be marked by changes in communication between the individual cells. What is communicated is not known, but by-products from photosynthesis would be a reasonable first guess.

Members of the Volvocales illustrate the problems of becoming larger with functional differentiation and a transition due to cell numbers (Michod 2007). There are at least two problems—costs to sexual reproduction, not shared by those that reproduce only vegetatively. First, there is a loss of photosynthetic yield due to sexual cell differentiation. Secondly, there is a reduction in overall motility. Only the largest colonies can bear the costs, and obtain the obvious benefits of sexual reproduction and overall gene mixing that it implies. Each sexually reproducing colony can now be regarded as a cooperative, even altruistic, entity and there must be communication as indicated between the individual cells to generate the synergistic interactions that benefit the colony as a whole.

The reduction in motility is actually a cost in potential homeostasis. The colonies are denser than water and need their flagellae to maintain their position in the lake in which they live. Being able to move means being able to access the optimal light sources. Movement also improves the potential for accessing minerals that are unlikely to be evenly distributed. At night-time there is a typical circadian pattern of *Volvox* movement upwards, presumably to search the layers of the lake near the surface, which may have higher mineral content.

Direct measurement of the motility of individual colonies does indicate that, as reproductive effort increases, motility declines. Michod (2007) regards fitness in these organisms then as the product of viability and fecundity. What drives cell groups towards becoming an individual is that the benefits of both specialization of vegetative functions (improved motility, higher photosynthetic yield, etc.) offset the initial costs of differentiation and reproduction. Fitness trade-offs often result in group fitness being higher than that of individual cells. Again, a form of synergy. Increasing fitness of the group then ensures that the fitness of the individual cells declines.

Cell clusters in yeast

Ratcliff et al. (2012) grew yeast in conditions in which multicellularity would be expected and observed the rapid evolution of clustering genotypes. The clusters exhibited no genotypic competition between the individual cell members and some division of labour was observed. They also reported that the rapid appearance of programmed cell death, leading in turn to propagation of the cell clusters that often assumed a kind of snowflake structure.

Size of bacterial colony changes behaviour

When I did my degree, the courses in microbiology concerned the behaviour of bacteria in free solution, commonly called planktonic cell populations. In the last 15–20 years or so increasing attention has been paid to the behaviour of bacteria in settled populations as biofilms. A biofilm starts with attachment of bacteria to a surface by secretion. This adhesion product is usually a polysaccharide or cellulose analogue. A signalling and response system is obviously required for surface recognition and subsequent secretion.

The signal to form a biofilm may be paucity of food. When faced with starvation conditions, bacteria alter the protein and lipid of the outer membrane, increasing both hydrophobicity and potential surface adherence. Further division in the film increases the size of the colony, and the sibling cells remain in close contact with each other and continue to secrete the matrix material.

There are a number of advantages to biofilm life. Organic materials may concentrate on surfaces, extracellular polymers can help concentrate nutrients from free solution, particularly if there is a flow of solution over the biofilm. A mixture of species can utilize waste excreted from their neighbours and if each species has different enzyme profiles they can utilize food that no individual on its own could use. Close association increases the chances of exchange of DNA and acquiring new genes. Furthermore, there is protection in a biofilm from noxious chemicals and other predatory damage. Although 50% of bacteria are motile and motility increases the potential chances of bacteria forming biofilms, flagellae are discarded upon surface adhesion. In a sense, a biofilm is analogous to a multicellular organism and benefits accrue again to those who occupy the biofilm.

The similarity to the Bak model comes with quorum sensing. Bacteria communicate with each other by signals that pass between them. Like multicellular plants and animals, these signals provide information that is sensed by receptors located in the outer membrane. The response can act to synchronize the population towards common goals. Quorum sensing is a particular aspect of communication (Waters and Bassler 2005). As its name implies, a minimal population number, a colony size, a quorum, is required in the biofilm. Continual production and release of signalling molecules reaches a threshold level and, when the quorum is reached, gene expression throughout the biofilm is altered. The signalling molecules are produced first by those individuals nearest the surface and, thus, the likely oldest members of the biofilm. Currently, the signals that are used are various small organic molecules and peptides.

The first example of quorum sensing was reported in the bacterium *Vibrio fischeri*. These bacteria populate a light organ pouch of a squid and produce luminescent light when the quorum is reached. The bacteria benefit, in turn, from rich nutrients in the pouch. The squid benefits from the luminescent light produced that increases its chances of catching prey.

The variety of signalling mechanisms uncovered in quorum sensing, illustrates the potential benefits for our multicellular plant progenitor, too. Again, it is distribution of function that seems crucial, but also there is an indication of reliability, in signal recognition. In *Vibrio*, for example, there are three auto-inducers for quorum sensing that act initially in parallel through the receptor stage. All lead to the same pathway, switching on *lux* genes that, in turn, generate light. Parallel pathways help provide reliability, a kind of fail-safe mechanism and something to be expected in multicellular plants. There

is evidence, too, that the squid that accommodates *Vibrio* eliminates cheating cells that fail to produce light, but benefit from the nutrients provided by the host.

In contrast, in *Pseudomonas*, there are two auto-inducers that act in parallel and there are three classes of responsive genes—those that are switched on by either inducer and those that are switched on only by both together. Different circumstances are thus sensed and specific patterns of gene expression correlate with these environments. In *Bacillus subtilis* there are two peptide inducers that either commit to competence or to sporulation. In *Streptococcus pneumoniae* a kind of on/off switch controls quorum sensing resulting from positive feedback in the mechanism. The particular gene circuits are then sequentially switched on.

In chemical identity there are a limited number of quorum sensing molecules. Thus, there is room for cooperative synergy between different bacterial species in the biofilm that both respond to the same signal. Is this not analogous to the behaviour of different kinds of cells in a multicellular organism? Thresholds between different cells in the same tissue in multicellular plants provide for flexibility in response to signals (Trewavas 2012).

Some other size-based transitions

Flowering plants can be grouped into those that flower at a defined time of year responding to day length and those that do not. The first are called photoperiodic and the latter, day neutral. Different cultivars of day neutral tobacco simply form flowers when they reach a critical size, determined as the numbers of nodes (McDaniel et al. 1996). If the plant is kept below this number and thus size, by continually removing the upper part of the stem, they can be kept permanently vegetative. It is thought that elements of hormonal communication are involved, but the Bak (1996) model indicates no qualitative variation is necessary, merely quantitative with an obvious threshold. Even photosynthetic products may be sufficient to tip the balance between the two states.

The shoot meristem is an embryonic region usually in annuals to be found on the top of the shoot. The meristem itself contains hundreds of cells and its function is the continued production of new leaves, which it does in continuous fashion with the positions of new leaf primordia determined on a Fibonacci series. Eventually, the meristem enters a new phase, the production of flowers. The appearance and specification of a new leaf is a radical change. The time period between the appearance of one leaf primordium compared with the next is called the plastochron. There is evidence that, in some plants, the length of the plastochron is determined by the size of the apical meristem. As cell division increases, a critical size is reached and a new leaf primordium is specified. Again, intensity of communication may be the defining step.

Is there a direction in evolution that increases multicellularity and complexity in behaviour?

Many consider that there has been a general direction, a progression, in evolutionary time. Something, it is thought, has been increasing from prokaryotes to eukaryotes, from single to multi-cells, but whatever it was, did it provide an underlying drive, an inevitable direction, about the general direction of evolution? Or is it all just random meandering of complex systems?

Darwin was in no doubt about an evolutionary direction and he considered that it was reflected in a greater degree of organization. Others have suggested that it is an increase in the ability to obtain and process information about the environment, or a degree of independence from the environment, or energy intensiveness, or even entropy reduction (McShea 1996). On the other hand, it is also generally accepted that the evolution of any specific organism or morphology is the product of a complex interplay of historical contingencies or accidents. This is a strong counter argument against the notion of a direction or pattern of evolution.

Despite the supposed stochastic nature of selection, coupled with a variable environmental context, overall general trends in complexity, size, individuality and diversity do seem to have arisen. Trees are obviously much larger than algal uni-cells and cover the earth's surface, while algae are limited to water or the surface of trees and sometimes rocks, like *Pleurococcus*. There is, then, one clue to the benefits that multi-cells bring. Demarcation of function increases complexity in behaviour and the potential occupation of new ecological habitats.

However, these benefits can only occur subsequently. Like that of meiosis and the subsequent fusion of gametes from different individuals, the benefits only occur once the original event has happened and sometime after, or so it is supposed. The initial event here was surely the production of haploid individuals able to be free living. Even some angiosperms can survive in the haploid state. From there fusion between different individuals to regain the diploid state is certainly understandable. No doubt this was a long evolutionary process, but the real mystery of evolution is that all have survived to the present day. Becoming multicellular and larger may have had benefits of some kind, but obviously not so overwhelming as to eliminate everything else.

Care has to be made not to confuse these trends in size or apparent complexity with what is commonly called 'The great chain of being' (Lovejoy 1936). The chain is constructed by placing organisms on an evolutionary tree according to how near they possess potentialities similar to ourselves. Vertebrates are considered on this idea as more advanced, more complex, than invertebrates, while mammals are more advanced than birds, for example. Self-evidently, plants are beyond the pale in this scheme (if they are mentioned at all), regarded as mere automatons, mere evolutionary simpletons provided only for our benefit. The great chain of being has a religious base seeing mankind as the ultimate top and the working out of God's plan, something on which evidence-based science cannot meaningfully comment.

The appearance of multicellular individuality requires communication

One simple way of seeing how a multicellular plant evolved is to propose that during the process of cell division of a uni-cell the two partners failed to separate. A mutation perhaps may have given rise to strings of cells or even a ball, much as Ratcliff et al. (2012) observed in yeast. Again, benefit is only gained in terms of demarcation of functions a long time after the initial event. An alternative sees two cells of different species accidentally joined through closeness of habitat. The stromatolite consisting of blue-green algae and bacteria is such an example, but these have existed for billions of years, and they are still blue-green algae and bacteria.

Survival of this new multi-cell will require it to behave as an individual, i.e. the new ability to stay together requires coordinated behaviour with both partner cells, and this requires new forms of communication and the appearance of new signalling systems. Even the earliest, multicellular algae acted as unitary individuals as they do today and selection would have involved aspects of the whole life cycle.

What is not often clear is the extent to which plant cells communicate with each other. Clear evidence of cell-to-cell communication on the details of cell status is provided by experiments on the developing fern prothallus. This tissue is generated by germination and mitosis of the single-cell spores released by the parent fern plant, and requires moist circumstances. The prothallus is one cell thick at its commencement and becomes heart-shaped, eventually generating either motile sperm cells or large egg cells. The planes of division to produce the three dimensional structure are controlled by both blue and red light (Dyer 1979).

The spore is a single cell and on germination produces a thin rhizoid. Two mitotic divisions of the spore cell give rise to a linear three-cell stage. Destroy the middle cell by squashing it or killing with an ultraviolet light micro-beam and what was cell number 3 in the line now reverts back to act like cell number 1. This original number 3 cell grows a rhizoid and commences the production of a new three-cell stage and with further division eventually a new prothallus. Obviously, the original cell number 3 receives signals from either cell 2 or 1 that provide the information on 3-ness. Interrupt that information and the programme resets to the cell number 1 stage, reiterating the programme of development. This is a defined programme of regeneration and presumably evolved because damage was common.

This very simple, but highly revealing experiment has profound consequences for understanding the nature of multicellular development. It suggests that each cell has unique information as to its identity and this information is conveyed to it by other cells. Presumably, however, cell number 1 also receives information that it is cell number 1 and if cell 2 is lost, it too regenerates the three-cell stage. So communication is two way.

The identity of that information remains unknown, but this situation is similar to notions in animal embryology of a field. Some consider an electrical possibility here, others direct movement of chemicals, peptides, oligonucleotides proteins, or nucleic acids or even attachment through adjacent plasma membranes via plasmodesmata, a tissue in plants that connects adjacent cells together. Whatever the process, it must also reflect the 'knowledge the cell has of itself' (McClintock 1984) because it is stage dependent too. Eliminate a single cell in the prothallus and there is no reversion. In that case, the unique characteristic is the stage of development that is then different for each cell. The stimulus or information conveyed can be relatively simple and lack obvious specificity.

Becoming multicellular and an individual while increasing in size

Multicellularity has evolved numerous times and is found even in the prokaryotes as well. Some blue-green algae (prokaryotes) like *Anabaena* consist of a string of cells with a specific cell type, the heterocyst, appearing every ninth, sometimes tenth, cell. The heterocyst is morphologically different, non-photosynthetic, and fixes nitrogen to form ammonia. The other cells are photosynthetic and provide the heterocyst with photosynthate, receiving in turn, fixed N, an excellent example of cooperation resulting from differentiation of two cell types. Nitrogen-fixing enzymes are highly oxygen sensitive and thus the two processes, photosynthesis and nitrogen fixation, work more efficiently when separated. So a cooperative synergistic endeavour between different cells may enable *Anabaena* to exist in a wider variety of environmental circumstance, outdoing competitors without these potentials. Heterocysts are induced by nitrogen starvation, so it is release from repression that is the stimulus, but internal communication ensures the heterocysts are spaced.

Modularity enables rapid evolution in size

One simple way to increase size rapidly during evolution is the repetition of certain basic units of growth. The process is called modularity and has occurred in the evolution of both animals and plants (Caroll 2001). Once the structure has been established, there is then the potential for some of the repeated modules to acquire different functions. Undoubtedly, this has happened in the evolution of higher plants. Above ground, angiosperms are constructed of repetitions of leaf plus bud, internodes, flowers, fruits, branches, and vascular bundles. Below ground, there are repetitions of root meristems, as a network of laterals develops. Further demarcation has occurred within this basic structure. Morphologists regard the petals and sepals of flowers as modified leaves; root systems possess fine roots and, again, many millions of root hairs (Arber 1950). The main innovation, which enabled modularity in plants, was the evolution of regional specification of semi-autonomous areas in the embryonic meristems of roots and shoots.

The onset of predation must have been one important driver towards multicellularity

Plants are the basis of virtually all food chains because they obtain energy from the sun. The present life-time of the sun, estimated at 5 billion years, certainly makes the process sustainable. Was a photosynthetic eukaryote the first eukaryote? I consider it most likely. The evolutionary separation between plant and animal cells is thought to have taken place at the single-cell stage. A reasonable scenario of this split sees the separation start when a plant cell developed the ability to eat other plants. With time, the burden of maintaining chloroplasts led to their loss, but the pentose phosphate pathway of photosynthesis was retained, enabling it to become a respiratory pathway as it is today.

What evidence indicates this potential route? One such 'cannibal' uni-cell is a photosynthetic dinoflagellate *Ceratium furca* that can ingest other protists (Smalley and Coats 2002). Other dinoflagellates can release toxins that kill small fish, which are then used as food.

The alternative evolutionary path is a eukaryotic animal eating blue-green algae and incorporating one algal individual by chance into its cytoplasm as a progenitor of a chloroplast to form the first eukaryote plant. Now, this animal cell has to acquire the pentose phosphate pathway. It makes more sense, perhaps, for eukaryotic plant cells to have evolved first because an abundance of plants would provide the primordial animal cell with plenty to eat.

The drive towards becoming a multicellular plant may simply issue from the convoy principle. Consider submarines as predators and merchant ships as plant cells. Convoys of ships were established in the last two world wars because it is equally difficult for a submarine to find a single ship on the large ocean as it is to find 30 in a convoy. Even when a single submarine did find a convoy, its ability to sink ships was limited by its own armament. Similarly, an early colony of plant cells joined together, rather than freely distributed, would have been more difficult for a predatory animal to find. Limited damage could be inflicted on one multi-cell by one uni-cell predator. Thus, evolutionary benefit accrues directly to those that stayed together—the combination increases fitness. Of course, the driving force of fitness increases if predators, too, are in abundance. Then, the more interesting question is whether multicellular plants gave rise to simple multicellular animals.

Evidence for the convoy principle in generating multicellularity has been published (Boreas et al. 1998). When a colony of *Chlorella* was mixed with a plant-eating, but small-mouthed flagellate, the appearance of clusters of eight *chlorollae* fused together rapidly formed. These observations confirm, in my mind, that predation is central to the formation of much evolutionary change.

How predation has changed plant behaviour

Predation has had a substantive effect on both plant evolution and behaviour. There has been an arms race between plants and animals ever since the two evolved separately. All plants have methods for killing unwary predators, the commonest is to poison them with natural pesticides, but there are a variety of others (mucilage, gum, indigestible lignin). Numerous other species produce sticky adhesive glands and exudates on leaves that capture insects and in many of these, proteases are secreted and partial digestion occurs (Spoomer 1999). The numbers of actual carnivorous plants are much greater than the few species referenced in text books. Certainly in higher plants these work very effectively.

The kinds of natural pesticide chemical employed damage nervous, digestive, reproductive and circulatory systems in predatory insects and sometimes larger animals. There are an estimated 100,000 natural pesticides. Occasionally, cyanide, amino acid analogues and other plant poisons, kill unwary humans too. Oestrogen analogues, like genestein, in soy are sufficiently strong to modify the human menstrual cycle; such chemicals will have much larger effects on insect sexuality. However, since predatory animals survive, predation will occur, regardless of chemistry, as predators find ways of defusing the chemical bombs they ingest.

Plan B for the herbivore-damaged plant is behavioural. Higher plants are modular in development. Lose some modules (leaf plus bud or root tip) and you can rely on others already developed, while you replace those lost. Dormant buds are activated to produce new leaves or shoots. In the root, pericycle cells initiate the production of new branch or lateral roots, but there is another critical point. Putting specific, but critical functions into one or two specialized tissues (such as animals do, via heart, nervous system, or brain) would be fatal because even limited predation could easily kill the whole plant. Thus, higher plants, like lower ones, have to remain largely unspecialized and apparently simple in comparison. This strategy then becomes the result of an active evolutionary decision to place survival above specialization.

The regenerative capacity of higher plants is quite extraordinary as exemplified by the number of ways in which many, but not all largely herbaceous plants can be regenerated. Most will be familiar with vegetative propagation from shoot cuttings. Many thousands of species possess this potential. About a thousand species can be regenerated from pieces of root and perhaps a few hundred from pieces of leaf. Many tissues can be grafted onto other related species. Bud grafts, for example, have been used for hundreds of years. In the laboratory, regeneration to whole plants can be derived from single cells, protoplasts (single cells without wall), pollen, or unfertilized ovules. Callus can be grown from wound tissue from almost any part of a plant and regenerated back to shoots or roots using changes in hormone balance. From thence, whole plants can be regenerated. Somatic embryogenesis is reported for a reasonable number of species, while others such as *Kalanchoe* simply produce new plantlets from leaf edges.

References

Arber, A. (1950). *The natural philosophy of plant form*. Cambridge University Press, Cambridge.

Bak, P. (1996). *How nature works: the science of self-organised criticality*. Copernicus Press, New York.

Boreas, M.E., Seale, D.B., and Boxhorn, J.E. (1998). Phagotrophy by a flagellate selects for colonial prey. *Evolutionary Ecology*, **12**, 153–164.

Carroll, S.B. (2001). Chance and necessity: the evolution of morphological complexity and diversity. *Nature*, **409**, 1102–1109.

Corning, P. (2003). *Nature's magic. Synergy in evolution and the fate of humankind*. Cambridge University Press, Cambridge.

Dyer, A.D. (1979). *The experimental biology of ferns*. Academic Press, London.

Gould, S.B. (2002). *The structure of evolutionary theory*. Belknap Press, Cambridge, MA.

Hoffmeister, M., and Martin, W. (2003). Interspecific evolution: microbial symbiosis, endosymbiosis and gene transfer. *Environmental Microbiology*, **5**, 641–649.

Lovejoy, A.O. (1936). *The great chain of being*. Harper and Row, New York.

McClintock, B. (1984) The significance of responses of the genome to challenge. *Science*, **226**, 792–801.

McDaniel, C.N., Hartnett, L.K., and Sangrey, K.A. (1996). Regulation of node number in day neutral *Nicotiana tabacum*: a factor in plant size. *Plant Journal*, **9**, 55–61.

McShea, D.W. (1996). Metazoan complexity: is there a trend? *Evolution*, **50**, 477–492.

Michod, R.E. (2007). Evolution of individuality during the transition from unicellular to multicellular life. *Proceedings of the National Academy of Sciences USA*, **194**, 8613–8618.

Poole, A., and Penny, D. (2001). Does endosymbiosis explain the origin of the nucleus? *Nature Cell Biology*, **3**, E173.

Prigogine, I. (1996). *The end of certainty*. Free Press, New York.

Ratcliff, W.C., Ford Denison, R., Borello, M., and Travisano, M. (2012). Experimental evolution of multi-cellularity.

Proceedings of the National Academy of Sciences USA, **109**, 1595–1600.

Rothschild, L.J., and Mancinelli, R.L. (2001). Extremophiles. *Nature*, **409**, 1092–1100.

Simonson, A.B., Servin, J.A., Skophammer, R.G., Herbold, C.W., Rivera, M.C., and Lake, J.A. (2005). Decoding the genomic tree of life. *Proceedings of the National Academy of Sciences USA*, **102**, Suppl. 1, 6608–6613.

Smalley, G.W., and Coats, D.W. (2002). Ecology of the Red-Tide Dinoflagellate *Ceratium furca*: distribution, mixotrophy, and grazing impact on ciliate populations of Chesapeake Bay. *Journal of Eukaryotic Microbiology*, **49**, 63–73.

Sneppen, K., Bak, P., Flyvberg, H., and Jensen, M.H. (1995). Evolution as a self-organised critical phenomenon. *Proceedings of the National Academy of Sciences USA*, **92**, 5209–5213.

Spoomer, G.G. (1999). Evidence of protocarnivorous capabilities in *Geranium viscosissimum* and *Potentilla arguta* and other sticky plants. *International Journal of Plant Sciences*, **160**, 98–101.

Trewavas, A.J. (2012). Information, noise and communication: thresholds as controlling elements in development. In Witzany, G., and Baluska, F., eds *Biocommunication in plants*, pp. 11–37. Springer-Verlag, Berlin.

Waters, C.M., and Bassler, B.L. (2005). Quorum-sensing, cell-to-cell communication in bacteria. *Annual Review of Cell and Developmental Biology*, **21**, 319–346.

Zhang, G., Dong, H., Xu, Z., Zhao, D., and Zhang, C. (2005). Microbial diversity in ultra high pressure rocks and fluids from the Chinese scientific drilling project in China. *Applied and Environmental Microbiology*, **71**, 3213–3227.

CHAPTER 6

Convergent evolution is common in plant systems

There is no new thing under the sun

(Ecclesiastes 1, 9)

⊃ Summary

Evolution can be considered to either have a direction or to be merely the result of the meandering of a complex system underpinned by random mutation. Convergent evolution would suggest, instead, that there are directions in the evolutionary process or that similar environmental contingencies generate similar solutions. A brief digression into human history and development would suggest that there is a direction, although often temporarily obscured. That direction is towards the construction of a suitable human niche in terms of satisfaction of basic life-long needs for food, water, and freedom from disease. The plant niche is often not referenced in the literature, but is constructed from a two-way flow of information between environment and organism. The environment and plant are to be regarded as a holistic integrated entity whose boundary encompasses both. Within that boundary, linkage may be substantial. The niche is constructed from the behavioural changes of the organism impacting on the environment as individual plants develop and subsequent environmental changes modifying the organism. The niche may indicate the potential for evolutionary convergence in plants. Convergent phenomena in many different aspects of plant life and behaviour are used to illustrate the potential for evolutionary direction. These cover aspects of physiological, molecular, morphological, parasitic, and even ecosystem characteristics. The notion that evolutionary change is first initiated by behavioural change and genetic assimilation is discussed. In all hierarchical systems, constraints are inevitable and these may indicate why convergent evolution is so common.

Introduction

In Chapter 5, some discussion was made as to whether there was direction in evolution or was evolution merely the random meanderings of a complex system. As in all situations where there is argument on both sides, aspects of both are probably nearer the truth. However, convergent evolution, in which there are many good examples in plants, could be used for both sides of the argument about direction, but I think it provides stronger evidence for the directional argument. Convergence can be used to contend that angiosperm plants and their behaviour are inevitable. Instead, it could be argued there are a limited number of environmental situations, so random meandering would simply repeat what has gone before. Then, this would not be random in the proper meaning of the word. This chapter enlarges knowledge of plant behaviour in describing convergent events.

Does human history repeat itself?

Giambattista Vico was an Italian philosopher and historian who lived in the seventeenth and

Plant Behaviour and Intelligence. First Edition. Anthony Trewavas.
© Anthony Trewavas 2014. Published 2014 by Oxford University Press.

eighteenth centuries. Although much of his work is rarely considered, his most well-known contribution concerning the history of civilization came in his book, *Scienza Nuova* (The New Science) originally published in 1725 and translated by Bergin and Fisch in 1948. Here, he argued that civilization (a term difficult to define, but supposedly obvious in practice) develops in a recurring pattern, the so-called Viconian cycles. Vico divided the development of civilizations into three political and social stages. The first was regarded as the divine, in which civilization used metaphors of human behaviour, such as the Gods of Olympus or Valhalla to help provide explanation of the natural world (e.g. Thor with his thunderbolts) and to cast light on aspects of human behaviour, too. The second stage was the heroic, god-made-flesh, good examples to be found in the Pharaohs of Ancient Egypt, many Roman (e.g. Nero) or Chinese Emperors, and, of course, the founding, idealized, individuals of major religions. Associated with these developments, the social structure lent itself to the prominence of monarchies and empires/emperors of all kinds. The final stage was the human phase, best described as the rational and sceptical phase, and governmental systems became democratic. Vico assumed that this stage would then, in due course, return to the first and largely poetic phase of human history. One can question the accuracy of Vico's divisions, they were, of course, based on limited appreciation of the variety of human society, but they do reflect some familiar aspects to human history and social development.

The crucial issue of Vico's notions is the repetitive aspect to human history that he proposed, the recurrence of social structures. It is perhaps this aspect that is probably most disputable, since many would see a very general progression and not a recurrence of stages, at least, yet. Vico may, in due course, be proved right and the reason for raising the issue is its relevance for understanding aspects of overall evolution, since there is an analogous dispute. Societies are systems, people connected to each other, much as cells are connected in the organism.

It is certainly the conclusion of many that the process of evolutionary change is largely random. For example, 'Darwinians have always argued

that mutational raw material must be random' (Gould 2002, p. 1276). Monod (1971) argued that man knows he is alone in the universe and only emerged by chance. 'It is widely accepted that that the evolution of any particular organism is the product of the interplay of a great number of historical contingencies. Rewind and replay the tape of life again and again and there is no predicting or reproducing the outcomes' (Carroll 2001). If the whole process of evolution could be rerun (a rewinding of the tape of history), the probability that the present situation that saw emergence onto the land, the evolution of mammals and trees and then finally humans is so small, as to be ignored—or is it?

If, in broad terms, we reran the tape of life, but inserted exactly the same history of environmental changes and contingencies, would we then have the same conclusion? The probability of repetition surely becomes much higher, the odds more weighted to recurrence (Box 6.1).

Box 6.1 Probability of repetition?

I use the word probability advisedly here, because probabilities are only completely accurate over infinite time and probability does not indicate when improbable events do happen, because there is no element of real time built into the concept. In fact, no-one has really estimated any probability of either evolutionary recurrence or that neo-Darwinian mechanisms (with random mutations) are the only evolutionary mechanism that functions. The limits of probability are also exemplified, by a simple thought experiment. Place a pencil on your desk and measure its position to the nearest nanometre. If you now calculate the probability that you could actually place the pencil in that exact position, to the nearest nanometre, it would be effectively zero, but you have just carried out an event that has effectively zero probability. Every time you put the pencil on your desk you have, to the nearest nanometre, carried out an event of zero probability. The key is the exactness of measurement. The probability that you have placed the pencil on your desk is 1; the probability that you have placed it on one half of the desk, rather than the other is 0.5; and so on. So when we talk about evolutionary convergence, it depends on the perceptions of similarity and function. Probabilities really do not come into it.

Direction in human history

We have a prime example of progress from human history as we know it. Is there a direction, an arrow? Consider the following. We have moved from caves to huts to environmentally controlled houses. We have replaced childhood death and human disease with vaccination, antibiotics, and medicine. We have replaced walking with innumerable means of individual and mass transport. We have replaced hunter-gatherer uncertainties for nutriment with reliable food supply from crop and animal domestication and distribution from mass markets. We have supplanted local gossip, limited human memory, and the need for human contact with innumerable alternative, often electronic, means of communication. We have replaced simple storytellers with mass entertainment. So the list continues. I have used the western lifestyle as indicant because I see that as the general desire of many people.

   What all these changes have in common is satisfying a biological need to optimize our environment to suit our biological selves. We are constructing an environment that is stable, and reflects our desire for a full and satisfactory life. There is a direction, progress, to what has obviously occurred in history. All this has happened despite numerous contingent events, famine, world wars, and plagues. Take any one century or any one country, and the arrow of progress can go backwards, but looked at over the period of written history, the appearance of direction is obvious. Progress will continue because mankind is a highly creative species—his only Achilles heel, in my view, xenophobia.

   If we reran the tape of history would it be any different? I think the same broad changes would happen. Fine details might be different, but not the obvious overall change. We have inverted the normal direction of history expected from the supposed Darwinian hypothesis of random evolutionary change and adaptation to an unyielding environment. We have done this, instead, by constructing our own environment and keeping nature at bay—a nature that would prefer child death of 99% to ensure increased biological fitness in the population and opposes all the creature comforts that accompany civilized life. We have discarded the human environment of 30,000 years ago and created one that best suits us.

Niche construction

There is, of course, a biological equivalent to what we as humans are doing and it is called niche construction. An organism can be decomposed into a set of characters, traits, or features, while its environment can be decomposed into arrays of factors. It is the connections between these that defines the niche. It is the functional changes between the organism and its environment leading to modification of its environment that defines niche construction (Odling-Smee 1988; Laland et al. 2001). All organisms modify their environment simply by being present, acquiring food, and excreting in its most general sense. However, the process is very obvious in plants and is complex, leading to an important understanding of plant behaviour. The construction of the niche in plants will be outlined later.

   The niche is readily recognized in root systems that modify so many characteristics of the soil environment as they grow (see Chapter 13, for an expanded view). The sessile nature of plants gives rise to greater environmental modification than animals because plants remain effectively in the same place and interact with the local environment on a permanent basis. Most animals, of course, simply move on and interact only transiently. When large numbers of trees become a forest, there are new even emergent properties that result (Bormann and Likens 1994). Forests exert substantial control on the temperature and humidity beneath the canopy; they control the run-off of water and the release of nitrate. They provide protection against wind damage.

Plant niche construction results from a two-way flow of information between organism and environment

A wealth of environmental information impacts on the growing plant, and modifies the way the shoot and the root grow. In turn, the resulting plant growth modifies the local environment in which it grows. The interaction between a plant organism and its surroundings is continuous, because development continues throughout the life cycle.

Plant development is inevitably plastic because this process of niche construction is continuous. Most higher animals have critical aspects of tissue specification, while enclosed in a more controlled environment in an egg or uterus, essential for an organism in which movement is so basic to lifestyle. There is very little room for plasticity in animal structure as a consequence. Instead, the overall structure tends to be highly specified, the limits of variation are much tighter. Not so in plants in which environmental impact must be accommodated and modified continuously.

The flow of information between the plant and its environment is thus a two-way flow, and one that continually changes as plants grow and develop. The seedling germinates, the environment modifies the behaviour; in turn, the behavioural change helps modify the environment, and so on. This process continues throughout the life cycle.

There is a common view that arises from experimental approaches. There are plants and then there are environments to be imposed on plants. It is considered that these are two conceptually independent entities. The reality, instead, is that a plant and its environment are always inextricably linked into one integrated holistic structure, whose boundary encompasses both the organism and its environment. The two are interlinked to varying degrees, with more interactions below ground than above, but still one unified whole. We cannot talk about a plant without, at the same, time detailing its precise environmental condition because of the integration of one with the other. However, it is this combination that is subject to evolutionary pressures. Plants are not, therefore, passive entities at the mercy of any environmental perturbation, but to an extent manipulating the environment for their benefit. How this is done will be considered in later chapters, some of it very surprising.

The challenge to the random meandering of evolution: evolutionary convergence. Are angiosperms inevitable products of evolution?

Conway-Morris (2003), in a refreshingly, challenging and well-argued text, argues powerfully for an alternative evolutionary perspective. 'The central theme of this book depends on the realities of evolutionary convergence: the recurrent tendency of biological organization to arrive at the same "solution" to a particular "need".' 'Its main, but not ultimate, aim is to argue that contrary to received wisdom, the emergence of humans is a near inevitability' (Conway-Morris 2003, p. xii). The use of the word 'need' is not too dissimilar to that of Lamarck who likewise stressed the requirement of need although the mechanism of reaching that 'need' would probably, after several centuries of critical knowledge, be regarded as very different. Chapter 21 extends what Lamarck actually said, in place of what is commonly assumed he said.

The notion of evolutionary convergence is certainly not new, but Conway-Morris provides a compendium of examples, which in sheer number are difficult to ignore. 'The best known example is the similarity between the camera-like eye of the octopus and that of any human . . . the camera-like eye has evolved independently at least six times'. The book is a compendium of similar events during mainly animal evolution, although plants do get several look-ins. There is a strong case here that challenges those who support the notion of a random meandering of evolutionary development.

What is meant by evolutionary convergence?

The critical element is that structural or life style patterns emerge from very different starting points in very remote lineages. What is important is to be sure that convergence has not resulted from a common ancestor, but in most cases, it is obvious that this is not the case. 'Convergence pervades the biological world. From anatomy to protein sequences, it appears at all levels of biological organization it permeates the evolutionary history of all groups of organisms' (Wray 2002).

Examples of convergence in plants

Plant biology is replete with examples of convergent evolution arising from polyphyletic sources and genetically remote groups. It would take a book to do justice to this topic. Instead, I have presented them more as a list. Those wishing for further information can follow the indicated papers. I do not claim to have identified all of them; there will be many more.

Multicellularity and early general morphology

There have been at least five (if not more) independent origins of multicellularity in plants from single-cell organisms (Niklas 2000). The most well-known, separate, multicellular lineages are the brown, red, and green algae. Green plants evolved, it is thought, only from the green algae. Despite substantial variations in the morphology of some of these lineages, it is common to find plants in all three groups with filamentous, foliar, tubular, kelp-like, and coralline habit. Kelps, members of the brown algae, possess trumpet cells that are similar to the conductive tissue, phloem, in higher plants and transport sugars from sun-lit tissue to that heavily shaded below. Similar problems give rise to similar solutions between entirely evolutionarily remote plants.

Some acellular species, like *Caulerpa*, can attain 20 m in length, but the general morphology, which encompasses substantial morphological differentiation, is very similar to that of many vascular land plants. However, this differentiation is attained without separation into discrete cells throughout the whole structure. The non-vascular structure of some of the brown algae, the blade-stipe-holdfast contains an intercalary meristem, strikingly similar to the arrangement of the leaf-stem-root in higher vascular plants.

Leaf functioning

From examination of 280 species of higher plants, Reich et al. (1997) concluded that, 'despite striking differences in climate, soils and evolutionary history among diverse biomes ranging from tropical and temperate forests to alpine, tundra and desert we found similar inter-specific relationships among leaf structure and function and plant growth in all biomes. Our results thus demonstrate convergent evolution and global generality in plant functioning, despite the enormous diversity of plant species and biomes.' The traits investigated included carbon assimilation rates, leaf lifespan, nitrogen and surface area to mass ratio. Using 108 species and pairwise correlations and convergence indices, Ackerley and Reich (1999) also concluded that 'the results of comparative analysis of leaf functional traits do provide strong additional support for broad patterns of convergence in leaf trait correlations'. This analysis indicates that there are strong inter-specific correlations among the leaf functioning traits examined, suggesting that, in very different plant taxa and biomes, high levels of evolutionary convergence are associated with rapid evolution and minimal constraints to selection pressures.

Convergence in leaf structure

Although we associate coniferous gymnosperms with needles, containing the photosynthetic chloroplasts, in one other gymnosperm, *Ginkgo* (Gingoales), flat-bladed leaves are produced like those in many higher angiosperm trees. However, angiosperms supposedly evolved from pines.

Origin of flowers

The Gnetales are one of the four extant groups of gymnosperms. There are some substantial similarities between the few species in this group and angiosperms. The Gnetales have separate male and female 'flowers'—the male with stamens, anthers, and a drop of nectar, the female with what might be reduced sepals and petals, but are actually bracts. The Gnetales carry out a double fertilization, in this case leading to two embryos; in angiosperms double fertilization leads to an embryo and an endosperm. Both groups have anatomical vessels similar in structure and ovules (the structure that develops into a seed) with two layers of tissue (integuments) covering their surface. On this basis, it has been a common although controversial assumption that members of the Gnetales were the ancestors of angiosperms and their flowers (Endress 1996).

Detailed molecular analyses of five homeotic gene sequences have, however, clearly indicated that the Gnetales are not sister to the angiosperms, nor is *Ginkgo* with its leaf structure. The angiosperms are much closer to the conifers, the major group of gymnosperms. The other characteristics that are similar are, therefore, between the Gnetales and the angiosperms are, instead, the result of convergent evolution (Frohlich 1999; Winter et al. 1999)

Convergent evolution of bat-pollinated and beetle-pollinated plants

Beetle pollinators seek out flowers for three interconnected reasons—edible rewards, mating, and a palatable physical temperature produced by thermogenesis (Bernhardt 2000). Beetle-pollinated flowers have evolved independently in 14 families of dicots and 6 families of monocots. Bats are attracted to flowers and, thus, pollinate them by scent. The chemical composition of eight bat-pollinated species belonging to six different flowering families exhibited a strong convergence in their volatile composition (Knudsen and Tollsten 1995). These families (Musaceae, Gesneriacae, Leguminosae, Lecythidaceae, Heliconiinae, Passifloraceae) are considered unrelated.

Reproductive convergence

The seed plants, fossil horsetails, and lycopods and ferns have converged reproductively, as well as vegetatively. Each has/had heterosporous reproduction producing separate male and female cells that combined in sexual reproduction. Present-day horsetails are homosporous. However, whereas ferns have separate male and female gametophytes, and a motile sperm, the fossil horsetails and lycopods had separate male and female cones. Present-day descendants of the lycopods still produce separate male and female cells in the same tissue called a strobilus, like that of fossil lycopods (Bower 1908).

Microbial eukaryotes

'Convergent evolution in microbial eukaryotes often involves very distantly related lineages with relatively limited repertoires of morphological features. These large phylogenetic distances weaken the role of ancestral developmental programmes on the subsequent evolution of morphological characters' (Leander 2008). Leander provides examples of convergent evolution in diverse ecosystems including planktonic environments, interstitial environments

and the intestinal environments of metazoan hosts. Some diatoms and the prorocentroid dinoflagellates are strikingly similar in cell size, construction (particularly the upper and lower siliceous plates connected by girdle bands), shape, anatomy, and photosynthetic ability, even though far apart in evolution. Distantly related lineages have evolved radially symmetrical cells with spiny projections.

Flexural and biomechanical convergence

Body plans (anatomy and morphology) in very different plant lineages can exhibit clear convergence (Niklas 2000). Since plants are photosynthetic eukaryotes, there are requirements to optimize structures that capture light, and enable exchange of mineral nutrients and water. The relationships between surface area, volume, and geometry of the body plan are thus crucial and choices can be constrained by the particular life style circumstances in which evolution has occurred. It is often difficult to distinguish between species based on general appearance, size, and internal structure. A critical feature of plants is the presence of a cell wall that has evolved independently and, thus, convergently many times. This biomechanical structure limits (as biomechanics does in many organisms) the potential for different body plans. As particular niches are occupied, convergence of body plan potentialities in very different lineages are likely as development interacts with the requirements of size, biomechanical constraints, geometry, and shape. These constraints are also detected in the biomechanical and anatomical features of leaves and petioles (Niklas 1991). Twenty-two species among dicots, monocots, and ferns were investigated and 'the convergence in mechanical designs among taxonomically distinct lineages is interpreted as evidence for selection of mechanical attributes of load-supporting structures like petioles'.

The tree lifestyle and cambial convergence

If one had to design an organism that optimized light collection, a branched structure with flat-bladed leaves would seem to be obvious. 'The tree growth habit (tall plants with a thickened single trunk branching well above ground level) evolved many times independently—in lycophytes, equise-tophytes, and lignophytes' (Niklas 1997; Donoghue 2005). These examples required the appearance of a cambium, a kind of internal skin that produced new cells by division from both faces in the lignophytes and, in the others, only to the inside of the cambium. Again, the cambium seems to have arisen independently and, thus, convergent in different lineages.

The tree habit required a change in the mechanical properties of the trunk to support the weight. The tree habit also evolved in the extinct Marattialean and Filicalean lineages, and in modern tree ferns. The latter plants lack a cambium and use instead a coat of entwined adventitious roots. Other fossil ferns constructed a 'trunk' and increased its girth from a mass of small stems enveloped by a mass of thickly entwined adventitious roots. 'Clearly the materials used to support stems differ among plant lineages—stiff leaf bases, periderm, girdling primary vascular bundles, draping roots or a stiff outer cortex- and virtually every type of plant organ has been employed at one time or another' (Niklas 1997). Niklas provides details of anatomical structure of various fossil trees and present-day trees, like palms, which provides both indications of anatomical difference, but convergence of the tree lifestyle in all cases.

The benefits of the woody perennial 'tree' lifestyle are immediately obvious. Increasing the height can substantially reduce competition for light, the primary plant energy source and, thus perhaps, the equivalent of animal food. However, the search for light requires, initially, full investment of all resources in growth. Only later, can the heavy use of resources in reproduction be introduced. Consequently, there is a juvenile period before perennial angiosperm flowering varying according to species between 2 and 10 years, and even longer in gymnosperms. The juvenile period enables the growing plant to construct a suitable morphology to fit the local environment, i.e. niche construction. When reproduction is finally embarked on, the benefit is a more reliable reproduction over many years compared with annuals in which a serious climatic variation can drastically reduce seed production and, thus, sibling numbers. Trees can store resources for eventual reproduction even years later.

The tree habit also re-evolved in the monocotyledons most notably the palms (which lack a cambium), but also in some members of the monocots in the Agavaceae, Iridaceae, Convalariaceae, and Xanthorrhoeacae.

Parasitic plants

There are at least 4000 species of parasitic higher plants distributed among 19 different flowering families. There are six different parasitic lifestyles indicating that the process has originated again by convergent evolution. These are holoparasites (lack chlorophyll), hemiparasites (partially photosynthetic for nutrition), obligate parasites (need a host to accomplish the life cycle), facultative parasites (host not needed for life cycle culmination), stem parasites (parasitize the stem), and root parasites (parasitize the root). All parasites use a haustorium, a specialized tissue and modified from a root, to penetrate the host tissue and connect their vascular system to that of the host (Nickrent and Musselman 2004). It is clear that some parasitic plants locate their prey through smelling the volatiles that are emitted by the host shoot. Others use chemicals in the soil to locate their prey.

Carnivorous plants

About 600 species of carnivorous higher plants are known in six angiosperm families including both monocots and dicots (Ellison and Gotelli 2001). The flypaper lifestyle of *Drosera* has evolved independently in five dicot families and pitfall traps (pitcher plants) in three dicot and one monocot family. 'Modern data supports multiple poly-phyletic origins of the carnivorous plants', which are thus the result of convergent evolution. The multiple origin of carnivory even with the Droseraceae suggests an adaptation to the low nutrient, bright, water-logged environments in which they normally occur. Many species produce adhesive regions on leaves and stems, and digest captured insects.

Nitrogen fixation

The familiar fixation of nitrogen by symbiotic bacteria in nodules has been reported in members of 10 flowering families covering 310 species (Bond 1967) that are regarded taxonomically as distantly related. Soltis et al. (1995) have stated that based on analysis of sequence data of Rubisco these families may be much closer together, suggesting perhaps a single origin of nodulation. However, only in the legumes (Fabaceae) are most family members, nitrogen fixers. The bacterial symbionts are *Rhizobium* species. The process of nitrogen fixation requires substantial changes in the structure of the bacterium as they become bacteroides implying the presence of unique sets of genes.

The symbiotic bacterium in eight other families of angiosperms (alders are a common example) is an actinomycete, notably *Frankia*. The numbers of genera of *Frankia* to the fewer numbers fixing nitrogen is very high, implying perhaps different origins of nitrogen fixation in the individual species. Anatomically, the nodules in rhizobial and frankial symbioses are different, but suggesting the nodule in both is convergent evolution. Cycads have nodules containing blue-green algae and a number of species have been identified as having nitrogen-fixing organisms in leaves, e.g. *Gunnera* using another blue-green alga. Clearly, these are convergent evolution.

C4 photosynthesis

The acquisition of carbon dioxide for photosynthesis through controllable pores (stomata) results in loss of water by transpiration. Although plants have evolved several mechanisms to alleviate this problem, one well-established solution, that of C4 photosynthesis, is estimated to have evolved 45 separate times starting some 20–30 million years ago, but the most recent being 4–5 million years (Sage 2004). C4 is found in three families of monocots and 16 families of dicots, and in 7500 species altogether. The evolution of C4 photosynthesis requires complex changes in the expression of genes governing photosynthesis, intermediary metabolism, and leaf anatomy and histology. Fifteen separate anatomical origins have occurred.

The basic mechanism of C4 replaces the initial use of Rubisco for CO_2 fixation by another enzyme, PEP carboxylase. This novel enzyme is found in specialized cells around the vascular tissue. The enzymatic product, phosphoglycerate, is transferred to mesophyll cells where it is broken down again to carbon dioxide, thus leading to the normal methods of carbon fixation occur through Rubisco. Because PEP carboxylase has a much higher affinity for carbon dioxide, this simple change increases the atmospheric carbon dioxide inside the leaf and, thus, reduces the loss of water in transpiration. Typical C4 plants are the tropical grass crops, such as maize, sorghum, or sugar cane and others. These plants can thus survive drier climates and experience improved mineral status. There are 4500, C4 species in the grass family.

Along with the general convergence of the phenomenon, molecular convergence has also been examined with indications of eight different evolutionary origins of the C4 PEP carboxylase in the grass family alone (Christin et al. 2007).

Convergence in desert species

The most well-known convergence here is between the new world Cactaceae and the old world Euphorbiaceae. The stems of both are succulent and store large amounts of water, they are little branched, and the stems often short and broad, reducing the surface to volume ratio. The stems are green and photosynthesize. Desert cacti bear spines that are modified leaves, while the euphorbs contain thorns that are modified branches. Both perform similar functions to help reduce predation and dissipate heat (Niklas 1997). A number of the Leguminosae exhibit stem swelling and greening if the leaves are experimentally removed indicative of likely responses to drought leading to premature leaf fall (Schmalhausen 1949). It is not difficult to see this as the evolutionary path adopted by present day arid climate species.

Ecosystem convergence

In regions of climatic similarity the vegetational aspect (physiognomy) often appears to be similar (Mooney and Duns 1970; Cody and Mooney 1978). One of the most fundamental lines of evidence that support the notion of convergent evolution has come from the study of comparative plant morphology.

Given analogous selective regimes, analogous phenotypic solutions will be forthcoming, regardless of the phylogenetic origins of the species involved. The Mediterranean climate type occurs in California, South Africa, Central Chile, and Southern Australia, as well as in the Mediterranean region itself. In all these five areas, the native vegetation has a similar appearance—a dense scrub dominated by woody evergreen sclerophyllous shrubs. The isolation of these geographic areas and the almost complete taxonomic dissimilarity between their resident floras indicate they have distinct evolutionary histories. The Mediterranean climactic style consists of high temperatures and poor water availability in the summer, and low temperatures and high water availability in the winter. Along with the unpredictability of these weather characteristics there are additional selection forces in fire, competition with other plants, predation, and mineral deficiencies, all of which interact in complex fashion with each other. The sclerophyllous shrubs may acquire water 8–27 m down in the soil from very deep roots, and have developed forms that serve to trap and conserve moisture.

Alpine ecosystems are further examples of convergence, since many species develop prostrate stems, small and hairy leaves, a response to often perpetual and strong wind, as well as mineral deficiency. Saline ecosystems see convergent evolution of species that are succulent in either stem or leaf.

The significance of convergent evolution for behaviour

Convergent evolution is certainly common in plants, in metabolism, structure, form, lifestyle, and even ecosystem. The reasons why this is so, need to be sought. The first of these, the importance of behaviour in selection, are best summarized by quotation from several authors. Ganong (1901) argued that the evolution of morphology in plants generally takes the line of least resistance. 'This means that when through a change in some condition of the environment, the necessity arises for the performance of a new function it will be assumed by the part (of the plant) most available for that purpose . . . because it happens to be set free from its former function by change of habit' (Ganong 1901, p. 429), i.e. behaviour.

A more modern statement that is similar in emphasis on behaviour is to be found in Mayr (1963). 'A shift into a new niche or adaptive zone is almost, without exception, initiated by a change in behaviour. The other adaptations to the new niche, particularly the structural ones, are acquired secondarily. With habitat and food selection-behavioural phenomena-playing a major role in the shift into new adaptive zones, the importance of behaviour in initiating new evolutionary events is self-evident'.

'It is the animal's behaviour that to a considerable extent determines the nature of the environment to which it will submit itself and the character of the selective forces with which it will be content to wrestle' Waddington (1975). Although the last two authors reference only animals (as though plants have not evolved), there is no reason to suppose the situation is in any ways different. However Waddington (1975) clarified his argument with a simple diagram, indicating how feedback enables organisms to modify their ecological niche, thus illustrating something already referred to above in this chapter.

This kind of selection is, of course, different from the more traditional and conventional view that centralizes attention only on the gene, and assumes a random meandering to the process of evolution. Convergence provides, instead, a kind of direction to evolutionary development, as pointed out by Conway-Morris (2003), and it is my contention that behavioural change is the initial reason for convergent phenomena when they occur.

Behaviour as the pacemaker of evolution

The emphasis on behaviour as a potential pacemaker of evolution directs attention towards the systems nature of cells, tissues, organisms, populations, etc. Expansion of this systems approach by Stanley (1975) provides potential explanation for apparent convergence in ecosystems, a higher systems level than single populations and would emphasize species behaviour.

Systems, as indicated in Chapter 3, are structured as a hierarchy of constraints. The lower levels are constrained in their behaviour by the higher levels in the system. On this basis, an ecosystem, composed of a network of interacting organisms, must provide some constraint on what individual organisms are acceptable in the ecosystem and thus can evolve. Is the necessity for integration, the basis for extinction? Those that cannot fit with others simply die off? Is convergence in ecosystem responsible for convergence in species properties and behaviour? The linkages connecting the organisms into an ecosystem are weaker than those connecting a species together and weaker again than those connecting the organism together. Nevertheless, they are still there and act to provide some constraint on potentially random meandering in evolution.

Of course, behaviour is inextricably linked with genes, as is everything in biology, but behaviour in the individual can easily change with environmental modification, whereas the genome may be more resistant to change and, in relative terms, is surely more stable. Behaviour is a phenotypic characteristic interconnected with niche. If particular kinds of behaviour provide a selective advantage to the individual then everything else about the organism, including its genes, is carried along with it, in a way similar to Sperry's conceptual wheel (Corning 2003, p. 175). Although a wheel going down hill normally does so only because it is circular, everything else on the wheel, tyres, axle, spokes, rims, etc., has no choice but to go down with it. They go along for the ride as it were.

Genetic assimilation starts with behavioural change

Corning (2003) in a challenging description of the importance of behaviour to understanding evolution indicates that it complements the classical natural selection viewpoint on selection of particular gene combinations. The notion of the importance of behaviour in natural selection is not new and Corning (2003, p. 182) lists the particular names applied to it—genetic assimilation, Baldwin effect, organic selection, holistic selection, internal selection, psychological selection, rational preselection, behavioural selection, and neo-Lamarckian selection. In all these descriptions, what changes first in evolution, is behaviour. If the novel situation persists, the population will change because,

over time, the new strategy **should promote the gene combinations that allow the strategy to develop with greater rapidity, higher probability, or lower cost.** Natural selection merely ratifies a behavioural adaptation that has already been tried and tested, but through non-genetic, potentially epigenetic and even behavioural means (Bateson 1963). Neo-Lamarckian evolution results from genetic assimilation. The extent to which these criteria apply to plants is a challenge dwelt on later in this book.

Neo-Lamarckian selection is implicated in habitat and dietary choices, adaptation, predator–prey interactions, and the formation of symbiotic conditions, all phenomena related to convergent evolution characteristics in plants considered in this chapter. Even plant breeding can be considered neo-Lamarckian because purposeful behavioural selection has been performed by the breeder that modifies the course of natural selection in other species that grow alongside it.

When convergence is discussed, it is always emphasized that it reflects the extent to which organisms are moulded by their environment, and end up with similar strategies. Virtually all multicellular organisms only survive within a limited temperature range; all have some requirement for access to water and oxygen. Couple this with the other fundamental requirements of multicellular life, such as the necessity for acquiring energy and other raw materials (organic food for animals, water, minerals, carbon dioxide for plants), sensing and dealing with other organisms (e.g. predation or finding prey), and finding mates. These requirements are similar in both animals and plants, and thus constraints on what can evolve and emerge regardless. Even random meandering through a genetic landscape acquires some boundaries within which life must be constrained.

Of course, there are severe limitations imposed by the nature of cells and their heritable equipment. Cells and organisms are very complex networks, genes, and proteins act only within constraints imposed by the rest of the network. The overall stability of the network in its many different manifestations during development constrains again.

Competition drives behavioural change and evolution?

The development of pollen as the male cell in angiosperms reflected occupation of drier regions of the earth surface. Possibly competition with other plants was the driving force to occupy drier climates or did the climate change instead? The evolutionary appearance of trees may reflect a response to competition, again; grow over your competition and reproduce only when that is satisfactorily achieved, but alternatives exist. If conditions are poor for seedling survival, then it makes sense for a lifestyle that year-on-year produces large numbers of seeds. The reliance on modular construction for change in size, and to resist predation and provide for phenotypic plasticity limit the evolutionary space for change.

Although most temperate plants may adopt a balance between the environmental parameters they perceive, there are occasions when one can become important almost to the exclusion of others. Plants can suddenly experience extreme depletion (starvation) of a specific mineral or water, for example. Mechanisms of adaptation are present, and are designed to counter the loss and continue development, albeit slowly. They are indicated later. If the environmental condition is prolonged, then this may drive convergent evolution with similar solutions adopted by those that experience it. Lack of water produces a typical xeromorphic adaptive response, well-characterized among many different angiosperm species for example.

Niklas (1994) examined the potential for evolution through complex domains of fitness and concluded that the number of equally efficient designs is proportional to the number and complexity of tasks that must be performed. When one factor overwhelms, then the efficient designs are few. Thus, for really low levels of water availability in deserts, the convergent evolution of the structures in the new world Cactaceae and the old world Euphoribaceae are to be expected. Both have expanded the stem at the expense of leaves that are either absent or vestigial. The swollen stem has now taken over the requirements for water storage and photosynthesis. This strategy is also mimicked when plants such as legumes have all their leaves removed; the stem expands and becomes photosynthetic (Schmalhausen 1949).

References

Ackerley, D.D., and Reich, P.B. (1999). Convergence and correlations among leaf size and function in seed plants: a comparative test using independent contrasts. *American Journal of Botany*, **86**, 1272–1281.

Bateson, G. (1963). The role of somatic change in evolution. *Evolution*, **17**, 529–539.

Bergin, T.G., and Fisch, M.H. (1948). *The new science of Gimbattista Vico*. Cornell University Press, New York.

Bernhardt, P. (2000). Convergent evolution and adaptive radiation of beetle-pollinated angiosperms. *Plant Systematics and Evolution*, **222**, 293–320.

Bond, G. (1967). Fixation of nitrogen by higher plants other than legumes. *Annual Review of Plant Physiology*, **18**, 107–126.

Bormann, E.H., and Likens, G.E. (1994). *Pattern and process in a forested ecosystem*. Springer-Verlag, Berlin.

Bower, F.O. (1908). *The origin of a land flora: a theory based upon the facts of alternation*. MacMillan, London.

Carroll, S.B. (2001). Chance and necessity: the evolution of morphological complexity and diversity. *Nature*, **409**, 1102–1109.

Christin, P.-A., Salamin, N., Savolainen, V., Duvall, M.R., and Besnard, G. (2007). C4 photosynthesis evolved in grasses via parallel adaptive genetic changes. *Current Biology*, **17**, 1241–1247.

Cody, M.L., and Mooney, H.A. (1978). Convergence versus non-convergence in Mediterranean climate ecosystems. *Annual Review of Ecology and Systematics*, **9**, 265–321.

Conway-Morris, S. (2003). *Life's solution. Inevitable humans in a lonely universe*. Cambridge University Press, Cambridge.

Corning, P. (2003). *Nature's magic; synergy in evolution and the fate of humankind*. Cambridge University Press, Cambridge.

Donoghue, M.J. (2005). Key innovations, convergence and success: macroevolutionary lessons from plant phylogeny. *Paleobiology*, **31**, 77–93.

Ellison, A.M., and Gotelli, N.J. (2001). Evolutionary ecology of carnivorous plants. *Trends in Ecology and Evolution*, **16**, 623–629.

Endress, P.K. (1996). Structure and function of female and bisexual organ complexes in *Gnetales*. *International Journal of Plant Sciences*, **157**, S113–125.

Frohlich, M.W. (1999). MADS about *Gnetales*. *Proceedings of the National Academy of Sciences USA*, **96**, 8811–8813.

Ganong, W.F. (1901).The cardinal principles of morphology. *Botanical Gazette*, **31**, 426–434.

Gould, S.J. (2002). *The structure of evolutionary theory*. Harvard University Press, Cambridge, MA.

Knudsen, J.T., and Tollsten, L. (1995). Floral scent in bat-pollinated plants. *Botanical Journal of the Linnean Society*, **119**, 45–57.

Laland, K.N., Odling-Smee, F.J., and Feldman, M.W. (2001). Niche construction, ecological inheritance and cycles of contingency in evolution. In Oyama, S., Griffiths, P.E., and Gray, R.D., eds, *Cycles of contingency. Developmental systems and evolution*, pp. 116–126. MIT Press, Cambridge, MA.

Leander, B.S. (2008). A hierarchical view of convergent evolution in microbial eukaryotes. *Journal of Eucaryotic Microbiology*, **55**, 59–68.

Mayr, E. (1963). *Animal species and evolution*. Harvard University Press, Cambridge, MA.

Monod, J. (1971). *Chance and necessity: an essay on the natural philosophy of modern biology*. Alfred A. Knopf, New York.

Mooney, H.A., and Duns, E.L. (1970). Convergent evolution of Mediterranean climate evergreen sclerophyll shrubs. *Evolution*, **24**, 292–303.

Nickrent, D.L., and Musselman, L.J. (2004). Introduction to parasitic flowering plants. *Plant Health Instructor*. doi:10.1094/PHI-I-2004-0330-01.

Niklas, K.J. (1991). Flexural stiffness allometries of angiosperm and fern petioles and rachises: evidence for biomechanical convergence. *Evolution*, **45**, 734–750.

Niklas, K.J. (1994). Morphological evolution through complex domains of fitness. *Proceedings of the National Academy of Sciences USA*, **91**, 6772–6779.

Niklas, K.J. (1997). *The evolutionary biology of plants*. Chicago University Press, Chicago, IL.

Niklas, K.J. (2000). The evolution of plant body plans. *Annals of Botany*, **85**, 411–438.

Odling-Smee, F.J. (1988). Niche-constructing phenotypes. In Plotkin, H.C., ed. *The role of behaviour in evolution*, pp. 73–133. MIT Press, Cambridge, MA.

Reich, P.B., Walters, M.B., and Ellsworth, D.S. (1997). From tropics to tundra: global convergence in plant functioning. *Proceedings of the National Academy of Sciences USA*, **94**, 13730–13734.

Sage, R. (2004). The evolution of C4 photosynthesis. *New Phytologist*, **161**, 341–370.

Schmalhausen, I.I. (1949). *Factors of evolution. The theory of stabilising selection*. Blakiston, Philadelphia, PA.

Soltis, D.E., Soltis, P.S., Morgan, D.R., Swenson, S.M., Mullin, B.C., Dows, J.M., and 1 other (1995). Chloroplast gene sequence data suggest a single origin of the predisposition for symbiotic nitrogen fixation in angiosperms. *Proceedings of the National Academy of Sciences USA*, **92**, 2647–2651.

Stanley, S.M. (1975). A theory of evolution above the species level. *Proceedings of the National Academy of Sciences USA*, **72**, 646–650.

Waddington, C.H. (1975). *The evolution of an evolutionist*. Edinburgh University Press, Edinburgh.

Winter, K., Becker, A., Munster, T., Kim, J.T., Saedler, H., and Theissen, G. (1999). MADS-box genes reveal that gnetophytes are more closely related to conifers than to flowering plants. *Proceedings of the National Academy of Sciences USA*, **96**, 7342–7347.

Wray, G.A. (2002). Do convergent developmental mechanisms underlie convergent phenotypes? *Brain, Behaviour and Evolution*, **59**, 327–336.

CHAPTER 7

Are angiosperms more complex than mammals?

It is always easier to destroy a complex system than selectively alter it.

(James 1997)

◌ Summary

It is a common assumption that organisms have increased in complexity during evolution, but what complexity involves is not often made clear. The corollary is that plants are simple organisms so that a judgement has been made about complexity and its measurement, although the comparator is usually not mentioned, presumably with mammals. The continued flow of energy through organisms may have been a driving force to increase the diversity of function and distribution of activities with organisms as time passes. McShea (1996) has considered the problem of complexity and suggested some criteria, whereby complexity might actually be comparatively assessed. These criteria are outlined and used as a comparison where possible between angiosperms and mammals, both often regarded as the most complex of their particular groups. The notion that plants are simple organisms is not supported by the use of these criteria. It is concluded that comparisons of complexity between organisms with very different lifestyles is not easy and subjective judgements from human bias are used, rather than an assessment made on detailed knowledge of their capabilities.

It is assumed that complexity has increased during evolution

Life in its least complex form started with a simple molecular system. Present-day organisms are, instead, large, well-organized, highly differentiated cellular societies and in plants, republics, that behave as integrated individuals. Intuitively, life has become more complex, but stating that it has does not explain what complexity is or why complexity has increased, if indeed it has. Is it more molecules, more cells, more connections, or more functions? Complexity is not an easy thing to measure.

It is relatively easy to see that a unicellular organism must be less complex than a multicellular one. There are numerous cell types in the multicellular organism, all of which need organization and control, but there is also a difference in behaviour as well. Unicellular organisms do, however, have some surprising capabilities, which will be described in Chapter 20.

Accepting that, indeed, organisms have become more complex, how has this happened? So far only two proposals have been made to explain the evolution of complexity.

The first is a passive tendency to evolve away from the current optimum of organism structure and comes from Maynard Smith (1969):

There is nothing in neo-Darwinism that enables us to pre-dict a long-term increase in complexity. All one can say is that since the first living organisms were presumably very simple, then if any large change has occurred in evo-lutionary lineage, it must have been in the direction of increasing complexity; as Thomas Hood might have said 'nowhere to go but up . . .' but this is intuition not reason.

The second is a non-random driven process that biases evolution towards optimizing size and com-plexity. That is, competition itself generates more complex behaviour to outwit the competition. Competition comes from two sources, either com-petition for mates and thus members of one's own species, or competition for food. The latter divides into two parts, either escape from predators, pests, or disease, or as a predator to out-compete other species or one's own species or out-manoeuvre the food itself. Whatever is used, the result is to increase functional diversity and thus complexity. These are versions of the Red Queen hypothesis. 'The rabbit runs faster than the fox, because the rabbit is run-ning for his life while the fox is only running for his dinner' (Dawkins 2006, p. 250).

The generation of complexity arising from predation

It is perhaps easier to see this process in animals and it started when one animal decided to eat another—the predator–prey relationship. If the prey acquired a behavioural mutation that enabled it to outrun the predator, then the predator can only survive well in this situation if it can match that change and im-prove its catching ability. The speed of movement is a complex issue itself, but in its very simplest terms, may boil down to the speed and accuracy of sens-ing, and the coordination through a central nexus of nerve cells, to a muscular apparatus. If the predator does match the change in the prey, then the prey has to generate improvements or face potential extinc-tion. I see this to-and-fro challenge between preda-tor and prey as a driving force, a kind of positive feedback situation that has greatly accelerated the rate of evolution in animals. In this case complex increases in sensory equipment, brain structure, and musculature become inevitable. Furthermore, the driver resulting from numerous disease pests, accelerated the evolution of an immune system.

Again, there is positive feedback between disease and organism, generating complexity.

However, with plants, the situation is different fundamentally, because the ubiquity of light provid-ed no evolutionary incentive for movement. Being the primary source of external energy on the planet has meant acting as the primary food source. The response by plants has been to intensify chemistry, to produce tens of thousands of natural pesticides, and make digestion difficult (if not disastrous), and in certain cases, such as the production of gums, mucilages, and lignin, almost impossible. It also meant moving to drier parts of the world not only to avoid the plant competition, typically found in forests, but also because such conditions minimize animal predation, too. One of the reasons for preda-tor–prey relations limited to animals is that the risk from eating natural pesticide in plants is avoided. The driver, of course, in plant chemistry evolution, comes from the predator acquiring detoxifying methods. Thus, new chemicals have to be acquired and synthesized.

It is much more difficult when making compari-sons of complexity within either mammals or plant groups. Is an angiosperm more complex than a fern, for example? Is a human more complex than a ma-caque? There are many fewer extant species of ferns than angiosperms, but ferns photosynthesize using leaf-like structures (fronds), they have a conduct-ing system that moves water and nutrients around, they produce rhizomes and live in a variety of plac-es, although many prefer tropical regions to grow in abundance, as do many angiosperms. Temper-ate ferns are also well known, often occupying dry places that angiosperms seem not to prefer and they can certainly cover upland hill sides, as bracken. They do require moisture for reproduction because motile sperms need water to swim in, to locate the archegonium containing the egg. Is pollen growth more complex than sperm motility?

Yet, intuitively, we would say angiosperms are more complex. They are able as a group to occupy a greater variety of environments, use pollen and many vectors for transferring it around, there are a greater variety of morphologies and they are more obvious, but do any of these mean they are more complex? The reason for asking this question is that there are implicit assumptions that the latest groups of organisms on the evolutionary scene must, therefore, be more complex than those that evolved before. Ferns are certainly an older group than angiosperms. Connected with this difficulty is the notion of progress in evolution, an idea again difficult if not impossible to assess.

An attempt to compare the complexity between different groups of organisms?

There is an intuitive relationship between complexity and diversity of function. An organism with many functions must have a multiplicity of control systems and increased function implies more genes. Comparing mammals with angiosperms means at its very simplest means trying to comparing complexity on comparable bases; comparing one with diversity of cell type movement, the other perhaps with chemistry.

I have made use here of the discussions on complexity by McShea (1991, 1996). He asks a fundamental question, whether a cat is more complex than a clam, for example, and if it is thought so, why? The reasons are difficult to specify, and they are equally difficult between angiosperms and ferns. The fact that angiosperms are abundant and, therefore, must be more complex, can be countered by pointing to the abundance of dinosaurs when progenitor mammals were just shrew-like creatures grubbing around in the dirt. On a size and numbers basis, the dinosaurs win. Posing the question of complexity then might lead to a different answer.

McShea (1996) provides a number of criteria whereby complexity might be assessed. These include the numbers of genes, cell types, organs, and finally, organisms in an ecosystem. The numbers of interactions among these parts, the number of levels in a causal hierarchy, such as in an organism (atoms, molecules, protein complexes, membranes, organelles, cells, etc.), or ecosystem, and finally, the interaction numbers and parts in a given spatial or time scale. Certainly on these bases, plant evolution has seen a considerable increase in complexity, from additional elements in photosynthesis to greater cytoplasmic complexity, from a single cell to at least 30 different cell types, and from a few thousand genes in a blue-green alga to over 15,000 in a eukaryotic alga, to 25–30,000 or more in angiosperms. However, gene sequences themselves

are not a clear indication *per se* of complexity because there are an increasing number of protein-modifying reactions identified in cells that can enormously increase the numbers of proteins with differing potential functions. It is more likely control of gene activity that leads to more complex behaviour.

Are angiosperms as complex as mammals?

A similar problem emerges with attitudes to plants. They are commonly assumed to be simple organisms in comparison with mammals, but isn't this judgement made because they do not seem to move or really do anything obvious? What is being used here is the imposition of human criteria on the behaviour of other organisms, something discussed in Chapters 1 and 2. We regard ourselves as complex and, therefore, judge other organisms on the basis of how similar their behaviour is to ours. This is dangerous territory. If behaviour is apparently absent or seems to be so, then inevitably that group must be simple because they don't have any. This is a recurring theme throughout this book—to get the reader to realize the bias inherent in making judgements on other organisms.

To try and make the assessment of complexity more meaningful, McShea (1996) has provided a set of reasonably objective criteria mentioned earlier and these are summarized in Box 7.1.

Box 7.1 McShea's criteria of complexity

McShea suggested four possible criteria that might be used to assess complexity, objects versus processes; hierarchy versus non-hierarchy. McShea considered that each of the four sections should be separately assessed, rather than making an overall judgement.

1. Numbers of objects. Genes, gene products, other molecules, cells, tissues, etc.
2. Numbers of interactions between these objects and processes such as physiological change and developmental processes that derive from them.
3. Levels of organization in a hierarchy, such as the simple hierarchy, molecules, organelles, cells, tissues, individual, population, etc.
4. Hierarchical process complexity considered mainly from a morphological perspective.

I have used McShea's criteria to test the notions of comparative complexity in mammals and angiosperms as an interesting exercise. It is unlikely that complexity can be meaningfully assessed with such disparate groups of organisms, but the information can be used to counter the notion that plants are simple. Angiosperms and mammals are assumed to be the 'highest' in the plant and animal kingdom. I have omitted humans from this discussion of mammals. I consider what marks humans as really different from other 'advanced' mammals, like a dolphin or chimpanzee, is the complexity of language (easily measured as numbers of words and concepts). In other words, social communication with other humans, enabling corporate intelligence to easily develop. As will be seen later (Chapter 19), it is extremely difficult to make comparative judgements about intelligence as well.

Comparisons based on gene numbers, gene products, cells, etc.

The numbers of genes in higher plants and mammals, based on sequence, are about the same, around 25–30,000. The current largest gene number is *Daphnia*, the water flea (Colbourne et al. 2011) with just over 31,000, but the water flea does have some unusual behaviour that may account for this high figure. Thus, potentially the numbers of protein products/cell are likely to be similar. Many more 'proteins', however, can be produced through post-translational modification. Higher plants and animals both contain about 1000 protein kinases, the primary modifying system. At least 10 other post-translational modifications of proteins are known to be present. However, what is more important is the way that genes are regulated and coordinated, a property of the upstream sequences. The coordinate complexity seems currently unknown.

Overlapping DNA sequences may also increase protein numbers. However, the heterozygosity of angiosperms is about 40% (Hamrich et al. 1979), whereas heterozygosity assessed from a number of mammalian species is about 5% (Nevo, 1978). This information suggests that there may be a much greater variety and, thus, complexity of protein sequence in cells of any plant species. There are about 250,000 angiosperm species and only 3000 mammalian species, increasing the number of potentially different gene products for plants as against mammals. Lilies with 100 pg DNA/cell nucleus may also have much higher amounts of DNA than mammalian cells. These plants have the potential for greater variety of controlling elements of gene products as a consequence.

The ability to accommodate the degree of heterozygosity indicated above suggests that ordinary cell circuitry must be sufficiently robust to tolerate more variation than perhaps found in mammals. In certain respects, even without elaborated organs to sense signals, angiosperms may be more sensitive to very low intensity signals. Some of the major signal transduction pathways are remarkably similar in both angiosperms and mammals. Both organism groups use cytosolic calcium, phospho-inositols, phospholipids of various kinds and cyclic nucleotides for signal transduction. Both groups use a network of about a thousand protein kinases.

Angiosperms synthesize many thousands of low molecular weight chemicals (natural pesticides, insecticides), not present in mammals to deter herbivory. The total number are estimated at about 100,000, but only about 100–1000 are found in any one individual (Ames and Gold 1999, and references therein). These should represent a history of predation or disease.

Furthermore, angiosperms are autotrophs and synthesize all their organic molecules from carbon dioxide, ammonia (or nitrate), and phosphate. Thus, there are many more synthetic pathways (for pesticides, amino acids, nucleic acid bases, lipids, vitamins, etc.), all of which are regulated by interaction and feedback. The main respiratory pathways are shared by both groups of organisms; the photosynthetic pathways are of course an exception. Actin/myosin, kinesin are used by angiosperms for streaming, chloroplast, and chromosome movements. Angiosperms do not use calcium phosphate for structural purposes, but have their own polymers, e.g. lignin/cellulose for support and they also possess pathways for secretion, endocytosis, packaging, and modification of chromatin.

Any balanced and current McShea-type assessment on this section must place angiosperms as higher in this category than mammals. Oddly enough their lifestyle may require much more control than mammals with homeostatic temperature that eliminates the needs for many additional controls (although see Chapter 12 for control of temperature in leaves).

Cell types, tissues and organs

There are about 30 recognizable cell types in an angiosperm, and about 100 or more, on average, in mammals. The distinction between a tissue and an organ and the definition of both are difficult, but I estimate at least 30 tissues or organs for an average mammal and about 15 for the average angiosperm. However, plants are self-organizing, modular organisms, and the numbers of organs, such as seeds, leaves, fruits, root meristems, easily reaches several thousand or more/individual plant. The degree of individual variation in number can be enormous. In herbaceous plants, like poppies, different individuals can produce a range of seed numbers, varying anywhere from a million down to two.

As a consequence, plants are sometimes regarded as metapopulations because the behaviour of the individual shoot branches or roots can respond locally to signals. Even in the absence of obvious external signalling, each of these modules can be demonstrably different. Different branches of trees can vary in flower number, and thus, fruit number and apparent growth rate. There is undoubted potential for a greater variety of epigenetic variation among the numerous branches and thus greater overall variety of behaviour compared with organisms limited to a few. Even if branches look morphologically similar this can disguise a much greater variety at the molecular level.

When trees are attacked by predatory herbivores an enormous variety of responses among the component leaves can be produced so that the predator is unable to determine whether the next leaf will be edible, or will kill or injure to varying degrees. In this case, each leaf of a tree will be different from any other (Karban and Baldwin 1997).

There are many more angiosperm individuals, even trees, than mammals and, indeed, there has to be. Plants are the basis of all food chains and a crude estimate of the ratio of photosynthetic processes (crudely plant) to respiratory processes (crudely plant plus animal) can be made from the ratio of oxygen to carbon dioxide in the atmosphere, a figure of about 666 to 1.

A simple example indicates the numbers. European beech forests cover only some 17 million ha of land, but contain 1.5–2 billion mature individuals, together with perhaps an order of magnitude more saplings (Petiti and Hampe 2006.) The potential variety of population gene products is thus much higher.

It is certainly the case that plants lack organs like the heart, brain, or liver. However, the primary difficulty in making a comparison in this respect arises because plants are the basis of all food chains, and predation to varying degrees is fact of life. High degrees of differentiation and development into tissues with very specific indispensable functions, such as heart or brain would be disastrous, because even slight predation could kill the whole plant. Regeneration after predation requires forms of negative feedback to replace lost tissues, but the circuit of control is not properly understood. Plasticity in structure, a common property of all higher plants, raises other issues of control.

The basic lifestyle is very different. Thus, it is unclear whether mammals can be regarded as more complex than angiosperms.

Numbers of signals

How discriminating plants are about their environment can be assessed by noting the remarkable list of physical, biological, and chemical characteristics to which plants are both sensitive. These are summarized in Box 7.2.

The number of signals to which angiosperms respond suggests signal transduction networks of substantial complexity. It is generally conceded that mammals use only five senses in total, but obviously they expand the sensitivity of some and use them in different ways, use of echolocation for example by bats. It should be appreciated that the intensity, direction, and length of all these plant signals are separately distinguished and acted upon accordingly. Even more complex is that many interact with and modify each other.

Box 7.2 Environmental signals to which many higher plants are sensitive and produce a defined response

- *Light:* red, blue, far red, green, and ultraviolet separately distinguished. Circadian, day length, and annual variations distinguished. Shade
- *Temperature:* hot, cold, circadian variation, and mechanisms for assessing numbers of days below or between certain temperatures. Freezing resistance
- *Mechanical:* wind, touch, tension, compression, sway, shaking, certain sound frequencies
- *Water:* drought, flooding, humidity, snow melt, osmotic signals, salinity
- *Gravity:* all angles distinguished and used. Branch weight, sensed and accommodated
- *Soil:* strength, resistance to root penetration, surface features, sand, clay, stones. Resource presence and distribution
- *Electrical signals:* action potentials. Potential differences
- *Volatile chemicals:* CO_2, O_2, H_2O, C_2H_4, NO. Specific organic volatiles distinguished by parasitic plants. Many organic volatile chemicals are perceived by plants indicating predation (herbivory) both within and between individual plants. Signals are perceived from neighbouring roots, but the identity is not known. Some parasitic plants sense a variety of unusual organic volatiles to home in on their prey.
- *Non-volatile chemicals:* potassium, cobalt, boron, nitrate, phosphate, calcium, pH (acid and alkali separately). Allelopathic chemicals. Herbicides, heavy metals
- *Biological:* cooperation, mutualism, disturbance, trampling, herbivory, parasitism, space, territoriality, competition. Presence, absence and identity of neighbours

There are known specific receptors for a number of these signals. An equal list of internal chemicals to which plants are sensitive can be constructed.

What is the reason for the difference? It is surely to do with the plant lifestyle. Higher plants are sessile—they stay in the same position. To deal with competition from other plants, a fairly exacting sense of the stable, local environment becomes important; some kind of image must form so that advantage can be made of unoccupied space. These signals are sensed because they contribute to the overall aim of the individual to increase fitness. Mammals, on the other hand, wander through many environments in none of which do they really require or need any amount of detail. Thus, the five senses are adequate for this purpose coupled with a central processing brain. However, in internal chemistry, mammals have at least 100 neurotransmitters, and a similar number of hormones. Although the number of what are called plant 'hormones' in angiosperms continues to increase, it is still an order of magnitude less being in the tens or thereabouts.

However, other circulating chemicals far outweigh the known list of plant hormones. Their number in total is not yet known, but I suspect is very large. We now know that in the phloem are found mobile proteins, nucleic acids, micro-RNAs of several kinds, polypeptides, many of which are concerned in communication because they modify shoot structure or initiate flowering or other changes in morphology to accommodate mineral imbalance. The numbers of other chemicals that circulate and that also have impact on development is much larger than known hormones. This group includes molecules like phosphate, nitrate, various carbohydrates, as well as numerous secondary products, amino acids many of which initiate defined changes.

Temperature control

Mammals maintain a reasonably constant internal temperature using negative feedback with a brain sensor and carbohydrate oxidation to provide heat. In trees certainly, the growing seasonal average leaf temperature remains remarkably and homeostatically uniform at about 21°C. This ability applies to trees ranging from the subtropical to the boreal conifer forests of the north (Helliker and Richter 2008).

Blood composition in mammals is also homeostatically regulated. Correspondingly, there is plenty of evidence for equivalent homeostatic regulation of the composition of the phloem (Smith and Milburn 1979; Weibull et al. 1990; Noctor et al. 2002; Pant et al. 2008). Some of the homeostatic circuitry in plants is partly understood as operating through osmotic regulation or phloem-based micro-RNAs.

Hierarchical structures

A similar hierarchical arrangement of molecules to cells, individuals, and populations holds for both angiosperms and mammals. As already mentioned, there may be more distinguishable cell types in a mammal, but plant shoot cells contain more cellular compartments in the chloroplast and vacuole, and in the root, vacuoles, and plastids.

Hierarchical interactions: complexity of connections

Another interesting comparison can be made by trying to assess the numbers of interactions or connections concerned in behavioural control between mammals and angiosperms within reasonable orders of magnitude. In mammals, the nervous system and brain coordinates the sensory systems that initiate muscular responses. Coordination depends on the ability of individual neurons to branch via dendrites and thus connect directly to 10^3–10^4 neurons through synapses and neurotransmitters. A mouse brain contains 75×10^6 neurons, and has 10^{11} synapses and probably 2×10^4 nerve endings. Crudely, then, the nervous system is composed of 10^{15} connections. I assume, here, that the nervous system in terms of interaction numbers, dominates other forms of cellular interaction, which would contribute a lot less to the total of interactions.

In a sessile, self-organizing, angiosperm different parts of the plant experience different environments and the response can be specific to that particular environmental locale. A branch experiencing greater light intensity, for example, can express greater rates of growth and organ formation. However, this response, in turn, is dependent on an integration of all the information (an assessment) coming from the rest of the individual plant and involves modification of the vascular system to ensure a greater supply of root resources. Overall control depends then on the complexity of cellular interaction.

Within an order of magnitude, a mature tree contains probably 10^{13} cells. [Assessment can be made from the measured surface area of mature trees and assuming, on average, a depth of 30–50 viable cells in all tissues (Whittaker and Woodwell 1967). There

are many dead cells in a mature tree, particularly in the trunk, which have to be ignored]. The average number of plasmodesmata/cell is about 1000 (Robards 1975). Thus, in a mature tree there could be of the order of 10^{16} cellular connections that contribute to the control of behaviour; not dissimilar to the critical connections of the largest land mammals. The important difference is that complexity of control and, thus, interaction is distributed throughout the tree, whereas it is more centrally located in the mammal.

The precision of the calculations above can obviously be queried, but within several orders of magnitude they are probably about right. However, I have included them to indicate that large organisms with different lifestyles at the end of the day require very large numbers of controlling connections for survival. A self-organizing structure like a tree requires equivalent amounts of information about behaviour to one whose control is largely subsumed in one dominant nervous tissue.

Are mammals then more complex than angiosperms?

This very brief collation of comparative information illustrates the difficulty in making assumptions about complexity of any kind. The transition from a uni- to multicellular state, surely required orders of magnitude increase in complexity of cellular controlling mechanisms to ensure cooperative cellular behaviour and differentiation. The complexity of these interactions is still unknown.

It would seem that both groups of organisms are elaborations of an evolutionary separation made over 2 billion years ago—one to photosynthesize and the other to eat the photosynthesizers, directly or indirectly. The latter decision required the organism to move to find its photosynthetic food. Thus, the distinction comes down to deciding whether mobile organisms (or I should say, mobile at our perception of movement) that evolved a special tissue, the nervous system, to control the movement, to be more complex than the self-organizing control systems of plants. At the unicellular level, the choice is equally stark. There are single motile animal cells using cilia to find usually plant food versus the highly elaborate and remarkable silica wall structures of photosynthesizing diatoms or the motility of some algae. Which is then more complex?

The supposition that animals are more complex, when it is made, simply represents human bias. We move around and thus invest an awful lot in suppositions of complexity in other organism that move. The reasonable conclusion is that both groups of organisms with different lifestyles are well adapted to their environments. Whereas plants could happily dispense with animals, we could not happily dispense with plants.

References

Ames, B.N., and Gold, L.S. (1999). Pollution, pesticides and cancer misconceptions. In Morris J., and Bate, R., eds, *Fearing food*, pp. 19–39. Butterworth-Heinemann, Oxford.

Colbourne, J.K., Pfrender, M.E., Gilbert, D., Kelley, W.T., Tucker, A., Oakely, T.H., and 64 others (2011). The ecoresponsive genome of *Daphnia pulex*. *Science*, **331**, 555–561.

Dawkins, R. (2006). *The selfish gene: 30th anniversary edition*. Oxford University Press, Oxford.

Hamrich, J.L., Linhart, Y.B., and Mitton, J.B. (1979). Relationships between life history characteristics and electrophoretically detectable genetic variation in plants. *Annual Review of Ecology and Systematics*, **10**, 173–200.

Helliker, R.R., and Richter, S.L. (2008). Subtropical to boreal convergence of tree-leaf temperature. *Nature*, **454**, 511–514.

James, R. (1997). *Commitment*. Del Rey, New York.

Karban R., and Baldwin, I.T. (1997). *Induced responses to herbivory*. University of Chicago Press, Chicago, IL.

Maynard-Smith, J. (1969). The status of neo-Darwinism. In Waddington, C., ed. *Towards a theoretical biology, Vol. 2*, p. 82. Edinburgh University Press, Edinburgh.

McShea, D.W. (1991). Complexity and evolution; what everybody knows. *Biology and Philosophy*, **6**, 303–324.

McShea, D.W. (1996). Metazoan complexity: is there a trend? *Evolution*, **50**, 477–492.

Nevo, E. (1978). Genetic variation in natural populations. Patterns and theory in 30 species of mammals. *Theoretical Population Biology*, **13**, 121–177.

Noctor, G., Gomez, L., Vanacker, H., and Foyer, C.H. (2002). Interactions between biosynthesis, compartmentation and transport in the control of glutathione homeostasis and signalling. *Journal of Experimental Botany*, **53**, 1283–1304.

Pant, B.D., Buhtz, A., Kehr, J., and Scheible, W-R. (2008). MicroRNA399 is a long distance signal for the regulation of phosphate homeostasis. *Plant Journal*, **53**, 731–738.

Petiti, R.J., and Hampe, A. (2006). Some evolutionary consequences of being a tree. *Annual Review of Ecology, Evolution and Systematics*, **37**, 187–214.

Robards, A.W. (1975). Plasmodesmata. *Annual Review of Plant Physiology*, **26**, 13–29.

Smith, J.A.C., and Milburn, J.A. (1979). Osmoregulation and the control of phloem-sap composition in *Ricinus communis*. *Planta*, **148**, 28–34.

Weibull, J., Ronquist, F., and Brishammer, S. (1990). Free amino acid composition of leaf exudates and phloem sap. *Plant Physiology*, **92**, 222–226.

Whittaker, R.H., and Woodwell, G.M. (1967). Surface area relations of woody plants and forest communities. *American Journal of Botany*, **54**, 931–939.

CHAPTER 8

Plant behaviour: first intimations of self-organization

Self-organisation is often associated with the spontaneous appearance of an ordered property of the whole that cannot be explained by the sum of the complexity of its elements.

(Sasai 2013)

⊃ Summary

Behaviours are the responses by organisms to environmental problems, whether these involve movement or not. These problems can be generalized and are uniform for most organisms; finding food, avoiding pests and predators, and locating mates. Behaviour and intelligence in all organisms underpins fitness, and that includes plants, too. Plants, however, explore and exploit their two environments, above and below ground, by growth rather than movement. A simple model, developed by Herbert Simon, is used to describe plant behaviour. The model indicates that plants do not grow randomly—their behaviour is rational. Most higher plants have clear needs in terms of acquiring light energy, minerals, and water, and their phenotype changes, to access patchily distributed resources. Further needs require resistance to both predators and disease. Behavioural responses to both are well established. Signalling mechanisms are basic to solving plant problems. Agnes Arber was a classical morphologist. Her description of behaviour is outlined, as are her research contributions, but the limitations of traditional morphology are indicated. The fundamental difference between plant and animal cells quoted by Arber lies in the necessary presence of the relatively rigid cell wall in plants. Nearly all the unique patterns of plant development and behaviour devolve from that one evolutionary acquisition, probably necessitated by sugar accumulation from photosynthesis. The notion that plants are merely populations of meristems is discussed and its limitations indicated. Visible plant behaviour, i.e. largely phenotypic plasticity, arises from the capability of self-organization that underpins plant development.

What exactly is behaviour?

Plant behaviour has been mentioned several times in previous chapters without indicating what exactly it is. A dictionary definition of behaviour indicates it is the response of an organism to a specific stimulus. On that basis, behaviour covers any change from the molecular to the whole plant. However, identifying molecular changes without specific technology is not easy and a satisfactory compromise for the ordinary reader is to appreciate that observable changes are anyway underpinned by molecular events inside tissues and cells.

Plotkin (1988), in the introduction to a text on behaviour and evolution, indicates the word 'behaviour' to be derived from the Latin *habere* meaning 'having possession of' or 'being characterized by'.

Plant Behaviour and Intelligence. First Edition. Anthony Trewavas.
© Anthony Trewavas 2014. Published 2014 by Oxford University Press.

These descriptions do, in fact, refer to some functions of the phenotype, but are not common descriptions of behaviour. Instead, animal behaviourists consider behaviour to refer to responses of the organism to environmental problems or environmental change. Some examples illustrate the description more clearly:

1. A bacterial cell swimming up a food concentration gradient.
2. Animal migration.
3. Betty the crow bending pieces of wire to hook up food from a narrow orifice (Weir et al. 2002) or some other detailed aspect of human creativity.

The implication here is of the organism, or ourselves, doing something as a response to new environmental situations. All of these responses involve movement on our time scale.

The limitations of our ability to perceive movement and regard it as an aspect of behaviour have already been referred to earlier. While I am sitting here wrestling with words to put down on paper, is this not my brain behaving? A brain on its own does not obviously move, but connect to an EEG machine and lots of neurones are clearly behaving, changing neural channels as different thought processes and ideas are examined. I regard behaviour as the organism dealing with the perpetual problems thrown up by its environment, regardless of whether movement in response is obvious or not. Behaviour and intelligence in all organisms underpins fitness and that includes plants, too. My view of intelligence, outlined later, is that it reflects a capacity to solve problems, particularly those that deal with survival. Those that solve them quicker or with greater skill than others are more intelligent. Intelligence varies between individuals, as well as species.

The major environmental situations requiring behavioural change are the acquisition of food, dealing with predation or disease, and finding mates or reproduction. Plants are no less subject to the same environmental problems, but because they are autotrophic and sessile, their behavioural solutions to these problems differ substantially from the way every animal behaves.

The words stimulus and/or signal also require brief comment because they will be used interchangeably.

Some ecologists use the word 'cue' instead. All of these three terms—stimulus, signal, or cue—I regard as representing meaningful information, because organisms recognize the information in the signals and adapt accordingly. If there is no recognition of the stimulus/signal, either the strength of the signal is inadequate to cross a threshold of sensitivity that would enable detection if it was stronger, or the organism possesses no sensory equipment to detect the information, whereas others will.

Do plants need behaviour?

A not uncommon view, held by some animal biologists, is that plants do not have behaviour (Silvertown and Gordon 1989).

I can justify the requirement for plants to behave, from a little known article by Herbert Simon (1956) that adequately answers this question. Simon's article was concerned with the question of rational choice and was an attempt to sort out an argument between economists. He constructed a very simple model of an organism that had one need—to acquire food. All organisms he argued must behave adaptively, i.e. rationally (with intelligence), and that although equipped with sensory equipment, the structure of the environment would be equally important in determining how they satisfied this requirement. Simon rejected any requirement to describe the totality of space, the environment, around the organism, merely describing the space that indicated the distribution of food.

The model organism was indicated to be capable of three different kinds of activity—resting, exploration, and food acquisition. The food space could be visualized as a surface over which exploration could occur. Simon (1956) considered that the rational way for an organism to behave is:

1. To explore its need surface, initially at random, watching for food.
2. When it senses food, to proceed to and consume it.
3. If the energy gained by the food is in excess of the energy expended in gaining it, then it can rest or do other things.

There is an important adjunct here and that is the storage capacity for food, which will determine the latitude with which this last requirement can be relaxed. Thus, this model organism has fixed aspiration levels and the nature of the environment limits its planning horizon. A choice of alternatives in exploratory searching by locomotion is simplified by the overall need to find food. The nature of the needs and the environment create a very natural separation between means and ends.

Simon places his model on a mathematical basis, but indicating that the chances of finding food must be described in probabilities. Equally, decisions about choices of paths to find food must be based on a balance of probabilities. The model is further examined using multiple goals (e.g. food and water), indicating that decisions have to be made with the minimum of complication. If two of the goals are randomly distributed, then Simon demonstrates that the time spent in exploration is increased by 50%, with four goals by two-fold, and so on.

Since it is unlikely that an optimal path for multiple goals can be constructed, a choice mechanism can probably only lead to a *satisficing* path, i.e. a path that will permit satisfaction at some specified level of all its needs. (Simon's article is known for the first use of this compromise word 'satisficing'.) This conclusion only holds if the need/satisfying points are independently distributed. If there is a negative correlation between them, then independent searching mechanisms and signalling systems will be necessary to trigger the exploration drives. Further exploration will only commence when its hunger or thirst, internally specified, thresholds are exceeded. If there are two basic requirements, one highly probable and the other much less likely, then obviously some priority decision mechanism must enter.

Simon finally points out that an organism that behaves completely at random leads to zero probability for survival. Furthermore, there must exist in the environment sufficient clues as to need-satisfying points.

I have introduced Simon's model here in some detail and will now indicate its relevance for plant behaviour. The plant equivalent of food is light to provide energy and minerals/water. I will illustrate this using the requirements of his model to a seedling growing under a wild, patchy canopy, in a soil known to be patchy in its distributions of minerals and water—a situation common for wild

plants. This environment is thus equivalent to Simon's patchy food environment for an animal, but indicates the different way plants approach the problems.

1. Plants explore their two environments, above and below ground, by growth; this is now the equivalent to Simon's animal locomotion or behaviour.
2. Plants cannot behave (grow) randomly or they would not survive; their behaviour must, therefore, be adaptive or rational.
3. Plants have clear needs—to gain shoot (light) and root resources (minerals and water) equivalent to Simon's food. Simple observation indicates that shoots grow towards rich sources of light, and roots towards rich sources of minerals and water. Often they will proliferate in these rich conditions. Random growth will only occur when there are no signals, but this really is Simon's exploratory behaviour.
4. The two-resource model fits the seedling better. A negative correlation must exist between shoot and root environment because both are entirely different. Signalling mechanisms must then be available for both resource sources and plants use these to grow towards richer sources.
5. There are other needs—a primary one is to deal with herbivory or disease, etc. Plants have complex mechanisms to resist or mitigate the damage. Separate sensing mechanisms must exist for these, both above and below ground.
6. Simon indicates that if there are two needs, and one is highly probable and the other of low probability, then a priority decision mechanism must be present. For plants growing in a poor light environment, growth resources are invested in the shoot at the expense of the root. If soil resources are poor then growth resources are invested in the root. Basic decision mechanisms are obviously present and, as will be seen in subsequent chapters, there are many more.

This brief discussion indicates that plants must express behaviour if they are to adequately gather necessary food resources and identifies growth as the basic equivalent of locomotion in animals. In general, plants grow, animals move—changes in growth to changing environmental signals are one form of plant behaviour. Specific alterations in growth in response to specific environmental signals are an important element in plant behaviour. The objectives of both animal and plant behaviours are the same. The ultimate goal is to optimize fitness, which should be distributed among individuals on a probability basis according to their capacity to solve problems, which is where intelligence comes in. Intelligence is based on how efficient a species becomes at doing the things they need to survive.

The decisions that initiate changes in behaviour when plant reserves fall below certain thresholds are not commonly discussed. Mechanisms for sensing the levels of reserves in plants, needs to be investigated.

Behaviour in plants is most easily seen as changes in form

The section above has indicated that changes in growth represent the equivalent to movement in animal behaviour. With alterations in growth, inevitably there are changes in phenotype or form. An early description of plant behaviour was proposed by the classical morphologist, Arber (1950; see Box 8.1). 'Among plants, form may be held to include something corresponding to behaviour in the zoological field' (Arber 1950, pp. 2–3).

She continues, 'The animal can do things without inducing any essential change in its bodily structure'—a bird pecking, to pick up seed, is the example used. Whereas in plants, the 'only available forms of action are either growth or the discarding of parts' (Arber 1950, p. 3). Her view, like many, was limited by her own interests and what information was currently considered in 1950.

However the texts by Pfeffer (1906) in particular were available, which did deal with a panoply of plant movements, and expanded on behaviour beyond growth and the discarding of parts. Cytoplasmic streaming and stomatal aperture control are two cases in point, the former working at visible rates and the latter not far behind. Chloroplast movement in response to light intensity and gradients inside cells is also behaviour; important to the functioning of photosynthesis and the gathering of light energy (i.e. food), and will be considered later.

Box 8.1 Agnes Arber

Agnes Arber was only the third woman to be elected to the Royal Society of London, but the first female botanist to achieve that status. She was the daughter of an artist and much of her early training in art enabled her to productively generate her own unique contribution to plant science. Her study by choice was comparative anatomy and morphology, and she published a number of books and articles, both on the monocotyledons and the history of Botanical Science. Although she graduated in the University of London she moved to Cambridge where she stayed subsequently. Despite her subsequent achievements and election to the Royal Society she was, in the 1930s, denied further laboratory facilities by the current departmental head. She then set up her own laboratory in her own house and continued her work, later becoming interested in philosophical aspects of morphology. Her most interesting book, from which I have quoted because I do regard her as being insightful in some respects, is *The Natural Philosophy of Plant Form*, published in 1950. The book is illustrated throughout with her own drawings.

I regard her as the last classical morphologist in the UK. She certainly became obsessed with Goethian philosophy and that comes through in the book. Morphology she considered to be the whole of the internal and external organization of the plant that governs its life history. 'It is the business of morphology to connect into one coherent whole all that belongs to the intrinsic nature of the living being'. Goethian approaches, certainly to plant study, I have always regarded as somewhat mystical rather than scientific. Morphology can be divided into idealistic morphology that uses comparative anatomy (as did Arber) and the stages of morphological development as its basis. However, it is indifferent to the mechanisms or processes by which such changes have been brought about. It relies instead on generalized and abstract conceptions. Realistic morphology, on the other hand, relies on anatomy, genetics, biochemistry, embryology, and the mechanisms that underpin morphologic or metamorphic change. It leads to more definite conclusions.

One of the great appeals of Arber's 1950 book are the large number of drawings of differing kinds of morphology (considered a necessary part of the philosophical appreciation) and her emphasis on the whole organism. It is the latter that is important for both behaviour and intelligence. There are still some who expound Goethian botanical philosophy (e.g. Antillo 2002), but it really is of historical interest only, so far as science is concerned.

However, to partly excuse Arber's oversight, there was no simple way then, in which time-lapse photography could be performed to make growth look similar to movement. Since plants do not possess a nervous system, a different timescale of life is to be expected. Furthermore, herbivore or disease resistance studies were in their infancy in 1950 when Arber was publishing, but are now regarded as important aspects of plant behaviour (Karban 2008). Both herbivory and infection act as signals that initiate detailed responses. However, the responses are largely molecular, being either accumulations of natural pesticides, volatiles to warn others of attack, or specific proteins to switch off infection. There may be few obvious visible changes, although leaf abscission in response to some damage can occur and leaf removal may lead to growth of new shoots from buds (Addicott 1982). It is, of course, the pest that usually changes its visible behaviour when consuming natural pesticides, since death is common.

The responses of sensitive plants like *Mimosa* to stimuli, mentioned in Chapter 2, are 'apparently' reversible changes in form. Again, the stimulus-response situation occurs here. In *Mimosa*, however, tiny increments of growth accompany each stimulation of response and the numbers of such responses is limited. Thus, there are differences even here with the bird pecking up seed, indicated by Arber as typical animal behaviour. However, Arber did dwell on obvious visible and important changes in shoot structure, but no less important are those in the root, to which she did not refer.

It is also not the case that animal movement always results in no change in the morphology, with muscle maintenance or muscle building from weight lifting an obvious example. I suspect that most animal movements are not without some molecular changes that may not be reversible; age takes its toll.

What fundamental difference between plants and animals elicits the difference in behaviour between plants and animals?

The possession of photosynthesis has already been discussed as a critical difference in Chapter 2. However, there is another difference that is a consequence of photosynthesis. Arber was aware of it when she quotes Thomas Huxley as saying 'The plant is an animal confined in a wooden case and Nature like Sycorax holds thousands of 'delicate Ariels' imprisoned within every oak' (Arber 1950, p. 196).

So far as I am aware, most photosynthetic organisms possess a cell wall. There are a few exceptions, of course. I suspect the reason, when it initially evolved, was to accommodate the problems caused by variable accumulations of sugars in photosynthesis. Without the wall, cytoplasm would expand uncontrollably due to osmotic uptake of water. However, with the wall, time for osmotic adjustments, if required, could be made and the structure maintained.

Once the choice of an outer, relatively rigid wall was made, enormous numbers of consequences followed. Animal cells are, with few exceptions, able to fold, move, contract, expand, and otherwise, change shape during embryological development. Once a cell wall intervenes, not only is overall movement rendered difficult, but contraction, folding, etc., become impossible. In multicellular plants, growth has to involve changes in wall structure as well as the cytoplasm. Growth takes place by adding, not interpolating, cells and tissues to those already there. Since overall movement of multicellular organisms whose cells are surrounded by a relatively rigid cell wall becomes difficult, the best way of exploiting the local environment is simply to grow into it; branching becomes essential as the primary means to occupy nutritionally abundant space. Growth and development have to continue throughout the life cycle adjusting the plant body to fit changing circumstances. Flowering can only be accommodated once a certain amount of growth and thus reserve accumulation has been accomplished. The association of behaviour with changes in growth and form become inevitable consequences.

The plant cell wall is a dynamic structure and does provide for a variety of functions in present-day angiosperms, including signal generation and mediation, transport, disease resistance, and structural stiffness (Cosgrove 2005). Different kinds of plant cell wall perform very different functions. These range from the thin, plastic cell wall of meristematic cells that permit cell division to dead secondary xylem that forms the basis of tree trunks.

The importance of the wall in plant behaviour cannot be over-emphasized because mechanical signalling then becomes crucial to both behaviour and development. Mechanical signals are of great importance. Each growing tissue generates a complex mixture of physical stresses and strains that are undoubtedly used as signals to control further growth and specify morphology. Biomechanics is of enormous relevance to understanding every aspect to plant development and behaviour (Niklas 1992; Trewavas and Knight 1994).

The modular plant and self-organization

Modularity refers to a very obvious higher plant characteristic. The plant body contains numerous shoot and root branches, repetitions of leaves, flowers, buds, and fruits, and was commented on as long ago as by Theophrastus, four centuries BCE, who wrote the first herbal. The modular habit is found even in multicellular algae. Repetitions of the modular structure, simplifies the genetic requirements for increasing size. Take an initial cellular and tissue programme, modify it slightly, and repeat it again and again. Some animals do exhibit obvious modular characteristics, segmented worms, the millipede and centipede, and segmented insects come obviously to mind. Higher plants are mostly all modular, but modularity is not generally used to describe mammalian morphology even though there are structures such as capillaries, which are repeated units (Vuorisalo and Tuomi 1986).

West-Eberhard (2003) broadens the definition of a module regarding it as discrete parts within a mature or developing organism that are integrated into a whole. On this basis the various plant tissues would be regarded as developmental modules, such as cortex, epidermis, xylem, phloem, etc., but these descriptions are not particularly helpful for understanding plant behaviour.

In this context Arber (1950, p. 136) clarifies the distinction between mammals and plants. 'One of the sharpest differences is that the individuality of the mammalian body is of a much more fixed character; that body consists of a limited number of members and organs which were already once and for all marked out in the embryo and which have no power of subsequent self-multiplication'. This consequence is inevitable in an organism in which coordinated movement is such a fundamental aspect of lifestyle. To these statements we can add the demarcation of function in most animals to particular tissues, such as heart, nervous system, alimentary canal. The critical specification of the numbers of tissues in higher animals occurs in the very earliest stages of embryological development and involves cellular movements. Consequently, these critical stages of development take place in a protected and controlled environment, either the egg or the uterus. The complexity of coordination required in mammals for movement provides enormous constraints on further evolution. Control operates through the nervous system that is both highly differentiated, but extraordinarily plastic too.

Are plants merely populations of meristems?

> In the animal body with its parts thus arranged in an ordered hierarchy there is no such thing as an indefinite succession of limbs and branches of limbs numerically unfixed and liable to impede one another but this is what we find among plants in which the urge to self-maintenance tends to an indefinite number of growing points and finds its expression in repetitive branching. (Arber 1950, p. 136)

The reference to growing points is, of course, to the enormous numbers of shoot buds that, when activated, can form, in turn, enormous numbers of branches. The growing points in the root are the pericycle cells, capable again when activated of generating huge numbers of growing branch roots when required. However, this statement can easily lead to suppositions that regard higher plants as merely populations of conjoined meristems exemplified in the philosophy of Goethe (to whom Arber was certainly a disciple).

White (1979) reiterates an ecological view in discussing plants as a meta-population and Firn (2004), more recently, also considers this one way to view a growing plant. The important difference is in the overall organization.

Self-organization is the key to understanding plant behaviour

Whereas a hierarchy of control seems obvious in animals, with an autocratic nervous system, purportedly acting as the conductor of the organ orchestra, in higher plants we are left with an obviously more democratic framework—a republic. The conductor is the whole organism, with the looser form of control on the behaviour of the modules implied by that statement (Kroon et al. 2005). Bearing in mind the inevitability of emergent properties in cells (Chapter 3), Addiscott, (2011) concluded that 'one of the characteristics of a biological emergent system seems to be the ability to confer self-organisation on an entity which may be larger than itself'. Plants exemplify the phenomenon of self-organization, the consequences of which are considered in greater detail in Chapters 10 and the following chapters.

Inevitable predation has prevented the more unitary kind of organization found in animals—lose one module and there are plenty of others that enable the organism to survive. Plasticity in the individual is a selectable character and ultimately derives from evolutionary processes, and is necessary. Obviously, genes do not specify exact forms, but instead merely provide the boundaries within which substantial phenotypic variation can occur (Sultan 2005). Phenotypic variation results from the response to local signals and they exhibit a much greater range of plasticity in form than animals (West-Eberhard 2003). Phenotypic plasticity can be regarded as the morphological expression of adaptation.

However, plasticity in plants can lead to suppositions that there really is no basic organization at all and this is most certainly incorrect. A local response does occur to a local signal, but it does so within the totality of a framework of information derived from the whole organism itself. If it did not, there would be no possibility of meaningful selection.

White (1979) quotes Erasmus Darwin (grandfather of Charles) as saying 'a tree therefore is a family or swarm of individual plants' and draws analogies with some sessile corals.

This statement by Erasmus Darwin was based on the observations that many isolated angiosperm shoots (cuttings) can be propagated to form a new plant. However, while many angiosperms can be propagated through shoot cuttings, many others cannot. Those that can be propagated through root cuttings (e.g. dandelion, chicory) are much more limited in number and there are many fewer again that can be propagated through leaf cuttings (e.g. *Begonia* sp.; Hartmann et al. 2002). For certain trees, e.g. rubber, branch propagation does not generate the important primary tap root meristem; only the weaker adventitious roots are regenerated. Branches of ivy or yew can remain as obvious branches in character and angle of growth after forming roots. Examining the regeneration of excised branches from *Araucaria* (a gymnosperm) it was observed that regenerants from the terminal apex exhibited normal branching, those from the first order lateral branches only branched in two dimensions, and second order laterals when regenerated, did not branch at all (Schmid 1992).

Simple appearances can thus deceive. A plant regenerant may look the same, but in detail be different. Comparisons have been made between regenerated cuttings of a particular species variant, to seedlings of the same species variant at a similar stage of development. Phenotypic variation was much larger in the regenerants than in seedlings of the same species (Schmid and Bazzaz 1990). This may not matter for the horticultural and agricultural requirements of propagation, but it does indicate that there are differences between the propagated shoot and the original shoot from which it derived. Erasmus Darwin's view indicated above is not correct in the way stated.

In my own view, the easy formation of adventitious roots in many cuttings is an evolutionary decision to two realities of plant life. Branches may touch the soil and by forming roots on that site propagate the individual as, for example, in *Rubus species*. In others increasing depth of soil around the stem provides for better anchorage.

Similarly, appearances can deceive for shoot bud behaviour. Buds on a stem can look superficially similar, too. However, the buds in different positions on the plant respond differently to different stimuli. Clearly, there is considerable molecular variation within similar tissues of the same individual (Gregory and Veale 1957).

Local signalling does involve self-organizing assessment by the whole plant: phosphate starvation as an example

The plant form in many dicotyledonous perennials can be very plastic, and this leads to interesting questions about organization, its control, and the extent of morphological plasticity. Arguments between proponents of morphological plasticity as against morphological stability or canalization were included in an interesting text edited by Sattler (1982). When the environment is coarse-grained, individuals with a largely invariant phenotype are favoured. When it is fine-grained, organisms with greater degrees of plasticity tend to be selected (Bradshaw 1965; Levene 1962). The distinctions between coarse and fine grain are somewhat arbitrary, but they are designed to distinguish more predictable from less predictable environments.

As indicated previously, plasticity induced by sensing a local environmental stimulus, is the result of a response assessed in some way by the whole organism. One well-investigated example illustrates the point. The necessary minerals needed for plant growth can be patchily distributed. Maps indicating this heterogeneous distribution of resources, this patchiness of minerals and water in natural soil were assessed using observed growth of tree seedlings (Bell and Lechowicz 1994). At least half of all world soils are rated as phosphate deficient. Even in agricultural soils to which phosphate is liberally applied, the free soil phosphate concentration is rarely above 10 μM (Richardson and Simpson 2011). This low concentration is caused by the precipitation or complexing of phosphate with calcium, aluminium, or iron, which are often abundant in soil. Another form of insoluble phosphate in soils is to be found as organic phosphate from dead plant and bacterial material. Since plants grow on these 'deficient' soils, they must have behavioural mechanisms for dealing with these problems. Fitness will be related to the ability of individual plants to solubilize phosphate from these insoluble sources, to sequester such phosphate away from competitors, and thus enhance its own growth relative to others.

The availability of free phosphate is sensed by the primary root cap (Svistonoff et al. 2007). On receipt of a very low phosphate signal, the growth of the primary root is either inhibited or ceases altogether. This information from the cap is conveyed to the shoot where it is sensed and it is known that it is the phosphate ion itself that is sensed. The transduction machinery in the shoot results in the synthesis of specific sRNAs (small oligonucleotide RNAs), and accumulation of sucrose that circulates and induces phenotypic, adaptive changes in the root system. The numbers of lateral roots are greatly increased, enhancing soil exploration and occupying and effectively sequestering soil space. Root hairs derived from single cells in the root epidermis act as the primary sites of phosphate absorption. The density of root hairs on lateral roots is greatly increased, too. Concomitantly, the root system starts substantial secretion of citrate and other organic acids to chelate the metals in the insoluble phosphate complexes, and to solubilize others by acidification. The secretion of phosphatase enzymes is also greatly increased to break down organic phosphates (Hammond and White 2011). In addition, strigolactone is secreted to attract fungal symbionts, such as Mycorrhizae, that absorb phosphate and donate it to the plant in exchange for carbohydrate.

Although plasticity in development occurs in the root system, where you would expect it to be, it is actually manipulated by the shoot in response to a root-detected signal; it is a whole organism response. Split root experiments in which different roots experience different phosphate environments, clearly demonstrate the response to low phosphate is a whole plant assessment (Thibaud et al. 2010).

As is typical of all multicellular organisms, messages pass throughout the whole organism to ensure some kind of integration of behaviour. From the fitness perspective, the changes in morphology are designed to increase soil exploration to rapidly contact new sources of potential soil phosphate and to deny these resources to others.

Local responses require whole organism assessment and are embedded in a life cycle assessment

De Kroon et al. (2005) point out that local stimulation by shading of specific nodes to a specific light source, for example, leads to local changes in plasticity of growth. Equally, a dormant bud can be induced to grow using a red microbeam focused on just the one bud. While indicating that phenotypic plasticity obviously involves those parts specifically stimulated, they also indicate that communication and behavioural integration of interconnected modules modifies the local response—a typical property of self-organizing systems. Any growing plant, it can be anticipated, experiences different environmental conditions in different parts of it. In that case, there has to be a localized response to the recognized external condition leading to phenotypic plasticity. Information arrives heterogeneously in space and intensity, and impacts heterogeneously on the individual plant. Phenotypic plasticity is the biological attempt to construct the individual phenotype best able to exploit it. Decisions are thus composite, reflecting the particular balance of information at the time.

Mammals, too, exhibit behavioural responses that are apparently local in response to local signals; the thickening of skin where continuously rubbed, the arm muscles on a weight lifter, the manipulation of the pupil aperture in response to light, but the integration of animal behaviour is evident and not disputed. Animals integrate behaviour through long-range electrical and chemical signals, and these changes take place within the context of the overall information state.

McNamara and Houston (1996) argue persuasively that the whole life cycle pattern is heritable and subject to selection. For higher plants, that necessitates optimizing the architecture to benefit the whole organism. Only by optimizing root and shoot proliferation, and the balance between and within them, can they maximize the capture of resources. Seed yield relates strongly to the level of captured resources gained throughout the life cycle. Seed number, in turn, provides the potential for siblings and, thus, ultimate fitness. Again, higher plants share their information throughout and local responses occur within the context of that information. They are integrated, not just a population of joined meristems, each capable of determining its own future independent of others.

References

Addicott, F. (1982). *Abscission*. University of California Press, Berkeley, CA.

Addiscott, T. (2011). Emergence or self organisation. *Communicative and Integrative Biology*, **4**, 469–470.

Antillo, A.O. (2002). *The will to create; Goethe's philosophy of nature*. The University of Pittsburgh Press, Pittsburgh, PA.

Arber, A. (1950). *The natural philosophy of plant form*. Cambridge University Press, Cambridge.

Bell, G., and Lechowicz, M.J. (1994). Spatial heterogeneity at small scales and how plants respond to it. In Caldwell, M.M., and Pearcy, R.W., eds, *Exploitation of environmental heterogeneity by plants*, pp. 391–414. Academic Press, New York.

Bradshaw, A.D. (1965). Evolutionary significance of phenotypic plasticity. *Genetics*, **13**, 115–155.

Cosgrove, D.J. (2005). Growth of the plant cell wall. *Nature Reviews Molecular Cell Biology*, **6**, 850–861.

Firn, R. (2004). Plant intelligence an alternative point of view. *Annals of Botany*, **93**, 475–481.

Gregory, F.C., and Veale, J.A. (1957). A reassessment of the problem of apical dominance. In Porter, H.K., ed. *Society for Experimental Biology Symposium XI. Biological action of growth substances*, pp. 1–20. Cambridge University Press, London.

Hammond, J.P., and White, P.J. (2011). Sugar signalling in root responses to low phosphate availability. *Plant Physiology*, **156**, 1033–1040.

Hartmann, H.T., Kester, D.E., Geneve, R.L., and Davies, F.T. (2002). *Plant propagation: principles and practices*, 7th edn. N.J. Prentice Hall, Englewood Cliffs, NJ.

Karban, R. (2008). Plant behaviour and communication. *Ecology Letters*, **11**, 1–13.

Kroon, H., de, Huber, H., Stuefer, J.E., and Groenendael, J.M., van (2005). A modular concept of phenotypic plasticity. *New Phytologist*, **166**, 73–82.

Levene, R. (1962). Theory of fitness in a heterogeneous environment. 1. The fitness set and adaptive function. *American Naturalist*, **96**, 361–378.

McNamara, J.M., and Houston, A.I. (1996). State dependent life histories. *Nature*, **380**, 215–221.

Niklas, K.J. (1992). *Plant biomechanics*. Chicago University Press, Chicago, IL.

Pfeffer, W. (1906). *The physiology of plants. A treatise upon the metabolism and sources of energy in plants*. Oxford at the Clarendon Press.

Plotkin, H.C. (1988). Behaviour and evolution. In Plotkin, H.C., ed. *The role of behaviour in evolution*, pp. 1–17. MIT Press, Cambridge, MA.

Richardson, A.E., and Simpson, R.J. (2011). Soil microorganisms mediating phosphorus availability. *Plant Physiology*, **156**, 989–996.

Sasai, Y. (2013). Cytosystems dynamics in self-organisation of tissue architecture. *Nature*, **493**, 318–326.

Sattler, R. (1982). Axioms and principles of plant construction. Proceedings of a Symposium held at the

International Botanical Congress, Sydney, Australia, 1981, Springer, Berlin.

Schmid, B. (1992). Phenotypic variation in plants. *Evolutionary Trends in Plants*, 6, 45–60.

Schmid, B., and Bazzaz, F.A. (1990). Plasticity in plant size and architecture in rhizome–derived and seed derived Solidago and Aster. *Ecology*, **71**, 523–535.

Silvertown, J., and Gordon, D.K. (1989). A framework for plant behaviour. *Annual Review of Ecology and Systematics*, **20**, 349–366.

Simon, H.A. (1956). Rational choice and the structure of the environment. *Psychological Review* **63**, 129–138.

Sultan, S.E. (2005). An emerging focus on plant ecological development. *New Phytologist*, **166**, 1–5.

Svistonoff, S., Creff, A., Reymond, M., Sigoillot-Claude, C., Ricaud, L., Blanchet, A., and 2 others (2007). Root tip contact with low-phosphate media reprograms plant root architecture. *Nature Genetics*, **39**, 792–796.

Thibaud, M-C., Arrighi, J.F., Bayle, V., Chiarenza, S., Creff, A., Bustos, R., and 3 others (2010). Dissection of local and systemic transcriptional responses to phosphate starvation in *Arabidopsis*. *Plant Journal*, **64**, 775–789.

Trewavas, A.J., and Knight, M.R. (1994). The regulation of shape and form by cytosol calcium. In Ingram D., and Hudson, A., eds, *Shape and form in plant and fungal cells*, pp. 221–233. Academic Press, London.

Vuorisalo, T., and Tuomi, J. (1986). Unitary and modular organisms: criteria for ecological division. *Oikos*, **47**, 382–386.

Weir, A.A.S., Chappell, J., and Kacelnik, A. (2002). Shaping of hooks in New Caledonian crows. *Science*, **297**, 981.

West-Eberhard, M.J. (2003). *Developmental plasticity and evolution*. Oxford University Press, Oxford.

White, J. (1979). The plant as a metapopulation. *Annual Review of Ecology and Systematics*, **10**, 109–145.

CHAPTER 9

The varieties of plant behaviour

All those adaptations are purposeful which contribute to its maintenance and insure its existence.

(Sachs 1887)

⊃ **Summary**

This chapter describes the varieties of behaviour exhibited by plants, all of which indicates a remarkable degree of sensory perception, assessment, forecasting, and purpose. Higher plants can discriminate among different environments and choose those that are more beneficial. Once decisions are initially made, they can be corrected after due assessment. Much research shows that plants have the ability to sense each other and avoid entanglement. Competition from other plants causes growth to be redirected away from competitors. Alternatively, phenotypic changes are used to outstrip competitors. Various chemicals can be sensed, including numerous volatiles, and growth can be directed along a gradient of them. Light or mineral gradients are equally used to direct to better growth resources. Behaviour to herbivores, disease pests, and various stresses can be modified by priming. On receipt of a first signal, subsequent responses are faster and larger in the primed plant. Habituation and conditioned behaviour have also been recorded. The ability to investigate, search, survey, examine, and discover is also reported in the literature. Much plant response requires an assessment of likely futures and is active, rather than passive. Phenotypic adjustment is slow, assessing a potential future is essential to avoid the response arriving when the original signal or environment has fundamentally changed. Such behaviour is purposeful, goal-directed, and probably intentional. Finally, plants can assess cost against benefits in situations that may require multiple possible decisions. Although phenotypic adjustment is considered irreversible, except for abscission, at the molecular level, behaviour is reversible.

Introduction

During the course of this book, various kinds of plant behaviour will be met and this chapter provides for a preliminary survey. Behaviour is generally described as the response to environmental signals and plants respond in various ways to those signals, from the molecular to the morphological. I have largely confined descriptions of behaviour to visible phenotypic changes, believing that such observations will be more familiar to the reader. However, all phenotypic changes have

to be underpinned by cellular and molecular controls. Some of these molecular controls are known and some are not. Signals indicating environmental change are perceived within a few seconds. Many such signals, but not all, initiate with rapid changes in cytosolic calcium, implying some kind of membrane perception involving protein receptors. Parallel and diversifying pathways of information flow issue from this initial perception. Certainly, some of this information arrives at the genome. Altered gene expression, epigenetic modifications, and modifications of chromatin structure underpin phenotypic change. Other lines of information flow result in modifying intercellular communication so that tissue and cell responses are coordinated. There is no doubt that coordinating phenotypic changes is complex and that only a limited degree of knowledge is currently available.

Behaviour is described as the ability of an organism to respond to signals in their environment. I have constrained molecular information here for reasons of space, but many molecular reviews can be found in the *Annual Reviews of Plant Physiology and Molecular Biology*. The intention of this chapter is simply to describe the range of plant behaviours so that the reader can get an impression of its width and what can subsequently be expected.

The ability to exhibit discrimination and choice

Discrimination and choice are terms normally used to describe aspects of the behaviour of intelligent organisms. Higher plants do discriminate amongst many factors in their environment and choose to respond to those that are immediately relevant. When clonal plants are given the choice, they do choose favourable habitats.

Calamagrostis canadensis is a wetland grass species commonly called bluejoint. It grows by underground rhizomes in which shoots appear at the nodes. A choice of habitats was provided to young growing plants of *Calamagrostis* by offering adjacent habitats separated into different compartments. The compartments were distinguished between competitive and non-competitive conditions, between warmer and colder temperatures or between light and shade, and even between cool soil and light, and warm soil and shade. Unsurprisingly, *Calamagrostis* chose to grow in the non-competitive, warmer and lighted conditions, where it could forage more adequately for the resources needed for growth (MacDonald and Leiffers 1993). These plants also discriminate between these conditions in combinations, again, choosing light plus warm soil in preference to others. The ability to exert choice is just as obvious.

Given the choice between growing into patches of grass or bare uncovered soil, *Elymus repens*

(couch grass) shows strong preference for the latter, where competition is minimal (Kleijn and Groendael 1999). *Hydrocotyle bonariensis* is a clonal dune plant known to grow in soils with considerable patchiness of competition and resources. Young plants were challenged with a large number of patches, some of which contained variable levels of competition from other grasses. *Hydrocotyle* skilfully avoided the competitive patches and, instead, adopted the most favourable in which to grow. The optimal foraging strategy was constructed by phenotypically changing their branching, internode distance, and direction of rhizome growth as they worked their way through the maze of competition (Evans and Cain 1995).

Given the choice between putting roots into soil containing competitors or unexploited soil, *Pisum sativum* (garden pea) chose the latter (Gersani et al. 1998). If these plants were unable to discriminate the difference between unoccupied soil and those containing competitors they would soon be eliminated by the fitter individuals.

In species with rhizomatous growth, the individual has the advantage of being able to search out their optimal habitat from a diverse range (Turkington and Harper 1979). Clones of individuals of *Trifolium repens* (white clover) were removed from their position within a permanent pasture and planted in other parts of the field. In none of these new positions within the pasture was growth as good as that from the original position in the field. The individual seeks out and optimizes its niche by trial and error. Information presumably resides in the individual that acts as an encoded memory that can be accessed to indicate when the developing niche is optimal or not. Again, the ability to discriminate between different kinds of environmental niche must be present (Trewavas 2003). When given the choice, roots chose not to grow into acidic or aluminium rich soils, or those containing saline (Salzman 1985).

Lianas, climbing plants found in the tropics, will not attach themselves to particular trees, even when brought into juxtaposition with them. These trees are those that are the least suited to the climbing characteristic of lianas; that is, they contain a smooth trunk and are umbrella-topped species (Brown 1874, p. 580). These observations are clear examples of the ability to discriminate, assess, and make a decision.

The ability to correct erroneous decisions

The ability to correct erroneous decisions is something found throughout the animal kingdom and the following indicates similar behaviour in plants.

Dionaea muscipula, commonly known as the Venus flytrap, is a carnivorous plant that grows in the mineral-poor wetlands of the east coast USA. It supplements the poor environmental soil conditions, particularly as regards N and P, and other food, by catching insects in a two-lobed trap that closes within seconds around an unsuspecting fly. Digestive juices are subsequently poured onto the trapped fly and the nutrients absorbed. However, *Dionaea* exercises choice over food. Although the trap immediately responds to an artificial stimulus, enclosing inert materials such as small stones or chalk, after assessment, it very rapidly opens again. Furthermore, the secretion of enzymes and other facets of digestion, which normally accompanies the capture of suitable food such as insects or, in the laboratory, small pieces of meat, is not initiated. The behaviour is judicious and shows the ability to discriminate. Although movement of the prey might have been inferred to be the stimulus to enzyme release, clearly this is not the case with small pieces of meat that are trapped and then digested (Darwin 1875).

The leaves of *Drosera rotundifolia* are covered in long glandular hairs that secrete a sticky gum mucilage. This is another insectivorous plant, found in wetlands with poor mineral possibilities in the soil. *Drosera* tentacles are activated when a small insect lands on them and becomes enveloped in the sticky gum. All of the leaf tentacles eventually bend over the prey and the leaf lamina bends too to ensure the prey is covered and remains trapped. Again digestive enzymes release nutrients to the leaf. Insect movement will of course bring it into contact with more tentacles but again movement to stimulate the tentacles into action is not the only signal. Placing an inert substance like a piece of moistened chalk on the leaf initiates some minor tentacle changes which quickly re-establish themselves in to the vertical plane against that of the leaf; that is, after assessment, they rapidly return to the position for

capture. Again *Drosera* is able to distinguish suitable food from unsuitable food. Darwin (1875) reported that the tentacles are sensitive to less than a few milligrams weight.

The ability to assess the nature and characteristics of signals or stimuli

Climbing plants use a tactile or touch stimulus to detect a potential support, and then wind around it. However, choices are made about the nature of the support (Darwin 1891, pp. 98–99). If a glass rod is offered as a support, there is initial winding, but then after assessment it unwinds and grows elsewhere; the glass rod is rejected. Presumably, there is recognition of the degree of smoothness. In describing the behaviour of tendrils of *Bignonia capreolata*, Darwin first found definite evidence that, during circumnutation, the tendrils always pointed to the darkest area of its environment. In the wild, this would represent the potential of a trunk in shade. He also reported that the tendrils often contacted a stick, but then unwound, and it could do this activity up to four times. Clearly, a discrimination and assessment process is in operation to find suitable supports. On offering a blackened glass tube or a blackened zinc plate 'the branches curled around the tube and abruptly bent themselves around the edges of the zinc plate but they soon recoiled from these objects with what I can only call disgust and straightened themselves'. While disgust is clearly Darwin's anthropomorphic assessment, there is clear assessment made by the plant about the character of the support.

Many other plants use tendrils that vary in their sensitivity to a touch stimulus amongst species. In sensitive species, 1–2 mg weight is sufficient to initiate coiling. In some very sensitive species the initiation of coiling can be observed in about a minute, although 10–30 min is more common. Coiling is due to contraction of the touched (ventral) side and extension of the untouched (dorsal; Jaffe and Galston 1968). Turgor pressure in plant cells is the result of accumulations of potassium chloride to a concentration of about 0.3 M in the cell vacuole, a large organelle that can occupy up to 90% of cell volume in mature cells. The tendril contraction results from a loss of turgor pressure. In the stimulated cells, potassium channels and probably chloride channels open in the vacuole and cytoplasm. Large amounts of potassium and chloride ions find their way with great rapidity into the wall. There may be some gain of potassium chloride in the dorsal cells. Even though touch sensing is the signal that causes coiling, a surprising observation reported many times is that water impacting on the tendril with considerable force fails to initiate coiling, even hail has no effect (Jaffe and Galston 1968). Discrimination between potential signals again.

Tendrils from the same plant or species recognize each other and will not coil around each other. Again, Darwin (1891, p. 131) states, 'I have however seen several tendrils of *Bryonia dioica* interlocked but they subsequently released each other'—the result of assessment again. I have observed the same property in vines that grow in my greenhouse. While they will coil around old woody parts of the vine, they will not do so on young stems and placing two tendrils across each elicits no reaction. There also seems a reluctance of tendrils from different species to coil around each other (Darwin 1891, p. 156). May be the surface is too smooth.

If the ventral side of a tendril is stimulated, followed immediately by stimulating the dorsal, the tendril fails to coil. However, if stimulating the dorsal side is delayed by 10 min the tendril now coils, although initially at a reduced rate, a similar property to that described for tropic bending. A memory process is involved here, obviously lasting some minutes. One significant property is that touching can initiate coiling, but if the object is removed the tendril uncoils and straightens, recovering its sensitivity. These observations are commonly reported. Darwin (1891) observed that with *Passiflora* tendrils, this false stimulus could be corrected 21 times before the tendril habituated and failed to respond further. Clearly, these plants exhibit error-correcting ability and a memory that is temporarily overridden by a stimulus, but resumes its original programme when occasion arises.

A similar example is reported in Brown (1874) of *Hoya carnosa* whose shoot circumnutates a circle of about a metre in search of a support. If a support is provided and the plant curls around it, and then the stick is removed, the shoot straightens and then continues its search for another support. There are clear examples of error correction in this section.

Ability to sense, position, and avoid entanglement with the parent plant

The light that passes through a leaf is enriched in the far red end of the light spectrum because of the absorption of red light in sunshine by chlorophyll. Many plants can sense this far red light and use it to change morphogenesis. A new developmental programme called shade avoidance results in longer, thinner stems, reduced leaf production, and positioning, etc., to be described later. An interesting example of this behavioural capability was described by Asa Gray (1872). He described how revolving *Passiflora* tendrils near the top of the plant avoided contacting their own stem. They do so because the growing apex bends away, allowing the tendril a reasonably free space to rotate across it, But it is more complicated than that. He continues 'If we watch these slender passion flowers which show the revolving so well, we may see that when a tendril sweeping horizontally comes round so that its base nears the parent stem rising above it, it stops short, rises stiffly upright, moves on in this position until it passes by the stem then rapidly comes down again to the horizontal position and moves on so until it again approaches and avoids the impending obstacle'. Clearly, there is coordination between both stem and tendril to avoid entanglement.

The ability to sense and grow along gradients of signals

Parasitic plants sense their prey, their host, through detecting chemical gradients released by the host. That of Dodder will be described in Chapter 26 (Runyon et al. 2006). Parasitic plants of the genus *Striga* (witchweed) grow in more tropical regions. These predators sense their prey in the soil through the release of strigolactone from crop and other plant roots that has been released by the host to attract mycorrhizae. A gradient of strigolactone is present in the soil, and the parasite can sense this gradient and grow up along it. Once the prey is reached, *Striga* attaches itself to the host roots. Nutrients are sequestered after penetration of the host and the formation of a conjoint vascular tissue structure.

According to a very early report in both *Nature* and *American Naturalist*, when living flies are pinned at a distance of about one cm from the leaf of the insectivore *Drosera*, the leaf actually bends towards the insect until it is reached, covered by the tentacles and then digested (Treat 1873; Anon 1874). This report merits repetition.

The ability to eliminate sensing of a repetitive signal: habituation

Some of the early research of the Indian scientist, Jagadish Chandra Bose, was described in Chapter 2 (also see Chapter 25). Bose (1906, 1912) made careful analysis of the electrical properties of a number of plants and observed both the phenomena of habituation (reduction or elimination of response with repeated stimulation), and enhanced memory of signal with increased number of stimuli. His research centred strongly around the sensitive plant *Mimosa pudica* whose leaves collapse suddenly if touched or are subject to sudden changes in electrical potential, cold, or light. Recovery of leaf turgor takes about 45–60 min from a single stimulus. The drop is due to a loss of turgor in motor cells. The stimulus also induces the formation of an action potential that is conducted along the phloem, part of the vascular system. Thus, information is transferred from regions of perception to motor cells that open vacuolar channels leading to a dramatic loss of potassium chloride. Recovery of turgor by actively re-pumping potassium chloride from the wall back into the vacuole takes about 45 min and requires cellular energy.

If the *Mimosa* leaf is subjected to continuous stimulation it has been found that after the preliminary fall, it re-erects itself in spite of the stimuli which are still acting upon it. (Bose 1912, p. 80, clearly indicating adoption of habituation after assessment.)

The ability to learn and prime a signal, increasing the response to its repetition: the potential of conditioned behaviour in plants

One of the familiar forms of behaviour in animals is the conditioned responses made famous by Pavlov. In these experiments, dogs were conditioned to salivate to the ringing of a bell by association between the sound of the bell and the provision of food.

Based on this description certain observations come within the framework of conditioned responses. A number of plant species, maybe all, can be primed by brief herbivory so that subsequent herbivore attacks are met with greater rapidity and greater strength of expression of the resistance mechanisms (Frost et al. 2008). Priming can last for years and there are reports that will be examined in Chapter 17, that priming can survive reproduction. Similarly, disease attack is underpinned by priming as well—a mild attack ensures greater rapidity and strength of resistance expression (Conrath et al. 2002). However, these two resistance pathways share numerous elements in common so that herbivory attack increases resistance to disease and vice versa (Koorneef and Pieterse 2008). In this sense, then, this is an example of conditioned behaviour. Priming is an obvious case of learning—learning about the environment and the learnt response can be remembered for many years. However, the learning here involves the whole plant because resistance involves the production of circulating molecules like salicylate, as well as the synthesis of numerous volatiles.

Attempts to obtain conditioned learning of membrane potentials using light/dark regimes in the plant *Philodendron* were not successful (Abramson et al. 2002). However, Bose (1906, 1912) reported that, in *Mimosa*, a slight stimulus with small response in leaf drop and electrical potential led to a much greater response from the same strength applied later, thus indicating sensitization or priming to a mechanical stimulus.

Leaves of higher plants contain apertures called stomata that allow the transit of carbon dioxide into the inner part of the leaf and water out as transpiration. Normally, stomates only open in daylight and shut at night, a well-established circadian mechanism. Opening is initiated by exposure to light, particularly wavelengths in the blue part of the spectrum. During drought, however, water conservation takes precedence, and stomates are partially or totally closed. One of the mechanisms that helps control stomatal aperture results from the accumulation of abscisic acid, a hormone that is synthesized in roots and leaves, once water depletion is experienced. Abscisic acid acts as a coordinating signal for further growth changes that see enhancement of root growth at the expense of the shoot.

Brief treatments with abscisic acid and repeated daily, subsequently entrained the responses of specific abscisic acid-regulated genes. Exposure to abscisic acid many days later after entrainment, ensured a more rapid and much greater response in the expression of these genes. Entrainment had initiated learning and set in place a priming memory. More significantly, the role of light in opening stomates was impaired in entrained plants. Exposure to light itself now initiated the synthesis of these specific genes associated with closure, whereas it had not done so previously. This is a clear example of a classical conditioned response (Goh et al. 2003).

The ability to investigate, search, survey, examine, observe, and discover

The most interesting example of the abilities in this section is described by Darwin (1891, pp. 95–96) with tendrils of *Bignonia speciosa*: 'the tendril . . . continually searches for any little crevice or hole in which to insert itself. I had two young plants and placed them near them posts which had been bored by beetles. The tendrils, by their own movement and by that of the internodes, slowly travelled over the surface of the wood and, when the apex came to a hole or fissure, it inserted itself. In order to effect this, the extremity for a length of a half- or a quarter-of-an-inch would often bend itself at right angles to the basal part. I have watched this process between 20 and 30 times. The same tendril would frequently withdraw from one hole and insert its point into a second hole. I have also seen a tendril keep its point, in one case for 20 hours and in another for 36 hours, in a minute hole and then withdraw. While the point is temporarily inserted, the opposite tendril (they come in pairs) keeps on revolving'.

For those that study root systems, aspects of these patterns of exploratory search behaviour will have some familiarity. What is unusual here is that the same behaviour is exhibited by the shoot or, in this case, tendrils. How such assessments are made by the tendril is not in any way clear, but there is a parallel with the social insects in which new nest sites are surveyed and assessed before a decision is finally made. Roots explore the soil and take particular avoidance action against obstacles in the soil. The root manoeuvres over stones with a particularly

characterized structure described later. The root search mechanism is designed to locate rich patches of mineral and water resource, which it can exploit and sequester, denying them to others. Once a patch is located, proliferation of lateral roots, fine roots, and root hairs is the likely consequence.

The ability to assess likely futures: active as against passive agendas

'Developmental processes are aimed at the future, they are directive towards supplying future structural and functional needs' (Russell 1946, p. 93). Being able to assess likely future situations could then adversely impact on fitness if the environmental event that caused commitment was no longer present. Many such examples of this future prediction behaviour will appear in subsequent chapters.

A number of plants are able to predict the potential loss of light from nearby competitors. This they do by assessing reflected far red radiation coming from the leaves of competitors. The phenotypic response is known as the shade avoidance strategy and importantly can be instituted before there is any loss of photosynthetic light. These plants are, thus, making a prediction of future shade and the loss of light that would involve. Some plants respond by growing away and, thus, in an alternative often opposite direction—one in which they can detect no likely competition. Others substantially increase the rate of growth of the stem and increase the internode length between leaves. The aim here is to outgrow and overgrow the opposition, and sequester the light for itself.

Below ground the opposite seems to be the case in which nearby competition is met by root proliferation, to remove minerals before they are removed by the competitor. Again, an assessment of the future is being made. There is a different schedule to deal with competition for energy (light) as against soil growth resources (minerals and water). The first is absolutely vital; the second can be stretched by storage or, in the case of water, root proliferation or deeper root systems.

Future assessment is also clearly made in the priming responses to herbivory and disease mentioned in the previous section. The prediction is of future episodes of attack. The costs of priming are low and can last years. Priming itself is either epigenetic in character or involves changes in chromatin structure. Similarly, future abiotic threats of adverse temperature change, drought, adverse soil status, and others are countered by preparing for them; again, another form of priming. Sudden dramatic changes in temperature, for example, can easily kill many leaves and, potentially, the whole plant. Milder changes in temperature lead to a development of resistance so that even future damaging impacts are properly countered and no longer kill. Similar resistance mechanisms to other future stresses are all known to occur. The individual plant thus comes, in part, prepared for what it is assumed is to follow in the future. Even if there are sudden changes in any of these stress conditions, repair mechanisms are available and, in the case of severe damage, fail safe mechanisms using new growth from buds or roots are available. Being modular is itself a prediction of future environmental challenge.

That these capabilities require a different assessment of plant behaviour by plant biologists was first made clear by Aphalo and Ballare (1995). In an eloquent article, these authors called for the concept of plant behaviour to be regarded as 'active', rather than 'passive'. They made the case that some plant biologists regarded plants as merely undergoing a standard development programme, occasionally interrupted by poor circumstance. Thus, plants are viewed as passive creatures at the mercy of the elements and whose behaviour is analogous to a piece of cork floating on the sea. Plants actively deal with their environmental situation, make credible assessment of the future, and prepare for them. Active properties require intelligent assessments if they are not to fail, something again to be found in subsequent chapters. Plants are self-organizing entities and behave analogously to social insect colonies, i.e. as swarm intelligence. They take in information, assess what it is, and then generate responses that benefit the whole organism.

I suspect that the common 'passive' attitudes applied to plant behaviour are engendered by common laboratory experience. Plants are made to perform to order by the experimenter, just as animals are made to perform in a circus ring. In wild conditions, the active pursuit of fitness provides a completely different perspective.

The ability to be purposeful and intentional in behaviour

Active behaviour is most easily defined as purposeful when it is goal-orientated (Rosenblueth et al. 1943; Russell 1946). For example, the return of seedling shoots or roots to the vertical in response to a gravitational signal when they are perturbed from the vertical position. An information loop is constructed from the signal to the responding cells to indicate the margin of error from the goal and to adjust behaviour accordingly. The general term is negative feedback (Trewavas 2007).

Although I have used gravi-tropism as an example, the actual goal is less clear because many roots grow at an angle to the gravity vector, as do most shoots and obviously branches. However, all seem to be gravi-sensitive. Other examples of more complex and less understood, purposeful (goal-directed) behaviour are the stem thickening that accompanies wind sway. The goal here is to adjust the strength of the stem or trunk to prevent damaging flailing of the branches and leaves in future gusty conditions. There is usually a degree of movement allowed in most trees, although limited.

Other goal-directed behaviour is the (indeterminate?) elongation of the leaf petiole in water plants like *Nymphaea*, which only stops when the leaf breaks surface. Some evidence indicates that the plant hormone ethylene accumulates in water grown petioles and declines when the surface is broken and in part this may be responsible. Russell (1946) includes several other good plant examples.

Obvious purposeful behaviour also arises from an integration of different signals. Charles Darwin (1880) showed experimentally how seedling roots sensed the signals of touch, light, moisture, and gravity resulting in sensory integration. Furthermore, he showed that growing roots could distinguish between these signals and decide which was the most crucial to respond to. Massa and Gilroy (2003) have amplified Darwin's observations on how roots avoid soil obstructions, such as stones, and also indicated how the root response is integrated between touch and gravity.

Behavioural intention

'By behaviour, I refer to all the actions directed toward the outside world in order to change conditions therein or to change their own situation in relation to these surroundings.' This definition of behaviour by Piaget (1979, p. 1), certainly describes the two-way signal and response exchange between the individual plant and its environment particularly in formation of the niche (see Chapter 8). However, Piaget's definition implies (more controversially) intention in behaviour.

My dictionary gives a definition of intention, as purpose or goal. In that case, do plants intend to resist herbivores, do they intend to respond to gravity, do they intend to resist the common stresses they experience? The purpose or goal of each of these behaviours is, of course, survival and the attempted optimization of fitness. On that basis, these behaviours must be intentional. Such statements merely indicate that plants are aware of their circumstances, and act to deal with those that diminish their ability to survive and/or reproduce, and thus diminish fitness.

Hull (1988) states baldly that he regards animal prey as intending to avoid predation. Scott-Turner (2007) discusses intentional behaviour at length in the context of the integrated behaviour of social insect colonies. Since, in Chapter 10, analogies between social insect colonies and plants will be made, intentional plant behaviour might only emerge at the whole plant level, and not with individual tissues or cells. Intentional behaviour becomes then, an emergent property, it results simply from all the interactions, all the signalling processes, between plant cells and tissues.

The notion of intentional behaviour could also conflict with the neo-Darwinist view of natural selection, which suggests organisms as being passive in the face of random selection. The alternative to simple selection from a systems framework and permitting intention, is powerfully argued by Gould (2002, p. 614 onwards).

The reason that controversy can surround the application of the word 'intention' to the behaviour of organisms surely arises from the fact that human intention commonly involves conscious action, and consciousness is judged on the basis that only very

similar organisms to ourselves can be conscious. However, on what basis, other than supposition, is it assumed that other organisms are not conscious and that consciousness is not widely distributed amongst living organisms? Chapter 25 amplifies discussion on this issue.

Plant behaviour involves assessment of costs and benefits

No wild plant could survive without a memory of its current perceived signals or without a cumulative memory that collates its past information experience, integrates it with present conditions so that the probabilities of potential futures could be assessed. The problems that wild plants face in their attempt to optimize fitness are numerous. The uneven distribution of light, minerals, soil structure and water, competition by other plants, variation in rainfall and wind, and variable degrees of damage by disease pests and herbivores, all have to be assessed. Flowers need to be positioned where pollination is optimal. The costs and benefits of any behavioural change in growth and development, and the resources to back it up, need assessment and appropriate optimizing decisions taken to redistribute internal resources amongst competing tissues. Wild plants are unlikely to have acquired a gross excess of all resources. What is given to one tissue will not be available to another. Trade-offs have to be estimated with care. Selection will not allow such redistribution decisions to be made at random and will be punitive on those that assess it incorrectly. Game theory deals with some of these situations and Chapter 17 describes them.

Trade-offs have to be assessed between root and shoot, between different shoots, roots, branches, or leaves, between vegetative and reproductive growth, and between vegetative growth and herbivore/disease resistance (Lerdau and Gershenzon 1997; Bazzaz 2000; Jong and Klinkhamer 2005). There will also be trade-offs in resources devoted to different abiotic stress conditions that will need careful assessment, because an excess resistance response to one will almost certainly diminish the capability to respond to another (Dinenny et al. 2008). An integration of numerous traits will generate an emergent intelligence that can provide for best fitness and problem solving in a variety of circumstances. Trade-offs require decisions; currently it is not known how they are made. Presumably, there must be some kind of threshold mechanism involved and there are indications amplified in Chapter 16.

Behaviour can be reversible

Although phenotypic change can be considered irreversible, this is not the case for various kinds of important chemicals (natural insecticides) synthesized by plants in response to herbivore attack. These exhibit a dynamic plasticity and many are easily reversible (Metlen et al. 2009). These observations indicate that Arber's statement that plant behaviour tends to be irreversible and animal behaviour is reversible is thus incorrect at the molecular level.

References

Abramson, C.I., Garrido, D.J., Lawson, A.L., Browne, B.L., and Thomas, D.G. (2002). Bioelectrical potentials of *Philodendron cordatum*: a new method for investigation of behaviour in plants. *Psychological Reports*, **91**, 173–185.

Anon. (1874). Notes. *Nature*, **9**, 332.

Aphalo, P.J., and Ballare, C.L. (1995). On the importance of information acquiring systems in plant–plant interactions. *Functional Ecology*, **9**, 5–14.

Bazzaz, F.A. (2000). *Plants in a changing environment*. Cambridge University Press, Cambridge.

Bose, J.C. (1906). *Plant response as a means of physiological investigation*. Longmans, Green and Co., London.

Bose, J.C. (1912). *Researches on the irritability of plants*. Longmans, Green and Co., London.

Brown, R. (1874). *A manual of botany*. Blackwood and Sons, Edinburgh.

Conrath, U., Pieterse, C.M.J., and Mauch-Mani, B. (2002). Priming in plant pathogen interactions. *Trends in Plant Science*, **7**, 210–216.

Darwin, C. (1875). *Insectivorous plants*. John Murray, London.

Darwin, C. (1880). *The power of movement in plants*. John Murray, London.

Darwin, C. (1891). *The movements and habits of climbing plants*. John Murray, London.

Dinenny, J.R., Long, T.A., Wang, J.Y., Jung, J.W., Mace, D., Pointer, S., and 4 others. (2008). Cell identity mediates the response of *Arabidopsis* roots to abiotic stress. *Science*, **320**, 942–945.

Evans, J.P., and Cain, M.L. (1995). A spatially explicit test of foraging behaviour in a clonal plant. *Ecology*, **76**, 1147–1155.

Frost, C.J., Mescher, M.C., Carlson, J.E., and Moraes, C.M., de (2008). Plant defence priming against herbivores: getting ready for a different battle. *Plant Physiology*, **146**, 818–824.

Gersani, M., Abramsky, Z., and Falik, O. (1998). Density-dependent habitat selection in plants. *Evolutionary Ecology*, 12, 223–234.

Goh, C.H., Nam, H.G., and Park, Y.S. (2003). Stress memory in plants: a negative regulation of stomatal response and transient induction of *rd22* gene to light in abscisic acid-entrained *Arabidopsis* plants. *Plant Journal*, **36**, 240–255.

Gould, S.J. (2002). *The structure of evolutionary theory*. Harvard University Press, Cambridge, MA.

Gray, A. (1872). *How plants behave*. American Book Company, New York.

Hull, D.L. (1988). Interactors versus vehicles. In Plotkin, H.C., ed. *The role of behaviour in evolution*, pp. 19–51. MIT Press, Cambridge, MA.

Jaffe, M.J., and Galston, A.W. (1968). The physiology of tendrils. *Annual Review of Plant Physiology*, **19**, 417–434.

Jong, T.J., de, and Klinkhamer, P.G.L. (2005). *Evolutionary ecology of plant reproductive strategies*. Cambridge University Press, Cambridge.

Kleijn, D., and Groenendael, J.M., van (1999). The exploitation of heterogeneity by a clonal plant with contrasting productivity levels. *Journal of Ecology*, **87**, 873–884.

Koorneef, A., and Pieterse, C.M.J. (2008). Cross talk in defense signalling. *Plant Physiology*, **148**, 839–844.

Lerdau, M., and Gershenzon, J. (1997). Allocation theory and chemical defence. In Bazzaz, F.A., and Grace, J., eds, *Plant resource allocation*, pp. 265–278. Academic Press, London.

MacDonald, S.E., and Leiffers, V.J. (1993). Rhizome plasticity and clonal foraging of *Calamagrostis canadensis* in response to habitat heterogeneity. *Journal of Ecology*, **81**, 769–776.

Massa, G.D., and Gilroy, S. (2003). Touch modulates gravity sensing to regulate the growth of primary roots of *Arabidopsis thaliana*. *Plant Journal*, **33**, 435–445.

Metlen, K.L., Aschehoug, E.T., and Callaway, R.M. (2009). Plant behavioural ecology: dynamic plasticity in secondary metabolites. *Plant Cell and Environment*, **32**, 641–653.

Piaget J. (1979). *Behaviour and evolution*. Routledge and Kegan Paul, London.

Rosenblueth, A., Weiner, N., and Bigelow, J. (1943). Behaviour, purpose and teleology. *Philosophy of Science*, **10**, 18–24.

Runyon, J.B., Mescher, M.C., and Moraes, C.M., de (2006). Volatile chemical cues guide host location and host selection by parasitic plants. *Science*, **313**, 1964–1967.

Russell, E.S. (1946). *The directiveness of organic activities.* Cambridge University Press, Cambridge.

Sachs, J., von (1887). *Lectures on the physiology of plants.* Clarendon Press, Oxford.

Salzman, A. (1985). Habitat selection in a clonal plant. *Science*, **228**, 603–604.

Scott-Turner, J. (2007). *The tinkerer's accomplice.* Harvard University Press, Cambridge MA.

Treat, M. (1873). Observations on the sundew. *American Naturalist*, **7**, 705–708.

Trewavas, A. (2003). Aspects of plant intelligence. *Annals of Botany*, **92**, 1–20.

Trewavas, A. (2007). A brief history of systems biology. *Plant Cell*, **18**, 2420–2430.

Turkington, R., and Harper, J.L. (1979). The growth, distribution and neighbour relationships of *Trifolium repens* in a permanent pasture. IV. Fine scale differentiation. *Journal of Ecology*, **67**, 245–254.

CHAPTER 10

The self-organizing plant: lessons from swarm intelligence

What is it that governs here? What is it that issues orders?
Foresees the future, elaborates plans and preserves equilibrium.

(Maeterlinck 1927)

⊃ Summary

Self-organization is a common terminology for describing biological phenomena. The developing brain and social insect colonies are used as examples. Small world networks are then described since these often underpin self-organization. Patterns of behaviour and activity are generated without an overall plan or planner in self-organizing systems. It is, instead, the interactions that generate order from the bottom upwards. Self-organizing capabilities maintain the social insect colony; they enable its growth and adaptation towards external influences. Trees are perfect examples of self-organization. There is no dictating overall plan or planner to control their growth and morphology. Robust behaviour may derive from modular development, obvious in trees and reflected in large numbers of colony workers in social insects. Flexibility results from being able to marshall groups of modules towards necessary objectives. Negative-feedback and feedforward controls operate to maintain both colonies and trees. Self-organizing systems are networks in which fairly simple rules between the components that make up the system can give rise to quite complex behaviour. A comparative assessment draws attention to analogous forms of behaviour in social insect colonies and large perennials like trees. Among these is quorum sensing that underpins the making of decisions. Social insect behaviour is described as swarm intelligence. Since trees act like colonies, although joined together, plant 'intelligence' is a suitable term to describe their behaviour, too.

Introduction

Maeterlinck (1927) made the comments in the title of this chapter on the behaviour of a social insect, the white ant. The organization and order of these colonies of ants, termites, and bees, now much studied, have fascinated scientists, engineers, and artists alike. How is it that without an overall plan, the colony survives, grows, adapts to environmental changes, and duplicates (reproduces) itself. We, ourselves, normally require detailed planning for such behaviour. Yet the same question should be asked about plants and, more particularly, large perennial plants. There is no one guiding tissue or overall plan. The quotation from Maeterlinck (1927) above is equally applicable to a deciduous tree.

From observation of the behaviour of colony individuals, has come the realization that simple rules of interaction between the individuals can generate some quite complex behaviour. Coupled with feedback and feedforward mechanisms, the colony adaptively responds to changes and needs to provide stability, and the requirements of selection and survival. The term 'swarm intelligence' to describe

Plant Behaviour and Intelligence. First Edition. Anthony Trewavas.
© Anthony Trewavas 2014. Published 2014 by Oxford University Press.

this collective behaviour was first used by Beni and Wang (1993) in respect of robotics. There is little doubt that, in robotics, studies of social insect colonies have paid off (Bonabeau and Theraulaz 2000).

The characteristics of self-organizing systems

Self-organization is a term increasingly used to describe pattern forming and organizational aspects of biological behaviour and development, but self-organization is rarely applied to anything in plant behaviour or development, even though plants clearly lack both a centralized brain and nervous tissue, and surely have to use forms of self-organization. Self-organization certainly describes the growth of the brain and social insect colonies, and some important properties emerge that can then be applied to the behaviour of the phenotypically plastic plant.

Self-organization in the developing brain

The growth and development of the mammalian brain is a model of self-organization. At the earliest stages of development, neural cells communicate with each other. As more cells are added, a complex network develops, with neural communications forming the links in the network. In this early stage, Edelman (1993) proposed that a form of neural Darwinism is used to lay down particular neural pathways. He pointed out that, although connections in the brain were very variable between individuals, behaviour would be similar, suggesting that pre-specified point-to-point wiring did not occur. Neural territories and maps are often unique to each individual. The selection of any particular group of neurones for pathway formation is effectively almost random, but experience reinforces the pathways of those that initially have a weak conductance at the expense of others. The preliminary networks were then reinforced by increased synaptic adhesion. Channels of information flow were thus deepened improving the quality of response.

Organization and structure thus emerge as a result of these purely local signals between the constituent cells. The connections form multiple feedback loops—some are positive and others negative. Organizational changes emerge as critical sizes (volumes) are reached initiating changes in structure (Trewavas 2007). Longer elements of communication are then constructed. This, in simple form, outlines what is an extremely complex process. Quite crucially, the growing brain emerges from a bottom-up approach; there is a clear absence of an overall leadership cell or tissue. Crucially, no individual cell or group of cells has any overview of the emerging structure (Scott-Kelso 1995; Ranganathan and Kira 2004; Sporns et al. 2004; Freeman 2005; Bassett et al. 2006; Chilton 2006).

Self-organization in social insects

Self-organization is also applied to describe much of the behaviour of social insects. Simple rules of interactions (meaningful communication) between the constituent organisms of the colony construct a network. Complex patterns can be generated without any knowledge of the overall pattern that the individual insects are constructing (Camazine et al. 2001). Pathways to food are initially laid down by exploration of individuals. Reinforcement of the pathway of ant movement is increased by the numbers using that pathway and is determined, in turn, by the density of food locations. Construction of termite nests involves very simple rules governing the behaviour of the individuals. The demarcation of bee behaviour using the hive dance floor and synchrony of firefly flashing all again follow fairly simple interactions. Bell (1984) drew an interesting parallel between ant foraging trails and a branched plant morphology. The analogy follows from reinforcement of trails that mimic food distribution.

Small world and scale-free networks

An important characteristic of all self-organized systems is that they are all networks. The components of the network whether they be cells, tissues, organs, or whole individual organisms connect together through meaningful and diverse communication. Similar self-organized systems can be found in social and economic networks (Trewavas 2006). The communicated information can be simple or complex, and communication usually involves multiple feedback loops. Many of these networks have a similar 'small world' and scale-free structure.

The designation of a particular kind of network structure was originally described and designated 'small world' based on the similarity between social networks, neural networks of *C. elegans*, and electricity generation control (Watts and Strogatz 1998). These network structures like those of the plastic plant, are mid-way between completely regular, unchanging structures, and those constructed at random.

In the brain, strongly integrated neural assemblies with multiple internal connections are connected to each other by neural channels with far fewer connection (dendrite) numbers. In these small world structures, the connections obey a simple power law distribution; there are many elements with a few connections (so-called connectors) and only a few elements with a lot (hubs). [A simple introduction to power laws and some of their potential value to plant biology can be found in Hunter (2003). Power laws do explain interesting phenomena such as metabolic rate variations with size and the extent of the circulation system in both animals and plants. There are also inferences to be made about ecosystems.] For example, in neural networks, the hubs are smaller numbers of neurones with many numerous dendritic connections to others forming a cluster, while the connectors are much larger numbers of neurones with far fewer dendritic connections (Barabasi and Oltvai 2004). Scale free describes a similar pattern of hub/connector organisation at different hierarchical levels in the network.

There are also indications of the 'small world' network structure in social insect colonies. In the beehive, the queen provides a relatively permanent hub. The connectors are clearly the working bees. The well-known waggle dance of a worker bee issuing information of appropriate food sources is a temporary hub. Information that indicates a need for either pollen or honey (nectar) collection operates via feedback processes within the hive and is indicated on the dance floor.

The 'small world' network structure optimizes information transfer, signal propagation speed, synchronizability, computational power, and thus increases the rate of learning, while also supporting segregated and distributed information processing, but they all rely on fairly simple rules.

Such 'small world' network structures seem to be common in biology. Protein–protein interaction networks are certainly 'small world', some proteins connect with a hundred others, while others may interact with only a few. Signal transduction and hormone networks are similar again, some hormones have numerous multiple interactions with many tissues (in plants, for example, auxin), while others are far more specialized and have more limited interactions, e.g. brassinosteroids. Metabolic flux networks also follow this typical pattern, with intense flux limited to certain discrete pathways.

Ecosystems are clearly self-organizing entities and form 'small world' networks, too. Some species are far more prominent than others (usually the generalists) and their removal has a much greater effect than others more specific (specialist) in either location or food source. Ecosystems form undoubted networks of interaction and experience multiple feedback loops, too (Scanlon et al. 2007). Certain ecosystems, although few in number, can be dominated by one or two species (e.g. wild wheat, mangrove, or *Salicornia* are largely free of other species), while in others, hundreds of species are found, with none dominant. The overall organization emerges, simply as a result of interactions between the individual species, from the bottom up, not top down. There is no overall guiding influence that dictates the final structure (Montoya et al. 2006; Rezende et al. 2007; Allesina et al. 2008).

Self-organization in plants

Self-organization refers to pattern-forming activities and the information for that pattern comes from within the system itself, without overall pattern specification. Any self-organized system is subject to environmental influences and will adapt to them. However, the pattern originates from simple rules between the components, the rules and interactions are local, and they are influenced by other parts of the pattern without there being any specifier of pattern. I have previously referred to this difference as akin to a democratic kind of organization (bottom up), compared with a dictatorship or military construction (top down; Trewavas 1986). The branching patterns or architecture of trees represent excellent examples of pattern formation, but other examples can be found in the distribution of vascular bundles in stems, or buds on stems or the distribution of root hairs on a root (Halle et al. 1978).

In an article published in 2008, I drew attention to some analogies between tree organization and that of social insect colonies (Trewavas 2008). In this chapter, I intend to expand that comparison. If the complex behaviour of colonies can emerge from quite simple interactions or rules then, by analogy, simple rules govern the behaviour of woody perennials. At the level of understanding required, information about these simple rules is not yet readily available. If the behaviour is analogous, then just as swarm intelligence applies to social insects, plant intelligence should be a term of equal applicability.

It is surely important to understand how all these leaves, branches, and roots, seemingly all with some degree of independence in behaviour (Kroon et al. 2005), are actually integrated to form the organism. All this is accomplished without any overall controlling tissue, organ, or nervous system? In this chapter, then, I wish to establish first that trees, in particular, have an organizational similarity to social insect colonies. Subsequently, it can be asked, 'What useful information can be got from viewing the tree in that way?', information that may help understanding.

I will use a deciduous tree, species unnamed as the comparator with information on bee, wasp, ant, and termite colonies as social insects (Seeley 1995; Turner 2000; Camazine et al. 2001). However, I sometimes have to ask for allowances on what information is available on trees and introduce material from smaller plants. Tree physiology, particularly of the larger kind is difficult to investigate and there is limited knowledge. Nevertheless, what is known is striking enough.

A further control that might exist in tree growth is information that comes from the structure itself. This process is called stigmergy and was first described in termite nests. It refers to the trace of a previous action or behaviour, which stimulates subsequent actions and thus that build on each other. Cambium might be a good example here; it is known that the long narrow TS shape of cambial cells is maintained by the pressure exerted by surrounding cells. However, cambial activity contributes to that pressure.

Reinforcement of pheromone trails left by ants are another example, continued depositing of mud by termites in building the mud nest and stimulated by previous termite pheromones are another. In situations like these, information derived from the size of the branch itself, may be determined by whether a bud remains dormant or grows.

Bifurcation phenomena also occur with self-organizing systems

One of the phenomena referred to earlier in this book was that of Prigogine's dissipative structures of systems behaviour far from chemical equilibrium (Chapter 3). With slight changes in the characteristics of the system, a node is reached in which the system can jump into one or other new states. Since one of the alternatives is chaos, sensibly there is only one potential surviving future when this event happens. Sudden changes like this are, of course, characteristic of the branching structure of trees and whether buds remain dormant or become active. A relatively simple description of bifurcation processes can be found in Dewdney (1991).

Analogous organizational and behavioural features between deciduous trees and social insect colonies

In this comparison I have assumed only a limited working knowledge of social insect colonies. Groups of workers are operating together, responding behaviourally to influences that arise within the colony and from outside. More details emerge within the comparison itself.

Structural analogies

1. *Both tree and colony are self-organizing systems.* There is no overall planning structure or determinant that specifies development.
2. *The emergent properties of a tree are numerous,* including the structure of the crown, the branching angles, and bud distribution and behaviour, as well as tissue interactions. A tree behaves as an integrated unit in growth, particularly with

regard to energy collection through leaves and storing resources. It is the connections throughout that provide for integration. Trees flower and then nurse the growing seeds to maturity. The emergent properties of the colony are its capability to gather and store different kinds of food, minimize energy use, nurse and feed the young, and ensure maintenance of the colony. The colony also behaves as an integrated unit in gathering food (Seeley 1995).

3. *Simple rules govern the branching patterns of trees,* the branch angles, the internode lengths and controls on which buds develop into branches and remain dormant (Jones and Harper 1987). These rules result from interactions between the constituent parts many of which are not understood, but must be mainly chemical in character. These rules of interaction change when the environment of the tree changes; the strength of the connections changes between the tissues. Simple rules determine the behaviour of individuals in a colony and the interactions are determined by chemical pheromones (Seeley 1995). The strength of connections between the hive organisms changes when some workers are required to collect pollen, rather than nectar.

4. *The tree is a modular entity with the modules performing different functions.* The active shoot structure consists of repetitions of very large numbers of active meristems, buds, leaves, branches, vascular tissues, and flowers with embryonic seeds as the reproductive entity. Below ground there are repetitions of adventitious roots and root hairs. The colony, too, is a modular structure consisting of thousands of identical workers, but with demarcated and different functions between them. A queen provides for more workers, and eventually drones and females. Modular construction provides for robust behaviour. Functions within the colony are distributed throughout the workers, just as different modules in a tree perform different functions. Flexibility arises because colony workers can be directed to different functions and perform different functions throughout their life. Flexibility in trees arises from the ability to increase numbers of roots or shoot branches according to requirements, thereby changing the balance of function. Loss of modules leads to

their replacement without destroying the functioning of either colony or tree.

5. *The swarm network can be constructed from interactions between the individual workers.* Alternatively, a network can be constructed from the different functions performed by the colony (Fewell 2003). It is feasible to construct similar functional networks for plant cells. As in a bee colony that acquires, stores, and uses resources, the acquisition, storage, and utilization of resources from both root and shoot could form one network. Another would arise from the network of hormone interactions, as well as sugars and metabolically-modified transported minerals such as amino acids.

6. *Hubs and connectors,* as in small world or scale-free networks described in Chapter 3, also exist in both colony and tree. In the colony, the foraging bee workers have fewer interactions with other hive workers than receiver bees that unload and distribute the nectar to empty cells and who must interact with many returning workers. The queen, likewise, providing pheromones to control hive and behaviour must interact with many workers, as do those that nurse the developing pupae. In the tree, the cambium and the main vascular elements are in connection with thousands of leaves, whereas a single leaf only connects with its specific vascular tissue.

Behavioural analogies

1. *Behavioural functions are differentiated.* The leaves, roots, and root hairs are concerned with foraging for carbohydrates, minerals, and water. Large numbers of colony workers forage for nectar, pollen, water, or plant or animal material. Others perform different functions for the nest, receiving nectar or pollen, or acting as guards or cleaners.

2. *Meristems provide for the production of new leaves and buds,* and the pericycle for new branch roots. The colony queen produces new workers.

3. *Both groups of organisms use fungi to help collect 'food'.* Mycorrhizal networks improve the acquisition of minerals and water, a constituent of 'food'. Some ant colonies use fungi to ferment plant material to make food.

4. *Trees store starch in twigs and branches* ready for use during the winter and to provision the activities of new meristems in spring. Colonies store nectar as honeydew, honey, or in specialized workers, as in honeypot ants, to enable survival during the winter and provision the nest in spring.

5. *Colony workers are used to direct the unloading of nectar and pollen.* Pollen forms the main source of N for growing worker larvae. Indication that the colony nest is currently replete with nectar (honey) because all appropriate cells are full is thought to result from measuring the delay in returning worker bees finding a receiver bee. If there are many unused storage cells then receiver bees have little difficulty in finding unoccupied cells and worker bees are unloaded quickly; if receivers have difficulty finding unused storage, then it will take time to find and fewer will be available to receive worker bees returning with honey. Simple feedback operates.

   Resources to be used for the growing meristems such as minerals and water can receive temporary storage in a vacuole and apoplast compartment (Sattelmacher and Horst 2007). A similar signalling mechanism might operate with respect to the shoot chloroplast for starch and the root vacuole compartment for minerals. The time taken to get sugars, minerals, and water into storage may act as feedback information to slow further acquisition. Photosynthesis is known to reduce activity to minimize starch accumulation if there is excess. Light energy is then simply dissipated as heat.

6. *Leaves and numerous buds are abscised every year or earlier.* Colony workers have a limited lifespan, and are replaced and removed from the colony. Numbers in both colony and tree are maintained by replication and some kind of feedback process.

7. *Leaves have mechanisms that control their internal temperature* (see Chapter 12) just as hives use worker bees to cool by fanning and distribution of water for evaporation. Termite nests have chimneys to help regulate temperature.

8. *When trees are short of water, root growth and branching is increased* at the expense of the shoot to increase its collection. When hives are short of water, more workers are directed to collect water at the expense of nectar and pollen collection. Both operate kinds of sensory systems using negative feedback to control water content.

9. *When trees are short of light they increase shoot growth at the expense of the root.* When colonies are short of nectar, hive workers are directed to increase collection of the material in shortest supply. In ant colonies, workers are transferred to other tasks when this situation of resource depletion is reached. Feedback must operate in all these situations to try and maintain a kind of homeostasis. Because this situation is one of information flow altering behaviour, it has been subject to theoretical analysis as a parallel-distributed model based on a simple Hopfield neural net (Gordon et al. 1992). It should be possible to use the same model for a tree.

10. *When trees are short of nitrate or NH_4, root exploration strategies are increased.* When hives are short of pollen, their source of N, more workers are directed to collect pollen.

11. *Gradients of light are used to inform the direction of branch growth and angle* so that subsequent leaves assume the best positions in the crown to collect light. Ants provide pheromone trails to provide directions for workers towards food. Bees use the waggle dance to provide directions to new sources. It is usually a few workers that lead the way and, thus, direct others on the right route to richer sources of nutrient.

12. *Rich sources of light or nitrate lead to increased branch growth,* and proliferation of leaves and branch roots to collect. Rich sources of flowers lead to more colony workers being recruited to collect the rich source of food and increased numbers of workers are involved.

13. *Hives use the dance floor to convey by symbolic language, new sources of food.* As a consequence, the flow of workers towards this source is increased and decreased towards lesser sources. The cambium acts to assess the productivity of individual branches, and either increases or reduces the vascular tissue elements to increase or decrease the flow of root resources (see Chapter 11). Likewise, the cambium or pericycle assesses the activity of root systems and

determines which shall receive more carbohydrate. The cambium acts like the dance floor for resource food direction.

14. *Foraging roots will follow a gradient of N and grow up it*, and shoots will follow a gradient of light. Rich sources, when contacted, lead to proliferation and, thus, increase flow of sugars, minerals, and water back into the body of the tree. Foraging ants will follow a pheromone trail to collect food, and reinforcement of this trail is determined by the numbers of ants so directed. The more ants that use the trail, the greater the return of food to the nest. Experienced foraging ants, lead naïve nest mates via contact in the right direction to food or a new nest site. Young ant workers are thus led or 'taught' by more mature workers how to get to rich sources of food (Morell 2009).

15. *Spatial recognition of the environment is pronounced in plants*, since they have the means to sense it in considerable detail. Above ground, leaves are sensitive to the direction of light and turn accordingly to the highest average intensity. The overall structure of the tree crown is equally sensitive to the direction of light and changes its overall morphology if overgrown (Chapter 18). Since this information must be sensed by the whole cambium, based on carbohydrate flow from leaves and branches, that tissue must possess some kind of map of the outside environment. The nature of the environment is learnt from the perceived signals and the information subsequently modifies growth and development.

   In honeybee foraging a great deal of information is acquired by the individual worker and conveyed to the nest. Information is gained and stored about the numbers of flowers within a certain area, the quality and ease of gaining the food available (the flower species involved, the distance, the numbers, the ease of collection). Decisions are made on which is the richest source out of a number of different local ones. Since it is highly improbable that all the types of flower structure that an individual can meet will, in some sense, be pre-programmed in the bee neural network, individual bees will learn to recognize what is and what is not a flower,

and learn to recognize particular kinds of flower structure (Gould and Marler 1987). The foraging workers learn as does the nest about the local environment.

16. *The ability to navigate a maze is shared between social insects and plants*. Below ground, root sensing mechanisms operate for nitrate, phosphate, oxygen, and water and other chemicals. Root direction and proliferation is changed accordingly. Likewise alien root systems are sensed and avoided or confronted. Mechanisms allow roots to take advantage of the most favourable mineral patches and, thus, can assess contextual information. Roots are also remarkably sensitive to obstacles in the soil and avoiding mechanisms are known. Roots will navigate to take avoiding action against a piece of string in the soil, for example (Falik et al. 2005). Other mechanisms use tactile stimuli (negative thigmotropism) in taking avoidance action. Roots or rhizomes are able to adjust the height from the soil surface at which they grow. They can maintain this soil surface position for considerable distance and times of growth. In short, root systems can optimally navigate a soil maze (Trewavas 2003). Through the mycorrhizal network, roots may gain information over a wider area and tree roots can extend themselves many tens of metres too.

   Bees must roam over larger areas of ground, leave a nest, and return. They process information and have good spatial memories recognizing natural scenes, necessary if they are to find their way back (Menzel et al. 1996; Dacke and Srinavasaan 2008; Dyer et al. 2008). Bees can learn to fly through mazes via spatial marks, transfer that memory of marks to new mazes, and use landmarks and landscape structure to estimate distance and hive position (Chittka et al. 1995; Zhang et al. 1996). In a sense, much of this can be predicted from observation that bees collect nectar and return from miles away to the same hive.

17. *Predicting future events*. Higher plants certainly make predictions about future events in their reaction to competitors for light and other stressful circumstances (Chapters 13 and 17). One interesting example is to be found in learning about water availability. When young trees

grown in barrels were subject to the provision of water once a year but at a predetermined but repeated time, they learnt to move their growth patterns progressively from the whole year to just the period when water was available (Hellmeier et al. 1997). The change in behaviour is slow, but plants work on a different time scale.

Individual bees were trained to extend their proboscis into a drop of sugar solution when it was offered. By providing the drop at defined intervals, the bees rapidly learn to predict when the next drop will appear and extend their proboscis in anticipation. Thus, they have a good sense of time, can predict the future, and have a memory of the past (Boisvert and Sherry 2006; Skorupski and Chittka 2006).

Ant colonies also learn about their nest site and acquire long-term memories of past experience, because frequent movement through nest sites progressively reduces the total emigration times. This memory can be lost if the interval between moves is greatly increased (Langridge et al. 2004, 2008).

18. *Seeley and Levien* (1987) *summarized the foraging capabilities and information gathering in hives* as follows. 'Indeed it is not too much to say that a bee colony is capable of cognition in much the same sense that a human being is. The colony gathers and continually updates diverse information about its surroundings, combines this with information about its internal state and makes decisions that reconcile its well-being with the environment'.

In a precisely similar fashion, a higher plant is equally capable. The tree gathers and continually updates diverse information about its surroundings, combines this with information about its internal state, and makes decisions that reconcile its well-being with the environment. The analogy with cognitive processes is equally valid.

19. *Both trees and colonies use quorum voting in certain circumstances.* There are many occasions in plant life when decisions have to be made, and trade-offs or cost-benefit analyses are common; between growth and reproduction, between assessments of rainfall and drought, between bud

dormancy and bud growth. Higher plants have to decide how to partition their resource use, either for the growth of shoot and root or towards storage of resources.

Bloom et al. (1985) provide an excellent analysis using an economic analogy that assesses costs and profit in terms of optimizing the use of carbohydrate currency for growth, storage, and fitness. Growth and resource storage contribute in different ways to:

(i) The eventual production of flowers.
(ii) To the provision of seed numbers.
(iii) Decisions between height and juvenility.

Decisions, therefore, are essential and some sort of majority voting, a quorum, would seem essential to ensure the decision goes one way or the other to divert resources. The decision is made in the best interest of the organism and its subsequent fitness.

However, other events have the characteristics of quorum voting, too. Cambium in trees is activated in springtime, as buds start to open and a stimulus of cambial activity moves down the trunk at about 25 cm/day (Thimann 1972). Although associated with auxin synthesis and obvious polar movement, application of auxin itself only caused activation over a few centimetres. The natural process acts contagiously until the whole of the trunk cambium is active and generating new vascular tissues.

The most well-known decisions that require some kind of quorum voting, and occur in trees that produce either separate male or female flowers. In some cases, the same individual is capable of producing either. The female flower uses four times more energy than the male. Female flowers tend to be produced in good soil, good growth, high ground positions, and generally beneficial environment. Male flowers become preponderant when some combination of the following are experienced: drought, weak light intensity, aberrant temperature regimes, loss of storage tissue, frequency of disease, and pests. Pollen in this case ensures the genotype is moved elsewhere.

Quorum voting occurs in colonies, too. The information obtained by returning bees about sources of food is conveyed in honeybee colonies by several kinds of waggle dance, a direct form of symbolic language. The dance conveys information by touching other bees with defined vibrations and movements, but is also acoustic defined by the characteristics of the buzz. The 'dance' conveys an integration of outside and inside information.

When the need arises for a new nest, a few explorer bees or scouts search for other nest sites. When such bees return with information, they convey this information on relative position to others by dancing. These, in turn, may also investigate, come back and convey to others by dancing until a quorum is reached on the best site before the collective decision is made to go (List et al. 2009). This is a typical example of feedforward control.

New nest sites for ants are investigated first by a few scouts who assess the level of suitability and convey that information quantitatively to others. In turn, these recruited workers will examine the new site and return, recruiting others until a quorum of approval results in a decision to move, led of course by scouts. If several sites are available then decisions must be made over which is the best. What constitutes the threshold or quorum for approval and changes the decision from 'no move' to 'move' is not understood. Poor sites, if all that is available, take longer for approval. Ant scouts actually measure the internal size of a new nest and assess the suitability of entrance ways (Franks 2008). This measuring capability is reminiscent of the ability of a plant root system to assess volume (McConnaughay and Bazzaz 1991).

Another form of quorum sensing in hives results in changes to nutrient acquisition between pollen and nectar. This is probably signalled on the dance floor.

If this model of quorum sensing is correct, then in trees a feedforward mechanism of recruitment seems essential, but what is to be recruited? Environmental information must accumulate initially in some meristems and epigenetic changes could ensure its stability, while the information was signalled to others. What signals are involved? Many years ago, plant hormones would have been identified as the factors involved and, of course, these may still contribute, but recently others have emerged.

The process of grafting of a scion on to a stock is a standard method of plant propagation, particularly among fruit trees. The choice of the two partners is determined by the characteristics of the final tree that is wanted. The root stock, for example, can convey features to the scion, such as an altered leaf structure, improved production or quality, or elevated resistance to pests and diseases. It is known that the homeobox protein RNA transcript, moves from the root stock through the graft union and modifies the behaviour of the scion (Kim et al. 2001). Likewise, mRNAs and non-coding small RNAs are found in the phloem and move throughout the plant, potentially DNA as well as proteins and peptides (references in Wu et al. 2013). The sRNAs are known to cause epigenetic changes in the DNA of cells that they enter, where they can cause gene silencing. This may be the basis of quorum sensing—molecules, rather than individual tissues—but recruitment will depend on numbers.

20. *Ants lay down pheromone trails to direct other ants toward food sources.* It is known from experiments that they optimize the trail that is shortest, optimizing energy expenditure for energy gain (Bonabeau et al. 2000). This trail is reinforced each time an individual ant moves along it. In this case, it is positive feedback that operates, more ants taking the trail means more will take it in the future.

This reinforcement of a pathway is similar to the mechanism proposed by Tsvi Sachs (1991) to describe the origins of auxin transport. When young leaves are in the process of formation they need to connect to the main vascular supply of the plant by forming their own vascular elements. Sachs (1991) suggested that auxin was synthesized initially in cells in the leaf tip and was eventually drained into the main vascular system. However, during its progress through some of these leaf cells, auxin induced its own transport mechanism in a kind of positive feedback. Auxin present in surrounding cells was thus drained into those that had advanced their transport more quickly. Thus, these cells claimed the majority of auxin in the leaf sufficient for them to become vascular elements and depriving others of that potential, which remained as photosynthetic leaf cells. This is, again, a case of positive feedback—a connecting line that is falteringly reinforced, each time auxin moves along it. Such behaviour might explain the cambial activation referred to above.

21. *A further interesting analogy emerges from trail geometry.* In following a trail, an ant quite frequently will miss the trail, but on coming back, needs to know the polarity of the trail if it is to continue in the right direction. Such information is essential if the energy expenditure on the collection of food is to be optimized. Ants can construct elaborate networks of trails throughout their environment. Investigation indicates that it is the branching angle that ants use to sense the polarity of the trail. A branching angle of 60° was found to be optimal in one direction (towards food) and 120° in the opposite direction towards the nest (Jackson et al. 2004). This angle of 60° appears in different transporting systems, such as tree branches and the vascular system in leaves as creating the most energy efficient structure either distributing or collecting resources (Leopold 1971; West et al. 1999).

22. *Plant behaviour operates on the same time scale as colony growth.* A major problem with the detection of plant behaviour has been the slow speed with which the phenotype changes are detected. The comparisons made between the time scale on which we operate and those of plants is, however, false. The comparison should be on the time scales of colony growth. On those times, plant behaviour is seen to be comparable. The slow patterns of growth of both result, in part, from the use of slower chemical and tactile communication, and the necessary accumulations of materials. Honey accumulation in hives is slow, as is that of pollen, and only direct measurements on a daily basis normally permits information of change to be gained. Visible alteration is, again, too slow to observe on any time less. Similarly, for the building of a termite nest, this can take years in total.

Reproductive analogies

1. *The new tree starts with a seed or seedling that replicates leaves and roots.* A new hive or nest starts with a queen that produces workers.
2. *Many trees have a juvenile period* in which only leaves, roots and branches are produced and resources are accumulated. Similarly, nests and hives have a period in which resources are built up and only workers produced.
3. *After the tree juvenile period has past, either an apical meristem or developing lateral bud can produce flowers.* In some plants, size seems to be the basis of this phase change (Poethig 1990). When colonies reach a certain size, the queen may lay virgin queen eggs as she receives less queen substance from attending workers. Drones are also produced and several hundred may be found in a large nest. With larger sizes part of the colony may swarm elsewhere with a new queen because fewer bees receive the pheromone in sufficient quantities from the queen to maintain the present nest.
4. *Many flowers are hermaphrodite containing both male and female cells.* The queen in a colony gives rise to both male drones and female queens. In both cases, there are more males than females
5. *Numerous pollen grains from individuals of the same species will land and fertilize the eggs in the ovary.* A colony queen mates with a number of different males up to 10.

Defence analogies

1. *Trees can be attacked by herbivores destroying leaves and buds.* Defence mechanisms use volatiles that mobilize other parts of the tree to initiate defence or attract parasites of the herbivore. Colony guards patrol the colony entry sites and a volatile alarm pheromone is used to rapidly increase workers to defence.
2. *Damaged or infected leaves can be abscised.* Damaged guards can be discarded and in ant colonies, are piled in one place or eaten.

Conclusion

Self-organizing systems have properties in common and this comparison has revealed a number.

Decisions are locally enacted, a common property of self-organised networks. The behaviour is described as 'distributed control'. Although, in many, if not all cases, the context of information arriving from the rest of the system contributes. Simple rules seem to operate in both trees and colonies that result in patterns of growth. Phenotypic change in trees is analogous to functional change in colonies. In both cases, feedback and feedforward operate to stabilize the system and enable change. In spring, workers are produced to gather food just as leaves likewise open to gather energy. Growth rates in colonies are slow like those in plants since both require an accumulation of resources. Quorums of one kind or another govern behaviour in both. The quorum can be generated contagiously or reflect an overall majority of tissues or cells that have made a decision one way, rather than another. External information is acquired and combined with that already present and decisions taken to benefit the community either colony or tree. The organizational analogies described here suggest that the particular structural arrangements of large numbers of modules and workers are those that provide for stability and robustness.

References

Allesina, S., Alonso, D., and Pascual, M. (2008). A general model for a food web structure. *Science*, **320**, 658–662.

Barabasi, A-L., and Oltvai, Z.N. (2004). Network biology: understanding the cell's organisation. *Nature Reviews Genetics*, **5**, 101–113.

Bassett, D.S., Meyer-Lindenburg, A., Achard, S., Duke, T., and Bullmore, N.E. (2006). Adaptive reconfiguration of fractal small world human brain functional networks. *Proceedings of the National Academy of Sciences USA*, **109**, 19518–19523.

Bell, A.D. (1984). Dynamic morphology. In Dirzo, R., and Sarukhan, J., eds, *Perspectives on plant population ecology*, pp. 48–66. Sinauer Associates, Sunderland, MA.

Beni, G., and Wang, J. (1993). Swarm intelligence in cellular robotic systems. In Dario, P., Sandini, G., and Aebischer, P., eds, *Robots and biological systems: towards a new bionics? NATO ISI series*, **102**, pp. 703–712. Springer, Berlin.

Bloom, A.J., Chapin, F.S., and Mooney, H.A. (1985). Resource limitation in plants an economic analogy. *Annual Review of Ecology and Systematics*, **16**, 363–392.

Boisvert, M.J., and Sherry, D.F. (2006). Interval timing by an invertebrate, the bumble bee, *Bombus impatiens*. *Current Biology*, **16**, 1636–1640.

Bonabeau, E., Dorigo, M., and Theraulax, G. (2000). Inspiration for optimisation from social insect behaviour. *Nature*, **406**, 39–42.

Bonabeau, E., and Theraulaz, G. (2000). Swarm Smarts. *Scientific American*, **282**, 72–79.

Camazine, S., Denounberg, J-L., Franks, N.R., Sneyd, J., Theraulaz, G., and Bonabeau, E. (2001). *Self-organisation in biological systems*. Princeton University Press, Princeton, NJ.

Chilton, J.K. (2006). Molecular mechanism of axon guidance. *Developmental Biology*, **292**, 13–24.

Chittka, L., Geiger, K., and Kunze, J. (1995). The influence of landmarks on distance estimation of honey bees. *Animal Behaviour*, **50**, 23–31.

Dacke, M., and Srinavasaan, M.V. (2008). Evidence for counting in insects. *Animal Cognition*, **11**, 683–689.

Dewdney, A.K. (1991). Leaping into Lyapunov space. *Scientific American*, **272**, 178–180.

Dyer, A.G., Rosa, M.G.P., and Reser, D.H. (2008). Honeybees can recognise images of complex natural scenes for use as potential landmarks. *Journal of Experimental Biology*, **211**, 1180–1186.

Edelman, G.M. (1993). Neural Darwinism. Selection and re-entrant signalling in higher brain function. *Neuron*, **10**, 115–125.

Falik, O., Reides, P., Gersani, M., and Novoplansky, A. (2005). Root navigation by self-inhibition. *Plant Cell and Environment*, **28**, 562–569.

Fewell, J.H. (2003). Social insect networks. *Science*, **301**, 1867–1870.

Franks, N.R. (2008). Convergent evolution. Serendipity and Intelligence for the simple minded. In Conway-Morris, S., ed. *The deep structure of biology*, pp. 111–128. Templeton Foundation Press, West Conshohocken, PA.

Freeman, W.J. (2005). NDN, volume transmission and self-organisation in brain dynamics. Journal of Integrative Neuroscience, **4**, 407–423.

Gordon, D.M., Goodwin, B.C., and Trainor, L.E.H. (1992). A parallel distributed model of the behaviour of ant colonies. *Journal of Theoretical Biology*, **156**, 293–307.

Gould, J.L., and Marler, P. (1987). Learning by instinct. *Scientific American*, **255**, 74–85.

Halle, F., Oldeman, R.A.A., and Tomlinson, P.B. (1978). *Tropical trees and forests—an architectural analysis*. Springer-Verlag, New York.

Hellmeier, H., Erhard, M., and Schulze, E.D. (1997). *Biomass accumulation and water use under arid conditions*. In Bazzaz, F.A., and Grace, J., eds, *Plant resource allocation*, pp. 93–113. Academic Press, London.

Hunter, P. (2003). The power of power laws. *The Scientist*, **17**, 22–25.

Jackson, D.E., Holcombe, M., and Ratnieks, F.L.W. (2004). Trail geometry gives polarity to ant foraging networks. *Nature*, **432**, 907–909.

Jones, M., and Harper, J.L. (1987). The influence of neighbours on the growth of trees. I. The demography of buds in *Betula pendula*. *Proceedings of the Royal Society London Series B*, **232**, 1–18.

Kim, M., Canio, W., Kessler, S., and Sinha, N. (2001). Developmental changes due to long-distance movement of a homeobox fusion transcript in tomato. *Science*, **293**, 287–289.

Kroon, H., de, Huber, H., Suefer, J.F., and Groenendael, J.M., van (2005). A modular concept of phenotypic plasticity in plants. *New Phytologist*, **166**, 73–82.

Langridge, E.A, Franks, N.R., and Sendova-Franks, A.B. (2004) Improvement in collective performance with experience in ants. *Behavioral Ecology and Sociobiology*, **56**, 523–529.

Langridge, E.A., Sendova-Franks, A.B., and Franks, N.R. (2008). How experienced individuals contribute to an improvement in collective performance in ants. *Behavioural Ecology and Sociobiology*, **62**, 447–456.

Leopold, L.B. (1971). Trees and streams: the efficiency of branching patterns. *Journal of Theoretical Biology*, **31**, 339–354.

List, C., Elsholtz, T., and Seeley, T.D. (2009). Independence and interdependence in collective decision making: an agent based model of nest site choice in honeybee swarming. *Philosophical Transactions of the Royal Society, Series B*, **364**, 755–762.

Maeterlinck, M. (1927). *The life of the white ant*. George Allen and Unwin, London.

McConnaughay, K.D.M., and Bazzaz, F.A. (1991). Is physical space a soil resource? *Ecology*, **92**, 94–103.

Menzel, R., Geiger, K., Chittka, L., Joerges, J., and Kunze, J. (1996). The knowledge base of bee navigation. *Journal of Experimental Biology*, **199**, 141–146.

Montoya, J.M., Pimm, S.L., and Sole, R.V. (2006). Ecological networks and their fragility. *Nature*, **442**, 259–269.

Morell, V. (2009). Watching as ants go marching-and deciding-one by one. *Science*, **323**, 1284–1285.

Poethig, R.S. (1990). Phase change and the regulation of shoot morphogenesis in plants. *Science*, **250**, 923–930.

Ranganathan, A., and Kira, Z. (2004). *Self-organisation in artificial intelligence and the brain*. Technical report, Georgia Institute of Technology. Available at: www.citeseerx.ist,psu.edu/viewdoc/download?doi=10.1.1.3.9668&rep/&type=pdf .

Rezende, E.L., Lavabre, J.E., Guimaraes, P.R., Jordano, P., and Bascompte, J. (2007). Non-random coextinctions in phylogenetically structured mutualistic networks. *Nature*, **448**, 925–928.

Sachs T. (1991). *Pattern formation in plant tissues*. Cambridge University Press, Cambridge.

Sattelmacher, B., and Horst, W.J. (2007). *The apoplast of higher plants: compartment, storage, transport and reactions*. Springer, Dordrecht.

Scanlon, T.M., Caylor, K.K., Levin, S.A., and Rodriguez-Iturbe, I. (2007). Positive feedbacks promote power law clustering of Kalahari vegetation. *Nature*, **449**, 209–216.

Scott-Kelso, T.A. (1995). *Dynamic patterns and the self-organisation of brain and behaviour (Complex Adaptive Systems)*. MIT Press, Cambridge, MA.

Seeley, T.D. (1995). *The wisdom of the hive*. Harvard University Press, Cambridge, MA.

Seeley, T.D., and Levien, R.A. (1987). A colony of mind: the beehive as thinking machine. *The Sciences*, **27**, 38–43.

Skorupski, P., and Chittka, L. (2006). Animal cognition: an insect's sense of time. *Current Biology*, **16**, R851–R853.

Sporns, O., Chialvo, D.R. Kaiser, M., and Hilgetaga, C.C. (2004). Organisation, development and function of complex brain networks. *Trends in Cognitive Sciences*, **8**, 418–426.

Thimann, K.V. (1972). The natural plant hormones. In Steward, F.C., ed. *Plant physiology 6B: a treatise: physiology of development*, pp. 3–372. Academic Press, New York.

Trewavas, A.J. (1986). Resource allocation under poor growth conditions. A major role for growth substances in developmental plasticity. In Jennings, D.H., and Trewavas, A.J., eds, *Plasticity in plants. Society for Experimental Biology Symposium, No. 40*, pp. 31–76. Cambridge University Press, Cambridge.

Trewavas, A. (2003). Aspects of plant intelligence. *Annals of Botany*, **92**, 1–20.

Trewavas, A. (2006). A brief history of systems biology. *Plant Cell*, **18**, 2420–2430.

Trewavas, A. (2007). Response to Alpi et al: plant neurobiology—all metaphors have value. *Trends in Plant Science*, **12**, 231–233.

Trewavas, A. (2008). Aspects of plant intelligence. In Conway Morris, S., ed. *The deep structure of biology*, pp. 68–110. Templeton Foundation Press, West Conshohocken, PA.

Turner, J.S. (2000). *The extended organism: the physiology of animal-built structures*. Harvard University Press, Cambridge, MA.

Watts, D.J., and Strogatz, S.H. (1998). Collective dynamics of 'small world' networks. *Nature*, **393**, 440–442.

West, G.B., Brown, J.H., and Enquist, B.J. (1999). A general model for the structure and allometry of plant vascular systems. *Nature*, **400**, 664–667.

Wu, R., Wang, X., Lin, Y., Ma., Y., Liu, G., Zhong, S., and 1 other (2013). Interspecies grafting caused extensive and heritable alterations of DNA methylation in *Solanaceae* plants. *PLoS One*, **8**, e61995.

Zhang, S.W., Bartsch, K., and Srinavasaan, M.V. (1996). Maze learning by honeybees. *Neurobiology of Learning and Memory*, **66**, 267–282.

CHAPTER 11

Self-organization: cambium as the integration assessor

The sinuous tenacity of a tree: finding the light newly blocked on one side, it turns in another. A blind intelligence, true.

(Hirshfield 2002)

⊃ Summary

Self-organizing systems are common in biology. Plants are self-organizing systems using communication between their constituent cells and tissues to generate organization. Thus, order in plant development results from bottom-up construction, rather than top-down. Communication in plants occurs by both competition and cooperation dependent on circumstances. Communication through the vascular system provides examples of both types. The behaviour of a simple two-shoot system derived from young legume seedlings in which competition clearly occurs between the two shoots is described. Whichever shoot becomes the most vigorous enables it to retain its competitive ability. A less vigorous shoot can become the most vigorous, if the original most vigorous shoot is restrained for several days. The cambium acts to dynamically alter vascular strand number responding to the requirements of vigorous shoots for more root resources and to decrease the active vascular strands for those less vigorous. Since the cambial cells are in communication with each other and form an inner skin underneath the bark, the cambium can act to demarcate the numbers of active vascular elements to all branches or roots. It can, therefore, act as an integration assessor. The mechanisms involved may be simple feedback, although comparisons between different branches also have to be made. Evidence for cambial integration is presented from observations on trees that experience a gravitropic signal. Different sides of the tree generate different kinds of cell to enhance the rate of regaining the vertical. Tension and compression as signals are indicated.

A growing plant is a 'small world' and self-organizing structure

A growing plant is clearly a self-organized network, there is no overall, top-down control specifying structure and morphology. Instead, overall structure is generated bottom-up, rather than top-down. The structure emerges as a result of communication between the various cells and tissues, and the local environment surrounding each growing point. The rules of interaction must be fairly simple. As growth continues, and new leaves and roots are added, they connect via newly-formed vascular tissue with the tissues that are already present. Communication is commonly conducted via the vascular system, but it can also pass from cell to cell via the adjacent cell walls or through plasmodesmata that connect the cytoplasm of adjacent cells. Sometimes communication within a single plant occurs through volatile compounds or electrically through the soil water.

The small world structure (see Chapter 10) is a suitable description of the levels of interaction (communication) between the parts of the plant. The meristematic regions at the tips of shoot, root, and branch self-evidently require intense communication between the constituent cells. Although meristems are embryonic structures, different regions have been shown to have different functions, either in maintenance, or cell specification, or initiating morphological change. These embryonic structures act to organize themselves and continually generate numerous differentiating cells. However, as cells mature to form stem and leaves, the intensity of communication and, thus, connection will diminish. A power law will operate—a few cells in the meristem with a lot of communication and many mature cells with a few.

Further evidence of self-organizing capacity comes from other meristematic properties. The meristem maintains itself despite continued cell division and the continual movement of cells out of the meristem itself. Meristems can maintain themselves for decades (Bowman and Eshed 2000; Reddy and Meyerowitz 2005; Traas and Moneger 2010). Even when damaged through deliberate incision, the resulting divided meristems (up to six) can regenerate into new autonomous meristems. Self-organization is evident.

The other features of small world organization arise from the fact that the main growing tissues communicate with each other through a relatively fast vascular system. Speedy processing of information and adjustment is therefore aided. Distributed information processing, a small world property, reflects the element of local control found in phenotypic plasticity.

The effects of critical size, changing development, and generating emergent properties, noted in brain development (Chapter 10) has its equivalent. Lateral roots appear as the root increases thickness. As the seedling grows, reduction in integrated communication diminishes and this may act to signal the production of first leaves too. Many plants reach critical sizes and then undergo a phase change to a flowering schedule (McDaniel et al. 1996). When the shoot meristem in day-neutral plants reaches a critical size it may commence flowering. Elements of control in these situations here might then simply result from size alterations in communication.

Types of overall communication

Competition and cooperation

Cooperation and competition between the tissues of a whole plant integrate together in a kaleidoscope of behaviours. The necessary resources for growth enter the plant through two different tissues and from two different environments. Roots provide minerals and water (resources), and synthesize and communicate various organic materials proteins, sRNAs (oligonucleotide hormones), proteins, peptides, and potential hormones like cytokinins, abscisins, etc., to the vascular system, and thus to the shoot. However, they need some of these resources themselves. Young leaves only transport carbohydrate to the rest of the plant when mature. As they grow they sequester carbohydrates from others.

However, the transport processes can be complex. Watson and Caspar (1984), for example, point to probable integrated physiological units that exist within plants. Using isotopically-labelled carbon, they were able to identify sectors in the shoot that are integrated in structure and in good communication with each other. Others were more remote and in weaker communication.

Individuals of different species can exist on a continuum from good or strong integration (as, for example, in many seedlings and some whole shoots) to highly localized and complex sectorialization that represent weak integration. Cohorts of branches, on a single individual plant, can differ enormously in fecundity and physiological properties. These reflect perhaps the integrated physiological unit.

One of the functions of the transported signals like auxin and kinins may be to cue the presence of growing tissues. Auxin synthesized in the young leaves of the growing shoot indicates to the root system that there are growing shoots above, and root growth should continue as a consequence. Cytokinins are synthesized in growing roots and signal the shoot to continue growth. These two hormones help integrate the overall growth pattern (Sachs 1991). However, many transported signals can also be subject to circulation from shoot to root and back again, and may be enzymatically-modified during movement. The process of cooperation is thus not simple.

However, cooperation easily slides into competition, a consequence of the two ports of entry of different, necessary resources placed in different environments. Increase the scarcity of one or other resource and multicellular plants have strategies to counteract. Two examples suffice.

If as a result of shading by competitors, some plants change their stem and leaf morphology. The growing stem becomes thinner, its elongation rate is increased, and leaves are produced in reduced numbers. Those that do grow increase their surface area, but reduce the numbers of cell layers. Root growth, correspondingly, is diminished. The shoot competes more strongly for the more limited carbohydrate of the individual. These adaptive changes are termed shade avoidance and are found in all shade-intolerant species (Aphalo et al. 1999).

The adaptive response is designed to produce a phenotype that either grows ahead of the opposition that is nearby, or out-grows a canopy overhead. Shade avoidance morphology can be induced before any loss of photosynthetic light. It is predictive of a potential future that has not yet happened and is an attempt to ensure it does not. Clearly, it is also a strategy for the individual plant to sequester the available light before the competition from other plants and to ensure the competition remains shaded.

However, the alternate developmental change occurs in water stress conditions. Here, the root increases its growth at the expense of the shoot and is thus able to sequester the 'lions share' of carbohydrate resources. The response is, again, clearly adaptive, rational, and designed to overcome the limitation of water by increased soil exploration. In larger plants, trees in particular, shortage of water leads to competition between leaves for the reduced supply, with abscission the fate for those that lose out. The goal is to re-establish the balance between the demands from transpiration with supply from the roots (Addicott 1982). Some internal sensor establishes the goal to be achieved. Thus, the behaviour can be described as goal-directed and purposeful (Trewavas 2009). The precise sensing and the internal arbiter that determines goal culmination is not known, but it has the form of a complex negative feedback phenomenon. Abscission ceases when the balance has been restored.

Evidence for cooperative and meaningful communication via vascular elements between root and shoot is indicated by the following:

1. The dependence of the shoot on the root for resources and vice versa. Isolated stems (after excision, for example) fail to grow until roots are regenerated, and this is similar for the isolated root.
2. Growth in the shoot is usually dependent upon some equivalent growth in the root. There is some plasticity in this dependence. The shoot to root ratio can vary up to 20-fold in wild plants growing in extreme conditions (Chapin 1980). In crop plants, five-fold variation is not uncommon in the literature.

The uptake of necessary resources by the root is not just dependant on root size. The transport systems for nitrate, phosphate, and water from outside express a degree of molecular flexibility. Transport can be increased by alterations in the numbers of proteins involved (Plaxton and Tran 2011).

Self-organization in decisions on branch formation and growth

Relatively simple experiments provide clues to the potential mechanisms involved in decisions on branching (Snow 1931; Novoplansky et al. 1989; Novoplansky 2003; Sachs 2006). These authors all used a similar system involving young, growing seedlings of pea and bean, in most cases provided with mineral salts. Normally, these seedlings have an apically-dominant main shoot that grows after the germination of the root. If this main shoot is removed, then the dormancy of two (cotyledonary) buds, located at the connection between the main shoot and the cotyledon, is broken, and they both grow out to form two new shoots. The behavioural response is obviously to compensate for herbivory of the main shoot.

However, it is the variation in size of these new shoots that intrigues. Either these two shoots may be effectively equal in size and thus vigour (vigour is considered to be equivalent to rate of growth) or they may show varying degrees of unequal size and vigour. The observations made here can be divided into two groups.

1. Shoots (branches) of about equal vigour:
   (i) Neither dominates the other. Both continue growth indefinitely.
   (ii) Shade one shoot and it grows more slowly and usually stops but remains alive; the other continues growth unabated.
   (iii) Shade both and growth continues in both but more slowly.
   (iv) Place one shoot in darkness and it eventually dies; the other grows vigorously.
   (v) Remove the one shoot that was growing in light. The shoot initially placed in darkness now recovers providing it has not died. Growth is now etiolated.
   (vi) Defoliate one shoot and its vigour is severely impaired compared to the unmodified shoot.
   (vii) Only slight perturbation can cause one shoot to obtain dominance over the other in an obviously finely balanced system.

2. Shoots (branches) of unequal vigour in light:
   (i) Second shoot is only slightly less vigorous and grows for some time.
   (ii) Second shoot is substantially weaker, ceases to grow, and dies.
   (iii) Remove vigorous shoot and the weaker shoot now grows indefinitely.
   (iv) Restrain vigorous shoot growth for 2 days, and the weaker shoot will overtake and remain dominant (see Figure 11.1).
   (v) Remove part of the cotyledons or remove mineral salts from the growth medium. Competition will be enhanced between the two.

This two-shoot system is an early seedling phase with both shoots dependent for some materials from the cotyledons. Water and abundant minerals (in growth medium) will probably only come from the root.

There are clear indications in these experiments that the two shoots compete with each other. If one becomes more vigorous, the vigour of the other is correspondingly reduced. If one of two equal shoots is in comparatively preferable circumstances compared with the other (e.g. more light), the differential in vigour is enhanced. Restrain the growth of the most vigorous shoot for only a few days and the other less vigorous shoot will permanently assume

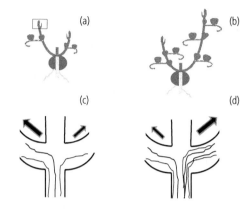

Figure 11.1 Control of shoot growth by the cambium. The two-shoot pea seedlings are shown diagrammatically (a,b). The primary shoot in (a) was restrained for 2 days (oblong). After removal of the restraint, it remained the minority shoot as indicated in (b). The probable distribution of vascular strands is only shown in proportion in (c) and (d). The restraint prevents further vascular development, whereas the unrestrained shoot develops more vascular tissue and gains more root resources as indicated by size of arrows. Adapted from Sachs (2006) and Novoplansky (2003).

the dominant vigour position (Figure 11.1). Simple feedforward mechanisms (= vigour) are surely responsible.

In these respects the seedling behaves like an integrated individual, organizing its branching pattern and vigour to take best advantage of the use of limited resources, mainly from the root. The properties above represent simple rules of self-organization.

Leaf and tree branch senescence mimics the comparative assessment of shoot behaviour observed in young legume seedlings

Arabidopsis plants form a rosette of leaves. Detach a leaf and place it in darkness; within a few days senescence, exemplified by loss of chlorophyll, is clearly visible. In separate experiments, cloth mitts were placed over one leaf to shade it on an intact growing plant. These mitt-covered individual leaves now rapidly show the typical symptoms of senescence and eventually die, like the detached leaf. If, on the other hand, the whole plant is shaded to the same extent and for the same period of time, no leaf senescence is visible (Weaver and Amasino 2001). Once again, the plant is conducting a comparative assessment and a decision is made to remove those leaves in poor positions, which seemingly cannot compete with others; or is it lack of comparative photosynthetic function? Note again, however, it is a whole plant assessment that is being made, and specific assessments and decisions are made about the behaviour of particular organs.

This comparative decision making can be seen in trees. Henrikkson (2001) used shading of individual branches to demonstrate a similar decision-making process. Shade one branch and impairment of growth is substantial, leading to sealing off and branch death within 2 years. Other unshaded branches grow more quickly as a consequence, again suggesting competition for resources. Shade the whole tree, however, to the same extent and only a minor reduction in overall growth is observed.

Honkanen and Haukioja (1994) used 20-year-old pine trees and removed 70% of needles, either from a single branch or from the whole tree to mimic herbivore (trophic) damage. They then measured the regenerated needle mass several years later in the two experimental treatments. When a single branch was defoliated, its growth in terms of needle mass was more retarded than when the whole tree was defoliated. Comparative defoliation is recognized and the ability to regain resources for needle regrowth, impaired when a single branch experiences loss of photosynthetic area. When a single branch is defoliated, it experiences a permanent change in its competitive ability to obtain resources from elsewhere in the plant.

Arbitration by the cambium: the cambium as the plant 'dance floor'?

Some important deductions from these data emerge about plant behaviour.

Individual plants behave as unified organisms, even very large ones. There may be enormous plasticity in the final structure, but there is clear reference to the whole organism in any decisions that are made about the behaviour and growth of individual branches. Forms of negative feedback may be responsible.

The overall ecological and evolutionary goal of any individual plant is to optimize fitness. Only if the overall behaviour of the individual is integrated

could this biological requirement be fulfilled. In other words, the morphology must be rational with respect to its environment. Branches contribute substantially to the accumulation of resources that relate to seed number and fitness in due course. No matter how plastic the structure, there has to be some overall principle that comes from self-organization. Sinnott (1960) summarizes much evidence that he calls correlation. Basically, many of these are indications of competitive ability among different organs, which confirm that plants act as whole individuals, not as clusters of largely independent 'plantlets' or ramets.

Clearly, something senses when the organ is functional. For both leaves and branches, the question is not whether it is synthesizing carbohydrate at all, but an **assessment** of the relative rate of carbohydrate production compared with other leaves and branches. It may not even be carbohydrate, but might be some other hormone-like chemicals whose synthesis mirrors that of carbohydrate. It may even be coordinated with the use of resources from the root. Whatever the assessment is, it has to take place over considerable distances within the stem or trunk.

The activity of the vascular system cannot be fixed because, as plants grow and new branches are better placed to gather light, **the resources of the vascular system must be redirected towards them and since there is competition, away from those which are now either shaded** or some other worse environment. Translocation of resources must be dynamic and adjusted to suit the conditions!

What is being competed for? Leaves and branches are connected directly via the vascular system to the root and, in these cases, competition among shoots is most likely for root resources for growth; i.e. water, minerals, and other synthesized materials. For roots, it is carbohydrate.

Dynamic redirection of translocation

It has been mentioned several times that branches die or leaves are abscised. Critical to those events is the essential sealing of the vascular system. A mechanism to control vascular function has to be in place to explain these observations. It is known that the phloem can be sealed either using a polysaccharide, callose, or protein aggregation; the xylem can be sealed by the formation of blocking tyloses. However, the critical thing is that these events of blockage are coordinated, suggesting that a signal must be involved to coordinate the action between the two types of vascular cells. Where does that signal come from? The most likely origin is the cambium.

The cambium is a kind of inner skin, a meristem that generates the phloem and xylem cells on either side to generate the vascular tissue. In stems and tree trunks, the cambial ring can be seen as surrounding the whole of the inner tissues, largely xylem and secondary xylem. The cambium generates the phloem towards the outside. Any simple observation of the way a tree trunk develops uniformly both in the horizontal and vertical directions indicates that the cambial cells must be in continuous communication with each other. It clearly acts as an integrated structure. Furthermore, interruption of the cambial ring by substantial removal of a sizeable chunk of stem leads to callus formation and regeneration of the cambial ring from both of the cut ends growing towards each other—obviously cambial cell communication again (Steeves and Sussex 1972).

If the cambium signals the coordination of the mechanisms that can specifically seal the two vascular tissues when required, it could also seal off a more limited number of vascular cells. Some strands could be blocked reducing the amounts of root (or shoot) resources donated to any branch, but thus releasing more resources for others that are more vigorous.

However, since the cambium is dynamic, it can increase the potential for well-placed branches to receive more vascular tissue resources by cambial division and cell development. This dynamic has been demonstrated. Sachs (2006) observed a greater number of vascular strands connecting the more vigorous branch in the simple two-shoot seedling system described above (see Figure 11.1).

Thus, the cambium has the facility of dynamically adjusting the vascular elements according to requirement. We know this dynamic is there, vascular elements damaged during winter can be regenerated by cambial activity in spring. The cambium has the potential to assess the rate of flow of materials through the adjacent vascular elements, since it will itself be dependent on these materials for its own behaviour and maintenance. Simple negative feedback from what is perceived, could control the potential for increasing vascular strands or blocking them. Since the cambium is a continuous tissue, it has the potential to comparatively assess the movement of materials into all branches and branch roots throughout the whole plant and adjust the supply. The underlying control will be self-organization, simple rules using feedback and feedforward to optimize the distribution of translocation.

The cambium may initiate the processes of leaf senescence, too. Very young leaves form their own vascular tissue and connect to the mature systems via cambial activity. Auxin may be one component important in this linking up (Sachs et al. 1993).

The cambium is acting as an integration arbiter and overall assessor. The two-way flow of materials in the adjacent vascular elements will be constantly assessed and redirected as necessary by formation of vascular tissue or its blockage. As Sachs (2006) expressed it, 'the cambium responds to the best branches . . . and ignores the weaker branches whose vascular tissues deteriorate without being replaced'.

The arbitration role of the cambium is also shown in tree gravitropism and wind sway

Wind sway, if allowed to occur uncontrollably, can damage leaves and, thus, photosynthetic area. The thickness of a growing plant stem or trunk can be increased when the plant sways frequently, when induced to do so by wind stimuli. Concomitantly, growth in height is reduced and competition for resources between the vertical and horizontal polarities of the stem or trunk occurs; i.e. the competition occurs between the shoot apical meristems and the cambial meristems. Wind sway is also known to increase the cell division activity of the vascular and cork cambium, and root growth. It is not known what determines the optimal trunk thickness or acceptable trunk movement in wind, but it has the characteristics of a complex negative feedback to a predetermined goal and is thus purposeful. Ethylene, a plant hormone, is associated with promoting stem thickness and the activity of the two cambiums, but its primary function, being gaseous, should be to synchronize the behaviour of all the cells in the tissue. In the absence of ethylene, the behaviour of the cells would be sporadic and slow the process. Hormones in plants act to synchronize cells to a common end, thereby accelerating development (Bradford and Trewavas 1994; Trewavas 2012).

Woody angiosperms and gymnosperms are capable of reorientating both the trunk and branches, when these are displaced from their original growth position (Niklas 1992, p. 420ff.). The signal is a change in the gravity vector. In a trunk or stem displaced from the vertical, the upper surface is under tensile stress, while the lower experiences compressive stress. For both trunk and branches, special kinds of secondary xylem are generated by the cambium called, generically, reaction wood. In a leaning trunk the cambium generates compression-generated reaction wood on the lower side that pushes upwards; tension wood is generated by the cambium on the upper part of the trunk and these cells contract. A push–pull mechanism operates in trunk reorientation. This is very obviously purposeful behaviour and reaction wood formation ceases once the vertical position is re-established. The cambium emerges again as a dynamic meristem, able to change development according to external and internal signals. Note that it can perform two different functions, although an integrated ring.

In gymnosperms, only compression wood seems to be formed and it was thought that the weight of branches was the stimulus, since the cells formed on the lower portion of the branch. In fact, experiments in which young branches were bent into different shapes, showed that compression wood always formed where the cells were under compression (Niklas 1992). Compression wood is formed regardless of the original upper or lower position on the branch. In angiosperms, capable of forming both tension and compression wood, the woods form, respectively, in areas under either tension or compression (see Box 11.1).

The stimulus that actually induces reaction wood formation is a change in the gravitational vector. Branches may have a pre-set angle to the gravity vector and use reaction wood to recover that angle when it is altered. Either the cambium senses the gravity vector or it is in direct contact with cells that

---

Box 11.1 Tension and compression signalling in plants

One of the consequences of having a cell wall constructed of various carbohydrate polymers and some protein is that cells are permanently joined together. This creates problems when cells expand and grow in particular, since the wall has to be sufficiently plastic to allow growth to occur at all. A further difficulty is that tissues consist of a population of cells that often grow or divide at variable rates (within limits) to each other, providing stresses within any growing tissue. It is possible to envisage nodal points of stress that are relieved by introduction of changes in local expansion and that might be used to specify overall morphology. It is thought, for example, that the cambial meristematic ring in trees, consisting as it does of horizontally thin cells, is maintained in this spatial configuration by the pressure exerted by the surrounding woody tissues. If the pressure is relieved by isolation of a fragment containing cambial cells, a callus is generated. Conversely, placing callus under pressure generates tissue that looks suspiciously like tree cambium (Steeves and Sussex 1972). A developmental nicety—the cambium maintains external pressure on to itself that in turn maintains its structure.

A further important issue is that what is called mechanical signalling becomes important in plant development. Stresses and strains are communicated to the cytoplasm of cells experiencing the signalling. If a plant tissue is bent, then on the inside of the bend there is compression and on the outside, tension. Seedling hypocotyls caused to move in this way express immediate changes in cytosolic calcium, a signal that initiates changes in growth rate and morphology (Knight et al. 1991).

Tension wood plays some interesting roles in plant development. In some corms (a monocot swollen, storage stem, like a bulb, but lacking the fleshy leaves) the new bud is on top of the corm, and continued growth and production of a new corm each season would place the successive corms and buds higher and higher, until they projected from the soil surface. To solve this problem contractile roots develop that pull the corms down in each season so that the new bud for next year remains at a similar level with regard to the soil surface. The aerial roots of some sub-tropical fig trees elongate until they reach the ground. By placing the end of such roots in soil in pots it was shown that the root contracts and pulls the pot upwards. Thus, the aerial roots, once penetrating the soil, contract and act like the guy ropes of a tent maintaining the upright position of the trunk (Niklas 1992).

can accomplish this task. The behaviour is goal-directed and thus purposeful.

Angiosperm branches in early development commonly form reaction wood only on the upper surface. In young plants, the branches are placed more vertically than they are later. With subsequent growth, the optimal capture of light requires a more horizontal branch position. Reaction wood is then used to push the branch down to form the more familiar, near horizontal branches of the mature tree and, thus, place its leaves more remotely from the shading of the upper branches—negative feedback again? What signalling system is used to accomplish this developmental change is simply unknown, but importantly, this mechanism increases the available photosynthetic area by reduction of self-shading. Presumably, the sensing of the relevant branch angle with respect to gravity, changes with age. As older branches increase in weight, reaction wood forms on the lower part to help maintain the horizontal position. Although this process is slow, nevertheless, it exhibits clear purposeful behaviour and whole plant response.

The cambium is, indeed, analogous to the bee hive dance floor

Earlier in this chapter the question was asked as to whether the cambium is analogous to the beehive dance floor. This is the place in the hive where information from outside the hive on food distribution is exchanged to initiate new behaviour in other members of the hive and hive integrity maintained. The cambium surely plays a similar role in plant behaviour and the evidence in this chapter strongly supports the analogy. Translocation is dynamic in that the numbers of vascular cells can be increased or decreased into already well-established tissues. The cambium is the tissue in which all sorts of external information and flow can be perceived and integrated into rational responses. Communication throughout the cambium attempts to optimize the distribution of resources to accommodate the differential and heterogeneous environment in which wild plants grow. The cambium will self-organize to optimize its functioning architecture based on continual communication of information throughout all the cambial cells and the differential information that requires arbitration of vascular tissue flow between different branches. The cambium is a complex network, the overall functioning will result in a series of emergent, integrated, but self-organized functional structures.

This behaviour of the cambium in solving the problems of branch distribution of resources is evidently intelligent in character. This chapter has illustrated starkly how little we actually know about this important meristem and it capacities, and surprisingly, despite its importance it attracts little attention at present at this level of investigation. Most research is pronouncedly molecular and progress can be expected there, but that is for another book, not this one.

References

Addicott, F.T. (1982). *Abscission*. University of California Press, Berkeley, CA.

Aphalo, P.J., Ballare, C.L., and Scopel, A.L. (1999). Plant–plant signalling, the shade avoidance response and competition. *Journal of Experimental Botany*, **50**, 1629–1634.

Bowman, J.L., and Eshed, Y. (2000). Formation and maintenance of the shoot apical meristem. *Trends in Plant Science*, **5**, 110–115.

Bradford, K.J., and Trewavas, A.J. (1994). Sensitivity thresholds and variable time scales in plant hormone action. *Plant Physiology*, **105**, 1029–1036.

Chapin, F.S. (1980). The mineral nutrition of wild plants. *Annual Review of Ecology and Systematics*, **11**, 233–260.

Henriksson, J. (2001). Differential shading of branches or whole trees: survival growth and reproduction. *Oecologia*, **126**, 482–486.

Hirshfield, J. (2002). Optimism. *Given Sugar, Given Salt*. Harper Collins, New York.

Honkanen, T., and Haukioja, E. (1994). Why does a branch suffer more after branch-wide that after tree-wide defoliation. *Oikos*, **71**, 441–450.

Knight, M.R., Campbell, A.K, Smith, S.M., and Trewavas, A.J. (1991). Transgenic plant aequorin reports the effects of touch and cold-shock and elicitors on cytoplasmic calcium. *Nature*, **352**, 524–526.

McDaniel, C.M., Hartnett, L.K., and Sangrey, K.A. (1996). Regulation of node number in day neutral tobacco: a factor in plant size. *Plant Journal*, **9**, 55–61.

Niklas, K.J. (1992). *Plant Biomechanics*. Chicago University Press, Chicago, IL.

Novoplansky, A. (2003). Ecological implications of the determination of branch hierarchies. *New Phytologist*, **160**, 111–118.

Novoplansky, A., Cohen, D., and Sachs, T. (1989). Ecological implications of correlative inhibition between plant shoots. *Physiologia Plantarum*, **77**, 136–140.

Plaxton, W.C., and Tran, H.T. (2011). Metabolic adaptations of phosphate starved plants. *Plant Physiology*, **156**, 1006–1015.

Reddy, G.V., and Meyerowitz, E.M. (2005). Stem cell homeostasis and growth dynamics can be uncoupled in the *Arabidopsis* shoot apex. *Science*, **310**, 663–667.

Sachs, T. (1991). *Pattern formation in plant tissues*. Cambridge University Press, Cambridge.

Sachs, T. (2006). How can plants choose the most promising organs? In Baluska, F., Mancuso, S., and Volkmann, D.,eds, *Communication in plants*, pp. 53–63. Springer-Verlag, Berlin.

Sachs, T., Novoplansky, A., and Cohen, D. (1993). Plants as competing populations of redundant organs. *Plant Cell and Environment*, **16**, 765–770.

Sinnott, E.W. (1960). *Plant morphogenesis*. McGraw Hill Book Co., New York.

Snow, R. (1931). Experiments on growth and inhibition. II. New phenomena of inhibition. *Proceedings of the Royal Society Series B*, **108**, 305–316.

Steeves, T.A., and Sussex, I.M. (1972). *Patterns in plant development*. Prentice-Hall, Englewood Cliffs, NJ.

Traas, J., and Moneger, F. (2010). Systems biology of organ initiation at the shoot apex. *Plant Physiology*, **152**, 420–427.

Trewavas, A.J. (2009). What is plant behaviour. *Plant Cell and Environment*, **32**, 606–616.

Trewavas, A.J. (2012). Information, noise and communication: thresholds as controlling development. In Witzany, G., and Baluska, F., eds, *Biocommunication of plants*, pp. 11–35. Springer-Verlag, Berlin.

Watson, M.A., and Caspar, B.B. (1984). Morphogenetic constraints on pattern of carbon distribution in plants. *Annual Review of Ecology and Systematics*, **15**, 233–258.

Weaver, L.M., and Amasino, R.M. (2001). Leaf senescence is induced in individually darkened *Arabidopsis* leaves but inhibited in whole, darkened plants. *Plant Physiology*, **127**, 876–886.

CHAPTER 12

Self-organizing capacity in leaf behaviour

Again spread out their leaves of glossy green.

(Clare 1835)

➲ Summary

Leaves are often in a dynamic state on the adult plant. Senescence and loss through abscission is the usual fate, although this can be accelerated by various environmental conditions, including shading. The evidence that internal leaf temperature remains relatively constant, and is in a form of homeostasis throughout the growing season and near the optimum of photosynthesis, is outlined. The factors involved in cooling or warming the leaf temperature are described. These are leaf position with respect to light, chloroplast movement, stomatal aperture, cuticular wax, trichome density; all are facets of leaf temperature homeostasis. These factors can change on demand and are easily adapted to maintain internal leaf temperature within a few minutes to several days. The interactions between these leaf characteristics form another example of self-organization and should be governed by fairly simple rules. These rules are currently unknown, although direct and sensitive manipulations might sense leaf temperature and convey that information to the relevant leaf cells. There is evidence that stomatal apertures communicate information to stomata on adjacent developing leaves, changing their stomatal density. Guard cell pairs on a single leaf are co-ordinately controlled in their behaviour as parts of much larger complexes or patches that behave differently to other patches when in receipt of an environmental signal. Such behaviour enables the leaf to exert fine control over overall transpiration and CO_2 uptake, and to control temperature.

Introduction

The collection of light energy and its conversion to sugars is fundamental to virtually all life on this planet. Leaves of one kind or another are the primary plant conduits for the collection of energy in many angiosperms. So it should be no surprise that aspects of plant behaviour are designed to optimize the capture of light energy, particularly in crowded environments where competition for light is at a premium. In some plants, stems replace this function (e.g. many cacti, brooms) and,

in yet others—parasitical plants in particular—leaves may be vestigial or absent.

Branches and leaves within a single individual can impede each other for light accession (Arber 1950). Seen from above, leaves are usually well-spaced in seedlings since they emerge at different angles to each other. Although a variety of factors determine the loss of dormancy in buds, in seedlings it is imperative that self-shading be minimized or absent. The leaves that are produced should gather as much light energy as possible. The likely reason is that only those buds whose threshold for red light/far red light is exceeded, actually grow out. If one bud is under a leaf, it will receive a higher balance of far red to red light as a consequence of the absorption of red light by chlorophyll in the leaf above (Finlayson et al. 2010; Reddy et al. 2013). This control on its own may directly prevent bud outgrowth, but this published current research also identifies abscisic acid as being the hormonal control on bud outgrowth and its synthesis being increased by a low red/far red light experienced under these conditions. With increasing height, some overlap becomes difficult to avoid, but in that situation, the top leaves are further away from the earliest and, thus, some sunlight with a high red/far red ratio gets through, enough perhaps to offset the extra far red light that comes from the leaves above.

For woody perennials these problems of impedance may become more acute. The distribution of leaves in a tree canopy is certainly complex but not in any way random (Monsi et al. 1973; Yamada et al. 2000). Even cursory observation indicates that branches adopt structures that place most leaves in reasonable positions to capture sunlight. Birches, for example, often use a weeping branch structure with a cascade of leaves.

When leaves become seriously shaded at least two adaptive choices are open. Internal modification of the photosynthetic system and metabolism to optimize collection of what light is available. Alternatively, a predetermined programme of senescence can be initiated. This developmental programme of apoptosis results in mobilization and recovery into the vascular tissue, and eventually into the main body of the plant of carbohydrate, mineral, and nitrogenous compounds from the leaf.

Shade acts as an environmental signal that initiates changes in leaf and branch behaviour (Finlayson et al. 2010). The leaves of a tree seedling at the bottom of a tropical forest may receive less than 1% of the light available in the highest canopy storey. In general, the adaptations described in the literature describe the difference between leaves grown only in light or shade. These adaptations of leaves grown in shade recognize the lower density of photons, which are sensed quantitatively during the development of the leaf. The surface area of the shade leaf is greatly increased, but the leaf is thinner with

reduced numbers of palisade layers, thus minimizing the use of growth resources (Lichtenthaler et al. 1981). They have a lower dry weight. There may be more chlorophyll to compensate for reduced palisade layers and there are reductions in the ratio of chlorophyll a to chlorophyll b. There are fewer stomata. Chloroplasts are increased in size. The orientation of the leaves and branches is changed more towards the horizontal (Givnish 1988). These behavioural changes are not all-or-none, many can be initiated in all-ready established leaves although the processes may take several days (Pearcy and Sims 1994).

Leaf senescence is commensurate with, or usually preceded by, the formation of an abscission zone commonly at the base of the leaf petiole (Addicott 1982). The development of this specialized zone of cells is initiated when an unfavourable assessment is made of the transport rates of root resources in and transport of leaf photosynthate out. As indicated in Chapter 11, the cambium may act as an integrating arbiter on which leaves will survive and which will not. How transport rates are assessed at the molecular level and used to initiate abscission zone development, is currently not known, but once initiated, hormones like ethylene are involved in synchronizing all the abscission zone cells to uniformly secrete wall hydrolases like cellulase into the wall and ensure a clean break. The synchronizing process controlled by ethylene, also ensures the production of β 1–3 glucans to block the vascular tissues, and other wound-induced polysaccharides and proteins to block the surface against fungal entry.

Leaf temperature is a holistic, homeostatically controlled phenomenon

The current processes of photosynthesis in many temperate plants appears to optimize at around 20°C. The $\delta^{18}O$ in cellulose is considered a proxy for leaf temperature and reflects the isotopic enrichment that accompanies transpiration in the leaf (Roden et al. 2000). Helliker and Richter (2008) in a ground-breaking paper analysed the $\delta^{18}O$ of cellulose in tree rings from trees ranging over 50° of latitude: that is, from the subtropical to boreal biomes. They concluded that, throughout the growing season, the average leaf temperature was maintained at 21.4 ± 2.2°C. This average leaf temperature was maintained in biomes whose average outside temperature throughout the growing season ranged from 12°C to 26°C. The external leaf and canopy temperature do not remain constant throughout the day, so clearly they will be subject to daily variations to an extent and most certainly at night. There will be some second-to-second changes in temperature in daytime. It is the functional plasticity of the photosynthetic molecular apparatus that works to maintain photosynthesis within this short time variation of temperature.

However, their surprising data indicate that these trees have an in-built temperature target that optimizes photosynthesis to an average ideal temperature. Clearly, the plants examined must possess the means to either warm or cool the leaf against the current temperature so as to achieve the average. Clearly, some form of self-organizing homeostat is working.

The factors cooling leaf temperature in warmer climates, or higher than average temperatures, are numerous

1. *Evaporation of water from the mesophyll cells inside the leaf.* The loss of water is controlled by the numerous stomata found mostly on the underside of the leaf.
2. *Changes in surface reflectance of sunlight.* At least two factors are involved here; the molecular nature of the cuticular wax, and the presence and/or density of trichomes or hairs on the leaf surface (Grant et al. 2003).
3. *Leaf shape and position.* Leaf shape determines the ease of airflow around the leaf and thus the movement of water vapour away from the stomatal aperture. Leaves that grow in full sunlight have a reduced surface area, in turn, reducing potential heat absorption.
4. *Angle of leaf to sunlight.* It has been known for over a century that a motor tissue called the pulvinus, connecting the petiole to the leaf blade can adjust the leaf blade angle to the vector of sunlight (Darwin 1880). The angle is known to vary through the day. A vertical position, with

respect to overhead sunlight, will reduce light and thus infra-red (heat) absorption, helping cooling. Correspondingly, placing the leaf blade at right angles to sunlight should help warming. Time lapse of leaves on some seedlings and trees indicates their movement in response to sunlight. Measurements of tree leaf angles in different light regimes confirms the operations of the pulvinus behavioural strategy (Muth and Bazzaz 2002). Some 'heliotropic' plants rotate the angle of the leaf continuously with the angle of incidence of sunlight.

5. *Chloroplast movements.* These organelles, concerned with light absorption and photosynthesis, do not assume a fixed position in mesophyll cells. Instead, their position is determined by the cell, and responds to light intensity and probably other environmental signals. Chloroplasts can spread in the cell to maximize light interception and, of course, heat absorption. Alternatively, they can move inside the cell and pile up in positions vertical to the polarity of sunlight reducing light exposure and obviously absorbing less heat from infra-red radiation. This process involves cellular actin and other contractile proteins. It is a feature of self-organization.

The factors helping to warm the leaf to a higher temperature in colder situations are similar

1. Reducing stomatal aperture and stomatal density will decrease evaporative cooling.
2. Moving leaves so that they align directly with the sunlight vector and retain it through the day.
3. Changes in wax composition, and increasing trichome and hair numbers will reduce reflectance and reduce air movement across the leaf by constructing a relatively, static boundary layer. Warmth generated by the leaf itself will be locally retained. Increasing pubescence all over the leaf will also help this process.
4. Increasing the number of leaves on a branch increases the branch boundary layer and decreases heat loss from the leaves by convection. As a consequence canopy temperatures can be increased by 5–9°C, depending on the species involved

(Michaeletz and Johnson 2006; Leuzinger and Korner 2007).

5. Overall branching patterns themselves can help to reduce overlap in the canopy, reduce self-shading, and help warming that become important in some environments (Honda and Fisher 1978).

Leaf characteristics contributing to homeostatic temperature control are all adaptive within several days at the longest and are critical aspects of behaviour

The above leaf parameters can be adaptively modified at different speeds when environmental factors change; they are all excellent examples of phenotypic and cell plasticity. It is presumed and based on present understanding that individual leaves respond to their particular conditions environmental conditions. Self-organization develops from the bottom-up, rather than top-down.

Leaf position, chloroplast movements and stomatal apertures respond within several minutes to various environmental changes (Prichard and Forseth 1988; Willmer and Fricker 1996; Takagi 2003). Cuticular wax composition and structure can be changed within 1–2 days (Skoss 1955; Baker 1971; Jetter and Schaffer 2001). Trichomes can be increased in number even on mature leaves and can develop in a few hours. The numbers of these are all under environmental control (Nagata et al. 1999; Perez-Estrada et al. 2000; Gan et al. 2007).

Leaf shape is well known to be adaptively modified during development (Gurevitch 1992; Tsukaya 2002), although modifications only occur early during leaf development, in a developmental window lasting about 1 day (Smart and Trewavas 1983).

The environmental features to which behavioural adaptation occurs, show considerable similarity. The angle of leaves in plants in forest sites respond within minutes to sudden changes in irradiance (Prichard and Forseth 1988). Temperature is also a critical factor in leaf angle optimizing photosynthetic processes through controlled movement (Fu and Ehleringer 1989). Trichome density increases during dry periods, and is strongly correlated with

temperature and irradiance. Higher irradiance and water stress increases the thickness of the cuticle and, thus, wax deposition (Skoss 1955). Stomatal density on developing leaves is modified by the light regime, the present carbon dioxide concentration, and the current availability of water. Adaptive variations have also been observed in stomatal size (Woodward 1987; Lake et al. 2001; Xu and Zhou 2008). The enormous variations in light, CO_2, and availability of water in wild circumstances potentially influence stomatal numbers. The shape of leaves is also adaptively modified by irradiance, water availability, and temperature. The leaf factors determining potential leaf temperature are clearly in a dynamic state and are adaptively restructured as the environment changes.

Self-organizing characteristics must be the basis of leaf temperature and canopy structures

This short discussion indicates that there are higher orders of control on canopy structure than just leaf area. There will be trade-offs between the need for constant temperatures for photosynthesis, and leaf and chloroplast surface area to provide yield anyway. Many other factors in canopy structure contribute to this homeostasis, leaf shape, leaf number, branch structure, stomatal frequency, root structure, etc. (Helliker and Richter 2008). Since photosynthetic yield will be an important element of fitness, overall canopy structure will thus be subject to selection.

However, the outstanding fact missing is how the overall control is exerted to provide for effective homeostasis. Some form of negative feedback must operate for the whole leaf to provide for effective homeostasis in temperature. Presumably, there must be interaction between trichomes, cuticular wax, leaf position, and stomatal aperture, for example. These features self-organize, so there must be fairly simple rules that govern the interactions between them all. Since it is the process of photosynthesis itself that is the recipient of the control of temperature then a reasonable guess is that by-products of photosynthesis, notably reactive oxygen species might be the coordinating signal. Alternatively, the ubiquitous cytosolic calcium might be the internal signal that sets the processes in train for each individual leaf, but these signals or rules, however, remain currently unknown.

In addition, communicative elements and self-organizing features must be present to account for the overall control of canopy structure, but again, these are also currently unknown. There are exciting challenges here for investigators of this most important phenomenon.

Stomata on one leaf communicate with those on developing leaves: leaf-to-leaf communication

An average mature tree may have well over 100,000 leaves arranged in different positions and experiencing different environments. Is the behaviour of all of these leaves in some way integrated holistically? Holistic integration evidently requires communication between all the leaves. A major insight originated into this problem has started with the recognition that stomatal density on mature leaves actually modifies directly the number of stomata on developing leaves and does so by communication (Lake et al. 2001).

Exposure of developing leaves to CO_2 concentrations, different from ambient CO_2, is known to alter stomatal density on the exposed leaf. With higher CO_2, stomatal density is lower; with lower than ambient CO_2, stomatal density is increased. Instead, in these experiments, Lake et al. (2001) placed cuvettes over mature leaves so that they could be exposed to different concentrations of CO_2. Developing leaves were left in ambient CO_2. When mature leaves were exposed to higher than ambient CO_2, the developing leaves had substantially reduced stomatal densities, as though they, too, had been exposed to higher than ambient CO_2. Similarly, when the mature leaves were shaded, but the developing leaves exposed to normal irradiance, the stomatal density of the developing leaves was, again, substantially reduced, thus mimicking the reduced stomatal density normally observed in shade. The implication is of an integrating signal synthesized by the mature leaves and conveyed to the developing leaf to ensure it is fit for the present environmental circumstances, even though the developing leaf may

not experience it. A self-organizing and integrating mechanism between leaves is at work here. A local stimulus gives rise to a less than local response.

What is communicated to mediate this particular response is unknown, although several hormones have been proposed as candidates, but communication in plants has become very complex. Proteins, nucleic acids, micro- or s-RNAs, polypeptides together with the classical hormones are all possibilities (Lake et al. 2002; Lough and Lucas 2006). The communication pathway in plants contains a multiplicity of signals that mimic in complexity those known to occur in mammalian organisms.

Although leaf-to-leaf stomatal density has been reported, in wild circumstances the communication signals will be modified by signals from other parts of the plant, together with other direct environmental influences. Again, these characteristics must involve a degree of self-organization and, thus, fairly simple rules of interaction. However, the net effect has to resolve itself into optimizing fitness. Similar considerations will be found to apply to root systems, too. Although there is plasticity in the behaviour of individual organs enabling the exploitation of local circumstances better, there is also a behavioural integration into an optimized whole indicating a hierarchy of controlling influences.

There should be no mystery here. Social insect colonies have exactly the same hierarchical characteristics in overall controlling mechanisms. There are direct rules governing organism interactions, but an overall control that stabilizes the colony constructed from these interactions themselves.

Guard cells form a self-organizing network optimizing gas exchange across a leaf

A consistent feature of biological systems is that they are a hierarchical series of networks that self-organize. The complex molecular network inside cells is enclosed by a network formed between specific cells and, in turn, a tissue network of all tissue cells, and thus upwards to the whole plant and populations. The situation is often compared with the well-known Russian dolls; a series of dolls of diminishing size found inside each other.

The internal photosynthetic cells in leaves are surrounded on both sides by an epidermis. Situated in this epidermis are large numbers of guard cell pairs that bound the stomatal aperture. Usually, the density of stomata is higher on the underside than the topside of a leaf. Guard cells control the size of the stomatal aperture size and, thus, manipulate the rates of CO_2 and water vapour transit, into and out of the leaf. Stomatal apertures do respond to changes in a great variety of environmental signals; red light, blue light, CO_2, humidity, abscisic acid, ozone, potassium, and calcium ions to indicate just a few (Willmer and Fricker 1996). The aperture closes from loss of turgor in the two surrounding guard cells. Closure is caused by rapid, massive movements of potassium and chloride ions out from the guard cell vacuole into the adjacent wall. Turgor is regained by active pumping of potassium chloride back into the vacuole, using ATP, that is, cellular energy. Closure can be complete in 10 min.

Complete stomatal closure is unlikely, however, to occur during the daylight hours. Instead, what is observed is that constant monitoring of the ambient conditions, incorporating the signals above, leads to changes in aperture. Thus, the aperture continually fluctuates in size through the day in an attempt to optimize water loss for maximal inward CO_2 flow for photosynthesis. Guard cells have to integrate together the numerous signals they perceive and make essential adjustments to aperture size.

Early studies on guard cell behaviour leant heavily on measurement of the stomatal aperture. Individual apertures were measured on large numbers and the results expressed as an average aperture. When the statistical standard errors of this average were calculated, they were found to be extremely wide. Initially, this result was assumed to be solely individual cell variation. The notion that stomata might communicate with each other was not considered. However, it is now known that these cells also construct a network from the known mechanical or hydraulic connections between adjacent stomata. Guard cell behaviour is also strongly influenced by the surrounding epidermal cells and there are direct influences on aperture from the mesophyll cells communicated by a vapour phase signal (Sibbernsen and Mott 2010; Peak and Mott 2011).

Evidence for communicative interactions between guard cells was uncovered when the behaviour of many thousands of guard cells in intact leaves could be visualized continuously. When leaves were signalled by, e.g. slight water loss, it was observed that, instead of a uniform response to aperture changes, it was extremely patchy with patches constructed from thousands of stomata responding differently in their aperture to others outside the patch (Mott and Buckley 2000; Peak et al. 2004; Mott and Peak 2007). As the signal continued, these patches were observed to be mobile moving across the leaf, could oscillate or disappear, or remain stable for hours, acting clearly as a self-organized collective. The patches exhibit rich, complex dynamics. Patches have been observed in natural conditions and in many species.

Peak et al. (2004) have recognized that the complex behaviour exhibited by patchiness can be simply modelled. The basic theoretical assumption is that an individual stomata acts as a simple cellular automaton; when acting as a collective of thousands, the patch becomes capable of hard problem solving. The cellular automaton is envisaged to be composed of one guard cell connected, and in communication with four others via mechanical and hydraulic connections.

The analysis starts with the state of the central stomata and those to which it is connected. There is no central control in any leaf that determines and directs all cells to behave in an identical manner. Instead, a collective self-organizes as a result of immediate connections within the unit and as a result of information transfer more loosely with others. The patch transfers information around itself. Emergent organization has to develop bottom-up, and does so as a result of the connections throughout the network. Patches develop from slight variations in starting conditions that when amplified by positive feedback help to synchronize the behaviour of local groups of guard cells. Almost certainly, patch formation enables the leaf to compute the optimal gas exchange rate to and from the environment it now experiences. Individual guard cells do not have sufficient information on their own to optimize gas exchange rates. Simple rules thus give rise to quite complex behaviour as found in social insect colonies.

Leaf senescence

The falling leaves, drift by my window. ('Autumn Leaves', Mercer, 1947.)

Leaf senescence is a familiar sight in deciduous trees in autumn, but leaf loss or turnover occurs in evergreens, too, quite often in spring. In many species, it is the leaf that perceives the shortening day length (photoperiod) in autumn, and initiates the familiar loss of chlorophyll and other molecular constituents of the chloroplast, mobilizing the materials back into the branch. While the signal is perceived by the leaf blade, communication of the signal to the base of the petiole initiates the construction of the few layers of cells that form the abscission zone.

Some trees form substantial amounts of red anthocyanin during senescence. The suggested reasons being to signal pests to stay away (particularly aphids) or to stunt local, potentially competitive seedlings by shading during autumn. Detached young leaves placed in darkness and kept moist, mimic the onset and progress of visible senescence, including loss of chlorophyll and proteins, with relevant amino acids being mobilized into the leaf vascular tissue. In some isolated leaves, anthocyanins are synthesized too. Loss of information arriving through the vascular system from the stem must be the signal. Up to a certain stage of development, senescence can be reversed if conditions change. In plants, like tobacco, the lower (shaded) leaves, frequently senesce. Remove the stem above these leaves and they re-green quickly. Clearly, this regeneration of the leaf has limits beyond which reversal is no longer possible. Probably, the sealing of the vascular tissue is crucial. The signals for regreening are possibly hormonal using cytokinins synthesized in root tissues, but this is probably simplistic—many signals must be involved.

Leaf senescence is a coordinated molecular process and the recovery of the materials is considered important for fitness (Lim et al. 2007). Numerous factors can induce premature senescence and leaf loss including nutrient deprivation, ultraviolet light, pest damage, drought, or shading. In certain environmental conditions, when lower leaves are slightly shaded, they are lost first and the resources mobilized back into the adult are used to provision the upper leaves to continue growth. Loss of leaf structure is initiated first in various patches within the leaf, which then spread outwards. The mesophyll cells are the first to be dissimulated. Leaf senescence is an example of programmed cell death, but has the characteristics of contagion from an initial point.

References

Addicott, F.T. (1982). *Abscission*. University of California Press, Berkeley, CA.

Arber, A. (1950). *The natural philosophy of plant form*. Cambridge University Press, Cambridge.

Baker, E.A. (1971). The influence of environment on leaf wax development in *Brassica oleracea*. *New Phytologist*, **73**, 955–966.

Clare, J. (1835). Water lilies. In Maguire, S., ed. *Flora poetica: the Chatto book of botanical verse* (2001). Chatto and Windus, London.

Darwin, C. (1880). *The movements of plants*. John Murray, London.

Finlayson, S.A., Reddy, S.K., Kebrom, T.H., and Casal, J.J. (2010). Phytochrome regulation of branching in *Arabidopsis*. *Plant Physiology*, **152**, 1914–1927.

Fu, Q.A., and Ehleringer, J.R. (1989). Heliotropic movements in common beans controlled by air temperature. *Plant Physiology*, **91**, 1162–1167.

Gan, Y., Yu, H., Peng, J., and Broun, P. (2007). Genetic and molecular regulation by DELLA proteins of trichome development in *Arabidopsis*. *Plant Physiology*, **145**, 1031–1042.

Givnish, T.J. (1988). Adaptation to sun and shade: a whole plant perspective. *Australian Journal of Plant Physiology*, **15**, 63–92.

Grant, R.H., Heisler, G.M., Gao, W., and Jenks, M. (2003). Ultraviolet leaf reflectance of common urban trees and the prediction of reflectance from leaf surface characteristics. *Agricultural and Forest Meteorology*, **120**, 127–139.

Gurevitch, J. (1992). Sources of variation in leaf shape among two populations of *Achillea lanulosa*. *Genetics*, **130**, 385–394.

Helliker, B.R., and Richter, S.L. (2008). Subtropical to boreal convergence of tree leaf temperatures. *Nature*, **454**, 511–514.

Honda, H., and Fisher, J.B. (1978). Tree branch angle maximising effective leaf area. *Science*, **199**, 888–889.

Jetter, R., and Schaffer, S. (2001). Chemical composition of the *Prunus laurocerasus* leaf surface. Dynamic changes of the epicuticular wax film during leaf development. *Plant Physiology*, **126**, 1725–1737.

Lake, J.A., Quick, W.P., Beerling, D.J., and Woodward, F.I. (2001). Signals from mature to new leaves. *Nature*, **411**, 154.

Lake, J.A., Woodward, F.I., and Quick, W.P. (2002). Long distance CO_2 signalling in plant. *Journal of Experimental Botany*, **53**, 183–193.

Leuzinger, S., and Korner, C. (2007). Tree species diversity affects canopy leaf temperature in a mature temperate forest. *Agricultural and Forest Meteorology*, **146**, 29–37.

Lichtenthaler, H.K., Buschmann, C., Doll, M., Fietz, H-J., Bach, T., Kozel, U., and 2 others (1981). Photosynthetic activity, chloroplast ultrastructure, and leaf characteristics of high-light and low-light plants and of sun and shade leaves. *Photosynthesis Research*, **2**, 115–141.

Lim, P.O., Kim, H.J., and Nam, H.G. (2007). Leaf senescence. *Annual Review of Plant Biology*, **58**, 115–136.

Lough, T.J., and Lucas, W.J. (2006). Integrative plant biology: role of phloem long distance macromolecular trafficking. *Annual Review of Plant Biology*, **57**, 203–232.

Mercer, J. (1947). Autumn leaves (song). Available at: http://en.wikipedia.org/wiki/Autumn_leaves_(song)

Michaeletz, S.T., and Johnson, E.A. (2006). Foliage influences forced convection heat transfer in conifer branches and buds. *New Phytologist*, **170**, 87–98.

Monsi, M., Uchijima, Z., and Oikawa, T. (1973). Structure of foliage canopies and photosynthesis. *Annual Review of Ecology and Systematics*, **4**, 301–327.

Mott, K.A., and Buckley, T.N. (2000). Patchy stomatal conductance: emergent collective behaviour of stomata. *Trends in Plant Science*, **5**, 258–262.

Mott, K.A., and Peak, D. (2007). Stomatal patchiness and task performing networks. *Annals of Botany*, **99**, 219–226.

Muth, C. C., and Bazzaz, F.A. (2002). Tree seedling canopy responses to conflicting photosensory cues. *Oecologia*, **132**, 197–204.

Nagata, T., Todokiri, S., Hayashi, T., Shibata, Y., Mori, M., Kanegae, H., and 1 other (1999). γ-Radiation induces leaf trichome formation in Arabidopsis. *Plant Physiology*, **120**, 113–120.

Peak, D., and Mott, K.A. (2011). A new vapour–phase mechanism for stomatal responses to humidity and temperature. *Plant Cell and Environment*, **34**, 162–178.

Peak, D., West, J.D., Messinger, S.M., and Mott, K.A. (2004). Evidence for complex, collective dynamics and emergent distributed computation in plants. *Proceedings of the National Academy of Sciences USA*, **101**, 918–922.

Pearcy, R.W., and Sims, D.A. (1994). Photosynthetic acclimation to changing light environments: scaling from the leaf to the whole plant. In Caldwell, M.M., and Pearcy, R.W., eds, *Exploitation of environmental heterogeneity by plants*, pp. 145–175. Academic Press, New York.

Perez-Estrada, L.B., Cano-Santana, Z., and Oyama, K. (2000). Variation in leaf trichomes of *Wigandia urens*: environmental factors and physiological consequences. *Tree Physiology*, **20**, 629–632.

Pritchard, J.M., and Forseth, I.N. (1988). Rapid leaf movement, microclimate and water relations of two temperate legumes in three contrasting habitats. *American Journal of Botany*, **75**, 1201–1211.

Reddy, S.K., Holalu, S.V., Casal, J.J., and Finlayson, S.A. (2013). Abscisic acid regulates axillary bud outgrowth responses to the ratio of Red to Far Red light. *Plant Physiology*, **163**, 1047–1058.

Roden, J.S., Lin, G., and Ehleringer, J.R. (2000). A mechanistic model for interpretation of hydrogen and oxygen isotope ratios in tree ring cellulose. *Geochimica et Geocosmica Acta*, **64**, 21–35.

Sibbernsen, E., and Mott, K.A. (2010). Stomatal responses to flooding of the intercellular air spaces suggest a vapour phase signal between the mesophyll and the guard cells. *Plant Physiology*, **153**, 1435–1442.

Skoss, J.D. (1955). Structure and composition of the plant cuticle in relation to environmental factors and permeability. *Botanical Gazette*, **117**, 55–72.

Smart, C.C., and Trewavas, A.J. (1983). Abscisic acid-induced turion development in *Spirodela polyrrhiza*. 1. Production and development of the turion. *Plant Cell and Environment*, **6**, 507–514.

Takagi, S. (2003). Actin-based, photo-orientation movement of chloroplasts in plant cells. *Journal of Experimental Biology*, **206**, 1963–1969.

Tsukaya, H. (2002). The leaf index: heteroblasty, natural variation and the genetic control of polar processes of leaf expansion. *Plant and Cell Physiology*, **43**, 372–378.

Willmer, C., and Fricker, M. (1996). *Stomata*, 2nd edn. Chapman and Hall, London.

Woodward, F.I. (1987). Stomatal numbers are sensitive to increases in CO_2 from pre-industrial levels. *Nature*, **327**, 617–618.

Xu, Z., and Zhou, G. (2008). Responses of leaf stomatal density to water status and its relationship with photosynthesis in a grass. *Journal of Experimental Botany*, **59**, 3317–3325.

Yamada, T., Okada, T., Abdullah, M., Awang, M., and Furukawa, A. (2000). The leaf development process and its significance for reducing self-shading of a tropical pioneer tree species. *Oecologia*, **125**, 476–482.

CHAPTER 13

Self-organization and behaviour in root systems

Plants search for food as if they had eyes.

(Justus von Liebig, quoted in Weaver 1926)

↺ Summary

The complexity of the soil structure is described and followed by a brief consideration of the failings of the concept of limiting factors in growth. The difficulties of observing root system behaviour are indicated. As the title quotation indicates, roots follow gradients of resources and proliferate where they find them. Thus, roots construct some kind of image of their root environment. The presence of a biological niche is most clearly indicated by root behaviour and the optimal niche is potentially recognized. Some basic root patterns are introduced including plants, like corn that clearly occupy space at first, by sending out horizontal roots that eventually grow vertically. The phenotypic responses to water shortage result in root proliferation that increases the search for water. Proliferation of root systems, mainly lateral roots, in patches rich with N and P is commonly observed, but does not occur with patches of K that are equally required. It is concluded that when this proliferation happens, it is as much to deny the resources to other competitor plants as increased uptake. Finally, it is indicated that soil space itself might be a resource in its own right. Auto-inhibition between roots might help construct a root system that spreads itself throughout the available soil.

Introduction

The theme highlighted in this book concerns the behaviour of angiosperm plants in effectively wild circumstances. It is in these situations that plants face the enormous variety of environmental problems that must be solved if they are to attempt to reach the ultimate and rarely achievable goal of optimal fitness. The aim is, of course, to provide the growing parent plant with the maximal resources to provision the maximal number of seeds. In these situations, the requirements to solve unexpected problems must elicit intelligent behaviour, i.e. learning and memory. The food to which Liebig refers in the title is at its most simple, minerals and water for the root system, and light for the shoot.

Liebig was the discoverer of the role of minerals in plant growth.

The complexity of the environmental soil situation indicates the problem for root systems

The root system of wild plants is rarely, if ever, examined for its behaviour. Indeed, the whole process is, of course, extremely difficult to do. Soil is the standard medium in which most plants root. Soils are complex and compositionally variable across the world, but a basic property is that they consist of particulate materials, mixtures of clay (fine particles of aluminium (Al) silicates, silica as sand, stones and gravel, and organic material composed of both decaying organic matter from dead plants, roots, and another portion containing living organisms, bacteria, fungi, and invertebrates). There is also substantial, but variable amounts of gas in-between the particles. The gaseous composition varies from atmospheric concentrations very near the surface, to an atmosphere with perhaps only 10% oxygen, higher levels of carbon dioxide than atmospheric, and other root-modifying gases like ethylene and nitrous oxide deeper in the soil. Light will penetrate only the very upper layers and temperature clines are also expected. Clay regions are composed of small particles and are difficult to penetrate, but on the other hand, they do hold water and minerals better. Water is a vital element, roots need some moisture for growth, but again, the amounts are dependent on the vagaries of climate and weather, and are only crudely predictable on a fine scale. All these soil conditions are sensed because roots change their behaviour when they are perceived.

Resources are patchily distributed

The soil is a particulate structure—ions, water, and gases can therefore diffuse only slowly. Local variation caused by burrowing animals, earth worms, other invertebrates, and microbes, and uneven depositions of dead organisms on the surface, rainfall and uneven soil surface generates, inevitably, a patchiness in the required resources for growth. Growing roots will meet a variety of different and unpredictable soil experiences because seeds can only germinate and grow where they are finally deposited. The degree of success with which any individual root or root system can solve its experienced problems, the greater its contribution to the ultimate goal of any plant, which is to optimize fitness. The accumulation of mineral resources is required not only for growth, but also to provision the carriers of the next generation, the newly-forming seeds. The greater the level of stored resources, the greater the potential fitness of the parent plants.

One crucial property governs much of root behaviour. Both N and K, but not P, are mobile ions in the soil. On a mobility scale in which water is 10, N is 10, K is 3, and P is 1. Different problem solving

is required for each of these vital materials. Search mechanisms are essential, as is the ability to follow detected gradients. The assumption when following a gradient is that there must be exploitable material at the end. Such behaviour thus requires an active assessment of a likely future.

Patchiness of resources requires plasticity in development. Shoot plasticity in response to environmental variation has been recorded for centuries (see references in Turkington and Aarssen 1984). Because the plant acts as a self-organized, but integrated structure, modification of either root or shoot, in turn modifies the growth and development of the other. Soil moisture distributions, serpentine soils, heavy metals including toxic Al, proportions of sandstone in parent material, stones, N, P, K, and other mineral distribution, herbivory by animals and nematodes, mutualistic and parasitical microbes, wind sway, all specifically affect root development and generate essential plasticity in development.

However, along with these signals, the growing plant deals with plant competition. The local soil must be occupied before others, and resources removed first to try and reduce subsequent competition. Search mechanisms must operate, and spread outwards from the shoot and the root to locate patchily distributed resources.

Although the soil is relatively static compared with the atmosphere above ground, there is still a dynamic on a daily basis, particularly as regards water and N. As other plants and organisms grow, develop, and metabolize, the root system must change in concert. However, above all, the root must also provide anchorage to enable the shoot to grow in a reasonably upright state.

Complexity in environmental interactions on growth: can there ever be an optimum environment?

My own estimate suggests that any root system is assessing at any one time some 20 or so obvious signals. Some of these necessitate estimates of the probable future conditions that are to be experienced because slow phenotypic responses mean that the conditions may have changed by the time the phenotypic change is instituted.

Limiting constituents for growth rates

Justus von Liebig (1803–1873) was one of the first scientists to apply evidence-based research to agriculture. His unique agricultural contributions were the identification of N as a basis for the first fertilizer combination, and for some appreciation of the nitrogen cycle. He also developed the law of the minimum, i.e. plant growth rates are dependent on the element least available, a law of limiting constraint.

Whether any element limits growth, however, depends on the balance of everything else (e.g. light, other minerals, water, etc.) that affects growth and development. The dose response effect of any individual mineral, for example, is non-linear, indicating the rapid onset of constraint for other materials required for growth. However, what is apparently defined agriculturally as deficient is relative to all the other minerals needed for growth. Keeping the 'deficient' mineral constant and changing the others eliminates apparent deficiency (Trewavas 1986). The suggestion is of a kind of balance in cellular metabolism that cannot tolerate gross differences between the minerals plants need for growth.

In 1937, White introduced the simple concept of balanced growth. He examined the growth of *Lemna minor* in media of different, but defined composition and in varying light conditions. He measured many simple criteria of good growth, chlorophyll content, protein, starch, frond number, fresh weight increase, etc. The necessity for balance could be clearly observed. For example, in media of low N, the best growth that provided balance between all the constituents measured was only found in low light. If he increased light intensity, growth was actually reduced. It would seem this time that an unequal provision of minerals and light distorts internal metabolism. An excess of light against necessary minerals leads to starch accumulation and other carbon-rich compounds like oxalate. Similarly, the concept of balance must apply to the mineral constituents provided or found in the soil.

These observations raise certain difficulties for plants in the wild. It is unlikely that anywhere near optimal amounts of light or the balance of minerals will ever be experienced. So many factors influence growth, resource accumulation, and thus final seed yield, that it becomes unlikely that wild plants can experience the optimal conditions. Self-organization ensures adjustments in phenotype and metabolism to best accommodate the situations as they arise. The seed yield of any individual must then reflect the plasticity with which each plants accommodates the uncertainty of what is experienced. Each plant is a system of interconnected tissues and connections with its environment, too. That, perhaps, is the real individual.

Root behaviour is difficult to observe, but is as complex as those of shoots: the root niche

The great difficulty with investigations of plant behaviour is that half of it occurs below ground and, thus, is largely invisible. Methods for examining the behaviour of the developing root system are quite limited. The problems with most of them are outlined by Mairhofer et al. (2012). These authors have used X-ray tomography to provide a series of images of plant roots growing in soil. Justifiably, this is a major, but expensive breakthrough in being able to monitor root behaviour in natural circumstances. However, these are early days with this technology.

Much root system structure can be deduced from the material published in the two books by Weaver (1926) and Weaver and Bruner (1927). Both books are free and available on the web. The methods used to investigate root structure were largely brute force. A trench several metres deep was opened up next to the plant in question and by careful removal of the soil with small picks, the root systems were slowly exposed. Drawings were then made and a grid placed on the drawing to indicate size.

These two books contain a wealth of information about root systems in different circumstances and on many species, but are rarely referred to. I have included a number of the drawings since they illustrate some basic aspects of plant behaviour underground. These are, of course, static pictures, lacking the dynamic we might expect from behaviour and the behavioural reasons for the structure have to be inferred. Furthermore, they are two-dimensional drawings, whereas a root system grows in three dimensions. Weaver had no way of projecting three dimensions at the time, but accepting those limitations, the drawings in Figure 13.1(a–d) illustrate some basic adaptive properties.

Figure 13.1(a) shows a month-old corn seedling and indicates that in this plant, all the early roots are near horizontal in growth, rather than vertical. Only later do some of these change direction and become vertical as shown in a 2-month-old corn plant (Figure 13.1(b)).

This behaviour is quite common in different species. The mechanism of this turn-down is not known. Is it a developmental switch requiring a certain number of cell divisions in the meristem; is it an assessment of distance from the shoot; or does it result from a change in the perception of the gravity signal? (The former can be rejected based on the root patterns in Figure 13.4.) This pattern of growth makes adaptive sense because it enables greater exploration of the local soil and its resource exploitation. It also increases anchorage ability of the shoot. Perhaps, most crucially, it occupies soil space before a potential competitor.

Figure 13.1(c) shows the root system of *Liatris punctate* (blazing star). Like many such root profiles

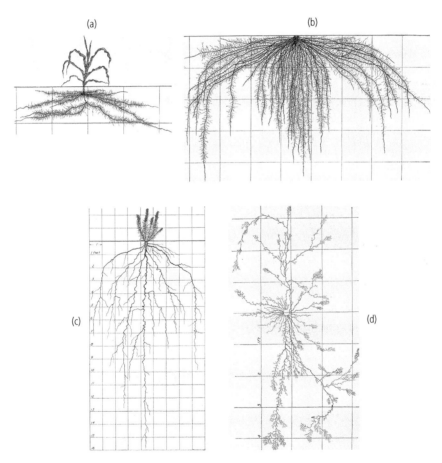

Figure 13.1 (a,b) Root systems of corn. (a) A corn plant at 5 weeks old. (b) A corn plant at 8 weeks old. The scale is the horizontal and vertical lines, and represent distances in feet. Roots are originally near horizontal, but gravitropically sensitive. By 8 weeks many have started to grow downwards and new secondary roots have appeared to fill in the middle space. Taken from Weaver 1926. (c,d). Branch roots possess separation, inhibitory-style and spatial 3D mechanisms. Scale bars are one foot. (c) Root system of Liatris punctata. Note depth penetration of 17 feet and how branch roots grow away from each other. (d). Top-down view of Opuntia camanchica. These roots run about an inch below the surface, implying a spatial recognition mechanism of depth. Opuntia competes with shallow grasses for rain showers so spread is essential. Note terminal proliferation and spread.

produced by Weaver, there are clear indications that the individual roots grow separately and almost away from each other. Do these root structures imply some kind of self-sensing and inhibitory mechanisms? If so, it is rarely, if ever, investigated. Figure 13.1(d) shows a top-down picture of roots of *Opuntia camanchica*. These roots are normally only about a few centimetres in depth, but spread over a wide area and terminate in lateral proliferation. Their supposed function is to gather rainwater fast, since they compete with grasses, but again, note the pattern of root spread. Is this auto-inhibition of root growth?

The construction of a root niche

The strategy of a developing root system is not only to forage for the necessary resources of water and minerals (Hutchings and Kroon 1994), but to create an equitable soil environment for its root systems to improve survival. This is behaviour and creates a specific environment, probably specific to the individual. It is called a niche and is constructed by obvious self-organization.

Like many organisms, plants help construct their own biological niche. The niche is more obvious and consistent for roots than shoots, because the environmental parameters of soil are a good deal more constant. The root niche is a complex and a dynamical structure. As the root grows through soil, it modifies the surrounding soil that, in turn, feeds back to modify further growth. The exchange of information between soil and root become effectively circular in character. What happens in the root has knock-on effects for the shoot, too. Thus, the niche, being individual in character, increases the distance between the genome and natural selection.

How roots construct the soil niche

From the earliest germination times, the root normally penetrates the soil. As it continues through growth, the tip secretes mucilage, various proteins, and chemicals. These chemicals are sugars, polysaccharides that act as mucilage and other mucilage-like compounds, amino acids, aromatic and aliphatic acids, fatty acids, sterols, phenolics, other secondary products, plant growth regulators,

and secondary metabolites (Badri et al. 2009). Enzymes are secreted, too. Among the enzymes are phosphatases that help release phosphate from organic forms, proteases and peptidases, chitinases, amylases, and invertases. Additional enzymes are released when root hairs die and their cellular contents leak into the soil.

Lateral roots are initiated by cell divisions in pericycle cells inside the root. Continued growth of the primordial lateral root requires digestion of the mature root cell walls ahead of them until they break through the epidermis of the main root. A number of digestive enzymes including cellulases will then be released. These enzymes together with associated microbes, often of specific classes of bacteria, help breakdown soil carbon-containing compounds, releasing carbon dioxide that is recycled through photosynthesis. Without that soil carbon breakdown, atmospheric carbon dioxide would probably run out within a decade (Priem 1998). Phosphate in soil is normally present in an insoluble form, precipitated by salts of calcium, iron (Fe), and Al. Numerous acids, like citrate, are secreted by roots to help chelate and release free soluble phosphates into the soil (Shen et al. 2011). By the time these secretions have acted, the subsequent root hairs absorb the released phosphate using a mixture of channels and transporters.

Other minerals and water are also absorbed by the root hairs. Typically, there is a shell of depletion of these resources around the root (Richardson and Simpson 2011). The typical root hair is a single cell, growing up to a centimetre in length and ephemeral in the extreme, maybe only lasting a week. Hairs are readily replenished and they greatly increase the root surface area for absorption. Once dead, the remains contribute to the soil structure. The root tip sloughs off cells as well, which contribute. Lateral roots penetrate the soil at a more horizontal angle and increase exploration and soil modification. According to environmental conditions there may be variable degrees of lateral root formation, each in turn modifying its local environment and releasing material as dying root hairs and lateral roots die off, too. Roots respire and use up oxygen, as do microbes. Soil oxygen is 10% or lower compared with the 20% above ground. Ethylene, evolved from both roots and microbes, accumulates in the soil. This plant hormone, in turn, modifies the extent of lateral root formation and can change the internal construction of roots making them aerenchymatous. Aerenchyma is characterized by large airspaces between many cells, while retaining the overall root structure. In flooded conditions, aerenchyma forms readily in roots. Channels are thus constructed throughout the root, through which air can be drawn down from the surface.

The root niche also encompasses many other organisms: interactions and conversations are very complex

There is a very complex chemical dialogue of growing roots with other soil organisms. The zone adjacent to the root surface is termed the rhizosphere, contains numerous microbes and fungi, and characterizes the zone of mineral depletion. Mutualistic associations form with beneficial bacteria, fungi, endophytes, and plant growth-promoting rhizobacteria. Parasitic interactions form with other plants, pathogenic microbes, and invertebrate herbivores.

Mutualistic associations are formed with diverse microbial genera. The molecular specifics of the recognition conversation between five different microbe species and the plant root have been described. More will surely appear with research (Badri et al. 2009). As a result of secretion of specific pheromones by the growing root, some microbes, termed endophytes, are attracted to the root. These microbes are able to swim through cracks that temporarily develop when lateral roots break through the epidermis. Endophytes can either fix nitrogen and may be rhizobial bacteria, as in legume symbiosis. They can also synthesize root growth regulators, or alter sugar-sensing mechanisms to mutual benefit. Growth regulators released by these organisms, can increase lateral root production, thus increasing numbers of cracks in the root through which additional microbes can enter. Endophytes live in the spaces between root cells, sometimes in cells, can move through young plants, and can also be found inside leaves, presumably having moved there from the root. Some also help to defeat pathogens that have entered.

Other bacteria (ectophytes) also generally colonize the outside of the root attracted by aliphatic acid signals secreted by growing roots. Sometimes, some of these bacteria may enter available root cracks, but many remain near or on the root surface. There are free-living rhizobia that may adhere to the root surface only.

However, the formation of the developing niche is dependent on probably 1000 other bacterial species, many of which participate in the nitrogen cycle or release phosphate from insoluble materials, a process called mineralization. By the provision of many secreted compounds, bacterial growth will be enhanced, and the plant root benefits by acquiring nitrate and ammonium ions released from these microbes. Because individual microbe species interact with each other in the compounds they use for growth and those they secrete, the process is a system that generates emergent properties, i.e. properties greater than the sum of the parts (Addiscott 2010). There is also competition between free-living microbes and between roots containing mycorrhizal symbionts for nitrogenous compounds that contribute to this complex system. Kaye and Hart (1997) list a number of amino acids and proteins that these symbionts are known to sequester.

Signals like strigolactone and flavonoids are secreted by roots that are clear pheromones, attracting both mycorrhizal fungi and swimming bacteria. The important fungi are the mycorrhizae that live in a symbiotic relationship with the root, helping to gain mainly potassium (K) and phosphate (P) for the plant and, in turn, receiving carbohydrates for their own growth (Parniske 2008; Smith and Read 2008). Eighty per cent of angiosperms form mycorrhizal collaborations. Water, zinc, and copper are also provided by the fungus and N in small amounts.

Outside the root, the mycorrhizae extend over enormous distances into the soil, forming a network involving other plant roots and hyphae, potentially the size of a wood and designated the 'wood-wide web' (Whitfield 2007). The root niche then extends well beyond the physical root structure. Another 4000 plant species actually parasitize the mycorrhizal network of others, gaining from the fungus the nutrients it has acquired from its host plants. Thus, some mature plants indirectly donate some of their photosynthate to young seedlings and orchids, e.g. under the forest canopy. Recent research suggests that the hyphal network also acts to communicate disease attack from one plant to its adjacent neighbour, thus enabling the neighbour to adopt a defence stance prior to infection (Song et al. 2010).

There are also strong indications that roots can secrete chemicals that inhibit the growth of roots of nearby plants and are used to distinguish its own roots from those of competitors. Evidence that plants are territorial has appeared. They guard their territory against competitors by behavioural changes and this is discussed in Chapter 18. There is also evidence that plants have preferences to be adjacent to other specific species that may be complementary in their resource requirements or symbionts.

There is a shoot niche, too

For the germinating shoot, the phenotype is dependent on the surroundings into which it grows. Plants can sense nearby vegetation by the detection of far red light and assume a particular kind of shoot structure with elongated stem and minimal numbers of leaves. If it is in clear soil, then the production of leaves shades the soil below. By shading, the humidity of the soil surface is increased and transpiration, mostly from the underside of the leaf adds to this. Shading also reduces soil temperature in sunlight and decreases wind speeds near the surface. As the shoot continues to grow, subsequent leaves may partially shade those below, and the reduced wind speed reduces the mixing of gases permitting areas of reduced carbon dioxide and higher oxygen. If leaves underneath the primary canopy are shed, they add nutrients to the soil and encourage surface roots where much immobilized phosphate is located. As the plant continues to grow, it modifies the light environment around for other plants. The annual loss of deciduous leaves or needles shades the soil, providing better conditions for germination, as well as returning minerals to the soil by decay or by ingestion by soil organisms that produce free nitrate and phosphate, in turn, for plant roots.

Conclusion on the plant niche

The plant niche is an extremely complex environment, contingently constructed using self-organization to optimize its nature and ensure temporary stability, and thus robustness. Is there a memory of the niche embedded somewhere inside the plant, which dictates what the optimum should look like or is it just a reactive structure (Trewavas 2003)? Currently, information favours the latter, but presumably conversations have some kind of prior specificity controlled by the plant. It may simply be a mixture of serendipity and knowledge that controls the niche, but the niche is an additional environmental feature whose contribution to fitness can only be guessed. This, together with the equally contingent and stochastic nature of the plant growth position, reinforces the difficulty. Common views of phenotypic plasticity simply ignore that of the much greater self-organization that develops below ground.

The niche is, of course, only one factor in the life cycle, which must in some way become the ultimate target of selection and crudely assessed as seed number. Can we envisage how the system self-organizes? The best way to view the complexity of the environment and the resulting accommodation of the plant is as a topological surface consisting of hills and valleys that are continually changing in shape and size as the environment alters. Surfaces constructed from just two environmental parameters have been published (Bazzaz 1996, p.91). What the surface would look like with 20 interacting signals or thousands more niche constituents cannot be conceived.

Is there a direct mapping one-to-one of this complex topological surface onto the molecular network and cells of the plant, leading to a reactive counterbalance by the plant itself? Would the external environmental network be matched in shape and form, the hills and valleys that would be present by the internal networks that construct the plant itself? Does one environmental network map onto an equivalent cellular network that compensates by manipulating itself to a predetermined structure? Mapping the internal and external networks in this way, Griffin (1976) described as awareness.

Other organisms contribute strongly to the root niche and thus selection must encompass these as well. If these organisms are not present, or present in only small numbers, then the individual plant, no matter its genotype, faces severe competitive difficulties with individuals that construct a full-blown root niche. A symbiotic arrangement will also be advantageous.

From this short discussion, it can be seen that it is the individual plant plus its capacity to form these relationships that becomes one agent of selection. The individual plant can be seen as a central focus of connections with many different facets of environment and other organisms and it is that upon which individual fitness is strongly based as well as the contingent factors in reproduction. Only at a population level can selection have more meaning. And yet Darwin was sure that meaningful selection took place at the individual level.

Self-organization constructs the plant phenotype to patchiness of water and minerals in the soil

Direct evidence for soil patchiness

Resources of water and minerals are patchily distributed in natural and even in agricultural soils. Although such uneven distributions seem, in some senses, obvious, actual measurements are rare. Direct measurements of soil patchiness for nitrate, ammonium, phosphate, and K were made in a small area in a US steppe region by simply sampling for these minerals along a line. Two to three orders of magnitude variation were recorded in the nitrogenous material, but only about an order of magnitude for P and K (Jackson and Caldwell 1993). These results were confirmed in measurements made at several times over a season and including measurements of soil moisture (Ryel et al. 1996). Within the span of one root system of a single plant, 10-fold variations in the nitrogenous compounds were observed, but less in P and K. There was substantial variation in these minerals throughout the season.

Root phenotypic change to water status

Growing plants sense their status as regards water availability and when a threshold is crossed, root proliferation is greatly increased. The effects of water, or lack of it, are illustrated in Figure 13.2(a,b), using corn plants of the same age. The dry soil type is indicated by Figure 13.2(a) and in a fully irrigated soil in Figure 13.2(b). The difference in proliferation

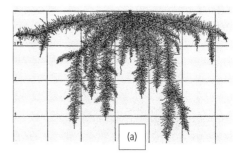

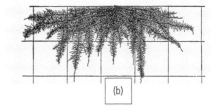

Figure 13.2 (a,b) Root systems of corn. The figures show 8-week-old plants grown either in dry land conditions (a) or in well-irrigated soil (b). Scale bars are in feet. Notice increased search for moisture by increased depth, but solubility and movement of minerals, and any symbiont establishment will also depend on moist soil. Taken from Weaver (1926).

is obvious and suggests either increased exploration or increased surface area for water uptake. 'They search for water as if they had eyes'?

Some plants store water in their stems, particularly those that grow in relatively dry climatic conditions. The sensing of water status has, in the past, been claimed to be located either in root or shoot. The most probable scenario is that both are involved.

A variety of mechanisms whereby water status is sensed and acted upon have been highlighted in a diverse literature. These mechanisms include a loss of turgor, changes in plasma membrane fluidity, changes in water activity, or protein–protein and protein lipid interactions (Chaves et al. 2003). To these can be added assessment of transit rates of water across aquaporins (plasma membrane-located water channels) and/or subtle changes in cytoplasmic gel structure and structured water (Trewavas 2009, 2012).

In reality, reliability in signalling is far more likely to be accurate if several cellular and tissue events contribute. Single signals are often noisy and corrupted in transmission. Several sensing locations will make for greater reliability and, thus, robustness. It is not necessary that the signals appear at the same time or, if they do, that the transduction mechanism operate at the same speed, because many transduction chains overlap and integrate giving rise to cross-talk.

One consequence of drought conditions is the accumulation of the plant hormone abscisic acid, which has multiple effects, but particularly on the diversion of carbohydrate away from shoot growth and towards root growth. Stomatal aperture can be diminished by abscisic acid, helping conservation of water, but reducing CO_2 in leaf flux and fixation to carbohydrate. Abscisic acid can be synthesized by both root and shoot tissues, but changes in other hormones and metabolites will undoubtedly accompany the process, and help construct the best decision to optimize survival and reconstruct the growth pattern.

Proliferation of roots in patches of N and P

The other primary resource to be obtained from the soil are minerals, the major ones being N (either as nitrate or ammonium), P, K, and a host of minor ones, chloride, zinc, copper, etc. It has been known probably for several centuries that roots of many, but not all, angiosperm plants proliferate in regions of the soil containing higher concentrations of minerals (Weaver 1926). Figure 13.3(a,b) shows, respectively, sugar beet and *Kuhnia glutinosa* (false boneset) growing through regions of clay and sand, and proliferating specifically in the regions of clay where a greater supply of minerals is probably present. However, other features of the soil environment may be responsible for the observed proliferation.

More recent demonstrations of this apparent behavioural adaptation were published in 1975 in which layers enriched with N, P, or K were tested (Drew 1975). [However, Weaver (1926) indicates that this was first reported in 1862 and perhaps reference to this paper, actually in German, would represent scientific justice.] Proliferation of lateral roots and increases in their length were observed with defined layers of N (both nitrate and ammonium ions) and P, but not K. Furthermore, despite

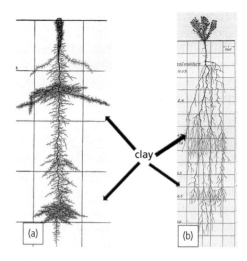

Figure 13.3 (a,b) Probable impact of mineral layers on lateral root proliferation. Root systems of sugar beet (a) and false boneset (b) growing through sand, and then layers of clay. Proliferation in clay is suggested by Weaver (1926) as due to higher mineral content. Weaver reports that proliferation in layers enriched in minerals were first reported in 1862, although commonly assumed to be recent.

lateral root proliferation, the growth of the main axis (the so-called tap root) remained unaffected. So the effects were specific to one tissue, rather than the whole root growth.

One surprising feature is that provision of normal N or P in soil layers to one-third, or even less, of a root system has little effect on overall shoot growth, compared with those in which the minerals are provided to the whole root system (Caldwell 1994). The suspicion is that transporter mechanisms up-regulate to increase mineral supplies to the shoot. Localized applications of even higher P concentrations led to the estimate that only 4% of the root systems need be exposed to obtain normal shoot growth. In part, this ability reflects metabolic adaptations—increased transporter activity, increased P recycling, and the greater involvement of pyrophosphatases in energy production (Yang et al. 2007; Plaxton and Tran 2011). In a parallel fashion, plants with half of their roots in dry soil showed almost no diminution of growth compared with controls with all their roots in well-watered soil (Zhang and Kirkham 1995). Clearly, higher plants have strong adaptive features, which compensate for deficiencies in different areas of the soil, as would be expected when resources are patchily distributed.

However, when comparisons were made between many different plant species, no clear relationship emerged between mineral uptake and lateral root proliferation (Caldwell 1994; Robinson 1994). Crop plants can exhibit frenetic proliferation of laterals in patches of N or P. These plants are characterized by high growth rates, high nutrient demand, and often an annual habit. The phenotypic effect on lateral root proliferation is enhanced when the parent plant is already deficient in N or P. Similar results were found for weeds like *Arabidopsis*. This plant has a 6-week life cycle and is a pioneer species, occupying bare ground in the wild, opened up by falling trees in a forest, but other species did not share these characteristics and, consequently, failed to respond to local heterogeneity in N by evident proliferation, or if they did, it was imprecise or much weaker in its positioning of proliferation (Fitter 1994). Plants in this latter group were usually genetically slow growers.

The foraging response to minerals is obviously confined to lateral roots, but the rest of the plant is involved. In the case of P, shoot signals in the form of transportable micro-RNAs are necessary to permit the essential changes in lateral root proliferation and the same seems to be the case with nitrate N (Hammond and White 2011; Ruffel et al. 2011). Recent studies have clarified an intimate relationship between nitrate and hormonal relations that help provide some understanding about phenotypic change (Krouk et al. 2011). Both N and P receptors sense the actual nitrate and phosphate molecules, rather than metabolized versions, and in the case of N (nitrate), a direct relationship has been found that results in modification of auxin transport.

Cells in the root cap sense environmental phosphate levels

Phosphate is an important element in plant nutrition and deficiency leads to substantive changes in the expression of thousands of genes (Calderon-Vazquez et al. 2011). When the root tip senses that the soil it is about to enter is low in phosphate, numerous adaptive changes in the phenotype are initiated. The growth of the main root axis is inhibited and may stop completely. The numbers of root hairs are increased and they assume a much greater

length. Furthermore, there is a proliferation of lateral roots originating from the pericycle. These can be intense in some species, with tertiary laterals forming on secondary laterals, the so-called cluster roots (Cheng et al. 2011). The surface area of the root enabling phosphate uptake is greatly increased, something that will benefit the uptake of other ions, such as Fe and K. Secretion is altered with acidification of the surrounding soil and, as indicated earlier, strigolactone secretion attracts mycorrhizal hyphae to form a symbiosis. All of these phenotypic changes take place in a root region well behind that of the tip itself.

The adaptation to low P is sure to improve search, to explore the territory around the root, rather than put resources from the shoot into deeper vertical penetration. The adaptation is entirely sensible; the original root has grown through a zone that is, relatively speaking, rich in phosphate. When the tip penetrates areas deficient in phosphate then the time has come to forage more actively in the soil in which adequate reserves of phosphate were first experienced.

That it is the extreme tip, the cap itself, that detects the low phosphate and reacts accordingly has been shown experimentally (Ticconni and Abel 2004; Svistoonoff et al. 2007). These authors confirmed the suggestions of others that, as soon as the extreme root tip encounters low phosphate, the phenotypic changes are set in train by a communicating signal involving the shoot as well. They also identified two mutations that permitted the continued growth of the main axis in low phosphate. The mutations turned out to be in two multi-copper oxidases that were expressed specifically in the root cap. Such results suggest that reactive oxygen species (ROS), e.g. hydrogen peroxide, may be acting as second messengers either inside cap cells or through the wall to other cells. Potentially, a large increase in auxin flow could act to inhibit root axis growth, but something else must apprise the shoot of the situation, too.

However, it does seem to be that phosphate itself that acts as a signal. Phosphite ($H_2PO_3^-$) acts as a phosphate surrogate. It is not metabolized to phosphate, but mimics phosphate in its biological effects and can repress typical phosphate deficiency responses in low phosphate (Ticconi and Abel 2004).

The implication is that there must be a protein directly binding phosphate that acts as a phosphate sensor and that also recognizes phosphite. Presumably, this protein must be present in the cap itself. One possibility is that it is the flux of phosphate that is sensed as it enters cells through transporters, implying some sort of counting mechanism. An alternative is that phosphate receptors sense the circulating level of phosphate and act on its decline, but this might be extremely slow and seems to be belied by observations that the phenotypic changes often start without measureable decline of root phosphate at all (Svistoonoff et al. 2007).

There seem to be several ways of mimicking these low phosphate-associated phenotypic changes. The most intriguing are the plants in which expression of a vacuolar proton-pumping pyro-phosphatase is increased (Yang et al. 2007)

Root proliferation is probably all about competition, not necessarily uptake for growth

Earlier it was indicated that N is very soluble and as freely moveable in the soil as water, whereas that of K is one-third that of N, and P one-tenth. The lateral root proliferation induced by N is not only unexpected, or if it is expected, why is there is no effective lateral root response to rich patches of K if the function of proliferation is essential to nutrient uptake (Robinson 1996)? An alternative reason for proliferation is to remove N before competitors do.

Mineralization to release P from insoluble forms is slow; partial deficiency is always likely for wild plants. Thus, competition is thus likely to be fierce for what is produced. Proliferation to outcompete the opposition is also to be expected. Failure to compete will be selected against when confronted with those root systems that do compete. However, weak competitors might survive by deciding against assessed strong competition and, instead, preferentially growing into unoccupied soil.

When sharing soil, the roots of each individual tend to avoid those of others (Caldwell 1994). Given the choice, plants place their roots in effectively, unoccupied soil (Gersani et al. 1998). These latter authors took advantage of an experimental manipulation that provides two largely equal root systems from the same plant. The roots were split between two containers of soil. In one container, increasing numbers of competitive plants were grown, while the other was left only to the initial split root of the parent plant. With the highest competition, the individual placed virtually all its new root in the unoccupied container. Clearly, a sensing of competition is present, as is the direction of growth away from competition. In the presence of competitors in an enclosed space, root growth of any individual is strongly diminished (Fitter 1994).

When a plant competes with its neighbour for water and mineral resources, it is effectively defending its local space. The most efficient method of defence of your own territory is to remove the resources before others do. Thus, the phenotypic change in root proliferation is likely to be a property of those plants that grow quickly and need to remove N before others do. This situation favours speed over efficiency and, as indicated, may be limited to fast-growing domesticated annual crop species or pioneer weeds. A larger surface area will also help K uptake.

Do slow-growing roots use a more efficient adaptation of uptake and transport mechanisms? Experiments using competition have tested this hypothesis. By using two different grasses fighting for the same patch of organic material, only one of which showed greater root proliferative response to N, it was observed that this latter plant gained greater amounts of N (Robinson et al. 1999). Soils with most diverse communities have lowest free N and greatest competition.

Illustrations of root structures under competitive circumstances are rare. Figure 13.4(a–c) illustrates the root systems of sunflowers grown spaced at 32, 8, and 2 inches (Weaver 1926).

At 32-inch separation there is unlikely to be much in the way of interaction with adjacent plants and Weaver (1926) reported these plants as being over 2 m tall and flowering. He also commented that the front roots had to be removed because of the intense network structure that developed. The roots extend over 5 feet on either side. At 8-inch spacing, competition has obviously had a profound effect on the extent of root growth and the maximum extent on either side is reduced to about 2 feet. Even smaller is the root system in plant separated only by 2 inches.

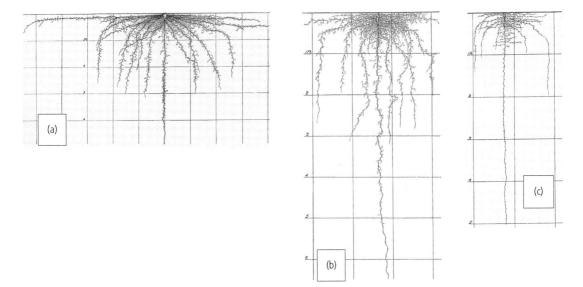

Figure 13.4 (a–c) Effects of competition. Sunflower planted at 32 (a), 8 (b), and 2 (c) inches apart. Scale bars = 1 foot. Shows a striking example of phenotypic plasticity, but competition much less effective on root structure than shoot, which was reduced 200-fold. Note developmental priority given to tap root (depth similar) and how roots continue to turn down, but over shorter distance. The turn-down signal is not related to root length.

Weaver (1926) provides quantitative information on the shoot material in these plants. The leaf area and dry weight are reduced 10-fold for the 8-inch separation and 100–200-fold for the 2-inch separation. In contrast, root depth remains approximately constant and lateral root spread only reduced four-fold for the most densely planted sunflowers. These data indicate then protection, a prioritizing of the root system against the shoot, and in the root system itself, there is priority given to the tap root, which as indicated reaches to almost the same depth in the three examples. Note also how the turn-down of roots towards gravity takes place in all cases, but the length at which turn-down starts is progressively reduced from 3 to 1.5–1 foot. So distance from the shoot/root junction is not invariable. These pictures are excellent examples of phenotypic plasticity.

One potential explanation for the priority of root systems comes from the known effects of strigol-actone on shoot branching. Strigolactone synthesis is substantially increased when soil impoverishment is recognized. The goal is the establishment of a symbiotic relationship with mycorrhizae discussed in greater detail in Chapter 17. The symbi-ont can more easily sequester limiting quantities of phosphate from the soil, provides these to the host, and in return receives carbohydrate. Concomitant with this, strigolactone circulates throughout the plant, will inhibit shoot growth, and in particular shoot branching (Gomez-Roldan et al. 2008; Umehara et al. 2008). However, note that this only occurs during mineral shortage. The mechanism of increasing strigolactone synthesis has yet to be described, although the receptor for strigolactone has recently been isolated (Smith 2013), but strigolactone is yet another circulating signal that will modify the phenotype.

How is a network of roots constructed?

The pictures of root growth shown in this chapter (Figure 13.1–13.4) indicate that roots space themselves. In vertically growing shoots, branches usually emerge at an angle to the shoot by growth of a lateral bud. Various signals come into play to ensure the maintenance of this branching pattern at angles to the main shoot. In contrast, one plant can have many main roots. To properly spread this root system around the soil suggests communication between the growing roots.

One possibility is for each root to construct a zone of inhibition around itself, preventing other roots from the same plant growing in the vicinity. Presumably, the secretion of inhibitory chemicals could explain the distribution. When roots are forced to grow close together, as in containers, they become pot-bound and suffer overall growth inhibition. By growing members of four different species in containers of a range of sizes, but with identical amounts of nutrient in each case, McConnaughay and Bazzaz (1991) reported that the larger the pot the greater the growth and seed output. The implication is that soil space is a resource on its own. Production of inhibitory chemicals by each root could also explain this result, but the problem is how does it avoid being inhibited itself? If this does not happen than a mechanism for estimating soil space has to be sought. It is not immediately obvious what it can be. These results on soil space were confirmed in experiments in which soil was partly filled either with glass beads or wire (McConnaughay and Bazzaz 1992). Many chemicals are secreted from the root, so any of these could potentially be responsible, if they act to inhibit root growth.

Other related, horizontally growing organs are the rhizomes and stolons. These are described as diagravitropic, a term that could be applied to horizontally growing tree roots, but usually is not. That scourge of the gardener—ground elder—sends its stolons horizontally just below ground level, and only forms roots and a shoot at nodes. Other familiar garden rhizomes are found in the Iris family (Iridaceae). Their behaviour is interesting, since rhizomes maintain their spatial position in the soil. If the rhizome is placed too high, effectively on top of the soil, new rhizome shoots tend to grow downward; if the rhizome is buried too deep the rhizome grows upwards until they reach a predetermined and, supposedly, optimal position in the soil. Rhizomes clearly have a three-dimensional sense of their position using a variety of environmental signals (Bennet-Clerk and Ball 1951; Maun and Lapierre 1984). These rhizomes must have fairly complicated sensing mechanisms, probably more than just light and gravity, and they have feedback controls that enable that optimal position to be regained if it is altered. The internal mechanisms that adjust the rhizome position in this way are not known.

Conclusion

The title of this chapter quoted Liebig as indicating plants searching for minerals as if they had eyes. This suggests that living roots construct a chemical image of their environment using specific receptors. The quality of soil is also sensed, as are its constituents, and the self-organizing structure adapts to what is perceived; roots thus learn about their surroundings. It is that learning that leads to problem-solving adaptation and obviously intelligent responses that accommodate to their state.

References

Addiscott, T.M. (2010). Soil mineralisation: an emergent process? *Geoderma*, **160**, 31–35.

Badri, D.V., Weir, T.L., Lelie, D., van der, and Vivanco, J.M. (2009). Rhizosphere chemical dialogues: plant microbe interactions. *Current Opinion in Biotechnology*, **20**, 642–650.

Bazzaz, F.A (1996). *Plants in changing environments*. Cambridge University Press, Cambridge.

Bennett-Clerk, T.A., and Ball, N.G. (1951). The diageotropic behaviour of rhizomes. *Journal of Experimental Botany*, **2**, 169–203.

Calderon-Vazquez, C., Sawers, R.J.H., and Herera-Estrella, L. (2011). Phosphate deprivation in maize and genomics. *Plant Physiology*, **156**, 1067–1078.

Caldwell, M.M. (1994). Exploiting nutrients in fertile soil microsites. In, Caldwell, M.M. and Pearcy, R.W. eds. *Exploitation of Environmental Heterogeneity by Plants*. pp. 325–349. Academic Press, New York.

Chaves, M.M., Maroco, J.P., and Pereira, J.S. (2003). Understanding plant responses to drought-from genes to the whole plant. *Functional Plant Biology*, 30, 239–264.

Cheng, L., Bucciarelli, B., Shen, J., Allan, D., and Vance, C.A. (2011). Update on white lupin cluster root acclimation to phosphorus deficiency. *Plant Physiology*, **156**, 1025–1033.

Drew, M.C. (1975). Comparison of the effects of a localised supply of phosphate, nitrate and ammonium and potassium on the growth of the seminal root system and the shoot in barley. *New Phytologist*, **75**, 479–490.

Fitter, A.H. (1994). Architecture and biomass allocation as components of the plastic response of root systems to soil heterogeneity. In, Caldwell, M.M.and Pearcy, R.W. eds. *Exploitation of Environmental Heterogeneity by Plants*. pp.305–325. Academic Press, New York.

Gersani, M., Abramsky, Z., and Falik, O. (1998). Density dependent habitat selection in plants. *Evolutionary Ecology*, **12**, 223–234.

Gomez-Roldan, V., Fermas, S., Brewer, P.B., Puech-Pages, V., Dun, E.A., Pillot, J.-P., and 9 others (2008). Strigolactone inhibition of shoot branching. *Nature*, **455**, 189–195.

Griffin, D.R. (1976). *The question of animal awareness*. Rockefeller University Press, New York.

Hammond, J.P., and White, P.J. (2011). Sugar signalling in root responses to low phosphate availability. *Plant Physiology*, **156**, 1033–1040.

Hutchings, M.J., and Kroon, H., de (1994). Foraging in plants: the role of morphological plasticity in resource acquisition. *Advances in Ecological Research*, **25**, 159–238.

Jackson, R.B. and Caldwell, M.M. (1993). Geostatistical patterns of soil heterogeneity around individual perennial plants. *Journal of Ecology*, 81, 683–692.

Kaye, J.P., and Hart, S.C. (1997). Competition for nitrogen between plants and soil microorganisms. *Trends in Ecology and Evolution*, **12**, 139–143.

Krouk, G., Ruffel, S., Gutierrez, R.A., Gojon, A., Crawford, N.M., Coruzzi, G.M., and 1 other (2011). A framework integrating plant growth with hormones and nutrients. *Trends in Plant Science*, **16**, 178–182.

Mairhofer, S., Zappala, S., Tracy, S.R., Sturrock, C., Bennett, M., Moony, S.J., and 1 other (2012). RooTrak: automated recovery of three dimensional plant root architecture in soil from X-ray microcomputed tomography images using visual tracking. *Plant Physiology*, **158**, 561–569.

Maun, M.A., and LaPierre, J. (1984). The effects of burial by sand on *Ammophila brevilugata*. *Journal of Ecology*, **72**, 827–839.

McConnaughay, K.D.M., and Bazzaz, F.A. (1991) Is physical space a soil resource. *Ecology*, **72**, 94–103.

McConnaughay, K.D.M., and Bazzaz, F.A. (1992). The occupation and fragmentation of space: consequences of neighbouring roots. *Functional Ecology*, **6**, 704–710.

Parniske, M. (2008). Arbuscular mycorrhiza: the mother of all plant root endosymbioses. *Nature Reviews Microbiology*, **6**, 763–776.

Plaxton, W.C. and Tran, H.T. (2011). Metabolic adaptations of phosphate –starved plants. *Plant Physiology*, **156**, 1006–1015.

Priem, H.N.A. (1998). CO_2 and climate: geological perspective. *Energy and Environment*, **9**, 659–672.

Richardson, A.E., and Simpson, R.J. (2011). Soil microorganisms mediating phosphorus availability. *Plant Physiology*, **156**, 989–996.

Robinson, D. (1994).The responses of plants to non-uniform supplies of nutrients. *New Phytologist*, **127**, 635–674.

Robinson, D. (1996). Resource capture by localised root proliferation: why do plants bother? *Annals of Botany*, **77**, 179–185.

Robinson, D., Hodge, A., Griffiths, B.S., and Fitter, A.H. (1999). Plant root proliferation in nitrogen-rich patches confers competitive advantage. *Proceedings of the Royal Society London, Series B*, **266**, 431–435.

Ruffel, S., Krouk, G., Ristova, D., Shasha, D., Birnbaum, K.D., and Coruzzi, G.M. (2011). Nitrogen economics of root foraging: transitive closure of the nitrate cytokinin relay and distinct systemic signalling for N supply vs demand. *Proceedings of the National Academy of Sciences USA*, **108**, 18524–18529.

Ryel, R.J., Caldwell, M.M., and Manwaring, J.H. (1996). Temporal dynamics of soil spatial heterogeneity in sagebrush-wheatgrass steppe during a growing season. *Plant and Soil*, **184**, 299–309.

Shen, J., Yuan, J., Zhang, J., Li, H., Bai, Z., Chen, X., and 2 others (2011). Phosphorus dynamics from soil to plant. *Plant Physiology*, **156**, 997–1005.

Smith, S.E., and Read, D.J. (2008). *Mycorrhizal symbiosis*. Elsevier, Amsterdam.

Smith, S.M. (2013). Witchcraft and destruction. *Nature*, **504**, 384–385.

Song, Y.Y., Zeng, R.S., Xu, J.F., Li, J., Shen, X., and Yihdego, W.G. (2010). Interplant communication of tomato plants through underground common mycorrhizal networks. *PLoS* 5, e13324.

Svistoonoff, S., Creff, A., Reymond, M., Sigoillot-Claude, C., Ricaud, L., Blanchet, A., and 2 others (2007). Root tip contact with low-phosphate media reprograms plant root architecture. *Nature Genetics*, **39**, 792–796.

Ticconi, C.A., and Abel, S. (2004). Short on phosphate: plant surveillance and counter-measures. *Trends in Plant Science*, **9**, 548–555.

Trewavas, A.J. (1986). Resource allocation under poor growth conditions. A major role for growth substances in developmental plasticity. In Jennings, D.H., and Trewavas, A.J., eds, *Plasticity in plants. Symposia of the Society for Experimental Biology, No. XXXX*, pp. 31–76. Company of Biologists Limited, Cambridge.

Trewavas, A.J. (2003). Aspects of plant intelligence. *Annals of Botany*, **92**, 1–20.

Trewavas, A.J. (2009). What is plant behaviour? *Plant Cell and Environment*, **32**, 606–616.

Trewavas, A. J. Information, noise and communication: thresholds as controlling elements in development. In Witzany, G., and Baluska F., eds, *Biocommunication of plants*, pp. 11–37. Springer, Berlin.

Turkington, R., and Aarssen, L.W. (1984). Local scale differentiation as a result of competitive interactions. In Dirzo, R., and Sarukha, J., eds, *Perspectives on plant population ecology*, pp. 107–128. Sinaure Associates, Sunderland, MA.

Umehara, M., Hanada, A., Yoshida, S., Akiyama, K., Arite, T., Takeda-Kamiya, N., and 6 others (2008). Inhibition of shoot branching by new terpenoid plant hormones. *Nature*, **455**, 195–200.

Weaver, J.E. (1926). *Root development of field crops*. McGraw Hill, New York.

Weaver, J.E., and Bruner, W.E. (1927). *Root development of vegetable crops*. McGraw Hill, New York.

White, H.L. (1937). The interaction of factors in the growth of *Lemna*. *Annals of Botany*, **1**, 623–647.

Whitfield, J. (2007). Underground networking. *Nature*, **449**, 136–138.

Yang, H., Knapp, J., Koirola, P., Rajagopal, D., Peer, W.A., Silbart, L.K., and 2 others (2007). Enhanced phosphorus nutrition in monocots and dicots over-expressing a phosphorus-responsive type1 H^+ pyrophosphatase. *Plant Biotechnology Journal*, **5**, 735–745.

Zhang, J., and Kirkham, M.B. (1995). Water relations of water-stressed, split-root C_4 (*Sorghum bicolor*) and C_3 (*Helianthus annuus*) plants. *American Journal of Botany*, **82**, 1220–1229.

CHAPTER 14

Self-organization in response to gravity

In tropistic movements, plants appear to exhibit a sort of intelligence; their movement is of subsequent advantage to them.

(Went and Thimann 1937)

⊃ Summary

The quotation that heads this chapter indicates the obvious relationship between advantage, intelligence, and fitness. The well-known bending of some seedling roots to a displacement of the gravity signal is considered. The anatomy of the root meristem is outlined and the mechanism of gravity sensing in the root cap columella is described. Auxin moves in seedling tissues in a polar manner and arrives in the root cap via the vascular tissue. In the cap, it progresses shootwards in the tissues outside the vascular elements. The Cholodny–Went theory describes root bending as resulting of a redistribution of auxin on the two sides of a gravitropically-stimulated root. The recent molecular evidence that relates auxin to gravitropic bending is described. Some of this evidence, which supports the Cholodny–Went theory, is discussed, and then critically examined. Other processes contribute to gravitropic responses than just auxin on its own and these can precede auxin redistribution. The sensitivity with which auxin acts to manipulate growth is discussed. There are also indications of complex growth control mechanisms from the individuality observed in root bending kinetics. There are at least two zones of gravitropic sensitivity in the root. The Cholodny–Went theory is an over-simplification of a group of mechanisms involved in growth orientation control. A complex soil environment will need equally complex mechanisms to control orientation if root systems work with optimal fitness. Potential contributions from other hormones and processes in the bending process might help explanation.

Historical background: roots and coleoptiles

The early experiments that initiated subsequent research on tropic signalling we owe to Darwin (1880). He had reported that removal of the root tip temporarily inhibited gravitropic sensitivity of the root stump. Coincidentally, and necessary to this story, he also did significant, but relevant work on grass coleoptiles. The grass coleoptile is a tubular tissue, enclosing the first leaves (Box 14.1). It is largely closed at the tip except for a guttation pore. In natural circumstances, the growth of the coleoptile is inhibited by light when it appears above the soil and the first leaves break through. The function of the coleoptile is not only protection of fragile leaf tissue but its conical tip and tubular structure, enables easier soil penetration.

Plant Behaviour and Intelligence. First Edition. Anthony Trewavas.
© Anthony Trewavas 2014. Published 2014 by Oxford University Press.

Box 14.1 The oat coleoptile

Darwin (1880) used canary grass seedlings to show that light was sensed in the coleoptile tip and influenced growth in coleoptile regions further down. The coleoptile as an experimental system had the advantage that, by the time it had reached a centimetre or more in length, cell divisions had ceased and growth was solely through cell elongation. Auxin in grass seedlings is derived from the seed endosperm as esterified conjugates. There are two vascular bundles on either side of the coleoptile and it is assumed that auxin conjugates travel up these to the tip. Guttation fluid, that forms when seedlings are grown under very high humidity, can be shown to contain auxin, and many amino acids and sugars. Guttation is assumed to help the upward flow of water from roots. The tip contains esterases that hydrolyse the conjugates and no doubt control how much auxin is released in the tip, and becomes available for polar transport. The tip thus acts as a redistribution centre. Thereafter, released auxin moves in a polar direction down the non-vascular tissues of the coleoptile. There have been thousands of papers on this one tissue.

The routine investigative treatment was to remove the tip surgically. The distribution site was removed and further auxin movement into the coleoptile tissue ceased. Continued polar movement depleted the coleoptile of auxin usually within an hour. Growth was slowed, although some continued. The distribution centre can regenerate within 3–4 hr, so sometimes a double decapitation was performed. By removing auxin from the tissue, growth becomes strongly dependent on applied auxin.

Darwin noted that covering the coleoptile cap to low levels of unilateral illumination inhibited phototropic bending. Light was sensed in the tip, but the effect of unilateral light was evidently expressed by tissues below the cap where bending occurred. These early observations indicated movement of an active substance(s) or influence(s) from the tip to this region. It is thought that auxin is the substance that moves from the tip to control unequal growth below.

These early observations had little impact for some 45 years until Frits Went made some striking progress. In searching for this active material, he excised the coleoptile tip, placed it on agar blocks and then applied the block asymmetrically to a coleoptile minus the tip. This caused bending of the coleoptile by acceleration of growth on the side to which the block was placed. An active substance had diffused from the tip into the agar and, by an increase in concentration, accelerated growth on that side. This substance was later identified as auxin or indole-3-acetic acid. Went and Thimann (1937) provided the first compilation of hormone effects in plants, and described the discovery and effective biological properties of auxin (3-indole-acetic acid). They are responsible for the quotation that introduces this chapter.

Although auxin appears to promote the growth of some shoot tissues under some circumstances, it also inhibits the growth of roots. A simplifying theory was proposed that, in light- or gravity-stimulated organs, unequal distributions of auxin between the two sides of the tissue generated tropic curvatures. This theory is commonly called the Cholodny–Went theory. A critical assessment of these early studies is available (Trewavas 1981) and will be expanded later with more recent information. Central to the problems with the Cholodny–Went theory is the use of tissues depleted of auxin. Many of the early formulations of theories about growth and bending assumed that results under these circumstances were easily applicable to plants with intact coleoptiles or roots.

Both tropic responses to gravity and light are common characteristics of many tissues in higher plants and, indeed, lower plants as well. Tropic movements are direct indications of adaptive behaviour that obviously improves fitness. They are of obvious direct benefit to the whole plant. Adaptive behaviour that improves fitness is rightly described as intelligent behaviour. The movement towards light places the shoot in a more advantageous position, increasing its capture of that vital plant food ingredient—light energy. In many shoots, responses to gravity also place the shoot in a preferable position as regards light collection. Very old experiments indicated that, in competition, light supersedes gravity as a signal.

The responsiveness of roots to gravity is, again, of obvious benefit, since it places the early root in a position to anchor the shoot, and sequester the necessary minerals and water. In the case of grasses where early roots are effectively horizontal, a number of main roots grow at the same time before turning downwards, once a certain degree of growth has been accomplished. However, the behaviour again provides obvious fitness benefits. A relationship emerges between intelligent behaviour and the fitness of the individual. However, the forms of the behavioural response to light and gravity are enormously variable between different species. Both light and gravity signals, once sensed, change the polarities of growth and development. More importantly, it reflects an ability of the plant to sense the strength of gradients of either and to act upon the intensity of that gradient.

The polar movement of auxin and canalization

Early investigations indicated that auxin is transported in the vascular system, but in cells outside this tissue, auxin movement is active, polar, and vertically downwards with a speed of about 1 cm/hr. Although the sites of synthesis of auxin are poorly defined, most is thought to be synthesized in the tips of young developing leaves in the shoot. This auxin eventually finds its way into the vascular system. Polar movement takes place by secretion of auxin from an upper cell and diffuses through the connecting wall to the cell below. Auxin is both synthesized and catabolized during its progress.

Indole-3-acetic acid is a weak acid. In the neutral cytoplasm, it is fully ionized, but in the wall compartment, with a pH of about 5.5, substantial amounts are present as the protonated uncharged and membrane permeable moiety. Thus, once present in the wall, auxin can simply partition into the cytoplasm of the cell below where it will remain trapped. The polar movement is continued via two separate groups of proteins. A family of facilitator proteins help increase the influx rate of auxin from the wall into the cell. A family of efflux, PIN proteins, secrete auxin from the basal membrane of the cell into the wall below, to continue the polar movement (Kramer 2006). The syntheses of both groups of proteins are thought to be auxin-dependent, thus enabling a kind of feedforward mechanism in the development of polar transport.

However, there are several difficulties with this theory of polar movement that Kramer (2006) highlighted. Secretion of auxin into the wall and movement by diffusion towards the next cell would not prevent uptake into surrounding

horizontally-placed adjacent cells. There is also a further problem with catabolism of auxin in the wall by oxidases. Auxin catabolism and conjugation inside the cell itself is also reported.

These difficulties can be offset by auxin inducing its own synthesis to maintain the amount as it is transported. Some weak evidence supports that possibility (Trewavas 2007). Furthermore, facilitators of auxin entry greatly reduce lateral diffusion by increasing auxin uptake by 10–15-fold into the next cell below, thus helping maintain auxin in a uniseriate stream (Kramer and Bennett 2006). What is surprising is that auxin movement does not involve plasmodesmata, the direct interconnecting strands of cytoplasm between cells.

Canalization of auxin movement

In very young leaves, auxin synthesis uses the above feedforward mechanism to generate polar movement and canalize it into channels that become vascular tissue. It is thought that cells in the extreme tip of developing leaves synthesize auxin. Adjacent cells receiving an auxin signal are likely to start synthesizing the necessary cellular apparatus, facilitator, and PIN proteins, to construct a transport stream. However, the rate at which individual cells do this will be variable, determined by molecular noise. Those that accomplish this synthesis first, will sequester more of the auxin from others, who will slowly be depleted and cease further synthesis. Thus, these cells, first into the development programme, gain more and more of the auxin, and establish a transport line, while others remain depleted.

Higher levels of auxin are known to induce vascular tissue formation and, thus, these transport streams help induce the typical reticulate network of vascular channels in the leaf. Other depleted cells assume a different programme becoming typical, photosynthesizing, leaf cells (Sachs 1991.) Thus, auxin movement and cell differentiation in leaves is a typical self-organizing system using feedforward activation and inhibition common in developing processes. One function of this vascular transport of auxin down towards the root, is to provide information to the root that leaf development is progressing, and that more roots are required to provision the growing leaves with soil resources (Berleth and Sachs 2001).

Molecular technology has now reached the stage where aspects of auxin transport, the proteins responsible, and potential concentrations of them can all be imaged (Benjamins and Scheres 2008). The use of mutants that are either insensitive to auxin or are deficient in auxin production indicate that both the presence and flow of auxin are essential to maintain root meristem development (Geidner et al. 2001; Wang et al. 2005). However, given the variation of individual cell behaviour in the root and the ubiquitous involvement of auxin in many plant processes, its role is more likely to enable cell differentiation processes to continue once they are established; i.e. its effects are permissive of cell differentiation, rather than inductive. Once a cell differentiation process starts, its continuation will be dependent on a continued flow of auxin. Good evidence supports the involvement of the polar flow of auxin in the development of other plant organs, which exhibit a pronounced growth and morphological polarity (Benkova et al. 2003).

Critical aspects of root behaviour are sensed by the root tip

The root meristem is a dynamic structure

In these present days, many longitudinal sections through the root meristem are displayed on the web (e.g. http://plantsinaction.science.uq.edu.au/edition1/?q=content/7-1-1-root-apical-meristems). In longitudinal section, the root meristem is constructed from two different cellular regions. The extreme, rootward end contains the root cap. Here, there are several rows of permanently dividing cells that form a meristem. The daughter cells from these rows are pushed outwards towards the extreme outer part of the cap, ceasing division as they mature. Eventually, many mature cap cells are sloughed off by soil particles and new ones added by the root cap meristem. There must be a simple feedback mechanism that adjusts cell numbers according to loss, because even in soil-less conditions the root cap is limited in cell number.

The more shootward part of the root meristem contains another meristem that consists of obvious files of cells that are highly cytoplasmic and are in the process of cell division. These files can be traced down to the root cap junction. The progressive fate of the cells in these files, as they increase their distance from the root cap junction, is well-known. These files produce the various root tissues as they mature. Further back from the meristem, division ceases, and cell specification and elongation become more pronounced. After initiation of cell elongation, a rapid five- or six-fold increase in cell length occurs. In roots of pea or maize, the distance from the root cap to the end of the extension zone is little more than 5 mm.

By the end of the extension zone, well-characterized cell types are easily detectable. In transverse section, these mature differentiated tissues are arranged as concentric rings. A central vascular core (xylem and phloem) is surrounded by an endodermis that controls water and movement of ions into the vascular tissue. Outside this is a ring of pericycle cells from which lateral roots emerge. Outside the pericycle are layers of cortex. The whole root is surrounded by an epidermis (Allan and Trewavas 1986).

However, detailed examination indicates that changes in rates of division, cessation of mitosis or rates of extension, or changes in cell volume with time are not synchronized processes between different cell types in larger roots, such as those of pea (Allan and Trewavas 1986). There are regions where virtually all cells are in division and in a more shootward direction, regions where they are in elongation, but the transition between these regions, often sees a mixture of the two. The growth of these roots as an organized morphological unit must be integrated at a higher level of the whole root itself. The root maintains a cylindrical shape that slowly with maturation increases its diameter. The elements that construct this integrated information are not known, but a variety of mechanical and chemical/electrical signals may be involved. Complex negative feedback processes must be present to ensure its success.

In between the root cap proper and the adjacent proximal meristem is a small area called the quiescent centre, in which division rates are extremely low. The function of the quiescent centre is considered important for cell specification, but how it functions in this regard remains obscure. Because the cells that abut the quiescent centre are the base of the obvious files of cells, these cells are designated as founder cells or initials. It is thought that many of these founders are effective stem cells embedded in a cellular and wall milieu that acts as a stem cell niche (Jiang and Feldman 2005).

Root responses to gravity signals: gravitropic behaviour

Tropic bending occurs in response to a new gravitational vector and is easily demonstrated, particularly in seedlings. Gravitropism enables organs and plants to order their development, and grow up or down or at an angle to the gravity vector as a consequence.

Darwin (1880) reported that excision of the extreme tip of the root caused a temporary loss of gravitropic sensitivity lasting several hours. Removal of just the root cap is sufficient. Gravitropic sensitivity regenerates within a day, even though a defined root cap has not regenerated. The root region where the response to gravity occurs is thus remote from the elongating region where differential growth is known to be generated. Signals of some kind are obviously transmitted from the cap to the elongating zone. These early observations suggest two questions that need answers: how is gravity sensed and what is known about how gravisensitivity is recovered after removal of the tip? The second question has failed to receive much in the way of answer other than cells in the stump accumulate starch and, in some way, redistribute auxin. The anatomical cap takes days to fully regenerate.

Gravitropism has attracted a substantial amount of research and Blancaflor and Masson (2002) and the short recent review (Moirta et al. 2011) summarize current understanding. Finally, the book edited by Gilroy and Masson (2007) describes current research on gravitropism and a variety of other tropisms.

Gravity sensing in the root cap: the columella

In the middle of the root cap are a group of cells, termed the columella, that contain numerous amyloplasts. These amyloplasts are subcellular bodies (probably modified plastids) containing very large numbers of starch grains and are held in a basket of actin-based microfilaments that are themselves attached to the plasma membrane. The attachment sites are thought to be coupled with mechano-sensitive channels, which can open when signalled. There is good evidence that these amyloplasts act as statoliths; they are much heavier than other constituents in the cytoplasm and, consequently, sediment under the action of gravity (Kiss et al. 1989; Leitz et al. 2009). In a vertically growing root, the statoliths are localized in the lower half of the columella cells. When the root is laid horizontally, these statoliths rapidly move in response to the altered gravity stimulus, deforming the endoplasmic reticulum as they do so and within several minutes are found on the new 'bottom' of the cell. Manipulated displacement of amyloplasts by applied magnetic fields leads to curvature and supports the role of amyloplasts as gravity sensors (Kuznetosov and Hasenstein 1996). Starchless mutants still respond to a gravity signal, but do so much more slowly.

The most critical demonstration that these columella cells are essential to gravisensing was shown by using laser ablation to specifically eliminate one or more stories of columella cells (Blancaflor et al. 1998). Eliminating the innermost columella cells had the greatest effect on the sensitivity of the root to gravity, while eliminating those at the lateral cap periphery had minimal influence. Elongation growth continued normally even with total ablation of the columella. When signalled, by placing the root horizontally, a normal root rapidly turns and reaches a vertical position. Those roots with specific tiers of inner columella cells ablated, failed to reach the vertical position, and would often only reach a curvature of 45°. There is a suggestion, here, of a quantitative change in sensing and indications of a holistic character to the columella cell family. Columella cells communicate with each other!

Events that happen in the columella on gravity stimulation

When the root is stimulated by placing it at 90°, the cytoplasmic pH of the columella cells becomes rapidly more alkaline and the associated cell wall compartment more acidic (Scott and Allen 1999; Fasano et al. 2001). These events take place within 2 min of stimulation. Inhibiting the alkalinization by photolysis of caged hydrogen ions in the columella cytoplasm, exerts a strong inhibition on the response to a gravitropic signal.

The alkalinization of the columella can be greatly prolonged by prior disruption of the actin filaments with a low dose of inhibitors, like lantrunculin B. Furthermore, such treatments greatly increase the gravitropic response measured by curvature. To detect this response, the seedlings were pretreated with inhibitor, then placed horizontally for 0.5 hr. They were then further rotated on a clinostat, a device that rotates the seedlings slowly through 360° and prevents further gravitropic stimulation. Curvatures greater than 90° were commonly observed after 5–6 hr on the clinostat and were much greater than controls. The suggestion is that by disrupting the actin filaments, the statoliths can sediment at greater rates than before. These results suggest that what the columella cells estimate is the rate of statolith falling, rather than its position inside the cell.

Additional changes in the columella are potentially changes in cytosolic Ca^{2+} (Plieth and Trewavas 2002). These were first observed by measuring the luminescence of seedlings transformed with a calcium-sensitive luminescent probe called aequorin. Although earlier work (Legué et al. 1997) had failed to detect such changes in cytosolic Ca^{2+}, they have now been reported to occur in the lateral root cap, rather than the columella. Imaging of luminescence has shown gravitropically-induced changes in cytosolic Ca^{2+} in the seedling petiole and hypocotyl, both organs sensitive to gravitational signals (Toyota et al. 2008).

The potential role of auxin in gravitropic curvature

Channels of auxin movement in the root

Many mutants of auxin transport and response have now been isolated, and common phenotypes are defects in gravitropic responses.

In the root, the evidence has long indicated that the polar movement of auxin is like an inverted fountain (Trewavas 1986). In seedlings, auxin is transported rootwards through the central vascular core, towards the extreme tip, and probably into, and then through the root cap, where it is redistributed to tissues on either side of the vascular core. In these outer tissues, auxin then moves shootwards,

particularly in the epidermis, a tissue thought to constrain growth. Thus the presence of facilitators in the lateral root cap and epidermis but not in the columella, clarified the likely pathway of auxin movement in gravitropic curvature (Swarup et al. 2005). The central columella core, the main gravity sensing zone, is not directly involved in auxin movement.

The Cholodny and Went theory of root curvature

Roots can be gravitropically stimulated by placing them horizontally and the root returns to the vertical position by relative unequal growth between the two sides of the root. The long established theory proposed by Cholodny and Went in the 30's (Went and Thimann 1937) suggested that auxin was redistributed between the upper and lower sides of the root to initiate unequal growth and thus curvature. Since auxin at most concentrations inhibits root growth (it promotes extension at very low concentrations), it was suggested that bending occurs by accumulation of auxin on the lower side relative to the upper, inhibiting lower side growth and thus causing bending. This theory became known as the Cholodny–Went theory of tropic bending (Went and Thimann 1937).

Ever since its early formulation, further investigation has given rise to both proponents and opponents of the theory, and a forum in 1992 was set up to allow both sides to state their case (Trewavas 1992). The major problem is not particularly the involvement of auxin, but an oversimplification of the theory to cover all eventualities. Auxin is 'a' factor in tropic bending and an important one, but it is not 'the' factor.

Molecular evidence supporting the Cholodny–Went Theory

Early evidence on the Cholodny–Went theory used radioactively-labelled auxin applied to roots subject to a gravitational signal. By careful sectioning and quantitative assay it was reported that more auxin was detectable in the basal region of a gravitropically-stimulated root. Attempted imaging of auxin redistribution in the root used a method that relied on an auxin promoter specifying a fluorescent protein probe (Ottenschlager et al. 2003). Although indicating auxin redistribution, this method has an inevitable lag period of about 1.5 hr before differences can be detected, and curvature is already well underway by this time (Blancaflor et al. 1998). Also there appeared to be little movement of auxin into the epidermis in the published pictures. The most recent development using a probe that detects free auxin in individual cells clearly indicates that redistribution can be detected in the predicted way in the upper and lower epidermis (Brunoud et al. 2012). One difficulty is that continuous imaging is not presently practicable, so that the dynamics of auxin movement during stimulation and bending cannot be observed in a single root.

Molecular advances have improved the imaging of auxin efflux transport carriers that secrete auxin from the basal plasma membrane of the cell (Estelle 1998; Blancaflor and Masson 2002; Friml et al. 2002). The efflux carriers are relocated on gravitropic stimulation towards what now becomes the basal plasma membrane of cells when placed in a horizontal position. However, this raises the issue of what controls the redistribution of these proteins. It cannot be auxin itself, unless there is an alternative method for moving auxin. These results suggest that other processes cause relocation of these proteins and that auxin redistribution is a secondary event.

The pathway of auxin movement from the vascular tissue to the epidermis involved the lateral root cap cells, but not the columella (Swarup et al. 2005). Clearly, an additional signal is required to convey information from the columella, where gravity is sensed, to the lateral root cap to redistribute auxin movement from these cells. Reactive oxygen species have been suggested as this signal. This pathway of auxin movement, avoiding the columella, is also supported by observations that ablation of the columella does not result in changes in growth rates in vertically growing roots (Blancaflor et al. 1998). A columella-less root should still leave auxin movement into the epidermis unaltered.

Auxin redistribution is not the primary control of gravitropic bending

In growing plant tissues, the rate of growth is modified by the pH of the cell wall and its free Ca^{2+} content. An increase in pH increases wall loosening, while Ca^{2+}, potentially through cross-linking pectins, counteracts this loosening. In shoots, auxin can increase secretion of H^+, while in roots it inhibits secretion, permitting alkalinization. This control is exerted through transient elevation of cytosolic Ca^{2+} (Monshausen et al. 2011).

The earliest event when roots are gravitropically stimulated is a change in the surface pH and the electrical field around the roots occurring in about 2–3 min (Weisenseel and Meyer 1997; Monshausen et al. 2011). The surface pH oscillates with time in individual roots as does the electrical field. Concomitant with these events is a redistribution of Ca^{2+} within the wall apoplast (Sinclair and Trewavas 1997). The concentration of Ca^{2+} can be 2–3 mM higher on the lower side of the root and should lead to growth inhibition (Bjorkman and Cleland 1991). The mechanism of Ca^{2+} movement is probably related to changes in H^+ movements and could also result from the change in the electrical field. These events themselves may account for the redistribution of PIN proteins and the movement of auxin from the upper surface to the lower.

By careful application of auxin to the extreme tip of a growing root, it was observed that a wave of activity moved rapidly back along the root cells increasing cytosolic Ca^{2+} in the cells as it passed (Monshausen et al. 2011). Waves of electrical change that increase cellular cytosolic Ca^{2+}, moving at about 1 mm/min, are not uncommon in Ca^{2+} signalling (Malho et al. 1998). These waves act to coordinate tissue responses.

What is then the role of auxin? Almost certainly it helps stabilize a growth pattern set in motion by other events, but its role is secondary, not primary.

Other problems with the Cholodny-Went theory

Is auxin a sensitive control of growth in root and shoot?

If auxin controls growth then it is to be expected it should be a sensitive constraint on growth itself (Trewavas 1987, 2007). In Figure 14.1, I have drawn a theoretical dose–response curve plotting the concentration of, say, auxin against a growth response. To get the dose–response curve on a suitable scale, I have compressed the concentration axis that would

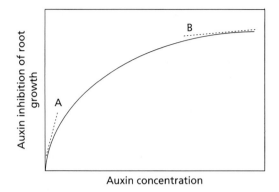

Figure 14.1 Diagrammatic variation of inhibition of root growth plotted against auxin concentration. The sensitivity of control is the asymptote to the curve, very high at A, very low at B. However, B seems the normal position for growth regulator control in intact plants.

normally span 60–100-fold change in concentration. The characteristics of this kind of dose–response are one of increasing decline in responsiveness as the concentration increases, indicating the constraint on the response arising from other cellular or tissue constituents involved in the response. The sensitivity to control, the effect of a small change in auxin concentration, can be judged by the asymptote to this curve as indicated in Figure 14.1.

For a sensitive control, the endogenous auxin concentration should be in region A and not in region B; a small change in concentration should have a large effect on growth. At A, auxin would, indeed, be the limiting factor in the response. Increased growth would be entirely dependent on this one molecule, or if in roots, growth inhibition. If, on the other hand, it is at B, then this indicates that many other processes in growth constrain and contribute to control.

The information from a number of investigations (Trewavas 1987) is that growth regulators like auxin, gibberellin, ethylene are usually in region B, rather than region A. In other words, numerous factors, perhaps unsurprisingly, are contributing to the growth process under examination (Trewavas 1987). Small changes in concentration of auxin in this case have little effect, but the best way to improve the sensitivity of control, is to lower the auxin concentration.

In the classical tissue, the coleoptile, the tip was removed and the tissue allowed to use polar movement to deplete it of auxin (Box 14.1). Virtually all the early auxin physiological studies on coleoptiles and the theories that derived from them, started off by depleting the tissue of auxin, thus making it effectively the limiting factor in growth. Growth becomes strongly dependent on applied auxin. By depletion, auxin is moved from region B of the dose–response profile to region A. The intact growing coleoptile is rather insensitive to applied auxin in agreement with these deductions suggesting it is, indeed, in region B and that other events do, indeed, contribute to control of growth (Went and Thimann 1937).

Seedling roots do grow fast and since auxin is known to be present in the root, it is presumably somewhere in region B, rather than A. In that case, depletion from the upper side of the root would seem to be more important than accumulation on the bottom since this will have a greater influence on growth. This problem has not yet been resolved. Mutants in which one or other growth hormones are eliminated has not helped resolve the situation on control sensitivity because, in a sense, they move the growth hormone misleadingly into region A, rather than recognizing it as being at B in normal tissues.

Control of growth and bending by other factors

Can a complex process be under the control of a single molecule? Even in extreme environmental circumstances a sensitivity analysis would reveal the contribution of other processes. Single molecule control is made less likely, bearing in mind that plants live in uncontrolled and uncertain surroundings. While auxin contributes to tropic bending, other processes must be present to ensure reliability. The recognition of other contributing factors was recognized by Went and Thimann (1937), but little further work has established what these are, although other hormones, like ethylene or abscisic acid are commonly quoted as contributing to gravitropic responses. Went and Thimann (1937) claimed there were food factors involved and also reported that starving coleoptiles, by removing the seed endosperm, made the coleoptiles more sensitive to auxin.

Complexity in growth responses by individual roots in response to gravity

Despite the experimental support, the Cholodny–Went theory fails to explain many actual patterns of growth on tropic stimulation. The discrepancy is not minor either. Various authors have used exacting video and computational methods to analyse the patterns of growth changes after gravity signalling in roots (Selker and Sievers, 1987; Ishikawa et al. 1991; Zieschang and Sievers, 1991). These authors and others have made detailed kinetic analysis of all parts of the growing regions of the root using attached minute beads or carbon particles. Measurements of the growth rates of the upper and lower surface in particular have been very valuable.

Substantial variation in growth characteristics occurs between individual roots on gravitropic stimulation, with only a minority settling down uniformly to regain the vertical position. The majority, instead, either show oscillations of growth, growth reversals, overshoot, and initial upward bending in some cases. Little consistent behaviour is found between the various parts of the growing region, which may exhibit acceleration, oscillations between acceleration, and inhibition, zero growth rate, and faster growth rates on the lower side, compared with the upper, which may also drop to zero, thus reversing initial bending characteristics and even continued variation in inhibition of growth rates. However, after an appropriate length of time, despite all the variation, most roots have recovered the vertical position. There can be considerable variation in the final time period required to achieve this. No simple pattern of change in growth rate occurs. It is not difficult to demonstrate that auxin is somehow involved in the responses to gravity. Auxin-insensitive mutants have clarified that situation as have inhibitors of auxin transport and elimination of transport proteins.

The reasons for the complexity of growth variability and response are perhaps not surprising. It is quite simply that there are many other processes involved to re-establish a vertical growth direction, than just auxin redistribution. It can be expected that these operate in complex non-linear fashion to control growth.

Monshausen et al. (2011) report that there is considerable variation in hydrogen ion extrusion from growing roots during normal vertical growth and this may be one agent causing the variations in growth pattern observed by the authors above.

Averaging masks the true variation

If the kinetics of gravitropic growth responses of 100 roots of maize or pea placed horizontally were averaged, the pattern would be very simple. The average would exhibit a smooth progressive change in the angle of growth ending up in the vertical position. The fact is averaging simplifies individual complexity, but the average is not the mechanism used by the individual root and, indeed shoot, responding to gravity or light. I have discussed this previously pointing out by analogy that averaging large numbers of games of chess would miss the basic essential element in the chess game, i.e. the individuality of the trajectory of any game (Trewavas 2003). In fact, the rules underlying chess could not be gained from the moves provided by averaged chess games, just as the true mechanisms that underpin gravitropic responses roots cannot be understood and will be missed from averaged responses. The emphasis in experimental work should probe the individual, even though that is, in some sense, an average of the cells involved.

The use of averaging in biology started as a result of the input of statistics, a useful procedure if you are comparing agricultural yields from different treatment because the yield, while being an average, is what is needed. However, I suspect its use in terms of mechanisms may mislead.

Regions other than the tip are gravisensitive

Not only is the root cap gravisensitive, but also the growing region, an observation clarified early by Keble et al. (1929). Removal of the tip still leaves the stump with a limited, but detectable gravisensing and response. The stump is simply slower to respond and, thus, less sensitive. The reasons why a statolith mechanism evolved may simply lie in the greater sensitivity that it confers on any root. It improves the accuracy with which growth responds and rapidity of response. Slow growing roots may then not need a cap-sensitive mechanism at all.

The presence of two gravisensitive regions in roots was directly demonstrated by Wolverton et al. (2002a,b), using a device that maintained a gravity stimulus of identical size on targeted segments of the bending root. Even when the tip was vertical, the expanding zone continued to respond and bend. They confirmed that the growing region responds more slowly to gravity. It is less sensitive than the columella cells in the cap, but could predominate in slow growing plants and organs.

How gravisensing occurs in the growing region is currently not understood, but among several proposals, the simple weight of the cytoplasm on the basal plasma membrane may be sufficient. A number of single-cell organisms and spores do sense and react to a gravity stimulus, and these organisms do not appear to possess statoliths so far as can be ascertained (Edwards and Roux 1998; Richter et al. 2001). An alternative suggestion is sensing of gravity by sedimentation of small ordinary plastids, but this has yet to be clarified.

Changes in sensitivity to auxin?

Finally, there is some evidence that applying a gravity stimulus changes the sensitivity of the responding region to auxin (Evans 1991). In addition, an auxin-independent component in growth bending seems also to be present. By soaking roots in relatively high (10^{-6} M) auxin concentration, vertical elongation can be completely inhibited. When such roots are placed horizontally, they exhibit strong gravitropism, sometimes even greater than untreated controls and often initially in the upward direction, before reversing and exhibiting normal responses (Ishikawa and Evans 1993). This important experiment contradicts the Cholodny–Went theory. There is further evidence that other growth hormones, cytokinins, ethylene, and abscisic acid may also contribute to altering the pattern of growth direction, and obviously may alter the sensitivity to auxin (Aloni et al. 2006; Kuswah et al. 2011). Cross-talk between the numerous hormones now identified in plants has been known for a long time. The integration of

these hormones, together with abiotic and biotic factors, and others yet to be discovered, will improve understanding (Santner and Estelle 2009). For example, a recent direct interaction between the nitrate receptor and auxin has now been clarified (Krouk et al., 2011). A systems approach is going to be essential to better understanding in the future for integrating so many contributing factors (Teale et al. 2008).

Roots can retain a memory of a gravitropic response for some hours

Darwin (1880) was also able to show that a growing root could remember a gravity signal even when the signal was no longer present. Under Darwin's growth conditions (his living room), bending took some 3–4 hr before it commenced. With different roots and more optimal present-day growth conditions, this bending in response to gravity can start within 10–15 min. However, Darwin placed the primary bean root horizontally, for 1–2 hr and then replaced them back to their vertical growth direction. In that case, sideways bending still occurred later in the direction in which the gravity vector had earlier been imposed. If the root tip was removed and the stump placed horizontally, detectable curvature was not observed. However, Darwin also placed roots horizontally then, well before any curvature started, removed the tip region and re-placed the de-tipped root vertically. Within several hours, the roots curved in the anticipated direction, indicating they had remembered the initial gravitational signal for some hours. The memory may be related to auxin transport, but other possibilities cannot be discounted. Just as there are delays until auxin has reached and modified the elongating zone, so there will be delays once the gravity stimulus diminishes.

Conclusion on auxin and gravitropism

The simple picture generated by Cholodny and Went has to incorporate a much greater degree of complexity. There is nothing simple about the actual processes of tropic bending, and it would be helpful if this complexity was recognized by those that write text books or teach elementary courses in plant biology.

What function does auxin actually perform? In due course, redistributions of auxin seem to occur and maybe the accumulation eventually overwhelms other factors that might disrupt a programme to regain vertical growth. However, placing the root in the horizontal position is also an artificial experimental treatment, unlikely to happen unless a seedling germinates, radical upwards. Furthermore, when roots are placed horizontally without support there may be a mechanical stress/signal that is generated by the weight that will complicate interpretation. Normally, roots growing through soil will be subject to milder and progressive changes in direction, probably when growing around obstacles and in ways less easy to mimic in the laboratory. There are, presumably, complex feedback phenomena in growth reorientation detectable as oscillations in reorientation bending. At the present time, these are little understood and may reflect our still impoverished understanding of growth itself. The constituents of growth, walls, ions, turgor, hormones, different cell and tissue types, root individuality, and a host of other known and unknown factors, interact with each other and thus form a complex network (Trewavas 1999; Forde 2009). Understanding the behaviour of complex networks is still in its infancy. The current reductionist approach has been valuable in providing information on many of the constituents involved, but the more difficult question of assembling the interactions into a testable whole, has yet to be started.

References

Allan, E.F., and Trewavas, A.J. (1986). Tissue dependent heterogeneity in the root apex of *Pisum sativum*. *Botanical Gazette*, **147**, 258–269.

Aloni, R., Aloni, E., Langhans, M., and Ullrich, C.J. (2006). Role of cytokinin and auxin in shaping root architecture: regulating vascular differentiation, lateral root initiation, root apical dominance and root gravitropism. *Annals of Botany*, **97**, 883–893.

Benjamins, R., and Scheres, B. (2008). Auxin; the looping star in plant development. *Annual Review of Plant Biology*, **59**, 443–465.

Benkova, E., Michniewicz, M., Sauer, M., Teichmann, T., Seifertova, D., Jurgens, G., and 1 other (2003). Local efflux dependent auxin gradients as a common module for plant organ formation. *Cell*, **115**, 591–602.

Berleth, T., and Sachs, T. (2001). Plant morphogenesis: long distance coordination and local patterning. *Current Opinion in Plant Biology*, **4**, 57–62.

Bjorkman, T., and Cleland, R.E. (1991). The role of extracellular Ca^{2+} gradients in gravitropic signalling in maize roots. *Planta*, **185**, 379–384.

Blancaflor, E.B., Fasano, J.M., and Gilroy, S. (1998). Mapping the functional roles of cap cells in the response of *Arabidopsis* primary root to gravity. *Plant Physiology*, **116**, 213–222.

Blancaflor, E.B., and Masson, P.H. (2002). Plant gravitropism. Unravelling the ups and downs of a complex process. *Plant Physiology*, **133**, 1677–1690.

Brunoud, G., Wells, D.M., Oliva, M., Larrieu, A., Mirabet, V., Burrow, A.H., and 5 others (2012). A novel sensor to map auxin response and distribution at high spatiotemporal resolution. *Nature*, **482**, 103–106.

Darwin, C. (1880). *The Power of Movement in Plants*. John Murray, London.

Edwards, E.S., and Roux, S.J. (1998). Influence of gravity and light on the developmental polarity of *Ceratopteris richardii* fern spores. *Planta*, **205**, 553–560.

Estelle, M. (1998). Polar auxin transport: new support for an old model. *Plant Cell*, **10**, 1775–1778.

Evans, M.L. (1991). Gravitropism: interaction of sensitivity modulation and effector redistribution. *Plant Physiology*, **95**, 1–5.

Fasano, J.M., Swanson, S.J., Blancaflor, E.B., Dowd, P.E., Kao, T-H., and Gilroy, S. (2001). Changes in root cap pH are required for the gravity response of the *Arabidopsis* root. *Plant Cell*, **13**, 907–921.

Forde, B.G. (2009). Is it good noise? The role of developmental instability in the shaping of a root. *Journal of Experimental Botany*, **60**, 3989–4002.

Friml, J. Wisniecwska, J., Benkova, E., Mendgen, K., and Palme, K. (2002). Lateral relocation of auxin efflux regulator PIN3 mediates tropism in Arabidopsis. *Nature*, **415**, 806–809.

Geidner, N., Friml, J., Stierhof, Y-B, Jurgens, G., and Palme, K. (2001). Auxin transport inhibitors block PIN cycling and vesicle trafficking. *Nature*, **413**, 425–428.

Gilroy, S., and Masson, P. (2007). *Plant tropisms*. Wiley-Blackwell, New York.

Ishikawa H., and Evans, M.L. (1993). The role of the distal elongation zone in the response of maize roots to auxin and gravity. *Plant Physiology*, **102**, 1203–1210.

Ishikawa, H., Hasenstein, K.H., and Evans, M.L. (1991). Computer based video digitiser analysis of surface extension in maize roots. *Planta*, **183**, 381–390.

Jiang, K., and Feldman, L.J. (2005). Regulation of root apical meristem development. *Annual Review of Cell and Developmental Biology*, **21**, 485–509.

Keble, F., Nelson, M.G., and Snow, R. (1929). The integration of plant behaviour. 1. Separate geotropic stimulations of tip and stump in roots. *Proceedings of the Royal Society Series B*, **106**, 493–498.

Kiss, J.Z., Hertel, R., and Sack, F.D. (1989). Amyloplasts are necessary for full gravitropic sensitivity in roots of *Arabidopsis thaliana*. *Planta*, **177**, 198–206.

Kramer, E.M. (2006). How far can a molecule of weak acid travel in the apoplast or xylem. *Plant Physiology*, **141**, 1233–1236.

Kramer, E.M., and Bennett, M.J. (2006). Auxin transport: a field in flux. *Trends in Plant Science*, **11**, 382–386.

Krouk, G., Ruffel, S., Guterriez, R.A., Gojon, A., Crawford, N.M., Coruzzi, G.M., and 1 other (2011). A framework integrating plant growth with hormones and nutrients. *Trends in Plant Science*, **16**, 178–182.

Kuswah, S., Jones, A.M., and Laxmi, A. (2011). Cytokinin interplay with ethylene, auxin, and glucose signalling controls *Arabidopsis* seedling root directional growth. *Plant Physiology*, **156**, 1851–1866.

Kuznetsov, O.A., and Hasenstein, K.H. (1996). Intracellular magnetophoresis of amyloplast and induction of root curvature. *Planta*, **198**, 87–94.

Legue, V., Blancaflor, E., Wymer, C., Perbal, D., Fantin, D. and Gilroy, S. (1997). Cytoplasmic free Ca^{2+} in Arabidopsis roots changes in response to touch but not gravity. *Plant Physiology* 114, 789–800.

Leitz, G., Kang, B-H., Schoenwaelder, M.E.A., and Staehelin, L.A. (2009). Statolith sedimentation kinetics and force transduction to the cortical endoplasmic reticulum in gravity sensing columella cells. *Plant Cell*, **21**, 843–860.

Malho, R., Moutinho, A., Luit, A., van der, and Trewavas, A. J. (1998). Spatial characteristics to calcium signalling: the calcium wave as a basic unit in plant cell calcium signalling. *Philosophical Transactions of the Royal Society Series B*, **353**, 1463–1473.

Moirta M.T., Nakamura, M., and Tasaka, M. (2011). Gravity sensing, interpretation and response. In Witzany, G., and Baluska, F., eds, *Biocommunication of plants*, pp. 51–66. Springer-Verlag, Berlin.

Monshausen, G.B., Miller, N.D., Murphy, A.S., and Gilroy, S. (2011). Dynamics of auxin-dependent Ca^{2+} and pH signalling in root growth revealed by integrating high resolution imaging with automated computer vision-based analysis. *Plant Journal*, **65**, 309–318.

Ottenschlager, I., Wolff, P., Wolverton, C., Bhalerao, R.P., Sandberg, G., Ishikawa, H., and 2 others (2003). Gravity regulated differential auxin transport from columella to lateral root cap cells. *Proceedings of the National Academy of Sciences USA*, **100**, 2987–2991.

Plieth, C., and Trewavas, A.J. (2002). Reorientation of seedlings in the earth's gravitational field induces cytosolic calcium transients. *Plant Physiology*, **129**, 78–796.

Richter, P.R., Lebert, M., Tahedl, H., and Hader, D-P. (2001). Physiological characterisation of gravitaxis in *Euglena gracilis* and *Astasia longa* studied on sounding rocket flights. *Advances in Space Research*, **27**, 983–988.

Sachs, T. (1991). *Pattern formation in plant tissue*. Cambridge University Press, Cambridge.

Santner, A., and Estelle, M. (2009). Recent advances and emerging trends in plant hormone signalling. *Nature*, **459**, 1071–1078.

Scott, A.C., and Allen, N.S. (1999). Changes in cytosolic pH within *Arabidopsis* root columella play a key role in the early signalling pathway for root gravitropism. *Plant Physiology*, **121**, 548–558.

Selker, J.M.L., and Sievers, A. (1987). Analysis of extension and curvature during the graviresponse in *Lepidium* roots. *American Journal of Botany*, **74**, 1863–1871.

Sinclair, W., and Trewavas, A.J. (1997). Calcium in gravitropism. A re-examination. *Planta*, **203**, S85–90.

Swarup, R., Kramer, E.M., Perry, P., Knox, K., Leyser, H.M.O., Haseloff, J., and 3 others (2005). Root gravitropism requires lateral root cap and epidermal cells for transport and response to a mobile auxin signal. *Nature Cell Biology*, **7**, 1057–1065.

Teale, W.D., Ditengou, F.A., Dovzhenko, A.D., Li, X., Molendijk, A.M., Rupeerti, B., and 2 others (2008). Auxin as a model for the integration of hormonal signal processing and transduction. *Molecular Plant*, **1**, 229–237.

Toyota, M., Furuichi, T., Tatsumi, H., and Sokabe, M. (2008). Cytoplasmic calcium increases in response to changes in gravity vector in hypocotyls and petioles of *Arabidopsis* seedlings. *Plant Physiology*, **146**, 505–514.

Trewavas, A. (1981). How do plant growth substances work? *Plant Cell and Environment*, **4**, 203–228.

Trewavas, A.J. (1986). Resource allocation under poor growth conditions. A major role for growth substances in developmental plasticity. In Jennings D.H., and Trewavas, A.J., eds, *Plasticity in plants. Symposia of the Society for Experimental Biology, No. XXXX*, pp. 31–76. Company of Biologists Ltd, Cambridge.

Trewavas, A. (1987). Sensitivity and sensory adaptation in growth substance responses. In Hoad, G.V., Lenton, J.R., Jackson, M.B., and Atkin, R.K., eds, *Hormone action in plant development—a critical appraisal*, pp. 19–39. Butterworths, London.

Trewavas, A.J. (1992). What remains of the Cholodny–Went theory. *Plant Cell and Environment*, **15**, 759–764.

Trewavas, A.J. (1999). The importance of individuality. In Lerner, H., ed. *Plant responses to environmental stresses from phytohormones to genome reorganisation*, pp. 27–50. Dekker Inc., New York.

Trewavas, A. (2003). Aspects of plant intelligence. *Annals of Botany*, **92**, 1–20.

Trewavas, A.J. (2007). A brief history of systems biology. *Plant Cell*, **18**, 2420–2430.

Wang, J-W., Wang, L-J., Mao, W-J., Cai, W-J., Xue, H-W., and Chen, X-Y. (2005). Control of root cap formation by micro RNA-targeted auxin response factors in *Arabidopsis*. *Plant Cell*, **17**, 2204–2216.

Weisenseel, M.H., and Meyer, A.J. (1997). Bioelectricity, gravity and plants. *Planta*, **203**, S98–106.

Went, F.W., and Thimann, K.V. (1937). *Phytohormones*. Macmillan Co., New York.

Wolverton, C., Ishikawa, H., and Evans, M.L. (2002). The kinetics of root gravitropism: dual motors and sensors. *Journal of Plant Growth Regulation*, **21**, 102–112.

Wolverton, C., Mullen, J.L., Ishikawa, H., and Evans, M.L. (2002). Root gravitropism in response to a signal originating outside of the cap. *Planta*, **215**, 153–157.

Zieschang, H.E., and Sievers, A. (1991). Graviresponse and the localisation of its initiating cells in roots of *Phleum pratense*. *Planta*, **184**, 468–477.

CHAPTER 15

Signals other than gravity

It is hardly an exaggeration to say that the tip of the root having the power of redirecting the movements of the adjoining parts, acts like the brain of one of the lower animals receiving the impressions of sense organs and directing the several movements.

(Darwin 1880)

⊃ **Summary**

There are many other signals that cause tropic changes in root behaviour. Touch is the signal most studied and the modifications of root structure used to either avoid or move across obstacles in the soil are described. Touch signals are sensed by the root cap and give rise to rapid changes in cytosolic calcium. Touch also modifies the columella cells reducing responses to gravity. The sensory system in the columella is reconstructed and represents a likely assessment of future potential signalling. Gradients of water are again sensed by the root cap, but a different transduction sequence is initiated to redirect growth. Again, the starch-containing columella cells acting as statoliths are degraded. Humidity gradients may use abscisic acid and not auxin to help manipulate growth. Roots are also sensitive to light and grow away from unilateral light. There are many other signals to which roots respond and most have never been investigated for their communication and growth-modifying character. Roots can respond in many different ways to signals and these are indicated. Darwin's 'root brain' is briefly described; he was fascinated by the way the tip responds to touch and gravity. Finally, the dispute concerning root regeneration between Darwin and Sachs was resolved by careful experiments removing defined portions of the root tip. Most surprisingly, three new root meristems can be regenerated if just the dividing cells in the meristem are removed. These experiments have consequences for supposed stem cells in the root meristems.

All tropic movements are essential to fitness

Even though Darwin wrote one whole book on plant behaviour, very little of this actually found its way into school or university curricula on plant biology. What I learned at school about root behaviour could be summarized in one or two sentences as roots growing vertically downwards in receipt of a gravity stimulus sensed in the extreme tip. Again

we can quote from Darwin 'In the case of radicles of several, probably of all seedling plants, sensitiveness to gravitation is confined to the tip which transmits an influence to the adjoining part causing it to bend to the centre of the earth' (Darwin 1880, p. 568). One of the reasons that students come away with the idea that plants are simple organisms is the almost naïve level at which gravitropic responses are taught and the often extreme simplification of many current text books. In many cases little more is taught than that one sentence by Darwin above; it may also be included with a brief summary of the Cholodny–Went theory (Chapter 14).

However, even Darwin recognized that root sensing and response to their environment is complex. 'Although it is impossible to modify in any direct way the attraction of gravity, yet its influence could be moderated indirectly in the several ways described' (Darwin 1880, p. 567). The 'moderating' stimuli that Darwin was referring to were moisture gradients (already reported by Sachs 1887), touch stimuli, wounding by a simple cut and light, all of which roots respond to, as described below.

All tropic responses are concerned with constructing a plant body that best fits its current environment. Tropic behaviours are essential aspects of plant behaviour conferring fitness and those best able to construct the optimal phenotype improve the probability of optimal fitness. Various difficulties emerge as roots grow through the soil and these have to be managed, while continuing the primary function of gathering resources and anchoring the plant.

How roots deal with soil stones: the sensation of touch and inter-relationship with gravity signals

Most soils contain a mixture of materials, including stones and other hard materials. The avoidance strategy roots used to manage obstacles was first investigated by Darwin (1880, pp. 129–130) 'in order to see how the radicals (roots) of seedlings would pass over stones, roots and other obstacles which they must incessantly encounter in the soil'. So he placed artificial surfaces like glass slides in front of the growing root. 'The delicate root cap when it first touched any directly opposing surface was a little flattened transversely; the flattening soon became oblique and in a few hours quite disappeared, the apex now pointing nearly at right angles to its former course'. 'The radicle then seemed to glide in its new direction over the surface pressing on it with very little force'.

This initial change in direction is accompanied by a pronounced curvature of the side of the root opposite to the touch stimulation that looks like a dog leg. A recent excellent demonstration of obstacle avoidance shows this unusual phenomenon quite clearly (Massa and Gilroy 2003; Monshausen and Gilroy 2009). Despite the continued growth of the root, the sloughing off of root cap cells, and the production of new cells from division entering the growth programme and others leaving it, this shape is maintained. The tip is maintained almost horizontally and thus is enabled to slide easily along the surface. More likely, it will tap along the surface since there is a circumnutatory oscillation associated with a gravity stimulus that enables frequent checks as to whether the edge of the obstacle has been reached. It is, again, the root tip that senses the process of touch and that information is, again, conveyed back to the growing region to assume this 'dog leg' shape. When the edge of the obstacle is reached, normal vertical growth is resumed. As it grows past the obstacle, the elongating region of the root may touch its edge. The side that touches the edge reduces its growth rate so that the root can actually construct a rectangular bend around the edge of the obstacle.

Darwin (1880) reported that fixing tiny pieces of card to various seedling roots cause growth to become completely spiral, an enhancement of a normal circumnutatory movement that many plants exhibit under experimental conditions. Darwin regarded this spiral pattern to be the result of a permanent touch stimulus. If, however, *Arabidopsis* roots are grown on a firm agar surface sloped at 45°, they exhibit a wavy type of growth pattern that is caused by a periodic reversion of rotation of the root tip (Okada and Shimura 1990). These roots generated a repeating right-to-left undulation across the vertical growth axis as they elongated, producing a regular sinusoidal pattern. It was supposed that the stimulus was a gravity- and touch-induced response to the medium surface as the root tip changed direction in an obstacle-avoidance manoeuvre.

On the agar slope the root responds to gravity and tries to grow vertically downward. However, this gravitational signal is then overridden by the touch stimulus from the hard surface. The tip lifts slightly from the surface and with circumnutatory movements, directs growth in a different direction. The touch signal is remembered for a period of time, but eventually the slow loss of touch memory enables the gravity signal to reassert itself and a new wave starts. Mutational analyses do indicate the involvement of proteins concerned with gravitropism in this response. However, the rotation ceased when the plants were returned to the normal vertical position with an inevitable reduction in touch sensing. When an obstacle was encountered, the rotation direction was quickly reversed, a means of finding a way around small obstacles.

How does touch over-ride a gravity signal?

A transient touch stimulation of the root cap cells strongly inhibited both statocyte sedimentation and thus subsequent gravitropic sensitivity (Massa and Gilroy 2003). Other root regions failed to respond to this touch stimulus. The touch stimulus itself usually institutes immediate changes in cytosolic Ca^{2+} (Knight et al. 1991 and Box 15.1). In turn, this change in cytosolic Ca^{2+} mobilizes changes in

reactive oxygen species, synthesized by NAPH oxidase, and alters cytoplasmic pH (Monshausen et al. 2009). Perhaps, the most intriguing observation is that the effect of an initial point of impact of touch spreads to other surrounding cells via a calcium wave and ROS diffusion, particularly through the cell wall. This transmission phenomenon explains how a slight touch stimulus on the outside affects columella cells and statocyte sedimentation.

Touch is regarded as a mechanical stimulus and such stimuli are ubiquitous throughout plant development. Cells are enclosed by a relatively rigid cell wall and touch will cause mechanical distortion of the wall and its attachment to the plasma membrane. The consequent change in the structure of the plasma membrane opens stretch-activated Ca^{2+} channels. A transduction sequence is initiated involving parallel paths of information that result in changes in gene expression, hormone movement,

---

Box 15.1 The significant role of cytosolic Ca^{2+} in signal transduction

Calcium is a chemical cross-linker; it can couple together disparate molecules in a non-covalent manner. Therein lies its advantage for cells that wish to provide for a signalling system that is transient in effect. An unusual feature of Ca^{2+} in the cytoplasm is that its free concentration is extremely low, commonly 50 nM. Overall, cellular Ca^{2+} is at least 1 mM. Most cellular Ca^{2+} is found in cellular organelles such as the endoplasmic reticulum or the vacuole or cell wall. These subcellular, membrane-bounded compartments contain Ca^{2+} channels, protein complexes, which when open can transmit a million molecules of Ca^{2+}/sec and thus allow Ca^{2+} to flow down its electrochemical gradient into the cytoplasm. These membranes also contain specific ATPases that can pump Ca^{2+} back into these stores. Transduction chains therefore require proteins, often receptors, in combination with other proteins that respond directly to signals and can open Ca^{2+} channels. Sometimes membrane potential and/or mechanical influences on membranes can cause channels to open, too.

In the cytoplasm there are numerous Ca^{2+} binding proteins (receptors) such as the large family of calmodulins, 100 or so Ca^{2+}-dependent protein kinases able to phosphorylate and activate or deactivate other proteins. Many of these will be structurally located within the cell. Ca^{2+}-sensitive phosphatases can reverse the transient effects of kinases. Altogether plant cells contain about a thousand protein kinases with varying degrees of specificity.

An unusual feature of cell cytoplasm is its gel-like nature generated by its composition, often 20–40% protein (Trewavas 2012). The consequence is that many proteins exist in large transduction complexes either pinned to membranes or specifically located in defined regions of the cell cytoplasm, usually very close to channels and ATPases. Others form transient complexes when signalled; again, these are usually membrane bound. Many of these complexes are attached to the plasma membrane and form a discrete protein layer lying under the plasma membrane (Trewavas 2011). There is, thus, a defined spatial character to Ca^{2+} signalling. With a specific location of receptors or Ca^{2+} dependent proteins, discrete regions of the cytoplasm can be activated. A specific and limited set of cytoplasmic activities can be switched on. There is a strong relationship of cytoplasmic Ca^{2+} with the processes underpinning polarity and polar growth.

Many plant hormones and other signals, e.g. red or blue light are able to transiently increase cytosolic Ca^{2+} and the resulting kinase activation can also modify gene expression, as well as more transient functions in the cytoplasm such as ion flow or secretion. Numerous biotic and abiotic signals can also produce Ca^{2+} transients with complex downstream events generated. A recent book (Luan 2011) summarizes much present knowledge.

The material in this box is expanded in Chapter 23.

and finally growth. Sensing of such mechanical stimuli is implicit in plant development because of the interaction of turgor pressure and the wall. Growth stresses and strains, and flexing of shoot or root initiate an effective inside-out touch stimulus (Haley et al. 1995).

By stimulating the root cap on the outside with tiny pressure pulses from a micropipette, Legué et al. (1997) demonstrated that cytoplasmic Ca^{2+} spikes lasting about a minute could be demonstrated in cap cells. Cells in the elongating region were also sensitive with much shorter spikes than those in the cap. These observations become important when considering how roots avoid inert objects in the soil.

When roots were constrained to bend approximately at right angles as can happen when the root encounters an obstacle in the soil, this signal initiates changes in cytosolic Ca^{2+} in the pericycle cells and the commencement of the formation of lateral roots. This process does not require auxin and blocking the Ca^{2+} change stopped root initiation (Richter et al. 2009).

Darwin (1880) reported that the tip would respond to a touch stimulus of about a 1/3rd mg weight difference between the two sides of the root. If both sides are touched concomitantly with this weight difference, as Darwin did, it suggests communication and assessment of some kind across the root. A decision is made over which touch signal to respond to. [There are other plant tissues that Darwin examined, such as tendrils, that will respond to a few micrograms, that is a millionth of a gram; more sensitive than the touch in our fingertips.] He was also able to show that the root tip exerted very little force on the obstacle, as also indicated by Massa and Gilroy (2003), and was unable to penetrate very thin tin foil.

Hydrotropism or osmotropism

Although Darwin examined the potential role of water or humidity gradients in directing root growth he was not the first to do so (Kiss 2007). Sachs (1887) described a very simple experimental situation that showed a response to water or humidity that clearly overrode gravity. He placed seedlings on the edge of a frame set at 45°, but covered in moist paper. Although the roots could have grown vertically downwards, they refrained from doing so and continued growing at 45°. Darwin had also shown that a touch stimulus will override a gravity signal and was able to demonstrate that humidity would do the same. The sensing of the humidity signal, he was able to show, again, was located in the tip region.

There the subject lay for nearly 100 years, the experimental problem seemingly being the inability to distinguish hydrotropism from gravitropism. However, the experimental situations of both Sachs and Darwin indicated that the plant root has the ability to integrate both signals and to make a decision, to override the other, when the necessity emerges.

In the presence of a gradient of moisture or humidity the growing root curves towards the source providing a straightforward assay, but complicated by potential gravity signals too. Using mutants that failed to respond to gravity clarified the hydrotropic response. These agravitropic mutants enabled the measurement of the minimal perception time for hydrotropism of about 2 min. However, cap removal at successive time intervals after osmotic signalling, with subsequent measurement of curvature on a clinostat, indicated that the memory of the signal took three times longer to develop than a gravity signal, indicative perhaps of a different pathway of communication to the elongating and curvature zone. The evidence at present indicates that this pathway of communication does not require auxin transport (Stinemetz et al. 1996; Kaneyasu et al. 2007).

Several anhydrotropic mutants have been isolated and these exhibit a normal gravitropic response (Eapen et al. 2003; Kobayashi et al. 2007). Such observations indicate that separate transduction and communication pathways are distinguishable from those interpreting a gravity signal. A realignment of auxin distribution does not control curvature of roots towards moisture. Current results indicate that abscisic acid may be involved in communicating the response to water or moisture. Degradation of the amyloplasts in the columella has been observed to occur after a hydrotropic stimulus (Eapen et al. 2005; Ponce et al. 2008). Thus, a moisture gradient response may directly reduce sensitivity to gravity as also happens with a touch stimulus.

The directing effect of light on root growth

Although Darwin indicated that roots will also curve towards a unilaterally imposed light signal, he did not investigate this further. Roots of many plants do respond to light signals. The difficulty as always is distinguishing a negative phototropism from gravitropism itself. Imposition of a unilateral blue light signal causes a negative curvature in a vertically bending root that can, in due course, be constrained by gravity. One way to investigate this phenomenon is to set up complex imaging facilities. The vertical position of the root is sensed and maintained in the vertical by rotation of the medium on which the root is grown. In that way, any gravitropic signalling is obviated. What is then measured is how much movement is needed to keep the root in the vertical position.

The latent period before a curvature response was detected was about 30 min, slower than a gravitational response itself, but most crucially it is, again, the root cap that detects the unilateral light applied. The degree of curvature is related to the fluence applied (Mullen et al. 2002). The root cap is also the site of location of phytochrome, the red light sensor in plants and in the root. Red light irradiation causes a weak positive phototropic response and there is some evidence of influence on lateral root production (Kiss et al. 2001, 2003; Salisbury et al. 2007).

Outstanding root signals yet to be clarified

There are numerous other tropic phenomena. Pfeffer (1906) listed thermotropism, chemotropism, rheotropism, galvanotropism, and autotropism. Mostly, these refer to the signal that causes changes in phenotype, but these have received little or no investigation. Tip sensing of phosphate was described in Chapter 13.

Over the last 130 years, many other soil signals have been added to the compendium of information a growing root must assess. These are bulk soil density, mechanical impedance determined by soil character, water content as distinct from moisture (especially important when soil mechanical and hydraulic properties are layered), temperature, aeration, mineral gradients, pH, elemental toxicities like aluminium, other roots, and volatile gases present in soils such as carbon dioxide, ethylene, nitric oxide, and oxygen. The latter called oxytropism was discovered as a result of experiments in space. Uncultivated soil is a complex mosaic in which variably distributed hazards (e.g. predators, adjacent plant roots, etc.) are accompanied by equally variable patchy resources. Each is usually presented to the growing root as gradients often varying in intensity and direction, in both space and time.

For the wild plant subject to natural selection and thus competition from its peers, the accuracy with which these signals can be sensed and acted upon will directly feed into survival and ultimate fitness. The growing root thus experiences a mosaic of different environments and different signals, which must be sensed, assessed, and sensible responses constructed. Many of the signals indicated previously are all sensed by the root cap and, probably, the columella. How these differing signals are integrated into a compatible response that attempts to optimize fitness is still only dimly perceived.

The dynamics of the growing root enable plants to construct a sensing system that fits the predominant signal

What is most invigorating about the present state of research here is the demonstration that the growing plant root simply changes the dynamics of the sensing system to fit the predominant signal that is perceived. The root cap is not a static entity, but one in which columella cells are continually produced and lost. There may be some stem cells here, but this seems unknown at present. With signals other than gravity, the statoliths are simply degraded in preference to an alternative sensing system without them. Clearly, a decision is necessary here about when gravity should be overridden compared with touch, humidity, or light. How that assessment is made is unknown. What the other sensing systems are in the columella seem unknown if they are, indeed, located here. The change in columella structure is most surely unexpected and entirely novel. Darwin (1880, p. 573) summarizes the situation, since he reported on the above four signals that influenced root growth. 'In almost every case we can clearly perceive the purpose or advantage of the several movements. Two or perhaps more of the exciting causes often act simultaneously on the tip and one conquers the other, no doubt in accordance with its importance in the life of the plant'. Thresholds probably help discrimination and response. The great emphasis on experimental analysis of gravity signalling is seen to be limited in scope in describing root behaviour. Roots do many more things than just grow downwards!

What kind of growth responses are available to a growing root?

The following responses by roots to signalling have all been reported.

1. Increased rate of growth.
2. Decreased rate of growth.
3. Stopping growth altogether.
4. Sealing off root from shoot resources, leading to death.
5. Change in direction of growth polarity through 360°.
6. Change morphological polarity of growth, either getting thinner or fatter.
7. Assume avoidance structure over stones.
8. Assume growth reductions when obstacles are sensed, rather than touched.
9. Regenerate damaged mature tissues through initiation of division and differentiation.
10. Regenerate damaged tip.
11. Initiate branch root growth.
12. Increase/decrease intensity of branching.
13. If the tip is irreversibly damaged, ensure that one lateral root takes over and changes polarity from horizontal to vertical.
14. Developing a structure for a symbiotic relationship in response to bacterial signals.
15. Circumnutation: wavy roots; reversion of circumnutatory direction.
16. Increasing/decreasing root hair number.
17. Contractile roots.

Darwin's root brain?

The title of this chapter contained Darwin's expression of delight over root behaviour and his analogy of a root brain. That was extraordinarily far-sighted. The statement by Went and Thimann (1937, p. 151)

relating tropic movements to a kind of intelligence has already been referenced in Chapter 14.

A plant 'brain' is certainly a metaphor because Darwin recognized that plants have no nerves or nervous system, and he makes this very clear. Darwin was struck by the behaviour he actually observed, and realized that there are strong analogous behaviours between plants and animals. What he certainly called into question were the common suppositions about 'vegetable' or 'carrot' as meaningful descriptions of plant behaviour, as I indicated earlier. Darwin's suggestion has been recently resuscitated as plant neurobiology, an area of study, particularly in root systems, which emphasizes electrical controls and electrical information as mediating many signals (Brenner et al. 2006).

Was Darwin's description of the root tip as like or analogous to a brain correct? Darwin was someone who usually chose his words with care and I think he certainly did so here. John Allman is a brain specialist who has been studying brain structure and behaviour for over 30 years and summarized the properties expected of a brain in his book (1998). He has very pertinent comments to make such as 'there would be little need for a nervous system in an immobile organism' for example, but only in animals is speed necessary because predators or prey move fast, too. In commenting on bacterial behaviour, Allman states that 'some of the most basic features of brains such as sensory integration, memory, decision making and the control of behaviour can all be found in these simple organisms'.

How do the Darwin root tip observations match to these 'brain' criteria?

1. Darwin had observed **sensory integration** among the three signals he investigated; gravity, humidity, and touch. Massa and Gilroy (2003) dwell at length in their excellent publication on the interaction between touch and gravity.
2. A touch stimulus was **remembered** for several hours, as were gravity and hydrotropic stimuli.
3. A decision was then made after an assessment of the strength of the three stimuli as to which was the most pressing stimulus to respond to; thus, **decision-making** was implicit.

4. Finally, there was **control of behaviour** to ensure that the response was matched to the information gained from the environment.

Darwin's metaphorical brain was accurate then even in 1880.

Reconciling the quarrel between Sachs and Darwin

Regeneration of root tips and other tissues indicates the limitations of auxin involvement in differentiation

Darwin (1880) reported that excision of the extreme tip of the root caused a loss of gravitropic sensitivity. If kept in favourable growth conditions, however, he observed that, within a few days, the extreme tip had regenerated and gravisensitivity was recovered. How much of the tip can be removed and regeneration of a kind of tip be recovered is important. In fact, the observation itself is surprising and it is necessary to explain why. Sachs (1887) disputed Darwin's observation, but Sachs removed more than just the extreme tip. We now know that both observations are correct, but Darwin's is much more significant as regards understanding plant behaviour.

One simple way to initiate regeneration is to specifically ablate (destroy) particular groups of cells and, thus, initiate recovery processes. This has been performed by ablating the quiescent centre itself. A detailed examination of cell type respecification using defined cell molecular markers was made as regeneration followed from ablation. Although there is an accumulation of auxin at the tip following the ablation, this may simply be required to maintain cell division and permit other regeneration processes to continue as a consequence. It was made clear that the polar movement of auxin that finally accompanied the formation of the regenerated tip reflected an inherent polarity in the cells responsible, rather than being induced by the polar movement of auxin itself (Xu et al. 2006).

More pertinent observations of pea root tip regeneration were made by careful removal of defined lengths of the root tip measured from the quiescent centre junction (Rost and Jones 1988).

Removal of 0.25 mm of the pea root tip led to complete regeneration of the growing meristem in 7 days without obvious microscopic difference between the regenerated root and a control. Removal of more than 1.5 mm of the root tip that is removal of all dividing cells, obviated tip regeneration altogether, but instead resulted in the generation of lateral roots close to the excision cut. Removal of 0.5 mm of the tip, that is, removing the great majority of dividing cells, led in a minority of roots to complete tip regeneration (as for 0.25 mm). However, in the majority, regeneration led to the production of two or even three new root meristems growing in the same longitudinal axis as the initial now excised root meristem.

How does this happen? The developing xylem cells are often arranged in what is called a tri-arch—a recognizable three armed structure. Once the xylem is cut across, it is possible that the end of each of these arms leaks auxin into the cut surface, inducing cell division from which a new meristem regenerates. In situations where only two meristems regenerate perhaps stochastic processes enable two to get going earlier than a third and that, once well started, a zone of inhibition prevents any later regenerative centre emerging. With the smallest removal of the tip (0.25 mm), the tri-arch nature of the xylem is less well-defined and thus only one organizing centre emerges.

Failure of the stem cell concept for root development

However, two other conclusions can be drawn from experiments on regeneration. First, the stem cell concept often applied to root and shoot meristems at this level fails. As in animal cells, discrete stem cells in the root meristem are supposedly capable of specifying all cell types in discrete tissues. Although cells that abut the quiescent centre may look like stem cells giving rise to files of cells, if such cells exist in the true meaning of the word, they are clearly distributed throughout the meristem enabling its regeneration. This conclusion was also recently reached again by examining the effects of root tip excision and subsequent regeneration (Sena et al. 2009). There is no particular environment in the extreme root tip that represents a stem cell niche.

Box 15.2 Remarkable regenerative capacities are common in many higher plants

The regenerative capabilities of many but not all higher plants are one of their less-than-usual properties. When plants tissues are damaged the wound is often covered by a proliferation of largely, undifferentiated cells called callus. Removal of callus from a number of different genera onto a rich nutritional medium containing auxin and, in certain cases, another hormone, cytokinin, can keep cells, at least on the surface of the callus, in continual division. Sometimes these cells can be turned into liquid or shake cultures. By changing the balance of auxin to cytokinins in growing callus, either root or shoot meristems can be observed to regenerate.

Ball (1952) made vertical incisions on a lupin shoot meristem and observed that up to six new shoot meristems regenerated. Such observations have important consequences for the assumptions of the presence of a few stem cells in the shoot meristem.

Even earlier work examined the regeneration of the cambial ring in root and, indeed, later in shoot tissue. By cutting off vertically a portion of the root that contained the cambium ring and observing ring regeneration or displacing the cut off piece to one side it was found that the cambial ring could re-establish its continuity, even though much was originally lost. From the cut surface, wound-induced callus formed, an essential first stage. It was observed that the ring was reformed by new cambial cells appearing progressively from either cut end and eventually meeting in the middle of the newly-produced callus. In other experiments, roots were vertically cut and put back together, but displaced horizontally. In these experiments a polarity in the direction of cambial regeneration was observed (Steeves and Sussex 1989).

Many single-celled algae can replace a portion lost by excision (Sinnott 1960). Even single cells of a few species that are isolated from a mature tissue can with the right culture conditions regenerate a completely new plant. Pieces of tissue (cuttings) of many plants, such as stem, root, leaf, hypocotyls, floral axis, flower, are able to regenerate whole plants as horticulturalists can testify (Sinnott 1960). Plants such as *Kalanchoe* or *Bryophyllum* are able to generate plantlets from the margins of leaves.

The second conclusion is that information that specifies cell and tissue identity must, in part, come from the residual cells in the stump. What regenerates, in this case, is after all another root meristem and not other potential possibilities, such as a shoot meristem, cambium, or bud. Some plant species (e.g. *Taraxacum*) are known that will regenerate shoots from root cuttings, but not those used in the experiments above. Many experiments demonstrate that regeneration of whole tissues and even whole plants can involve very tiny numbers even just one cell as initiator; the process is not understood.

Similar conclusions to the above for roots hold for the regeneration of young leaves. *Monstera* grows leaves that eventually develop holes or tears as they expand. It is known that cells on the edges of these tears are respecified to form leaf epidermal cells, not those of root or stem. Regenerative properties are common in plants (Box 15.2).

These regenerative properties are most probably a response to the inevitable predation by insects (and others). How any plant is able to recognize lost tissues and initiate appropriate recovery to rebalance its morphology is not understood. Any individual plant must contain information about its whole phenotypic condition coupled with a mechanism that recognizes tissue loss and institutes relevant tissue recovery. Current views stress the importance of plant hormones and undoubtedly these are involved in the process of recovery but clearly more than that is involved.

References

Allman, J. (1998). *Evolving brains*. Freeman & Co, New York.

Ball, E. (1952). Morphogenesis of shoots after isolation of the shoot apex of *Lupinus albus*. *American Journal of Botany*, **39**, 167–191.

Brenner, E.D., Stahlberg, R., Mancuso, S., Vivanco, J., Baluska, F., and Volkenburgh, E., van (2006). Plant neurobiology: an integrated view of plant signalling. *Trends in Plant Sciences*, **11**, 413–449.

Darwin, C. (1880). *The movements of plants*. John Murray, London.

Eapen, D., Barroso, M.L., Campos, M.E., Ponce, G., Corkidi, G., Dubrovsky, J.G., and 1 other (2003). A *no hydrotropic response* mutant that responds positively to gravitropism in *Arabidopsis*. *Plant Physiology*, **131**, 536–546.

Eapen, D., Barroso, M.L., Ponce, G., Campos, M.E., and Cassab, G.I. (2005). Hydrotropism: root growth responses to water. *Trends in Plant Science*, **10**, 1360–1365.

Haley A., Russell, A.J., Wood, N., Allan, A.C., Knight, M.R., Campbell, A.K., and 1 other (1995). Effects of mechanical signaling on plant cell cytosolic calcium. *Proceedings of the National Academy of Sciences USA*, **92**, 4124–4128.

Kaneyasu, T., Kobayashi, A., Nakayama, M., Fujii, N., Takahashi, H., and Miyazawa, Y. (2007). Auxin response but not its polar transport, plays a role in hydrotropism of *Arabidopsis* roots. *Journal of Experimental Botany*, **58**, 1143–1150.

Kiss, J.Z. (2007). Where's the water? Hydrotropism in plants. *Proceedings of the National Academy of Sciences USA*, **104**, 4247–4248.

Kiss, J.Z., Mullen, J.L., Correll, M.J., and Hangartner, R.P. (2003). Phytochromes A and B mediate red-light induced positive phototropism in roots. *Plant Physiology*, **131**, 1411–1417.

Kiss, J.Z. Ruppel, N.J., and Hangartner, R.P. (2001). Phototropism in *Arabidopsis* roots is mediated by two sensory systems. *Advances in Space Research*, **27**, 877–885.

Knight, M.R., Campbell, A. K., Smith, S.M., and Trewavas, A.J. (1991). Transgenic plant aequorin reports the effects of touch and cold and elicitors on cytoplasmic calcium. *Nature*, **352**, 524–526.

Kobayashi, A., Takahashi, A., Kakimoto, Y., Miyazawa, Y., Fujoi, N., Higashtani, A., and 1 other (2007). A gene essential for hydrotropism in roots. *Proceedings of the National Academy of Sciences USA*, **104**, 4724–4729.

Legué, V., Blancaflor, E., Wymer, C., Perbal, G., Fantin, D., and Gilroy, S. (1997). Cytoplasmic free Ca²⁺ in *Arabidopsis* roots changes in response to touch but not gravity. *Plant Physiology*, **114**, 789–800.

Luan, S. (2011). *Coding and decoding of calcium signals in plants*. Springer, Berlin.

Massa, G., and Gilroy, S. (2003). Touch modulates gravity sensing to regulate the growth of primary roots of Arabidopsis thaliana. *Plant Journal*, **33**, 435–445.

Monshausen, G.B., Bibikova, T.N., Weisenseel, M.H., and Gilroy, S. (2009). Ca²⁺ regulates reactive oxygen species production and pH during mechanosensing in *Arabidopsis* roots. *Plant Cell*, **21**, 2341–2356.

Monshausen, G.B., and Gilroy, S. (2009). Feeling Green: mechanosensing in plants. *Trends in Cell Biology*, **19**, 228–235.

Mullen, J.L., Wolverton, C., Ishikawa, H., Hangartner, R.P., and Evans, M.L. (2002). Spatial separation of light perception and growth response in maize root phototropism. *Plant Cell and Environment*, **25**, 1191–1196.

Okada, K., and Shimura, Y. (1990). Reversible root tip rotation in *Arabidopsis* seedlings induced by obstacle-touching stimulus. *Science*, **250**, 274–276.

Pfeffer, W. (1906). *The physiology of plants*, vol. 3, transl. A. J. Ewart. Clarendon Press, Oxford.

Ponce, G., Rasgado, F., and Cassab, G.I. (2008). How amyloplasts, water deficit and root tropisms interact? *Plant Signalling and Behaviour*, **3**, 460–462.

Richter, G.L., Monshausen, G.B., Krol, A., and Gilroy, S. (2009). Mechanical stimuli modulate lateral root organogenesis. *Plant Physiology*, **151**, 1855–1866.

Rost T.L., and Jones, T.J. (1988). Pea root regeneration after tip excision at different levels; polarity of new growth. *Annals of Botany*, **61**, 513–523.

Sachs J., von (1887). *Lectures on the physiology of plants*, transl. H. Marshall Ward. Clarendon Press, Oxford.

Salisbury, F.J., Hall, A., Grierson, C.S., and Halliday, K.J. (2007). Phytochrome coordinates *Arabidopsis* shoot and root development. *Plant Journal*, **50**, 429–439.

Sena, G., Wang, X., Liu, H-Y., Hofhuis, H., and Birnbaum, K.D. (2009). Organ regeneration does not require a functional stem cell niche in plants. *Nature*, **457**, 1150–1153.

Sinnott, E.W. (1960). *Plant morphogenesis*. McGraw Hill Book Company Inc., New York.

Steeves, T.A., and Sussex, I.M. (1989). *Patterns in plant development*. Cambridge University Press, Cambridge.

Stinemetz, C., Takahashi, H., and Suge, H. (1996). Characterisation of hydrotropism: the timing of perception and signal movement from the root cap in the agravitropic pea mutant *Ageotropum*. *Plant and Cell Physiology*, **37**, 800–805.

Trewavas, A.J. (2011). Plant cell calcium, past and future. In Luan, S., ed. *Coding and decoding of calcium signals in plants*, pp. 1–7. Springer-Verlag, Berlin.

Trewavas, A.J. (2012). Information, noise and communication: thresholds as controlling elements in development. In Witzany, G., and Baluska, F., eds, *Biocommunication of plants*, pp.11–36. Springer, Heidelberg.

Went, F.W., and Thimann, K.V. (1937). *Phytohormones*. Macmillan Co., New York.

Xu, J., Holhuis, H., Heidstra, R., Sauer, M., Friml, J., and Scheres, B. (2006). A molecular framework for plant regeneration. *Science*, **311**, 385–388.

CHAPTER 16

Behavioural characteristics of seeds: elements of dormancy

If you can look into the seeds of time and say which grain will grow and which will not, speak then to me.
(Shakespeare, *Macbeth*, Act 1 Scene 3)

⊃ **Summary**

The phenomena of seed behaviour largely hinge around dormancy and its breakage. Some unusual characteristics of this process are indicated in the range of different chemicals that induce germination, as well as some plant hormones. Similar variation has been observed for a number of processes of development. It is indicated that the strategy of bet-hedging underpins much variation in dormancy breakage patterns, so as to ensure that some seeds are always available to take advantage of good growth conditions. The particular and complex characteristics of seed dormancy, and its breakage in the wild oat are outlined. There are distinct indications of different phases in the wild oat seed during dry storage that are not understood. Finally, the apparent synchronizing characteristics to the effects of plant hormones are outlined. Explanation of these phenomena might be found in the effects of noise in genetic circuitry, in particular, for transcription factors that are involved in controlling the specific gene products that are necessary for the germination process to commence. Above all, these data suggest that individual seeds act in their behaviour like individual cells.

Background

Crop seeds are the basic elements of human diet. Both religious and historical reference has been made to seeds throughout history and the quote in the title is a good example.

Karban (2008) and Silvertown (1998) indicate that germination per se should not be regarded as an aspect of behaviour. The process, it is stated, is ontogenetic, representing the unfolding of a developmental programme. Dormancy and its breakage however is behaviour.

A seed normally consists of two dormant meristems, the root and the shoot. Plant development is a trajectory, a continuum, from a single-celled zygote to the fully mature, but still-growing adult. As this programme progresses, the potential for plasticity of all kinds increases enormously as new dormant meristems are added to the maturing tissues of the stem and roots. However, in the seed with just two meristems, the only potential for plasticity will be in its timing of germination, but this is still behaviour and quite complex at that.

Any plant is at its most vulnerable when germination commences. For those germinating on the soil surface, temperature and moisture variation can be substantial, insect, slug, and bird predation is common. Some burial is preferable and tree seeds are often released prior to leaf fall so that they are covered. However, deeper burial in the soil can be common with the seed then fully hydrated. In the imbibed state there are further hazards. The seed must maintain its vital activities, respire, replace proteins and lipids damaged by free radicals, and carry out DNA repair. The reserves of starch, oil and protein will then be slowly metabolized and less becomes available for provisioning the young seedling. If the seed is buried too deep, the seedling may not have enough reserves to grow and penetrate the soil surface.

What breaks seed dormancy?

Most seeds, when shed, have undergone variable degrees of drying (5% for the grasses, 20% for many oil seeds). They are initially dormant, when placed in good conditions with the optimal temperature and moisture for germination. Dormancy is subject to maternal influences; the position in the caryopsis may be critical. Dormant states may require specific signalling to break them and recommence their programme of development, while for many others, time itself is sufficient to lead to eventual germination. These signals have a recognizable ecological basis, they are designed to try and ensure germination takes place in what will be the most equitable environment for seedling and juvenile growth. They therefore involve an element of prediction of what the future environment might actually be.

Seeds of some species can exist imbibed in soil for periods up to at least a century and only germinate when conditions are right. Germination can depend on flashes of light (usually red light), sudden increases in nitrate, and accumulation of soil gases, such as ethylene. In addition, specific variations in temperature that cue the month of the year, often for early or late summer when rainfall can be expected (Simpson 1990). Some seeds respond to specific chemicals in their environment. Other seeds can count the number of cold days (monitoring the progress of winter) and germinate when a threshold has passed. In some, fire is a stimulant to germination. Yet others can mark the passage of years and exhibit a discrete flush of germination, localized around a specific month each year for up to 10 years. In this latter case, there is a progressive loss of synchrony in the germination rates (Barton 1961; Simpson 1990).

Laboratory research has shown that, in many different seed types, dormancy may be broken by an array of apparently unrelated chemicals. These include various solvents, like ethanol and chloroform, respiratory inhibitors such as azide, carbon monoxide, and cyanide, reagents that react with sulfydryl groups in proteins (iodoacetate, mercaptoethanol), nitrogenous compounds (urea, thiourea, nitrite), reducing agents (methylene blue, hydroxylamine), oxidants (carbon monoxide, hypochlorite), various acids (malonate) (Roberts 1964, 1969, 1973; Simpson 1990; Bewley and Black 1994). I know of no research that tries to understand these remarkable observations.

If a dormant, but imbibed seed is placed under conditions not conducive to germination (high temperatures or sudden lack of water or reburial, for example), the seed generates a new molecular phenotype, called secondary dormancy (Baskin and Baskin 1980; Symons et al. 2006). In this state, the seed can remain dormant for many years even under good conditions for germination. Secondary dormancy is a rational strategy, again, for dealing with sudden adverse environments and is only slowly lost. This, too, is obviously behaviour. I suspect that buds exhibit an equivalent to secondary dormancy in seeds (Box 16.1)

Dormancy is a simple way for plants to hedge their bets against an uncertain future

Bet-hedging (spreading ones bets) is a simple way of reducing ultimate risk, i.e. of losing everything. For many organisms, if not most, life is a gamble against circumstance and ways must be sought for reducing ultimate risk. Hedging one's bets, that is, switching between different phenotypes, facilitates survival and persistence in a fluctuating environment. Bet-hedging is found in organisms ranging from bacteria to humans, and in bacteria the process is clearly adaptive (Hubertus et al. 2009). Because of their lifestyle, plants that experience fluctuating environments have three obvious strategies:

1. Either to produce huge numbers of siblings on the basis that some will survive.

Box 16.1 There is also plasticity in the dormancy of isolated resting buds.	

There are some similarities in the situation of dormant seeds with one aspect of the behaviour of the greater duckweed, *Spirodela polyrhiza*. This plant is a monocot that grows on the surface of freshwater ponds, generating new fronds (leaves) from an internal, but simplified meristem. Under poor light or temperature conditions in the wild, a single plant can generate a number of what are called turions, which represent a single isolated resting bud (Smart and Trewavas 1983). Experimentally, turions can be easily induced by the hormone abscisic acid, but these germinate as soon as the abscisic acid is removed. Turions induced in the wild usually have to overwinter before germinating. Turions are small, pigmented fronds with cells that lack a vacuole, are full of starch and with thicker cell walls as well as modified ion flux status. Turions sink to the bottom of the pond (or medium) to survive cold conditions. During germination in the spring, bubbles of gas form that enable the turion to float. However, just like seeds, the turion responds to a variety of light, hormone, or temperature signals that cause germination. This, too, is obviously behaviour, but exhibited by a structure directly formed from vegetative tissue.

Although most duckweeds cover the surface of ponds by vegetative replication, they can certainly flower and produce seed. In the wild, flowering is infrequent. Interestingly, flowering in duckweeds can be induced by a variety of light treatments and an array of organic chemicals (salicylic acid, EDTA, pipecolic acid, linolenic acid, polypeptides, nor-epinephrine) and some inorganic chemicals such as copper. Flowering is an ontogenetic process, but like other features of the developing plant, clearly plastic in its ability to respond to an array of signals (Pieterse 1982; Kozaki et al. 1991; Fujioka and Sakurai 1997; Yamaguchi et al. 2001).

2. If few are produced, provide enormous protection during the vulnerable period of development and growth.
3. Generate different phenotypes, one of which will survive the difficult times. The risks will almost certainly be higher, the more extreme the circumstances.

Plants exhibit combinations of these strategies

Production of huge numbers of seeds are common for plants that have grown in good circumstances—a single poppy plant can produce a million seeds, yet few will find suitable places for germination and most will be eaten by an army of herbivores. The alternative strategy is perhaps exemplified by the coconut. Only a relatively few coconuts are produced by individual trees. A strong fibrous cover and a hard shell protects the embryo against most herbivores and the milk inside provides both nutrient and water when a suitable place is reached for germination of the embryo. Generally, this happens when the nut is washed ashore, but what signal is perceived to initiate germination seems unknown. As for individual growing plants, bet-hedging is the strategy that produces enormous numbers of dormant buds during development. Self-evidently, this is a critical aspect to plant behaviour both in the individual and in the seed.

Yet there is a difficult aspect to understand. Take any batch of wild seed and place it under germination conditions. The result is often good germination, but a certain portion of seed will still not germinate. Most of the remaining, ungerminated seeds are viable and obviously dormant, and can germinate in succeeding years under the same good growth conditions. On the basis that fitness requires the maximal number of growing seedlings, such a strategy does not make evolutionary sense, until it is appreciated that for plants that grow in variable circumstances, the future environment still has a certain probability of being uncertain, no matter how good the present conditions actually are. If all seeds are dormant, then good growth conditions can be missed; if all germinate, then they may all subsequently die. Seed dormancy then protects against an unpredictable future and is a clear example of phenotypic plasticity. At an ecological level, dormancy is a factor dependent on what other seeds are actually doing. Dormancy is, therefore, a necessary strategy to deal with a variable environment.

Most wild seed is distributed in a dry and dormant state. Seeds are dried because they are broadcast onto the soil surface, and a delay is advantageous until rains ensure the seed becomes imbibed and the soil wet. The additional dormancy built into the seed increases the probability that germination will not occur until the seed is in a more suitable environment.

For certain ecosystems, some form of dormancy is crucial. The obvious examples are those of deserts, where rains may only appear sporadically over years. However, dormancy helps species avoid disease epidemics, fire, overgrazing, and drought. Soils can contain a seed bank of potentially viable seed built up over many years. Even Darwin reported that a teaspoon of soil contained in total some 400–500 small seeds that germinated on his windowsill.

Dormancy was recognized early on as a problem in cultivation. Current cereals no longer produce obviously dormant seed—it has been bred out.

Two broad categories of bet-hedging behaviour are theoretically posed

Conservative bet-hedging involves seed lines that:

1. germinate with reduced variance to either good or bad conditions, or
2. germinate well in good conditions but very badly in poor conditions.

These differences reflect the likely degree of variability of the environments in which the seeds are shed. Diversified bet-hedging, on the other hand, involves increasing the phenotypic variance among individual seeds of the population, some responding very well to good growth conditions and the others responding well to very poor growth conditions (Philippi and Seger 1989). Investigations on desert seeds indicate only weak support for the ideas (Philippi 1993)—the situations look to be more complex. Bet-hedging has also been suggested to explain the timing of flowering in some plants (Simons and Johnston 2003).

Timing in wild oat dormancy: a plant behavioural system with analogies to mammalian memory

Avena fatua, the wild oat, is something young men are supposed to sow. It is a pernicious and skilful weed, difficult to eliminate from fields once it is established, damaging both crop yield, value, and purity. Once shed from the parent, seeds can be easily covered in soil and there they remain in an imbibed, but fully dormant state, germinating sporadically over the next decade. The characteristics of dormancy are strongly analogous to some characteristics of mammalian memory. Wild oats produce seed with long or short versions of dormancy. Dormancy can be reinforced or overridden, and loss of memory might be likened to breakage of dormancy. Both memory and dormancy are modified by a variety of signals with a complex interplay of environmental characteristics (Trewavas 1987a,b; Simpson 1990).

Complexity of wild oat dormancy, a challenging biological system

The environmental conditions of the parent plant are critical to the subsequent expression of dormancy and there is a complex interplay with specific wild oat lines (Simpson 1990). Different inbred lines have been used to explore the behaviour of individual genotypes. Even though inbred, the seeds from any line can be extremely variable in behaviour, with deeply dormant lines still producing a substantial minority of seeds that exhibit no dormancy at all.

These deeply dormant lines also are quite individual in their response to maternal environmental conditions. In some, a warm maternal environment of 28°C produces completely non-dormant seed; moderate temperatures such as 20°C generate a mixed population, half dormant, half non-dormant and cool temperatures produce a totally dormant population. In others, warm temperatures produce either mixed populations or completely dormant seed. These maternal environmental conditions also interact in complex fashion with other maternal environmental conditions, such as water supply and are again individual to the genotype. Water stress itself can produce dormant, non-dormant, or mixed populations, but this is modified, in turn, by the maternal temperature and germination temperature states. Treated in one particular way, seed may germinate only at 4°C, but not at 20°C, treated in another way it may germinate at 20°C. Maternal nutrient status adds a third factor to this complex melting pot. In the field, of course, variable environmental conditions of climate and soil make dormancy an entirely plastic character.

What is striking, here, is how analogous these events are to sensory assessment, a form of learning from experience. Complex assessments are being made as the seed develops that will provide in some way for ultimate fitness of the line. Many of these assessments can clearly be regarded as epigenetic and, indeed, may not involve direct modifications of the genome at all. Instead, what we are dealing with is a variety of inter-convertible cellular network states from which, ultimately, germination can be reached.

In the imbibed state, measurements indicate that dormant seeds respire and synthesize protein at a rate anywhere from 50 to 100% that of non-dormant seed. Thus, the dormant state lasts much longer than the general turnover rates of all the cellular macromolecules. Information survives the complete turnover of its constituents. Again, this is analogous to memory; long-term memory certainly exists well beyond the turnover rates of all the cellular brain molecules.

Even if the seed is maintained in a dry condition with only about 5% of the water of a fully imbibed state, there are progressive changes in the capabilities for germination suggesting a synchronizing process is involved (Trewavas 1987a,b). However, the interpretation is complex. If such dry seed (or imbibed, but ungerminated) seed is placed under poor germination conditions, secondary dormancy is invoked, analogous to reinforcement of mammalian memory.

The fundamental mystery of dormancy: plasticity that signals its end

Dormancy finishes when the schedule leading to germination becomes dominant over that of dormancy. A threshold is passed, but what this threshold consists of is not yet understood. However, environmental conditions that modify germination in many species are as complex as those in the wild oat. A few-fold variations in several environmental factors can convert a dormant to a non-dormant seed and vice versa, and the length of time already spent in the dormant state is critical.

In the laboratory, gibberellin, a plant growth substance or hormone, can be used to break the dormancy of wild oat, but usually it requires 3–4 orders of magnitude higher concentration when the seed is new, compared with when it is aged and kept in the dry state. A variety of different chemicals can be used to break dormancy in the wild oat. When the seed is fresh, ethanol and chloroform can break dormancy, but after intermediate periods of time, respiratory inhibitors, such as azide or cyanide, electron acceptors, such as nitrate or nitrite, will induce germination. Even mechanical effects, such as solidification of agar as a medium for germination can curtail dormancy (Simpson 1990).

However, some dormant genotypes of the wild oat lose dormancy in response to azide or nitrate, others do not. Some respond to high temperatures for germination, others do not. Some respond to water stress, others do not. Only semi-dormant lines respond to thiourea to break dormancy. Exogenous gibberellin can break dormancy, but seeds in which endogenous gibberellin has been eliminated, can still break dormancy. The behaviour is complex, but probably matches the degree of environmental variation experienced by seeds. There is no obligatory molecular sequence that leads to germination; it can be approached from a variety of directions.

Dormancy is thus not a single molecular condition, but instead an enormous variety. Any one of these molecular states can be occupied by any individual seed. An interlinking group of molecular networks may account for this condition and its properties.

What deductions about seed dormancy are credible?

Despite the relative simplicity of the system, a seed, there is clear complexity in its underlying behaviour. This view is in contrast to a simple concept that relies on the presence of some inhibitory substance that is slowly degraded. Dormancy is not a static process, but a progressive series of changes that can eventually lead to germination, with the proviso that the seed can be returned at any time to secondary dormancy.

Could dormancy simply be the result of a state of unfinished development? Winter aconite actually sheds seeds that have not completed embryogenesis and need several months of development before germination can occur. However, the fact that dormancy can effectively be lost in the dry state (5% moisture) as in after-ripening conditions, argues against this possibility for other seeds. There is a limit on what metabolic changes occur in the dry state that lead to germination (Leopold 1999). A low rate of hydrolase activity is to be expected in 5% moisture. I have suggested that protein phosphatase might be one of those enzymes. In that case, protein phosphorylation system states might control the dormant state by manipulating protein/protein interactions that underpin control networks (Trewavas 1987b).

Plasticity in signalling is found in other plant behaviours

In 1992, I published a table that compared the range of factors inducing regeneration in callus or epidermal layers, promoting root formation, and cell division in shoot buds or affecting abscission with those causing breakage of seed dormancy (Trewavas 1992). The treatments turned out to be remarkably similar. These treatments were osmotic pressure, various minerals, sugars, plant hormones (usually at least four of them), various organic compounds, polyamines, and amino acids, fatty acids, phenols, light, pH, CO_2, temperature, and mechanical effects. The table indicates that there can be redundancy in the signals that initiate behavioural change. Many different environmental signals cause a similar physiological event. Redundancy in signalling should improve both reliability and accuracy.

Dynamical systems theory would view recognizable stages of development as attractors, conceived as a kind of vortex into which the molecular network will drop from different regions around the vortex (Sole and Goodwin 2000; Kaufmann 2008). On this basis, there is probably only one or two possible attractors that operate at any particular stage of development. Thus, the signals merely act to push the undeveloped state into the vortex, from whatever particular molecular state it is currently in. These data fit a pattern exemplified by the *Fucus* zygote, in which gradients of at least 14

experimental and environmental signals applied across the zygote can be used to specify polarity of germination and direction of rhizoid formation (Trewavas et al. 1984). Seed dormancy breakage is thus not particularly unique in the variety of treatments that can initiate it. A similar variety of stimuli can be constructed for induction of leaf senescence, stomatal closure, breakage of apical dominance, and stem and leaf growth (Trewavas 1992). One potential unifying factor maybe that many of these treatments can be expected to induce transients of cytosolic Ca^{2+} in the cells of the tissues involved.

Induction of cell synchrony may determine how plants control behaviour

Figure 16.1(a) shows the germination profiles of a gibberellin-deficient tomato seed when supplied with different amounts of gibberellic acid (Bradford and Trewavas 1994). Very obviously, there is substantial variation in the sensitivities of the individual seeds of the population in response to gibberellic acid. This is summarized in Figure 16.1(b) that suggests a normal distribution in gibberellic acid sensitivity in the seed population. This variation suggests a bet-hedging strategy, but the process of germination has within it the characteristics of positive feedback. Once started the process is driven forwards.

However, a real surprise is the width of variation in the sensing of gibberellic acid by this seed population. A more than 400-fold increase in gibberellin concentration was required to induce germination of the least sensitive 10% of the seed population to the most sensitive 10%. At low concentrations, a few seeds germinate, but as the concentration increases, more and more seeds germinate. For a single seed, the decision whether to germinate occurs over a very narrow increase in gibberellic acid concentration. The variation in numbers germinated, reflects a population response and cannot be directly related to what happens in the individual seed. Equivalent width of dose–responses was reported for very large numbers of auxin-dependent growth effects (Trewavas 1992). Potentially, the equivalent argument holds. The width of dose–response curves is related to variation in sensitivity of the individuals in the populations used for investigation

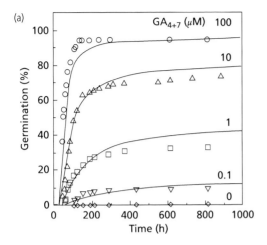

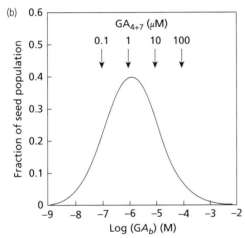

Figure 16.1 (a) Germination profiles of gibberellin deficient tomato seed against levels of added gibberellin, GA_{4+7}. (b) Suggested distribution of sensitivity of these seeds to added gibberellin among the population. Copyright American Society of Plant Biologists, published with permission from Bradford and Trewavas, 1994.

Box 16.2 Dormancy breakage in potatoes

Potato is again a good example of the effect of unrelated chemicals on bud break. Chemical treatments that work include 2-chloroethanol, carbon tetrachloride, bromoethane, thiourea, ethyl bromide, carbon disulphide, trichloroethylene, glutathione, thiocyanate, cyanamide (Denny 1926; Coleman 1983, 1988; Northcott and Nowak 1988; Wiltshire and Cobb 1996). Many of these will probably alter membrane permeability properties and may increase cytosolic calcium, but the measurements have not been made. Ethylene may inhibit dormancy breakage in potato.

in potato, which is less than 10-fold (Ranjan and Kaur 1954). Potato is another good example of the effects of unrelated chemicals breaking dormancy (Box 16.2).

Does variation in the gibberellin content affect the breakage of dormancy in the tomato seed indicated in Figure 16.1. This is certainly possible. Even in humans, hormone levels can vary 10–50-fold between different healthy, reproducing individuals (Williams 1956). It is thought that compensatory mechanisms enable the organism to survive such variation. It is the network of inter-relationships that are responsible. The hierarchy of levels of which the organism is composed exert increasing constraint as the levels of the hierarchy go upwards (Chapter 3).

The variation in sensitivity to gibberellin in this seed line can be explained by 'reliable' noise in genetic circuitry

I have indicated previously that one of the most puzzling features of the effects of exogenously added growth regulators (and probably internal growth regulators, too) is their capacity to synchronize cells and tissues towards a response (Trewavas 1982, 1987a,b, 1991). Synchronization suggests that the underlying mechanisms involved are probabilistic, rather than mechanistic. The most well-known example is cell division in which the numbers of cells leaving the first stage, called G0, and entering the mitotic cell cycle are determined by the strength of stimulus (Smith and Martin 1973). The explanation

and reflects essential phenotypic variability for organisms that must survive variable environmental conditions.

The observation of width in response is common for behavioural responses involving growth regulators like gibberellic acid, but oddly enough, not for the kind of artificial chemical indicated above that caused breakage of bud dormancy noted above, where a few-fold change may be sufficient for full induction of the change in behaviour (Trewavas 1992). A good example of the latter is the effect of ethylene chlorohydrin on breaking bud dormancy of this phenomenon requires recognition that cells have a threshold that they must cross before entering the cell cycle. These thresholds, however, vary stochastically in the population. Very likely, the threshold has the characteristics of positive feedforward; that is, a small stimulus becomes greatly amplified to drive the cell into mitotic activity. It is certainly possible that some environmental conditions could modify the threshold value.

The solution is the recognition of the stochastic nature of the threshold. Noise in genetic circuitry is well established. This simply means that for individual cells there is substantial variation in gene products, the result of inevitable errors encountered in any process that requires a number of molecules to get together to perform a cellular function. I have summarized much of this evidence recently (Trewavas 2012). There are many situations in plants where behaviour depends on single cells, the fertilized embryo is one, others, for example, are the pericycle where only one or two cells act to initiate a lateral root, pollen grains, guard cells are another, it is also thought that a single cell provides for the origin of a leaf.

Some transcription factors are found in single numbers/cell; the potential for error in replication numbers of these factors/cell must be enormous. Seeds are derived from a single cell, the embryo. Molecular noise will affect aspects of this individual cell as it is formed by fertilization. Assume that the products of probabilistic variation once established in this single embryo cell are maintained throughout the whole process of embryogenesis to seed formation. Assume also that some of these are in transcription factors necessary for germination. In other words, the variation in the first embryonic cell is a proxy for the final seed. Then, in certain respects, a population of seeds with certain different properties, i.e. degrees of dormancy, is to be expected. The breakage of dormancy in a whole seed becomes probabilistic just as it does for the cell entering the cell cycle and, indeed, a host of other processes, such as the formation of lateral roots, the response of individual guard cells to signals and, indeed, amylase formation by cereal aleurone cells (Trewavas 2012).

Figure 16.2 indicates diagrammatically the probability of a specific gene being switched on or off

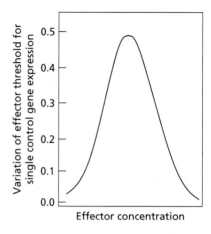

Figure 16.2 Suggested distribution of thresholds of effector concentrations among a population of single cells. This characteristic behaviour is exhibited by guard cells, pericycle cells, and aleurone cells, and it is suggested here to occur in the zygote and, thus, influence in the same way a later population of seeds (Trewavas 2012).

in individual cells (Levens and Gupta 2010; To and Maheshri 2010). What varies stochastically among the individual cells is the threshold that has to be crossed to switch the gene on. Note the similar normal distribution here and in seed germination (Figure 16.1(b)) and other plant cell types exhibiting similar behaviour (Trewavas 2012). Such probabilistic mechanisms surely contribute to many aspects of plant development. Noise then becomes a reliable way of ensuring variety in response, essential for plants experiencing an uncertain environment.

References

Barton, L.V. (1961). *Seed preservation and longevity*. Hill, London.

Baskin, J.M., and Baskin, C.C. (1980). Ecophysiology of secondary dormancy in seeds of *Ambrosia artemisiifolia*. *Ecology*, **61**, 475–480.

Bewley, D., and Black, M. (1994). *Seeds, physiology of development and germination*. Plenum Press, London.

Bradford, K.J., and Trewavas, A.J. (1994). Sensitivity thresholds and variable time scales in plant hormone action. *Plant Physiology*, **105**, 1029–1036.

Coleman, W.K. (1983). An evaluation of bromoethane for breaking tuber dormancy in *Solanum tuberosum*. *American Journal of Potato Research*, **60**, 161–167.

Coleman, W.K. (1988). Dormancy release in potatoes. *American Journal of Potato Research*, **64**, 57–68.

Denny, F.E. (1926). Second report on the use of chemicals for hastening the sprouting of dormant potato tubers. *American Journal of Botany*, **13**, 386–396.

Fujioka, S., and Sakurai, A. (1997). Conversion of lysine to L-pipecolic acid induces flowering in *Lemna paucicostata* 151. *Plant and Cell Physiology*, **38**, 1276–1280.

Hubertus, J., Beaumont, E., Gallie, J., Kost, C., Ferguson, G.C., and Rainey, P.B. (2009). Experimental evolution of bet hedging. *Nature*, **462**, 90–93.

Karban, R. (2008). Plant communication and behaviour. *Ecology Letters*, **11**, 727–729.

Kaufmann, S.A. (2008). *Reinventing the sacred*. Perseus Books Group, New York.

Kozaki, A., Takeba, G., and Tanaka, O. (1991). A polypeptide that induces flowering in *Lemna paucicostata* at a very low concentration. *Plant Physiology*, **95**, 1288–1290.

Leopold, A.C. (1999). Learning from seeds. *Seed Science Research*, **9**, 111–116.

Levens, D., and Gupta, A. (2010). Reliable noise. *Science*, **327**, 1088–1091.

Northcott, D., and Nowak, J. (1988). Effects of hydrogen cyanamide on seed potato. *Potato Research*, **31**, 95–103.

Philippi, T. (1993). Bet hedging germination of desert annuals: beyond the first year. *American Naturalist*, **142**, 474–487.

Philippi, T., and Seger, J. (1989). Hedging ones evolutionary bets. *Trends in Ecology and Evolution*, **4**, 41–45.

Pieterse, A.H. (1982). A review of chemically induced flowering in *Lemna Gibba* G3 and *Pistia stratiotes*. *Aquatic Botany*, **13**, 21–28.

Ranjan, S., and Kaur, R. (1954). Respiratory responses in potato tubers as an index of the effect of ethylene chlorohydrin and ammonium thiocyanate. *Journal of Experimental Botany*, **5**, 414–420.

Roberts, E.H. (1964). A survey of the effects of chemical treatments on the dormancy of rice. *Physiologia Plantarum*, **17**, 30–43.

Roberts, E.H. (1969). Seed dormancy and oxidation processes. *Society of Experimental Biology Symposium*, **23**, 161–192.

Roberts, E.H. (1973). Oxidative processes in seed germination. In Heydecker, W., ed. *Seed ecology*, pp. 189–216. Butterworths, London.

Silvertown, J. (1998). Plant phenotypic plasticity and non-cognitive behaviour. *Trends in Ecology and Evolution*, **13**, 255–256.

Simons, A.M., and Johnston, M.O. (2003). Sub-optimal timing of reproduction in *Lobelia inflata* may be a conservative bet-hedging strategy. *Journal of Evolutionary Biology*, **16**, 233–243.

Simpson, G.S. (1990). *Seed dormancy in grasses*. Cambridge University Press, Cambridge.

Smart, C.C., and Trewavas, A.J. (1983). Abscisic acid-induced turion formation in *Spirodela polyrrhiza* L. I. Production and development of the turion. *Plant Cell and Environment*, **6**, 507–514.

Smith, J.A., and Martin, L. (1973). Do cells cycle? *Proceedings of the National Academy of Sciences*, **70**, 1263–1267.

Sole R., and Goodwin, B. (2000). *Signs of life. How complexity pervades biology*. Perseus Books Group, New York.

Symons, S.J., Simpson, G.M., and Adkins, S.W. (2006). Secondary dormancy in *Avena fatua*. Effect of temperature and after ripening. *Physiologia Plantarum*, **70**, 419–426.

To, T-L., and Maheshwari, N. (2010). Noise can induce bimodality in positive transcriptional feedback loops without bistability. *Science*, **327**, 1142–1145.

Trewavas, A.J. (1982). Growth substance sensitivity: the limiting factor in plant development. *Physiologia Plantarum*, **55**, 60–72.

Trewavas, A. (1987a). Sensitivity and sensory adaptation in growth substance responses. In Hoad, G.V., Lenton, J.R., Jackson, M.B., and Atkin, R.K., eds, *Hormone action in plant development—a critical appraisal*, pp. 19–39. Butterworths, London.

Trewavas, A.J. (1987b). Timing and memory processes in seed embryo dormancy—a conceptual paradigm for plant development questions. *Bioessays*, **6**, 87–92.

Trewavas, A.J. (1991). How do plant growth substances work? II. *Plant Cell and Environment*, **14**, 1–12.

Trewavas, A.J. (1992). Growth substances in context: a decade of sensitivity. *Biochemical Society Transactions*, **20**, 102–108.

Trewavas, A.J. (2012). Information, noise and communication: thresholds as controlling elements in development. In Witzany G., and Baluska, F., eds, *Biocommunication of plants*, pp. 11–37. Springer-Verlag, Berlin.

Trewavas, A.J., Sexton, R., and Kelly, P. (1984). Polarity, calcium and abscission: molecular bases for developmental plasticity in plants. *Journal of Embryology and Experimental Morphology*, **83** Suppl., 179–195.

Williams, R.J. (1956). *Biochemical individuality*. Keats Publishing, New Canaan, CT.

Wiltshire, J.J.J., and Cobb, A.H. (1996). A review of the physiology of potato tuber dormancy. *Annals of Applied Biology*, **129**, 553–569.

Yamaguchi, S., Yokoyama, M., Iida, T., Okai, M., Tanaaka, O., and Takimoto, A. (2001). Identification of a component that induces flowering of *Lemna* amongst the products of α-ketol linolenic acid (FIF) and norepinephrine. *Plant and Cell Physiology*, **42**, 1201–1209.

CHAPTER 17

Games plants play

At the heart of game theory lies a complex optimization problem, where an individual's best strategy depends on what strategies other members of the population are using.

(Szathmary and Hammerstein 2004)

⊃ Summary

Game theory is constructed on the basis that individuals interact with each other, often competitively, and that selection occurs at the individual level. Various games are described, such as tit-for-tat, prisoner's dilemma, etc., that lead to different outcomes. Games that plants play require both self-recognition and the capacity to make decisions. It also requires learning, memory, and assessment capabilities. Game theory involves fence-sitter plants and the 'tragedy of the commons' scenario. The potential for soil space to be a resource may be an influence, modifying interpretation of games, although separate species respond differently to access of soil space. However, most plants do not act alone, but with extra symbiotic partners. These are mycorrhizae and other bacteria that have an intimate relation with the root. These other partners modify competition and can create mutual networks that allow transfer of minerals, water, and information on disease and herbivores. However, as in the prisoner's dilemma game, cheaters may occur. In a number of cases, it is known that the host punishes cheaters that take resources, but do not reciprocate with a normal symbiotic contribution. Shoots also play games over plant height, leaf movements, and finally reproduction. Game theory describes the behaviour of plants under competition, and provides further evidence for learning and memory that underpin intelligent behaviour.

What is game theory?

Darwin's original hypothesis for evolution envisaged over-production of members of any species. As a result, competition for food and mates was intensive. Those that survived produced most progeny. Darwin saw adaptation as a means whereby any individual improved its fitness. Two sources are commonly quoted that provided the bedrock of Darwin's (and of course Wallace's) hypothesis. First were Malthusian prophesies of human disaster from over-reproduction and, secondly the economic system existing during Darwin' life. The competition between businessmen for survival and economic success provided a direct metaphor for natural selection. Adam Smith, in the eighteenth century, had proposed competition as a cause of business adaptation and efficiency. It was surprising that little dialogue occurred between economics and biology at the time, but there has been a distinct resurgence in the notion of basing business organization on biology in the last 30–40 years. One product of that exploration has been the recognition that game theory introduced by Neumann and Morgenstern (1944) provides a point of contact for both biology and economics.

One difficulty for biologists in accepting game theory was that, until the middle of the 1960s, development of any trait was regarded only in terms of its benefit to the species at large. It was, of course, Darwin's original contention that selection occurred between individuals. The introduction of game theory came from the realization that selection did occur between individuals (Maynard-Smith and Price 1973). Game theory provides for a number of different strategies for any individual when facing a competitor. As in the economic analogy, businessmen are expected to strive for success for good or ill of the society in which they live, regardless of the overall effects. So it is for the populations of animals and plants. Traits can be selected between individuals or demes that would be deleterious, if embedded in the whole population. That might explain the enormous variation in the wild of any population. In such a theory, however, it is essential to specify the organisms involved, their possible interactions, and how success of one depends on the behaviour of others.

What game theory indicates about plant behaviour

Very few plant ecologists have used game theory, although some examples are given later of the few that have. This is surprising given the fact that competition is well established and that game theory deals directly with competition. Competition is discussed at length by plant ecologists, mainly in reference to community structure, but I suspect the mathematical procedures involved tend to limit interest. Biologists, in general, do not relish equations and often regard them with suspicion. However, a typical game of action and reaction that constructs the contest mathematically can be a decision tree. The branch points represent objective decision situations. The branches represent the alternative actions available. Which branch is taken requires assessment of past issues, coupled with assessment of the likely future when the decision is made.

In economic theory, the participants are assumed to be acting rationally using the human brain, although that assumption has often proved wrong. In biological game theory, one approach has been to assume that natural selection has already predetermined the responses. The alternative, and surely correct alternative, is that the organism assesses the situation and reacts accordingly. That ability to assess and make a decision is what marks organisms as intelligent. That is why I have included game theory in this book. Genes can only set the boundaries of behaviour; there is plenty of behavioural plasticity allowed within those boundaries.

There are several game-specific theories that are also relevant. The 'Nash equilibrium' is a combination of strategies, such that each players strategy is the best response to the others strategies. Such games imply recognition of others and, thus, self. (Evidence for self-recognition among plants is indicated in Chapter 18). The best response is one that maximizes the individuals gain against a fixed combination of strategies used by the other. The Nash equilibrium is strongly associated with evolutionary stable strategies (ESS) which constrain interpolation by behavioural mutants (Maynard-Smith and Price 1973). It is possible that such strategies give rise to apparently stable community structures, such as are found in single species *Salicornia*, mangrove, or wild wheat communities.

There is another game that leads to cooperation among, for example, kin. This is called 'tit-for-tat' (Axelrod and Hamilton 1981). The game simply requires the first interaction between individuals to be cooperative. Subsequent interactions are then required to copy or recognize, and respond cooperatively, to whatever the first individual does. It is recognized to take place between close family members and can give rise to altruistic behaviour, as described later by Givnish (1982) with respect to plant height. The situation described by Dudley and File (2007) regarding kin recognition would also fit in this category of cooperation, since competition is reduced among sibling roots in *Cakile edentula*. Donahue (2003) had shown earlier that siblings of great lakes seed rocket grown together produced many more seeds than when grown in mixtures of siblings from other mothers.

Signalling for tit-for-tat in plant shoots presumably involves the recognition of shading by adjacent siblings, the initial cooperation being protection in the seedling stage against wind, frost, or some such other physical problem? There are also excellent examples of cooperation between unrelated species, such as those for symbiosis, higher plants with mycorrhiza or nitrogen fixation. In these, cooperation occurs as a result of a tit-for-tat sequence of messages between the partners. Some of the signals are known, although the conversation is complex.

Finally, the game which has exercised many in this area is called the 'prisoners dilemma' (Axelrod and Hamilton 1981). In this game, each player out of two does better for itself if it cheats, rather than cooperates, but the combined pay-off for cooperation is greater than the combined pay-off for cheating—hence, the dilemma. Such a procedure can account for the evolution of symbiotic state and, as will be seen, plays a significant role in the interactions between plants.

Games below ground and between two players

The basic requirements for games between plants: learning and memory

Competition requires communication in some way between the individual plants (self-recognition) and other organisms that are part of the game; recognition of self, at least in roots, seems well established, leading to greater proliferation in the presence of non-self, aliens, or strangers. The association of con-generics with each other indicates additional relationships (Kelly et al. 2008).

The individuals involved also require the ability to make decisions according to circumstance. Decisions require the ability of an individual plant to learn about its environmental circumstances, about the adjacent organisms that it can sense, and to remember what those circumstances are for periods of time. Learning in plants, as in other non-neural organisms, involves perception of a stimulus, activation of a transduction pathway, and a subsequent change in behaviour; the flow of information in individual cells has been altered (Ginsburgh and Jablonka 2009). When the signal stops, however, a physical or chemical trace of the activated transduction pathway should remain, and this acts as a memory of the initial stimulus and its pathway. By this means, a threshold of response has been lowered, so that on subsequent signalling either the signal required is lower than before, or, the response is quicker or it is stronger.

Examples of learning and memory, in response to environmental signals of other organisms or circumstances, are indicated in Chapters 9, 11, 18, 21, and 26 amongst others. Learning implies forms of latency and recall. The mechanisms involved are multiple, but the basic elements in changing information flow can be seen by comparison with neural organisms. All forms of intelligent behaviour start with networks, whether they be neural or cellular networks, involving protein phosphorylation and other post-translational methods to alter protein activity. Through these modifying processes the state and connections within the network can be altered. Chapters 22 and 23 describe some of the cellular mechanisms involved.

Games played between competitor plants under laboratory conditions

In what follows I have not used mathematical equations that are common to all game theoretical analysis. Instead, I point out where game theory may be useful. The benefits of mathematical approaches are that equations can make predictions, which can then be tested. For example, Vincent and Brown (1984) indicated that the effects of competition (via the operation of a game between individuals) leads to a later flowering time than plants without competition, but as a consequence, ensures greater seed production. There is evidence that such behaviour occurs. If such behaviour becomes incorporated through genetic assimilation and ends up as directly heritable, then not only is this behaviour leading evolutionary change, it also indicates why some species will flower later than others. In addition, it will indicate the particular circumstances under which it may have been initiated.

One simple approach to examining how plants compete was examined by constructing 'fence-sitter' plants (Gersani et al. 1998). These simple experiments involved the construction and use of a number of leguminous plants with two equal and, thus split, root systems. The two roots of the plant were grown in separate pots and thus became a fence sitter. To assess the effects of increasing competition, in one half of all the split root pots, variable numbers of competitors from the same species were also planted. In the other, the split root owned all the soil. Root weight and numbers of both treatments were estimated after a period of growth. The response was quite clear—the greater the number of competitors, the more the fence-sitter placed its new roots in the unoccupied pot. The total amount of root hardly differed from a fence-sitter grown in the absence of competition. Individual plants can then make a comparison of soil circumstances and reward roots that grow in unoccupied ground with more shoot resources.

The total seed production of the fence-sitter hardly varied with the degree of competition in the adjacent pot. Those plants confined to single pot and the soil it contained, and thus subject to increasing competition, exhibited substantive and increasing reductions in seed number. Feasibly, lowered nutrient level in the competitive space or root secreted chemicals might be the signal that determines this kind of competitive behavioural response.

An alternative suggestion is based on notions of idealized free distributions introduced by Fretwell (1972). The assumption is that organisms distribute themselves in weakly competitive situations, so that no individual has a higher per capita population growth rate than any other. In that case, behaviour is based on density-dependent habitat selection. Plants proliferate roots to maintain sufficient acquisition of resources regardless of other neighbouring plant root systems.

'Tragedy of the Commons' scenario

The positioning of roots in game theory can be strongly determined by the position of the roots of a competitor, if the competitor can be recognized. This model predicts that plants that share each other's soil space will suffer Hardin's 'Tragedy of the Commons' (Hardin 1968). In common soil space, each plant attempts to gain the maximal amount of nutrient for itself and from the competitor, by increased root proliferation and orientation of developing roots towards the neighbour's space. In comparison to plants on unoccupied soil, competitive individuals will experience reduced reproductive output because of the extra resources devoted to the roots. Failure to participate in this game, however, could mean ceding resources and benefits to others. It would mean even greater reproductive loss. This version of game theory was constructed

from the behaviour of animals that compete with each other for food in a constrained area.

The assumption is that whole plant fitness governs behaviour. In that case, it is better to occupy a neighbour's soil space and gain resources there, than continue to proliferate with your own root system. In due course, those resources within the locale of the individual's root system will probably be acquired anyway. There is little or no benefit to competing with your own root system, but there certainly is to competing with your neighbour.

This game theory version in plants was tested by using a very simple device (Gersani et al. 2001; Maina et al. 2002; O'Brien et al. 2005). A soil box with a removable partition dividing it in two was constructed and one plant placed on either side of the partition. With the partition in place, each plant individual **owned** its own soil and did not experience competition. Remove the partition and each plant has double the soil available, but now faces competition and has to **share** its soil space with another plant.

Owners and sharers, indeed, did conform to game theory predictions using soybeans as the trial plant. Plants constrained their own root production when no competitors could be sensed, but increased root production when they sensed the competition and, moreover, turned their roots in the direction of the competitor in a form of confrontation. Owners **increased** their seed yield, while in sharers, seed yield was **reduced**. This game requires plants to recognize themselves and to recognize the other competitor plant as alien. Different signals and, thus, different responses are required in the two situations.

These results suggest that different roots and parts of a plant respond to their soil opportunities in a way that optimizes and benefits the whole plant. 'Thus plants may be more sophisticated and share more in common with animals in their non-cognitive behaviours than previously thought' (Gersani et al. 2001). Other things being equal and the plant acting as a coordinated whole, it should first proliferate roots into unoccupied soil, next into those of a conspecific competitor and, finally, into soil that is already occupied by its own root systems. Plants that fail to compete hand over the soil resources to plants that over-proliferate their roots and sequester available soil space for themselves.

The most efficient way to compete is to sequester resources from the soil before your neighbour does. The situation is similar in character to the 'tragedy of the commons'; a statement referring to the sequestration of all land resources by one individual on the basis that if he/she doesn't take it, others will.

Is soil volume a potential resource?

In their discussion Gersani et al. (2001), however, do raise an alternative view—soil volume is a resource, too. The evidence that plants do perceive soil space was documented some years before. Species, it was found, responded differently in both vegetative and reproductive tissues to physical soil space, independent of minerals and water. For example, one species increased allocation to reproductive tissues, relative to vegetative tissues with increased soil volume. Another increased reproductive output in smaller volumes (McConnaughay and Bazzaz 1991). These results indicated that, again, plants do not respond naively to variations in nutrients; other factors are equally important in determining root architecture. However, if volume is a perceived resource, then perhaps roots of a single individual separate themselves apart from each other, because of self-inhibition by secreted inhibitory chemicals (Caffaro et al. 2011). Any root secreting an inhibitory chemical to separate roots runs the risk of inhibiting its own growth!

The issue of soil space or volume in the owner/ sharer experiments was taken up by others (Hess and Kroon 2007; Semchenko et al. 2007) who considered that the issue of space in the experimental procedure created difficulties in the owner/sharer interpretation. On this basis, it was argued that the increase in soil volume in going from owners to sharers was sufficient in itself to account for the changes in root biomass, although less likely for the reductions in reproductive output. When more soil is available, it was argued, root systems simply grow into it, regardless of the presence of others. This is surely unlikely, given that plant-to-plant competition is established. It also contradicts the striking evidence for spatial root segregation and territory guarding in plants (Schenk et al. 1999), a subject to be expanded in Chapter 18.

The 'tragedy of the commons' scenario has, however, been demonstrated for three different kinds of legume, but the effects of increased soil space are not predictable on reproductive capacity, as indicated above. An extension of the competitive game (O' Brien and Brown 2008) indicated how the criticisms could be incorporated without a basic change in the game theory predictions.

Incorporating the third partner in games that roots play: mycorrhizae

Mycorrhizal basics

A general criticism of all the game theory experiments in the above sections is that the plants are grown either in sand, vermiculite, or some other artificial soil. The reasons for doing so are certainly reasonable, measuring root mass is made much easier, compared with disentangling roots from actual soil. Roots grown in natural soils however form symbiotic and mutualistic relations with a host of other organisms and these undoubtedly modify the relationships between root systems of different species. There are two kinds of mycorrhizal symbiotic states, arbuscular- and ecto-mycorrhizae (AM and EM).

Secretion of strigolactone by roots acts as a pheromone to attract growing mycorrhizal fungi. In phosphate deficient soils, strigolactone synthesis is increased, thus accelerating the formation of the cooperative game to be undergone. The formation of the AM symbiosis is only completed after a complex conversation of recognition, penetration and introduction into plant cells, only some of which is understood. If the conversation is correct, it assures the plant that the fungal organism is beneficial. Defence mechanisms are thus not initiated. Some of the fungal conversation signals involve various lipochito-oligosaccharides (Maillet et al. 2011). Recognition enables the fungus to continue a complex process of penetrating the root. Living root cells are entered to form an arbuscule that sets up nutrient exchange processes.

Once perceived by the plant root, these fungal signals often increase lateral root formation. The surface area available for symbiotic interaction is enhanced. Increased lateral root production, with reduction in the growth of the main root, is also a common response to phosphate-deficient soils and is sensed by the root tip itself. Arbuscular mycorrhizae form a fine network of hyphae that penetrates throughout the local soil taking up P, copper, zinc, and N, transferring them to the root cells in exchange for carbohydrate and some vitamins (Smith and Smith 2011). In the arbuscule, phosphate is transported across the root cell membrane to the host by a specific phosphate transporter, usually induced in the plant by colonization. Elimination of this transporter gives rise to much smaller AM nodules and more necrosis.

There is considerable emphasis on P in mycorrhizal studies because of its immobility in the soil, but the symbiotic state also enables greater drought resistance and improved resistance against pathogenic fungi and bacteria. Drought resistance is helped by transport of water through the mycorrhizal network. The improved resistance is not yet understood.

Plant cooperation through mycorrhizal networks: new transfer of information

Perhaps the most important consequence is that two or more different species of plant can share a common mycorrhizal network, thus providing the potential for communication between each. This is a very fruitful area for investigation. Song et al. (2010) have demonstrated that the communication network can convey resistance signals from one plant to another. They infected one partner with a pathogen and observed that the other partner increased the synthesis of a number of proteins concerned with defence mechanisms. Additionally, Babikova et al. (2013) have shown that information on aphid attacks can be transferred through the same mycorrhizal network to adjacent plants. Attacked plants generate volatile methyl salicylate that repels aphids and attracts aphid parasitoids. Adjacent, connected, but unattacked plants were observed to increase volatile repellent production.

Can plants enforce mycorrhizal cooperation?

Plant roots are usually colonized by several mycorrhizal species. Providing nutritional benefits can be costly and, thus, the expectation is that some species

---

> **Box 17.1 Examples where host plants enforce compliance on cheaters**
>
> Rhizobia in legume nodules that fix nitrogen poorly or not at all are faced with the sanction of a reduced oxygen supply by the host. The result of punishment is a markedly reduced fitness of the rhizobium species (Kiers et al. 2003). In both the *Yucca* and *Glochidion* tree mutualism between flowers and moth pollinators, the moth provides for pollination, but lays an egg in the flower that, on hatching, has a ready supply of food for its larva. In this case, compliance of one to two eggs/plant ovary is imposed on the obligate pollinator. While the developing seeds provide food for the moth larvae, flowers containing more than one or two moth eggs/ovary are aborted (Pellmyr and Thompson 1992; Goto et al. 2010). Fig wasps normally carry pollen to a new flower and lay eggs inside the ovary and the larvae feed on some of the developing seeds or ovules. If eggs are laid by a non-pollinator, either the flowers are aborted or very few eggs were allowed to develop (Jander and Herre 2010). Again, signal recognition mechanisms designed to count numbers of insect eggs, or to assess concurrent pollination with egg laying or to assess insect species must be present. The final stage of abortion is likely due to over production of ethylene.

could cheat, effectively become free riders, by gaining host carbon advantageously, but providing little in the way of phosphate in return. This would be a clear-cut case of the 'prisoners dilemma' game referred to earlier. In that case, one solution would be for the host plant either to force genuine symbiotic behaviour on the cheater or to punish them. A number of cases where the host plant either enforces compliance on the cheater or punishes them with reduced fitness are known (Box 17.1).

Alternatively, do market conditions operate to enforce cooperation?

The alternative is to create a market in which recognition of the supply of phosphate by individual hyphae is matched by the supply of carbon to the symbiont. The degree of co-operativity of any individual mycorrhizal species to the host can be assessed from the plant growth response, the costs of carbon/P transferred and/or resource hoarding by the fungus. Investigations showed that the most cooperative fungi transferring more P, received substantially more carbon as a consequence; up to 10-fold more (Kiers et al. 2011). This particular game is clearly in the tit-for-tat structure and its economic parallel is in trade between nations (Leigh 2010). However, in uncooperative mycorrhizae, experimentally providing more carbohydrate did not elicit the greater transfer of P. Instead, this partner hoarded P as polyphosphate. The implication is that mycorrhizal fungi and plants will discriminate between each other on the basis of their reciprocal carbon supply, and cooperative provision of P and other nutrients. A market operates.

Can any individual specie or plant provide sanctions against free-loading mycorrhizae?

In different species, mycorrhizae can range from cooperation to outright parasitism. A fungal species that was attacked by the specific host plant or denied everything by the host can easily acquire resources from elsewhere. The sanctions or punishment administered by host plants to deter free riders could be costly in terms of resources. However experimentally, it is difficult to define a free rider because mycorrhizae provide multiple benefits to the host. Mycorrhizae may not provide extra phosphate but instead help in other respects; most notably in reducing herbivory, disease and in tolerating drought better (Kiers and Denison 2008; Song et al. 2010). Furthermore, it is not known what conversation takes place between the different mycorrhizal species attached to the same plant. There is evidence that a mycorrhizal symbiont that finds its carbohydrate supply diminishing will reduce its phosphate uptake.

Mycorrhizae alter competitive behaviour between individual plants and even between plant species

Direct tests have been made of the effects of a variety of mycorrhizal species on the competitive abilities between two different species—a legume and a grass. Competitive ability was assessed quantitatively as shoot mass in different planting ratios of the two species. The quality of the soil and the species of mycorrhizae present both relaxed plant-plant competition (Wagg et al. 2011). Perhaps the more interesting observations arise from species competition that results from sharing a common mycorrhizal network (CMN) through which information and nutrients can flow (Walder et al. 2012). By establishing a CMN with just one mycorrhizal species between flax and sorghum, it was found that flax plants acquired 80–90% of the total P and N, and that most carbohydrate to the symbiont was supplied by the sorghum. In game theory, this would surely be regarded as flax cheating on the combination. However, with a CMN established with a different myorrhizal species there was a better balance of resource acquisition between the two.

The introduction of a third symbiotic partner in competition between individual plants makes for substantial complexity in behaviour. Individual roots may link up to common or single or multiple species mycorrhizal networks. Ecological interpretations based on the assumption that competition operated solely between individual plants has to be reassessed. With a third fourth, fifth . . . nth partner, explanations of complex community structure require increased understanding.

Ectomycorrhizae also form complex and wood-wide networks underground

Ectomycorrhizae are fungal symbionts primarily attached to perennial plant roots, particularly those of trees. *Rhizopogon* species are the predominant symbiont. The first appearance of symbiosis is the construction of a sheath of hyphae around the root. Subsequently, hyphae penetrate the wall space between epidermal and cortical cells where symbiotic exchange occurs. Again, a complex recognition process involving a conversation between root and fungus is essential (Martin et al. 2001). In these cases, the network of hyphae seem able to provide the plant with a variety of minerals not just P, although again P is emphasized because much root growth is limited by the immobility of this ion in soil (Smith and Read 2008).

The common mycorrhizal networks (CMN) can be enormous, being even woodland-wide. When a woodland-wide network was mapped, it was observed that there was a relationship between tree size and the numbers of connections to the network. Thus, the network had the characteristics of being scale free with small world properties (Beiler et al. 2010). With the evident size of such a network, the potential for intelligent capability is increased, but again, the presence of these symbionts alters the basic assessments of competition and game theory between just two individual plants.

Incorporating another third partner in games roots play: the root microbiome

Plant roots associate with numerous bacterial species that, qualitatively, are different to the microbe diversity found in the soil. Bacteria associate with the outside of the root, the so-called rhizosphere, while other species penetrate through cracks in the root (often opened when lateral roots break through) to become endophytes. Some of these endophytes fix atmospheric N_2 to synthesize ammonia and glutamate, in the much same way as rhizobial bacteria do in legume nodules. In return, they gain resources for growth and division, and are free from predation by protozoa. Others may contribute to host growth in alternative ways and yet others may be free riders, effective cheaters who benefit, but contribute nothing back. However, all endophytes require recognition processes by the host root, or they will be regarded as pathogens and subject to the full force of plant defence mechanisms. Microbes attached to the root surface, and thus in the rhizosphere, are likely to express recognition signals, too.

The microbial complexity of these two compartments has recently been assessed. Each contains at least 500–600 different bacterial species (Bulgarelli et al. 2012; Lundberg et al. 2012). The bacteria in these compartments improve resistance against disease, but like all mutualisms, there are costs to the plant too. An interesting possibility is that a qualitative change in the rhizosphere bacterial population opens plants up to pathogenic attack. (There is an interesting parallel with human beings that equally contain about a thousand different bacterial species in their gut that are thought to change qualitatively if the host becomes diseased.)

In game theory terms, it is the nature of the cooperation that is the issue. The common legume/rhizobial species cooperative mutualism perhaps illustrates the complexity of the game. There are many different strains of rhizobia that can enter a nodule and they do so in a morphologically altered state, called a bacteroid. However, these different species can vary as much as 10-fold in their provision of fixed N, but each demanding similar amounts of carbohydrate from the host. Other species of rhizobia either reproduce poorly in the nodule or even act as parasites. Other rhizobial species are endophytes, living in the spaces between cells or occasionally occupying cells, providing some N and receiving some carbohydrate. In addition, there are free-living rhizobia unable to colonize nodules at all.

If different strains live inside the same nodule, then those that fix N efficiently and enable better host growth and carbohydrate supply benefit other strains that perform poorly or not at all. Either these efficient rhizobia act altruistically, or the others act to cheat and are thus free riders. This is a typical prisoners-dilemma situation for the host (Kiers and Denson 2008). From present studies it would seem that the host is aware of the situation.

Discrimination does not take place at the first stages of recognition for entry, since poorly performing, but closely-related rhizobia still enter. Presumably, these strains have eavesdropped on the recognition process and acquired the necessary bacterial plasmid with the information. For those that perform N fixation poorly in a nodule, host sanctions involve reductions in oxygen supply as punishment. In addition, it is known that some hosts assesses the N fixed and provide carbohydrate on a *quid pro quo* basis; the more N, the more C provided. Other hosts can exclude particularly harmful rhizobial species, the implication being that the recognition conversation failed at some stage. The behaviour of the host can be perceptive and active.

Among the rhizosphere microbes, pseudomonds appear to be particularly useful, since they produce toxins to inhibit protozoal predation and also damage pathogenic bacteria thus benefiting the host. How many other rhizospheric bacteria are beneficial, is not known.

Games operate continuously between the roots of different individuals and symbiotic and mutualistic microbes: the conclusion

Game theory involves competition between individuals. Competition forms the basis of selection and evolution starts with changes in local populations or demes. The fitness of any individual is comparative determined by the capabilities of other members of the deme. So what relevance do game theories, between roots, have to selection? The root is a critical part of development of the individual, but only part. The state of the shoot is just as crucial; plants are integrated entities. The games between roots under one set of environmental circumstances will be crucial, but in others trivial. From the plant root point of view, the games are one step removed from reproduction, a phenomenon that takes place in the shoot. The condition of the shoot will vary in the same way, and under one set of circumstances shoot and root cooperate, under others they compete.

A basic criticism of much past plant ecological research is that, for ease of estimate, only modifications of the shoot were considered. However, the shoot and the root are inextricably linked together. Games involve behaviour and yet the behaviour, although apparently played between two individuals, actually involves many more organisms that are only indirectly part of the individual plant.

If the network below ground, like all networks, possesses emergent properties, then root behaviour must carry a higher level of uncertainty of behaviour between two individuals and that, in turn, must carry through to the shoot. The possibility is that a group of individuals linked together through the mycorrhizal network will, in turn, express an overall emergent property in terms of interaction, reproduction, and survival. Important lessons for behaviour and selection must then be assessed. With the evidence that congeneric pairs tend to be found in natural populations, the potential for direct communication of information through the root system becomes one additional way in which these pairs establish themselves (Liebold 2008). The corollary is that non-generic pairs, if formed, are inhibited, with neither partner doing well or the state remains completely neutral.

There are, of course, serious difficulties in examining how the root network contributes to overall behaviour. The serious difficulties that confront the rhizologist who wishes to obtain day-to-day assessments of what is actually happening below ground are multiple. Observing roots in soil as they grow looks likely to have been (expensively) and partly solved using magnetic resonance imaging, nuclear magnetic resonance, or computer tomography (Schulz et al. 2012). These technologies may replace mini-rhizotrons and ^{14}C labelling previously used (Trumbore and Gaudinski 2003; Strand et al. 2008), but even the limited studies available indicate how uncertain even basic knowledge on root system behaviour is, let alone their interactions in effective natural soil coupled with the symbiotic network, too. However, the interactions that do occur require conversations of varying degrees of complexity, and decisions to be made on the basis of that conversation. How those decisions are made in the framework of a mass of perceived external information and with the ultimate goal of fitness is what makes for intelligent behaviour, but solution and understanding is still a long way off.

The games shoots play

For the shoot, the scenario is entirely different to that of the root. The external environment is much more variable. Physical signals, e.g. wind, touch, rain, light, are plentiful and variable as are the biotic signals, such as herbivory, volatile organic chemicals and disease. These two environments, root and shoot, face the individual plant with a conundrum—how to deal with environmental variability in the shoot with better environmental predictability in the root and attached to effectively a third tissue, the mycorrhizal network. Yet the individual plant must still remain a complex, but integrated entity with differential decisions for both parts that must integrate to an overall decision on fitness.

Shoot decisions on growth and development have to be made as priorities, based on an assessment of the presented signals and with a measure of prediction as to what the future will actually look like. Shoot phenotypic plasticity is slow to develop so the element of prediction is likely to be more difficult for the shoot than the root given the greater, future, environmental variability. However, decisions have to be made for a projected future, otherwise the alternative, producing a new phenotype for a condition that no longer exists, is hardly likely to impact favourably on fitness.

The basic function of the shoot is to photosynthesize, to project and position leaves on a growing stem, and to adjust the plane of the leaf with regard to the direction of sunlight. The primary goal of game theory in shoots has been to examine the conclusions of what follows when certain rules operate. If a game is to be played then the plants must be close enough to interfere in some way with each other, a condition common in the wild, but not so for cultivated plants. Game theory has investigated shoot and leaf competition, although the number of papers are limited.

Game theory and plant height

Givnish (1982) examined the different heights achieved by forest herbs. He pointed out that, in the understory, light is limiting and yet herbs of very differing maximal heights are to be found. Those species that gain light resources best can, of course, gain even more light, water, and minerals. The competitive game that Givnish constructed implied a likely trade-off between the benefits of providing leaf area and the structural costs of providing for an ever-increasing stem height to support them. These costs increasingly diminish those available for seed production. The photosynthetic advantage gained from superior height, however, should depend on the density of surrounding foliage; a competitor can overtop others, gain more resources, and shade competitors. Givnish (1982) made measurements on large numbers of forest herbs, and found an excellent correlation between the foliage density and the final height.

Plants in dimly lit habitats tend to produce monolayers of leaves and, thus, intelligently avoid self-shading:

Leaves are not that stupid. Leaves are positively phototactic at low light levels and tend to arrange themselves so as to avoid overlap. Since mutual shading may often be the most important way in which plants interact trophically, it may be profitable to study leaf height as an expression of altruism. However for short, conspecific

herbs to exclude competitors from a highly productive site, they must possess means other than competition for light to eliminate opposition, such as root competition. (Givnish 1982)

In forest gaps, the shape of the gap determines the spatial distribution of diffuse and direct light (Ackerley and Bazzaz 1995). By measuring the mean orientation of the crown of a number of young tree seedlings, an excellent correlation was observed with the orientation of diffuse light in the gap. These seedlings can sense the optimal light direction and place leaves and growing branches to maximize collection. An effective monolayer of leaves with virtually no overlap was indicated and these data confirm those of Givnish (1982) above.

In a further analysis of the competitive games for shoots, it was indicated that in a multispecies canopy, a 'tragedy of the commons' appears (Schieving and Poorter 1999). The overall yield of the canopy is less than it could be because individual plants maximize their own gain in resources at the expense of others. In good light conditions, investment in height improves access to light, but bears increasing costs in the construction and maintenance of the stem. This game theoretic model can be generalized to account for the variations in height between different perennial plants competing with each other for light and soil resources. It can also explain the long juvenile periods in trees (Falster and Westoby 2003). These latter authors investigated a number of game theory assessments and concluded that only one explained the presence of leaves in a canopy at different heights. In this case, foliage height increases with leaf area and decreases with an increase in the costs of/height increment and crown depth. Only when reasonable access to light is gained, is reproduction initiated.

Leaf distribution and game theory

Leaves provide for the capture of external energy and are the equivalent of food to an animal. However, leaf populations are in a dynamic state undergoing birth, maturity, and death, followed by abscission. Even evergreen bushes and trees have an annual turnover. A recent approach has been to use game theory to understand the canopy structure itself (Hikosaka and Anten 2012). In this model, the leaf area index (LAI, leaf area/unit ground area) was predicted to increase with an increasing degree of inhibition and light interception between genetically-distinct neighbours. This implies most crucially that clonal plant stands with genetically identical daughters have a different LAI structure. These authors included the fact that it matters on the plant where leaves fall from, because those highest on the plant capture more energy than those that are lower down and partially shaded. Their model accounts more accurately for observations on canopy structures with competition between the various individuals. The model has yet to include the change in orientation of branch structure with age.

Game theory and reproduction

Game theoretic models also appear in many different areas of reproductive strategies and in internal competition (Jong and Klinkhamer 2005). There are conflicts that result in trade-offs between plant size and reproduction particularly in monocarpic species that die after flowering. There are also trade-offs as a result of competition between seed size and seed number. Larger seeds have a better chance of producing a surviving seedling. However, larger seeds reduce the number that can be provisioned and, thus, reduce the possible environments that could be occupied. How this decision is reached and judged is not known, but all trade-offs require decisions to be made.

There are also conflicts between the requirements of the maternal plant, between the growing individual seeds and between individual seeds as well (Zhang and Hang 2000). Either way the situation is regarded as competitive and thus subject to game theory analysis. In these situations, seeds may provide 'begging' signals to the maternal plant, requesting more resources, while the maternal plant is in a conflict situation as to how many seeds are produced and their eventual size. Recall that half of the seed's genome is foreign to the maternal plant with cross-pollination. These opposing situations require bounds to be placed upon them with decisions made within these boundaries. The molecular nature of decision-making presumably reflects the structure of the complex molecular network inside the plant at the time. There seems to be no research trying to access the understanding of decision making.

Conclusion on game theory and competition between individuals

Competition self-evidently occurs between individual plants in many, but not all environmental situations and the strength of the competition may vary too. A simplistic attitude to competition supposes that it is like a trial of strength—an either/or situation, winners and losers—and yet communities consist of a great variety of different individuals and species, a situation that does not lend itself to such naïve assessments. There are certainly some species that dominate some communities, but more rarely is there only one. What game theory indicates is that, in competition, there is a variety of behavioural outcomes, not just one. Some of these behaviours require cooperation, as well as competition, and with interpolation of a third or more symbiotic species both of fungi and bacteria, it is hardly surprising that the outcome is complex.

The common mycorrhizal networks may transfer information slowly, but this may be commensurate with the time-scale of phenotypic change in the individual plants involved. What occurs is a complex conversation of signals whose ultimate result is the common problem of survival by all the individuals concerned. These require organisms that can solve the problems that recur of variable nutritional availability. Those must end in reproduction and the over-arching requirement of fitness through it all. Problem solving is, of course, the acme of intelligent behaviour aided, in this case, by an established outside symbiotic network whose behaviour is only just beginning to be perceived.

It is common in the ecological literature to find discussion of trade-offs between all sorts of phenotypic characteristics, between, for example, shoot and root, between vegetative and reproductive requirements, between seed size and number, between dormancy and germination, and a host of others. Clearly, there are also trade-offs in symbiosis and what the symbiotic partner provides. Yet there is very little consideration of how such trade-offs are governed. Decisions have to be made, implying thresholds are crossed when one form of behaviour is selected in favour of another. These decisions are, of course, made by the individual plant. Aside from hand waving, often about hormones, the mechanisms are in no way clear.

References

Ackerley, D.D., and Bazzaz, F.A. (1995). Seedling crown orientation and interception of diffuse radiation in tropical forest gaps. *Ecology*, **76**, 1134–1146.

Axelrod, R., and Hamilton, W.D. (1981). The evolution of cooperation. *Science*, **211**, 1390–1396.

Babikova, Z., Gilbert, L., Toby J. A., Bruce, T.A.J., Birkett, M., Caulfield, J.C., and 3 others (2013). Underground signals carried through common mycelial networks warn neighbouring plants of aphid attack. *Ecology Letters*, **16**, 835–843.

Beiler, K.J., Durall, D.M., Simard, S.W., Maxwell, S.A., and Kretzer, A.M. (2010). Architecture of the wood-wide web: *Rhizopogon* spp. genets link multiple Douglas-fir cohorts. *New Phytologist*, **185**, 543–553.

Bulgarelli, D., Rott, M., Schlaeppi, K., van Themaat, E.V.L., Ahmadinejad, N., Assenza, F., and 9 others (2012). Revealing structure and assembly cues for *Arabidopsis* root-inhabiting bacterial microbiota. *Nature*, **488**, 91–95.

Caffaro, M., Vivanco, J., Boem, G., and Rubio, G. (2011). The effect of root exudates on root architecture in *Arabidopsis thaliana*. *Plant Growth Regulation*, **64**, 241–249.

Donahue, K. (2003). The influence of neighbour relatedness on multilevel selections in the great lakes seed rocket. *American Naturalist*, **162**, 77–92.

Dudley, S.A., and File, A.L. (2007). Kin recognition in an annual plant. *Biology Letters*, **3**, 435–438.

Falster, D.S., and Westoby, M. (2003). Plant height and evolutionary games. *Trends in Ecology and Evolution*, **18**, 337–343.

Fretwell S.D. (1972). *Population in a seasonal environment*. Princeton University Press, Princeton, NJ.

Gersani, M., Abramsky, Z., and Falik, O. (1998). Density dependent habitat selection in plants. *Evolutionary Ecology*, **12**, 223–234.

Gersani, M., Brown, J.S., O'Brien, E.E., Maina, G.M., and Abramsky, Z. (2001). Tragedy of the commons as a result of root competition. *Journal of Ecology*, **89**, 660–669.

Ginsburg, S., and Jablonka, E. (2009). Epigenetic learning in non-neural organisms. *Journal of Bioscience*, **34**, 633–646.

Givnish, T.J. (1982). On the adaptive significance of leaf height in forest herbs. *American Naturalist*, **120**, 353–381.

Goto, R., Okamoto, T., Kiers, T., Kawakita, A., and Kato, M. (2010). Selective flower abortion maintains moth cooperation in a newly discovered pollination mutualism. *Ecology Letters*, **13**, 321–329.

Hardin, G. (1968). The tragedy of the commons. *Science*, **162**, 1243–1248.

Hess, L., and Kroon, H., de (2007). Effects of rooting volume and nutrient availability as an alternative explanation for root self/non-self discrimination. *Journal of Ecology*, **95**, 241–251.

Hikosaka, K., and Anten, N.P.R. (2012). An evolutionary game of leaf dynamics and its consequences for canopy structure. *Functional Ecology*, **26**, 1024–1032.

Jander, K.C., and Herre, E.A. (2010). Host sanctions and pollinator cheating in the fig tree-fig wasp mutualism. *Proceedings of the Royal Society Series B*, **277**, 1481–1489.

Jong, T., de, and Klinkhamer, P. (2005). *Evolutionary ecology of plant reproductive strategies*. Cambridge University Press, Cambridge.

Kelly, C.K., Bowler, M.G., Pybus, O., and Harvey, P.H. (2008). Phylogeny, niches, and relative abundance in natural communities. *Ecology*, **89**, 962–970.

Kiers, E.T., Duhamel, M., Beesetty, Y., Mensah, J.A., Franken, O., Verbruggen, E., and 9 others (2011). Reciprocal rewards stabilise cooperation in the mycorrhizal symbiosis. *Science*, **333**, 880–882.

Kiers, E.T., and Ford Denison, R. (2008). Sanctions and cooperation and the stability of plant-rhizosphere mutualisms. *Annual Review of Ecology and Systematics*, **39**, 215–236.

Kiers, E.T., Rousseau R.A., West, S.A., and Denison, R.F. (2003). Host sanctions and the legume rhizobia mutualism. *Nature*, **425**, 78–81.

Leigh, E.G. (2010). The evolution of mutualism. *Journal of Evolutionary Biology*, **23**, 2507–2528.

Liebold, M.A. (2008). Return of the niche. *Nature*, **454**, 39–41.

Lundberg, D.S., Lebeis, S.L., Paredes, S.H., Yourstone, S., Gehring, J., Malfatti, S., and 10 others (2012). Defining the core *Arabidopsis thaliana* root microbiome. *Nature*, **488**, 86–90.

Maillet, F., Poinsot, V., Andre, O., Puech-Pages, V., Haouy, A., Gueunier, M., and 8 others (2011). Fungal lipo-chito-oligosaccharide symbiotic signals in arbuscular mycorrhiza. *Nature*, **469**, 58–63.

Maina, G.G., Brown, J.S., and Gersani, M. (2002). Intra plant versus interplant competition in beans: avoidance, resource matching or tragedy of the commons. *Plant Ecology*, **160**, 235–247.

Martin, F., Duplessis, S., Ditengou, F., Lagrange, H., Voiblet, C., and Lapeyrie, F. (2001). Developmental cross talking in the ectomycorrhizal symbiosis: signals and communication genes. *New Phytologist*, **151**, 145–154.

Maynard-Smith, J., and Price, G.R. (1973). The logic of animal conflict. *Nature*, **246**, 15–19.

McConnaughay, K.D.M., and Bazzaz, F.A. (1991). Is physical space a soil resource? *Ecology*, **72**, 94–103.

Neumann, J., von, and Morgenstern, O. (1944). *Theory of games and economic behaviour*. Princeton University Press, Princeton, NJ.

O'Brien, E.E., and Brown, J.S. (2008). Games roots play: effect of soil volume and nutrients. *Journal of Ecology*, **96**, 438–446.

O'Brien, E.E., Gersani, M., and Brown, J.S. (2005). Root proliferation and seed yield in response to spatial heterogeneity of below ground competition. *New Phytologist*, **168**, 401–412.

Pellmyr, O., and Thompson, J.N. (1992). Multiple occurrences of mutualism in the yucca moth lineage. *Proceedings of the National Academy of Sciences USA*, **89**, 2927–2929.

Schenk, H.J., Callaway R.A., and Mahall, B.E. (1999). Spatial root segregation. Are roots territorial? *Advances in Ecological Research*, **28**, 145–180.

Schieving, F., and Poorter, H. (1999). Carbon gain in a multispecies canopy: the role of specific leaf area and photosynthetic nitrogen-use efficiency in the tragedy of the commons. *New Phytologist*, **143**, 201–211.

Schulz, H., Postma, J.A., van Dusschoten, D., Scharr, H., and Behnke, S. (2012). 3D reconstruction of plant roots from MRI images. *Proceedings of the International Conference on Computer Vision Theory and Applications (VISAPP)*, pp. 1–9. Springer, Berlin.

Semchenko, M., Hutchings, M.J., and John, E. (2007). Challenging the tragedy of the commons : confounding effects of neighbour presence and substrate volume. *Journal of Ecology*, **95**, 252–260.

Smith, S.E. and Read, D.J. (2008). *Mycorrhizal Symbiosis*. Academic Press, London.

Smith, S.E., and Smith, F.A. (2011). Roles of arbuscular mycorrhizas in plant nutrition and growth: paradigms from cellular to ecosystems scales. *Annual Review of Plant Biology*, **62**, 227–250.

Song, Y.Y, Zeng, R.S., Xu, J.F., Li, J., Shen, X., and Yihdego, W.G. (2010). Interplant communication of tomato plants through underground common mycorrhizal networks. *PLoS ONE*, **5**(10), e13324.

Strand A.E., Pritchard, S.G., McCormack, M.L., David, M.A., and Oren, R. (2008). Irreconcilable differences: fine root life spans and soil carbon persistence. *Science*, **319**, 456–458.

Szathmary, E., and Hammerstein, P. (2004). Obituary: John Maynard Smith (1920–2004). *Nature*, **429**, 258–259.

Trumbore, S.E., and Gaudinski, J.B. (2003). The secret lives of roots. *Science*, **302**, 1344–1345.

Vincent, T.L., and Brown, J.S. (1984). Stability in an evolutionary game. *Theoretical Population Biology*, **26**, 408–427.

Wagg, C., Jansa, J., Stadler, M., Schmid, B., and Heiden, M.G.A., van der (2011). Mycorrhizal fungal identity and diversity relaxes plant-plant competition. *Ecology*, **92**, 1303–1313.

Walder, F., Niemann, H., Natarajan, M., Lehmann, M.F., Boller, T., and Wiemken, A. (2012). Mycorrhizal networks: common goods of plants share unequal terms of trade. *Plant Physiology*, **159**, 789–797.

Zhang, D-Y., and Hang, X-H. (2000). Costly solicitation, timing of offspring conflict and resource allocation in plants. *Annals of Botany*, **86**, 123–131.

CHAPTER 18

Competition and cooperation between individual plants for mates and territory: the recognition of self

Sexual reproduction is the chef d'oeuvre, the masterpiece of Nature.

(Darwin 1800, quoted in Smith and Arnott 2005)

⊃ Summary

Although it is common to find competition for mates in many animal species, similar competitive capabilities are rarely recognized in plants. However, competition for the fittest mates in plants occurs through a variety of discriminating chemical and developmental mechanisms, notably pollen competition to first enter the ovary, to self/non-self-incompatibility mechanisms and others. Potential cooperative behaviour between plant species has been observed in which pairs of species seem to prefer to grow adjacent to each other. The use of volatiles in cooperatively helping protect neighbours against herbivore attack has been reported. Competition for space between trees occurs particularly with close neighbours and leads to crown asymmetry. The strong indications are that crown asymmetry is adaptive behaviour and thus can be regarded as intelligent behaviour. Root systems in a number of species have been shown to have the unusual properties of self-recognition. It is thought that self-recognition operates through physiological coordination. Recognizing one's self is of value in that, with a plastically developing plant, self-competition among growing roots is reduced and internal resources saved.

Competition for mates

Competition for mates is well-known in certain animal groups. Often it is the highly decorative males that compete with each other through elaborate signalling displays. There is also a second signalling conversation between male and female whether it be chemical (scent), visual, vocal, or physical. Alongside this is a clear territorial aspect. Males that control the largest territory also control the largest numbers of females and available food. In this chapter how plants conduct some of their competition and potential cooperation for mates and food is described. Both behaviours require the ability to recognize self and non-self.

The structure of mating in higher plants

Darwin (1858) in his origin of species failed to discuss mate competition in plants, probably because it was not immediately obvious how it could occur, but it does. The title quote from Charles Darwins' grandfather, Erasmus Darwin, fronted an article that indicated how sexual reproduction increased the variety available for evolution to work on compared with asexual reproduction.

Plant Behaviour and Intelligence. First Edition. Anthony Trewavas.
© Anthony Trewavas 2014. Published 2014 by Oxford University Press.

Fertilization in angiosperms takes place between the male cell located in the pollen, and the egg or ovum located in the ovary, usually embedded in the flower. In lower plants, such as ferns, the sperm is motile and swims in surface water towards the egg cell on a haploid structure, the prothallus, attracted by specific chemical gradients. The angiosperms evolved this different method of fertilization, called siphonogamy, as a response to the occupation of drier climates, several hundred million years ago by angiosperm ancestors. No doubt, competition for land and the resources within it was the evolutionary driver, since there had to be some reason to occupy less clement conditions. The male cell is enclosed in a growing pollen tube whose growth is directed by gradients of specific pheromones towards the ovary and the eggs. The path of the pollen tube in the stigma can be elaborate, involving numerous changes in direction. Pollen tubes secrete a number of hydrolytic enzymes and the passage of pollen to the ovary may involve partial digestion of female tissues to enable penetration. Being (effectively) a single cell, the tube can grow surprisingly fast, up to 10 cm/day.

Many higher plants are hermaphroditic and can self-pollinate. However, self-pollination is an insurance, a fallback, if all else fails; a form of bet-hedging. Usually, there are processes that mitigate against immediate self-pollination and these enable forms of competition to emerge between pollen grains. However, since plant behaviour is different to that of animals, competitive behaviour to ensure only the fittest mates manage fertilization, is likely to be different too. Communication is involved, some of it complex. In general, the numbers of flowers produced by any individual is usually related to the previous life-cycle success. When conditions are very bad, many perennial plants may flower abundantly as a last resort and a precedent to death. A prediction about the potential future has thus been made, although how this is signalled is not understood.

Pollen is classed as the male cell, but often pollen contains three nuclei, only one of which is concerned with fertilizing the egg. The vegetative nucleus is responsible for the synthesis of proteins necessary for the growing pollen tube, while the third nucleus is involved in the formation of a triploid structure, the endosperm, which becomes a repository of stored material in the seed. Pollen tubes germinate when they adhere to the often-viscous secretions of the stigma.

However, the grasses in particular use a dry stigma. On attachment of the grass pollen to the stigma, a drop of liquid forms at the junction into which the pollen tube grows (Sanchez et al. 2004). Specific lipids are necessary for penetration. Application of these lipids to leaves enables pollen tubes to, most unusually, penetrate and grow through them, too. The mechanisms of penetration are not understood, but digestion of surfaces and walls may occur.

Mate selection is optimized in a variety of ways

1. *Pollen viability and growth rate:* anyone who has observed pollen growth *in vitro* on defined media, knows how extraordinarily variable are both germinability and the rate of growth among the individual pollen grains. In this case, selection certainly operates because the vegetative nucleus, that is deeply involved in the growth and germination of the pollen tube, is of the same genotype as the sexual nucleus. Clearly, competition takes place as pollen tubes grow down through the style towards the ovary. Those that arrive at the ovary first, have a choice of eggs for fertilization. Usually, they do not fertilize the nearest, but grow within the ovary, assessing the eggs (?) before a choice, a decision, is finally made. The implication is that the fastest growing pollen may be considered the fittest and because the nearest ovum is not the first to be fertilized, this suggests selection must operate after assessment of the females.

2. *Self-incompatibility:* up to 50% of angiosperms are described as self-incompatible (Franklin-Tong 2008). Pollen from flowers of the same plant are rejected. The aim is to cause out-breeding, even though the individual is structurally hermaphrodite. A variety of mechanisms underpinning self-incompatibility are known to exist, but the end is the same, a rejection of self-pollen arriving on the stigma of the same individual (Zhang et al. 2009). Only pollen from another individual can grow unhindered. Self-pollen is usually killed

in the style or its growth is severely constrained, accomplishing the same goal if foreign pollen is available. If not, then in these cases, like tobacco, self-fertilization occurs as a fallback position (Graaf et al. 2006).

The mechanism of recognition clearly requires self-awareness or self-recognition, a distinguishing of self from alien, a phenomenon that recurs in root recognition. As the pollen tube penetrates the stigma and style, it comes into contact with the extracellular matrix of the style that contains numerous proteins secreted by the pistil (Sanchez et al. 2004). For self-recognition, proteins synthesized by a particular genetic locus (the S-locus) are involved. Specific proteins synthesized by the self, interact with others synthesized and secreted by the female tissue, and the combination causes pollen tube death in the incompatible state. The obvious implication is that each individual of a species produces its own specific S-locus protein. Is this a parallel situation with the capabilities of an immune system?

A complex conversation between female and male tissue is conducted as pollen tubes grow through the pistil

Some of the proteins in the extracellular matrix of the pistil are concerned with a chemotropic guidance of the pollen tube to its destination. However, pollen from another individual will have a different genome to the maternal plant. Even if it is allowed to grow, compatibility can still be a problem, simply because of normal genetic variation. Thus, a probable consequence is that the conversation with the proteins in the pistil selects out pollen tubes that are more compatible with the maternal environment.

Over 750 genes concerned with ion flux, i.e. channels, transporters, ATPases, and exchangers, which are critical to pollen tube growth, are specifically expressed in the male cells (Sze et al. 2006). Fairly obviously, the combination of so many specific proteins expressed in the male cell argues for a stringent discrimination and complex conversation with the maternal tissue. Some mismatching of proteins in the conversation can then misdirect the growing pollen tube. In addition, different recognition proteins are likely involved in all the different stages of fertilization—stigma penetration, pollen tube growth in the transmitting tube, transmitting tissue exit, ovary guidance, and pollen tube/egg reception, as well as final fusion itself. Multiple and complex signals are involved, and the pistil acts as a platform on which selection, and thus fitness, can clearly operate. One unusual feature of the growing pollen tube is a gradient of cytoplasmic Ca^{2+} that is high in the tip and oscillates in intensity with a frequency of about 1 min. Localized alteration of this gradient in the tip leads to defined changes in the orientation of pollen tube growth (Malho and Trewavas 1996).

3. *Addition of more pollen often improves fertilization rates*: addition of more pollen often increases fertilization rates, even though the pollen is not of the same species and is not involved in fertilization. The mechanism is not understood, but the implication is of overwhelming the female discrimination mechanisms (Moore and Pannell 2011).

4. *The stigma is not receptive as the same time as pollen release*: another method used to discriminate against self-pollen is timing. Pollen is often released (anthesis) days before the stigma becomes receptive to pollen. Again, the method discriminates in favour of alien pollen.

Abortion of seeds and fruits

Even when fertilization has been successfully accomplished, the complex conversation continues between seeds in pods or fruit, and the parent plant. The maternal plant bears the cost of provisioning seeds whose genome is half foreign to itself. In many plants, seeds are provisioned by the photosynthetic products of only a limited number of leaves. There is, thus, limited resources available for seed production which demands both organic N and P, as well as carbohydrate, minerals, and others. Competition can be expected if many ovules are fertilized, more than can be accommodated by the resources assessed as available by the parent plant. Thus, competition can be expected to continue between the developing seeds themselves. At some stage, the maternal plant must make an assessment of how many seeds it can provision and control the diversion of resources to those seeds that are favoured (Sadras and Denison 2009).

Although ultimately seed size is a phenotypic character that varies within a range; there is a trade-off between numbers and size. The larger the seed, the more likely is its chances of survival in germination and growth. The relationship between seed size and fitness of seeds is, however, hyperbolic. There are limits to the value of increasing seed size. On the other hand, large numbers imply the possibility of greater distribution. Thus, the maternal plant assesses the future possibilities of the environment, and decides at some stage between size and numbers. How this trade-off is decided is not known. In the competition stakes in the ovary, early fertilized seeds have an advantage and in some species siblicide is used; the dominant seed kills off others, thus sequestering all the resources available.

However, abortion of immature fruits and seeds is common. The implication, again, is that this must be the result of a complex conversation between the parent plant and the developing embryos, and those that do not match up to the requirements of the conversation are simply aborted. As with pollen tubes, there will be conflict because of differing genomes and relatedness to the maternal plant. Extensive collected data indicate that in numerous species the seed to ovule (egg) ratio varies from 0.1 to 1, suggesting either differing degrees of discrimination or the extent of selfing (Shankar et al. 1988). The low seed to ovule ratio might imply lack of pollen, but this is unlikely. Maternal discrimination is more probable and embryos that eventually fail in the conversation are aborted.

About 30% of angiosperms have some form of dioecy

Separate male and female flowers on individual plants of some species have been known ever since Theophrastus produced the first herbal in the fourth century BC. He described the necessity of dusting the female date plant with pollen from the male to get improved fertilization.

There is quite a mix of different sex types, as indicated in Table 18.1. In dioecious species any individual is capable of producing male or female flowers

Table 18.1 Sex types in angiosperms.

Sex kind	% of all species
Hermaphrodite	72
Monoecious	5
Dioecious	4
Andromonoecious	1.7
Gynomonoecious	2.8
Hermaphrodite + one other sex type	7
Monoecious + separate male and female plants	3.6
Other mixed kinds	3.9

Hermaphrodite: male and female tissues in the same flower.
Monoecious: male and female flowers separate but on the same individual.
Dioecious: male and female flowers on separate plants.
Andromonoecious: plants with both hermaphrodite and male flowers.
Gynomonoecious: plants with both hermaphrodite and female flowers.

dependent on the environmental circumstance. In N-rich areas, females are preponderant, whereas in N-poor areas, males are preponderant (Heslop-Harrison 1957). Seeds produced on maternal plants do so in regions of good soil fertility and environmental circumstances that are likely conducive to good germination and growth of siblings. However, in some species the individual can switch between these in different years (Korpelainien 1998). There are contributions to a change in sex from photoperiod, light intensity, and temperature.

Thus, there is an assessment by the plant and a decision made on the balance of information obtained, as to which sexual flower is to be developed. The supposition is that within a locale of the female plant rich in N and other good growth conditions, distributed seeds are more likely to enjoy reasonable germination and growth conditions. Male plants produced in regions of poor N, ensure that the genetic capabilities are transferred elsewhere where conditions might be better. Again, both of these behaviours are predictive of a potential future.

Is there an indication of the mechanisms involved in these sex transitions? One assumption has been a change in the balance of hormones, but the literature on this issue is confusing when different species have been investigated. The ability to change between sexes suggests, perhaps, epigenetic controls operate.

Conclusion on mate selection and competition

Hermaphroditism is obviously a fail-safe mechanism—in the last resort, fertilize yourself, but under what circumstances would such a situation be beneficial, given the value of cross-fertilization. I suspect it has much to do with colonization, group living, and the sessile trait. Any individual remote from others is likely to find cross-pollination more difficult. With self-pollination, a group of individuals could rapidly be formed. Once in a group, however, the benefits of cross-pollination emerge and, thus, mechanisms are in place to ensure this is used preferentially. Populations will not be static in location, but move as environmental variation directs.

The mechanisms involved in mate selection are complex and require detailed conversations that are largely chemical in character. Such conversations replace the more obvious visual and chemical conversations that are found in the higher animals and birds. Mate selection in plants will be no less stringent towards the value of cross-fertilization. The advantages of cross-breeding are well known in crops and are used to advantage in agriculture. Crop lines that are selfed for some four or so generations often exhibit big reductions in height and yield. Crossing two of these lines together, results in recovery of height and fitness yield, a process known as hybrid vigour.

Most higher animals have elected to separate male and female organisms, although some can change gender. This facility surely reflects the ability of animals to move to find mates, although how recognition takes place in many lower animals is rarely considered. If mates are dispersed, then pheromones are used as attractants.

Cooperation or confrontation between individual plants?

Cooperation surely means sharing space

If there is cooperation between plants then it might be expected to reflect in non-random co-occurring species in communities; pairs of individuals should be apparent when distribution of individuals in a community is mapped. One detailed analysis has indicated this is the case (Kelly et al. 2008; Liebold 2008). The evidence suggests that relatively close species in a carefully analysed forest do occur in pairs, rather than being randomly distributed. The authors suggest that these observations indicate the preponderance of the niche concept and that the pair-wise structure reflects slight variations in sensitivity to available water. However, these data also indicate 'that the closely related members of congeneric pairs must interact (communicate) with one another differently than members of randomly selected species' (Kelly et al. 2008). There are numerous interpretations of what this communication, information transfer, might be. The possibilities range from a complimentary network of mycorrhizae, a complimentary morphology or chemicals that are recognized, and protect each other against herbivores or disease. Even complimentary exploitation of minerals is possible. The suggestion of water availability by the authors as the answer seems unlikely because it is insufficiently exact for what is observed.

Cooperation may also mean protection

Protection of one plant by another is not in any way fanciful. There are enormous areas of communication that are conducted by the release of volatile chemicals. In forests, up to 36% of fixed carbon is released as volatile organic chemicals and many act as signals. Concentrations drop off rapidly from the source as the diffusion front moves outward and, of course, it spreads in all directions, but the ability to detect a diffused signal at a distance is determined by the concentration of receptors, as well as distance from the source. The volatile signal can easily be disrupted by wind. However, wind speeds are lower near ground surfaces because of higher shear or frictional forces, and in a canopy can be very low. Communication by diffusion of volatile signals is familiar within the animal world ourselves included. Some insects can detect diffused volatile pheromones over several kilometres.

Some of the released plant volatiles are involved in pollination mechanisms attracting invertebrates and some vertebrates (Baldwin et al. 2006), but others are volatiles released by plants and trees attacked by herbivores or disease pests, and these can be detected by their nearest neighbours. Consequently, the neighbour can be primed against attack. Once this was realized, it gave rise to a popular description of 'trees talking to each other', although more realistically, it is a form of eavesdropping (Baldwin et al. 2006).

When plants are attacked by herbivores, defence mechanisms are activated by mechanical signals that involve electrical signalling (Wildon et al. 1992). Specific chemical signalling by the herbivore's salivary chemical composition is also used (Wu et al. 2008). These signals initiate the operations of specific jasmonate-dependent transduction pathways and circulating salicylates and peptides that alert the rest of the plant to potential damage (Jander and Howe 2008). Some of these defence chemicals are volatiles that are sensed by neighbours and enable these plants to prime their defence systems to reduce the potential spread of the pest (Engleberth et al. 2004). In addition, these released volatiles can be sensed by the attacked individual itself, so that parts of the plant that are poorly served by the vascular system, and thus recognition of the alarm signal in salicylate, can also be primed against attack (Frost et al. 2007).

Plants emit characteristic signatures of volatiles when attacked by specific pests that also act as a kind of burglar alarm (Moraes et al. 2004). These specific signals are recognized by parasitoids of the pest who are attracted to them and help destroy the pest (Moraes et al. 1998). The volatile signature can also act as a repellent to predatory moths (Ryan 2001), but surrounding plants access the signals again, too. These herbivore–plant interactions also help to determine community composition (Poelman et al. 2008; Dicke 2009) and influence the distribution of predator species, too. The extent of communication is still being uncovered, but indicates that communication potential between plants is becoming extremely complex as it is also between predators and plants. Communication of signals aiding herbivore resistance might help explain the pair-wise distribution of plant species in forests described earlier.

Competitive interactions: the adaptive nature of tree crown asymmetry

Crown asymmetry describes the overall morphology of trees in competition. Tree architecture has

a strong influence on fitness and is determined by the arrangement of buds and branches and the angles at which branches are to be found. It is modifications of these in different species that create the overall species shape. In a landmark study, Halle et al. (1978) analysed such patterns in tropical trees and came up with 23 different architectural and fractal-based models, based on the behaviour of the apical meristems and activity of potentially dormant buds in the tree. Because of the nature of the subject matter, trees are rather long-term research, and experimental work has been quite limited, but there is enough to draw some important conclusions.

The branching pattern of an isolated, usually deciduous, tree exhibits a characteristic species pattern such that many are recognizable without the need for further identifying factors. The characteristic branching patterns derive from rules of growth that determine branching angles and internode lengths. Internal assessment, based on environmental and other internal information, determines which buds develop on branches into new growth points or branches, or which remain dormant. These intrinsic patterns can be overridden by neighbouring trees. The crown refers to the characteristic dome-like structure that marks the outer ends of all the branches and leaves.

On an isolated tree, the crown is centrally placed over the main trunk. It is a common observation that trees growing near their neighbours show a displacement of the crown, relative to the lower trunk and away from the neighbour; the crown becomes asymmetric (Brisson 2001; Muth and Bazzaz 2002a, 2003). Observations indicate that tree crowns were displaced away from large neighbours, close neighbours, and shade tolerant neighbours; or if in a group, were positioned towards a gap (Franco 1986). As neighbour size increased, the precision with which crowns were shifted to avoid competition increased, too.

Some notion of how this is accomplished can be deduced from experiments on young birch trees planted close together for four years (Jones and Harper 1987). Every year numerous growth parameters were estimated, including bud numbers, lateral branch numbers, and net bud production, and these were estimated each year until the trees grew close to their neighbours and their branches penetrated the crown of their neighbours. Those branches that penetrated into the crown of the neighbour exhibited a much-reduced number of buds and a much higher death rate of buds, which had been formed. The branches were shorter, too. These authors concluded that a bud is much more influenced by its environment than its position on the tree. Clearly, resources for growth have been removed from these branches presumably by re-direction of the vascular system controlled by the cambium as indicated in Chapter 11.

Flexibility in crown structure and shape appears to reduce competition. In very crowded environments, the crown asymmetry was also weighted towards the average direction of sunlight in addition to close neighbours (Rouvinen and Kuuluvanen 1997).

When tree branches do approach each other, a gap between them is often common and is thought to be due to a touch stimulus. Sometimes, this gap is also assumed to be abrasion, but evidence for this stronger stimulus seems to currently be missing. The positioning of leaves between neighbours approaching this gap often sees a lack of overlap between the two in a kind of complimentary spatial distribution. Analogously, in young seedlings growing in a forest gap, leaf overlap was minimal in the individual (Ackerley and Bazzaz 1995).

The signalling involved in crown asymmetry obviously does involve light distribution and intensity (King 1998). Conflicting clues were provided to young seedlings of either a high or low R/FR stimulus. This light regime was designed to mimic shade avoidance signalling or a signal from ordinary photosynthetically active radiation (PAR). The crown grew towards PAR rather than the red light signal (Muth and Bazzaz 2002b). Even in young seedling trees, transplanted into canopy openings in forests, there was little or no leaf overlap in the young crown (Ackerly and Bazzaz 1995). Thus, there is strict and sensitive control of which buds are permitted to grow. Furthermore, the crown was aligned with the direction of diffuse radiation, rather than direct radiation.

A number of authors have commented on the more luxurious growth of tree branches on the edges of groups (Stoll and Schmid 1998; Muth and

Bazzaz 2002a). A displaced crown is considered to optimize light collection by branch positioning under reduced light circumstances. It has long been thought that, in isolated trees, the branch structure maximizes leaf exposure to light with minimal overlap (Honda and Fisher 1978). The branching pattern and leaf distribution of one specific tree species, *Terminalia*, is very close to the maximum effective leaf area for photosynthesis.

The change in crown structure is considered to be of considerable adaptive value because it has a significant effect on tree performance (Smith and Brewer 1994; Vincent and Harja 2008). Crown plasticity was observed to confer competitive superiority in all potential situations examined. The probable mechanism lies in the hands of the cambium. Stoll and Schmid (1998) compared the growth increments of edge tree branches in the sun or the shade of these trees, with those in the centre of a group. The growth pattern revealed was familiar in that growth of sun branches > centre branches > shade branches. There is clear competition between sun and shade branches of the edge tree with the shade branch doing worse than branches in total shade in the centre. This familiar result was, in Chapter 11, ascribed to control of the direction of root resources by the cambium assessing the yield of photosynthate from different branches, and increasing or decreasing the amount of active vascular tissue accordingly. One branch benefits in a competitive situation, whereas none do when light distribution is even.

The tree is a typical self-organizing structure. Simple rules are used to govern a pattern of development in an isolated tree, but development is not fixed; at each stage an assessment must be made of both the local environment and information coming through the tree itself. The decision will either be to continue as before or to adjust the rules of behaviour to accommodate the new circumstance. All this has to involve continual learning about the environment and a memory of the learnt processes to make the adjustment long term. The critical point is that the crown acts as an integrated entity which speaks of extensive communication throughout. The tree adapts its structure to the circumstances and does so in a way that can only be regarded as intelligent.

Competition and cooperation in root systems: knowledge of self and non-self, and the defence of territory

The potential for root systems meaningfully communicating with each other is certainly better. The soil environment is likely more stable, particularly for communication and not only by volatiles, but diffusible chemicals, too. There will also be better potential for more accurate communication, for the accuracy of information transmission for all kinds of signalling. Indications of root-to-root communication can be found in older literature, but only more recently has interest recovered.

Obvious communication can be seen from root excavation analyses of desert shrubs, such as *Parthenium argentatum* (guayule). Excavations of two planted individuals clearly show that the roots of each grow down, but very clearly away from the other individual, leaving a clear soil zone between the two (see picture published in Schenk et al. 1999).

Direct demonstrations of self-identity were reported using root observation chambers and two desert plants *Ambrosia* and *Larrea*, grown from local Californian seed (Mahall and Callaway 1991, 1992, 1996). The observations suggested that two mechanisms were involved. When two individuals of *Ambrosia* contact the roots of each other, there was an immediate decline in growth rate, leading to complete cessation within a few days. When the roots of the same individual contacted each other, no such inhibition of growth was observed. Intriguingly genotypes of *Ambrosia* from a different geographic region failed to recognize those collected from California. Self-recognition also occurred if the plants were vegetatively cloned, a process obviously requiring separation of the daughter clones for some months. In that case, it was found that the daughter clones now regard each other as alien. The mechanism of this recognition process remains a mystery, but distinction between vegetatively-cloned individuals is remarkable. The discrimination is obviously as good as using vision. However, a similar capability to recognize self is present in reproduction.

Larrea root systems inhibited the growth of both *Larrea* and *Ambrosia*. The suggestion, in this case, is allelopathy; that is, the production of growth inhibitory, small molecular weight, secreted chemicals.

However, unless there is some distinction in the kind of chemical produced between individuals, the secretor is going to inhibit the growth of its own roots. Allelopathy as a concept works well between different species, but not between individuals of the same species.

However, this phenomenon of self-recognition in root systems is widespread. Schenk et al. (1999) list 13 species in which intraspecific spatial segregation of root systems has been observed and Novoplansky (2009) describes several more. Schenk et al. (1999) also provide excavation diagrams for a number of species. Plants are clearly acting territorially and guarding their own space that may also be a resource in its own right. Could this simply be guarding resources in situations where they are in short supply or is it an assessment of the future resource availability?

The notion that soil space itself is a basic plant resource has received some support. I have mentioned it in Chapter 17 (see also Bazzaz 1996). The suggestion is that increased soil volume allows roots to space themselves farther apart, indicating potential self-inhibition of growth if roots are too close (Chapter 13). Whatever the reason, the observations that morphological changes depend more on the identity of neighbours than local resource distribution, seems likely to come down strongly to self and non-self root recognition (Caldwell 1996; Huber-Sannwald et al. 1997) 'This study is one of the first to document that rhizome and root contact of a clonal plant with its neighbours may induce different clonal responses depending on the species of neighbour' (Huber-Sannwald et al. 1997).

A further dimension to self and non-self recognition has arisen from simple experiments on competition that used seedlings of a genetically uniform line of *Pisum sativum*, the green pea. Pea seeds contain two cotyledons that enclose an embryo. Excision of the first root or shoot leads to regeneration of two more roots and two more shoots through the breakage of dormancy of two dormant cotyledonary buds. By experimental manipulation, plants with either two roots or doubles with two shoots and two roots were constructed (Falik et al. 2003). These seedlings could remain as they are and were referred to as INTACT. If the seedling was cut in half vertically through the two cotyledons and used immediately, the two daughters were designated as

TWINS. If instead, they were individuals from another twin separation and grown separately for a period, they were designated as ALIEN.

These seedlings were arranged so that each target root faced a self on one side and a non-self root, an alien, on the other. Although there were slight increases in root variables noted between the two roots of a separated twin, indicating loss of physiological coordination, there was substantial increases in root length and numbers of lateral roots when the adjacent partner was an alien. Furthermore, the roots in this latter combination, exhibited a distinct vectorial behaviour being turned towards the other individual. Similar observations were made on a number of different species of plant (Falik et al. 2006).

Similar observations were made on a grass species, but here the separation period of twins was greatly lengthened. Within 60 days of separation individuals originally from the same plant, now sense each other as aliens increasing both root production and vectorial distribution towards each other (Gruntmann and Novoplansky 2004). The suggestion is that physiological signals throughout a connected plant coordinate the recognition of self, but there must be other signals that pass between roots of the self and the alien that lead to a reaction that looks like confrontation (Novoplansky 2009). One good possibility is that excision of the partner in the original alien production leads to epigenetic changes in gene expression or modifications of the switch mechanisms that control recognition.

Similar placement effects in roots was noted in a clonal plant between either a connected or separated parts of the clone (Holzapfel and Alpert 2003). When connected through a runner, the roots from each adjacent node were observed to exploit soil areas more remote from each other. When that connection was severed, much more root was placed between what were originally the adjacent nodes. Again, this indicates that a severed clone now regards other clones as aliens, even though originally genetically identical. Feasibly, epigenetic changes accompany severing, thus leading to alien recognition. Self- and non-self-discrimination can have significant effects on clonal growth and architecture leading to clump and tussock formation (Herben and Novoplansky 2008).

Self-identity and kin recognition

Dudley and File (2007) indicate that kin recognition may also occur through their root systems, since they reported that kin, as immediate siblings from the same plant, showed a reduced root formation compared with unrelated members of the same species described as strangers. More intriguingly, kin recognition possibly involved root secretions, whereas self/non-self-recognition did not (Bierdrzycki et al. 2010). There is, of course, a problem with exudate recognition as kin signals. First, if the signal is the same, how does the plant distinguish itself from others of the same kin. Secondly, exudates would have to change qualitatively as siblings part company with earlier kin and go their own way to become strangers.

For those that find self-recognition in plants surprising, there is direct evidence that such capabilities occur in fungi (Poulsen and Boomsma 2005) and as reported in Chapter 20 in bacteria.

References

Ackerley, D.D., and Bazzaz, F.A. (1995). Seedling crown orientation and interception of diffuse radiation in tropical forest gaps. *Ecology*, **76**, 1134–1146.

Baldwin, I.T., Halitschke, R., Paschold, A., von Dahl, C.C., and Preston, C.A. (2006). Volatile signalling in plant–plant interactions: talking trees in the genomics era. *Science*, **311**, 812–815.

Bazzaz, F.A. (1996). *Plants in changing environments*. Cambridge University Press, Cambridge.

Bierdrzycki, M.L., Jilany, T.A., Dudley, S.A., and Pais, H.P. (2010). Root exudates mediate kin recognition in plants. *Communicative and Integrative Biology*, **3**, 28–35.

Brisson, J. (2001). Neighbourhood competition and crown asymmetry in *Acer saccharum*. *Canadian Journal of Forest Research*, **31**, 2151–2159.

Caldwell. M.M. (1996). Exploiting nutrients in fertile soil microsites. In Caldwell M.M., and Pearcy, R.W., eds, *Exploitation of environmental heterogeneity in plants*, pp. 325–344. Academic Press, New York.

Darwin, C. (1858). *The origin of species by means of natural selection*. John Murray, London.

Dicke, M. (2009). Behavioural and community ecology of plants that cry for help. *Plant Cell and Environment*, **32**, 654–665.

Dudley, S.A., and File, A.L. (2007). Kin recognition in an annual plant. *Biology Letters*, **3**, 435–438.

Engleberth, J., Alborn, H.T., Schmelz, E.A., and Tumlinson, J.H. (2004). Airborne signals prime plants against herbivore attack. *Proceedings of the National Academy of Sciences USA*, **101**, 1781–1785.

Falik, O., Reides, P., Gersani, M., and Novoplansky, A. (2003). Self/non-self discrimination in roots. *Journal of Ecology*, **91**, 525–531.

Falik, O., de Kroon, H., and Novoplansky, A. (2006). Physiologically mediated self/non-self root discrimination in *Trifolium repens* has mixed effects on plant performance. *Plant Signaling and Behaviour*, **1**, 116–121.

Franco, M. (1986). The influence of neighbours on the growth of modular organisms with an example from trees. *Philosophical Transactions of the Royal Society London Series B*, **313**, 209–225.

Franklin-Tong, V.E. (2008). *Self-incompatibility in flowering plants. Evolution, diversity and mechanisms.* Springer, Berlin.

Frost, C.J., Appel, H.M., Carlson, J.E., De Moraes, C.M., Mescher, M.C., and Schultz, J.C. (2007). Within-plant signalling via volatiles overcomes vascular constraints on systemic signalling and primes responses against herbivores. *Ecology Letters*, **10**, 490–498.

Graaf, B.H.J., de, Lee, C., McClure, B.A., and Franklin-Tong, V.E. (2006). Cellular mechanism for pollen tube growth inhibition in gametophytic self-incompatibility. In Malho, R., ed. *The pollen tube*, pp. 201–221. Springer-Verlag, Heidelberg.

Gruntmann, M., and Novoplansky, A. (2004). Physiologically mediated self/non self discrimination in roots. *Proceedings of the National Academy of Sciences USA*, **101**, 3863–3867.

Halle, F., Oldeman, R.A.A., and Tomlinson, P.B. (1978). *Tropical trees and forests: an architectural analysis.* Springer-Verlag, New York.

Herben, T., and Novoplasnky, A. (2008). Implications of self/non-self discrimination for spatial patterning of clonal plants. *Evolutionary Ecology*, **22**, 337–350.

Heslop-Harrison, J. (1957). The experimental modification of sex expression in flowering plants. *Biological Reviews*, **32**, 38–90.

Holzapfel, C., and Alpert, P. (2003). Root cooperation in a clonal plant: connected strawberries segregate roots. *Oecologia*, **134**, 72–77.

Honda, H., and Fisher, J.B. (1978). Tree branch angle: maximising effective leaf area. *Science*, **199**, 888–889.

Huber-Sannwald, E., Pryce, D.A., and Caldwell, M.M. (1997). Perception of neighbouring plants by rhizomes and roots: morphological manifestations of a clonal plant. *Canadian Journal of Botany*, **75**, 2146–2157.

Jander, G., and Howe, G. (2008). Plant interactions with arthropod herbivores: state of the field. *Plant Physiology*, **146**, 801–803.

Jones, M., and Harper, J.L. (1987). The influence of neighbours on the growth of trees. 1. The demography of buds in *Betula pendula*. *Proceedings of the Royal Society Series B*, **232**, 1–18.

Kelly, C.K., Bowler, M.G., Pybus, O., and Harvey, P.H. (2008). Phylogeny, niches and relative abundance in natural communities. *Ecology*, **89**, 962–970.

King, D.A. (1998). Relationship between crown architecture and branch orientation in rain forest trees. *Annals of Botany*, **82**, 1–7.

Korpelainin, H. (1998). Labile sex expression in plants. *Biological Reviews*, **73**, 157–180.

Liebold, M.A. (2008). Return of the niche. *Nature*, **454**, 39–41.

Mahall, B.E., and Callaway, R.M. (1991). Root communication among desert shrubs. *Proceedings of the National Academy of Sciences USA*, **88**, 874–876.

Mahall, B.E., and Callaway, R.M. (1992). Root communication mechanisms and intracommunity distributions of two Mojave Desert shrubs. *Ecology*, **73**, 2145–2151.

Mahall, B.E., and Callaway, R.M. (1996). Effects of regional origin and genotype on intraspecific root communication in the desert shrub *Ambrosia dumosa*. *American Journal of Botany*, **83**, 93–98.

Malho, R., and Trewavas, A.J. (1996). Localised apical increases of cytosolic calcium control pollen tube orientation. *Plant Cell*, **8**, 1935–1949.

Moore, J.C., and Panell, J.R. (2011). Sexual Selection in Plants. *Current Biology*, **21**, R176–R182.

Moraes, C.M., de, Lewis, W.J., Pare P.W., Alborn, H.T., and Tumlinson, J.H. (1998). Herbivore-infested plants selectively attract parasitoids. *Nature*, **393**, 570–573.

Moraes, C.D., de, Schultz, J.C., Mescher, M.C., and Tumlinson, J.H. (2004). Induced plant signalling and its implications for environmental sensing. *Journal of Toxicology and Environmental Health Part A*, **67**, 819–834.

Muth, C.C., and Bazzaz, F. (2002a). Tree canopy displacement at forest gap edges. *Canadian Journal of Forestry Research*, **32**, 247–254.

Muth, C.C., and Bazzaz, F. (2002b). Tree seedling canopy responses to conflicting photosensory cues. *Oecologia*, **132**, 197–204.

Muth, C.C., and Bazzaz, F. (2003). Tree canopy displacement and neighbourhood interactions. *Canadian Journal of Forestry Research*, **33**, 1323–1330.

Novoplansky, A. (2009). Picking battles wisely; plant behaviour under competition. *Plant Cell and Environment*, **32**, 726–741.

Poelman, E.H., van Loon, J.J.A., and Dicke, M. (2008). Consequences of variation in plant defense for biodiversity at higher trophic levels. *Trends in Plant Sciences*, **13**, 534–540.

Poulsen, M., and Boomsma, J.J. (2005). Mutualistic fungi control crop diversity in fungus growing ants. *Science*, **307**, 741–744.

Rouvainen, S., and Kuuvulvainin, T. (1997). Structure and asymmetry of tree crowns in relation to local competition in a natural mature forest. *Canadian Journal of Forest Research*, **27**, 890–902.

Ryan, C.A. (2001). Night moves of pregnant moths. *Nature*, **410**, 530–531.

Sadras, V.O. and Denison, R.F. (2009). Do plants compete for resources? An evolutionary viewpoint. *New Phytologist*, **183**, 565–574.

Sanchez, A.M., Bosch, M., Bots, M., Nieuwland, J., Feron, R., and Mariani, C. (2004). Pistil factors controlling pollination. *Plant Cell*, **16**, S98–S106.

Schenk, H.J., Callaway, R.M., and Mahall, B.E. (1999). Spatial root segregation: are plants territorial? *Advances in Ecological Research*, **28**, 145–180.

Shankar, R.U., Ganeshaiah, K.N., and Bawa, K.S. (1988). Parent-offspring conflict, sibling rivalry and brood size patterns in plants. *Annual Review of Ecology and Systematics*, **19**, 177–205.

Smith, C.U.M., and Arnott, R. (2005). *The genius of Erasmus Darwin*. Ashgate Publishing Company, Farnham.

Smith, W.K., and Brewer, C.A. (1994). The adaptive importance of shoot and crown architecture in conifer trees. *American Naturalist*, **143**, 528–532.

Stoll, P., and Schmid, B. (1998). Plant foraging and dynamic competition between branches of *Pinus sylvestris* in contrasting light environments. *Journal of Ecology*, **86**, 934–945.

Sze, H., Frietsch, S., Li, X., Bock, K.W., and Harper, J.F. (2006). Genomic and molecular analyses of transporters in the male gametophyte. In Malho, R., ed. *The pollen tube*, pp. 71–93. Springer, Berlin.

Vincent, G., and Harja, D. (2008). Exploring ecological significance of tree crown plasticity through three dimensional modelling. *Annals of Botany*, **101**, 1221–1231.

Wildon, D.C., Thain, J.F., Minchin, P.E.H., Gubb, I.R., Reilly, A.J., Skipper, Y.D., and 3 others (1992). Electrical signalling and systemic proteinase inhibitor induction in the wounded plant. *Nature*, **360**, 62–65.

Wu, J., Hettenhausen, C., Schuman, M.C., and Baldwin, I.T. (2008). A comparison of two *Nicotiana attenuata* accessions reveals large differences in signalling induced by oral secretions of the specialist herbivore *Manduca sexta*. *Plant Physiology*, **146**, 927–939.

Zhang, Y., Zhao, Z., and Xue, Y. (2009). Roles of proteolysis in plant self-incompatibility. *Annual Review of Plant Biology*, **60**, 21–42.

CHAPTER 19

The nature of intelligent behaviour: cognition or adaptation?

The measure of intelligence is the ability to change.

(Albert Einstein 1934)

➲ Summary

There is a common public perception that regards intelligence as limited to human beings, to do with language and success in mental tests of various kinds. This subjective view, unfortunately, clouds the ability to see its biological base and enable a better understanding of what intelligent behaviour involves. Whereas today IQ tests are used with trivial problems to be solved, 50,000 years ago these problems involved survival and, thus, fitness. That is the real context of intelligent behaviour and concerns all organisms other than humans who live in wild circumstances. Intelligent human behaviour has been broadened into multiple intelligences ranging from physical to logico-mathematical intelligence. This radical view has implications for human evolution, particularly notions of group evolution. A suggestion of physical intelligence removes the common view of intelligence as supposedly always intellectual in character. The capacity for problem solving, as a descriptor of intelligence, is suggested by several authors as the most common descriptor of intelligence given by numerous qualified psychologists and is considered to be present throughout the living world. Other definitions of intelligence can be summarized as the ability to succeed in achieving biological goals in variable environments, i.e. adaptation. Further psychological discussion makes clear the relationship between adaptation and intelligence. It has been argued cogently that species be regarded as intelligent. Intelligence in this case, is then a holistic, emergent quality of populations and species as it is for individuals.

What is intelligence?

What exactly intelligence is has become a cause for controversy. In this book, I will spend some time stating what other biologists and, of course, psychologists make of it. There is a public view of intelligence, but this is based on a common, usually undefined, perception. This perception refers only to human intelligence because that is as far as public knowledge goes. The word gets confused with all sorts of attributes like cleverness or IQ; smart is perhaps a better synonym. The derivation of the word intelligence comes from the Latin, *interlegere*; basically meaning, to choose between. As a descriptor that is not a bad assessment, because choice implies many things. It implies recognition of two or more different, sometimes conflicting, circumstances—an assessment of the situation and the necessity of a decision in favour of an assessed future behaviour that is beneficial.

Plant Behaviour and Intelligence. First Edition. Anthony Trewavas.
© Anthony Trewavas 2014. Published 2014 by Oxford University Press.

Assessments of human intelligence have got in the way of understanding the biology

Intelligence is an aspect of behaviour; it may well account for most behaviour. In fact, there are many (of the public) who think that only humans are intelligent and express surprise if they find equivalent behaviour elsewhere in the biological world. For other organisms, intelligent behaviour can only be expressed within the confines of their behavioural capabilities. If the essence of intelligent behaviour can be identified, stripped of the particular way humans express it, then the potential for understanding intelligent behaviour, whether it exists in other organisms, for example, or how it evolved can be investigated.

I do not consider it credible that intelligent behaviour suddenly emerged with the present version of *Homo sapiens*. There is really nothing in human biology that does not have similar, but maybe simpler characteristics elsewhere in the living world. Humans have complex language but Griffin (1976, 1984) made clear that other organisms, including some invertebrates, communicate meaningfully and, in previous chapters, some examples have emerged in plants.

Scientists have generally assumed that most animals cope with the challenges they face solely by following behavioural instructions from their genetic heritage or their individual experiences. But to account for the flexibility with which many animals adapt their behaviour to changing circumstances, would provide an enormous number of specific instructions to provide for all likely contingencies. If on the other hand, an animal thinks about its needs and desires and about the probable results of alternative actions (decisions), fewer and more general instructions are sufficient'. (Griffin 1984, preface vii)

Thinking is the difficult issue here for plant biology, but although thinking is often confined to the properties of brains, brains themselves are themselves just very complex integrated networks. Unless one thinks that there is some kind of vital force embedded in nerve cells, then an equally complex network constructed in any other way should be capable of thinking. However, removal of the need for special instructions to account for every circumstance is equally applicable to plants. Generalized responses should be sufficient.

The reason that intelligence is so interwoven in the public mind with human intelligence surely comes from its history. In the very early 1900s, educational psychologists were interested in trying to identify children with special educational needs. In turn, that required some sort of test that would enable identification of these children. The earliest published test, the Binet–Simon test for French children, was later modified by Lewis Terman (at Stanford University) to form the Stanford–Binet IQ (intelligence quotient) test supposedly assessing cognitive abilities. IQ has, of course, entered our language, but unfortunately the test became more than just trying to assess children with educational difficulties. It is supposedly used to try and segregate those with high IQ, from those like myself of a somewhat lower order. These early attempts on defining intelligence were followed by Spearman's 'g' factor that supposedly indicated facets of overall brain behaviour and intelligence, not just cognitive abilities.

IQ has caused most controversy. When tested on a population, a bell-shaped curve is usually seen. The relationship between IQ and achievement is not strong, but most controversy has surrounded the heritability of IQ with attempts to partition the supposed contributions of environment and heritability (Wahlsten 1990). As a biologist and an individual, I regard such attempts as largely meaningless, since neither the specific influences of inheritance or environment can actually be known for the individual. Intelligence is a property of the phenotype; genes and environment are inextricably inter-twined and this is what Wahlsten concludes. However, Wahlsten's article should be read by many plant biologists, as a useful reminder that environment impinges enormously on development. It should remind investigators that laboratories, growth rooms, and greenhouses provide one kind of environment only, and that those are remote from the variable and often stochastic situation in the wild.

Tests to sort out whether people can perform advanced mathematics or become prolific musical composers, magnificent painters, or compelling novelists are not necessary, they sort themselves out. I am one of those that has no extraordinary ability at any of these subjects, but I appreciate and enjoy those that do.

Gardener's different intelligences

A refreshing attempt to better assess human intelligence only was made by Gardener (1983). His different approach underlined the cultural relativity of intelligence. What is considered intelligent behaviour in one society is not considered so in another. That immediately raises questions about the public view of intelligence—is it not just a western cultural view of intelligence? The question of cultural influences in IQ tests has long been raised, but I doubt that a test could be designed that did not, in some way, express cultural influences.

Gardener's main contribution, for which he clearly has some support, was to extend the notion of familiar human intelligence to physical, emotional, musical, spatial, and logico-mathematical intelligence, and others. Unfortunately, western culture emphasizes only the last of these particularly as intelligence. Other cultures differ. In reality, logico-mathematical intelligence is just one of the capabilities of a complex brain that is demarcated effectively into different regional capacities. Those with greater logico-mathematical abilities, extraordinary though some are, probably just have much greater numbers of dendrite connections in these brain regions. By that means the flow and integration of information in those brain regions is greatly increased compared with others. Including a physical intelligence, as Gardener does, now removes the constraint of cognition as the only form of intelligence.

It seems to me that Gardener's novel approach is of great value in understanding human evolution. If, indeed, humans did evolve, like many primates in smallish groups, then those groups that contained individuals, each of whom excelled in one or more of Gardener's attributes and also covered all of the intelligences posed, would surely have superior group intelligence compared with those that lacked one or more. That raises the issue of human group selection as detailed by Wilson (1994). Group selection could then account for the present maintenance of such capabilities in present human societies, but what applies to one group can also apply to another group of animals or even plants.

In an enlightening section entitled 'What is an intelligence', Gardener (1983, p. 60) states 'To my mind, a human intellectual competence must entail a set of skills for problem solving to resolve genuine problems that he or she encounters'. What Gardener is saying, as have others, is that basically, intelligence is the capacity for problem solving. Intelligence can either be thought of as a cognitive ability or what a cognitive ability enables people to do; that is, to solve problems. If, of course, it requires a human to outpace a predator then physical intelligence comes into its own. Some consider creativity to be the touchstone of intelligence, but creativity is simply problem solving. The only difference is that the people set their own, often-intellectual, problems to be solved. Creativity is still just problem solving.

However, is problem solving any different to adaptation? By adaptation I mean an acquired modification in any organism that enables them to survive and reproduce better. Adaptation is a term applicable to any organism. Adaptation has two forms. We can consider an organism adapting to its environment by behavioural modifications (adaptive plasticity) or we can reference adaptation as a heritable part of the phenotype (heritable adaptation). The first meaning is the one that is considered here and this form of adaptation improves fitness. The second is probably some behavioural change acquired long ago in the past and now heritable through genetic assimilation. This form is what we mean, when we say birds are well-adapted for flight.

Adaptive plasticity is induced as a result of a problem faced by the organism in question and is a partial solution. Those that provide the better or quicker solution are the more intelligent, are the more skilled, have adapted better, and are therefore fitter. The connection with fitness has been lost in both the public assessment and, indeed, the largely psychological assessment of human intelligence. An IQ test consists of a set of problems that have to be solved. The candidates adapt to the IQ situation by solving the problems posed to them, but it is, at best, remote from the likely problems faced 50,000 years ago by early *Homo sapiens*. Those that adapt more quickly and more exactly we consider are the more intelligent. Gardener's broader view is that intelligence is really a holistic attribute covering all aspects of behaviour of the organism in question and surely in contrast to the reductionist approach implicit in IQ assessment.

Legg and Hutter (2007) list 70 definitions of intelligence and provide the following summarizing conclusion.

Intelligence:
- Is a property that an individual agent has as it interacts with its environment or environments.
- Is related to the agent's ability to succeed or profit with respect to some goal or objective.
- Depends on how able the agent is to adapt to different objectives and environments.

Putting these key attributes together produces an informal definition of intelligence.

'Intelligence measures an agent's ability to achieve goals in a wide range of environments. Features such as the ability to learn and adapt, or to understand, are implicit in the above definition as these capacities enable an agent to succeed in a wide range of environments' (Legg and Hutter 2007). Earlier chapters in this book have indicated how plant behaviour in many different environmental circumstances and thus plant intelligence, agrees with this description. The measure of intelligence is the ability to change.

A further novel approach that generated much discussion was provided by Liam Hudson (1967) with his emphasis on divergent and convergent thinking. This approach was a valid attempt at the time to point to faculties possessed by some who invariably did badly in the standard IQ test, but could exercise considerable imagination as detected by simple testing. The standard question 'how many uses can you suggest for a nail or a brick' certainly demonstrated vast differences between individuals. I used some of the questions in Hudson's book on my own students as a suitable way in tutorials of indicating the wide variety of capabilities possessed by human beings and the necessity of critical thinking about intelligent behaviour. Again, notice the emphasis on problem solving. Those who do well in this test adapt to the situation that is posed by the problem. Intelligent behaviour is inextricably linked to the environment that calls it forth and does not exist in its absence. I should add that I am very bad at Hudson's test.

The Sternberg and Detterman (1986) assessment of human and other organism intelligence: intelligence advances into other organisms

The psychologist Sternberg has published a wealth of papers and at least two books on intelligence. I suspect he has published more on intelligence than any other psychologist. A truncated list of publications is to be found in Sternberg (2006), a standard text on cognitive psychology. The final chapter covers the areas of human and artificial intelligence, and its history and problems.

In 1986, Sternberg and Detterman edited a short book in which 24 psychologists were asked to briefly answer the question 'What is Intelligence'. The results were collated, analysed and then published. The investigation was an effective repeat of a similar question posed in 1921 to 14 educational psychologists whose assessments were then published in the *Journal of Educational Psychology*.

Sternberg and Berg (1986) analysed all 38 statements, using 27 potential attributes of intelligence. The commonest terms by far, and stated by more than half of the psychologists, were 'problem solving, followed some way behind by decision making and abstract reasoning'. Abstract reasoning is commonly, but incorrectly, assumed to be largely limited to human beings. However, observations on crows indicate that they, too, can reason abstractly in solving some quite complicated problems (Clayton and Emery 2008). It is simply not known how many organisms can reason abstractly and on what basis, other than supposition, do we assume other organisms cannot think abstractly. Is abstract thinking not just a feature of complex networks? How complex, is the question.

Early humankind faced familiar problems, such as gathering food, avoiding predators, finding suitable mates, assessing likely futures. They solved those problems with the attributes evolution had made available to them—a large brain. This is where psychologists and the public have lost a sense of what intelligent behaviour is about. These basic biological problems are no different to those faced by all organisms, but these organisms use whatever evolution has provided to enable them to acquire food, avoid being eaten, or find mates. Plants, of course, face the same difficulties and use a great variety of means to deal with the problems, i.e. to solve them. Intelligent behaviour is required by all.

Cognition is the way organisms with large brains approach problem solving. Mankind has sacrificed numerous abilities, such as running as fast as cheetahs, flying like a bat or using echolocation in favour of large brain solutions, but to argue that only organisms with nervous systems can be intelligent is to ascribe an almost vitalist quality to nerve cells—artificial intelligence indicates its falsity. The fundamental requirement of intelligence is a complex network capable of controlling its own behaviour. The brain is one such network, the cell is another.

The most revealing part of Sternberg and Berg (1986) comes in the introduction written by Sternberg (1986a):

Across organisms, one can view intelligence within the context of the evolution of species, of the genetics of a single species or within the interaction between interspecies evolution. For example one might consider how insects differ from rats in their intelligence.

Within organisms one can view intelligence in terms of structural aspects of the organism or in terms of process.

Furthermore it is possible to look at the interaction between structure and process.

An integrated biological viewpoint would take into account the interaction of biological factors across and within organisms.

Sternberg carefully separates the question of human intelligence from intelligence in other organisms and clearly accepts the latter.

However Sternberg (1986b) also contributes his assessment of intelligence as one of the 24 contributors. 'Intelligence must be understood in terms of the interaction of the individual with the environment'. The environment sets the problems that intelligence is needed to solve; the two are indissolubly linked. So the holistic character to intelligence binds both environment and organism together. Again 'a capacity to solve problems' is a short descriptor of intelligence and encompasses both environment and organism.

Thompson (1990), another psychologist, directs this descriptor into adaptation.

Intelligence is the apt application of information, technique or structure to the situation of the individual. Adaptation is the apt application of information, technique or structure to the situation of a phyletic individual. Intelligence is a teleonomic (i.e. goal-directed or purposeful) concept. To say that an individual is intelligent is to make a value judgement concerning the quality of the design of its behaviour. We judge the intelligence (adaptability) of an individual by watching it apply its knowledge to the various situations it encounters. If it repeatedly applies the appropriate technique from its repertoire to each situation it encounters, we say its behaviour is intelligent (adapted). Intelligence is well-designed behaviour . . . Adapted behaviour is well-designed behaviour.

This definition forms the basis of plant intelligence. It is adaptation of the individual solving its local problems by phenotypic plasticity and if we could monitor is sufficiently well, metabolic and genomic plasticity, too.

Sternberg (1986a) emphasizes the holistic nature of intelligence. 'In striving to find a single dependent variable that adequately captures the complexity of a phenomenon, one can lose the phenomena or reduce it to something that bears only the vaguest resemblance to the phenomenon in all its richness'. Reductionist approaches simply lose this holistic character or at least render it unrecognizable. Intelligence is a holistic property. It is an emergent property—the result of the integration of behaviour and environment. I used a similar definition to describe plant intelligence (Trewavas 2004). Intelligence contributes to fitness. Problem solving involves the whole organism and, in some organisms, interconnected groups of them, such as swarm intelligence.

The problem in gaining recognition of these simple statements is the failure of many outside psychology to remove the human bias on the characteristic of intelligence. Thompson places the failure squarely on causal mentalism. That is, behaviour results solely from thoughts, feelings or to personal attributes, such as sentience. We recognize our own mental processes and the way that we use them in the various attributes of our behaviour, including intelligence. The assumption then becomes that, if an organism lacks these other attributes, if it does not display sentience (self-awareness), it cannot likewise be intelligent. The immune system both learns and has an obvious memory. Yet the word intelligent is rarely applied to it, even though learning and memory are the basic elements in intelligence.

It isn't referred to as intelligent because we do not think the immune system is sentient, a different characteristic from intelligence.

Because we cannot know directly (because of language problems) whether other organisms do have feelings, thoughts, and sentience (causal mentalism), then it seems that only the most recent version of *Homo sapiens* can be intelligent; not a biologically defensible position. We cannot communicate with Neanderthals or *Homo erectus*, or even earlier hominoid versions, so it is not known whether they had emotions, feelings, sentience, etc. However, given the concern showed by some of these hominoid ancestors concerning the treatment of the dead it is at least possible or likely that they did (Dobzhansky 1967). Sentience is self-knowledge, self-awareness, and in a short article the case has been argued for its ubiquitous nature (Trewavas and Baluska 2011).

Subjective intelligence

Warwick (2000), an artificial intelligence (AI) expert that actually experiments upon himself, has taken this situation further. AI, now a subject for substantive investigation, does not involve cognitive or sentient processes. What is necessary is a complex network (for AI, a silicon-based version) and, in addition, as we shall see later, one able to control its own information flow. However, Warwick marks the transition away from the assumption that only humans are intelligent, to looking at intelligence in other species. Warwick (2000) cleanly separates the phenomenon of intelligence from the way different species express such behaviour. Human intelligence is expressed with another nearly unique human attribute—language, i.e. complex signalling, but to require all other organisms to express intelligent behaviour by a complex language is subjective. AI, swarm intelligence, and other intelligent genomes, immune systems, etc., indicates that many no longer recognize the human constraints on intelligent behaviour. It is necessary to point out that the word 'intelligence' was formulated when knowledge of behaviour was limited only to humankind. As knowledge increases, so our perceptions change.

Intelligence is subjective in terms of the group by which it is being viewed. (Warwick 2000, p. 12)

The success of a species depends on it performing well in its own particular environment and intelligence plays a critical part in its success. (p. 9)

Just as the way in which other creatures perceive the world is quite different from the way humans perceive it, so intelligence, which is inextricably linked to the senses, reflects each creature's physical attributes.

Attempting to make comparisons between species is fraught with problems, comparisons are made between characteristics that humans regard as important. Such a stance is of course biased and subjective towards human intelligence. (p. 160)

Warwick also reiterates the description of intelligence as 'a capacity for problem solving.' In all the discussion of human intelligence by psychologists, it seems to me that the fundamental point of fitness has often been missed.

Conclusion on intelligence

The conclusion in this book is that intelligence is quite simply the capacity for problem solving. Capacity reflects variability in its aspect between individuals. The means of solving the problem is determined by the capabilities that evolution has provided, but eliminating the human bias is fundamental. All organisms act intelligently within their environment. If they did not, they would not be here, but for plants, different timescale and greater emphasis on the molecular in behaviour have always been a barrier to the ready recognition of both behaviour and intelligence in these organisms.

Are species intelligent?

As an indicant of how imaginative some scientists can be, I have included at the end of this chapter on intelligence, something that few in both the plant and animal area would ever have considered. Whether species could be intelligent? The value of investigating this hypothesis, is that it highlights that intelligence is not just about humans, but about all species. If true, it has some radical consequences for understanding behaviour and evolution.

Schull (1990), in a formidable article, approaches this difficult question and his article is followed by a substantial discussion by his psychological peers who range in assessment from A to Z—from complete agreement to complete disagreement.

For some considerable time, the formal analogy between a paradigm individual and its species group has been drawn (Hull 1976; Damuth 1985). The appearance of a new species is like the birth of an individual, speciation is analogous to reproduction, and extinction is like death (Stanley 1975). Species development and subsequent evolution are considered analogous to learning. Evolution occurs by trial and error, the form of individual learning described by Thorndike (1911). Each species must retain some element of memory of its optimal ecological niche and recognition of other individual species members and their behaviour.

The organization of evolution is hierarchical, genes give rise to other genes, organisms give rise to other organisms and species give rise to other species. Whatever is considered in the process of evolution must be related by descent; species certainly come into that category. Stanley (1975) has indicated that the major features of evolution could only occur by there being a hierarchical level in the organization above species in evolution; this higher level in the hierarchy is described as species selection, analogous in mechanism to natural selection at the organism level. If, however, speciation is random as claimed (Mayr 1963), then natural selection cannot be regarded as playing a major role in determining the overall course of evolution; instead, it might be natural selection among species. If species are recognized as intelligent, however, this facility, variable among species, might also be a determinant of overall evolutionary patterns—the more intelligent would likely come to the fore. The rate of large scale evolution can be considered proportional to the rate of speciation and the intensity of species selection.

It is with this background that the article by Schull (1990) can be assessed as to whether species can be regarded as intelligent. Learning and memory are clearly both present and Schull (1990) re-emphasizes the issue. As indicated earlier the intelligence of any individual organism is judged by watching it apply its knowledge, gained by learning and memory, to repetitively solve problems in the situations it encounters (Thompson 1990). Adaptation is also a teleonomic concept and an apt application of information, technique, or structure to the situation of a phyletic individual. Just as intelligent behaviour is well designed, so is adapted behaviour (Thompson 1990) and if phyla repeatedly apply the relevant technique to the situation it encounters, they are both well adapted and intelligent. The necessary procedures for identifying both adaptation and intelligence are the same. If we now collapse the timescale for species behaviour to that of the individual then what is referred to as an intelligent individual is shared by the species as well.

'Plant and animal species are information processing entities of such complexity, integration and adaptive competence that they should be considered to be intelligent' (Schull 1990). Their adaptive achievements certainly rival those of the animal and electronic systems commonly described as intelligent. Information is processed at the individual level, in demes, in communities and in species. The numbers of individuals in any species can vary enormously usually dependent on the size of the individual. I estimate that for single-cell organism species (bacteria, protozoans, plankton, etc.), there are about 10^{20} individuals. Single species of small, short-life cycle, dicot weeds, 10^{15} individuals; mouse or rat species, 10^{12}; and even ourselves 7×10^9 individuals. I cannot find estimates for numbers of individuals of each grass species in the pampas, savannah or steppes, but given the area covered it must be very large. If each individual differs from any other phenotypically then the variation in potential for information processing is certainly massive. There are, of course, obvious differences between species and individual, not only in the timescale. The individual is probably the most integrated in terms of strength, variety, and complexity of connections, which form the organismal network. Between individuals (that construct the species) the connections are limited mainly to competition and reproduction and are thus weaker. While each of these connections can be strong, the variety is much smaller.

Individuals adapt just as species adapt. Variation, followed by natural selection, continually alters the biological profile of the species. Most surprisingly, current concepts of brain development emphasize both variation and selection; different neural networks give rise to identical behavioural traits in complex brains (Edelman 1993). The brain is a self-organizing structure that changes development when certain sizes are reached (Scott-Kelso 1995; Sporns et al. 2004; Freeman 2005). Individuals integrate information by reason of the historical information gained and contributed by peripheral organs. In species, it is the generation-by-generation turnover of populations, communities, demes, and individuals that allow for the adaptive pooling of information gained from the interactions between the organisms, and between the organism and the environment. However, it is not individuals that evolve, only demes or species, and a new individual eventually contributes to its deme.

Schull (1990) uses Wright's (1982) adaptive landscape metaphor to explore how species behave and why they need intelligent behaviour. Wright (1982) envisioned an evolutionary adaptive landscape as a series of hills and valleys with the hills representing fitness peaks. It has become a popular means of understanding species change. Movement across this adaptive landscape is more readily accomplished by numerous demes than whole species, but if demes do stumble upon particular fitness characteristics then they climb to higher fitness peaks and replicate in greater numbers. Emigrants then carry the combination of fitness-improving characteristics elsewhere. The fitness of any individual is, of course, a relative property to the particular deme in which the individual is located. Smarter individuals would find much quicker ways of reaching the fitness peak. The way to accomplish this is by genetic assimilation (the Baldwin effect) described briefly in Chapter 6.

Bateson (1963) illustrated the important role of somatic change in selection and the necessity of building an evolutionary theory that would account for adaptation and phylogeny, as well as mutation or redistribution of genomes. Consider what happens when important environmental situations change. Individuals that exhibit greater plasticity can learn to adapt more quickly by behavioural alterations. These will increase in number if the environmental shift continues. Thus, in the long run, the mere prevalence of the shift should promote the selection of organisms with the relevant characteristics to develop with greater rapidity, higher probability, or lower cost. Later selection thus ratifies an adaptation that has already been tested through non-genetic possible epigenetic means. This then implies either insight or generating the perception

that this group of organisms has an uncanny ability to predict future situations and make the prior and necessary genetic changes. As Bateson (1963) points out, when we meet a new problem we deal with it by trial and error learning or by insight. Genetic assimilation enables organism to adjust apparently without any delay and, thus, acts like insight. Given the degree to which phenotypic plasticity is so much embedded in the development of any individual higher plant, these mechanisms are of extraordinary relevance. Do they help account for the striking rates of speciation in the angiosperms?

Does this mechanism of species change, also account for any features of known evolution? Conway-Morris (2003) has summarized the extraordinary number of times morphological adaptation seems to repeat itself during aeons of evolution and the examples in plants have been summarized previously (Chapter 6). In any stressful situation (such as paucity of water), in which the intelligent response by a species is likely to far outpace anything that random mutation (dullard approach?) can come up with, then the intelligent solution will win out. Given the morphological constraints of the organisms involved, then the intelligent solution is likely to replicate itself even on different continents.

References

Bateson, G. (1963). The role of somatic change in evolution. *Evolution*, **17**, 529–539.

Clayton, N.S., and Emery, N.J. (2008). Canny Corvids and political primates. In Conway-Morris, S., ed. *The deep structure of biology*, pp. 128–142. Templeton Foundation Press, West Conshohocken, PA.

Conway-Morris, S. (2003). *Life's solution. Inevitable humans in a lonely universe*. Cambridge University Press, Cambridge.

Damuth, J. (1985). Selection among species: a formulation in terms of natural functional units. *Evolution*, **39**, 1132–1146.

Dobzhansky, T.G. (1967). *The biology of ultimate concern*. Rapp-Whiting, London.

Edelman, G. (1993). Neural Darwinism: selection and reentrant signalling in higher brain function. *Neuron*, 10, 115–125.

Einstein, A. (1934). *The world as I see it*. Querido Verlag, Amsterdam.

Freeman, W.J. (2005). Neurodynamics volume transmission and self-organisation in brain dynamics. *Journal of Integrative Neuroscience*, **4**, 407–421.

Gardener, H. (1983). *Frames of mind*. Basic Books, Inc., New York.

Griffin, D.R. (1976). *The question of animal awareness*. Rockefeller University Press, New York.

Griffin, D.R. (1984). *Animal thinking*. Harvard University Press, Cambridge, MA.

Hudson, L. (1967). *Contrary imaginations*. Pelican Books, London.

Hull, D.L. (1976). Are species really individuals. *Systematic Zoology*, **25**, 174–191.

Legg, S., and Hutter, M. (2007). A collection of definitions of intelligence. *Frontiers in Artificial Intelligence and Applications*, **157**, 17–24.

Mayr, E. (1963). *Animal species and evolution*. Harvard University Press, Cambridge, MA.

Schull, J. (1990). Are species intelligent? *Behavioural and Brain Sciences*, **13**, 63–108.

Scott-Kelso, T.A (1995). *Dynamic patterns: the self-organisation of brain and behaviour*. MIT Press, Cambridge, MA.

Sporns, O., Chialvo, D.R., Kaiser, M., and Hilgetag, C.C. (2004). Organization, development and function of complex brain networks. *Trends in Cognitive Sciences*, **8**, 418–425.

Stanley, S.M. (1975). A theory of evolution above the species level. *Proceedings National Academy of Sciences USA*, **72**, 646–650.

Sternberg, R.J. (1986a). A framework for understanding conceptions of intelligence. In Sternberg, R.J., and Detterman, D.K., eds, *What is intelligence*? pp. 3–15. Ablex Publishing Corporation, Norwood, NJ.

Sternberg, R.J. (1986b). Intelligence is mental self government. In Sternberg, R.J., and Detterman, D.K., eds, *What is intelligence*? pp. 141–149. Ablex Publishing Corporation, Norwood, NJ.

Sternberg, R.J. (2006). *Cognitive psychology*. Thomson-Wadsworth, Belmont, CA.

Sternberg, R.J., and Berg, C.A. (1986). Definitions of intelligence. A comparison of the 1921 and 1986 symposia. In Sternberg, R.J., and Detterman, D.K., eds, *What is intelligence*? pp. 155–163. Ablex Publishing Corporation, Norwood, NJ.

Sternberg, R.J., and Detterman, D.K. (1986). *What is Intelligence*? Ablex Publishing Corporation, Norwood, NJ.

Thompson, N.S. (1990).Why would we ever doubt that species are intelligent? *Behavioural and Brain Sciences*, **13**(1), 94.

Thorndike, E.L. (1911). *Animal intelligence: experimental studies*. MacMillan, New York.

Trewavas, A.J. (2004). Aspects of plant intelligence: an answer to Firn. *Annals of Botany*, **93**, 353–357.

Trewavas, A.J., and Baluska, F. (2011). The ubiquity of consciousness, cognition and intelligence in life. *EMBO Reports*, **12**, 1221–1225.

Wahlsten, D. (1990). Insensitivity of the analysis of variance to heredity environment interaction. *Behavioural and Brain Sciences*, **13**, 109–120.

Warwick, K. (2000). *QI. The quest for intelligence*. Piatkus Ltd., London.

Wilson, D.S. (1994). Reintroducing group selection to the human behavioural sciences. *Behavioural and Brain Sciences*, **17**, 585–654.

Wright, S. (1982). Character change, speciation and the higher taxa. *Evolution*, **36**, 427–443

CHAPTER 20

Brains and nerve cells are not necessary for intelligent behaviour

It is puzzling that primitive organisms that lack any kind of nervous system show sophisticated behaviours that we assume require a nervous system. Many examples noted in the past belie this assumption.

(Bonner 2010)

⊃ **Summary**

The notion that brains and nervous systems are necessary for intelligence is dubbed brain chauvinism. Organisms cannot rely alone on simple reflexes in complex environments; there is insufficient room in the genome for solutions for all to be encoded. Organisms learn from experience and apply that knowledge to future challenges. Learning is central to all intelligent behaviour. If reason is profiting from experience to modify current behaviour, then most organisms are capable of reason whether it be simple or complex. Examples of current behaviour being modified in this way are described for slime moulds in its response to food sources and discrimination between food sources to provide an optimal diet. Slime moulds also learn the frequency of applied electric shocks and anticipate future ones. Observations on *Amoeba* and *Paramecium* indicate a capability for learning and, thus, profiting from experience. *Stentor* has been observed to express a variety of behaviours according to the stimulus and previous experience. This single-celled organism is therefore capable of simple reasoning. Cooperative hunting was observed in *Amoeba*. The potential inherent in large aggregated communities of bacteria is pointed out and several examples quoted. Bacterial intelligence is also claimed for signal transduction assessments. Communication in bacteria, that is meaning-based communication permitting colonial identity, intentional behaviour (e.g. pheromone-based courtship for mating), purposeful alteration of colony structure (e.g. formation of fruiting bodies), decision making (e.g. sporulation), and recognition and identification of other colonies, are credited with and resulting from a bacterial social intelligence and wisdom.

The problem with brain chauvinism

Plants are obviously organisms that lack both a nervous system and a brain. So do many other organisms in the single cell class and this chapter illustrates their capability for intelligent behaviour.

The supposition that only humans can be intelligent has been (understandably) described as brain chauvinism (Schull 1990; Vertosick 2002). Brains are good at solving problems, but they hold no monopoly on this capability. There is observable behaviour in single cells, which those scientists who observe them strongly argue are intelligent. They fit the scenario of problem solving and learning in certain cases.

Brain chauvinism derives from three assumptions (Vertosick 2002).

1. Because nerve cells are a late evolutionary occurrence, intelligence must therefore be a late adaptation to survival. Anything earlier in evolution cannot therefore be intelligent.
2. Because only multicellular animals have nervous systems, only multicellular animals can reason, i.e. profit from experience to modify current behaviour.
3. Because the human brain is but the latest of evolutionary models to appear, the human brain is the apogee of biological intelligence. However, the human brain is, in essence, nothing more than an amorphous, decentralized but self-organizing society, composed of a trillion cells.

Brain chauvinism arises from our assessment that we are the most intelligent organisms on the planet and the right confirmed given by religious belief (Biblical Genesis, for example) to dominate nature. It does, however, lead to very inconsistent treatment of the natural world based on our estimate of the similarity of the behaviour of other organisms to our own and a confusion of intelligence with consciousness and internal thinking. As Vertosick (2002) indicates, we happily kill dumb tunas, but object to the killing of smart dolphins, we do not ascribe souls to apes (how can we know?), and generally the invertebrate population gets short shrift. The use of the words 'dumb' and 'smart' indicate our subjective judgement of their value, but how much do we know of tuna behaviour anyway? The possibility that plants may be intelligent is guaranteed to raise vigorous antagonism and the notion that bacteria may express intelligent behaviour is viewed with indifference or even alarm. Yet a soldier defusing a bomb is considered to be intelligent; bacterial species defusing an antibiotic bomb are not.

No organism can survive on dumb reflex to environmental situations. Given the variety of circumstance, the number of dumb reflexes that would have to integrated into our genome is imponderably large. 'Organisms learn from experience and apply that knowledge to future challenges. Learning is central to all intelligent behaviour' Vertosick (2002, p. 9). In an interesting and challenging text, Vertosick (2002) provides indicative pointers to intelligence in many organisms and species, including bacteria. He goes further and identifies pattern recognition as one basis of biological intelligence. Whereas brains do it well, most organisms do it as well. Even seeds recognize the pattern of temperature or light variation in their environment as do the buds on trees and respond accordingly, and so do bacteria.

The fundamental quality that drives all behaviour is the need to optimize fitness. I rarely see fitness in any discussion of intelligence particularly by psychologists. Behaviour is a holistic quality and so is intelligence. Networks also fail to get included. Whatever is done in biology deals at some stage with networks. Organisms and populations are networks. Networks capable of controlling and manipulating their own information flow to generate beneficial behaviour, are intelligent. What is required of the network is the ability to capture the dynamic multidimensional structure of the environment. This can be achieved by constructing internal network patterns, moulded by controlling network connection strength. Internal representations of this network situation can then govern behaviour. Indeed intelligence can be defined as learning the old patterns so they can be applied to generate new ones.

Intelligent behaviour in slime moulds and social amoebae

Physarum

Physarum polycephalum is a slime mould. Individuals consist of a large, single multinucleate cell—a plasmodium—that uses pseudopodia for movement. The plasmodium consists of networks of protoplasmic veins and tubes; like amoeba it surrounds its food and ingests it. Under poor conditions, such as drought, it can enter a dormant phase, but can resume its movement and search for food once conditions improve. Lack of food is used to signal the entry to a reproductive state in which spores are formed.

When *Physarum* was presented with a labyrinth or maze, in which food was located at two different ends of the maze with four different pathways between them, the plasmodium forms a single thick tube that connects both sources, but always connects by the shortest route (Nakagaki et al. 2000). The authors state 'this remarkable process of cellular computation, implies that cellular materials can show a primitive intelligence'. *Physarum* is a light-avoiding organism and can be damaged by strong light. When challenged with two sources of food, but with partial illumination of the shortest path, the tubular structure now adopts the minimum risk path, the shortest route in darkness (Nakagaki et al. 2007). When the food sources were increased in number and positioned between geometrically-shaped structures, the tubular network, the plasmodium, again assumed the form that connected the food sources via the mathematically shortest routes. Again, the authors concluded that 'the plasmodium tube network is a well-designed and intelligent system' and exhibits 'behavioural intelligence' (Nakagaki et al. 2004).

The travelling salesman problem consists of finding the optimal solution in cost and efficiency to a tour of a number of towns, cities, or stations (Bonabeau et al. 2000). Human transport networks require a robust optimum solution to the salesman problem using trade-offs between efficiency, fault (risk) tolerance, and cost. Biological networks almost certainly require optimal solutions to these same trade-offs in terms of efficient investment of energy into gaining food, but minimizing the potential for damage. *Physarum*, in foraging for food, adaptively forms such a self-organizing network of plasmodial tubes by adopting minimal path length and optimal tube thickness. This process minimizes the energy outlay to maximize energy gain. This simple organism is solving problems that improve its fitness.

When a small plasmodium of *Physarum* was challenged with food sources placed at positions that were a similitude of the major cities around Tokyo, the slime mould mycelium resolved into a network of thin tubes. This network optimally connected the food sources together, thus mimicking the actual rail network between these cities, indicating their connecting routes were optimally placed and basically self-organized (Tero et al. 2010).

The morphological network of higher plant root and shoot branches, and leaf patterns are considered to represent the optimal solution to gathering resources in both environments at the time. The molecular mechanisms involved, that require an assessment of energy outlay against energy gain to elicit this structure, are unclear in higher plants.

When *Physarum* was subjected to a limited series of shocks, it learnt the frequency pattern and changed behaviour in anticipation of the next one to come, even though this last shock was not yet given. Remarkably, this memory stayed in the slime mould for several hours. A single renewed shock, after a lengthy unstimulated period, left the slime mould, again, anticipating another shock in the behavioural pattern it had learned previously. Again, this 'hints at the origin of intelligence' (Ball 2008; Saigusa et al. 2008).

A fundamental nutritional problem that besets all organisms is how to acquire the optimal supply of appropriate nutrients for growth and development. An optimal diet for *Physarum* was determined by offering hundreds of plasmodial fragments 35 different diets, which varied in the amounts of carbohydrate and protein. The organism can survive just on carbohydrate, but grows much more densely when the protein content of the diet outweighs carbohydrate. Diets based heavily on protein, cause breakage into plasmodial fragments.

To estimate how well *Physarum* itself can optimize its food supply, the organism was presented either with various food pairings or with a clock face of 11 different combinations of carbohydrate to protein (Dussutour et al. 2010). In these two cases, the plasmodium selected and connected with the food sources that 'in precise proportions' provided the optimal diet for growth. This simple brainless organism is, thus, capable of selectively foraging among different food sources to provide an optimal diet. It is thus capable of solving complex nutritional problems.

The trade-off between speed of information processing and accuracy with which it is acted upon is commonly discussed in animal behaviour. *Physarum* was presented with tasks that required difficult or easy discrimination between separate food sources, and success was assessed by plasmodia that connected with the highest quality food (Latty and Beekman 2010). To make the tasks more diffi-cult, conditions of stress were also imposed in some experiments. When the discrimination required was difficult, individuals tended to make faster, and more inaccurate and costly decisions. With easy dis-crimination tasks, stressed individuals made slower decisions than unstressed individuals.

Social Amoebae

A few animals, ants, termites, beetles, and fish are known to perform forms of agriculture. That is, they cultivate plants or fungi to provide food for themselves. *Dictyostelium* is a social amoeba that exhibits an alternation of developmental phases be-tween free-living amoebae and a slug formed from aggregates of amoebae. In the free-living state the single amoebae live on bacteria and, when these are in short supply, signals are released that cause amoebal aggregation into the slug. The slug is capa-ble of movement looking for better environments, but if these are not available the slug forms a fruit-ing body producing spores that are released and distributed. Upon spore germination the amoebic state is recovered to feed on bacteria.

Investigation shows that *Dictyostelium* possesses a primitive farming system and that includes dis-persal and harvesting of bacterial food (Brock et al. 2011). When bacterial food becomes short, not all the bacteria are consumed. Instead, a number are stored in amoebae and are distributed in the spore. Upon germination the bacteria are released and thus seed a new crop of bacteria that provides for food.

Intelligent behaviour in other protozoa

The examination of intelligence in animals of all kinds was first compiled by Romanes (1892). Some of his material is very familiar in present-day terms, particularly the obvious intelligent behaviour of members of the Crow family. However, Romanes (1892) was systematic and collected observations throughout the animal kingdom, although some are classed as anecdotal. His section on protozoa was brief, but he stated at the outset that 'no-one can have watched the movements of certain infuso-ria without feeling it difficult to believe that are not

actuated by some amount of intelligence' (p. 18). In a book on intelligence, a definition is attempted. 'Reason or intelligence is the faculty which is con-cerned with the intentional adaptation of means to ends.' Note the emphasis on adaptation. Intention implies the ends are beneficial.

Romanes describes his own observations on two rotifers very different in size, but both having pincers. The smaller attached itself to the larger whereupon the larger underwent a series of violent jerks that within several minutes managed to fling the smaller off. Much of the remaining chapter on protozoa quotes extensively from an article by H. J. Carter FRS published in the *Annals of Natural His-tory* and concerns the behaviour of rhizopods (pro-tozoa using pseudopodia, like amoeba). This article describes the choice made by one rhizopod that rec-ognized its preferred habitat through a watchglass and crawled over the edge to find it.

Two other early texts cover similar areas of pro-tozoa by Binet (1897), the same psychologist who later generated what might be regarded as the first IQ test in 1911 (Chapter 19). The second much more detailed is a large book by Jennings (1923). Both books record a fascinating array of different kinds of unanticipated, unexpected, and complex behav-iour concentrating on protozoa, although Jennings (1923) deals also with some coelenterates. These single-cell organisms can perceive and act upon an array of specific stimuli similar in scope to our own; signals such as light, mechanical signals of touch and vibration, chemicals, mild electrical fields, and gravitational signals. These organisms will move towards rewarding circumstances and away from damaging ones. There is also discrimination in the kind of food they will ingest. *Amoeba* can distin-guish between a euglena cyst and a grain of sand, and will surround and engulf the first with its pseu-dopodia, but ignore the second. Is this an example of simple taste? The behaviour is reminiscent of that described in Chapter 9 by the Venus flytrap that dis-criminated in behaviour between a piece of chalk and that of an insect.

Jennings (1923) reports two sets of intriguing ob-servations of amoebic behaviour. First, an individ-ual attempting to engulf a round cyst by a variety of different pseudopodial movements, even losing contact at one stage, but resuming the attempt. The organism persisted for 15 min and then gave up. Presumably, there is a time memory involved. The second observations concern a predatory *Amoeba* attempting several times to engulf a second *Amoeba* that keeps moving away. Although being caught several times, the intended prey manages to finally escape. Obviously, a short-term memory seems to be in operation by the predatory *Amoeba* and may finally stop when error recognition occurs. Ilse Walker (2005) describes some remarkable amoebic behaviour. When encountering innocuous objects, the organism flows around them; for irritating objects, it retracts the pseudopods. On sensing prey, the cytoplasm ceases current movement, then accelerates cytoplasmic flow towards and around the prey. She also describes cooperative hunting from 2–4 amoebae, with the pseudopodia of all four forming a complete encirclement. 'It perceives, recognises, chooses and ingests a variety of prey that is not much short of the resource choice of higher animals, it recognises its own kind and engages in cooperative behaviour' (Walker 2005), obviously self-aware. Some amoebae and other protists build protective, enveloping cases from gathered material (Hansell 2011). Complex behaviour? Of course—how else can it be described and what signal transduction and conversation has to be used to enable this behaviour.

Paramecium is a swimming protozoan that is known to have the ability to reverse direction when it bumps into an obstacle. Considerable numbers of investigations indicate its capability to learn. Stevenson-Smith (1908) confined paramecia to tubes narrower in diameter than the length of the protozoan. Whereas it required minutes to learn originally how to turn under these circumstances, with practice this was reduced to a few seconds. Armus et al. (2006) used positive reinforcement provided by electrical stimulation to reinforce light signals, and demonstrated clear training and thus discrimination learning in paramecia.

Didinium is a swimming, carnivorous protozoan that can perceive moving protozoans and aim a dart, a trichocyst, to kill or immobilize its mobile prey. Once the prey is damaged or killed, *Didinium* locates and consumes the organism. It is not clear how this is accomplished, how movement is detected. *Didinium* will target *Paramecium aurelia*, but not *Paramecium bursaria* (Binet 1897, p. 63). This is an advanced level of discrimination.

More complex behaviour has been observed in the infusoria, including the observations that different behaviours can be exhibited on receipt of the same stimulus and under the same conditions (Jennings 1923, p.170 onwards). *Stentor roeseli* is tubular in shape, containing an open apical mouth surrounded by active cilia that by their coordinated movement waft particles of food to the inside of the cell. The basal part of the cell is surrounded by secreted gelatinous material that fixes the whole structure to a surface.

Aim a fine jet of water at the mouth and the cell contracts into the tube, only to reappear shortly after and continue feeding. A second jet of water produces a much-reduced effect and subsequent ones have no effect. The cell has adapted to a mild touch stimulus, it has habituated. However, increase the stimulus and it contracts again. There is a degree of assessment occurring here about the meaning of the signal and the operation of a simple memory.

However, more complex behaviour has been observed (Jennings 1923). Experimentally, a stream of innocuous, carmine particles was poured into the mouth of *Stentor*, with the following observations. The cell responded initially by bending the mouth to one side to avoid these particles. The organism exercises choice. It repeated this action of bending several times if the initial bending failed. If the stream continued, the cilia reversed direction to drive the particles away. If this procedure continued to fail to stop the particles entering the mouth, the cell contracts into the tube. After a short time, the cell can re-emerge and try again to feed normally. If the carmine particle stream is continued, the contraction periods increase in length. Eventually, if the stream continues, then the *Stentor* cell exhibits violent contractions to break the adhesion of the foot and swims away. Finally, landing on another surface, *Stentor* slowly explores and examines the surface, and when a suitable site is chosen, oscillatory movements of the body are observed while mucus is rapidly secreted to form a new adhering tube. These varieties of behaviour seem to me to involve, choice, learning, assessment, and memory, and are clearly adaptive. Several times particular problems were satisfactorily solved. The same stimulus gives rise to different behaviours.

Grasse (1977, p. 213) in a more recent text describes unexpected behaviour in *Arcella*, another protozoan. This protozoan also uses pseudopodia for movement. *Arcella* individuals are covered by an apical shell (like a beret). If the organism finds itself inadvertently upside-down, initial attempts are made using the pseudopodia to right itself. If that fails, a bubble of gas is generated internally to change the centre of gravity and the pseudopodia used to right itself. In rich cultures of amoebae, sometimes some are impaled on a thorn. Two methods of getting themselves off this structure have been observed. Either the organism splits in two, and each goes its way or, instead, a line appears in the cytoplasm that divides the cell up to the thorn-like structure and the organism can thus fall off.

Albrecht-Buehler (2013) in a short article summarizes the need for cell intelligence based on 30 years of his own observations and concludes that single crawling mammalian cells, like phagocytes, act intelligently. His primary evidence is that single cells are able to measure both space (angles, distances, curvatures) and time (duration), and thus can acquire abstract information from these assessments.

If an organism reacts in a certain way under certain conditions and continues this behaviour, no matter how disastrous the effects its behaviour, is surely unintelligent. If, on the other hand, it modifies its behaviour in such a way to improve both its survival and contribute to its fitness, then the behaviour is surely intelligent. Intelligent behaviour is to be found even in the protozoa.

Conclusions on protozoal behaviour for intelligence

One important conclusion is that behaviour is completely constrained by structure. In one sense, this should be obvious. We cannot fly like a bird because structurally we do not have feathered wings or see like a bat because we do not, as an individual, use echo location. Amoebae are constrained by what evolution has given them, pseudopodia. I am unable to conceive what additional forms of behaviour they could exhibit given their cellular constraints. Intelligent behaviour, therefore, has to be judged

within the structural constraints. *Stentor* has a more complex structural system, but one that allows a variety of behaviours. *Didinium* can target moving objects.

'Intelligence is held to consist essentially in the modification of behaviour in accord with experience.' 'It is difficult to draw a line separating the regulatory behaviour of lower organisms from the so-called intelligent behaviour of higher ones,' (Jennings 1923, p. 334). These are not 'in most instances simple reflex motions, they are movements adapted to an end' (Binet 1897, p. 64). 'These movements are not explained by the simple phenomena of irritability.'

Bacterial intelligence: complex communication, networks and an ability to predict future events

Bacteria are regarded by many as critical to the maintenance of life on earth. They are also the 'simplest' free-living cell. Bacteria are found everywhere, even in the most extreme habitats. Each of us lives with at least a thousand species symbiotically in our intestine and one of those, *Escherichia coli*, has proven to be the commonest species for thousands of laboratory investigations. The notion that a population or species of bacteria act intelligently, a kind of swarm intelligence, is being voiced, quite frequently in the literature. A bacterial species in total is like other species of organism, an enormous information processing system that constructs a complex network. Leaving aside the networks inside cells, the connections between cells are of at least three or even four different kinds, and these create a network too.

Bacteria are perfectly capable of living as free individual cells. Many species are motile and can respond chemotactically to chemicals in the medium. Conditions of starvation or being plated out on hard surfaces, or an imbalance of nutrients, signal enormous numbers of bacteria (10^9–10^{12} cells) to cooperatively self-organize into collectives with highly structured morphologies and obvious intercellular communication (Ben Jacob et al. 1998, 2004, 2006). The colony patterns are thought to represent strategies for survival under environmentally-challenging conditions and are described as social intelligence. At least three different kinds of morphotypes have been recognized, dependent on the specific environmental conditions (Ben Jacob et al. 2006).

These morphs originate from travelling waves of motile bacteria that enable cells to find confining environments and to collapse into them thus ensuring close permanent contact (Park et al. 2003). The communicating elements used to help form these structures range from simple molecules to polymers, peptides, complex proteins, and genetic material. The colony is capable of collective sensing, distributed information processing, and collective gene regulation. Ben Jacob et al. (2006) regard these properties as indicating both cognitive functions and a social intelligence.

The other common bacterial collectives are biofilms. These result from the aggregation of smaller numbers of cells together. Once a threshold in number of cells in the biofilm is exceeded, a major change in colony behaviour can be detected. These changes are initiated by quorum sensing (Bassler 2002; Taga and Bassler 2003).

The first recognition of quorum sensing was observed with the onset of luminescence from a biofilm of luminescent bacteria. Quorum sensing for virulence, sporulation, biofilm formation itself, and mating have all been reported. Quorum sensing is achieved through the production, release, and subsequent detection of signal molecules called autoinducers. Some signals are sensed on the outside of the cell. Others can be transported inside the cell and sensed there. The combination of signal systems changes the response of the whole collective.

Although most biofilms are composed of the same species, some do involve mixtures of species and, thus, all members listen in to what is now, a different conversation. The implication is that many bacteria can sense members of their own species and thus have self-recognition and this has now been reported (Gibbs et al. 2008). *Chlamydomonas*, a motile green alga, secretes compounds that mimic bacterial signals and interfere with quorum sensing in bacteria (Teplitiski et al. 2004).

The second communication process that supports the notion of bacterial intelligence is chemotactic signalling. Chemotaxis enables many bacterial species to swim up towards sources of nutrient, it can

perceive and follow along a gradient. Alternatively, it can swim away from damaging materials. Bacteria are small and are easily knocked off course by Brownian motion. So to continue a direct course towards or away from any chemical for little more than 1 or 2 sec requires a constant reassessment of their position. 'How do they do this? The answer is that they have a sort of short term memory that tells them whether conditions are better at this instant of time than a few seconds ago' (Bray 2009, p. 7).

It is known that bacteria can sense up to some 50 different chemicals using proteins embedded in the outer membrane. A further network of some 12–14 proteins, are involved in the interpretation and transduction of the signals to control the swimming direction. The numerous signals to which free swimming bacteria respond have, as their molecular basis, a network of protein kinase and phosphatases (a two component system). Many transduction processes occur in parallel with cross-linking between the pathways. Subsequent integration of the information from different signals provides the optimal response.

Hellingwerf et al. (1995) describe the complex and unexpected properties of this kinase/phosphatase network and have designated it accordingly as a 'phospho-neural' network. Meetings have been held on neural networks in bacteria. There are many analogous properties between these molecular networks and the behaviour of those constructed from neurons. The well-characterized components of both networks act as logical operators. Bacterial two-component systems often use modular proteins with a large variety of input/output domains yet strikingly conserved transmission domains. Coupled with cross-talk between the few dozen two-component systems organized into a neural type-network provides bacteria with a 'rudimentary form of intelligence' (Hellingwerf 2005). The 'phospho-neural' network can auto-amplify, an obvious learning process resulting from signal amplification and generating associative responses and memory effects, all characteristics typical for neural networks (Hoffer et al. 2001). Bacteria that auto-amplify this network, respond more quickly or more extensively to a signal that has previously been perceived in the past. One of the main challenges of studying this 'phospho-neural' network is 'to outline the extent of intelligence-like behaviour, the network can generate' (Hellingwerf 2005). Bijlsma and Groisman (2003) describe the interactions between the different parallel pathways as enabling bacteria to make 'informed decisions'.

In commenting on bacterial behaviour, Allmann (1999, p. 5) stated 'some of the most basic properties of brains such as sensory integration, memory, decision making and the control of behaviour can all be found in these simple organisms'. Allmann's area of study is the brain and, like many, he finds bacterial behaviour referred to in this quotation as impressive, but no more impressive than that exhibited by higher plants.

The *sine qua non* of behavioural intelligence systems is the capacity to predict the future—to model likely behavioural outcomes in the service of inclusive fitness. This logic is already evident in a primitive sense in *Escherichia coli*: information transduced by environmental sensors directs behavioural responses in a manner that increases the probability of the attainment of bio-energetic resources in the next moment. (La Cerra and Bingham 1998)

Plants also exhibit these behaviours but in much more complex fashion.

The final known form of communication between bacteria is via exchange of genetic material usually in the form of plasmids. It is this capability that primarily led Vertosick (2002) to regard bacterial populations as acting intelligently, i.e. solving problems. This is a kind of swarm intelligence; it is most obvious in the production of resistance to antibiotics. The phenomenon is of course adaptation and there has been considerable disagreement about the way that it is produced (Ben Jacob et al. 2006). The rapid spread of antibiotic resistance to penicillin among different species of bacteria, occurred by communication; an exchange of plasmids containing lactamase genes. 'Staphylococcus saw a solution to the penicillin holocaust by standing on the shoulders of other lactamase producing species. And we now have a name for the Darwinian adaptation exhibited by communicating networks: intelligence' (Vertosick 2002, p. 49).

Ben Jacob et al. (2004) regard the conglomerate of these shared communications to indicate that the conversations between bacterial cells can be linguistically divided both into semantic exchanges of communications and pragmatic dialogues. These communications represent 'meaning-based communication permitting colonial identity, intentional behaviour (e.g. pheromone-based courtship for mating), purposeful alteration of colony structure (e.g. formation of fruiting bodies), decision making (e.g. sporulation) and recognition and identification of other colonies-features we might regard associated with bacterial social intelligence'. In further statements they argue that such communication is an investigative route to uncover 'the foundations of cognition in bacteria' and 'bacterial wisdom' (Ben Jacob 1998; Ben Jacob et al. 2006).

If organisms are exposed to repetitive circumstances, there is a fitness advantage to pre-empting the change by responding more quickly when the environment starts to change. Certain bacteria, such as *E. coli*, undergo a predictable set of environmental changes in the human gut, for example, if they are ingested. 'Cells that can efficiently learn such correlations, are able to express the energy-extracting metabolic pathway at the appropriate time, giving them a sizeable fitness advantage over their competitors' (Tagkopoulos et al. 2008). This predictive potential was investigated theoretically, using modelled biochemical networks in bacteria, but constructed as analogues to neural networks. Later investigations of the use of repetitive oxygen and temperature variations demonstrated the learning capacity (Tagkopoulos et al. 2008). These authors conclude that 'biochemical networks evolving randomly under precisely defined complex habitats capture the multi-dimensional structure of diverse complex habitats by forming internal representations that allow prediction of environmental change'.

Mitchell et al. (2009) demonstrated the same predictive capacity in both *E. coli* and yeast. The natural temporal order of expression for the changes in position in the gut and, for yeast, changes in fermentation were both embedded in the wiring of the regulatory networks. These capabilities, they consider, are analogous to classical Pavlovian conditioning, a process that requires learning about the congruence of a signal and reward, and a recognition that, in using food as a reward, the organism is making a reasoned or intelligent assessment that would increase fitness in the wild. Using *E. coli* that had been bred for many generations in the laboratory (i.e. effectively domesticated) indicated that this facility was no longer present.

References

Albrecht-Buehler, G. (2013). Cell intelligence. Available at: M www.basic.northwestern.edu/g-buehler/FRAME.htm

Allmann, J.M. (1999). *Evolving brains*. Scientific American Library, New York.

Armus, H.L., Montgomery, A.R., and Jellisoni, J.L. (2006). Discrimination learning in paramecia (*Paramecium caudatum*). *Psychological Record*, **56**, 489–498.

Ball, P. (2008). Cellular memory hints at the origins of intelligence. *Nature*, **451**, 385.

Bassler, B.L. (2002). Small talk¨cell-to-cell communication in bacteria. *Cell*, **109**, 421–424.

Ben Jacob E., Becker, I., Shapira, Y., and Levine, H. (2004). Bacterial linguistic communication and social intelligence. *Trends in Microbiology*, **12**, 367–372.

Ben Jacob, E., Cohen, I., and Gutnick, D.L. (1998). Cooperative organisation of bacterial colonies: from genotype to phenotype. *Annual Review of Microbiology*, **52**, 779–806.

Ben Jacob, E., Shapira, Y., and Tauber, A.I. (2006). Seeking the foundations of cognition in bacteria: from Schrödingers negative entropy to latent information. *Physica A*, **359**, 495–524.

Bijlsma, J.J.E., and Groisman, E.A. (2003). Making informed decisions: regulatory interactions between two-component systems. *Trends in Microbiology*, 11, 359–366.

Binet, A. (1897). *The psychic life of micro-organisms*. Open Court Publishing Company, Chicago, IL.

Bonabeau, E., Dorigo, M., and Theraulaz, G. (2000). Inspiration for optimisation from social insect behaviour. *Nature*, **406**, 39–42.

Bonner, J.T. (2010). Brainless behaviour: a myxomycete chooses a balanced diet. *Proceedings of the National Academy of Sciences USA*, **107**, 5267–5268.

Bray, D. (2009). *Wetware; a computer in every living cell*. Yale University Press, New Haven, CT.

Brock, D.A., Douglas, T.E., Queller, D.C., and Strassmann, J.E. (2011). Primitive agriculture in a social amoeba. *Nature*, **469**, 393–396.

Dussutoru, A., Latty, T., Beekman, M., and Simpson, S.J. (2010). Amoeboid organism solves complex nutritional challenges. *Proceedings of the National Academy of Sciences USA*, **107**, 4607–4611.

Gibbs, K.A., Urbanowski, M.L., and Greenberg, E.P. (2008). Genetic determinants of self- identity and social recognition. *Science*, **321**, 256–259.

Grasse, P.-P. (1977). *Evolution of living organisms*. Academic Press, London.

Hansell, M. (2011). Houses made by protists. *Current Biology*, **21**, R485–R487.

Hellingwerf, K.J. (2005). Bacterial observations: a rudimentary form of intelligence? *Trends in Microbiology*, **13**, 152–189.

Hellingwerf, K.J., Postma, P.W., Tommassen, J., and Westerhoff, H.V. (1995). Signal transduction in bacteria: phosphoneural networks in Escherichia coli. *FEMS Microbiology Reviews*, **16**, 309–321.

Hoffer, S.M., Westerhoff, H.V., Hellingwerf, K.J., Postma, P.W., and Tommassen, J. (2001). Autoamplification of a two component regulatory system results in learning behaviour. *Journal of Bacteriology*, **183**, 4914–4917.

Jennings, H.S. (1923). *Behaviour of the lower organisms*. Columbia University Press, New York.

La Cerra, P., and Bingham, R. (1998). The adaptive nature of the human neurocognitive architecture. An alternative model. *Proceedings of the National Academy of Sciences USA*, **95**, 11290–11294.

Latty, T., and Beekman, M. (2010). Speed accuracy trade-offs during foraging decisions in the acellular slime mould *Physarum polycephalum*. *Proceedings of the Royal Society series B*, **278**, 539–545.

Mitchell, A., Romano, G.H., Groisman, B., Yona, A., Dekel, E., Kuplec, M., and 2 others (2009). Adaptive prediction of environmental changes by microorganisms. *Nature*, **460**, 220–224.

Nakagaki, T., Iima, M., Ueda, T., Nishiura, Y., Saigusa, T., Tero, A., and 2 others (2007). Minimum risk path finding by an adaptive amoebal network. *Physical Review Letters*, **99**, 068104.

Nakagaki, T., Kobayashi, R., Nishiura, Y., and Ueda, T. (2004). Obtaining multiple separate food sources: behavioural intelligence in the *Physarum* plasmodium. *Proceedings of the Royal Society, Series B*, **271**, 2305–2310.

Nakagaki, T., Yamada, H., and Toth, A. (2000). Maze solving by an amoeboid organism. *Nature*, **407**, 470.

Park, S., Wolanin, P.M., Yuzbashyan, E.A., Lin, H., Darnton, M.C., Stock, J.B. and 2 others (2003). Influence of topology on bacterial social interaction. *Proceedings of the National Academy of Sciences USA*, **100**, 13910–13915.

Romanes, G.J. (1892). *Animal intelligence*. Kegan Paul, Trench, Trubner and Co. Ltd., London.

Saigusa, T., Tero, A., Nakagaki, T., and Kuramoto, Y. (2008). Amoebae anticipate periodic events. *Physical Review Letters*, **100**, 018101.

Schull, J. (1990). Are species intelligent? *Behavioural and Brain Sciences*, **13**, 63–108.Smith, S. (1908). The limits of educability in *Paramecium*. *Journal of Comparative Neurology and Psychiatry*, 18, 499–510.

Taga, M., and Bassler, B.L. (2003). Chemical communication among bacteria. *Proceedings of the National Academy of Sciences USA*, **100**, 14549–14554.

Tagkopulos, I., Liu, Y.-C., and Tavazoie, S. (2008). Predictive behaviour within microbial genetic networks. *Science*, **320**, 1313–1317.

Teplitski, M., Chen, H.C., Rajamain, S., Gao, M.S., Merighi, M., Sayre, R.T., and 3 others (2004). *Chlamydomonas reinhardii* secretes compounds that mimic bacterial signals and interfere with quorum sensing regulation in bacteria. *Plant Physiology*, **134**, 137–146.

Tero, A. Takagaki, S., Saigusa, T., Ito, K., Bebber, D.P., Fricker, M., and 3 others (2010). Rules for biologically inspired adaptive network design. *Science*, **327**, 439–442.

Vertosick, F.T. (2002). *The genius within. Discovering the intelligence of every living thing*. Harcourt Inc., New York.

Walker, I. (2005). *The evolution of biological organisation as a function of information*. pp.90–99. Editora INPA, Manaus.

CHAPTER 21

Intelligent genomes

Genomes functioning as true intelligence systems which can be readjusted when conditions require.

(Shapiro 1991)

⊃ Summary

Barbara McClintock's identification of transposons heralded much new understanding of the complexity involved in the control of gene expression. Her information indicated that the cell is the master of the genome and not, as commonly assumed, the reverse. The evolutionary emphasis on random changes in mutation and selection among enormous numbers of individuals a few of which have more desirable characteristics needs reassessment. Adaptive information processing, particularly as applied in natural complex systems is crucial. Evolution may be led by behavioural changes followed by either reversible modification of DNA sequence or, finally, the nucleotide sequence itself. However, cells and organisms act as integrated entities. One part of the whole cell cannot be elevated at the expense of others. Cells and organisms are effectively complex regulatory networks through which information flows. Fundamental to all these concepts is the notion of biological information, the processing of information, its interpretation, and how that impacts on the DNA sequence itself. Learning and memory are both exemplified by epigenetic phenomena. The change in attitude is illustrated by descriptions of McClintock's insights as indicating either the intelligent genome or genetic intelligence (Shapiro 1991; Thaler 1994) that fits precisely with the theme of this book. Finally, Lamarck's writings, much misquoted in the past, has returned to construct a grander view than the modern synthesis. I have included extensive quotation from Lamarck to indicate that he actually predicted much of what is presently understood.

McClintock's insight: the cell not the gene is the biological determinant

We first met Barbara McClintock in Chapter 1. Whatever reason took Barbara McClintock originally to study plants is not actually recorded, but her emotional contact is clear. 'I start with the seedling and I don't want to leave it. I don't feel I know the story if I don't watch the plant all the way along. So I know every plant in the field. I know them intimately and I find it a great pleasure to know them' (Keller 1983). That pleasure sustained her through the lean years; it reflected a sure embrace of the natural word in its very being. One of my previous PhD students described her plants as her babies. The connection can be very strong.

McClintock's intimate knowledge of the maize plant (US corn, *Zea mays*) and her discriminating observations of some of its behaviour led her to the Nobel prize podium. What she had uncovered were novel genes, often called jumping genes, but now called transposons; stretches of DNA that moved around the genome within the time frame of the individual organism. Stress conditions, in

particular, caused enhanced transposon movement. When transposons jumped, they frequently
altered the expression of some genes or even eliminated the expression of others. The genome was
not then the stable entity many had supposed ever
since Watson and Crick's discovery of the structure
of DNA! There are indications that about one-half
of the plant genome originated from transposable
elements.

The quotation from McClintock (1984) that I used
as a title to Chapter 1 stated: 'a goal for the future
would be to determine the extent of knowledge the
cell has of itself and how it uses that knowledge in a
thoughtful manner when challenged'. Put in different terminology, McClintock is asking:

1. How much of their current molecular and physiological situation, cells can assess (or know).
2. How they can then use that information to sensibly deal with environmental change in a way that
   enhances survival and thus improves fitness.

The quotation indicates a deep understanding
and insight into plant behaviour. McClintock was
not afraid to use anthropomorphic words, such as
knowledge or thoughtful, believing as she did that
one should approach biology with a completely
open mind. Her creative, open approach contrasts
with the rigidity that some other scientists would
use to condemn such sentiments. Her attitude was
recorded by Keller (1983), 'There's no such thing as
a central dogma into which everything will fit—any
mechanism you can think of you will find—even if
it is the most bizarre form of thinking. Anything.
So if the material tells you "it may be this", allow
that. Don't turn it aside and call it an exception, an
aberration. So many good clues have been lost in
that manner'.

In commenting on her Nobel speech, Thaler
(1994) described McClintock's award as directing
attention towards the evolution of genetic intelligence. Shapiro (1991) described it as 'genomes
functioning as true intelligence systems which can
be readjusted when conditions require'. These two
latter scientists understandably concentrated on
the genome because McClintock received her Nobel prize for the discovery of transposons. Note the
use of the term intelligence by these two leading
scientists; if a genome can behave intelligently then

the description equally applies to the organism in
which this genome is located as well.

Waddington and epigenetics

Conrad Waddington (1977) was an animal embry-
ologist and very substantive biological thinker. For
many years, he was Head of the Genetics Department at the University of Edinburgh and, as with
all strong personalities, no stranger to controversy.
In his last book, he described scientific dogma as
the conventional wisdom of the dominant group,
which he conveniently abbreviated to cow dung.
McClintock was posing a new paradigm and like
all paradigm changes, the early going can be rough.

While recognizing the value of controversial challenge, Waddington's characterization is perhaps a
touch unfair. All revolutionaries require the an-
vil of an established conventional view on which
they can hammer out their new understanding and
prove themselves against conventional resistance.
Waddington coined the term epigenetics to indicate
heritable changes that occur without changes in
the DNA sequence. Just as important is Waddington's epigenetic landscape, a topological surface
structure formed by the connections between the
molecules that construct the cell and his introduction of the term genetic assimilation. Waddington
found these notions of value in thinking about the
processes of development.

Further evolution of the McClintock paradigm of an unstable genome

The presence of transposons in numerous genomes
is now well accepted, but does our understanding
stop there? Is the gene the inviolable entity that
classical genetics assumes? Does an apparent stable
trait represent a stable DNA sequence? Does the cell
or plant decide that the genome can remain stable
for now, but when needs arise, simply change, ef-
fecting a kind of learning? The study of epigenetics
in which transposons are just one good example,
has continued apace in recent years. The term is
now used to describe heritable changes that survive
meiosis, as well as mitosis, and encompasses a variety of mechanisms.

Molinier et al. (2006) treated plants with 'stressful' conditions, such as UV light or bacterial infection, and observed that these treatments elevated genome rearrangements. These alterations continued for at least four generation—longer was not examined, but clearly a heritable change had occurred as a result of environmental stress. McClintock (1984), again in her Nobel speech, referred to a number of chromosomal rearrangements she had observed in response to stress. Thus, to quote again, 'the examples chosen illustrate the importance of stress in instigating genome modifications by mobilizing available cell mechanisms that can restructure genomes'. The cell controls the genome, not as commonly assumed the other way round.

Epigenetic modifications of inheritance

Epigenetic changes in the genome have received heightened attention in recent years. In addition to transposon changes, other mechanisms involve methylation of cytosines in DNA, histone post-translational modifications (chromatin marks), small inhibitory RNAs, paramutation, and nucleosome rearrangements (Henderson and Jacobsen 2007; Chen et al. 2010; Zaratiegui and Martienssen 2012). Changes in chromatin structure attract a great deal of current research investigation, particularly plant histone modification. Phosphorylation of histone H1 was first reported over 30 years ago and its relationship to the cell cycle indicated (Stratton and Trewavas 1981).

Epigenetic modifications are responsible for long-term memory changes in plant development, such as in vernalization or hybrid vigour (Grozmann et al. 2011) and for environmentally induced changes in behaviour that lead to heritable change in the offspring (Boyko and Kovalchuk 2011; Paszkowski and Groosniklaus 2011). DNA methylation is extensive in the *Arabidopsis* genome and methylation variations in discrete parts of the genome seem to be probably responsible for phenotypic variations that characterize wild populations. With behavioural changes being the initial event, the epigenetic state that follows may simply be transitory, thus enabling genetic mutations that arise to fix this new state in a genetic, rather than an epigenetic context (Eichten and Borevitz 2013.) This process

is genetic assimilation and is led by behavioural changes (Chapter 19).

An apparent alteration of heritable changes by particular environments, not even particularly stressful ones, is not uncommon in plants. There are many such reports in the past that are now given more credence by the extensive recent studies. There are well-established reports of the effects of moderate changes in temperature, soil mineral changes, and effects of various chemicals inducing heritable changes in morphological characteristics that have been observed to last from 5 to 12 generations, or even longer in the absence of the inductive environmental treatment (Highkin 1958; Hill 1965; Moss and Mullet 1982; Francis and Jones 1989; Meins 1989; Ries et al. 2000; Cullis 2005). I suspect that virtually all 'stressful' environmental conditions will induce genome rearrangements or other epigenetic modifications, but that does not necessarily lead to visible heritable changes in the progeny.

Durrant's radical experiments

Perhaps the most well-known in this category of environmentally-induced heritability are those originally reported by Durrant (1962) in flax and reviewed in Cullis (2005). Treatment of a single generation of flax with particular nutrient conditions changed the branching habit, and other morphological changes in height and weight. These changes were inherited by the siblings that did not receive the unusual soil mineral mixture. It took at least 12 generations in normal soil conditions for these morphological changes to slowly revert to the original, untreated, parental type. The suggestion from present studies is that sensitive regions of the genome that are concerned in the response to signals from outside, are also able to undergo re-arrangements or epigenetic modification that increase offspring variability in response to signalling.

Molinier et al. (2006) observed that all their plants responded to the enhanced rearrangement. Thus, the cellular events that cause rearrangement are inevitably epigenetic; they are not directly the result of some randomized mutation in the DNA sequence that then increases DNA rearrangements. The slow reversion of the altered morphology to wild-type flax, reported by Durrant (1962), suggests that this phenomenon, too, is not a permanent change in DNA sequence of appropriate genes. The answer must lie in the control of expression of particular genes associated with the particular trait that survives reproduction.

Inheritance of plant environmental experience is widespread

The potential for inheritance of environmentally-induced characters has always been present in plants, because of their life cycle characteristics. Vegetative growth of shoot meristems precedes the formation of reproductive cells that are subsequently formed from these vegetative cells. In some, vegetative experience goes on for many years before reproduction. Reproductive cells are thus derived from vegetative cells that have been directly exposed to environmental challenges of all kinds. Plant growth is pronouncedly modular and, in mature perennials, thousands of shoot meristems or modules are subject to potential changes during their vegetative history.

It is well known in horticultural circles that some growing shoot modules can undergo recognizable spontaneous and continuous alteration in behaviour. The changes that are easily identifiable are in pigmentation, but many others, often developmental, are known, producing what are called sports or chimeras (Neilson-Jones 1969; Tilney-Bassett 1986).

These module changes are not usually alterations in DNA sequence, because most do not survive sexual reproduction. They are, therefore, probably epigenetic. The sport can, instead, be maintained by vegetative propagation. However, the consequence is important. Sports were easily identified because of obvious visible changes. Molecular sports may only be detected under certain critical behavioural circumstances. For example, a mature tree contains thousands of branches with enormous numbers of buds, many of which remain dormant. A large number of these can harbour epigenetic changes. Even in growing modules without detailed examination, sports may easily be missed. It is not uncommon for different branches to produce different amounts of fruit or different senescence characteristics of leaves. These are rarely, if ever, investigated further.

However, environmental treatments can, indeed, change heritability, even if sometimes limited to a few generations. Recent important advances indicate that there is much hidden genetic variation, which can be revealed under stressful conditions, and a mechanism centralized around a heat shock protein, *Hsp* 90, has been observed (Queitsch et al. 2002; Sangster et al. 2008).

It has also been noted that sibling plants can express different morphologies as a result of parental, usually maternal, experience (Galloway 2005; Galloway and Etterson 2007). Numerous previous reports of this phenomenon are referenced in Galloway (2005). These authors showed that offspring life history, i.e. annual versus biennial, is influenced by the maternal light environment. What the parent plant experiences is passed on, because if the environmental experiences remain relatively constant, the siblings that have 'remembered' parental experience will benefit, as against those parents and siblings that don't. These influences can last for a number of generations and convincing studies indicate improvements in sibling fitness. Inheritance of parental experience has a meaningful biological and evolutionary relevance and is analogous to learning by human adults that is passed onto their children. Again, these sibling changes may be epigenetic, rather than DNA nucleotide sequence changes.

Epigenetic changes may last centuries

Perhaps the most prominent example at present is the peloric variant of the toadflax (*Linaria vulgaris*) flower (Cubas et al. 1999). Whereas the normal toadflax flower possesses a bilateral symmetry, in the peloric flower the symmetry has become radial and tube-like. Linnaeus first reported this variant over two centuries ago and regarded it incorrectly, as it turns out, as a different species. The change to the peloric condition can be unstable and revert to its original non-peloric form. Peloric flowers are known to exist in a number of plant species and are common in certain plant groups. Like toadflax they are stable through reproduction (Darwin 1876; Busch and Zachgo 2007).

Because Linnaeus first reported the toadflax peloric variant some 250 years ago, it is clearly a variation that has either been stable for that period of time or continually recurs. The gene *cycloidea*, whose product is essential for dorsoventral symmetry in flowers has been identified. In toadflax both the peloric and wild-type *cycloidea* DNA sequences are identical. However, in the peloric variant (or mutant) the *cycloidea* gene has had appropriate DNA bases methylated and, thus, silenced (Cubas et al. 1999). In other plants, like *Antirrhinum*, transposon shifts can silence *cycloidea* and these shifts, of course, can result from stressful environments.

The biological reasons for the origin and long-term continuation of the epigenetic peloric variants are not known. Flower morphology strongly interrelates with pollinator behaviour, so the evolutionary advantage of keeping the peloric state unstable may reflect, at some time, rapid changes in pollinator populations (Busch and Zachgo 2007). This is a theme that needs further investigation. In particular, the extent to which insect pollinators might have directly influenced flower structure through initial epigenetic or other modifications to provide easier pollen and nectar collection needs to be investigated. An early attempt quoting mechanical influences of bees on flower structures that eventually become heritable was made by Henslow (1888). Although Henslow's views and those of others like him were dismissed in the twentieth century, there is a resurgence of interest following from better knowledge of how unstable the genome can actually be and from proposed mechanisms like genetic assimilation or stabilizing selection (Schmalhausen 1949; Waddington 1957).

Genes learning and genes remembering: epigenetic learning in non-neural organisms

Do these epigenetic examples above indicate that 'genes learn by experience' (Bird 2007)? Are epigenetic changes the equivalent of a genetic memory? The experiments previously described certainly suggest this to be the case. Memory and learning are of potential advantage to organisms that live in a variable, but repetitive environment. When signals are likely to recur and the adaptive responses to these signals are costly, it is beneficial to reduce the cost by memorizing them.

Ginsburg and Jablonka (2009) indicate that learning is a kind of adaptive plasticity. These authors define two types of non-neural learning.

1. In **sensitization**, the learning process results in an organism in which the magnitude of a behavioural response follows a subsequent signal. Demonstrations that plants experience a learning process are readily easy to establish, since some processes require two signals for their response (see references in Trewavas 2009 and Chapter 26). Provision of one institutes a memory period in which another signal has to be provided to initiate a response. Many such phenomena are known. The memory may be seconds to days. Other convincing examples are the priming of plants that have experienced disease or herbivory. When there is recurrence of the stressful condition, the defence responses occurs much more quickly and are greatly enhanced. This memory can last for years. Similarly a long-term, trainable, memory of water depletion (Ding et al. 2012) and vernalization, the memory of winter, are other examples that use chromatin modifications and result in sensitization. Chromatin modifications form the basis of some cases of long-term memory in neural systems (Levenson and Sweatt 2005). 'Chromatin remodelling is thus intimately linked . . . to neural activity survival and ultimately the integrated regulation of behaviour' (Tsankova et al. 2007).

2. The alternative is **habituation** in which repetitive signalling leads to a reduction in response so that irrelevant signalling is now ignored and is easily demonstrated in *mimosa*, other plant movements and hormone effects (Bose 1906; Meins 1989).

The complex network that constructs the cell imposes these epigenetic changes on one specific part of the cell; its genome. The words 'thoughtful' and 'knowledge' about cellular behaviour suddenly look much more realistic than they did before, but if the genome can exhibit these properties of intelligence how much more so can the whole organism.

As Bird (2007) indicates, in respect of epigenetic DNA modifications, this 'deliciously Lamarckian flavour has proved difficult to resist as a potential antidote to genetic determinism'. Steven Gould (2002, p. 632 onwards) regards the emphasis on

DNA sequences of genes, as mere book-keeping about evolutionary change. Phenotypes, organisms, and groups of organisms are the real subjects of evolutionary change. In appropriate environmental and organism situations, modifications of heritability by selection can be induced at any of those system levels. The common emphasis on genes as the causal mechanism of both evolution and development neglects the cellular input that McClintock emphasized. 'A decision to privilege the level of genes plays into the strongest of all Western science: our tradition of reductionism and the desire to explain larger scale phenomena by properties of the smallest constituent particles' (Gould 2002, p. 634). Reductionism has yet to resolve the issue of network emergent properties.

Heritability and behaviour: the neo-Lamarckian approach

The name of Jean Lamarck will surely be familiar to many readers. He was a French biologist who worked in Paris during and beyond the French revolution. His most well-known text *Philosophie Zoologique* was published originally in 1808 and 50 years before Darwin's *Origin of species*. There is an English translation of this text by Hugh Elliott and published in 1914. In addition, Elliott provides a 90-page explanatory introduction.

A further text of considerable value was authored by Packard (1901). This latter book is part biography, part translation, and part explanations of Lamarck's scientific contributions, including comparisons with the substance of ideas of the Darwin's—Erasmus and Charles. Translators are in a unique position to explain the author's real meaning. My assessment is that Elliott, Packard, and even Lamarck himself is rarely read, despite frequent reference to Lamarck in the scientific literature. His name has normally been referenced to indicate that Lamarckian ideas are wrong and Darwin is right. These claims are commonly made by those whose knowledge of what Lamarck actually said is second- or third-hand, or even more remote.

Lamarck was an undoubted leading thinker and biologist of his time, and his suggestions have to be placed in that context. He proposed and defended the doctrine of organic evolution at a time when any such heretical idea was opposed not only by the church and the general public, but also by the leading scientists of the time. Like all influential thinkers, he attracted great criticism as well, usually from lesser individuals. When Darwin's *Origin of Species* was published in 1859, the facts of evolution became more generally accepted, as was Darwin's mechanism of natural selection. The reason that Darwin is credited with the concept of evolution is not because he was the first to suggest evolution. Many others, including Lamarck and Darwin's grandfather, Erasmus Darwin, had suggested the possibility and the idea of evolutionary change goes back even to early Greek philosophers. Darwin was not even the first to suggest natural selection, as he himself acknowledged in later reprints of the *Origin of Species*. Others had made the point that there was unequal survival among progeny and the better suited to the environment (the fitter) increased the chances of offspring survival.

However, Darwin is rightly credited with substantiating the idea of evolution because for the first time he provided a detailed argument based on enormous amounts of evidence that left little doubt at the time as to its validity in the mind of any unbiased individual. In one sense, it is easy to make passing reference to natural selection, as did Patrick Matthew in his book of 1831 on Naval Timbers and Arboriculture. However, the common reader of the appropriate paragraphs in Matthew's book would simply not have regarded them as in any way challenging fundamental beliefs about the origin of species; they remained only a passing suggestion, even if the reader recognized what was said as being essentially correct. It is only overwhelming evidence that focuses the attention on one theme. As Darwin found, however, the more convincing and stronger your argument the greater the opposition from those unwilling to change entrenched attitudes. It is the reaction by those who read the text at the time, which is most revealing about its strength. Some of the evidence for evolution Darwin had gathered in his long trip around the world. Other evidence he acquired from an enormous correspondence with all kinds of individuals and that also included his reading of Lamarck. Darwin changed his mind a number of times about Lamarckian views.

Lamarck certainly provided many important ideas, some of which current evidence indicates are incorrect. However, I have included the following quotations translated by Packard to indicate how wrong some of the views are, about what Lamarck said or thought (1901):

Nature has successively produced the different living beings by proceeding from the most simple to the most compound . . . and becomes complicated in a most remarkable way (p. 241).

I do not mean by this to say that the existing animals form a very simple series but I claim that they form a branched series irregularly graduated and which has no discontinuity in its parts; if it is true that owing to the extinction of some species there are some breaks (p. 243).

It follows that the species which terminates each branch of the general series is connected at least on one side with other species which inter-grade with it (p.243).

Nature has progressively created the different special organs also the faculties that animals enjoy p. 243).

As the individuals of one of our species are subjected to changes in situation, in climate, mode of life or habits, receive influences which gradually change the consistence and the proportion of their parts, their form, their faculties, even their structure, so that it follows that all of them participate in the changes to which they have been subjected (p. 243).

Very different situations and exposures cause simple variations in the individuals there which live and successively reproduce under the same circumstances, produce differences in form which become essential to their existence so that at the end of many successive generations, these individuals which originally belonged to another species become finally transformed into a new species distinct from the other (p. 244).

Species then, have only a relative stability and are invariable only temporarily (p. 247).

We know it is the strongest and the best armed which devour the weaker, devour the smaller (p. 248).

The influence of circumstances is really continuously and everywhere active on living beings as its effects only become recognisable at the end of a long period' (p. 252).

In the plants where there are no movements and consequently no habits so-called, great changes in circumstances do not bring about less great differences (than in animals) in the development of their parts (p. 255).

All botanists know that plants transplanted from their natal spot (the wild) into gardens gradually undergo changes, which in the end make them unrecognizable' (p. 215).

Is not wheat a plant brought by man to the state wherein we actually see it which otherwise I could not believe. Who can now say in what place its like lives in nature (p. 215)?

I have introduced the above statements because they indicate that Lamarck did not consider species immutable, regarded evolution as a branched structure, recognized extinction, and emphasized that a change in circumstances was responsible for evolutionary change. He also recognized that populations were naturally controlled from over-abundance with the stronger surviving. Furthermore, Lamarck was streets ahead of other thinkers at the time and clearly recognized that huge intervals of time were involved in the process of organic evolution. There is also, oddly enough, a recognition of genetic assimilation mechanisms.

There are many other aspects to Lamarck' writings to whom due credit is surely necessary. The main problem has been the caricature of Lamarck's statements about wants or needs interpreted by some as indicating that animals strove to change their structure, but to quote Packard again (1901, p. 300) 'In all the examples given he intimates that owing to changes in environment, leading to isolation in a new area separating a large number of individuals from their accustomed habitat, they are driven by necessity or new (physiological) needs to adopt a new or different mode of life'. Such a view hardly differs from what is currently understood to be sympatric speciation.

One consequence to Lamarck's substantive contributions from the publication of Darwin's *Origin of Species* was that further scientific reference to Lamarck's arguments for evolution disappeared. Instead, debate about Lamarck narrowed to one 'law' proposed by Lamarck, which is commonly summarized as 'the inheritance of acquired characters'. As indicated in the previous sections above, elements of this proposal are now appearing in the scientific literature. Actually reading the relevant chapter VII in Lamarck's book and Elliott's long introduction, it is quite obvious to me that Lamarck viewed these acquisitions of characters as very long term and reflecting no more than the familiar, that organisms are remarkably well-adapted to their environments. Even Darwin at times was a convinced Lamarckian on certain issues and with good reason. The hints to look at artificial selection, that Darwin used to such good effect in the *Origin of Species*, he surely derived directly from Lamarck who, 50 years before, pointed out the remarkable changes in both birds and dogs that artificial selection had managed. What both Darwin and Lamarck lacked were suitable mechanisms that could account for inheritance and adaptation. Only in the twentieth century did better understanding of inheritance emerge.

With the rediscovery of Mendel's simple genetics experiments by Bateson de Vries and Corenn in 1900, with the development of genetics and, finally, with Muller's description of mutations induced by X rays, the modern synthesis was created in the 1930s. The 'modern synthesis', acting on the limited knowledge of the time, ascribed all evolutionary mechanisms simply to random mutation and natural selection of appropriate mutated organisms. This paradigm was sometimes expounded dogmatically—the inverse of the open-minded, exploratory spirit that characterizes the true scientific approach. Lamarck's 'acquired character' proposal was often pilloried by those who clearly had not read or who misquoted *Philosophie Zoologique* or Eliott's long analysis. Cannon (1959), in a colourful text, points to the enormous errors of fact, and statement by the great and good at the time about Lamarck.

Lamarck's books were major contributions to understanding biology at the time they were written. As discussed earlier, increasing numbers of observations suggest the environment can modify plant heritability thus supporting one of Lamarck's suggestions. Even if these 'heritable' changes only last for five generations that is long enough to start substantially modifying local population heritability and gene pool. For the peloric flower at least in toadflax, there may be centuries of stability thus altering local populations of toadflax, but in turn modifying the spectrum of other plants in the local environment.

Lamarck's second proposal on behaviour and evolution

The second proposal by Lamarck on behaviour rarely receives any attention at all.

It is not the organs, the nature and shape of the parts of an animal's (plants) body that have given rise to its special habits and faculties; but it is its habits (behaviour), mode of life and environment that have in the course of time controlled the shape of its body the number and state of its organs and lastly the faculties which it possesses.

Note the use of the words 'in the course of time' as indicating Lamarck's understanding that changes had to be long term. Lamarck's book was a zoological text, but he included statements (and a book) on plants, too, and I have put the word 'plant' in brackets above to indicate the relevance of this statement to the subject matter of this book. Lamarck did not recognize plants as having behaviour, but behavioural modifications can lead the path anyway in evolutionary change.

Unfortunately, for Lamarck's second proposal there is no mechanism known at present whereby a relevant environmental change could directly cause changes in the nucleotide sequence of DNA coding for genes and that would adjust the plant body plastically. Reference instead has been made to epigenetic changes, which do account for them.

Lamarck has received a more reasoned appraisal in recent years. In part, this is because the modern synthesis and the simple gene-based ideas that underpin it, have themselves been subject to strong reappraisal and have been found wanting. The first of these reappraisals has become known as evo-devo. This area of investigation emphasizes evolution as resulting from changes in the regulation of gene expression during development, rather than random mutations in the mature adult (Oyama et al. 2001). The original supposition had been that the enormous diversity of plant morphology and development would result from a correspondingly large number of different kinds of genes and, in particular, in their sequence. However, sequencing has, in contrast, revealed the similarity of DNA sequences between species that are far apart in evolutionary terms.

The first book on epigenetic inheritance was published in 1995 detailing the mechanisms known at the time and, of course, referring appropriately and accurately to Lamarckian proposals (Jablonka and Lamb 1995). An updated version has also been published (Jablonka and Lamb 2006).

Some significant experiments in bacteria were reported in 1988 that provide the potential for rapid evolutionary change by a kind of evo-devo mechanism. Initially, these controversial experiments suggested directed mutation, but on reappraisal, is now called adaptive mutation (Cairns et al. 1988; Foster, 2004; Stump et al. 2007). The experimental observations were simple. Bacteria were used that had a mutation in the genomic region that prevented the use of lactose. However, when these mutants were incubated in solutions of lactose, relatively large numbers of revertants appeared able now to metabolize and live on lactose.

The actual mechanism is still a matter of debate. Foster (2004) provides a reasoned update with a balance of evidence suggesting increased error-prone DNA replication by an unusual error-prone DNA polymerase (polymerase IV). Higher rates of mutant production in the regulation of lactose utilization were the consequence. However, mutations were not directly limited to the lactose system genes. The stressful condition, instead, had increased a more general rate of mutation in siblings and some of these were enabled to now use lactose. What this suggests is that stressful conditions in both plants and bacteria, and feasibly numerous animal species (Jablonka and Lamb 1995) cause increased mutation of gene regulation, thus accelerating the appearance of some sibling individuals able to better tolerate the stressful state.

The end of this section is taken by Lamarck himself. 'It is not enough to discover and prove a useful truth but that it is necessary also to be able to propagate it and get it recognised' (Lamarck 1914, p. 404). Darwin, of course, had his immediate supporters; Lamarck did not.

The cell not the gene, because the cell integrates all information

'Future attention will be centred on the genome as a highly sensitive organ **of the cell** that monitors its genomic activities and corrects common errors, senses unusual and unexpected events and responds to them often by restructuring the genome' (McClintock 1984). Are cells the prisoner of their genes or is it the alternative that might be interpreted from McClintock's statement that genes are prisoners of their cells? The answer, of course, is neither. The cell is an integrated system and its survival depends on all its constituent parts.

What the evidence in this chapter shows, is that apart from genomic intelligence, plants learn about the features and characteristics in their environment. It is a genuine process of learning because it affects future behaviour and can be remembered for extended periods of time, even passed down to subsequent generations. All this accomplished by organisms that have no neural systems.

References

Bird, A. (2007). Perceptions of epigenetics. *Nature*, **447**, 396–398.

Bose, J.C. (1906). *Plant response as a means of physiological investigation*. Longmans Green and Co., New York.

Boyko, A., and Kovalchuk, I. (2011). Genome instability and epigenetic modification–heritable responses to environmental stress? *Current Opinion in Plant Biology*, **14**, 260–266.

Busch, A., and Zachgo, S. (2007). Control of corolla monosymmetry in the *Brassicaceae iberis amara*. *Proceedings of the National Academy of Sciences USA*, **104**, 16714–16719.

Cairns, J., Overbaugh, J., and Miller, S. (1988). The origin of mutants. *Nature*, **335**, 142–145.

Cannon, H.G. (1959). *Lamarck and modern genetics*. Manchester University Press, Manchester.

Chen, M., Lv, S., and Meng, Y. (2010). Epigenetic performers in plants. *Development Growth and Differentiation*, **52**, 555–566.

Cubas, P., Vincent, C., and Coen, E. (1999). An epigenetic mutation responsible for natural variation in foral symmetry. *Nature*, **401**, 157–161.

Cullis, C.A. (2005). Mechanism and control of rapid genomic changes in flax. *Annals of Botany*, **95**, 204–206.

Darwin, C. (1859). *The origin of species by means of natural selection*. John Murray, London.

Darwin, C. (1875). *The variation of animals and plants under domestication*, Vol. 1. Murray, London.

Darwin, C. (1876). *The variation of animals and plants under domestication*, Vol. 2. Murray, London.

Ding, Y., Fromm, M., and Avramova, Z. (2012). Multiple exposures to drought 'train' transcriptional responses in *Arabidopsis*. *Nature Communications*, **3**, 740.

Durrant, A. (1962). The environmental induction of heritable change in *Linum*. *Heredity*, **17**, 27–61.

Eichten, S., and Borevitz, J. (2013). Epigenomics: methylation's mark on inheritance. *Nature*, **495**, 181–182.

Foster, P.L. (2004). Adaptive mutation in *Escherichia coli*. *Journal of Bacteriology*, **186**, 4846–4852.

Francis, A., and Jones R.N. (1989). Heritable nature of colchicine induced variation in diploid *Lolium perenne*. *Heredity*, **62**, 407–410.

Galloway, G. (2005). Maternal effects provide phenotypic adaptation to local environmental conditions. *New Phytologist*, **166**, 93–100.

Galloway, L.F., and Etterson, J.R. (2007). Transgenerational plasticity is adaptive in the wild. *Science*, **318**, 1134–1136.

Ginsburg, S., and Jablonka, E. (2009). Epigenetic learning in non-neural organisms. *Journal of Biosciences*, **34**, 633–646.

Gould, S.J. (2002). *The structure of evolutionary theory*. Belknap Press of Harvard University Press, Cambridge, MA.

Grozmann, M., Greaves, I.K., Albert, N., Fujimoto, R., Helliwell, C.A., Dennis, E.S., and 1 other (2011). Epigenetics in vernalisation and hybrid vigour. *Biochimica Biophysica Acta*, **1809**, 427–437.

Henderson, I.B., and Jacobsen, S.E. (2007). Epigenetic inheritance in plants. *Nature*, **447**, 418–424.

Henslow (1888). *The origin of floral structures through insect and other agencies*. Appleton and Co., New York.

Highkin, H.R. (1958). Temperature induced variability in peas. *American Journal of Botany*, **45**, 626–631.

Hill, J. (1965). Environmental induction of heritable changes in *Nicotiana*. *Nature*, **207**, 732–734.

Jablonka, E., and Lamb, M.J. (1995). *Epigenetic inheritance and evolution. The Lamarckian dimension*. Oxford University Press, Oxford.

Jablonka, E., and Lamb, M.J. (2006). *Evolution in four dimensions*. MIT Press, Cambridge, MA.

Keller, E.F. (1983). *A feeling for the organism. The life and work of Barbara McClintock*. W.H. Freeman and Co., New York.

Lamarck, J. (1914). *Zoological philosophy*, transl. Hugh Elliott. MacMillan, London.

Levenson, J.M., and Sweatt, J.D. (2005). Epigenetic mechanisms in memory formation. *Nature Reviews Neuroscience*, **6**, 108–118.

Matthew, P. (1831). *On naval timber and arboriculture with critical notes on authors who have recently treated the subject of planting*. Black, Edinburgh.

McClintock, B. (1984). The significance of the responses of the genome to challenge. *Science*, **226**, 792–801.

Meins, F. (1989). Habituation: heritable variation in the requirement of cultured plant cells for hormones. *Annual Review of Genetics*, **23**, 395–408.

Molinier, J., Ries, G., Zipfel, C., and Hohn, B. (2006). Transgeneration memory of stress in plants. *Nature*, **442**, 1046–1049.

Moss, G.I., and Mullet, J.H. (1982). Potassium release and seed vigour in germinating bean seed as influenced by

temperature over the previous five generations. *Journal of Experimental Botany*, **33**, 1147–1160.

Neilson-Jones, W. (1969). *Plant chimeras*. Methuen, London.

Oyama, S., Griffiths, P.E., and Gray, R.D. (2001). *Cycles of contingency: developmental systems and evolution*. MIT Press, Cambridge, MA.

Packard, A.S. (1901). *Lamarck, the founder of evolution: his life and work*. Longmans Green, London.

Paszkowski, J., and Grossniklaus, U. (2011). Selected aspects of transgenerational epigenetic inheritance and resetting in plants. *Current Opinion in Plant Biology*, **14**, 1–9.

Queitsch, C., Sangster, T.A., and Lundquist, S. (2002). Hsp90 as a capacitor of phenotypic variation. *Nature*, **417**, 618–624.

Ries, G. Heller, W. Puchta, H., Sandermann, H. Seidlitz, H.K., and Hohn, B. (2000). Elevated UV-B radiation reduces genome stability in plants. *Nature*, **406**, 98–101.

Sangster, T.A., Salathia, N., Lee, H.N. Watanabe, E., Schellenberg, K., Morneau, K., and 4 others (2008). Hsp90 buffered genetic variation is common in *Arabidopsis thaliana*. *Proceedings of the National Academy of Sciences USA*, **105**, 2969–2974.

Schmalhausen, I.I. (1949). *Factors of evolution. The theory of stabilising selection*. Blakiston Co., Philadelphia, PA.

Shapiro, J.A. (1991).Genomes as smart systems. *Genetica*, **84**, 3–4.

Stratton, B.R., and Trewavas, A.J. (1981). Phosphorylation of histone H1 during the cell cycle of artichoke. *Plant Cell and Environment*, **4**, 419–426.

Stump, J.D. Poteete, A.R., and Foster, P.L. (2007). Amplification of lac cannot account for adaptive mutation to lac $^+$ in *Escherichia coli*. *Journal of Bacteriology*, **189**, 2291–2299.

Thaler, D.S. (1994). The evolution of genetic intelligence. *Science*, **264**, 224–225.

Tilney-Bassett, R.A.E. (1986). *Plant chimeras*. Edward Arnold, London.

Trewavas, A. (2009). What is plant behaviour? *Plant Cell and Environment*, **32**, 606–616.

Tsankova, N., Renthal, W., Kumar, A., and Nestler, E.J. (2007). Epigenetic regulation in psychiatric disorders. *Nature Reviews Neuroscience*, **8**, 355–367.

Waddington, C.H. (1957). *The strategy of the genes*. Allen and Unwin, London.

Waddington, C.H. (1977). *Tools for thought*. Jonathan Cape, London.

Zaratiegui, M., and Martienssen, R.A. (2012). SnapShot: small RNA mediated epigenetic modifications. *Cell*, **151**, 456–457.

CHAPTER 22

Cellular basis of intelligent behaviour

Because of their high degree of interconnection, systems
of interacting proteins act as neural networks to respond
to patterns of extracellular stimuli.

(Bray 1995)

⊃ Summary

Cellular proteins have a broad range of functions that provide a springboard for understanding how cells express intelligent behaviour. The major proteins and processes in signal transduction have switch-like activity from receptors to cytosolic Ca^{2+}, and then further amplification occurs via protein kinase and phosphorylation. The potential for creativity (novelty) in transduction sequence has been demonstrated from a consideration of different energy levels in proteins. Cyclic enzymes of different kinds can also be shown to have switch-like characteristics, as do allosteric proteins in combination with an activator. Boolean language underpins computer design and some Boolean operations mimic known transduction steps. Nerve cells often have a switch-like character to them and simple neural networks composed of a few neurones have been modelled and shown to exhibit important properties, such as pattern recognition, computation, and memory. Some transduction sequences bear similarity to simple neural networks and use of chemical diodes, all-or-none chemical reactions linked together, exhibited similar behaviour as the neural net. Logic circuits that describe certain developmental behaviours have been reported. The concept of mutual information has been used to determine the 'bits' of information that underpin transduction events in single cells. In most cases, a single bit, an on/off function was detected. More cells provide for greater numbers of outcomes. Finally, Manfred Eigen's (Nobel Prize winner) assessment of learning, memory and intelligence in single cells is described.

Introduction

Two previous chapters, 19 and 20, have outlined the nature of intelligence and the evidence that intelligent behaviour can be observed in organisms and cells that do not possess a nervous system. These next two chapters indicate the potential mechanisms whereby intelligent capacities, that is a capacity to solve problems, can be found in such organisms, referring to the simplest; that of the cell itself. Since the main engines of cells are proteins, inevitably discussion hinges around these as providing for

understanding. 'Many aspects of cell behaviour display a capacity for information processing that is independent of the genome and hence is controlled by sets of proteins' (Bray 1995).

The remarkable range of protein properties in cells

Behaviour is generally elicited by changes in signalling. The complex mess of information arrives both from outside the plant and outside the cell, and is interpreted by proteins.

Plant Behaviour and Intelligence. First Edition. Anthony Trewavas.
© Anthony Trewavas 2014. Published 2014 by Oxford University Press.

In the unicellular organisms whose behaviour was outlined previously, there is no coordinating nervous system. Instead, protein circuits replace these and provide for quite surprisingly complex behaviour. It is the proteins that perform the main activities of the cell and translate the flow of information into cellular responses. In the more complicated cells of higher plants, many thousands of proteins are involved in the assessment and transduction of signals. A common figure suggests at least 5% of genes encode proteins that are directly involved in processing information, but these merge seamlessly with other groups of proteins that perform motor activities.

Furthermore, many of these proteins undergo post-translational modification, increasing the number of discrete protein activities involved. Other proteins act as nucleation sites for the formation of signalling complexes. Some protein complexes function like miniature motors, others rotate with ion fluxes or cause cytoplasm to stream, others carry vesicles on predetermined protein tracks to different regions of the cell, while yet others separate chromosome pairs during division or spin fibres of cellulose into the cell wall. It would be difficult to disentangle these from proteins directly involved in reacting to signals, since many changes in behaviour involve them intimately.

Cellular proteins interact with each other to form enormous and complex networks. The degree of connectedness of the proteins involved is crucial, since this provides the network of interrelationships that starts with the cell and leads to tissues, organs, and finally whole plant behaviour. 'The imprint of the environment on the concentration and activity of many thousands of proteins is in effect a memory trace, like a random access memory containing ever changing information about its surroundings' (Bray 1995). Critical to understanding cellular behaviour is the strength of connections between proteins since modifications in the strength of connection underpin many changes in cellular behaviour.

The cytoplasm is a plethora of different states of organization

The cytoplasm, where much of cellular interpretation occurs, is 20–40% protein; some membranes are up to 80%. The cytoplasm is highly structured in a gel-like form, interspersed with regions of greater fluidity (Pollack 2001). Gel-like cytoplasm is found in the cortical region of cells directly under and attached to the plasma membrane (Trewavas 2012). The gel structure owes much to actin proteins that acts as nucleation sites interacting directly, usually in microfilament form, with a very large family of actin binding proteins. These, in turn, help organize others into semi-permanent structures. The gel structure imposes order on water molecules, and these can interfere and slow protein diffusion. The disruption of structured water will then free up and increase interaction rates, but structured water itself being of low entropy is able to provide energy to drive cellular processes when the structure collapses. These concepts are expanded Chapter 23.

Other proteins are often found in large complexes that are located in particular regions of the cell and many are often pinned to a membrane, either through lipid rafts or integral membrane proteins. These complexes will often contain receptor proteins. Such complexes are constructed to speed up information transfer events; for example, the active sites of kinases and substrates can be close together. On receipt of a signal, induced changes in conformation occur stepwise through the signalling complex, but branching can also occur, too.

This is quite simply biological solid state circuitry, as found in computer wiring. Other complexes form on signalling and are often hinged around specific proteins (such as PH or SH proteins). These proteins are usually attached to the plasma membrane. The formation of the complex is diffusion limited. Microfilaments usually find attachment sites on the plasma membrane, although these are in a dynamic state; also microtubules sometimes attach here.

Molecular noise enables creative protein conformations and novel transduction sequences to be constructed: a novel potential for cellular learning

Our understanding of the way transduction proteins behave has undergone substantive change recently (Smock and Gierasc 2009). The conformation of individual proteins is in constant flux, exploring energy landscapes that enable sampling from an ensemble of different structures. Upstream proteins that are present in transduction circuits remodel this energy landscape in downstream proteins, changing conformations by interaction and enabling exploration of new energy landscapes. How well any sequence performs at the individual protein level, depends on the particular conformation expressed by the downstream proteins. The conformations that enable signalling are usually considered to be in the commoner, that is the lower, energy states. However, with molecular noise complicating the issue, the potential for change to a higher energy state, must be present and occur frequently. If the protein is in a higher energy state, then signalling through those individual proteins may temporarily cease. There are, however, lag periods of variable length before different conformation/energy configurations are assumed. In this state, the altered configuration may then be sequestered to act upstream of proteins in a different transduction sequence altogether. With an ensemble of conformations, only some of which are currently used, there is clearly the potential for novel information processing to occur.

For any protein kinases that are ubiquitous members of many transduction sequences, an environmentally-induced new conformation could lead to changes in phosphorylation specificity. Different serines or threonines could be now be phosphorylated, activating different sites on a previous substrate. There is the potential for activating or inactivating novel protein substrates too with substantive signalling consequences. There is, therefore, a ready potential for creating new pathways, but at the minimum it represents learning and learning is the basis for intelligent behaviour.

Signal transduction processes use molecular changes that act like switches

Some of the molecules involved in processing environmental information in plant cells are known. There are signal receptors, cytosolic Ca^{2+}, inositol phosphates, protein kinases, and other signalling proteins. Each of these can have the biological characteristic of acting like an on/off switch. Positive feedback in the transduction chain will also act like a switch.

Receptors either have a chemical binding site or a ligand that recognizes the signals, such as light. Receptors may also be clustered and amplify signals so that one active receptor can, in turn, activate many downstream proteins. If receptors are clustered together the accuracy of signalling is improved as well (Bialek and Setayeshgar 2005). If the receptor is a protein kinase activated by the signal, then the potential for activating other receptors by phosphorylation is present. The decay rate of the active state of the receptors can specify the characteristics and stability of the external signal. Protein complexes in the synapses of the brain have a similar but more complex processing ability (Bray 2009). An occupied receptor contains substantive information about the external signal, because other proteins interpret its occupied state. In contrast, the non-activated receptor may contain no useful information. In information terms, receptor occupation acts like a switch.

The resting cytosolic concentration of Ca^{2+} in the cytoplasm is too low to influence cellular events. On receipt of mechanical influences, touch, light, temperature, disease organism, hormones, etc., in plant cells, channels (specific protein conduits) open in one or other membrane systems that contain many orders of magnitude higher concentrations of Ca^{2+}. A single channel protein can conduct a million atoms of Ca^{2+}/sec and cytosolic concentrations can increase by several orders of magnitude within a few seconds. In the cytoplasm or nucleus, the transient effect of the Ca^{2+} signal is prolonged by activation of many Ca^{2+}-dependent enzymes, including importantly protein kinases (Luan 2011). Enzymes that remove Ca^{2+} from the cytoplasm come into operation quickly to truncate the Ca^{2+} transient and enable continued signal detection.

Inositol phosphates are released on receptor occupation and signalling by enzymatic degradation of plasma membrane lipids, and can initiate a series of metabolic changes, including release of Ca^{2+} from various cell storage sites. Phosphatases rapidly deplete what is a transient switch–like character.

Protein kinases and phosphatases act to alter network connections via phosphorylation

In neural networks, learning results from the formation of new dendrites, thus opening up new channels through which information can flow. Analogously, phosphorylation modifications do the same to the metabolic network. Protein kinases use ATP to phosphorylate and, thus, change the activity of other cellular proteins or other protein kinases. The modification can be reversed by specific protein phosphatases.

Clarification on control functions using protein phosphorylation was greatly accelerated by theoretical and practical studies (Chock and Stadtman 1977; Shachter et al. 1984). These authors explored some of the amplification potential (switch-like character) in a simple protein kinase/phosphatase system. They also explored the amplification inherent in coupled protein kinases, i.e. one protein kinase phosphorylating and activating another protein kinase, with both under dephosphorylation control by protein phosphatases. Such cascades of protein kinases are known to be present in both plant and animal cells as mitogen-activated protein kinases (three protein kinases in a cascade) and these are part of the transduction sequences involving control of plant behaviour (Rodriguez et al. 2010). They are also subject to additional phosphorylation too by other protein kinases such as MEK1 (MAP kinase kinase kinase kinase). Amplification by a single protein kinase may be several-hundred-fold; in the cascade it is of the order of 100,000-fold—a clear switch-like capability. The advantages of using a kinase cascade are not only greater amplification, but the more proteins that are involved in a transduction sequence, enables greater possibilities for control by other molecules. On the other hand, more proteins in the sequence increase the potential damaging consequence of interference from molecular noise.

There are at least a thousand protein kinases in both plant and animal cells. Some kinases are enzymatically specific for only a few proteins, others can be very promiscuous, phosphorylating 50 substrate proteins or more. A typical hub and connector distribution exists as noted for cellular proteins in total (Chapter 3). There are recognizable classes of protein kinase (Trewavas 2000) and up to a hundred protein kinases that are activated either directly or indirectly by cytosolic Ca^{2+}. Other kinases act as receptors.

Some protein substrates are phosphorylated on only one amino acid side chain (serine, tyrosine, or threonine), while others can be multiply phosphorylated. Different kinases, located in different regions of the cell, may pick on one serine; others may pick on another. Many protein substrate serines or threonines remain unphosphorylated, so leaving a potential for new modification of activity under appropriate (creative) circumstances as indicated earlier. Many phosphorylation sites are situated on the protein surface and a change in conformation of the substrate protein may be all that is necessary for the creation of new signalling events. In addition to phosphorylation there are other ways of changing protein activity by post-translational modification. There are, in total, some 10 different protein modifications currently known that modify protein activity. These capabilities increase the effective number of genomic products beyond that of the DNA sequence.

Other switch-like capabilities in cellular processes

A number of processes in cells that are cyclic in character as, for example, the phosphorylation/dephosphorylation cycle or electron donor/acceptor cycle have been shown to exhibit switch-like and bistable characteristics (Okamoto et al. 1988; Jackson 1993).

There is often acute sensitivity to allosteric activation of specific proteins by signals, a 2–3-fold change in concentration in a signal molecule can be sufficient for a full change in activity.

Computers are based on on/off switch-like processes: Boolean logic language can be applied to biological circuitry and signal transduction

Present-day computers function by processing information. Very large numbers of transistors form the basis of the chip circuits, and these act as on/off or yes/no devices. The memory of these devices is measured in bits, short for binary digit. A simple on/off device contains one bit of information. Computers use electronic gates as ways of controlling and manipulating the flow of information. The simplest element is a simple logic gate that has two outputs—either zero or one. Which of the two outputs operates is dependent on the information arriving at the input stage of the gate.

More complex gates have multiple inputs with different combinations of bit values. The output will again be high or low, depending on the type of operation performed. Logic circuits are constructed from the interactions of numerous single gates to provide more complex computation. When very large numbers of gates are connected together, the output can be used for eventual computation and with larger numbers again, artificial intelligence. While a cell is not a computer, there are very useful parallels in seeing how transduction networks might be constructed using these logical principles.

George Boole devised the binary system of numeration in the nineteenth century and developed a language that is now used to construct logical operations by present-day computers.

The commonest computer operations are called AND and OR. The AND operation says if, and only if, all inputs are on, then the output will be on. The output will be off, if any of the inputs are off. The OR operation says if any input is on, the output will be on. Biological parallels for the AND gate are, of course, genes that require all transcription factors to be attached to the promoter region or a receptor kinase. The OR gate is again a gene that has a promoter that needs only one transcription factor, although having other regions of the promoter that can accept other transcription factors.

There are two operations that have the same logic as above, but with an inverted output. The NAND operation says if, and only if, all inputs are on, the output will be off. The NOR operation says if any input is on, the output will be off. There is a variation on the OR logic called Exclusive OR or XOR. Exclusive OR says the output will be on if the inputs are different. Another one, the inverter or NOT operation, says that the output will be opposite in state to the input. The NAND operation can be considered equivalent to some protein phosphatases, which when activated inhibit current phosphorylation circuits. Other more complex logic circuits are mentioned later.

Transduction networks are analogous to simple modelled neural nets and act like chemical neurones

The interactions in transduction networks inevitably generate emergent properties that we see as the coordinated responses to specific signals. Nerve cells are also known to exhibit all-or-none switch-like activity, and this feature has been used to model simple neural networks and examine their behaviour (McCulloch and Pitts 1943; Hopfield 1982; Hopfield and Tank 1986). Simple networks, constructed from only 3–4 neurons and connected to each other by modelled dendrites with an input and an output, had quite complex properties. These networks displayed a memory, error correction, time sequence retention, and a natural capacity for solving optimization problems.

The transduction reactions that use second messages and enzymes form a densely-connected network of considerable complexity. There are analogies between this network and the modelled neural networks constructed by Hopfield and parallel distributed process networks (PDPN) used in the computer simulation of cognitive tasks such as symbol recognition (Bray 1990).

PDPN learn by changing the strength of connections in the individual pathways so that the balance of information arising at a focal point enables prioritizing of responses. Protein kinase networks have the same capability. Phosphorylation changes the effective connection strength between the protein components, as well as acting like computer switches.

Bray (1990) points to three advantages of such PDPN structures within biological transduction networks.

1. Cells are able to recognize combinations of environmental signals, increasing the diversity of cell behaviour.
2. A PDPN can stabilize signal transduction against fluctuations in the cellular concentrations of signalling molecules. In bacterial cells, variations of 10–15-fold have been observed in protein

constituents between individual cells (Taniguchi et al., 2010).

3. The potential for the construction of logic circuits that can amplify weak signals, integrate signals or responses, control natural rhythmic processes, or store information.

The molecular processes that underpin some of these logic circuits have been identified in cells. Many logic circuits use negative feedback and feed forward controls on signal processing and these act as switches, toggles, or timers (Bray 1990, 1995; Nurse 2008). Such control mechanisms are essential to developing cellular responses and, in turn, whole organism behaviour. There are probably thousands of negative feedback controls in any cell, necessary to maintain some sort of internal homeostasis, or at least a sufficiently constant cellular milieu for optimal functioning.

Chemical diodes act as alternative modelling devices

Chemical diodes have been constructed that are similar in behaviour to any biochemical switch or modelled neurone. These are threshold devices changing effectively from 0 to1 at a given value of an input variable (Hjelmfeldt et al. 1991, 1992, 1993; Hjelmfeldt and Ross 1994). In earlier work, these authors showed that bi-stable chemical reactions, coupled by mass transport, could be used to store and recall patterns when the connection weights were chosen using a Hebbian rule. This rule describes how synaptic efficacy in neural systems increases, as a result of persistent stimulation by a presynaptic cell on a post-synaptic cell. These authors adapted the Hebb learning rule to specify how much the weight of the connection between two diode units should be increased or decreased in proportion to the product of their activation. One way in which cells use this Hebbian potential for learning, is when a protein kinase in a transduction sequence feeds back on partial activation to increase the activity of another earlier in the circuitry. A MAP kinase cascade is a good example. These authors found that coupling together a number of these chemical diodes produced a stack memory, a simple calculating and adding device, and pattern recognition.

These authors further simulated homogeneous chemical systems, where each 'neuron' or chemical diode was composed of a set of cyclic chemical reactions thus forming what they termed 'chemical neurons'. These were cyclic coupled chemical reactions, such as the phosphorylation/dephosphorylation cycles between a number of kinases and phosphatases, or other metabolic on/off switches. These models had direct relevance to cellular behaviour. When coupled together in different configurations, a programmable network was constructed that could store (remember) patterns. That is, the network was able to recognize (that is assess) patterns similar, but not identical to the stored patterns. These investigations indicate the potential available and help to explain how some of the described cellular properties can follow from phosphorylation cyclic systems. Coupled with the switch-like characteristics of all the transduction molecules, a simple 'neural network' capable of realistic assessment of incoming information, is potentially present in every cell. Coupled chemical neurones in appropriate combinations can exhibit some of the logical operations indicated by Boole previously, thus emphasizing the potential computational character to the way living cells respond to signals (Arkin and Ross 1994).

Both cells and nervous systems use frequency modulation of signals for transduction

Nerve cells use frequency modulation according to the strength of stimulus. When the stimulus is increased, the nerve responds by an increase in frequency of its action potentials.

In both animals and plants, oscillations of cytosolic or organelle Ca^{2+} have been observed and, in some of these, the frequency of oscillation is determined by the strength of stimulus, indicating frequency modulation (Berridge et al., 1998; Berridge 2005; Ehrhardt et al. 1996; Pierson et al. 1996; Allen et al. 2001).

Single cell analysis has revealed that cytosolic Ca^{2+} elevation may also be responsible for causing frequency modulation in other molecules. On elevation of cytosolic Ca^{2+} in yeast, a transcription factor Crz1 is dephosphorylated by a specific protein phosphatase. This protein undergoes bursts of nuclear localization, coordinating the expression of some 100 genes (Cai et al. 2008). The frequency of nuclear bursts is determined by the size of the cytosolic Ca^{2+} signal.

The potential identification of logic circuits for developmental and physiological functions

Gene regulatory networks are one of the two contributory factors that lead to the construction of the phenotype; the other being the cellular environmental circumstances in which the regulatory network operates. Regulatory networks are composed of subcircuits each of which defines a specific regulatory task. Organize these subcircuits into various groupings and different operations emerge (Davidson 2010). These are discussed again in Chapter 23.

Those subcircuits currently identified include signal-mediated switches, inductive signalling, AND logic circuitry, spatial repression, feedback, reciprocal repression of state, community effect circuits, boundary maintenance, binary cell fate choice, and discontinuous transcriptional choice to signal intensity or duration. The associated topological structure of each sub-circuit is described by Davidson (2010). Mathematical modelling of some of these sub-circuits, has indicated the function they actually mediate. Much of the regulatory structure and control is hierarchical.

While these analyses are based on animal development and some are clearly different to those in plants, the approach to gathering a language that will provide an understanding of the construction of living organism indicates the direction in which future plant molecular studies must develop. Theoretical analyses and practical investigations go hand-in-hand together.

Mutual information and real assessment of information constraints

A central concept in information theory is mutual information. This quite simply measures the correlation between the input and output in terms of bits 'and provides a measure of how much a cell can learn about external signals' (Mehta et al. 2009). Cells and organisms constantly probe their environments, and actively adapt their metabolism and genetic circuitry. The crucial requirement is that interpretation of the signals should provide some degree of faithfulness about the external information experienced, even when molecular noise tends to destroy this information. The 'bit' is the standard unit of information and 1 bit indicates a yes/no answer; it distinguishes between two equally probable states. N bits provides for 2^n solutions, thus 2 bits provides for four outcomes, etc. Assessment of bit numbers has been made in a number of situations, all of which are instructive.

Steveninck et al. (1997) estimated that a single neurone could transmit about 2.5 bits of information; about five possible outcomes. Coupled together with other neurones, that respond slightly differently, the information available is substantially increased. A much higher degree of information becomes available about the stimulus.

The formation of a bacterial quorum leading to a change in behaviour by the quorum, requires the synthesis and secretion of auto-inducers by bacterial cells. In *Vibrio harveyi*, three auto-inducers are known; two are specific to *Vibrio*, the third is synthesized by many bacterial species. Each inducer transduction pathway uses kinases, but all of these can end in the induction of the same quorum-sensing transcription changes (Mehta et al. 2009). The information obtained by quorum-sensing, participating cells, was found to be dependent on the state of the internal transduction pathways of these molecules. If the kinase levels of each transduction channel were the same, each auto-inducer on its own was estimated to provide no more than 0.6–0.8 bits; insufficient to indicate the presence of the auto-inducer.

One way to increase information transmission was either:

1. To greatly increase the production of one auto-inducer.
2. To increase the receptor number of one channel.
3. To increase the kinase activity of one channel.

In any of these situations, 1.5–1.7 bits was transferred, sufficient for about three outcomes and enabling recognition of the two specific auto-inducers.

The gradient of morphogen in a developing insect embryo is used to specify the initiation of different tissues. In terms of a specific gene product, the gradient provides only about 1.7 bits of information

(Gregor et al. 2007; Tkacik et al. 2008). It is known that there are three potential outputs from this gradient for the gene product—no change in gene expression, one intermediate expression, and one full expression. Thus, the gradient with 1.7 bits is sufficient to specify the outcomes.

The signal transduction pathway of tumour necrosis factor (TNF) has been examined in some detail for its ability to induce the synthesis of two specific proteins (Cheong et al. 2011; Thomas 2011). Measurements showed that the pathway in a single cell and as currently known, simply transferred 0.92 bits of information. The only information the cell gains is whether TNF is present or not. The signal transduction channel for these two proteins is shared for most of the steps in a tree type model with branching near the end. The shared sequence it was thought produces a bottleneck in information flow. These authors were also able to measure the channel capacity; that is the maximum amount of information that could be transferred through the transduction sequence and estimated it to be 1.26 ± 0.13 bits. The difference between that observed and the maximum is probably the effect of molecular noise.

One important piece of information was the finding that a group of cells conveys more information. 14 cells, for example, conveyed about 1.8 bits of information for TNF. That is nearly four outcomes and enables some discrimination between different TNF concentrations. The variety of cells involved, presumably varying in their sensitivity, enabled a larger number of potential outputs. Similar figures of about one bit were found for epidermal growth factor, platelet-derived growth factor and G protein-coupled receptors (Cheong et al. 2011).

The surprising feature of all these measurements is how little information is actually transferrable about a signal for individual cells. In the case of some, it is a receptor bottleneck that constrains information flow. In others, a bush-like transduction arrangement, an arrangement that uses different but parallel transduction channels, can theoretically increase information flow. In the TNF example case, it can elevate information flow to 1.26 bits and with time integration can take this up to 1.64 bits. Individual cells vary in the time taken to respond, too. In most cases, for a single cell, however, many

transduction pathways seem to operate in a yes/no configuration—above a threshold, the output is fully switched on. With many more cells operating, and with the differential effects of noise and cell variation, discrimination between different concentrations is possible. What this suggests is that a quantitative response by a tissue to an increasing strength of signal, originates from all-or-none responses exhibited by the constituent cells whose sensitivity to the signal is variable.

Plant tissues are composed of cells whose sensitivity or threshold of response is variable and a response to noise in their genetic circuitry

In Chapter 16, it was indicated that plant growth substances or hormones apparently acted as synchronizing agents. The higher the concentration of applied hormone used, the greater the number of cells responding. The explanation is similar to that above. Each cell responds to a signal in an on/off manner, but then each cell varies from its neighbour in the threshold sensitivity with which it goes from off to on. In that case, a dose–response situation originates from the sensitivity variations of the cells within the tissue. Thresholds become crucial elements in understanding behaviour of single tissues. For tissues that are derived originally from single cells such as seeds, even perhaps whole leaves, even perhaps the whole plant itself, the same consideration applies (Bradford and Trewavas 1994; Trewavas 2012). The dose–response character for plant growth hormones is a synchronizing effect, it is probabilistic.

Direct evidence for stochastic probabilistic responses to light was reported by Nick et al. (1993). Using a microbeam of red light they were able to irradiate small patches of cotyledon cells to induce purple anthocyanin production. Considerable cellular spottiness was observed, particularly at intermediate values of red light. Saturating light intensities switched on all cells. The activation of phytochrome, the red light sensor, provides just one bit of information for anthocyanin synthesis for any individual cell.

However, since other processes are induced by phytochrome activation, there may be more bits required. Different cells in a tissue may produce a different, but on/off response, to the same signal. Phytochrome-induced change in cytosolic Ca^{2+} may use other cells than those making anthocyanin. Certainly cellular spottiness in response to touch has been detected (Shacklock et al. 1992; Knight et al. 1993).

Other cell types, aleurone cells secreting amylase in response to gibberellin, pericycle cells producing lateral roots in response to auxin and guard cells, whose stomatal aperture is controlled by abscisic acid, are all responsive to this on/off signalling coupled with variation in cellular threshold of response (Trewavas 2012).

Cellular information, learning, and memory

'We need to know how information is gathered from the environment, from other cells and from the short and the long term memories in that cell, how it is either used or rejected or stored for later use' (Nurse 2008). Information is conveyed as messages between molecules, but only starts to exist when it is received and interpreted; 'Information is only that which can be understood' (Kuppers 1990, p. 32). We are still a long way from understanding the construction of the cellular circuitry for information transfer for many cellular processes. It is not known how accurate the transfer and receipt of information is within the whole plant, when signals are issued from one tissue and perceived by another. Other problems concern how information is used to maintain cell integrity, the generation of temporal and spatial order, and the process of morphogenesis. In short, areas of ignorance are abundant and rife. If a language of information structure, usage, and management could be constructed, it might be much more similar between organisms than their genomic sequence might imply.

Memory is a store of information that can be accessed when needed, although in what form memory resides in cells, is usually not stated. Learning at its simplest, must be the acquisition of the information that is found in the store. However, all signals leave an information trace within them that must modify subsequent signals that arrive provided they arrive with a certain period of time. Plants are replete with many such examples (summarized in Trewavas 2009). For instance, tendrils require the signals of both touch and blue light to respond by curling. But if the touch signal is given on its own, the curling response can still be elicited by a subsequent and separate blue light treatment provided it is given within several hours (Jaffe and Shotwell 1980). In different plant signalling systems, the memory may last anywhere from less than a minute to many months.

Manfred Eigen's assessment of learning in single cells

The questions posed previously in this chapter are not new. In 1966, the problems of information handling, memory, and learning in simple dynamic systems, but not exceeding the complexity of the single cell, were investigated (Eigen and De Maeyer 1966). The aim was, of course, to separate the meaning of these concepts from nervous systems. It was also to investigate how learning, memory, and intelligence could be defined for these simpler systems. Another of their aims was 'A fundamental study of the mechanism of any kind of process which is intelligent at the molecular level, e.g. the storage, readout and transfer of information, the processing of information in logical operations implemented in molecular interactions and generation of specific patterns of interaction' (Eigen and de Maeyer 1966, p. 245). In Eigen's view (Manfred Eigen was a Nobel Prize winner), adaptation characterized learning and was 'the ability of a system to respond in a new, improved or different way as a result of experience' (Eigen 1966). Learning and memory are inextricably linked. A memory of past behaviour can only be acquired if it is first learnt. Learning is regarded as the basis of intelligence (Thorpe 1963). Eigen's characterization of learning, memory, intelligence, and adaptation fits perfectly with the behaviour of plants.

References

Allen, G.J., Chu, S.P., Harrington, C.L., Schumacher, K., Hoffman, T., Tang, Y.Y., and 2 others (2001). A defined range of guard cell calcium oscillation parameters encodes stomatal movements. *Nature*, **411**, 1053–1057.

Arkin, A., and Ross, J. (1994). Computational functions in biochemical reaction networks. *Biophysical Journal*, **67**, 560–578.

Berridge, M.J. (2005). Unlocking the secrets of cell signalling. *Annual Review of Physiology*, 67, 1–21.

Berridge, M.J., Cobbold, P.H., Cuthbertson, K.S.R., Downes, C.P., and Hanley, M.R. (1988). Spatial and temporal aspects of cell signalling. *Philosophical Transactions of the Royal Society of London, Series B*, **320**, 325–343.

Bialek, W., and Setayeshgar, S. (2005). Physical limits to biochemical signalling. *Proceedings of the National Academy of Sciences USA*, **102**, 10040–10045.

Bradford, K.J., and Trewavas, A.J. (1994). Sensitivity thresholds and variable time scales in plant hormone action. *Plant Physiology*, **105**, 1029–1036.

Bray, D. (1990). Intracellular signaling as a parallel distributed process. *Journal of Theoretical Biology*, **143**, 215–231.

Bray, D. (1995). Protein molecules as computational elements in living cells. *Nature*, **376**, 307–312.

Bray, D. (2009). *Wetware. A computer in every living cell*. Harvard University Press, New Haven, CT.

Cai, L., Dala, C.K., and Elowitz, M.B. (2008). Frequency modulated nuclear localisation bursts coordinate gene regulation. *Nature*, **455**, 485–490.

Cheong, R., Rhee, A., Wang, C.J., Nemenman, I., and Levchenko, A. (2011). Information transduction capacity of biochemical signalling networks. *Science*, **334**, 354–358.

Chock, P.B., and Stadtman, E.R. (1977). Superiority of interconvertible enzyme cascades in metabolic regulation: analysis of multicyclic systems. *Proceedings of the National Academy of Sciences USA*, **74**, 2766–2770.

Davidson, E.H. (2010). Emerging properties of animal gene regulatory networks. *Nature*, **468**, 911–920.

Ehrhardt, D.W., Wais, R., and Long, S.R. (1996). Calcium spiking in plant root hairs responding to rhizobium nodulation signals. *Cell*, **85**, 673–681.

Eigen, M. (1966). Chemical means of information storage and readout in biological systems. In Schmitt, F.O., and Melnechuk, T., eds, *Neurosciences Research Symposium Summaries*, Vol. 1, pp. 268–278. MIT Press, Cambridge, MA.

Eigen, M., and Maeyer, L.C.M., de (1966). Summary of two NRP work sessions on information storage and processing in bimolecular systems. In Schmitt, F.O., and Melnechuk, T., eds, *Neurosciences Research Symposium Summaries*, Vol. 1, pp. 245–266. MIT Press, Cambridge, MA.

Gregor, T., Tank, D.W., Wieschaus, E.F., and Bilaek, W. (2007). Probing the limits to positional information. *Cell*, **130**, 153–164.

Hjelmfeldt, H., and Ross, J. (1994). Pattern recognition, chaos, and multiplicity in neural networks of excitable systems. *Proceedings of the National Academy of Sciences USA*, **91**, 63–67.

Hjelmfeldt, A., Schenider, F.W., and Ross, J. (1993). Pattern recognition in coupled chemical kinetic systems. *Science*, **260**, 335–337.

Hjelmfeldt, A., Weinberger, E.D., and Ross, J. (1991). Chemical implementation of neural networks and Turing machines. *Proceedings of the National Academy of Sciences USA*, **88**, 10983–10987.

Hjelmfeldt, A., Weinberger, E.D., and Ross, J. (1992). Chemical implementation of finite state machines. *Proceedings of the National Academy of Sciences USA*, **89**, 383–387.

Hopfield, J.J. (1982). Neural networks and physical systems with emergent, collective, computational abilities. *Proceedings of the National Academy of Sciences USA*, **79**, 2554–2558.

Hopfield, J.J., and Tank, D.W. (1986). Computing with neural circuits: a model. *Science*, **233**, 625–633.

Jackson, R.C. (1993). The kinetic properties of switch antimetabolites. *Journal of the National Cancer Institute*, **85**, 539–545.

Jaffe, M.J., and Shotwell, M. (1980). Physiological studies on pea tendrils. XI. Storage of tactile sensory information prior to the light activation effect. *Physiologia Plantarum*, **50**, 78–82.

Knight, M.R., Read, N.D., Campbell, A.K., and Trewavas, A.J. (1993). Imaging calcium dynamics in living plants using semi-synthetic recombinant aequorins. *Journal of Cell Biology*, **121**, 83–90.

Kuppers, B-O. (1990). *Information and the origin of life*. MIT Press, Cambridge, MA.

Luan, S. (2011). *Coding and decoding of calcium signals in plants*. Springer-Verlag, Berlin.

McCulloch, W.S., and Pitts, W. (1943). A logical calculus of the ideas immanent in nervous activity. *Bulletin of Mathematical Biophysics*, **5**, 115–133.

Mehta, P., Goyal, S., Long, T., Bassler, B.L., and Wingreen, N.S. (2009). Information processing and signal integration in bacterial quorum sensing. *Molecular Systems Biology*, **5**, 325.

Nick, P., Ehmann, B., Furuya, M., and Schafer, E. (1993). Cell communication, stochastic cell responses and anthocyanin patterns in mustard cotyledons. *Plant Cell*, **5**, 541–552.

Nurse, P. (2008). Life, logic and information. *Nature*, **454**, 424–426.

Okamoto, M., Sakai, T., and Hayashi, K. (1988). Biochemical switching device realising McCulloch-Pitts type equation. *Biological Cybernetics*, **58**, 295–299.

Pierson, E.S., Miller, D.D., Callaham, D.A., Aken, J., van, Hackett, G., and Hepler, P.K. (1996). Tip-localised calcium entry fluctuates during pollen tube growth. *Developmental Biology*, **174**, 160–173.

Pollack, G.H. (2001). *Cells, gels and the engines of life*. Ebner and Sons Ltd, Seattle, WA.

Rodriguez, M.C.S., Petersen, M., and Mundy, J. (2010). Mitogen-activated protein kinase signaling in plants. *Annual Review of Plant Biology*, **61**, 621–649.

Schacter, E., Chock, P.B., and Stadtman, E.R. (1984). Regulation through phosphorylation/dephosphorylation cascade systems. *Journal of Biological Chemistry*, **259**, 12252–12259.

Shacklock, P., Read, N.D., and Trewavas, A.J. (1992). Cytosolic free calcium mediates red light-induced photomorphogenesis. *Nature*, **358**, 753–755.

Smock, R.G., and Gierasch, L.M. (2009). Sending signals dynamically. *Science*, **324**, 198–203.

Steveninck, R.R., de R., van, Lewen, G.D., Strong, S.P., Koberle, R., and Bialek, W. (1997). Reproducibility and variability in neural spike trains. *Science*, **275**, 1805–1808.

Taniguchi, Y., Choi, P.J., Li, G-W., Chen, H., Babu, M., Hearn, J., and 2 others. (2010). Quantifying *E. coli* proteome and transcriptome with single molecule sensitivity in single cells. *Science* **329**, 533–538.

Thomas, P.J. (2011). Every bit counts. *Science*, **334**, 321–322.

Thorpe, W.H. (1963). *Learning and instinct in animals*. Methuen, London.

Tkacik, G., Callan, C.G., and Bialek, W. (2008). Information flow and optimisation in transcriptional regulation. *Proceedings of the National Academy of Sciences USA*, **105**, 12265–12270.

Trewavas, A.J. (2000). Signal perception and transduction. In Buchanan, R., Jones, R., and Gruissem, W. eds, *Biochemistry and molecular biology of plants*, pp. 930–988. American Society of Plant Biologists, Chicago, IL.

Trewavas, A. (2009). What is plant behaviour?. *Plant Cell and Environment*, 32, 606–616.

Trewavas, A. (2012). Information, noise and communication: thresholds as controlling elements in development. In Witzany G., and Baluska, F., eds, *Biocommunication of plants*, pp. 11–37. Springer-Verlag, Berlin.

CHAPTER 23

Cell organization and protein networks

The cell is like a table in which decision makers debate a question and respond collectively to the information put to them.

(Levy et al. 2010)

⊃ **Summary**

Biology is based on systems. Systems are a set of constituents densely linked to each other. Systems exhibit emergent properties that simply result from the connections between the constituents. Just as brains are systems of nerve cells, cells are systems of macromolecules. Evidence that the cytoplasm is an integrated structure is described. The cytoplasm is a gel and this implies the presence of structured water built around protein molecules that reduces the movement of ions and proteins. Transient elevations of cytosolic Ca^{2+} during transduction are thought to modify parts of its gel-like nature with far reaching consequences for access of protein kinases to protein substrates. Basic protein interaction analysis reveals a structure of hubs and connectors, and a power law distribution of linkages among proteins. There is striking organizational similarity between the network configurations of brains, higher plants, and cells that leads to robustness and behavioural plasticity. Interaction maps between all cellular proteins in some organisms have been constructed, including those involving protein kinases and phosphatases. Some common motifs of protein–protein interaction have been described. Robustness to loss of particular constituents has been shown to involve multiple pathways of response. These provide a fail-safe mechanism that protects against the disorganizing effect of extreme noise in protein production. The strength of connections between proteins is important, since modification of the strength will determine the direction of the flow of information from signals.

Introduction

In trying to understand the nature of intelligent behaviour in non-neural organisms, it is important to start at the simplest, the cell itself. Clues about cellular information processing can be gained by looking at what features seem important in brains themselves, since both process information. During development, brains self-organize their structure by means of what are probably simple rules. However, even in mature brains, neurogenesis continues, nerve cells are replaced in an unexpected dynamic particularly in areas that are rich in neural stem cells. However, the overall organization, the overall structure, remains, and the major dynamic is found in changes between nerve cells through growth or decay of dendrites. Certain areas of the brain emphasize certain traits, such as speech, or vision, or pleasure. Areas that increase their interconnection see greater information flow through those regions. Because of the multitude of connections between neurons and glia within the brain, the brain is a system, a network of relationships, whose properties emerge holistically as a consequence. However, brains are hierarchically organized and at a lower level a modular structure emerges both in function and structure (Bassett and Gazzanuga 2011). Thus they are scale free networks too.

Cells have many analogous features to brain and, in this chapter, most of them are indicated. These should eventually provide better understanding of the capabilities that individual cells possess. Cells are self-organized during the process of cell division and the self-organizing features of higher plants has already been referenced in Chapters 10–14. Cells are organized together by communication and just as brains use about a 100 molecules as neurotransmitters, plants use many such different molecules, both large and small, to attain integration into a defined individual. The analogy really is between the brain and the whole plant, both are the entities performing computation and intelligent behaviour.

Networks structure biology and the cell: every object that biology studies is a system of systems

Quite frequently through this book reference has been made to networks. Just as the brain is a complex network of interrelated cells, cells are complicated networks of molecules. The operations of both are dependent on maintaining that network structure, something easy to demonstrate. Homogenize the cell, crush the brain, and all signs of vital activity disappear.

The cell is an organized, hierarchical, and dynamical structure, commonly called a system. Systems are only held together by connections between the constituent parts. Connections are easily demonstrated—change one constituent and observe the effects on others.

In cells, it is the macromolecules, proteins, and nucleic acids that, together with water, provide for organization. Lipids and proteins help construct the numerous membranes inside and outside the cytoplasm. The plasma membrane may be up to

40% protein, but up to 80% in the mitochondrion. In plant cells, proteins and polysaccharides linked together, construct the wall. The dynamics of a system are achieved by changing the connections between the constituents and changing the constituents. Both have been referenced in the previous chapter.

As well as detailing the nature of individual constituents and the constituents as they change, it is necessary to comprehend the nature and specificity of the connections. Only with specific connections between the cellular constituents can information flow occur in a coherent way.

Networks, by their nature, behave as integrated entities or systems. In a sense, everything is connected to everything else and these, in turn, are connected to the outside environment. A change in any single constituent takes place within a systems context that equally determines what response in behaviour finally emerges. Such behaviour can be counter-intuitive, but each system can be constructed from recognizable sub-systems or modules that can then be arranged hierarchically in order of supposed complexity, and this is true of both the brain and the cell (Bassett and Gazzaniga 2011). All systems exhibit emergent behaviour, unique properties possessed only by the whole system or sub-system. Emergent behaviour originates solely from the connections between the constituents and, thus, places limits on analytical or reductionist approaches.

The sub-system may be simple—aggregates of enzyme sub-units to form a fully functional enzyme, or interaction of calmodulin, a Ca^{2+}-binding protein that interacts with many other proteins to generate novel enzyme activity and behaviour, for example. These are all examples of emergent behaviour, unpredictable by merely examining the behaviour of the individual components. Alternatively, the sub-system may be complex. Cyclins, crucial components of the cell cycle, interact with hundreds of other proteins, and produce intricate design and control features that underpin mitosis and meiosis.

Networks or systems are endemic in organisms, ecosystems, sociology, economies, and political systems, and account for most of their known properties. Recognition of their network structure can be traced back easily to the early nineteenth century and from highly insightful individuals even earlier (Trewavas 2006). It is only recently, however, that systems biology as a cellular discipline has emerged and this we owe to the enormous technical advances in genome sequencing, the technology of gene identification, protein separation, and identification. The nuts and bolts of cells are now largely understood. There is always a natural limit anyway to the understanding that derives from analytical approaches and the current degree of analytical detail indicates that for further progress in understanding the system there is 'no way but up'. The other advance has been the enormous jump in computing power. Detailed models can now be constructed and predictions of behaviour made that can then be translated into the laboratory for testing.

The cytoplasm is an organized structure

One obvious feature of a functioning brain is its defined anatomical structure. The whole is integrated anatomically, as well as functionally. The same is true for cells and the crucial part called the cytoplasm. Cytoplasm can contain anywhere from 20% to 40% protein; water is the other major constituent. Cytoplasm, when in a gel form, must organize the water to which the protein constituents are bonded. Much of this will be hydrogen bonding and, thus, capable of easy change. Evidence for a discrete organized cytoplasmic structure comes from simple, but profound experiments in which single cells of *Euglena gracilis*, an alga, or the fungal hypha of *Neurospora* were centrifuged (Zalokar 1960; Kaempner and Miller 1968). The organelles and endoplasmic reticulum were pelleted, but the clear solution left contained no detectable protein or enzymes. Clearly, the cytoplasm had been centrifuged down and, therefore, represents a completely organized structure. Even after centrifugation the cells remained viable (Srere 2000).

Further evidence for organized cytoplasmic structures came with the detection of metabolons (Burbulis and Winkel-Shirley 1999; Winkel 2004). Metabolons are considered to encompass all the major metabolic pathways and they consist of aggregates of all the enzymes that perform the metabolic processes. Metabolons speed up metabolism by enabling the substrate molecules to be passed from enzyme active site to enzyme active site without becoming free in solution. Furthermore,

polyribosomes whose function is the synthesis of proteins are localized to specific cellular positions and are clearly not free in the cytoplasm (Luby-Phelps 2000). The cytoplasm is penetrated throughout by a network of microtubules, microfilaments, and intermediate filaments to which many other proteins are attached. Of especial interest is a layer of gel-like cytoplasm, which is attached to the inside of the plasma membrane. Its structure is crucial for morphogenesis of cells in large plant cells like the unicellular alga *Acetabularia* whose uni-cell is about 1 cm in length (Goodwin and Patermichelakis 1979). Other evidence appears later.

The cytoplasm is a highly organized and structured, gel-type, network

The cytoplasm is commonly referred to as gel-like. The common gels that are most familiar with readers are in food processing. These are made from a 5% solution of partly degraded collagen producing, what is called, gelatin. The 'gel' is liquid at one temperature, thus indicating disorganization, with molecules mostly free in solution. When the temperature is lowered, reducing the movement of the collagen fragments in solution, the gel sets. A simple organization of the fragments is established (Kozlov 1983; Carvagal and Lanier 2006). Some of the linkages between the constituent fragments of collagen have been uncovered and they involve backbone hydroxyprolines as major contributors.

Equally important is the nature of water in a gel. It does not run out of a gel and is clearly no longer in the familiar liquid state, but is organized in some way by the collagen fragments. Organization requires interactions between the water molecules. Each water molecule is a simple dipole. By the nature of the atomic structure of both hydrogen and oxygen that make up the water molecule, the larger atomic nucleus of oxygen provides a greater attractant for the bonding electrons with hydrogen. Consequently, oxygen has a net negative charge, while hydrogen acquires a net positive charge. Electrical attraction between these charged groups in adjacent water molecules forms what is called a hydrogen bond. These hydrogen bonds are weaker than the covalent bonds in water itself. However, hydrogen bonds in large numbers can help confer stability on macromolecules such as nucleic acid and proteins.

Ice is a crystalline array in which virtually all the water molecules connect one with the other adjacent water molecules through their hydrogen bonds. In ordinary liquid water, hydrogen bonding is largely destroyed by the independent movement of the water molecules. A collagen gel need only contain 5% of collagen to form; other gels can form with very much less gelling agent, down as low as 0.01% (Trewavas 2012). In this case then, the gel must involve substantial hydrogen bonding between the water molecules. It is thought that this organized gel structure lies somewhere between the crystalline structure of ice and the disorganized structure of liquid water. Even more interesting is that a gelatin gel does not freeze at –15°C; it resists the formation of the defined ice structure. That observation has interesting potential to understand the freezing resistance of many plants in semi-arctic regions that withstand temperatures of –40° to –50°C.

Cytoplasmic gel structure and phase transitions

Just as synthetic gels can undergo a change in state by warming them, so that they become liquid, then the same facility must be available for the cytoplasmic gel, although temperature is less likely to be the solubilizing signal. However, some of the deleterious effects of heat shock might find explanation in gel disruption. All protein molecules in solution maintain what is called a vicinal layer of water around themselves. There are many amino acid side chains in proteins that are easily capable of forming hydrogen bonds with water molecules, thus organizing the water around them, but in addition, there is the strong likelihood of hydrogen bonding with the carbonyl and imino groups of the protein peptide bond with water too (Ling 1992; Pollack 2001). Each protein is then expected to have a coat of water molecules and these, in turn, have available H and OH from these water molecules available for H-bonding to other water molecules. In that case, there is the potential for additional layers of water to form around each protein molecule attached to the vicinal layer. Pollack (2001) suggests up to 10 layers.

Such structures have fairly profound consequence for the behaviour of the cytoplasmic gel.

The viscosity will be somewhere in between ice and pure liquid, and the diffusion rates of hydrated ions like potassium (K^+) and chloride (Cl^-) will be slowed. Once they have penetrated through the layers of water, they will become electrostatically attached to the charged side chains on the protein molecule. Removal of these ions will be slow because the layers of water surrounding them will inhibit diffusion. Ling (1992) reported that if he cut the cells he was investigating, K^+ and Cl^- only leaked out through the cut surface when proteins did. Interactions between different protein molecules will be hindered, too, by these layers of water. Such observations indicate why metabolons are essential cytoplasmic structures for rapid metabolism. A certain proportion of cellular ions will then only become free when the gel structure is broken. The cytoplasm will consist of regions constructed of different degrees of gel organization. Overall organization becomes apparent, important for cellular circuitry.

Actin is a small protein that polymerizes into filaments and is an important protein used for contractile processes inside cells. It is able to bind probably upwards of a 100 proteins most notably myosin. Actin gels can be formed with only 0.1% actin and actin is thus able to organize water at that degree of dilution into a gel. When ATP is added the gel contracts and expels water, indicating that contraction causes stronger and closer interactions between the actin molecules. When calcium ions are added at low concentrations, the actin gel disintegrates and viscosity is greatly decreased; the gel has undergone a phase transition.

Ca^{2+} performs particular functions inside cells and controls gel behaviour

Through its positive charge, Ca^{2+} can form charge interactions with macromolecules that contain negatively charged side chains, such as proteins or polysaccharides. Nucleic acids preferentially bind magnesium ions. Calcium is known as a labile cross-linker because it can connect together two proteins with overall net negative charge, but in a linkage that is not covalent, only electrostatic and, thus, easily broken. Once a signal is perceived through a receptor in the plasma membrane, it is a common observation in plant cells for information flow to include a transient elevation of cytosolic Ca^{2+} (Luan 2011).

Actin gels are disrupted by increasing cytoplasmic Ca^{2+}, because Ca^{2+} can temporarily bind two protein molecules together, eliminating the structured water between them. Viscosity of the gel will be lowered, thus enabling interaction of proteins with each other and the release of bound ions. Pollack (2001) suggests a fairly simple unzipping mechanism to explain the process, whereby structured water layers are disrupted. It is not only actin gels that will be disrupted. Most proteins carry a net negative charge. Thus, one consequence of transiently elevating cytoplasmic Ca^{2+} may simply be to disrupt gel structures by binding protein molecules transiently together, expelling water. In turn, gel disruption may allow some protein kinases to gain access to their protein substrates to activate or inhibit them by phosphorylation, when these were previously prevented by structured water. Alternatively, disruption may allow protein phosphatases to remove phosphate groups and modify protein substrate activity. This mechanism is separate from activating the numerous Ca^{2+}-dependent enzymes inside cells. However, this gel disruption establishes a new circuitry necessary in signal transduction.

The specific structure and properties of protein networks

Basic network structures

Further evidence that the cell is a highly organized structure has come from numerous investigations into cellular protein networks; the interactions between the 20,000 or so proteins that are found in any cell. The study of these cellular networks should hopefully lead to an understanding of control and design structures among proteins. They should report on resilience, robustness, and elements of structural stability that are common observations of cellular behaviour. The topology is crucial to understanding the flow of information necessary to modify cell and organism behaviour, just as it is in brains.

Early analysis suggested that many networks (cells, ecosystems, Internet) exhibit a particular kind of structure that helps contribute to its stability. It was the observation of social networks that gave rise to its description as 'small world' (Strogatz 2001). This descriptor referred to a network located between two extremes. Either it was a fully connected network (everything connected with everything else and entirely rigid in behaviour) or at the other extreme, a network whose connections were at random. The critical requirement is the ability of information flowing through the network from any one node, to reach any other using a short path length.

Scale-free networks were first suggested from studies of the Internet, but have also particular relevance to cell molecular networks (Barabasi and Albert 1999; Barabasi 2009). There is a crude division of components into two categories based on the numbers of connections that any individual component possesses. Some that are referred to as hubs (nodes) have many connections, others with fewer are called connectors (links), and if only one or two links, they are described as edges. The distribution of connections obeys a simple power law arrangement. That is, there are far fewer hubs than there are connectors or edges. Hubs are more important to network stability. This style of structure of hubs and connectors is found in both the anatomical and the functional aspect of brain function (Bassett and Gazzaniga 2011).

Both small world and scale-free networks have much in common as descriptions and both structures are applicable to an analysis of the metabolic networks in organisms (Fell and Wagner 2000; Jeong et al. 2000). The links between clusters of hubs and clusters of clusters (i.e. modules) exhibit a similar power law distribution as the links between individual hubs themselves (Song et al. 2005). Thus, its scale-free structure. This structure might also be described as nested—one kind of network structure existing within another greater network embodying a similar overall scale-free structure.

Ecosystem and economic networks have a similar kind of network structure too (Bascompte 2009; Schweitzer et al. 2009). In the networks between pollinators and flowering plants, nestedness enables a greater biodiversity to be contained in a relatively stable condition and reduces competition (Bastolla et al. 2009; Sugihara and Ye 2009).

An important advance was the description of a cartography, a map drawing exercise, of complex networks with particular reference to metabolism (Gulmera and Amaral 2008). The authors draw attention initially to road maps that indicate connections between cities, towns, and villages. These habitations they describe as nodes and are recognized as such according to the functions they fulfil. They further identify on a network map what are called 'functional modules' and these are similar to different map regions encompassing a number of nodes.

In the case of metabolism, functional modules can be recognized by the extent of connections between nodes. Good examples of functional modules would be those that hinge around pyruvate or acetyl CoA as hubs that have very large numbers of connections and are central to many modules. These functional modules connect together crucial metabolic pathways involving carbohydrates, amino acids, TCA cycle, lipid metabolism, and the production of ATP. More peripheral modules may be connected to these crucial modules by only single molecules. In examining 12 different organisms from three different super-kingdoms, it was found that 80% of the nodes in these modules connect to other nodes in the same module. Nodes with different roles outside the modules are however affected by different evolutionary constraints and pressures. Remarkably, it was found that metabolites that participate in only a few reactions, but that connect different modules, are more conserved, than nodes whose links are mostly within a single module. In a sense, the distinction becomes obvious. The module itself is able to accept a degree of internal variation or buffering, but the module connectors, being much fewer in number, cannot so easily be replaced or modified.

The architecture of protein networks

Advances in technology have now enabled the construction of what are called interactomes. The interactome describes the potential interactions between all cellular proteins. Yeast protein interactome networks have been constructed both *in vitro* and more spectacularly *in vivo* (Tarassov et al. 2008; Yu et al. 2008). Both forms of interactome exhibit the network structures described above of small world, scale-free, and self-similar structures, but both

indicate differences, reflecting the possible formation of transient structures in the *in vivo* assessment. One large research investigation aims to report all the connections within complex brains, a research enterprise called the 'connectome'.

The protein kinase/phosphatase network (Beitkrutz et al. 2010) has also been characterized. The reported structures revealed similar kinds of network structure, as those above, with scale-free and small world construction. However, these 'phosphorylomes' also indicated that many text book pictures of kinase/phosphatase networks were incorrect—there is very extensive and unexpected cross-talk between signalling pathways. Kinases contain much higher levels of internal phosphorylation compared with other kinase substrates. The implication is that numerous kinases phosphorylate each other.

This observation of extensive cross-talk between different signalling pathways was confirmed by examining the effects of specific inhibition of selective kinases and observing the changes in overall protein phosphorylation. There was extensive depletion of phosphorylation sites in many proteins with selective inhibition of just one kinase, but enrichment in others. There is obviously strong metabolic dependency between the protein kinases and phosphatases. Protein kinases and phosphatases also have stronger genomic relations with each other than with other proteins. There is substantial collaboration in the cell decision equipment. The interconnections indicated suggest that just as neurons in brains have numerous dendritic connections, so does the protein kinase circuitry in cells. The analogy in information processing between brains and cells is strengthened.

There are unifying organizational arrangements in biological networks

The cellular protein network has an intensely democratic structure suggesting that decisions are cooperatively spread throughout the cellular network. Levy et al. (2010) refer to this cooperation 'as like a table in which decision makers debate a question and respond collectively to the information put to them'. With millions of cells cooperating together in tissue behaviour, and tissues cooperating together in this democratic debating system, the seeds of intelligent behaviour become finally visible. It hardly needs saying that brains act holistically in the same way. Decisions are formulated initially at lower levels, and exchanged democratically and only when information has finally passed through the various anatomical regions and been assessed, do decisions emerge.

Genome scale interaction maps have also been constructed again in yeast for about 75% of the genes present (Costanzo et al. 2010). This enormous advance was only accomplished with the cooperative endeavour of over 50 scientists and required the production of double mutants in every combination of the 4000 non-lethal genes, a total of 5.4 million mutants. Each mutant was assessed for its effect on fitness. The detailed displayed networks revealed a functional map in which genes involved in similar processes cluster together in coherent subsets. The network structure again indicated functional cross-connections showing a kind of pleiotropic cellular wiring diagram. Co-expression networks for a limited number of genes in *Arabidopsis* and Rice have been published (Ficklin et al. 2010; Mutwil et al. 2010).

Sub-systems, modules, and motifs in the brain, the higher plant and in cells: unifying organizational arrangements emerge in all active biological systems

The entire brain system can be decomposed into sub-systems, modules, or motifs. In the temporal domain, these reflect perhaps long- or short-term memory, but anatomically and thus spatially, they reflect a structure built of columns or cortical mini-columns. Each of these 'column' or 'mini-column' modules contain higher levels of connection to other elements within the same module than to others outside. This kind of compartmentalization reduces the interdependence of modules and, thus, helps provide robustness. Modularity favours and facilitates behavioural adaptation, without adversely perturbing the rest of the system. In addition, not only is there a hierarchical modularity of brain connection, but also brain regions perform distinct roles, either as hubs of high connectivity or as provincial nodes of low connectivity.

There is also striking organizational similarity between the brain and the higher plant. The temporal behaviour (inducing memory) of plant behaviour can be short, as in electrical changes or long as in genomic events. Anatomically, the similarity should also account for aspects of plant behaviour. The modular plant is constructed of regions like buds and meristems, where local cellular interconnection is strong, and other areas—the stem or mature root—where the connections are fewer. These parallel the columns and mini-columns in the brain, and the provincial nodes of low connectivity in the brain. The reduction of interdependence between meristems and buds then provides for robustness just as provided by the modular structure in brains. By leaving these meristems with a degree of independence, local behavioural adaptation is facilitated, but brains still act holistically, as does the higher, self-organizing plant. Just as brains are hierarchically arranged so is the higher plant. Of course, again, like the brain, different tissues perform different functions.

There is also a striking organizational similarity with the cartographic analysis of metabolism referred to above, with the organization of the brain and the higher plant. Functional modules are recognized and the great majority of nodes within them are connected to other nodes in the same module. However, modules are connected together often by one or a few molecules. Such a structure tends again to provide robustness in function.

The hub and connector model is also similar in organizational structure. Some proteins like cyclins underpin central processes in division and connect with hundreds of other proteins; in contrast, others are enzymes that deal with the tail end of synthesis of some specific molecule and connect with very few. Some protein kinases, such as snf-1 kinase or Ca^{2+} or cyclic AMP kinases, phosphorylate many proteins. Others select only a few for phosphorylation.

Similar organizational structure emerges from complex genetic networks, at least in *E. coli*. These, again, seem to be built at a first approximation from a limited number of recurring motifs (modules) controlling different genes. It seems not to be necessary to know how each protein works. Instead, it is merely sufficient to include information on whether one protein activates another protein, or activates a gene directly or inhibits it, and at what concentration (Alon 2007). Shen-Orr et al. (2002) indicate the common appearance of feedforward motifs, responsible, for example, for keeping the hundreds of proteins in the cell cycle in synchrony and progression (Santos and Ferell 2008). Additional motifs include cross-interactions between different transcriptional factors and operons. Cross-interactions between densely overlapping regulons and larger motifs involve up to 15 proteins (Heath and Kavraki 2009).

It would seem from the evidence above that complex networks are stabilized by the structures described involving modules, hubs, and connectors, and the distribution of links that hold them together. There may, therefore, be a similarity in structure and, if it could be derived, a symbolic language, in all such networks. It may be that these structures are the only ones that provide for network stability, flexibility, and robustness, and act to unify all such biological networks.

The most detailed network analysis in development is provided by Davidson (2010). Here, again, fairly simple logic circuits form the basis of regulation of particular genes and these are grouped in various more complex structures that are hierarchically arranged. They were discussed in Chapter 22. The construction of the process of development is becoming clearer. Some of these circuits have the Boolean logic gate designation, but others involve more complex aspects of feedback, signal induction, and repression, community effects on cell-to-cell communication, signal-mediated switches, and boundary maintenance.

Robust behaviour in protein networks

Biological systems require the ability to be robust in the face of environmental uncertainty. Robustness is taken to mean that important molecules or functions from groups of molecules linked together remaining relatively constant under many environmental circumstances (Wagner 2005). Functions must be maintained, at least within certain limits, even when structural molecular variation is common (Barkai and Leibler 1997; Trewavas 2006; Shinar et al. 2009; Gunawardena 2010; Shinar and Feinberg 2010). Several sources of robustness have emerged varying in their degree of resistance to change.

Networks themselves do possess some resistance to change by virtue of the connections between the constituents (Waddington 1977). Perhaps this was most easily seen in the use of control theory in which it was found that the flux of material through a pathway varied little with quite substantive changes in the enzyme levels of particular steps, the consequence of the pathway being a simple joined network (Wagner 2005; Trewavas 2006). The only way found to increase flux rates through the whole pathway was to increase the levels of all the enzymes involved.

Negative feedback tends to maintain function as well and many pathways do have the first step regulated by the final product. Other forms of robustness emerge in the demonstration that blocking individual steps in metabolism simply leads to the rerouting of the flux elsewhere through the metabolic network (Ishii et al. 2007). One of the commonest forms of robustness emerges from phosphorylation or methylation of enzymes and proteins (Barkai and Leibler 1997; Shinar and Feinberg 2010). This process can involve bi-functional enzymes (containing both kinase and phosphatase activity), but can also use separate protein kinases and protein phosphatases under certain conditions.

All these behaviours have parallels with the brain and with the higher plant. Robustness derives from the modular structure and the capability of regeneration and, thus, rerouting of development.

Commensurate with robustness, networks can also be fragile in response to elimination of one or more critical (hub) components (Csete and Doyle 2002). In yeast, for example, lethal mutations occur for only 20% of genes, but suggesting their identification as hubs. Furthermore, the regulatory systems are particularly vulnerable. Cancerous cells can arise as the result of change in a single regulatory component, such as *ras*; others require many other genetic alterations before becoming oncological.

The strength of connections between constituents is also crucial to network behaviour

Network studies are still at an early phase. It is not just the connections between constituents that are important, but the strength of those connections too. Information flow is dependent on the strength of connections and is redirected as they are modified. Measuring affinities of molecules one for the other remains difficult, particularly *in vivo*, but is necessary for accurate modelling. In ecological networks, the process is somewhat easier to accomplish by changing the numbers of one contributing organism and measuring the stability of the whole; that is performing a sensitivity analysis. In similar fashion, specific protein kinases can be targeted and knocked out by especially designed inhibitors accompanied by *in vivo* measurements of overall performance. However, the likely re-routing of information flow through other kinases may make understanding difficult. It is to be expected that the strongest affinity would occur between a kinase and its specific substrate(s). Maerkl and Quake (2007) have developed an elegant technique to assess transcription factor-binding strength by measuring the trapping of molecular interactions. This technique can be adapted and used elsewhere to study the strength of interactions *in vivo*. There are, of course, thousands of connections between the molecules of any one cell that indicates the size of the challenge that remains. The strength of connections between two nerve cells is important in changing the path of information flow, and developing learning and memory.

Self-organizing structures determine their own stability and control

Cells and developing brains, and indeed networks of all kinds in biology are self-organizing. The structure emerges by growth and usually on the basis of fairly simple rules. This kind of self-organization is certainly very obvious in higher plants, but becomes less clear in higher animals because the brain apparently and centrally controls behaviour. This, of course, is not the case. The brain merely processes information from sensory systems, combines this with previous experience and passes the processed information onto the thousand or so muscles involved that manipulate movement. On its own the brain can do little.

However, other self-organizing systems process the information that they receive in the same way. The processing this time is performed throughout the whole network where it combines with prior information and experience. The response issues from the whole, whether this be cell, organism, higher plant, or ecosystem. Thus, the title of this chapter reflected the normal means whereby a self-organized structure, that has no centralized information processing, behaves in response to outside signalling. Interactions between decision makers within the network are like debate and the majority view prevails—a kind of cooperative democratic control that involves the whole. In higher plants, the immediate interactions can be local, but nevertheless the whole is involved in the response. These networks thus manipulate their own information flow and behaviour; they qualify as intelligent on that basis. In all respects the colonies of social insects exhibit a similar organizational similarity. They work on quorum voting, they demarcate specific groups of workers to specific tasks and communicate using forms of symbolic language. Above all self-organization emerges as the result of bottom-up interactions and a hierarchical arrangement.

Conclusion on network structure and function

There are some remarkable similarities between the anatomical and functional behaviour of the brain and the cell. Both are biological information processing systems that self-organize and, in architecture, there are similarities, too. Both seem based on scale-free organization and, clearly, a power law specification of frequency of hubs and connectors. Both are modular in structure and contain recognizable motifs in structure. In addition, changes in connection between nerve cells and transduction molecules alter the pathways of information flow. No doubt, a more detailed examination would provide many more points of similarity. The indication is that, perhaps, all biological networks that involve processing of information should exhibit a similar structural and probable functional basis, whether they be individual cells, organisms, populations, or ecosystems. The properties of resilience and robustness might then originate from the same structures. Do these represent lessons for economic activities, and for human population, structure, and behaviour?

References

Alon, U. (2007). Simplicity in biology. *Nature*, **446**, 497.

Barabasi, A.-L. (2009). Scale free networks: a decade and beyond. *Science*, **325**, 412–413.

Barabasi, A.L., and Albert, R. (1999). Emergence of scaling in random networks. *Science*, **286**, 509–512.

Barkai, N., and Leibler, S. (1997). Robustness in simple biochemical networks. *Nature*, **387**, 913–917.

Bascompte, J. (2009). Disentangling the web of life. *Science*, **325**, 416–419.

Bassett, D.S., and Gazzaniga, M.S. (2011). Understanding complexity in the human brain. *Trends in Cognitive Science*, **15**, 200–209.

Bastolla, U., Fortuna, M.A., Pascuel-Garcia, A., Ferrera, A., Luque, B., and Bascompte, J. (2009).The architecture of mutualistic networks minimizes competition and increases biodiversity. *Nature*, **458**, 1018–1020.

Beitkrutz, A., Choi, H., Sharom, J.R., Boucher, L., Neduva, V., Larsen, B., and 14 others (2010). A global protein kinase and phosphatase interaction network in yeast. *Science*, **328**, 1043–1046.

Burbilis, I.E., and Winkel-Shirley, B. (1999). Interactions among enzymes of the *Arabidopsis* flavonoid biosynthetic pathway. *Proceedings of the National Academy of Sciences USA*, **96**, 12920–12934.

Carvagal, P.A., and Lanier, T.C. (2006). The unfolded protein state revisited. In Pollack, G.H., Cameron, I.L., and Wheatley, D.N., eds, *Water and the cell*, pp. 235–252. Springer, Dordrecht.

Costanzo, M., Baryshnikova, A., Bellay, J., Kim, Y., Spear, D., Sevier, C.S., and 47 others (2010). The genetic landscape of a cell. *Science*, **327**, 425–431.

Csete, M.E., and Doyle, J.C. (2002). Reverse engineering of biological complexity. *Science*, **295**, 1664–1668.

Davidson, E. (2010). Emerging properties of animal gene regulatory networks. *Nature*, **468**, 911–920.

Fell, D.A., and Wagner, A. (2000). The small world of metabolism. *Nature Biotechnology*, **18**, 1121–1122.

Ficklin, S.P., Luo, F., and Feltus, F.A. (2010). The association of multiple interacting genes with specific phenotypes in rice using gene coexpression networks. *Plant Physiology*, **154**, 13–24.

Goodwin, B.C., and Pateromichelakis, S. (1979). The role of electrical fields, ions and cortex in the morphogenesis of *Acetabularia*. *Planta*, **157**, 1–7.

Gulmera, R., and Amaral, L.A.N. (2008). Functional cartography of complex metabolic networks. *Nature*, **433**, 895–900.

Gunarwardena, J. (2010). Biological systems theory. *Science*, **328**, 581–582.

Heath, A.P., and Kavraki, L.E. (2009). Computational challenges in systems biology. *Computer Science Review*, **3**, 1–17.

Ishii, N., Nakahigashi, K., Baba, T., Robert, M., Soga, T., Kanai, A., and 23 others (2007). Multiple high-throughput analyses monitor the response of *E. coli* to perturbations. *Science*, **316**, 593–597.

Jeong, H., Tombor, B., Albert, R., Oltval, Z.N., and Barabasi, A-L. (2000). The large scale organisation of metabolic networks. *Nature*, **407**, 651–654.

Kaempner, E.S., and Miller, J.H. (1968). The molecular biology of *Euglena gracilis*. IV. Cellular stratification by centrifuging. *Experimental Cell Research*, **51**, 141–149.

Kozlov, P.V. (1983). The structure and properties of solid gelatin and the principles of their modification. *Polymer*, **24**, 651–666.

Levy, E.D., Landry, C.R., and Michnik, S.W. (2010). Signaling through cooperation. *Science*, **328**, 983–984.

Ling, G.N. (1992). *A revolution in the physiology of the living cell*. Krieger Publishing Company, Malabar, FL.

Luan, S. (2011). *Coding and decoding of calcium signals in plants*. Springer-Verlag, Berlin.

Luby-Phelps, K. (2000). Cytoarchitecture and physical properties of cytoplasm, volume, diffusion, and intracellular surface area. *International Review of Cytology*, **192**, 189–220.

Maerkl, S.J., and Quake, S.R. (2007). A systems approach to measuring the binding energy landscapes of transcription factors. *Science*, **315**, 233–237.

Mutwil, M., Usadel, B., Schutte, M., Loraine, A., Ebenhoh, O., and Persson, S. (2010). Assembly of an interactive correlation network for the *Arabidopsis* genome using a novel heuristic clustering algorithm. *Plant Physiology*, **152**, 29–43.

Pollack, G.H. (2001). *Cells, gels and the engines of life*. Ebner & Sons, Seattle, WA.

Santos, S.D.M., and Ferrell, J.E. (2008). On the cell cycle and its switches. *Nature*, **454**, 288–289.

Schweitzer, F., Fagiolo, G., Sornette, D., Vega-Redondo, F., Vespignani, A., and White, D.R. (2009). Economic networks: the new challenges. *Science*, **325**, 422–424.

Shen-Orr, S.S. Milo, R., Mangan, S., and Alon, U. (2002). Network motifs in the transcriptional regulation network of *Escherichia coli*. *Nature Genetics*, **31**, 64–68.

Shinar, G., and Feinberg, M. (2010). Structural sources of robustness in biochemical reaction networks. *Science*, **327**, 1389–1391.

Shinar, G., Rabinowitz, J.D., and Alon, U. (2009). Robustness in glyoxylate bypass regulation *PLoS Computing Biology*, **5**, e1000297.

Song, C., Havlin, S., and Makes, H.A. (2005). Self-similarity of complex networks. *Nature*, **433**, 392–395.

Srere, P.A. (2000). Macromolecular interactions: tracing the roots. *Trends in Biochemical Sciences*, **25**, 150–153.

Strogatz, S.H. (2001). Exploring Complex Systems. *Nature*, **410**, 268–276.

Sugihara, G., and Ye, H. (2009). Cooperative network dynamics. *Nature*, **458**, 979–980.

Tarasov, K., Messier, V., Landry, C.R., Radinovic, S., Molina, M.M.S. Shames, I., and 4 others (2008). An *in vivo* map of the yeast protein interactome. *Science*, **320**, 1465–1470.

Trewavas, A.J. (2006). A brief history of systems biology. *Plant Cell*, **18**, 2420–2430.

Trewavas, A. (2012). Information, noise and communication: thresholds as controlling elements in development. In Witzany, G., and Baluska, F., eds, *Biocommunication of plants*, pp. 11–37. Springer-Verlag, Berlin.

Waddington, C.H. (1977). *Tools for thought*. Jonathan Cape, Ltd., London.

Wagner, A. (2005). *Robustness and evolvability in living systems*. Princeton University Press, Princeton, NJ.

Winkel, B.S.J. (2004). Metabolic channeling in plants. *Annual Review of Plant Biology*, **55**, 85–107.

Yu, H., Braun, P., Yildirim, M.A., Lemmens, I., Venkatesan, K., Sahalie, J., and 28 others (2008). High quality binary protein interaction map of the yeast interactome network. *Science*, **322**, 104–110.

Zalokar, M. (1960). Cytochemistry of centrifuged hyphae of *Neurospora. Experimental Cell Research*, **19**, 114–132.

CHAPTER 24

Instinct, reflex, and conditioned behaviours: characteristics of plant behaviour?

Instinct is a makeshift: an admission of helplessness before the problem of reality.

(Leo Frobenius 2006)

⮌ Summary

A common belief is to regard plant behaviour as like a reflex—fixed and unchangeable, but plants, like all organisms, have to assess costs and benefits of any change in behaviour. Jacques Loeb, an early botanist, introduced the notion of forced reactions or tropisms as a set of reflexes that make for fixed behaviour in both plants and animals. However, the machine-like quality that Loeb gave to organism behaviour is easily shown to be wrong because machines require exacting precision in their parts if they are to function. The real destruction of Loeb's forced reactions, however, came after Williams' extensive compilation in 1956 that summarized the enormous degrees of variation in tissue structure, organization, and chemistry in normal, reproducing, animal organisms. Similar variations are seen in all kinds of plants. Extensive variation at the molecular level between individuals is compensated by organization at higher levels that reduces the extent of variation in behaviour. Instinctual mechanisms that governed understanding of behaviour in animals have received extensive criticism. Developmental systems theory has provided critiques of both behaviourism and instinct, and they provide crucial insights into plant behaviour. Whether conditioned behavioural responses exist in plants are difficult to establish, but the effects of growth-promoting bacteria on disease and herbivory resistance might provide a potential for this kind of behaviour.

Assumptions about plant behaviour that may mislead

A common view of plants is to suppose their behaviour is either what might be called instinct, reflex, or some other invariant mechanical process. Reflex is considered to be an invariable reaction to a simple stimulus. Since this attitude is not uncommon, I have included this chapter to indicate both its history and its falsity. What I can suggest is that, in any organism, the identical molecular and physiological state, the identical stimulus, and the identical environment would lead, possibly, to an identical response, but since this can never happen it can be rejected and much evidence indicates its falsity. It almost certainly derives from experimental conditions in which the experimenter becomes part of the environment of the plant and drives the organism into the required behaviour.

Instead, what is meant by some as reflex plant behaviour is that, for example, in response to unilateral light, plants of most species will grow towards it, i.e. they exhibit the same response, but what is meant by the same response? Nothing is indicated in the word 'towards' about the variation in trajectory of response or the variation in response time involved, or the variation between different individuals and species. Given the importance of light (energy) to plant survival, is this process of 'growing towards' fundamentally different to lions chasing gazelles? Both require food to survive, and while lions chasing food often fail, it is only in the broadest of outline that the chase can be regarded as the same every time. In fine detail, each is unique. This is a common aspect of the way our brains work; we note the outlines, rather than the details, but nature notes the details and is hard on those whose details are uncompetitive.

The difficulties in achieving the 'same' response in a plant can also be illustrated. A cooperative enterprise between 10 different laboratories attempted to obtain entirely reproducible growth among inbred genotypes of *Arabidopsis*. Apparently identical growth conditions were used between these laboratories. Similarities or variations at the molecular and morphological level were assessed (Massonnet et al. 2010). Metabolite profiles showed a strong genotype × laboratory interaction and variation. Transcriptome data revealed considerable plant-to-plant variation, but inter-laboratory variation was not greater than intra-laboratory variation. After much investigation, it was concluded that small variations in growing conditions (often light) and handling of plants could account for significant differences between laboratories. Perhaps the crucial conclusion from this study was how sensitive plants actually are to their precise growing conditions, particularly to light and touch stimuli. Furthermore, variation in the individual plant is clearly established, the stuff of selection.

Bearing in mind the degree of growth control in present-day laboratory conditions, wild conditions by comparison must give rise to much greater variation and this, indeed, is the case. It is a common observation when dealing with crop plants that results in the laboratory often fail to translate into the field. This was particularly noticeable some 40 years ago with attempts to control growth chemically. The root/shoot weight ratio is a good example, and a parameter fundamental to the health and fecundity of the individual. Under laboratory conditions, the root to shoot ratio under the same conditions can vary between different individuals from about 0.7- to 2-fold, inclining, it should be added, towards notions of high heritable control of development. For field crops, however, the variation can be up to 7–8-fold (Bolinder et al. 2002). Chapin (1980) reports variations of up to 20-fold for plants in the wild. The degree of plasticity can be enormous.

Development and, thus, behavioural change is controlled by multiple causes, including the state of the plant at the immediate present. Deficits in water or minerals increase the root to shoot ratio very substantially, even up to 5-fold in the laboratory. Light deficit decreases the root to shoot ratio. Herbivory or disease, change it yet again.

The basic elements of plant construction arise through interactions within the individual, as well as those outside. The developing organism is reconstructed, contingently reassembled, every time from its zygote. All stages of development are subject to environmental influences to varying degrees. There is, therefore, no predetermined blueprint written in the genes. Heritability estimates, sometimes used to prop up ideas that distinguish between the contribution of genes or environment to development, measure only the proportion of variation in a specific population under specific circumstances, which can be ascribed to genetic differences (Lewontin 2001). Genes set the boundaries to behavioural plasticity; they do not determine the exact forms behaviour makes of the individual, but epigenetics has complicated that gene-centred view again.

In the laboratory, the investigator becomes part of the organism's environment and manipulates the behaviour of any organism for his/her own purpose. The endeavour is to make a complex situation simple, but even intelligent humans can be made to behave simply. Anyone that has not had a drink for 3 days will likely drink when offered. Is this behaviour determined, instinct, or reflex? Is it intelligent? I consider it is the latter, because drinking solves the problem of thirst. It is also something that, in the wild, would increase fitness.

When I used to take my children to the zoo we always tried to see the lions. Usually, they were asleep. So next time you go, you make sure the lions are moving and arrive at feeding time, but still they do not do much, except perhaps roar, and pace up and down. They grab the piece of offered meat, eat, and go back to sleep. If your sole assessment of lion intelligence was based on those observations, you would surely conclude these were dumb animals and little more intelligent than a single bacterial cell growing in a laboratory medium. However, we do know from those marvellous films taken on the African veldt that lions are highly intelligent animals. When you observe five or six lionesses engaged in carving out a single prey and, by unseen communication and coordination, successfully execute the hunt, assessment of their intelligence changes entirely. These are, indeed, highly intelligent animals in the wild.

Apply those considerations exactly to plants. If the experience with plants is only in the laboratory, then it may not be surprising that the judgement is dumb creatures. However, that may also apply to plants grown at home in greenhouses, even the garden; all these are artificial circumstances controlled by man. Only when the plant is in control can anything else be expected.

The context of any response contributes directly to what is observed. If we return to the plant growing towards light, that is phototropism, then the surrounding environment will change the situation. If there was approaching shade from another plant, then the characteristics of the phototropic response would probably be different. If the seedling was a *Syngonium* seedling it would make a beeline for the darkest region present to seek out a vertical trunk to grow up (Ray 1987). If the lions are full they do not eat again, just as a plant in full light grows straight up and no longer bends tropically. Context is critical. Ecologists often attempt to construct more challenging environments. Laboratory investigation is invaluable for describing the bits and pieces, the molecules, the simple physiology, but given that intelligence is a teleonomic property that requires a wild environment for its expression, the laboratory will never provide complete answers. Intelligent behaviour will only be detected if there are problems to be solved and, indeed, solutions that matter, which initiate selection and fitness in the wild.

The failure of reflex to describe behaviour that requires decisions in situations of choice

Reflex is an invariant response to a simple, usually single, stimulus. In humans, it is commonly associated with the involuntary phenomena of the knee jerk or eye blink. Some consider true reflexes to require a nervous system that would obviate lower organism behaviour. The behaviour of *Stentor* or *Paramecium* is not in any way invariant as indicated in Chapter 20. *Paramecium* can swim in all directions in response to a stimulus and there was renewed discussion some years back about learning in this organism (Gelber 1957; Armus et al. 2006; and references in these papers).

It is impossible to apply the concept of reflex to *amoeba*. The behaviour is formless, undefined, not held within narrow bounds by structural constraints since pseudopodia continually form and reform elsewhere in the cell. In fine detail, *amoeba* can never do exactly the same thing twice. Jennings (1923) points out that if an animal is presented with both food and a dangerous situation, both conditions of which it is sensitive to, it must be able to make a decision between these two possibilities and, consequently, such behaviour cannot be reflex—it requires assessment.

The situation is no different in higher plants—a root growing into soil containing both salt and necessary nitrate must assess the balance between cost and benefit. Plants with rhizomes show considerable preference for soil without salt when given free choice and can also help connected neighbours that are growing in salt conditions (Salzman 1985; Salzman and Parker 1985). Assessing the trade-offs, the costs and benefits occurs in every aspect of plant behaviour.

Forced reactions and Jacques Loeb

Early researchers like Jennings, Romanes, and Binet (Chapter 20) observed behaviour in single cells that they regarded as intelligent. The reason that these observations largely disappeared I put down to two reasons—the tropism ideas of Loeb (1912, 1918) and the rise of Watson's behaviourism in animal research. Behaviourism denied any mental inputs to behaviour. It tended to regard all forms of animal behaviour as occurring either in response to a set of rewards or punishments, and stated that behaviour could be described without recourse to notions of physiological or mental control. It has a certain similarity to those of Loeb. Because Loeb was a well-known plant biologist and produced interesting studies on plant regeneration, his views should be considered here.

Jacques Loeb considered that all life could be reduced to a physicochemical process and, consequently, argued that all biological behaviour was forced and thus determined. He dispensed with free will (no choice) and assumed that all behaviour was a mixture of reflexes or what he called tropisms. In arch-reductionist fashion, he espoused the total validity of mechanistic, machine-like principles. Loeb's experimental justifications were observations that if you placed some lower animals (hydroids) in experimental environments with unilateral light sources, after several days many showed behavioural properties similar to those in some plants—they grew towards the light.

Loeb called these responses tropisms in animals, after the more well-known term in plants. Thus, he describes tropisms to gravity, chemicals, touch, flow, as well as light in animals. He showed an obvious fascination with simple machines and describes in one chapter, one such device that has two photocells and is able to orientate its movement according to a light source. Parallels were drawn between the behaviour of this machine, the behaviour of certain moths, and of course tropic movements in plants.

The popularity of Loeb's views at the time and those of the behaviourists, I suspect was because they chimed with popular political attitudes that justified class segregation (poverty is the fault of the poor), justification of capitalism from Darwinian selection and the later use of social Darwinism to justify experiments on prison and mental home inmates. Human behaviour, like intelligence, was pre-determined and behaviour was heritable, instinctive, and thus supposedly invariant.

I regard Loeb's texts as largely naïve. His assumption that organisms were some kind of machine can be easily disproved. Machines have an extremely low tolerance of variation in the parts from which they are constructed. Imagine, if you can, a clock in which you try to insert a cogwheel that is slightly too big or has too many teeth on it. The clock will not function, but variation in organisms of the same species is the basis of natural selection.

There are two sets of evidence that disprove Loeb's reflexive or forced behaviour.

Noise introduces great variation in cellular and organism behaviour

Single-cell organisms are not identical in behaviour and molecular noise is one likely reason—there may be others. Molecular noise is inevitable in biological systems. Living cells use thousands of processes that are probabilistic in character requiring two or more molecules to come together in a crowded cellular environment. Life simply survives because the tendency of randomizing processes is offset by correcting statistical forces—a larger number of molecules working together tend on average to counteract individual stochastic events (Trewavas 2012).

The simplest molecular circuitry uses gene activation, transcription, translation, and that immediately exposes the cell to probabilistic events that can destabilize it. During transcription, DNA can change its structure; individual transcription factors can drop off or change conformation. The polysome requires many additional factors to synthesize a protein, and many of these have to arrive within discrete periods of time to function and, of course, can fall off the translating mRNA. The result—premature termination or even mistranslation. Ion channels are known to be noisy from direct observation, sometimes open, sometimes closed, and when they receive an opening signal, the response is merely to be more often open than closed.

As a consequence of molecular noise, there is a high degree of variation in the molecular content (copy number) of proteins between individual bacterial cells (e.g. Elowitz et al. 2002; Pearson 2008; Taniguchi et al. 2010) and many reports confirm the enormous degree of variation in copy number that can exist between individual cells produced at the same time in the same culture. Observations of transcription in single cells show that it comes in bursts and is not continuous; far from it (references in Trewavas 2012).

Such molecular variations can explain the individuality in chemotactic swimming in bacteria (Spudich and Koshland 1976). However, swimming continues despite the individual variation in its rate. The chemotactic programme is thus robust. Negative feedback of various kinds is one reason for robustness. The copy number variation applies to single immune cells, as well as those in bacteria and yeast, and will thus be the case for all single cells, including those in plants, generating behavioural diversity (Shalek et al. 2013).

Noise can be useful as well. In yeast, membrane bound signalling molecules are able to recruit proteins from a cytoplasmic pool using positive feedback mechanisms, and a noisy and limited cytoplasmic copy number of proteins. As a consequence, one end of a yeast cell ends up with more critical protein than another and this spontaneously establishes a polarity for future development (Altschuler et al. 2008). This noisy variation is found useful in organ behaviour, too. Plant lateral roots develop from one or two pericycle cells, and spontaneous root production occurs as noise variation in the progenitor cells (e.g. Forde 2009, 2014). Many other acts of development in plants, start, or rely on the behaviour of one or two cells (e.g. root hairs, guard cells, the fertilized embryo, potentially leaves, too). With epigenetic activities guiding the development of such tissues, there is substantive room for variation in final tissue and, thus, whole plant behaviour.

Can noise be reduced? Negative feedback is one mechanism that helps, but almost certainly there are limits. An alternative is to increase the copy number of proteins. Some proteins are only found as a few copies/cell, sometimes less than ten. Error is obviously more serious in these than protein copy numbers in the thousands. To decrease the standard deviation of protein distribution by half between separate cells would require a 16-fold increase of signalling proteins (Lestas et al. 2010). In cascades of protein kinases, such as MAP kinases, a five-step transduction sequence requires 25 more bursts of synthetic activity than a single step, to maintain the same capacity to reduce noise. Parallel signalling systems can instead improve noise suppression because each independent pathway contributes independent information

about the upstream state. 'Making a decent job is 16 times harder than a half decent job' (Lestas et al. 2010). Cells are not machines; they survive and function with huge amounts of variation in the constituents.

William's compilation of variation in more complex organisms

Noise probably helps generate variations in overall morphology and tissues. Williams (1956), in a novel compilation, recorded variations in tissue sizes in normal, healthy reproducing human beings, and some other mammals. His records indicate variations of up to 20- and sometimes 50-fold. Variations of 5–10-fold in many biochemicals and even larger variations in some hormones were reported, too. Compensation for variations results from the many hundreds of negative feedbacks built into the circuitry. It is the structure of the system itself that enables this robust character. Feedback acts to accommodate the variation and enable the organism to survive despite the variation. Those with small stomachs simply eat more often, for example, but with more detailed specification, individual constraints obviously emerge. Someone at the lower end of the 95% percentile on height is unlikely to run as fast as someone at the top end and so on.

Equal degrees of variation are seen in plants. For annuals I have seen variations of 100-fold in the size of the same cultivar of poppy plants in flower. Consider the degree of variation in height and volume in trees that produce flowers and seed. Mineral contents determined by what is in the soil can vary 100-fold, as well, and yet plants will not vary in growth to the same extent. Individual seeds can vary enormously in the production of particular enzymes.

Early rejection of Loeb's mechanist views

A major problem was that Loeb was content to observe the tropic reactions of organisms at merely two time points; he never investigated what changes went on in between. Weiss (1959) reported in his 1926 PhD thesis, on the resting positions of the *Vanessa* butterfly. The insects always settled with their heads away from a uni-directional light source, a supposed forced behaviour according to Loeb. However, Weiss observed that each insect chose its own individual path to reach that position. The behaviour was not forced or machine like; each individual recognized the source of light but used it only to reference the final position.

Since Loeb did use plants as his formulation of forced reactions, his formulation can be rejected based on observations in plants themselves. Seedling roots of a number of dicot species tend to grow vertically downwards. Place such seedlings horizontally and after 5–6 hr most roots will be growing vertically downwards, again. However, the path of curvature and growth changes towards that final growth position is seemingly unique for each seedling as indicated in Chapter 14 (Selker and Sievers 1987; Zieschang and Sievers 1991; Ishikawa et al. 1991). Perhaps more challenging is the onset of gravisensitivity. When placed with the embryonic root downwards, 95% of seedling roots grew downwards, i.e. sensitive to the gravity vector, but when placed with the embryonic root upwards, only 25% did; the rest grew randomly in all directions (Ma and Hasenstein 2006).

The evidence suggests that individual shoots exhibit similar degrees of variation (Firn and Digby 1980) in response to unilateral light. When they do respond to unidirectional light, the individuals can vary between 5 and 40 min before a response commences (Rich and Smith 1986). Thus, Loeb's hypothesis fails on the very basic experimental evidence on tropisms that he used to construct the notion in the first place. Since individuals exhibit their own unique trajectory in response to signals, Loeb's hypothesis is perhaps akin to assuming that because chess games begin, and end with usually the same moves of pawns and mating of the King, every game itself is a mechanical repetition of exactly the same moves in between. Every plant is an individual and individuality is the substance of natural selection. All that Loeb had shown was that light was something to which some animals, and most plants have a sensing and response (transduction) system to light. The crippling limitations of mechanistic attitudes lie not in the behaviour of the organism, but in its simplistic description (Griffin, 1976).

Instinct and behaviourist issues; the developmental alternative and crucial understanding of plant learning

The concept of instincts in animal behaviour was most notably championed by Lorenz and Tinbergen. Lorenz (1977) has provided a suitable summary of his position on this issue. Instinctive acts are highly stereotyped, co-ordinated movements by the neuromotor apparatus that he claims are genetically fixed. Lorenz recognized that there is learnt behaviour, and behaviour he divided into instinct and learning.

Instinct and behaviourism can interlink into a generalized view that sees animals as largely robots programmed by selfish genes, and the almost continual argument over gene-centred attitudes to morphology and behaviour. It takes little more to see the behaviour of lower organisms and other organisms, like plants, as classed in the same light. No choices, no decisions, all forced, all instinct. Whole books have been written on this topic (Oyama 1985) so I can only briefly refer to them, but these perceptions bear directly on plant behaviour and intelligence, and so it is necessary to assess their validity.

Lehrmann's critique of instinct

The notion of animal instinct has been subject to withering criticism by both Lehrmann (1953), Schneirla (1966), and the more recent developmental system theory approaches (Oyama 2000). Johnston (2001) provides a more up-to-date assessment of Lehrmann's contribution. The critiques hinge around the omission, by Lorenz, of information, available at the time, concerning behaviour of newly-hatched chicks or newborn rodents.

When newly hatched, chicks will peck for grain, supposedly an instinctual behaviour. Lehrmann summarizes the evidence that the behaviour is actually learnt in the egg itself and, thus, during development. Contractile movements of adjacent developing tissues become laid down as neural pathways in the developing nervous system that codes for pecking so that pecking may appear to be instinctive when the chick is hatched. Behaviour cannot, therefore, be parcelled up easily into instinct or learning, these two are intertwined and end up simply as behaviour resulting from development. West-Eberhard (2003, p. 111) quotes another example in the developing human foetus. Retinal ganglion cells mimic the action of light by sending bursts of action potentials. These enable correct nervous connections to be made in the developing eye so that the newborn can use their eyes immediately. Again, not instinct, just part of development.

Here, we meet a fundamental difference between plant and animal development. There is a period of similarity in which the single-cell plant embryo undergoes development into the seed, but thereafter with the onset of germination, development continues in the shoot and root meristems. There are now similarities with Lehrmann's concern with learning in development. What forms in the root meristem is a sensitive root cap columella that varies in structure according to the signals that it perceives are present in the environment. With continual development the columella cells are, in turn, continually replaced. The dynamic of cell division in the cap ensures that eventually all cells are replaced and in fast-growing roots replacement is fast. In Chapter 15, I indicated that other signals, to which a root needs to respond, change the sensing equipment, degrading the starch amyloplasts so as to downgrade the gravity signal response equipment. In that way, the new columella structure now can respond to touch or humidity gradient or anything else in the soil structure that requires a difference in behaviour.

However, this learning process is applicable to gravity, too. In the developing embryo in the pod, the putative root meristem is full of starch, but with the maturation of the seed this starch has disappeared (Sievers et al. 2002). Only with normal germination does starch reappear and the root become gravisensitive. This period of time commonly requires some 12 hr in reasonable temperatures.

However, this amyloplast sensitive equipment is only formed as a result of perception of a standard gravity signal itself. The observations that if seeds are germinated with the root vertically upward, that 75% the roots grow in all directions indicates what is commonly known in gravitational research; that exposure to a 180° angle to gravity is a very insensitive gravity signal (Ma and Hasenstein 2006). This 75% have not formed the gravisensing equipment

in the columella because under these conditions, the strength of the gravity signal is either too weak on cells which are known to respond best at angles of 135° or it cannot be sensed from this vertical position. The columella response system is a dynamic and its capability to respond is learnt from what it experiences. Imbibed seeds normally learn to respond to gravity, a pervasive signal, it is not a reflex response.

That gravity is sensed in plant roots without proper amyloplasts has been known for some time from research on starchless mutants (Caspar and Pickard 1989; Kiss et al. 1989). Amyloplasts do increase the sensitivity of the root to gravity, but they are not essential if growth is slow and a response to gravity can be slow. In their absence, gravisensing and response still occurs, but simply more slowly. What mechanism is used to stimulate the formation of the gravisensing equipment in the first place? Two potential mechanisms suggest either sedimentation of large plastids or the weight of the cytoplasm on the plasma membrane.

What has prevented recognition of this obvious information is the simple and uncritical way in which text books and teaching deal with the subject matter. The notion of fixed responses causes equal trouble. Offer a starving man food, how variable will be the response? However, for those plants that must grow quickly because they are annuals and either weeds or crop plants, or their equivalents, a rapid response of soil penetration is essential. These species are surely the equivalent of the starving man. The research emphasis on such plants also interferes with perception of behavioural variation among many other species.

Similar learning potential obviously occurs in the shoot. These also search for light primarily to get there before others and sequester the source, and by shading, do down the competition, not only because they will need light in due course. Seedlings with big seed reserves may rarely use all their seed reserves, and they can dispense with some of it and still maintain the same stem growth rate. Assessment is again clouded by using a pioneer weed, *Arabidopsis* as the standard experimental material. Its minimal height guarantees it will be overgrown. Similarly, in the shade response syndrome, the stem grows more quickly even though there is no loss of photosynthetic light. The aim is to shade the opposition. The shade response, the production of leaves and internode thickness is clearly altered, and this pattern starts with changes in the shoot meristem itself. The meristem is a flexible learning tissue because it is in continuous development.

Lehrmann (1953) emphasizes in his critique, that the zygote does not contain some kind of miniature homuncular plan of future behaviour, and that most biologists do not think of the gene as some kind of entelechy that purposefully pushes development in one direction. Behaviour is not usually associated with the newly-formed single cell zygote, but is certainly expressed by the adult. However, as development commences, the embryo is increasingly subject to maternal and environmental influences. Certainly in mammals, maternal influences such as thalidomide, lithium ions, too many litter mates, or a scarcity of food produce a different phenotype. There must be complex communication between mother and foetus that is little understood.

The course of development in plants starts with the zygote, but further development is also subject to maternal influences that change the seed phenotype and, in certain cases, the adult phenotype, too. These have all been mentioned in Chapter 16. The maternal environmental conditions influence the decision of developing seeds on the eventual timing of germination (to grow immediately or to wait, to remain dormant) and include the maternal signals of carbon dioxide levels, competition with other plant species, day length, fungal infection, growing season length, light quality, mineral nutrition, position in the ovary, defoliation, seed moisture, sunlight intensity and length, temperature, and time of seed maturation. Clearly, this mass of information is learnt, assessed and coupled (in some unknown way) to produce different seed phenotypes (Baskin and Baskin 2000).

From the single cell zygote onwards, environmental information has laid down molecular and physiological channels in the cellular network of the seed that finally impacts on timing mechanisms. This is clearly a good case of learning, but indirect learning passed onto the seed. Is this, in any way, really different in any meaningful way to Lehrmann's example of chick pecking?

Lorenz's book refers to the response by plants to light although under the heading of adaptation. Earlier (Chapter 19), it was concluded that adaptation is learning, it benefits the plant. I have placed discussion on this in Box 24.1.

The recognition of kin

Lorenz is, perhaps, most well-known for the phenomena of imprinting. Young goslings, when immediately hatched, follow anything that moves (mainly Lorenz himself) and stayed fixated on this. Imprinting is really part of a general aspect of kin recognition and is learnt. It is essential for animals to recognize their own species to enable mating (Krebs and Davies 1987). Plants do use kin recognition, too, and this was considered in Chapter 18.

Conditioned behaviour

The classical Pavlovian conditioning is not as it seems

One of the familiar forms of behaviour in animals is conditioned responses made famous by Pavlov. In these experiments, dogs were conditioned to salivate to the ringing of a bell by association between that and the provision of food. Two things mitigate against detecting conditioned behaviour in higher plants. First, plants use a single source of energy, the sun. Animals are heterotrophs and must seek their often variable supplies of food in a great variety of situations. Thus, they are open to learning by association. Secondly, and more problematic, is that plant behaviour appears largely as a result of changes in development, a continuous process of change. In a sense, you do not deal with the same plant twice because of changing development. Whereas Pavlov's dogs, unitary organisms, are in another sense the same stable organism throughout, although, of course, they continue the developmental cycle.

However, conditioned responses in animals are not as they are commonly portrayed (Rescoria 1988). 'Conditioning involves the learning of relations among events. It provides the animals with a much richer representation of the environment than a reflex tradition would ever have suggested.

Box 24.1 Lorenz, light, and plant behaviour

Lorenz (1977, p. 64) mentions the effect of light on plants regarding it as a form of adaptation:

'When a plant growing in darkness stretches upwards so as to give its leaves more light this is by no means solely due to environmental influences but also to an inbuilt genetic program which has evolved by the years through trial and success (presumably Thorndikean trial and error learning?) and is now available to be used in particular circumstances. It is as if the plant has been told, if the light is inadequate, extend yourself, until satisfactory illumination is achieved'.

The language is quaint and almost anthropomorphic. What Lorenz may be referring to is the increased elongation of some plant shoots placed in shade or darkness. There are usually morphological changes in such circumstances and in numerous species, which increase stem height at the expense of thickness, increase apical dominance, producing longer internodes and fewer leaves. The shoot gains more resources than the root. The phenomenon is known as the shade avoidance syndrome. There are, however, shade tolerant plants; some of these increase leaf area with a concomitant change in leaf anatomy.

There are three families of light receptors in plants, phytochromes, phototropins, and cryptochromes. Phytochromes sense light in the red end of the spectrum, phototropins and cryptochrome in the blue region. A single light receptor would provide only a kind of crude on/off switch. Families of receptors with different properties, enable a much more detailed assessment of the spatial distribution of light and help to construct an image of light distribution on the recipient plant through sensing by individual cells. Is there integration of that image through cell communication? Additional receptors enable the receipt of more information.

There are five phytochromes (A–E) that detect red light and induce the morphological events described in shade avoidance. These proteins contain a linear tetrapyrrole light-sensing cofactor. When red light is absorbed the protein structure rearranges to induce the active form of phytochrome. Far red light reverses this activation. Many red light-dependent behavioural events are modulated by the ratio between the red and far red absorbing forms of phytochrome. Under a canopy chlorophyll absorbs in the red region and thus the ratio of transmitted far red light/red light is increased. Once this altered ratio is sensed and assessed, a decision is required as to whether to invoke the shade avoidance response. Reflected sunlight from leaves is also enhanced in the far red too, so the far red/red ratio is also used to detect nearby and competitive neighbours, and to assess the likelihood of becoming a victim of future direct shade. The individual plant must therefore make a cost/benefit assessment and assess how close is the neighbour, and how quickly it is growing. Some seedlings of plants like *Portulaca* that grows along the ground will grow in the opposite direction to another plant and do so well before it loses any photosynthetic light (Novoplansky 1991). They grow away from the potential source of light competition, but no doubt with the eventual aim of shading the others. There are benefits to being above the rest not only in light acquisition, but in greater stability of soil temperature and reduction of wind speed. Shade avoidance is, indeed, an adaptive process, but a programme that can be summoned when need arises. It is not a reflex phenomenon. Shade avoidance will depend on other environmental characteristics.

In some single celled algae (e.g. *Mougeotia*) it can be shown that phytochrome is aligned spatially, possibly in the plasma membrane, so as to optimize the sensing of light gradients and direction. The situation is less clear in higher plants, most sensing ought to be epidermal or near epidermal; it would be advantageous if phytochromes were spatially aligned to optimize the sensing of the spatial distribution of light. Lorenz does not mention phototropism in which the blue sensitive phototropins are the primary sensory receptors involved. Phototropism is a clear case of adaptive behaviour and maybe the most sensitive light-sensing process in biology responding to 0.5 sec of light at a fluence rate of less than 10^{-2} nm/m^{-2} (Ellis 1987). Cryptochrome also responds to blue light. Roots of many plants are sensitive to light and grow away from it.

Organisms adjust their Pavlovian associations only when they are surprised'. The situation of surprise indicates high information content. The critical point here is the learning of the relations among different events.

Conditioned behaviour in plants?

Attempts to obtain conditioned learning of membrane potentials using light/dark regimes in *Philodendron* was not successful (Abramson et al. 2002).

There are, however, many relationships between different signals that indicate how plants learn about their environment. There is a remarkable complex of interactions between red and blue light on phototropism that informs the plant on its particular state of illumination (Curry 1969). A multitude of signals affect stomatal closure (Willmer and Fricker 1996). Much plant behaviour involves changes in growth and growth patterns, and all the major requirements, water, minerals, light, and other abiotic stimuli already impact on growth, making it difficult to identify a supposedly neutral signal that plants could be conditioned, too. Pavlov used a bell as the neutral signal information to gain the conditioned response of salivation.

Disease and herbivory resistance offer some potential for conditioned learning

The best potential at present for looking for this form of learning comes in the areas of disease and herbivory resistance. Plants are subject to a multitude of disease organisms and about 10,000 insect herbivores. Resistance is usually systemic, rather than local, and that implies the circulation of materials throughout the plant.

Currently, three transduction resistance pathways have been identified.

1. Disease induces the synthesis and circulation of salicylate that prime other tissues against further attack.
2. Herbivore damage induces the jasmonic acid pathway.
3. Ethylene, a plant hormone, which influences both (1) and (2).

These potentially separate transduction pathways interact (cross-talk) with each other. Disease attack can down-regulate herbivory resistance and vice versa (Koornneef and Pieterse 2008). Plants respond with a particular blend of these key transduction pathways that varies greatly in quantity, composition, and timing. Along with these generalized defences there is selectivity in response to the particular organism experienced. Vos et al. (2005) used different combinations of bacterial and fungal disease organisms, caterpillars, thrips, and aphids, and analysed the invaded plant transcripts produced in response. Although sets of transcripts in common were induced, each separate pest produced some transcripts unique to itself.

Large numbers of growth-promoting bacteria, associated with the root systems, actually induce systemic resistance to many fungi, bacteria, and viruses, and even in the presence of pathogens (Loon et al. 1998; Kloepper et al. 2004). The application of both treatments together can be investigated using split root treatments—one half pathogen, one half growth-promoting bacteria. Invasion by growth-promoting bacteria is acting to condition resistance.

The growth-promoting bacteria synthesize a variety of compounds, some are small and volatile, like butane diol, others larger molecular weight species. These rhizosphere bacteria also help plants tolerate abiotic stresses like drought and excess salinity, and again alter behaviour (Yang et al. 2009). A particular response, either to herbivory or disease pests, can be induced by all kinds of different treatments. This phenomenon seems to be present in many aspects of plant development, but this example offers the best potential for a kind of conditioned learning response.

A potential conditioned response with abscisic acid and gene expression and response to light has previously been referenced in Chapter 9.

Conclusion on Lorenz and Loeb, and the notion of determinate or forced development

Genes influence development, but do not dominate it. The phenotype in plants is highly variable not predetermined. To ascribe to genes, overall control of certain kinds of behaviour, as did Lorenz, simply ignores the obvious equal impact of environment in all processes of development even inside eggs, pods, or uterus. A critical example occurs in the sensing mechanisms in the root columella. Because this structure is continually changed by division and thus cell development, it is reconstructed each time to accommodate the priority signal whether it be gravity, humidity touch, or other signals yet uncharacterized. The notions of central, overall controls, a kind of autocracy that manipulates behaviour is easy to conceive, but wrong in practice, particularly for self-organizing plants. Systems thinking requires assessing all the available inter-actions so that the totality of the system can really be conceived. This is the message of developmental systems theory (Oyama 1985).

Plants are not complex machinery, they are complex life.

References

Abramson, C.I., Garrido, D.J., Lawson, A.L., Browne, B.L., and Thomas, D.G. (2002). Bioelectrical potentials of *Philodendron cordatum*: a new method for investigation of behaviour in plants. *Psychological Reports*, **91**, 173–185.

Altschuler, S.J., Angenent, S.B. Wang, Y., and Wu, L.F. (2008). On the spontaneous emergence of cell polarity. *Nature*, **454**, 886–889.

Armus, H.L., Montgomery, A.R., and Jellison, J.L. (2006). Discrimination learning in *paramecia* (*P. caudatum*). *Psychological Record*, **56**, 489–498.

Baskin, C.C., and Baskin, J.M. (2000). *Seeds: ecology, biogeography and evolution of dormancy and germination*. Academic Press, New York.

Bolinder, M.A., Angers, D.A., Belanger, G., Michaud, R., and Lavediere, M.R. (2002). Root biomass and shoot to root ratios of perennial forage crops in eastern Canada. *Canadian Journal of Plant Science*, **82**, 731–737.

Caspar, T., and Pickard, B.G. (1989). Gravitropism in a starchless mutant of *Arabidopsis*. *Planta*, **177**, 185–197.

Chapin, F.S., III (1980). The mineral nutrition of wild plants. *Annual Review of Ecology and Systematics*, **11**, 233–260.

Curry, G.M. (1969). Phototropism. In Wilkins, M.B., ed. *The physiology of plant growth and development*, pp. 243–273. McGraw-Hill, London.

Vos, M., de, Oosten, V.R., van, Poecke, R.M.P. van, Pelt, J.A., van, Pozo, M.J., Mueller, M.J., and 5 others (2005). Signal signature and transcriptome changes of *Arabidopsis* during pathogen and insect attack. *Molecular Plant Microbe Interactions*, **18**, 923–937.

Ellis, R.J. (1987). Comparison of fluence–response relationships of phototropism in light and dark-grown buckwheat. *Plant Physiology*, **85**, 689–692.

Elowitz, M.B., Levine, A.J., Siggia, E.D., and Swain, P.S. (2002). Stochastic gene expression in a single cell. *Science*, **297**, 1183–1186.

Firn, R., and Digby, J. (1980). The establishment of tropic curvatures. *Annual Review of Plant Physiology*, **31**, 131–148.

Forde, B.J. (2009). Is it good noise? The role of developmental instability in the shaping of a root system. *Journal of Experimental Botany*, **60**, 3989–4002.

Forde, B.J. (2014). Glutamate signalling in roots. *Journal of Experimental Botany*, **65**(3), 779–787.

Frobenius, L. (2006). *Storia della civilta africana*. Adelphi, London.

Gelber, B. (1957). Food or training in *Paramecium*. *Science*, **126**, 1340–1341.

Griffin, D.R. (1976). *The question of animal awareness. Evolutionary continuity of mental experience*. Rockefeller University Press, New York.

Ishikawa, H., Hasenstein, K.H., and Evans, M.L. (1991). Computer-based video digitizer analysis of surface extension in maize roots. *Planta*, **183**, 381–390.

Jennings, H.S. (1923). *Behaviour of the lower organisms*. Columbia University Press, New York.

Johnston, T.D. (2001). Towards a systems view of development. An appraisal of Lehrmann's critique of Lorenz. In Oyama, S., Griffiths, P.E., and Gray, R.D., eds, *Cycles of contingency*, pp. 15–25. MIT Press, Cambridge, MA.

Kiss, J.Z., Hertel, R., and Sack, F. (1989). Amyloplasts are necessary for full gravitropic sensitivity in roots of Arabidopsis thaliana. *Planta*, **177**, 198–206.

Kloepper, J.W., Ryu, C-M., and Zhang, S. (2004). Induced systemic resistance and promotion of plant growth by *Bacillus* spp. *Phytopathology*, **94**, 1259–1266.

Koornneef, A., and Pieterse, C.M.J. (2008). Cross talk in defence signalling. *Plant Physiology*, **146**, 839–844.

Krebs, J.R., and Davies, N.B. (1987). *An introduction to behavioural ecology*. Blackwell Scientific Publishers, Oxford.

Lehrmann, D.S. (1953). A critique of Konrad Lorenz's theory of instinctive behavior. *Quarterly Review of Biology*, **28**, 337–363.

Lestas, I., Vinnicombe, G., and Paulsson, J. (2010). Fundamental limits on the suppression of molecular variations. *Nature*, **467**, 174–178.

Lewontin, R. (2001). Gene, organism and environment. In Oyama, S., Griffiths, P.E., and Gray, R.D., eds, *Cycles of contingency*, pp. 55–67. MIT Press, Cambridge, MA.

Loeb, J. (1912). *The mechanistic conception of life*. Belknap Press, Cambridge, MA.

Loeb, J. (1918). *Forced movements, tropisms and animal conduct*. J.B. Lippincott Co., Philadelphia, PA.

Lorenz, K. (1977). *Behind the mirror*. Methuen and Co. Ltd, London.

Ma, Z., and Hasenstein, K.H. (2006). The onset of gravisensitivity in the embryonic root of flax. *Plant Physiology*, **140**, 159–166.

Massonet, C., Vile, D., Fabre, J., Hannah, M.A., Caldana, C., Lisee, J., and 22 others (2010). Probing the reproducibility of leaf growth and molecular phenotypes: a comparison of three Arabidopsis accessions cultivated in ten laboratories. *Plant Physiology*, **152**, 4142–4157.

Novoplansky, A. (1991). Developmental responses of *Portulaca* seedlings to conflicting spectral signals. *Oecologia*, **88**, 138–140.

Oyama, S. (1985). *The ontogeny of information.* Cambridge University Press, Cambridge.

Oyama, S. (2000). *The ontogeny of information.* Duke University Press, Durham, NC.

Pearson, H. (2008). The cellular hullabaloo. *Nature,* **453,** 150–153.

Ray TS. (1987). Cyclic heterophylly in *Syngonium. American Journal of Botany,* **74,** 16–26.

Rescoria, R.A. (1988). Pavlovian conditioning. It's not what you think it is. *American Psychologist,* **43,** 151–160.

Rich, T.S.G., and Smith, H. (1986). Comparison of lag times in plant physiology. *Plant Cell and Environment,* **9,** 707–709.

Salzman, A.G. (1985). Habitat selection in a clonal plant. *Science,* **228,** 603–604.

Salzman, A.G., and Parker, M.A. (1985). Neighbours ameliorate local salinity stress in a heterogeneous environment. *Oecologia,* **65,** 273–277.

Schneirla T.C. (1966). Behavioural development and comparative psychology. *Quarterly Review of Biology,* **41,** 283–302.

Selker, J.M.L., and Sievers, A. (1987). Analysis of extension and curvature during the graviresponse in *Lepidium* roots. *American Journal of Botany,* **74,** 1863–1871.

Shalek, A.K., Satija, R., Adiconis, X., Gertner, R.S., Gaublomme, J.T. Raychowdhury, R., and 12 others (2013). Single-cell transcriptomics reveal bimodality in expression and splicing in immune cells. *Nature,* **498,** 236–240.

Sievers, A., Braun, M., and Monshausen, G.B. (2002). The root cap structure and function. In Waisels, Y., Eshel, A., and Kafkafi, U., eds, *Plant roots: the hidden half,* 3rd edn, pp. 51–76. Marcel Dekker Ltd., New York.

Spudich, J.L., and Koshland, D.E. (1976). Non-genetic individuality: chance in the single cell. *Nature,* **262,** 467–472.

Taniguchi, Y., Choi, P.J., Li, G.-W., Chen, H., Babu, M., Hearn, J., and 2 others (2010). Quantifying *E.coli* proteome and transcriptome with single molecule sensitivity in single cells. *Science,* **329,** 533–538.

Trewavas, A. (2012). Information, noise and communication: thresholds as controlling elements in development. In Witzany G., and Baluska, F., eds, *Biocommunication of plants,* pp. 11–37. Springer-Verlag, Berlin.

Loon L.C., van, Bakker, P.A.H.M., and Pieterse, C.M.J. (1998). Systemic resistance induced by rhizosphere bacteria. *Annual Review of Phytopathology,* **36,** 453–483.

Weiss, P. (1959). Animal behaviour as system reaction: the orientation towards light and gravity in the resting postures of butterflies (*Vanessa*). In *General systems: year book of the Society for General Systems Research,* Vol. 4, pp. 1–44. English translation of a paper in *Biologia Generalis* 1, 167–248.

West-Eberhard, M.J. (2003). *Developmental plasticity and evolution.* Oxford University Press, Oxford.

Williams, R. (1956). *Biochemical individuality.* Wiley and Sons Ltd, London.

Willmer, C., and Fricker, M. (1996). *Stomata.* Springer, Berlin.

Yang, J., Kloepper, J.W., and Ryu, C-M. (2009). Rhizosphere bacteria help plants tolerate abiotic stress. *Trends in Plant Science,* **14,** 1–4.

Zieschang, H.E., and Sievers, A. (1991). Graviresponse and the localisation of its initiating cells in roots of *Phleum pratense. Planta,* **184,** 468–477.

CHAPTER 25

Intelligence and consciousness

Not just animals are conscious but every organic being,
every autopoietic cell is conscious. In the simplest sense,
consciousness is an awareness of the outside world.

(Margulis and Sagan 1995)

⊃ **Summary**

Consciousness is a term rarely applied to other animals and never to plants, but Margulis indicates its likely ubiquity in all organisms. Assessment of signalling may be the clearest indication of conscious activity, but assessment in plants is not understood. In bacterial swimming, assessment and memory involves a limited number of proteins whose interactions and modifications by phosphorylation or methylation construct a simple assessment system. This simple system is obviously a model for more complex organisms with much greater numbers of proteins involved. 'Do cells think' is the title of a paper that examines some unusual behaviour of yeast in response to two distinct signals given at the same time. The authors indicate a higher order of control is operative in such cells, which is not presently understood. However, the recognition of awareness in other organisms is disguised by the imposition of human criteria on their behaviour. Can social insect colonies be considered conscious? Since nervous systems are strongly associated with consciousness in animals the plant nervous system characterized by Bose is briefly described. Action potentials are not uncommon transduction pathways in plants. They lead to changes in cytosolic calcium that can mediate the response, and provide for long-term learning and memory. Herbivore damage induces electrical signals, which initiate defence mechanisms. Are immune systems conscious? They learn and remember and are aware in the Margulis conscious sense. Are they the consciousness of the body?

Introduction

The title of this chapter is to be found in an informative book by Lynn Margulis and her son Dorian Sagan (1995). It is an attempt to start the intricate dissection of something often considered to be unique to human beings, consciousness. However, no statement concerning consciousness in any other organism than ourselves is currently open to investigation or refutation by any experimental treatment that is known. Whatever consciousness actually is cannot be established objectively, because it is personal to the individual. The only reason the term exists is because we have this feature of our mental activity, the internal self-referencing, thoughts, images, self-observation, thinking as though one part of the brain is observing another. We convey that process to others by means of language and it is on that basis that we consider humans are conscious, i.e. they are sentient. Religious attitudes describe it as the soul, but the inadequacy of communication with virtually most other species means we cannot assess whether they are conscious and probably never will. All that can be judged is whether their

Plant Behaviour and Intelligence. First Edition. Anthony Trewavas.
© Anthony Trewavas 2014. Published 2014 by Oxford University Press.

behaviour is consistent with their being conscious. Only on supposition can we deny it for other species. Trewavas and Baluska (2011) provide evidence that consciousness can be regarded as ubiquitous in all of biology.

Autopoiesis is a fundamental property of living systems

Autopoiesis is a left-over life property from Chapter 3. There I included Jacques Monod's emphasis on teleonomy. 'Teleonomy is that of being objects, endowed with a purpose which they show in their structure and execute through their performances. Rather than reject this idea (as certain biologists try to do), it must be regarded as essential to the very definition of all living being' (Monod 1971, p. 20). Purposive behaviour in plants was first indicated by Sachs (1887, p. 601), 'All those adaptations of the organism are purposeful which contribute to its maintenance and insure its existence'. Virtually all plant behaviour comes in that category of being purposeful. Autopoiesis originated because its creators, Maturana and Varela (1980), felt that teleonomy was a programme imposed on the individual by the species during evolution. So they included what they felt was equally crucial to life, the maintenance of organization. Autopoiesis derives from the Latin 'auto' as self and 'poiesin' as making. The individual acts as a unitary organism and 'Through their interactions and transformations, continuously regenerate and realize the network of processes that produced them' (Maturana and Varela 1980, p. 79).

98% of all the atoms of the human body are replaced within 1 year. From measurements of average turnover rates of protein and ribosomal RNA in plants this replacement rate will be similar (Trewavas 1970, 1972). Again, on average, each cell in the human body repairs about a million bases/day in DNA responding to oxidative damage or external radiation sources, and leaves one uncorrected mutation. The thoughts you have today as images in the brain and your consciousness, and based on molecules, will have been completely replaced next year by equivalent new molecules. How well ordered that process is will determine how much you remember.

Two kinds of consciousness

Consciousness does indicate intention, it does deal with things or events, it relies on memory and the associated process of learning, but is not a simple copy of experience. There are also the clinical aspects of consciousness, criteria concerned with alertness, motivational behaviour, orientation, and self-awareness.

Edelman (1992) has suggested two kinds of consciousness. Primary consciousness is the familiar properties of heart rate, respiration rate, digestive contractions, hormone release, etc. We are aware of them, but do not control them. Higher order consciousness starts with perception through the sense organs and then control of muscular activities that drives the response. Perception, assessment, response—these are fundamental behaviours for all organisms. Assessment is the issue and perhaps the equivalent of consciousness in all.

Even the simplest organisms perceive their environment through sensory mechanisms and respond accordingly. 'The biological self, incorporates . . . facts, experiences, and senses impressions, which may become memories. All living beings perceive their environment, not just animals but plants and microbes too. To survive, an organic being must perceive- it must seek or at least recognize food and avoid environmental danger'. 'Certainly some level of awareness and of responsiveness owing to that awareness, is implied in all autopoietic systems' (Margulis and Sagan 1995, pp. 32 and 122).

'The Conscious Cell' (Margulis 2001): what is assessment?

Lynn Margulis is famous for her symbiotic theory of life. Mitochondria and chloroplasts were originally free-living bacterial and blue-green algal symbionts that have in the passage of time become critical organelles in eukaryotic cells. Her hypothesis has been well corroborated by DNA analysis. Margulis considers that the evolutionary antecedent of the nervous system is microbial consciousness. Thus, the eukaryotic cell that contains these symbionts is, by definition, conscious too. Her hypothesis also includes a consideration of the origin of neurotubules also acquired through the symbiotic route.

Escherichia coli, originally isolated from the human gut, swims by means of motors that drive six flagellae by rotation. There are two kinds of swimming—smooth when the flagellae trail uniformly behind the cell and chaotic tumbling when the direction of rotation is reversed (Sourjik 2004). Each cell has 10 to 12 receptors in its outer membrane, which sample its surrounding medium for chemicals, usually either food or toxins. The tumbling process is used to comparatively assess the present concentration of a desirable commodity like sugars, amino acids, or toxins, with a previous assessment using the specific receptors. This checking period lasts a few seconds. After assessment, swimming then continues in the direction of food or away from toxins. These few seconds represent its memory that, when accessed, controls behaviour.

Strictly speaking, *E. coli* possesses neither a nervous system or a brain but it does have what could be described as a centralised intelligence system. At a simple level it does what bigger brains do. It integrates information from sensory mechanisms that detect salient features of the environment. It has central decision-making machinery that encodes and analyses information about its past and present, and enables it to chart its course into a well-chosen future. And it has the equipment-the behavioural effector systems-to execute the plan. (Lacerra and Bingham 2002, p. 15)

The basis of this intelligent process is derived from a fairly simple system of interconnected proteins and does involve protein modification through phosphorylation and methylation. The connections in this assessment network are transiently modified to adjust the procedures of tumbling and smooth swimming. Phosphorylation is used because rapidity of response is essential. The bacterial cell thus exhibits awareness of its surroundings. Consciousness at its simplest is thus a system, a network property. However, these proteins are embedded in a much larger network of other proteins that create the cell, and its sensing and motors in the first place.

Eukaryotic cells are an order of magnitude more complex than the common bacterial cell and the variety of their behaviour increases accordingly (Chapter 20). Again, the assessment process depends on a densely connected network of proteins, which are structurally and strategically located inside the cell. However, with many more potential interactions between proteins and numerous post-translational modifications, the complexity of behaviour is greatly increased. These data provide definite clues about the nature of assessment, the consciousness equivalent in plants, and complete the consideration of such behaviour in cells described in Chapters 22 and 23. Jennings (1923, p. 336) asks, 'Is the behaviour of lower organisms of the character which we should naturally expect and appreciate if they did have conscious states of undifferentiated character and acted under similar conscious states in a way parallel to man'. He concludes they do. When such cells, for example, draw away from unpleasant circumstances can we conclude they do not experience pain? Our behaviour would be similar. That question has, of course, no answer and never will. Jennings was merely trying to indicate the evolutionary origins of what is called consciousness.

'Do cells think?'

Ramanathan and Broach (2007) ask this question in a well-argued and provocative paper. They point to a large number of examples of single cells, where genetically identical individuals maintain a range of phenotypes in a uniform environment. Most notable among these are trypanosomes and others that generate antigenic variants in an infection population. *Candida albicans*, a fungus that infects humans can express a number of phenotypic variants. It can change virulence by altering antigenicity, or alter antifungal resistance or sensitivity to macrophage ingestion. Even *Escherichia coli* can switch into a quiescent state that increases resistance to antibiotics. The optimum switching rate between phenotypes should be proportional to the probability that the environment will change, too.

Slow behavioural changes in plants in response to environmental signals raise an issue here of some importance. When the new phenotype starts to emerge after signalling, it may be unsuitable for the present environment. If the environment changes frequently, then fitter individuals need to maintain a memory of the frequency of changes it has experienced in the past and adjust behavioural responses accordingly. Such a record can be deposited in protein phosphorylation states or epigenetic modifications, and should involve thresholds that are superseded when critical numbers of environmental changes have been recorded (Chapter 16). Even *Bacillus subtilis* can manage to remember previous starvation conditions some time after they have been experienced, and changes phenotypic switching accordingly (Suel et al. 2006).

Yeast cells (*Saccharomyces cereviseae*) respond to a number of environmental signals that are interpreted by several well-characterized transduction pathways. Cells can adjust osmolarity in concentrated sugar solutions or respond to mating pheromones for sexual reproduction. The transduction pathways involve well-established cascades of protein kinases and MAP kinase cascades and act like a switch. Some of these critical kinases are shared between the osmolarity and mating transduction pathways. When responding to the mating pheromone it switches off the osmolarity pathway and *vice versa*. In the presence of both signals, some cells switch on the pheromone pathway, while others switch on the osmolarity pathway. The proportion of each type is dependent on the relative strength of the two signals provided. Yeast cells are, in some way, weighing the odds of the signals that are received and adjusting the proportions of each phenotype to better fit the environment. This higher level of information processing 'begins to approach the complexity of a true thought process' (Ramanathan and Broach 2007), something normally identified as cognition. Bear in mind that the cellular system is hierarchical in its construction. This higher order process must work at the pinnacle of the system properties. Again, there is an indication of the mechanisms involved in the process of assessment used during plant behaviour. Systems behaviours become crucial to understanding.

However, the understanding of cognition or thinking may need reassessment. 'A cognitive system is a system whose organization defines a domain of interactions in which it can act with relevance to the maintenance of itself. Living systems are cognitive systems and living is a process of cognition. This statement is valid for all organisms with and without a nervous system' (Maturana 1980). A statement made before the information above was published, but looks to have predicted it.

The evolutionary continuity of consciousness and perception

From the viewpoint of an evolutionary biologist it is reasonable to assume that the sensitive embodied actions of plants and bacteria are part of the same continuum of perception and action that culminates in our most revered mental attributes. 'Mind' may be the result of interacting cells. Mind and body perceiving and living are equally self-referring, self-reflexive processes already present in the earliest bacteria. (Margulis and Sagan 1995, p. 32)

A greater variety of terms are used to describe the behaviour of more complex organisms, such as motivation, appetite, drive, purposive behaviour (West Eberhard 2002). Again, these behaviours do describe what we observe in other organisms and about which assumptions are made. They are, of course, nuances of behaviour that we recognize in ourselves, but in essence are equally relevant to all organisms. *Hydra viridis* is a small multicellular coelenterate, and yet both Jennings (1923) and Bray (2009) refer to *Hydra* as sometimes being hungry and at other times full, because in the latter case it then ignores offered food.

Do plants intend to avoid the competition for light? They behave as though they do when they obviously grow away from competition. We do not use the word hungry for that circumstance, but is there a real difference in essence between a starving man and an etiolated plant? In both cases, the imperative is to find food or perish. The phenotypic mechanisms used by both to deal with this situation reflect what evolution has given them—movement in one case, growth (a form of movement) in the other—but oddly enough the molecular mechanisms look very similar since circulating sugar levels may be the crucial signals (Morkunas et al. 2012). A crucial kinase, snf 1 kinase, is activated by starvation and energy-depleting stress conditions in both plants and animals. Once activated, it enables energy homeostasis and thus survival, by up-regulating energy-conserving and energy-producing catabolic processes. It also limits energy-consuming anabolic metabolism. In addition, these enzymes manipulate and control normal growth and development as well as metabolic homeostasis at the organismal level. The plant uses a whole system assessment that is complex and used to change behaviour, mankind uses a more focused assessment to control hungry behaviour, the brain, but who can say one is not conscious and the other is.

West Eberhard (2002) describes the interesting example of salmon feeding, which under the watchful eye of a predator makes many more mistakes. Its behaviour swings between 'fear' and the necessity of feeding. It is an example of the use of the conflict between speed and efficiency. When the slime mould *Physarum* was hurried to make decisions, mistakes increase (Chapter 20).

Both organisms are finding their attention is modified by external circumstances. Attention reflects the ability to concentrate on one issue at a time, and if two are present one will supersede the other or they may simply alternate. Plant roots get round the issue of two signals by changing the sensing apparatus, which is in continual flux anyway (Chapter 15). There have to be choices, perceptions, decisions and can we add in desire, fear, and hunger? Jennings (1923) uses all these terms for simple organisms and the obvious answer is whether he was right to do so is that we simply do not know. These characteristics of behaviour are easy to see in our conscious selves and they are terms derived from our experience, but some features of all of these appear in some way or another in single cells and some of them in plants, too. It should be feasible to place a plant under stressful circumstances and see how many errors in behaviour emerge.

The natural world can be divided into human existence, other animals, plants and then single cells, but such classification hides the general truth that these divisions tend to merge at their boundaries. Animal life with its central direction of a society of cells, plant life with its organized republic of cells and cells with their organized republic of molecules (Whitehead 1938, p. 157). Like all true republics, plants will assess and vote by the majority view, controlled by a tissue quorum. The whole plant is equivalent to the animal brain.

In conclusion, in this section I agree with Kevin Warwick, artificial intelligence expert. 'I believe that dogs and cats are conscious in their own way and bees, ants and spiders are conscious, not as humans but as bees, ants and spiders. I cannot say that a robot with a computer for a brain is not

conscious because its brain is not like mine and because it thinks in a different way to me' (Warwick 2000, p. 184). I will add to Warwick's statement that 'plants are conscious in their own way, not as humans but as plants', although there is no obvious way at present in which that can ever be accessed. Assessment, mentioned frequently in this chapter and arising from the connections between cells and molecules, hierarchically arranged in a complex system structure, may represent the plant equivalent of thinking. Those conclusions should hold for any network system sufficiently complex.

Is a social insect colony sufficiently complex to acquire a recognisable consciousness?

In Chapter 10, I indicated the distinct analogy in organizational structure between social insect colonies and large plants, such as dicot trees. In this discussion about consciousness, is it possible to conceive that colonies also possess a kind of consciousness? The component individuals through connections with each other form an obvious system whose emergent property is the colony, self-sustaining, and self-organizing; that is, swarm intelligence.

Although much of the original investigations on social insects concentrated on bees, ants also construct substantial colonies involving many thousands of workers. Colonies of ants not only gather information, they evaluate, deliberate, consensus build, face choices (and implement one of them), and they are sensitive to context. They hunt for new nest sites, assess their suitability from size and entry ways, and decide its use from quorum sensing. A threshold number must agree to the site after inspection (Franks 2008). Workers search for food and engage others to follow to this food site. Individual experienced ants teach other, less mature, individuals the directions to new nest sites (Franks and Richardson 2006). More experienced and knowledgeable individuals do the tuition (Stroeymeyt et al. 2011). They communicate all this information by pheromones.

The colony is certainly regarded as behaving intelligently. That is, it has the capacity to solve problems engendered by its environment (Franks 2008). Perhaps most crucially, the individuals are not credited with intelligence, but it is only the connections between the individuals that give rise to colony intelligence. Ant colonies acquire long-term memories of past experience because frequent movement to different nest sites progressively reduces the total move time (Langridge et al. 2004). The colony seems self-aware because the individual workers do not attack others in the nest, but will raid others nearby of the same or other species. The colony is certainly aware of its environment, as are those of bees and termites, and on that basis has a kind of consciousness, an awareness of the outside world, but it is a form of consciousness that we cannot at present access.

Individual bees in a hive obtain a map of their external circumstances and communicate it to others symbolically. This map is reinforced by repetition of flights. An effective image of the local area is thus slowly constructed, then resides in the colony. A memory of the acquired information presumably lasts as long as the individual workers continue collecting, but must then decline as workers die off. Does this provide a very simple model of how a brain functions?

Central to these concepts of consciousness is recognition of self and non-self. In colonies, members generally do not attack each other, but will do so against other colonies and hive intruders. It is thought that the recognition of non-self, which is what this represents, is the result of exchange of recognition signals between all individuals using again a chemical, a pheromone. When under attack, other pheromones are released that call other workers to deal with the invasion. Recent work suggests that, in some wasp colonies, facial recognition is also involved (Tibbetts and Lindsay 2008).

Conclusion on consciousness

In 1902, Charles Minot stated, in a speech to the American Association for the Advancement of Science, 'A frank unbiased study of consciousness must convince every biologist that it is one of the fundamental phenomena of at least all animal life if not, as is quite possible, of all life. Consciousness is a device to regulate the actions of organisms to accomplish purposes which are useful to organisms and are thus teleological'. This statement places a different perspective on how we assess plant life.

After a detailed description of insectivorous plant behaviour, Lauder-Lindsay (1876) stated 'that unless we re-define the term consciousness we must regard some form of it as occurring in both animals and plants that are destitute not only of brain but of a nervous system . . . to regard mind and all its essential or concomitant phenomena as common in various senses or degrees to plants, the lower animals and man'.

The nervous mechanism of plants

The title of this section is taken from a little-known book by J. C. Bose published in 1926. Altogether, Bose published about 12 volumes describing his research on plants, at a time (early twentieth century) and place (India) where very little science operated. His research gained recognition with a knighthood and being elected a Fellow of the Royal Society London. Bose has already been mentioned in Chapter 2 as one of those remarkable people that science is often blessed with. Because nervous systems tend to dominate discussion about consciousness and intelligence, I have included reference to his work here. Plants do not have a defined nervous system in terms of neurons and synapses that connect through a central brain. The lack of a defined nervous system does not exclude a complex system built on electrical conduction, something that has given rise to confusion in the past to some (Alpi et al. 2007).

Bose' extensive experimental information on plant nervous systems also required the construction of highly sensitive equipment, unique for the time, and that enabled so much to be uncovered. His prime experimental material was the touch-sensitive *mimosa*. He was able to demonstrate that the leaf droop after touch excitation was communicated by an action potential through the petiole to motor cells in the pulvinus. A massive efflux of potassium chloride from the vacuoles of these motor cells, results in a loss of turgor. Recovery takes about 45 min and, during this period, the potassium chloride is actively pumped back into these motor cells using cellular energy. However, Bose worked on other cells and species than Mimosa, so much of what he found can be generalized.

The benefits that animals gain by nerves and brains, is speed of connection between sensing system and muscular response. The brain provides for assessment and for awareness. It is part of the animal lifestyle of eat or be eaten that has accelerated the evolution of this apparatus. Predator and prey combined in an evolutionary dance of increasing speed.

Some of the information on the plant nervous system that Bose established

Bose clearly established the details of this nervous system in plants and he frequently compared the electrical system in plants with that in animals using the terms freely and rightly, in my mind, of both nerve and nervous system. The prime conductive tissue of action potentials he found to be the phloem and he identified this vascular tissue as the plant equivalent to a nerve by constructing a delicate voltage-detecting electric probe that penetrated the petiolar tissues to defined depths. He also isolated the nerves (phloem strands) from some plants and demonstrated their conductivity.

Transmission of the action potential is slower than those in defined nerves, but anyone who has observed the touch-induced leaf droop in Mimosa will know that the response is over in a very few seconds. A cold ring applied around the conductive tissue slowed the movement of the action potential. Further work established that, as in the animal synapse, conduction works only in one direction at the junction of the nervous tissue with the motor tissue.

By careful construction of further highly sensitive equipment, Bose observed the latent period after stimulation to be 0.08 sec and the velocity of transmission of the action potential in thin petioles to be about 400 mm/sec, intermediate between those of higher and lower animals. In the stem it can be as low as 5 mm/sec. In other plants, such as *averrhoa*, indirect stimulation electrically applied or when applied at a distance, led to an increase in turgor in remote tissues.

The pulvinus of Mimosa he found to consist of four different effector regions and stimulation of just one can give rise to torsional movements. There is a definite connection between the nerve end in each quadrant of the pulvinus at its centre and the corresponding subregion of the petiole. When the intensity for peripheral stimulation is adequate, the afferent impulse reaching the pulvinus becomes reflected along a new path and becomes an efferent impulse. A reflex arc is thus formed at the centre. This is considered different to mammals where the afferent and efferent impulses in a reflex arc are carried by separate nerves. However, Bose contends that there may be two kinds of phloem in Mimosa, which may conduct differently, one being afferent, the other efferent, thus mimicking the nervous organization of the reflex arc in animals.

Bose also reported that the heliotropic movements of leaves in which the leaf blade is positioned at right angles to the direction of light, was brought about by transmission of nervous impulses from the perceptive pulvinar region to the motor tissue of the same organ. Leaf movement was caused by contraction of the proximal and expansion of the distal side of this organ.

Bose (1926) draws several conclusions from his detailed studies.

Vascular plants possess a well-defined nervous system (p. 218).

Conduction can be modified experimentally in the same way as in animal nerves.

The conducted excitation may, therefore, be justly spoken of as a nervous impulse and the conducting tissue as nerve.

It is possible to distinguish afferent or sensory impulses from efferent or motor impulses just as in animals and to trace the transformation of one into the other to form a reflex arc.

'The observations involve the conception of some kind of nerve centre', but Bose admits no structure corresponding to the nerve ganglion of the animals has ever been detected in Mimosa.

Why did Bose' research largely disappear from scientific view?

Given the volume of work produced by Bose, it is always surprising that very little of it found its way into textbooks on plant physiology. There are undoubtedly some simple reasons. Mimosa and the Venus flytrap, whose trap was likewise controlled by an action potential, were considered as virtually unique and thus not relevant to most plants. The primary research emphasis in the 1930s was centred instead on crop plants and agriculture. The isolation of auxin in the early 1930s gave rise to a potential for chemical control of plant communication, growth, and thus yield. It is easier to modify plant development by adding a chemical than using complex electrical equipment. So the chemical approaches won out and the electrical ones all but disappeared, but even so Bose indicated, in his enormous compendia of data, that most of his results were applicable to these crop plants, as well. However, another reason was the behaviour of plants themselves. Any reason for electrical conduction was not obvious. Why it was asked did plants need rapid responses, they are slow to visibly respond. They don't get up and walk away.

Electrical fields took over this area of research

However, some took up the challenge in a different way. In the 1930s there was considerable interest in electrical fields. Could these provide explanation of embryonic fields, particularly in animal embryology or the meristem? Lund and Rosene (1947) provided summaries of several decades of study and measurement on bioelectric potentials in plants. These measurements showed that, for example, potential differences of 100 mV or thereabouts could be detected between the top and bottom of plant organs, such as the coleoptile. When the tissue was laid on its side, the new top and bottom rapidly assumed an equivalent potential difference, the so-called geoelectric effect. Potential differences they found existed everywhere—across plants, across organs— the plant was surrounded by electrical fields. Roots were found to have defined electrical fields around them and these could oscillate with periodicities in minutes (Scott 1957; Shabal et al. 1997).

Any mystery that might have surrounded these was quickly dispelled once it was indicated that these probably reflected no more than the differential accumulation of ions in plant cells across the plasma membrane (Scott 1967). The difference can be large up to -200 mV, compare that with a nerve cell at -70mV. Most research on electrical fields initially identified potassium ions in particular

as being differentially regulated or accumulated across the plasma membrane.

Recent understanding has improved the perspective of the plant nervous system

Part of the reason for the oddity label applied to Mimosa was that the only thing affected seemed to be the turgor pressure. The sundew is another plant in which action potentials are used to help catch insect prey and in which relatively rapid movement occurs again using turgor pressure changes. If electrical conduction had greater relevance than just changing turgor pressure surely some other event should follow, a change in development for example?

Appreciation of the role of cytosolic Ca²⁺ in controlling many aspects of signal transduction: the missing link?

A slow accumulation of data starting in the 1980s indicated that cytosolic calcium was carefully regulated in plant cells at a very low concentration, about 100 nM (Trewavas 1985). Elevation by two to three orders of magnitude to a concentration of 10–100 µM could activate many numerous Ca^{2+}-dependent proteins and kinases in plant cells. Many of these proteins could modify transcription and translation, and change connections within cellular networks. What substantially propelled understanding forward was the development of an entirely simple method of measuring cytosolic calcium in plant cells using the Ca^{2+}-sensitive luminescent protein aequorin (Knight et al. 1991, 1993). When Ca^{2+} increased the plants luminesced. Very quickly it was found that numerous signals, such as touch, cold, light, oxidative signals or chemical elicitors of defence, and most signals to which plant respond could induce typical cytosolic Ca^{2+} transients in less than a second and lasting some 20–30 sec. Furthermore, imaging the luminescence and thus Ca^{2+} dynamics indicated self-propagating waves of Ca^{2+} elevation from the point of impact to thousands of responsive cells or as small cell clusters.

The speed with which a calcium signal could be induced, indicated that in contrast to the apparently slow response of plants, the initial impacts inside cells was equivalent to the speed of response to those in animal cells. Plant cells were far more sensitive to signals than had been appreciated. The reason the response is slow is because it often involves growth. Social insect colonies respond relatively slow compared with the speed of the workers because hive change involves slow parameters like honey accumulation. Reproduction, polarity, and circadian processes also used oscillations in cytosolic calcium to control their processes (Trewavas 2011).

Electrical signals, cytosolic calcium, and responses to herbivores

Herbivory is one of the commonest problems faced by all higher plants. There has been an arms race between insect herbivores and plants for probably 300 million years. In response to herbivore damage, plants synthesize compounds that are toxic, repellent, or anti-digestive for defence. Many of these chemicals are termed natural pesticides. Some are used by mankind to deal with insect pests. The activation of at least three resistance pathways occurs after recognition of attack. These involve signal transduction sequences that hinge around the synthesis of jasmonates, salicylate, and ethylene, although these pathways on their own are insufficient to generate resistance. Different herbivores elicit different profiles of expressed proteins from the prey plant and the kinetics of induction of the known three transduction pathways, which also cross-talk, are often specific to the herbivore (Vos et al. 2005). There can be considerable variation even between individuals of the same species in the resistance mechanisms, at the early stages of recognition of herbivore attack (Wu et al. 2008). Specific recognition chemicals that identify the herbivore are recognized through the unique chemical composition of the saliva of the herbivore (Mithofer and Boland 2008). The production of specific classes of emitted plant volatiles attracts the attention of parasitoids of the herbivore or act as repellents, but what starts it all off?

When herbivores commence feeding, the initial event, that of wounding, generates action potentials that propagate over considerable distances within the plant, and institute defence mechanisms including the synthesis of anti-digestive protease inhibitors and jasmonate (Wildon et al. 1992; Fisahn et al. 2004). The action potential results in a transient increase in cytosolic Ca^{2+} some 20–50 msec later. Blockage of the cytosolic Ca^{2+} entry by inhibitors prevented synthesis of specific jasmonate dependent proteins involved in defence reactions. The subsequent reactions involve induction of protein kinases including protein kinase cascades and oxidative reactions (Howe and Jander 2008).

However, the most intriguing is that the action potential can be initially propagated along the surface of leaves to others nearby and probably also through the phloem. The transmission is primarily through glutamate receptor-like, sensitive channels (Christmann and Grill 2013; Mousavi et al. 2013). Addition of glutamate to plant cells elicits Ca^{2+} transients and membrane depolarization (Dennison and Spalding 2000; Vincill et al. 2012). Like animal glutamate receptors, the effect of opening the channel permits the entry of K^+ ions, as well leading to depolarization.

These unexpected observations intrigue because glutamate is a neurotransmitter in animal brains. Here, glutamate is concentrated in cellular vesicles and these are localized in the presynaptic region of the neuron. On receipt of an action potential and attendant depolarization in the presynaptic cell, the glutamate is released from vesicles and travels across the synapse to the post-synaptic neuron, where it binds to glutamate receptors in the plasma membrane inducing cytosolic Ca^{2+} transients and depolarizing the post-synaptic cell leading to a further action potential. Glutamate is thus central to brain function involving learning and memory.

The attacks by herbivores on plants result in a learning process called priming, which is remembered for very long periods of time, even beyond reproduction. Its molecular basis is probably epigenetic. The memory can be accessed on future attacks, leading to a quicker and more robust answer to the herbivore (Frost et al. 2008). Volatile chemicals released by plant cells on herbivory can actually have a bigger effect on adjacent undamaged plants (Engelberth et al. 2004).

Glutamate has more specific effects on root systems causing changes in growth and lateral root formation when applied to the tip (Forde 2014). Most intriguingly, the transduction pathway involves MAP 3 kinase and probably MEK1 as it does in animal cells. There is a clear interaction between nitrate, the nitrate receptor, and the influence of glutamate.

It is extraordinary that the basic elements of signalling and memory events are shared between higher animals and higher plants, the latter in the absence of a defined nervous system.

Action potentials are involved in a variety of processes in plants (Fromm and Lautner 2007). How many of these involve glutamate and its receptors in plants, is not known.

Are immune systems intelligent, conscious or both?

The human immune system depends on both learning and memory. In simple outline, learning starts when the immune system detects a new antigen. Through trial and error processes, a kind of Thorndikean learning, the cell with the optimal antibody for this antigen is selected among a number of less optimal possibles and enormously replicated. The memory can last for a lifetime or disappear within a year or less. The immune system involves local contact, cooperation and direct recognition between several kinds of B- and T-cells, and uses information transfer, feedforward in replication and negative feedback to stabilize active cell populations. There may be epigenetic carry-over of resistance between generations. It is sometimes described as the molecular consciousness of the human body.

There are two kinds of immunity—innate and adaptive—and it is the adaptive form that has all the characteristics of swarm intelligence. It is self-organizing, lacks a central control, is initially imperfect in recognition, which is improved by trial and error, operates in stable overall fashion, adapts to changes in input giving a diversity of response and whose coordinate activity gives rise to evident intelligent behaviour (Timmis et al. 2010). The important feature to notice is that the immune system does not directly involve nerve cells. Instead of the collection of social insects in a colony, we now have a colony of interacting cells constructing a highly intelligent system.

Plants also have a complex immune system

Disease pests attacking plants seem to induce unique combinations of proteins that are equally responsible for resistance (Loon et al. 2006). The signalling is highly specific and seems tuned to the individual pest. Once attacked, the learning response is remembered and, again, it is primed for very considerable periods of time. As with herbivory, further attacks are then dealt with more quickly and more robustly (Conrath 2011). Priming results from:

1. Endogenous eliciters, signals arising from damage *per se*.
2. Molecular signatures arising from disease microbes.
3. Specific patterns of pathogen related damage.
4. Colonization by growth promoting bacteria.
5. Treatment with β-aminobutyric acid.

The initiation of priming is a learning process and priming can be remembered for years in perennials. The system is very obviously intelligent because it helps solve a problem of continued attack by pests and in showing such specific awareness agrees with Margulis definition of being conscious. The whole organism is involved.

More recent work has shown clearly that the primed state can be passed onto siblings and for several generations, suggesting epigenetic processes, DNA methylation, and siRNAs are likely involved with the learning process that controls specific methylases (Pieterse 2012).

Priming takes place against abiotic stimuli too

Perhaps the most extraordinary aspect of this process is the priming against abiotic stimuli. Treating plants with the amino acid, β-aminobutyric acid, not only primes against disease, but also primes against drought and salt stress—a process involving abscisic acid (Jakab et al. 2005). Large numbers of growth-promoting bacteria are associated with normal root systems and, surprisingly, induce systemic resistance to many fungi, bacteria and viruses even in the presence of pathogens (Loon et al. 1998; Kloepper et al., 2004). The growth-promoting bacteria produce a variety of compounds some of which are volatile, like butane diol. These on their own induce resistance mechanisms, but there is a range of small and large molecular weight chemicals that do so as well. Most significantly, these rhizosphere bacteria also help plants tolerate abiotic stresses like drought and excess salinity, and thus again alter behaviour (Yang et al. 2009).

References

Alpi, A., Amrhein, N., Bertl, A., Blatt, M.R., Blumwald, E., Cervone, F., and 30 others (2007). Plant neurobiology, no brain, no gain. *Trends in Plant Science*, **12**, 135–136.

Bose, J.C. (1926). *The nervous mechanism of plants*. Longmans, Green and Co Ltd, London.

Bray, D. (2009). *Wetware. A computer in every living cell*. Yale University Press, Newhaven.

Christmann, A., and Grill, E. (2013). Electric defence. *Nature*, **500**, 404–405.

Conrath, U. (2011). Molecular aspects of defence priming. *Trends in Plant Science*, **16**, 524–531.

Dennison, K.L., and Spalding, E.P. (2000). Glutamate gated calcium channels in *Arabidopsis*. *Plant Physiology*, **124**, 1511–1514.

Edelman, G.M. (1992). *Bright air, brilliant fire. On the matter of mind*. Penguin Books, London.

Engelberth, J., Alborn, H.T., Schmelz, E.A., and Tumlinson, J.H. (2004). Airborne signals prime plants against herbivore attack. *Proceedings of the National Academy of Sciences USA*, **101**, 1781–1785.

Fisahn, J., Herde, O., Willmitzer, L., and Pena-Cortes, H. (2004). Analysis of the transient increase in cytosolic Ca^{2+} during the action potential of higher plants with high temporal resolution: requirement of Ca^{2+} transients for induction of jasmonic acid biosynthesis and PINII gene expression. *Plant and Cell Physiology*, **45**, 456–459.

Forde, B.G. (2014). Glutamate signalling in roots. *Journal of Experimental Botany*, **65**(3), 779–787.

Franks, N.R. (2008). Convergent evolution, serendipity and intelligence. In Conway-Morris, S., ed. *The deep structure of biology*, pp. 111–126. Templeton Foundation Press. West Conshohocken, PA.

Franks, N.R., and Richardson, T. (2006). Teaching in tandem running ants. *Nature*, **439**, 153.

Fromm, J., and Lautner, S. (2007). Electrical signals and their physiological significance in plants. *Plant Cell and Environment*, **30**, 249–257.

Frost, C.J., Mescher, M.C., Carlson, J.E., and Moraes, C.M., de (2008). Plant defence priming against herbivores: getting ready for a different battle. *Plant Physiology*, **146**, 818–824.

Howe, G.A., and Jander, G. (2008). Plant Immunity to Insect herbivores. *Annual Review of Plant Biology*, **59**, 41–66.

Jakab, G., Ton, J., Flors, V., Zimmerli, L., Metraux, J-P., and Mauch-Mini, B. (2005). Enhancing *Arabidopsis* salt and drought stress tolerance by chemical priming for its abscisic acid responses. *Plant Physiology*, **139**, 267–274.

Jennings, H.S. (1923). *Behaviour of the lower organisms*. Columbia University Press, New York.

Kloepper, J.W., Ryu, C.-M., and Zhang, S. (2004). Induced systemic resistance and promotion of plant growth by *Bacillus* spp. *Phytopathology*, **94**, 1259–1266.

Knight, M.R., Campbell, A.K., Smith, S.M., and Trewavas, A.J. (1991). Transgenic plant aequorin reports the effects of touch and cold-shock and elicitors on cytoplasmic calcium. *Nature*, **352**, 524–526.

Knight, M.R., Read, N.D., Campbell, A.K., and Trewavas, A.J. (1993). Imaging calcium dynamics in living plants using semi-synthetic recombinant aequorins. *Journal of Cell Biology*, **121**, 83–90.

Lacerra, P., and Bingham, R. (2002). *The origin of minds*. Harmony Books, New York.

Langridge, E.A., Franks, N.R., and Sendova-Franks, A.B. (2004). Improvement in collective performance with experience in ants. *Behavioural Ecology and Sociobiology*, **56**, 523–529.

Lauder-Lindsay, W. (1876). Mind in plants. *British Journal of Psychiatry*, **21**, 513–532.

Loon L.C., van, Bakker, P.A.H.M., and Pieterse, C.M.J. (1998). Systemic resistance induced by rhizosphere bacteria. *Annual Review of Phytopathology*, **36**, 453–483.

Loon, L.C., van, Rep, M., and Piertese, C.M.J. (2006). Significance of inducible, defence-related proteins in infected plants. *Annual Review of Phytopathology*, **44**, 135–162.

Lund, E.J., and Rosene, H.F. (1947). *Bioelectric fields and growth*. University of Texas Press. Austin, TX,

Margulis, L. (2001). The conscious cell. *Annals of the New York Academy of Sciences*, **929**, 55–71.

Margulis, L., and Sagan, D. (1995). *What is life*? Weidenfield and Nicolson Ltd, London.

Maturana, H.R. (1980). Biology of cognition. In Maturana H.R., and Varela, F.J., eds, *Autopoiesis and cognition. The realisation of the living*, pp. 2–58. Reidel Publishing Co., Dordrecht.

Maturana, H.R., and Varela, F.J. (1980). Autopoiesis. The organisation of living. In Maturana H.R., and Varela, F.J., eds, *Autopoiesis and cognition*, pp. 73–155. Reidel Publishing Co., Dordrecht.

Minot, C.S. (1902). The problem of consciousness in its biological aspects. *Science*, **16**, 1–12.

Mithofer, A., and Boland, W. (2008). Recognition of herbivore-associated molecular patterns. *Plant Physiology*, **146**, 825–831.

Monod, J. (1971). *Chance and necessity. An essay on the natural philosophy of modern biology*. Alfred A Knopf, New York.

Morkunas, I., Borek, S., Formela, M., and Ratajczak, L. (2012). Plant responses to sugar starvation. In Chang, C.-F., ed. *Carbohydrates—comprehensive studies on glycobiology and glycotechnology*, pp. 409–438. Intech, Croatia.

Mousavi, S.A.R., Chauvin, A., Pascaud, F., Kellenberger, S., and Farmer, E.E. (2013). Glutamate receptor-like genes mediate leaf-leaf wound signalling. *Nature*, **500**, 422–426.

Pieterse, C.M.J. (2012). Prime time for transgenerational defense. *Plant Physiology*, **158**, 545.

Ramanathan, S., and Broach, J.R. (2007). Do cells think? *Cell and Molecular Life Sciences*, **64**, 1801–1804.

Scott, B.I.H. (1957). Electrical oscillations generated by plant roots and a possible feedback mechanism responsible for them. *Australian Journal of Biological Science*, **10**, 164–179.

Scott, B.I.H. (1967). Electric fields in plants. *Annual Review of Plant Physiology*, **18**, 409–418.

Shabal, S.N., Newman, I.A., and Morris, J. (1997). Oscillations in H^+ and Ca^{2+} ion fluxes around the elongation region of corn roots and effects of external pH. *Plant Physiology*, **113**, 111–118.

Sourjik, V. (2004). Receptor clustering and signal processing in *E. coli* chemotaxis. *Trends in Microbiology*, **12**, 569–576.

Stroeymeyt, N., Franks N.R., and Giurfal, M. (2011). Knowledgeable individuals lead collective decisions in ants. *Journal of Experimental Biology*, **214**, 3046–3054.

Suel, G.M., Garcia-Ojalvo, J., Lieberman, L.M., and Elowitz, M.B. (2006). An excitable gene regulatory circuit induces transient cellular differentiation. *Nature*, **440**, 545–550.

Tibbetts, E.A., and Lindsay, R. (2008). Visual signals of status and rival assessment in *Polistes dominulus* paper wasps. *Biology Letters*, **4**, 237–239.

Timmis, J, Andrews, P., and Hart, E. (2010). On artificial immune systems and swarm intelligence. *Swarm Intelligence*, **4**, 247–273.

Trewavas, A. (1970). The turnover of nucleic acids in *Lemna minor*. *Plant Physiology*, **45**, 742–751.

Trewavas, A. (1972). Determination of the rates of protein synthesis and degradation in *Lemna minor*. *Plant Physiology*, **49**, 40–46.

Trewavas, A.J. (1985). *Molecular and cellular aspects of calcium in plant development*. Springer, Berlin.

Trewavas, A.J. (2011). Plant cell calcium, past and future. In Luan, S., ed. *Coding and decoding of calcium signals in plant cells*, pp. 1–6. Springer-Verlag, Berlin.

Trewavas, A.J., and Baluska, F. (2011). The ubiquity of consciousness. *EMBO Reports*, **12**, 1221–1225.

Sachs, J.V., von (1887). *Lectures on the physiology of plants*, transl. H. Marshall Ward. Clarendon Press, Oxford.

Vincill, E.D., Bieck, A.M., and Spalding, E.P. (2012). Ca^{2+} conduction by an amino acid-gated ion channel related to glutamate receptors. *Plant Physiology*, **159**, 40–46.

Vos, M., de, Oesten, V.R., van, Poecke, R.M.P., van, Pelt, J.A., van, Pozo, M.J., Mueller, M.J., and 5 others (2005). Signal signature and transcriptome changes of *Arabidopsis* during pathogen and insect attack. *Molecular Plant—Microbe Interactions*, **18**, 923–937.

Warwick, K. (2000). *QI. The quest for intelligence*. Piatkus, London.

West Eberhard. M.J. (2002). *Developmental plasticity and evolution*. Oxford University Press, Oxford.

Whitehead, A.N. (1938). *Modes of thought*. Free Press, New York.

Wildon, D.C., Thain, J.F., Minchin, P.E.H., Gubb, I.R., Reilly, A.J., Skipper, Y.D., and 3 others (1992). Electrical signalling and systemic protease inhibitor induction in the wounded plant. *Nature*, **360**, 62–65.

Wu, J., Hettenhausen, C., Schuman, M.C., and Baldwin, I.T. (2008). A comparison of two *Nicotiana attenuata* accessions reveals large differences in signalling induced by oral secretions of the specialist herbivore *Manduca sexta*. *Plant Physiology*, **146**, 927–939.

Yang, J., Kloepper, J.W., and Ryu, C-M. (2009). Rhizosphere bacteria help plants tolerate abiotic stress. *Trends in Plant Science*, **14**, 1–4.

CHAPTER 26

Intelligent foraging?

In a state of nature, each is confined to that particular station and kind of nutriment which it can seize from other plants by which it is surrounded.

(Darwin 1875)

⊃ Summary

The link between foraging for resources and competition is well established in the experimental literature, but is complicated by obvious cooperative interactions between plants. Competition is critically assessed and may be more limited than commonly assumed. Competition is likely under some circumstances, and the patchy distribution of light above ground, and resources of minerals and water below ground has been well established. However, identifying responses to limiting resources in wild plants has proven difficult. Even small-scale physical variation can interfere with fitness. Foraging theory is well established in animals, but less well in plants. The same sequence, search, encounter, and decision, apply equally to plants and animals. Some above ground foraging involves clonal plants and some of these have the capacity to veer away from competition. A simple procedure using a rosette type structure to summarize behavioural traits and intelligent behaviour is indicated. Potential complications from different lengths of memory are indicated. The Charnov model, which relates energy investment and energy gain deals with optimal animal feeding in a patchy environment and ought to be relevant to plant behaviour. This model could be applied to root systems by equating mineral uptake (absorption, transport, and metabolism) to energy gain. Extensive research on Dodder (*Cuscuta*), a parasitic plant, indicates it has the capability to assess the likely return of resources from a host many days before such resources are exploited, a behaviour that can only be regarded as intelligent. Dodder forages in accordance with the optimal Charnov model.

Introduction

What is more important (about domestication) is that the plants are exposed as little as possible to struggle with other plants and are thus enabled to exist under diversified conditions. In a state of nature each is confined to that particular station and kind of nutriment which it can seize from other plants by which it is surrounded (Darwin 1875, p. 243).

Two important deductions come from Darwin's statement. First, domestication complicates deduc-

tions about plant behaviour. Secondly, foraging and competition for resources are intertwined and Darwin's statement recognized a central issue. If there were unlimited resources of light, minerals and water in the soil, and no herbivores or disease, then competition would not exist. The more reduced the level of resource, the stiffer the competition for what is actually there, or so it is supposed. How well established is Darwin's assessment on competition? Isn't competitive ability just one behavioural trait among a number? In the extreme situation of resource limitation, competition might be a dominant characteristic, but in those situations, such as deserts, there are few species and, often, they can be well spaced.

Obvious cooperation occurs between different species (Kelly and Bowler 2002). There may be complementarity in resource requirements (e.g. Tilman 1982) mitigating competition. Also, there is probably variation in resource requirements throughout seasons, plants do grow at different times of the year (Goldberg and Novoplansky 1997). Increasing evidence also indicates how plants communicate with each other through common mycorrhizal networks, which can form between different species (see Chapter 17) and obviously another aspect of cooperative behaviour. Not only are there mutual benefits to be gained from mineral uptake by mycorrhizae, but such networks help early seedling establishment and influence community composition. Furthermore, these networks can help transfer signals that enable close partners in the network to set up disease and herbivore resistance, and to transfer allelopathic chemicals (Babikova et al. 2013).

Volatile chemicals are produced by many, if not all plants, and are used by herbivores to locate their prey, but on attack the composition changes, often attracting parasitoids and repelling further herbivore attack. These volatile chemicals are also transmitted aerially and can help nearby plants to develop resistance, as well as protection—cooperative behaviour again?

Individuals of wild species vary enormously in their phenotypes and, thus, genotypes (Linhart and Grant 1996). This variation can be extremely small scale in distance, from a few centimetres upwards. Burdon (1980), for example, isolated a large number of clones of *Trifolium repens* from a single field and cultivated them in the laboratory. He observed that, on average, each differed from any other in at least six traits. This degree of variation could suggest complementarity in resource requirement or equally, complementarity in phenotype minimizing resource competition.

While there are numerous environmental signals to which plants respond and generate different phenotypes, there are others that complicate foraging for necessary resources, such as N or P. These include soil moisture levels, serpentine soils, the degree of wind exposure, date of snowmelt, proportion of sandstone in parent material, grazing, topography, disturbance, stage of succession in old fields, and trampling (references in Turkington and Aarsen 1984). Herbivory, disease, and other physical and chemical factors of the environment add to the difficulties, and surely complicate supposed resource competition. The large number of such variables surely accounts for the high variability of the genetic make-up of a wild species. Each individual will encounter a mixture of these variables in quantity and quality, and the only way to ensure survival of some is to build in enormous capability in the whole population—bet-hedging rules.

Probably at least 40 signals or more (including specific chemicals) are known to be sensed and assessed. The number of potential environments experienced by the individuals of a population has to be enormous, but if only half of the signals are individually sensed, the transduction machinery that combines these together to construct an optimal phenotype throughout the life cycle is daunting. The numbers of such signals continues to increase in the research literature. Dealing with that complexity requires intelligent assessments.

Competition for resources by some plants certainly occurs

Goldberg and Barton (1992) described competitive ability as the suppression of other plants, or an ability to avoid or to tolerate suppression. However, competition for resources, light, minerals, or water may only be one aspect of competitive ability. These authors summarized the results of about 100 papers published within a single decade to indicate the substantive research interest in competition. There is certainly variation between different species in competitive ability and there are influences on community structure as a consequence, but competition between individuals of the same species (intraspecific competition) was not usually stronger than that between different species. These observations indicate that competitive ability is one facet of behaviour; others clearly compensate in different environments. Individuals vary in their ability to resist herbivory, for example.

Small-scale variation in resources in any environment

If competition for resources can occur, then it is valuable to know something of their distribution in wild conditions. That competition for light occurs is most clearly indicated by the numerous species that exhibit the shade avoidance behavioural trait. For others, the presence of a family of light receptors in plants indicates that light must be sensed and acted upon, although there is no reason to think the response uniform. Much will depend on the habitat that the plant normally experiences. Others tolerate low light or provide for other adjustments in low light, such as increased leaf size and some for life-style reasons grow towards darker regions. To any wild plant, light gaps are a common experience and these can be patchily distributed. The likely spatial variations for light have been detailed for a number of environments (Ballare 1994). The phenotypic response to these variations attempts to optimize fitness within the constraints of the particular environment. Problems have to be faced, and that requires assessment of what is present and then decisions on how to deal with them. That ability to optimize how the plant grows and continues its life cycle is surely a clear indicator of the likely variation in intelligent behaviour among individuals and species. Intelligence and fitness are inextricably linked.

The situation is much less clear in the soil. Some indications of the possible distribution of resources below ground can be gained from the resource contour maps provided by Bell and Lechowicz (1996), although these were determined indirectly from plant growth.

The distribution of roots in field soils is very uneven, sometimes reflecting perhaps corresponding variations in soil structure and resources. The distribution of minerals, gases, water, and micro-organisms (including mycorrhizae) is probably variable and uneven. Roots sense a great variety of parameters of the physical structure of the soil and respond by phenotypic changes (Caldwell 1996).

Laboratory investigations have shown that roots (usually lateral roots) proliferate in rich patches of N or P. Caldwell (1996) analysed root density in various kinds of field soil, and found little or no correlation between the N and the P in the same sample. In laboratory experiments, other things being equal, the morphology of the roots of one species is influenced more by the presence of different neighbouring root systems, than local resource distribution (see references in Huber-Sannwald et al. 1997). Caldwell (1996) also reported on experiments with field plots containing mainly three different species (a shrub and two different grass species), and micro-injected P into various parts of the soil and examined the subsequent root distribution. He noted that root proliferation did not always happen in regions of high P, that the proliferation in soil microsites could be influenced by the roots of other species, that there was a tendency of roots of different species to avoid one another and that there was no relationship between root length and nutrient acquisition.

Establishing seedling-scale environmental heterogeneity experimentally can, however, affect subsequent fitness (Hartegerink and Bazzaz 1984). Seeds were germinated in homogeneous soil, or (1) adjacent to a small stone above the soil, or (2) below the soil, (3) adjacent to a localized nutrient patch, or (4) adjacent to a localized sand or soil compactions from a footprint. Compared with those that germinated without these difficulties, the growth of those on heterogeneous conditions was severely impaired in the presence of stones, either on the soil surface or below the soil, and by compacted soil. These influences continued through to the yield of seed and reduced fitness was a consequence. These authors concluded that such small-scale stochastic variation easily overrides any genetic determinants of fitness. These obstacles clearly interfere with the foraging ability of the seedlings at the earliest life stages, but these represent only part of the environmental contingency that a growing plant has to deal with.

Darwin's assumption of seizure of resources, as being the basis of competition and, thus, community structure, and of course, selection, may only be a part of the story and it might turn out to be minor with further investigation. The problem, as always, is that in biology we deal with complex systems, and it is hardly practicable in such systems to abstract one part of the system and credit it with overall control. If nothing else, control theory demonstrated the futility of that reductionist approach with regard to the molecules inside cells (Trewavas 2006), but it is equally apparent that ecology can fall into the same trap. I have indicated before that intelligence is a whole system property that includes the connections with the environment and is identified as the capacity for problem solving. Like all such systems, there is no 'limiting factor' except perhaps for very extreme circumstances. Systems have a way of compensating for deficiencies in one area by increasing those in another. Identifying the capacity in plants to express intelligent behaviour is an attempt to indicate the coherence in behaviour by problem solving and its congruity with the environment.

The basis of resource foraging

Foraging theory is well advanced in animal studies (Stephens and Krebs 1986). The first serious applications of foraging theory to plants are those of Kelly (1990, 1992). I have referenced her pioneering research on a number of occasions (Trewavas 2005), as well as that of Charnov (1976) considered later.

Foraging for resources implicates the following necessary sequence of steps: search; encounter; and decision.

Search

Sensory systems are required to detect potential resources. The etiolation programme of some seedlings is a familiar example, but not all plant species express it. In those that do, it represents a search programme for light and is assumed to have evolved in those plants in which seeds were buried and germinated some time later. In this programme, stem elongation gains the lion's share of growth resources with the minimal resources given to leaves, vascular tissue, and roots. If the constraint on seedling resources is exacerbated by removing part of the seed reserve, then within limits, the seedling stem maintains the same length, but it is thinner, suggesting competition between the vertical to horizontal components of growth.

Many shoots searching for the best light source when light is unevenly distributed, exhibit circumnutatory behaviour. Comparative assessments of light gradients are assessed across the large circle

of the rotation and used eventually to direct future growth. Tendrils also exhibit circumnutatory movements designed to search for suitable supports and some seem able to detect a support made from plant material, presumably through reflected light (Trewavas 2005).

Below ground, roots can be demonstrated, to exhibit some circumnutatory behaviour in growth. Perhaps in light soils this improves the search for resource gradients. Lateral roots may also be used to increase the soil space searched. Particular phenotypes are adopted for the search programme with emphasis on root proliferation in searching for water. Low N or P also increases root growth with a concomitant reduction in shoot growth suggesting a kind of negative feedback control over shoot/root ratio. It is assumed that increased root growth and branching acts to increase the searching for resources, although this has not been convincingly established.

Encounter

Once light is encountered, two requirements emerge. The ability to detect the polarity of gradients of light (circumnutation is involved there) and then to grow along the gradient until an optimal light intensity is gained. For leaves that access light, the leaf blade is usually set vertically to its average direction by a motor organ, the pulvinus. Alternatively, the leaf blade moves commensurate with the changing direction of light through the day. Since the pulvinus is shaded by the leaf blade, presumably its positioning of the blade is determined by the light minimum, rather than the optimum. In the soil, it is probably the root cap that assesses mineral content and water gradients, and provides instructions for lateral root development and other phenotypic changes.

Decisions

These are made after an assessment of whether the resource is sufficient for foraging, or if it is, how much effort is to be invested in acquiring it. For light, the requirement is to assess whether the detected light source is optimal. For climbing plants, the decision is whether the support is suitable.

Darwin (1891) observed that some climbing plants will attempt to use a glass rod for support, but on failure they will unwind and search elsewhere. In the case of Dodder, to be described later, decisions are taken after a rapid assessment of the likely reward of resources from the prey. If these are assessed as insufficient, the predatory Dodder looks elsewhere.

The models used in foraging theory are optimality models; they are based on the assumption that those individuals that acquire food with the greatest efficiency are likely to be better able to survive the Darwinian battle of over-production and selection. They raise questions about how various choices are to be evaluated and the constraints on decision.

Foraging theory currently seems absent in plant studies. It does need more investigation.

General foraging responses

The foraging shoot

Extensive investigation of experimental work of resource foraging has been summarized (Hutchings and Kroon 1994). Much of the experimentation has involved mimicking the supposed patchy distribution of resources and examining how plant behaviour was altered.

For above-ground investigations it has been common to use what are called clonal plants. These grow by repetition of above-ground stolons or horizontally-growing rhizomes below ground. At each node, leaves, buds, and roots may be developed. From a number of experimental investigations, it is clear that the majority of such growing plants can take discrete avoidance action when the plant perceives patches of another plant, such as grass. Quite simply, those that do, veer away. Potentially, that response is similar to a shade avoidance programme and is generated before any loss of photosynthetic light. The new rhizomes are selectively placed outside the patches of grass and if grown within the patch of grass, the internode length is much longer. That can be interpreted as speeding a retreat from competition (Evans and Cain 1995).

Furthermore, such clonal plants grow better when presented with strong contrasts in the nutrient status of the patch, than when nutrients are provided in uniform distribution (Wijesinghe and Hutchings 1999). How that is sensed and then acted upon, is not clear, but it is unusual. It is as though the growing plant needs time to accommodate (digest?) rich resources and a patchy distribution better fits some internal oscillation in resource usage.

At one time, it was thought that in all clonal plants, the internode length was directly modified by nutrients and light. When encountering good growth conditions, the internode length was short and the obvious interpretation is that growth is then more limited in an area of high resource potential to sequester the resources that are present. When encountering an area where resources are scarce or poor, internode length was increased implying an emphasis now on searching for better conditions. However, not all clonal plants show such changes and, instead, the only uniform response is increased branching in nutrient rich conditions (Kroon and Hutchings 1995). This, again, suggests that clonal plants have previously adapted to a variety of environmental circumstances of which resources are just one factor.

The foraging root

Root responses by proliferation in nutritionally rich areas are variable and this was discussed in more detail in Chapter 13. Although most species do show some increased root biomass in nutrient rich areas, others do not. The placement of roots is affected by neighbouring plants, requiring recognition of self and non-self. Also there are simple stochastic elements usually in lateral root growth (necessary exploration?), as well as soil quality variation and available space. There is a competitive feature that depends on size—larger, more mature root systems, it is assumed, acquire resources more easily (Schenk 2006; Cahill and McNickle 2011).

Root profiles and architecture are the result of numerous interactions, as well as the need for foraging. Despite substantive research, whether plants are more limited by soil nutrients than light seems to remain unanswered (Schenk 2006). Once shoot competition was removed, no effect of nutrient heterogeneity in the soil on root distribution was observed, although again, conflicting results can be found in the literature. Species-specific mechanisms are in place, which can complicate any attempt at interpretation. Root systems can show considerable plasticity in absorptive capacity, total surface area, mass-to-surface area ratios, rooting density, the timing of growth and replacement, stochastic root production, and architecture. It's not just the amounts of N or P.

It is notable that a common approach that simply measures the biomass or distribution of root systems in the soil, rarely measures the actual uptake of N, P, or K. However, measuring the absorptive capacity, and coupled transport and storage systems would reveal more useful information, although difficult to obtain. It is not possible to simply equate root size with increased absorptive capacity.

In temporally variable environments, it does seem that plastic individuals are superior competitors, suggesting why plasticity arose in the first place. As a generalization, species that invest more in roots, occupy areas with low productivity; those that invest more in shoots occupy areas with high productivity, although there are plenty of exceptions. Competition for resources is not the only factor involved in phenotype construction.

Intelligent integration of behavioural traits provides a potential solution to foraging conflicts

Part of the answer to the complications in foraging outlined above can be resolved by identifying more clearly how to assess intelligent behaviour in plants. Warwick (2000) produced a simple way of describing animal intelligence. He used a rosette structure like a pie chart, in which all the known characteristics of intelligent behaviour were approximately quantified. Each intelligence facet was incorporated into the pie with its size determined by its quantification. Intelligent behaviour is thus not one behavioural property, but an integrated compilation of many.

A similar compilation can be made for the plant behavioural traits that underpin plant intelligence too (Trewavas 2005). The behavioural traits of leaves, for example, include flexibility in leaf weight/area, speed of new leaf production, sensitivity to shade, flexible operation of photosynthesis, ability to

control internal leaf temperature, herbivore resistance, and stomatal sensitivity to opening and closing signals. Those for roots are absorptive capacity, total surface area, mass-to-surface area ratios, rooting density, the timing of growth and replacement, stochastic root production and architecture, root hair production, sensitivity to shortage of minerals, ability to attract mycorrhizae, and rhizosphere bacterial population. Those for the stem include wind sway response, response to shade, ability to redirect root resources to shoots, demarcation schedules, responses to gravity, area/volume ratio, extent of secondary tissues, and control of bud dormancy. There are, no doubt, many more.

When placed in a rosette with the size of each segment dependent on its degree of plasticity, then it would surely become apparent that plants differ between individuals and between species in the emphasis each places on the size of each trait. Warwick showed each rosette could be distorted in one direction or another reflecting the individual's particular capabilities.

There is, of course, an additional complication in using the above parameters and in resource competition. Intelligent behaviour is used to solve problems. That requires learning and the ability to store information as a memory, which can be accessed later. The capacity for either learning or memory is probably variable between individuals and species. Memory has become a commonly used word in the plant literature, but without the recognition that a memory cannot be acquired, without it being first learnt.

In animals, much memory resides in a conserved differentiated neural cell. Consequently, its molecular and neural characteristics tend to have some similarity between different animals. In the simplest case, the formation of a new dendrite, a new connection in the neural system, acts as both learning and memory (Kandel 2001). However, in more advanced neural systems, more connections and increased strength of connections, redirect information flow during the learning process and provide for memory.

However, memory also resides in immune systems and there is much greater variation here, and the mechanism is different. Antigens are sensed and the learning process involves trial and error processes, amplifying up the cells containing the optimal antibody. Long-term memory instead resides in a few cells and, when needed, is amplified by cell replication, but once established, the pathway of information flow is redirected towards generating defence. Cell variation may account for the variable length of memory.

In plants, the learning process is largely molecular and, again, the aim is to increase information flow through a defined pathway. The variation that occurs is determined by the nature of the response, but the memory of it can last for just a few seconds to minutes, hours, and then months or longer; it simply depends in what part of the cellular apparatus the memory is deposited. A few examples are indicated below, others can be found in other chapters or in some of the articles I have published (Trewavas 2003, 2009).

Some memories lasting several hours to days

All tropic stimuli generate memories of variable length. Place a seedling horizontally for a short period. On returning to the vertical, both shoot and root will indicate they have remembered the gravity stimulus by bending in the stimulated direction for a time (Leopold and Wetlaufer 1989). Brief exposure (30 sec) to unilaterally placed blue light of very low intensity induces phototropic bending. If light of equal intensity is shone from the other side within 65 min of the first signal, then the second signal overrides the first (Nick and Schafer 1988; Nick et al. 1990). If the second signal was given 90 min after the first, a minor temporary interruption in developing curvature development was observed, but then the response to the first signal took over. A memory of the first signal had been implanted only temporarily overridden by the second. In addition, and in the same way, after 90 min an imposed gravity signal could not be reversed. The authors conclude that, although curvature results in response to light and gravity, the gravity-induced memory is different to that of the light. The mechanisms of the long-term memory here are not known, but the temporary interruption indicates it can be accessed.

Tendrils require two signals to wind around a support—blue light and touch. When the tendril is touched in darkness, the second signal can be given later and thus estimates can be made of how long the touch signal is remembered. The touch memory is stored for up to 2 hr (Jaffe and Shotwell 1980). In the etiolated condition, cereal leaves are rolled up and need a brief exposure to red light to unroll them. Isolated leaves respond in this way, but need calcium in the medium to unroll. These two requirements can be separately applied. If red light is given first, Ca^{2+} can be given up to 4 hr later to cause unrolling. Some activated state is remembered for up to four hours (Viner et al. 1988).

Similarly, a hyperosmotic shock normally induces a cytosolic Ca^{2+} transient of short duration in cultured cells. If, however, the shock is administered in the absence of exogenous Ca^{2+}, the transient fails to appear until extracellular Ca^{2+} is returned to the medium. The separation of shock and Ca^{2+} administration can last up to 20 min (Takahashi et al. 1997).

A longer-term memory involving Ca^{2+} is involved in the induction of flax epidermal meristems (Verdus et al. 1997). These epidermal meristems could be induced by drought or wind treatment, both of which increase cytosolic Ca^{2+} transiently, but induction also required, a depletion of seedling Ca^{2+} for 1 day before these treatments became effective. Once established, the memory of the inductive signals lasted for at least 8 days.

Electrical memory lasting seconds

The Venus flytrap (*Dionaea*) is an insectivorous plant, familiar to many because it uses a trap constructed from two hinged leaves that are induced to close on an unfortunate fly using an action potential. The sensing tissues are two short hairs that initiate electrical change and both must be touched to initiate closure. Touch one and the other has to be touched within 20 sec for trap closure. The first, in some way, causes accumulation of a sub threshold electrical potential that is additive when the second signal is given (Volkov et al. 2009).

Memories lasting months to years

Vernalization is the process whereby a reproductive meristem in some grasses requires a prior cold treatment for some weeks, before flowering. The memory of this cold treatment can last for up to a year (Sung and Amasino 2006; Goodrich and Tweedie 2002). Priming against herbivores and disease was mentioned in the previous chapter; these memories can last years and are clearly accessible.

Other examples of priming-like behaviour result from a mild initial treatment that leads to much greater resistance to an increased signal imposed later. The first signal is thus remembered and is accessible. Pretreatment with low levels of cadmium leads to resistance to much higher concentrations experienced later on (Brown and Martin 1981). Similarly, for cold temperatures, pretreatment with a lower than ambient, but not freezing temperatures, enables greater resistance to later freezing exposure (Kacperska and Kulesza 1987). An initial mild drought stress, enables increased resistance to a prolonged drought imposed subsequently (Bartels and Sunkara 2005). For saline conditions, a pretreatment with low concentrations of salt increases resistance to much higher concentrations met subsequently (Amzallag et al. 1990). In each case, imposition of the later stress on untreated plants is usually sufficient to kill.

The length of time these memories last suggests chromatin changes of some kind are involved and thus probably similar in mechanism to much long-term memory in animal nerve cells. A memory is instituted that can be accessed months to years later.

The variability of memory length indicated here would complicate assessing the notions of competition for N and P. Once N and P are sensed, how long does the memory of that signal last? It will surely be longer than the actual resource itself.

Is the Charnov model applicable to plant foraging?

In 1976, Eric Charnov (1976) described a model that indicated how an animal could forage in an optimal fashion when feeding in a patchwork of food. What Charnov derived is shown in Figure 26.1a.

This model relates the net energy gained from a food source, whether it be a patch of grass or a host, to the energy investment required to get that energy. The relationship should be optimal. In that case, each curve that relates a feed line indicates the organism should stop when the curve slope reaches a critical value and that is indicated as the asymptote to each curve. Basically, when the marginal capture rate of energy in the patch or host falls below the average capture rate for the habitat, then for optimal feeding behaviour, the animal should leave the patch. A number of examples of animal feeding situations have been shown to follow this pattern of behaviour. How animals make that assessment is not known.

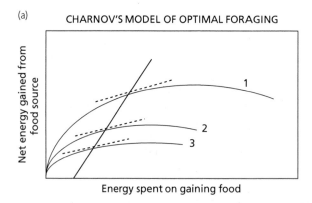
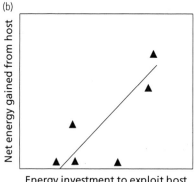

Figure 26.1 (a) Simplified version of Charnov (1976) model of optimal foraging. The Charnov model indicates that the optimal energy investment in feeding is indicated by the asymptote (dotted line) to the feed line. On different sizes of food a straight line connects the points of contact of the asymptotes as shown. Failure to grow through zero indicates errors in foraging. (b) Diagrammatic results of exploitation of six different hosts by Dodder. Energy investment was measured by coil length of parasite around host. Net energy gained was measured as increase in fresh weight after 28 days. Coiling is complete within three days. Net energy transfer to parasite starts after four days. Note that Dodder assesses energy return from host before actual energy transfer starts. The Charnov model works for Dodder. Adapted from Kelly (1990).

Since it is assumed that plant resources above and below ground are patchily distributed, this theory could have relevance to understanding aspects of plant behaviour.

Important foraging lessons from a parasitic plant

Dodder (*Cuscuta* sp.) is a well-known parasitic plant. It is barely photosynthetic and has no root. Thus, when the seed germinates, it has to find a host quickly if it is to survive. It is a host generalist able to gain resources from a variety of different species. Being a member of the Convolvulacae, which contains many twining species, it is able to wind around a potential host. Coiling finishes in about 3 days under experimental conditions. Haustoria (infective pegs) penetrate the host from Dodders inner surface and link up with the host's vascular tissue, thus gaining the resources that would normally go to provision the host. Transfer of resources starts some days after coiling has completed (Kelly 1990). Presumably, touch sensing operates to indicate on which side of the parasite, haustoria should develop and penetrate. Either the peg digests its way in or uses additional higher turgor pressure to break through the turgor pressure of cells of the host.

However, carbohydrates, water, and organic N are not the only thing to be transferred. In recent years, it has become apparent that both proteins and mRNA, as well as sRNA species circulate in the host phloem. These macromolecules can also cross the parasite/host divide and are found in parasitizing Dodder (Roney et al. 2007). So far, some 27 mRNA species are transferred from the host and many of these code for regulatory proteins (Westwood et al. 2009; Leblanc et al. 2012). Specific sRNAs, synthesized by the host, can seriously interfere with parasitic development and represent one way of reducing parasite damage (Alakonya et al. 2012).

The fact that some hundreds of mRNAs, and over a thousand proteins, circulate in the phloem and seem able to penetrate cells via plasmodesmata indicates a degree of coherence to the growing plant and can counteract the notion that phenotypic plasticity only involves local tissues and control (Atkins et al. 2011).

Dodder is able to detect its host by sensing the volatile chemicals released from potential host plants (Runyon et al. 2006). The supplementary information in this paper provides a video showing how Dodder captures its prey. The seedling germinates and the thin shoot appears, and starts to circumnutate, that is, it undergoes **search**. Detection of the host causes a progressive change in the angle of rotation towards the host, but rotation continues as the parasite continues to grow; this is equivalent to **encounter**. Clearly, circumnutation enables the seedling to assess the spatial direction of the host volatiles, since it is able to assess volatile concentration across the whole circle of nutation. Once that direction is clarified, a final and straightforward lunge is used to attach itself to the host stem; that represents **decision**. The stem direction has been accurately identified. A decision is made at that point to stop rotating and lunge for the stem. Dodder does not seem to parasitize itself indicating self-recognition.

Dodder must then have receptors for these host volatiles and if Dodder has them, then given the exchange of information between host and parasite, they are likely to be present in the host plants, too. If root systems have the ability to detect alien root systems, then receptors for root-emitted chemicals, which includes volatiles may have been adapted and used by Dodder as it evolved. Many, if not all higher plants, emit an enormous range of volatile chemicals, many during reproduction. No doubt, in past times, some of these were designed to repel herbivores or to attract parasites of herbivores.

Dodder grows more vigorously in patches of mixed hosts by parasitizing two different hosts. The order in which these hosts were parasitized makes a difference to the overall growth response (Kelly and Horning 1999). However, there is no doubt that Dodder makes decisions about which plants it parasitizes, when given the choice. Out of 10 potential hosts in field conditions that it could survive on, only two were parasitized (Kelly et al. 1988; Kelly 1992). Thus, Dodder exhibits discrimination. Could discrimination be based on volatile recognition or is there brief contact with a potential host to make an assessment. Sodium may be important to Dodder to help maintain its turgor pressure so sensing, which host has more sodium could lead to distinguishing between hosts.

Breakage of the Dodder shoot in the wild does occur and leaves two viable plants. The shape of a clonal individual is altered affecting the probabilities of encounter with other patchily-distributed living resources (Kelly et al. 2001). The level of breakage reflected the nature of the habitat in which Dodder grew, but is presumably important in improving overall species parasitization. The Dodder colony should not waste resources on the exploitation of poor hosts when richer ones are available, since seed number relates to stored resources and thus to fitness.

This situation is analogous to patch exploitation. The individual host is equivalent to a patch of resource. Dodder grows better on those that are more productive. The decisions made by Dodder can represent a model of the capabilities of other plants to exploit resources efficiently. Resources are sensed before exploitation implying decisions to exploit or ignore, if warranted.

Charnov's marginal value model operates in Dodder

A detailed investigation of sensing and assessment by Dodder revealed some surprising features (Kelly 1990, 1992). The results are diagrammatically shown in Figure 26.1b.

1. When Dodder encounters a suitable host, the coiling process is rapid and finally complete within 3–4 days. The growth of haustorial initials lags well behind and the earliest possible uptake of resources from the host only takes place only when coiling is complete.
2. Recognition of a host may take place through flavonoids and other compounds in the host bark. Specific receptors and signal transduction processes must be involved. Could volatile release also contribute?
3. Many potential hosts are rejected within a few hours. Crucially decisions are made within this very short time period based on an assessment of host productivity.
4. Coiling represents an investment of energy by the parasite to gain resources.
5. The relationship between coiling and host quality was assessed experimentally by measuring the numbers of coils and biomass accumulation by the parasite from a variety of hosts over a growing season.
6. Using different species it was shown that the coil length (the energy invested) was linearly related to the net energy gained, expressed as biomass/unit coil length.
7. Thus, the assessment period caps the amount of energy that will be used to gain resource from the host. An assessment of the likely reward is made before any uptake of resource from the host.
8. Larger plants produced more seed and are thus fitter. Discrimination and choice of host are thus crucial for fitness.
9. Dodder actively exerted resource choice, even with the same host species. While 60% of known hosts were rejected in a few hours, hosts that had been fertilized with increasing amounts of N, greatly reduced rejection.

To summarize, Dodder senses its prey and assesses a likely return in resources before actually accessing the host resources. A prediction of the future resource gain is made. The assessment also compares the outlay of energy in coiling and the likely energy acquired. Accurate assessment leads to larger and fitter plants.

The Charnov model is illustrated in Figure 26.1a Figure 26.1b shows the equivalent situation in Dodder using a number of different hosts as different patch qualities. The investment of energy and that gained is linearly related. On this basis, Dodder optimally forages.

Since it is unlikely that Dodder has capabilities unique in the plant kingdom, energy investment and assessment of resources when patchily distributed may be present in normal photosynthetic plants. Assessment when further light or root resources are no longer profitable to be gained from any one patch can also be made. Dodder's behaviour is surely what is to be expected for an intelligent organism. It can assess its likely energy expenditure for its likely energy gain.

Problems with using the Charnov model for plant foraging

Although the Charnov model is well accepted in animal behaviour studies, there are difficulties with its application to other higher plants. With one parasitic seedling and one food source, an optimization mechanism can be feasibly teased out. It is far more problematic with numerous food sources, resource variability, and symbiotic partners. There are differing forms of N in the soil, too; N may exist either as nitrate, ammonium, or degraded proteins. Root systems as indicated previously also exhibit other behaviours, they react to those of aliens and change patterns of growth, acting antagonistically (Cahill and McNickle 2011). To get the Charnov model to fit ordinary growing plants, it might be better to use mineral uptake as a proxy for energy gain.

There is a trade-off between mineral transport efficiency in the plant and uptake efficiency (Fitter 1987). Transport proteins concerned with uptake into root cells are inducible. Finally, higher plants are modular organisms, they have multiples of leaves and roots, and most of these live in different environments around the plant. Many of these environments will be sub-optimal and in the soil will be variably shaped. Decisions have to be made on a whole plant basis as to how much to devote to any one of them at any one time. In wild plants there is unlikely to be an abundance of all resources at the same time, one or more will constrain the overall growth rate. To an extent, compensation against a variable environment can occur through storage of minerals when they are in abundance. I indicated in Chapter 11 that the cambium might act as arbitrator of root resource distribution.

What the experiments on Dodder reveal is an unexpected sensitivity and ability to optimize that solves a fundamental problem for Dodder. However, Dodder is a higher plant and that capacity for problem solving is undoubtedly intelligent behaviour, a facility that is likewise present in other higher plants. If there is to be a direct translation of the experiments from Dodder to higher plants, then at the best it could be examined using one root and perhaps one mineral.

Some further work on the Charnov model

One attempt to capitalize on the Dodder experiments used a sorghum root system (Gleeson and Fry 1997). The biomass of the root system was equated to energy investment; the rate of mineral uptake considered either analogous to the energy gained or to the time taken to move between patches. Using four defined patches of increasing mineral content, only the fine root mass exhibited an increase related to mineral content and thus to an increased potential return/unit of root mass invested. There was a very high degree of variation between individuals in total root tissue and as the authors stated, if only overall root content had been measured there would have been no meaningful relationship between root tissue and mineral distribution. Given the degree of variation in root systems indicated above this is hardly surprising, but mineral uptake was what should have been measured.

The notion of optimal solutions with regard to the Charnov method has, more recently, been revived again for root systems (McNickle and Cahill 2009; McNickle et al. 2009). It was observed that roots spent longer in rich patches than less rich ones, the travelling times between patches varied according to the predictions of the Charnov model. Thus, the analogy with Dodder might hold for individual roots or just fine roots under certain circumstances. Since the shoot deals with just one resource, light, the Charnov model might better fit this circumstance than below ground investigations.

Conclusion

There is much to be gained by regarding the plant as an intelligent system, not only in foraging, but in all sorts of behavioural responses. Many of these have been indicated throughout this book. There is certainly a better need for understanding systems properties and behaviour, and the consequences of self-organization. There is also an important need to recognize the limitations that come from laboratory research and how experimentalists often become part of the plant environment.

Earlier in this book I indicated that plants gain information about their environment, combine this information with their present condition, and after assessment make a behavioural decision that benefits the whole plant. The process is analogous to cognition. Assessment is the result of the activities of complicated networks in cell and tissues. The behaviour described in this chapter is a fine example of these more general plant processes. In its capacity for solving the problems of optimizing resource acquisition, it is properly described as intelligent. What is least understood is the mechanism of assessment.

Finally, I finish with another statement from Barbara McClintock who was introduced in Chapters 1 and 2. 'There is no such thing as a central dogma into which everything will fit- any mechanisms you can think of you will find-even if it is the most bizarre form of thinking. Anything. Don't turn it aside and call it an exception, an aberration. So many good clues have been lost in that manner' (Keller 1983). Plant intelligence is one of those categories described by some as aberrations, but when properly investigated will start to reveal how a complex non-neural organism derives intelligent behaviour from the systems structures within itself. The challenge is there. What is needed is the devotion of open-minded, imaginative individuals to take the challenge up.

References

Alakonya, A., Kumar, R., Koenig, D., Kimura, S., Townsley, B., Runo, S., and 6 others (2012). Interspecific RNA interference of SHOOT MERISTEMLESS-like disrupts *Cuscuta pentagona* plant parasiticism. *Plant Cell*, **24**, 3153–3166.

Amzallag, G.N., Lerner, H.R., and Poljakoff-Mayber, A. (1990). Induction of increased salt tolerance in *Sorghum bicolor* by NaCl treatment. *Journal of Experimental Botany*, **41**, 29–34.

Atkins C., Smith P., and Rodriguez-Medina C. (2011). Macromolecules in phloem exudates–a review. *Protoplasma*, **248**, 165–172.

Babikova, Z., Gilbert, L., Bruce, T.J.A., Birkett, M., Caulfield, J.C., Woodcock, C., and 2 others (2013). Underground signals carried through common mycelial networks warn neighbouring plants of aphid attack. *Ecology Letters*, **16**, 835–843.

Ballare, C.L. (1994). Light gaps: sensing the light opportunities in highly dynamic canopy environments. In Caldwell M.M., and Pearcy, R.W., eds, *Exploitation of environmental heterogeneity by plants*, pp. 73–111. Academic Press, New York.

Bartels, D., and Sunkara, R. (2005). Drought and salt tolerance in plants. *Critical Reviews in Plant Science*, **24**, 23–58.

Bell, G., and Lechowicz, M.J. (1996). Spatial heterogeneity at small scales and how plants respond to it. In Caldwell M.M., and Pearcy, R.W., eds, *Exploitation of environmental heterogeneity by plants*, pp. 391–411. Academic Press, New York.

Brown, H., and Martin, M.H. (1981). Pretreatment effects of cadmium on the root growth of *Holcus lanatus*. *New Phytologist*, **89**, 621–629.

Burdon, J.J. (1980). Intra-specific diversity in a natural population of *Trifolium repens*. *Journal of Ecology*, **68**, 717–735.

Cahill, J.F., and McNickle, G.G. (2011). The behavioural ecology of nutrient foraging in plants. *Annual Review of Ecology and Systematics*, **42**, 289–311.

Caldwell, M.M. (1996). Exploiting nutrients in fertile soil microsites. In Caldwell M.M., and Pearcy, R.W., eds, *Exploitation of environmental heterogeneity by plants*, pp. 325–347. Academic Press, New York.

Charnov, E.L. (1976). Optimal foraging, the marginal value theorem. *Theoretical Population Biology*, **9**, 129–136.

Darwin, C. (1875). *The variation of animals and plants under domestication*, Vol. 1. John Murray, London.

Darwin, C. (1891). *The movements and habits of climbing plants*. John Murray, London.

Evans, J.P., and Cain, M.L. (1995). A spatially explicit test of foraging behaviour in a clonal plant. *Ecology*, **76**, 1147–1155.

Fitter, A.H. (1987). An architectural approach to the comparative ecology of plant root systems. *New Phytologist*, **106**, 61–77.

Gleeson, S.K., and Fry, J.E. (1997). Root proliferation and marginal patch value. *Oikos*, **79**, 387–393.

Goldberg, D.E., and Barton, A.M. (1992). Patterns and consequences of interspecific competition in natural communities: a review of field experiments with plants. *American Naturalist*, **139**, 771–801.

Goldberg, D.E., and Novoplansky, A. (1997). On the relative importance of competition in unproductive environments. *Journal of Ecology*, **85**, 409–418.

Goodrich, J., and Tweedie, S. (2002). Remembrance of things past: chromatin remodelling in plant development. *Annual Review of Cell and Developmental Biology*, **18**, 707–746.

Hartegerink, A.P., and Bazzaz, F.A. (1984). Seedling-scale environmental heterogeneity influences individual fitness and population structure. *Ecology*, **65**, 198–206.

Huber-Sannwald, E., Pyke, D.A., and Caldwell, M.M. (1997). Perception of neighbouring plants by rhizomes: morphological manifestations of a clonal plant. *Canadian Journal of Botany*, **75**, 2146–2157.

Hutchings, M.J., and Kroon, H., de (1994). Foraging in plants: the role of morphological plasticity in resource acquisition. *Advances in Ecological Research*, **25**, 159–238 .

Jaffe, M.J. and Shotwell, M. (1980). Physiological studies on pea tendrils XI. Storage of tactile sensory information prior in the light activation effect. *Physiologia Plantarum*, **50**, 78–82.

Kacperska, A., and Kulesza, L. (1987). Frost resistance of winter rape leaves as related to changes in water potential and growth capability. *Physiologia Plantarum*, **71**, 483–488.

Kandel, E.E. (2001). The molecular biology of memory storage. A dialogue between genes and synapses. *Science*, **294**, 1030–1038.

Keller, E.F. (1983). *A feeling for the organism. The life and work of Barbara McClintock*. W.H. Freeman and Co., New York.

Kelly, C.K. (1990). Plant foraging: a marginal value model and coiling response in *Cuscuta subinclusa*. *Ecology*, **71**, 1916–1925.

Kelly, C.K. (1992). Resource choice in *Cuscuta europaea*. *Proceedings of the National Academy of Sciences USA*, **89**, 12194–12197.

Kelly, C.K., and Bowler, M.G. (2002). Coexistence and relative abundance in forest trees. *Nature*, **417**, 437–440.

Kelly, C.L., Harris, D., and Perez-Ishiwara, R. (2001). Is breaking up hard to do? Breakage, growth and survival in the parasitic clonal plant *Cuscuta corymbosa*. *American Journal of Botany*, **88**, 1458–1468.

Kelly, C.K., and Horning, K. (1999). Acquisition order and resource value in *Cuscuta attenuata*. *Proceedings of the National Academy of Sciences USA*, **96**, 13219–13222.

Kelly, C.K., Venable, D.L., and Zimmerer, K. (1988). Host specialisation in *Cuscuta costaricensis*: an assessment of host use relative to host availability. *Oikos*, **53**, 315–320.

Kroon, H., de, and Hutchings, M.J. (1995). Morphological plasticity in clonal plants: the foraging hypothesis reconsidered. *Journal of Ecology*, **83**, 143–152.

Leblanc, M., Kim, G., and Westwood, J.H. (2012). RNA trafficking in parasitic plant systems. *Frontiers in Plant Science*, **3**, 203–233.

Leopold, A.C., and Wetlaufer, S.H. (1989). Springback in root gravitropism. *Plant Physiology*, **91**, 1247–1251.

Linhart, Y.B., and Grant, M.C. (1996). Evolutionary significance of local genetic differentiation in plants. *Annual Review of Ecology and Systematics*, **27**, 237–277.

McNickle, G.G., and Cahill, J.F. (2009). Plant root growth and the marginal value theorem. *Proceedings of the National Academy of Sciences USA*, **106**, 4747–4751.

McNickle, G.G., St Clair, C.C., and Cahill, J.F. (2009). Focusing the metaphor: plant root foraging behaviour. *Trends in Ecology and Evolution*, **24**, 419–426.

Nick P., Sailer, H., and Schafer, E. (1990). On the relation between photo- and gravitropically induced spatial memory in maize coleoptiles. *Planta*, **181**, 385–392.

Nick, P. and Schafer, E. (1988). Spatial memory during the tropism of maize (*Zea mays*) coleoptiles. *Planta*, **175**, 380–388.

Roney, J.K., Khatibi, P.A., and Westwood, J.H. (2007). Cross species translocation of mRNA from host plants into the parasitic plant Dodder. *Plant Physiology*, **143**, 1037–1043.

Runyon, J.B., Mescher, M.C., and De Moraes, C.M. (2006). Volatile chemical cues guide host location and host selection by parasitic plants. *Science*, **313**, 1964–1967.

Schenk, H.J. (2006). Root competition: beyond resource depletion. *Journal of Ecology*, **94**, 725–739.

Stephens, D.W., and Krebs, J.R. (1986). *Foraging theory*. Princeton University Press, Princeton, NJ.

Sung, S., and Amasino, R.M. (2006). Vernalisation and epigenetics: how plants remember winter. *Current Opinion in Plant Biology*, **7**, 4–10.

Takahashi, K., Isobe, M., Knight, M.R., Trewavas, A.J., and Muto, S. (1997). Hypo-osmotic shock induces increases in cytosolic calcium in tobacco suspension cultured cells. *Plant Physiology*, **113**, 587–594.

Tilman, D. (1982). *Resource competition and community structure*. Princeton University Press, Princeton, NJ.

Trewavas, A (2003). Aspects of plant intelligence. *Annals of Botany*, **92**, 1–20.

Trewavas, A. (2005). Green plants as intelligent organisms. *Trends in Plant Science*, **10**, 413–419.

Trewavas, A. (2006). A brief history of systems biology. *Plant Cell*, **18**, 2420–2430.

Trewavas, A. (2009). What is plant behaviour? *Plant Cell and Environment*, 32, 606–616.

Turkington, R., and Aarsen, L.W. (1984). Local scale differentiation as a result of competitive interactions. In Dirzo R., and Sarukhan, J. eds, *Perspectives on plant population ecology*, pp. 107–128. Sinauer, Sunderland, MA.

Verdus, M.C., Thellier, M., and Ripoli, C. (1997). Storage of environmental signals in flax: their morphogenetic effects as enabled by transient depletion of calcium. *Plant Journal*, **12**, 1399–1410.

Viner, N., Whitlam, G., Smith, H. (1988). Ca^{2+} and phytochrome control of leaf unrolling in dark grown barley seedlings. *Planta*, **175**, 209–213.

Volkov, A.G., Carrell, H., Baldwin, A., and Markin, V.S. (2009). Electrical memory in Venus flytrap. *Bioelectrochemistry*, **75**, 142–147.

Warwick, K. (2000). *QI. The quest for intelligence*. Piatkus, London.

Westwood, J.H., Roney, J.K., Khatibi, P.A., and Stromberg, V.K. (2009). RNA translocation between parasitic plants and their hosts. *Pest Management Science*, **65**, 533–539.

Wijesinghe, D.K., and Hutchings, M.J. (1999). The effects of environmental heterogeneity on the performance of *Glechoma hederacea*: the interaction between patch contrast and patch scale. *Journal of Ecology*, **87**, 860–872.

Index